# TRAINING & DEVELOPMENT YEARBOOK 2001

## CAROLYN NILSON

PRENTICE HALL

Printed in the United States of America

10 9 8 7 6 5 4 3 2 1

ISSN 1049-3875

ISBN 0-13-028143-3

9 780130 281432    90000

**ATTENTION: CORPORATIONS AND SCHOOLS**

Prentice Hall books are available at quantity discounts with bulk purchase for educational, business, or sales promotional use. For information, please write to: Prentice Hall Special Sales, 240 Frisch Court, Paramus, New Jersey 07652. Please supply: title of book, ISBN, quantity, how the book will be used, date needed.

**PRENTICE HALL**
**Paramus, NJ 07652**
On the World Wide Web at http://www.phdirect.com

# WHAT THIS BOOK WILL DO FOR YOU

The *Training & Development Yearbook 2001* is the most comprehensive, varied, wide-ranging, accessible collection of high-interest, high-priority information and verified data of importance to the field. Both the organization of the book and the way in which current ideas and developing trends are presented are carefully designed to start you immediately thinking about meaningful change and point you in the right direction to accomplish it. As you read and become familiar with its contents, you will find that the *Yearbook:*

- Synthesizes the most recent best practices for you,
- Provides contact information for people you can call on for help,
- Focuses your thinking,
- Spurs you into action,
- Pushes your personal performance, and
- Enables you to help your company succeed.

In this *Yearbook,* editor's comments written from the perspective of a seasoned training manager, experienced instructional designer, and consultant quickly focus your thinking and suggest the essential issues you'll need to consider as you read further. Having a highly respected and widely published trainer review the published literature defining the field helps you to sort out your thinking and develop your own up-to-date platform for action. Succinct analysis of the kernel of creativity inherent in an idea, experience, report, or program lets you slash away the superficial and extraneous information that constantly bombards you in books, journals, the media, and online.

Thousands of documents comprise the base of material for this book. The unique concept of a yearbook such as this is that only the best practices and most relevant current thinking and reporting are chosen for this book. Because of this, you can finally throw away those shelves 'full of old magazines, journals, dog-eared downloads, and newsletters. Your annual record of the training and development field is right here in this one volume, on your desk, always at hand for ready reference. The *Yearbook* contains detailed lists of organizations, conferences, seminars, training centers, publishers, publications, reference books, and Websites providing you with a one-stop directory of names, addresses, Websites, telephone and FAX numbers vital to your work. Our Trainer's Almanac, Section 6, is the most comprehensive and information-rich reference on the market today.

This *Yearbook* is built upon the solid conviction that individuals want to be able to help make their companies successful—to do meaningful work that contributes to overall productivity and performance—and build your own career in the process. The specialized field of training and development has traditionally taken the lead in designing and delivering programs that help people learn better ways to do work, and it will continue to carry the banner for workplace learning. Today, however, things are not as simple as they seemed in the past:

- Fewer people are listed as employees on corporate rosters; outsourcing is common everywhere and training consultants are thriving. Leadership for learning is a major challenge.

- Classroom training is changing: There are not as many people to fill up classrooms, budgets are tighter for out of town training trips, and companies are looking for ways to combine time- and money-saving technology-delivered training with classroom training.

- There are growing relationships between the big picture of social and political changes and the smaller picture of why and how workplace learning must take place. Actions in Washington, in state capitals, and in political and cultural centers around the globe affect how trainers do their jobs.

- Advances in the capabilities of computing and telecommunications, satellite and Internet transmission, combined with decreasing prices of personal computer and peripheral hardware have tended to broaden the resource base and to individualize the accessing and choosing of information which forms the foundation for learning. Trainers are struggling with quality issues in both instructional design and training delivery in the online learning environment.

- The explosion of "e-everything" happened this year. Our skills for personal communication are changing because of this. How we interact in e-jobs, e-commerce, and e-learning challenges our personal and career growth in ways we are still discovering.

- Global connections with fellow workers and colleagues on the periphery of a business (such as professors, suppliers, and even competitors) drive individuals to enter into working and learning relationships with even more people.

- Intellectual capital and knowledge management present opportunities for training managers.

- Worker stress the 24/7 work environment, an increasingly litigious society, and gun violence add to the reasons trainers need to help preserve "high touch" in a "high tech" environment.

- Those who design, deliver, support, and manage training are particularly challenged to stay focused on learning in the midst of an advertising, entertainment, and information onslaught.

- Those who evaluate the learning event itself, as well as the results of training, must understand business results and added value in addition to simply determining what has been learned.

The *Training & Development Yearbook 2001* reflects the current continued broadening of the training field and the need for trainers to think more inclusively and strategically as training departments dwindle and stabilize after several recent years of corporate downsizing. The wider conceptual base of this *Yearbook* can bring you more quickly in touch with the current range of ideas in the field and encourage you to take action with the confidence of being well informed. Among other current trends and developments included in the *Training & Development Yearbook 2001* are:

- Growth opportunities for trainers in times of change—knowledge management, performance consulting, e-learning.

- Boosting individual and organizational performance for stability and growth.

- Assessing training needs, both for individuals and for the enterprise as a whole.

- Nuances in the experiences with the latest technological directions in training, such as delivering lessons online, instructional Websites, distance learning, virtual universities, and better administrative software.

- New and better tools for Web-based and online learning.

- New kinds of training delivery sites, including combinations of "high touch" and "high tech."

- Corporate collaborations for increased learning, both within companies and with others outside of companies.

- Special training challenges of home-based employees and contingent workers.

- Successful welfare-to-work legislation affecting training program design and workplace learning.

- The push for design quality standards in e-learning.

- Training that leverages and maximizes the benefits of global workplace diversity.

- How to build flexibility, better decision making, and creativity into your training programs.

- How leadership is changing; new views of organizations and teams.

- Knowledge as strategy; managing, protecting, sharing, and increasing intellectual capital.

The trainer's familiar systems development framework that begins with analysis and ends with evaluation is as critical today as it has ever been because it provides a way for you to think about identifying and solving problems within whatever large or small workplace environment you work. As the issues around performance and performance support, productivity, organizational learning, and the "enterprise" as a whole are debated, it's important for you to take off from a base of experience in systems thinking. And, of course, in all such debate, what you as an individual can bring to technology is the important relationship, not the other way around.

The entries in the *Training & Development Yearbook 2001* are fit within the systems framework beginning with those focused on analysis issues relative to the learner and ending with ideas and experiences in evaluation. Rather than simply choosing "interesting topics" at random, the entries in this *Yearbook* have been cited in relationship to each other and to the broad training and development field through the instructional systems design framework. Around this structure, the opening section on managing training places today's management challenges within the big-picture issues from knowledge management to global interconnectivity. Helping you to recognize and benefit from these system relationships is an important reason why this book was written.

The *Training & Development Yearbook 2001* provides models, case studies, data, insight, applications, and a host of individuals to inspire and encourage the kind of innovative thinking and informed risk-taking that trainers must do in order to continue to improve individual and organizational performance and help your company compete. Entries in this book feature committed employees, leaders, and team members in small companies, entrepreneurial operations, mid- and large-size companies, non-profit and government agencies, consultants, academics, writers, gurus, and just plain folks with good ideas. The scope of *Training & Development Yearbook 2001* is purposely broad, encompassing the strongest influences, most interesting ideas, and best practices in America's training and development scene as the new year 2001 begins. Our *Yearbook* is not affiliated with any organization or other commercial venture. We have been free to choose references from the widest possible field, and include them based only on their merits. We have intentionally searched a range of sources from the general business press representing diverse viewpoints on matters of concern to trainers, and we have purposely included in our literature base the publications of numerous professional associations who have important things to say about training. The breadth of our base of ideas and experience far surpasses any similar publication. Our efforts on your behalf are made with one goal in mind—to provide you with the most complete information about workplace learning in this calendar year.

Think of this book not just as a compendium of information, but in addition and more importantly, as a creative source of new ideas for the year 2001—ideas that drive learning, personal performance, and go right to your company's bottom line.

# ABOUT THE EDITOR

Carolyn Nilson, Ed.D., is a veteran trainer with a wide experience base in traditional and state-of-the-art training assignments. Among the corporations and agencies she has served as consultant in training design are: American Management Association, The ARINC Companies, AT&T, Chemical Bank, Chevron, Dun & Bradstreet, Martin-Marietta, Nabisco, National Institute of Education, National Occupational Competency Testing Institute, National Westminster Bank, New Jersey Bell, New Jersey State Department of Education, New Jersey Department of Labor, US Department of Education Office of Vocational and Adult Education, and The World Bank.

Dr. Nilson was a Member of the Technical Staff at AT&T Bell Laboratories where she was part of the Standards, Audits, and Inspections Group of the Systems Training Center. In this capacity, she developed, implemented, and promoted quality standards in course design and delivery throughout AT&T; she was the Bell Labs' representative on a corporate instructional design team. At Bell Labs, she received commendations for her work one-to-one with technical professionals for whom English was a second language. She also taught the Bell Labs' train-the-trainer course.

She held the position of Manager of Simulation Training at Combustion Engineering, where she managed the training operation and created high-level computer-based training for an international base of clients in various fields of the chemical process industry. At CE, she was a member of a corporate training design team where her specific contribution was design of a performance support system in learner evaluation using expert system technologies.

Dr. Nilson was Director of Training for a systems consulting firm with a broad-based Fortune 500 clientele in the New York City metropolitan area. In this position, she supervised a staff of training consultants and was responsible for training analysis, design, development, implementation, and evaluation across a range of corporations.

She has been a faculty member for Padgett-Thompson seminars, the Ziff Institute, the Center for the Study of Work Teams, the U.S. Armed Services Training Institute, and USAID's Management Development Initiative in Cairo, Egypt. She is an active member of the American Society for Training and Development (ASTD) where she was part of a grass-roots planning task force in the area of human resources development skills and strategies. She was ASTD's guest host for an online nationwide teleconference on dealing with change. She has been a speaker at national conferences of ASTD, the American Management Association, and at a regional conference of the International Society for Performance and Instruction. She received her doctorate from Rutgers University with a specialty in measurement and evaluation in vocational and technical education.

Her work has been featured in *TRAINING Magazine, Training & Development, Successful Meetings, Entrepreneur,* and *Fortune.* She is the author of numerous training papers, speeches, articles, and manuals; her writings are selling worldwide to a diverse customer base. Four of her books currently appear in amazon.com's "50 Bestselling Training Books." She is a Schwartz Business Books 1995 "Celebrity Author" (Milwaukee, WI), on the 1996 "This Year's Bestsellers" list of the Newbridge Book Clubs (Delran, NJ), and has been featured as a talk show guest on "Money Radio" (Pomona, CA). Her books have been used throughout the country in management seminars of the American Management Association. She has been the editor of Prentice Hall's *Training & Development Yearbook* for the past six years. Her books have been chosen by Macmillan's Executive Program Book Club, the Newbridge Book Club, the Training Professionals Book Club, and the *Business Week* Book Club. Among her other books are:

*How To Start A Training Program,* ASTD, 1999

*The Performance Consulting Toolbook,* McGraw-Hill, 1999

*How To Manage Training,* Amacom, 1998

*More Team Games for Trainers,* McGraw-Hill, 1997

*Games That Drive Change,* McGraw-Hill, 1995

*Team Games for Trainers,* McGraw-Hill, 1993

*Training for Non-Trainers,* Amacom, 1990; and Spanish edition, 1994

*Training Program Workbook and Kit,* Prentice Hall, 1989

# ACKNOWLEDGMENTS

Great appreciation for their ideas and implementation skills goes to the many hundreds of individuals who are mentioned in this 2001 edition of the *Training & Development Yearbook*. These are the persons whose writing, strategizing, planning, problem solving, points of view, and program expertise are featured in this book. Their names and affiliations are listed in the expanded citations on pages where their work is featured, and a big thank you goes out to them for moving the field forward through another year of change and growth. Also, names you will not find elsewhere are Noel Nilson, Bert Holtje, Herbert Burtis, and John Ferris, the most important men in my daily life, whose support, steadfastness, forbearance, humor, bread and circuses sustain me on the journey of creating a book, especially one such as this. To Eric, Jeffrey, Kristen, and Bob, I send hugs and kisses across the miles for your genuine interest in and enjoyment of my work, and for your encouragement throughout the project. To Betsey, Sari, Charlotte, Alex, Pearl, Jeanne, Marnie, Carla, and Lisa who also love reading and writing, and who share ideas with me, I thank you too for your support and enthusiasm in my sisterhood of learners, communicators, and trainers.

My Postmaster, Howard Wisell, and his assistant Bev Fallon were a critical link in the production process, as were my favorite bookstore owners, Meg and Jim Schmidt and their friendly and persistent team at the Corner Book Store, Winsted, Connecticut. I miss your smiling faces. Ruth Dwyer, librarian, keeps Sandisfield reading. To them also, thank you for caring for and believing in books.

In addition, a special thank you again goes to Katherine M. Franklin of Colebrook, Connecticut for your excellent detail work with Section 6, *The Trainer's Almanac*. Your reliability, research skills, your initiative, tenacity, accuracy, and dogged determination to get every item documented, every source checked were great gifts to me. Your creative work with book reviews in Sections 1 and 2, was again outstanding.

And finally, my team at Prentice Hall in Paramus, New Jersey deserves a standing ovation for seeing this project through another year with more demands for teamwork to get it to market: Executive Editor, Ellen Schneid Coleman rallied us all to keep us going forward; Barry Richardson, Senior Editor with many hats, deftly juggled ideas, details, and personalities, keeping me engaged in the game of beating the clock; Gloria Antaramian guided the paperwork through the editorial process and did a hundred other things that only she knows. Judy Weiss-Brown and Jo-Anne Kern, in the Marketing organization, Sandy Hutchison and Anna Yudina in Creative, and Beth Carey in Sales dealt with all the details of matching book to reader. Eve Mossman in Production and Susan Peluso and Janet Kirkland in Book Manufacturing, along with compositor Joe Gorman, did magical feats of scheduling and coordination, and turned a tricky manuscript into a book. Susan Sherman, Manager of Sub-Rights, steered us swiftly and surely through legal waters. An enhanced book, wider in scope, and in the hands of our readers sooner than ever before is the result of pulling together. We should all be proud of what we've done again this year.

Those outside of the Prentice Hall family who have been especially helpful in the development of this particular book or bringing it to market are:

Istvan Banyai, Illustrator
*The New Yorker*
New York, NY

Yvonne Burnside, Permissions Manager
*Across the Board*
The Conference Board
New York, NY

Daphne Ben Ari, Permissions
*Forbes* and *Forbes ASAP*
New York, NY

Karen Caldwell, Editorial Assistant
Society for Human Resource Management
Alexandria, VA

The Rev. Ernest L. Bengston
Colebrook Congregational Church
Colebrook, CT

Maureen Canon, Marketing Product Manager
*e-Learning*
Advanstar Communications
Santa Ana, CA

Jill Casner-Lotto, Vice President
for Policy Studies
Work In America Institute
Scarsdale, NY

Lori Cefus, Permissions Manager, Research
ASTD Benchmarking Service
Alexandria, VA

Kelly Champion, Permissions
*Fortune*
New York, NY

Nancy Dann, Permissions Administrator
*The Systems Thinker*
Pegasus Communications
Waltham, MA

Courtney Diffley, Permissions
*SHRM Legal Report*
Society for Human Resource Management
Alexandria, VA

Susan Dobak, Promotion Manager
*e-Learning*
Advanstar Communications
Santa Ana, CA

Margaret Driscoll
IBM
Westwood, MA

Christy Eidson, Assistant Editor
*Across the Board*
The Conference Board
New York, NY

Denise Fenrick, Permissions Assistant
Society for Human Resource Management
Alexandria, VA

Patricia A. Fitzpatrick, Permissions Manager
*MIT Sloan Management Review*
Cambridge, MA

Sandra Genova, Marketing Director
Generation21
Golden, CO

Deborah Keary, Director
SHRM Information Center
Society for Human Resource Management
Alexandria, VA

Ronda Lathian, Editorial Administrator
*Workforce*
ACC Communications
Costa Mesa, CA

Susan LeClair, Permissions Editor
*U.S. News & World Report*
New York, NY

Lawrence Lipsitz, Editor
*Educational Technology*
Englewood Cliffs, NJ

Alex Lumb, Permissions Manager
*Harvard Business Review*
Boston, MA

The MASIE Center
Saratoga Springs, NY

Jo Mattern, Permissions
*Fortune*
New York, NY

Andrea Medley, Permissions
*Fortune*
New York, NY

Leigh Montville,
Senior Permissions Coordinator
Conde Nast
New York, NY

Patrick Murphy,
Senior Permissions Assistant
John Wiley & Sons
New York, NY

Michael McDermott, Author
*Continental* Airlines Magazine
Carmel, NY

Brian McNally, Permissions Editor
Pohly & Partners
Boston, MA

Sabrina Paris, Manager
Permissions and Electronic Publishing
AMACOM Books/AMA Publishing
New York, NY

Drew Pawling, Permissions
*Harvard Management Update*
Boston, MA

Robin Reader, Customer Service
Copyright Clearance Center
Danvers, MA

Julie Richards, Permissions Assistant
*Forbes* and *Forbes ASAP*
New York, NY

Cheryl Lynn Rogers, Permissions Director
*MS.*
New York, NY

Diane Ruhlander, Editor
*e-Learning* Magazine
Santa Ana, CA

Karen Silber, Permissions Editor
The Bureau of National Affairs
Washington, DC

Debbie Sklar, Managing Editor
*e-Learning* Magazine
Santa Ana, CA

Valerie Small, Periodicals Coordinator
ASTD
American Society for Training & Development
Alexandria, VA

Steven M. Smith, Director of Communications
International Association
of Conference Centers
St. Louis, MO

Lyle Steele, Permissions Manager
*Business Week*
New York, NY

Jeremy Stratton, Permissions Editor
*TRAINING Magazine*
Bill Communications Inc.
Minneapolis, MN

Matt Tews
Training Supersite
*www.trainingsupersite.com*

Stacy Van der Wall, Editorial Assistant
Society for Human Resource Management
Alexandria, VA

Sal Vittolino, Director, Communications
Modis Professional Services
Jacksonville, FL

Becky Wilkinson, Permissions Manager
*Lakewood Report on Technology
for Learning* newsletter
Minneapolis, MN

Mark Worth, Account Representative
Copyright Clearance Center
Danvers, MA

# CONTENTS

# INTRODUCTION

## OVERVIEW

This is the twelfth edition of the *Training & Development Yearbook,* the latest in a series of what has become the respected annual review of the field of workplace learning. In a field exploding with new information, practices, and ideas, a tool is needed to organize that information, make it accessible and easy to find, and, most of all, to put it into perspective. This comprehensive volume is that tool. It is the only book of its kind—wide in scope, inclusive of hundreds of organizations, featuring the current experiences and ideas of more than a thousand businesses and individuals, based on primary information sources from 120 different publications and publishers. We show you what's working, who's doing it, and how they're getting results—corporations, colleges, government agencies, online universities, associations, consultants, start-ups.

## WHY A YEARBOOK SERIES?

This yearbook series is envisioned as a year-by-year archive of the most important writing on training and development during any twelve-month period. Synthesizing the best ideas and practices of the field in the form of a yearbook provides the reader with an organized and coherent view of the profession at the start of the new year. Since literature on workplace learning and performance is being created continuously and is proliferating around the globe in both quantity and depth, on paper and, electronically, the most meaningful way to organize and archive it is chronologically in the yearbook series. Over time, with a complete collection of yearbooks, we can trace any particular subject or company for a better understanding of the trends that inform the knowledge work of today. The series provides historical perspective of the field; the current volume provides perspective for work in the year ahead.

## WHAT'S SPECIAL ABOUT THIS TWELFTH EDITION

Research for this *Training & Development Yearbook 2001* involved reading thousands of journal and magazine articles, books, research studies, monographs, directories, newsletters, newspapers, conference proceedings, websites, and government documents. Analysis of these sources has produced a "best practices" compilation of ideas and experiences which define the field for a full twelve-month period and provide a unified foundation of ideas to start the new year.

The training field is in particular flux these days, with fewer staff required to do more work, with strategic business decisions being pushed down lower and lower out of the executive suite, with more outsider involvement in all aspects of training and training management, with old ways of delivering training being questioned, with computer and communications technology being used to support individual and organizational learning, and with global effects on training operations.

This book defines the field of training in the context of societal as well as professional influences—influences on the broader field of training that include competency and career development, infrastructure and design challenges of e-learning, performance improvement, and the development and management of intellectual capital. This book is much more than a reference document: it not only includes the essence of the best practices literature of the field, but it also explains the issues contained in that literature and places the highest level training debate within a framework that trainers can readily understand.

Entries in this year's *Training & Development Yearbook* are presented in a content structure that highlights the most important issues in each of the major training functions: management, needs analysis, instructional design, training delivery, and evaluation. Editor's comments focus each of the 94 major entries. A comprehensive introduction is included for each of the six major sections of the book. The most obvious trends and challenges of the field are given meaning for the trainer in this time of change. The ideas are structured within a systems development framework familiar to most trainers and managers. Each section of content is complete within itself. Each could stand alone as a book within a book. Taken together, these sections provide a powerful platform for developing a vital, relevant, value-adding, successful training program for 2001—a program designed to improve individual and organizational performance.

Approximately 250 books, authors, articles, databases, publishers, and publications have been cited within the text, illustrating the important dialogue within the field. In addition, 120 primary source publishers and publications are listed alphabetically in the following pages for quick and complete reference. Additional publishers who are primarily seminar or conference providers, as well as professional associations and non-profit agencies who also publish newsletters, journals, or other publications, are listed in Section 6, *The Trainer's Almanac,* providing hundreds more sources of printed information.

The publishing industry's long-held standards of excellence, the practice of peer review, editorial and fair use ethics, the rule of copyright law, standards of style and expression, sales and marketing practices that historically have put the consumer first, all make the information contained in this book an objective, verified and accurate representation of facts and ideas. The World Wide Web as a source of information, in contrast, is still struggling with these fundamental checks and balances. A yearbook and a yearbook series is what no Website can ever expect to be. Our *Trainer's Almanac,* alone, contains 934 entries, all of which feature multiple fields of data, compounding the quality of information at your fingertips.

## WHO SHOULD READ THIS BOOK?

Training consultants, coordinators, managers, directors, multimedia specialists, instructional designers, instructors, performance specialists, knowledge officers, and CEOs: This yearbook is committed to helping trainers with all sorts of titles and job descriptions in companies of all sizes to design and build the knowledge infrastructure of their companies. It is for those learning and performance consultants who advise and listen, coach, negotiate, facilitate, and chart strategic directions. It is for men and women inhabiting the skin of the traditional trainer who are now required to stretch the limits of their organizational creativity, their personal and professional commitment to learning, and their capacity for making systems work in the deepening and broadening of a business's knowledge base.

## WHAT IS COVERED IN THIS BOOK?

Because this is a yearbook, the content which we've chosen to include represents new ideas, experiences, challenges, and insights apparent in a year's worth of business literature. This literature base includes references from literally hundreds of primary sources. If a subject or company does not seem to be represented in this information base, it is probably because the underlying ideas and practices were not particularly new this year, or not part of the public or professional literature base, or not particularly indicative of a trend anticipated for year 2001. This book concentrates on annual best practices as seen through a thorough, focused, annotated literature review of the immediate past forming a foundation for the immediate future.

The content is organized within a systems framework, recognizing that change and development must occur within a structure that relies especially on analysis of a business's as well as a learner's needs, a process of intentional design, an appropriate delivery method, and the use of evaluation and feedback. Content of this book recognizes that trainers must formulate business goals within a learning and performance context, and must view the development and delivery of training as a means to add value to the company through knowledge. Literature reviewed includes some publications not generally considered as part of the field. This is because we believe that societal trends and political actions have an impact on corporate directions and should be considered as important framers of workplace learning and performance improvement.

Specifically, more than 300 topics of unique interest have been categorized into the following major sections:

- Section 1: Training Management
- Section 2: Needs of Learners
- Section 3: Training Program Design
- Section 4: Training Program Delivery
- Section 5: Evaluation of Training

A complete listing of topics is found in the book's Table of Contents, with additional detail in the introductions to each section. A comprehensive master index in the back of this book will direct you to individuals and companies, concepts, and topics elaborated on throughout the book. In all, 94 entries make up Sections 1 through 5.

## SPECIAL FEATURES

In a literature review of this size, all content does not fall neatly into "article" form. Therefore, within the first five sections of the book, you'll find the following special features:

- **Abstracts:** An abstract is a brief summary of an information source, often an article from a journal or magazine, newspaper or newsletter. This book contains 18 abstracts.

- **Article Reprints:** Articles have been chosen from a wide variety of relevant publications. This book contains 38 article reprints, plus 18 other reprints placed in other categories.

- **Book Reviews:** Among the many fine business books from many publishing houses, 7 were selected from 2000 to review. In some cases, a book chosen for relevance to training and development is also a business best-seller; in other cases, it is not. Their inclusion here means that their authors had something particularly new or developmental to contribute to the field of workplace learning in this twelve-month period. Only the latest publication dates are eligible to be included in *Training & Development Yearbook 2001*. This year's books reviewed here are:

*Common Knowledge: How Companies Thrive By Sharing What They Know* by Nancy M. Dixon (Boston: Harvard Business School Press, 2000), $29.95. Nancy M. Dixon is an Associate Professor of Administrative Sciences at The George Washington University.

*The Social Life of Information* by John Seely Brown and Paul Duguid (Boston: Harvard Business School Press, 2000), $25.95. John Seely Brown is Chief Scientist at Xerox Corporation and Director of the Xerox Palo Alto Research Center (PARC). Paul Duguid is a Research Specialist in Social and Cultural Studies in Education at the University of California at Berkeley.

*The Monk and the Riddle: The Education of a Silicon Valley Entrepreneur* by Randy Komisar with Kent Lineback (Boston: Harvard Business School Press, 2000), $22.50. Randy Kosimar is a virtual CEO who has worked with companies such as WebTV and TiVo. He was CEO of LucasArts Entertainment and Crystal Dynamics, CFO of GO Corporation, and one of the founders of Claris Corporation. Kent Lineback is a writer, producer, and consultant.

*Instructional Design for Web-based Training* by Kerri Conrad and TrainingLinks (Amherst: HRD Press, 2000), $34.95. Kerri Conrad is a Principal with TrainingLinks, a Colorado-based corporate education and instructional technology consulting company. *www.traininglinks.com*

*Executive Coaching with Backbone and Heart* by Mary Beth O'Neill (San Francisco: Jossey-Bass Inc., Publishers, 2000), $30.00. Mary Beth O'Neill is a Senior Consultant for LIOS Consulting Corporation at the Leadership Institute of Seattle at Bastyr University.

*Performance Scorecards: Measuring the Right Things in the Real World* by Richard Y. Chang and Mark W. Morgan (San Francisco: Jossey-Bass Inc., Publishers, 2000), $32.95. Richard Y. Chang, PhD, is President and CEO of Richard Chang Associates, Inc., Irvine, CA., a diversified consulting and publishing company. He is also past-president of the American Society for Training & Development (ASTD), and a judge for the Malcolm Baldrige National Quality Award. Mark Morgan is a Senior Consultant for Richard Chang Associates, Inc., an examiner for the Malcolm Baldrige National Quality Award, and former instructor at Florida Institute of Technology and University of Central Florida.

*The Knowing-Doing Gap: How Smart Companies Turn Knowledge into Action* by Jeffrey Pfeffer and Robert I. Sutton (Boston: Harvard Business School Press, 2000), $27.50. Jeffrey Pfeffer is the Thomas D. Dee Professor of Organizational Behavior at Stanford University's Graduate School of Business. Robert I. Sutton is Professor of Organizational Behavior at Stanford University's School of Engineering. Sutton is also Co-Director of the Center on Work, Technology, and Organization.

- **Case Studies:** A case study focuses on a specific good idea, program, policy, or strategy practiced this year by a particular organization, individual, or group of companies. In each instance, specific and useful approaches are described and explained. This book contains 14 case studies. Companies and organizations represented in the case studies this year are:

| | |
|---|---|
| Aetna Financial Services | Modis Professional Services |
| Bell Atlantic | MASIE Center |
| Boeing | NJ Department of Labor |
| Cisco Systems | Park Avenue Bank |
| Conference Board | PriceWaterhouseCoopers |
| Dell Computer | QUALCOMM |
| Department of Defense | Rutgers University FMO |
| Gateway | Ryder Systems |
| GTE | Storage Technology |
| Hay/McBer | Time Warner AOL |
| Hewlett-Packard | US West |
| IBM | Visteon |
| International Association of Machinists | Volvo |
| International Space Station | Weyerhaeuser |
| McDonalds | Work In America Institute |
| Merck & Company | Xerox |

- **Research Summaries:** Many agencies, professional organizations, and companies engage in research projects that reflect the field of workplace learning. Results of such research often point toward new directions in policy and practice. In this book, 17 research studies are summarized; in some cases, sponsors have collaborated in doing studies. Throughout the book, numerous research studies have been referenced.

## THE TRAINER'S ALMANAC

*The Trainer's Almanac* is a book within a book, organized as a directory of various sources of particular interest to persons responsible for creating policies and programs that facilitate learning. It contains hundreds of names, addresses and telephone numbers, e-mail and Website addresses—approximately 1000 key citations. All these have been updated since the previous edition of the *Training & Development Yearbook*. The Almanac is your verified, one-stop reference for current listings of the most important information you need to know, presented in directory format.

Sections of the *The Trainer's Almanac* include listings of:

| | |
|---|---|
| • Professional Organizations | • Nonprofit Organizations |
| • Training Conferences, including a year 2001 calendar of 59 conferences | • Training Research and Reference Sources |
| | • Training Journals, Magazines, and Newsletters |
| • Worldwide Conference Centers | • Ratings of Training Websites |
| • Training for Trainers | |

## HOW TO GET A COPY OF AN ITEM CITED IN THIS YEARBOOK

Three major sources of information are easily accessible for getting reprints of articles and documents referenced in the *Abstracts, Articles, Case Studies,* and *Research Summaries* in this yearbook. These sources are:

- The publication or publisher of the cited item, whose addresses and telephone numbers are listed in the following several pages;

- Websites of publications from which sources are referenced;

- The Information Center of the American Society for Training and Development (ASTD), 1040 King Street, Box 1443, Alexandria, VA 2313, 703/683-8184; ASTD's Website is *www.astd.org.*

- The Information Center of the Society for Human Resource Management (SHRM), 1800 Duke Street, Alexandria, VA 22314; 800/283-SHRM; SHRM's Website is *www.shrm.org.*

Back issues of publications are usually available for a modest fee, and research services such as those provided by ASTD and SHRM charge a reprint fee based on the length of the record and the database from which it comes. Quantity reprints can be had at a discount through reprint offices of the publications from which they originate. Another source of training information, including some sources referenced in this *Training & Development Yearbook* is Lakewood Publication's training Website, *www.trainingsupersite.com.*

ASTD and SHRM maintain staff who can help you seek and find information. These two major online sources for published articles and documents in the broad field of training and development make available topics in areas such as learning organizations, individual learning, performance systems and supports, technologies to enhance learning, and methodologies for assessing needs, designing instruction, delivering training by whatever medium, and evaluating training organizations, systems, programs, courses, materials, and learning events. Customer service personnel, librarians, and technologists on staff can direct you to many kinds of resources and guide you through online searching for information related to what you read here in the pages of this yearbook. Public, college, and university librarians can also direct you to reprint services available locally. Books, of course, are available at libraries, through publishers listed here, at book stores, and online from amazon.com and Websites of publishers and megabookstores.

# ADDRESSES OF PUBLISHERS AND PUBLICATIONS USED AS SOURCES
## IN *TRAINING & DEVELOPMENT YEARBOOK 2001*

The 120 primary publishing sources listed here are in addition to approximately 100 different secondary sources referenced at the end of many article reprints in sections 1 through 5 of this *Yearbook*. Nearly 1,000 additional listings are included in section 6, "The Trainer's Almanac." This is the most comprehensive publication in the field, representing the ideas, practices, models, personalities, challenges, and opportunities in training and development in its evolution at the beginning of calendar year 2001.

**ACC Communications, Inc.**
245 Fischer Avenue B-2
Costa Mesa, CA 92626
714/751-1883

*Across the Board*
The Conference Board
845 Third Avenue
New York, NY 10022
212/759-0900

*Advanstar Communications Inc.*
131 W. First St.
Duluth, MN 55802
888/527-7008

**AMACOM**
P.O. Box 1026
Saranac Lake, NY 12983
518/891-5510

**American Management Association International**
1601 Broadway
New York, NY 10019
212/586-8100

**American Productivity & Quality Center (APQC)**
123 North Post Oak Lane
Houston, TX 77024
713/681-3705

**American Society for Training and Development (ASTD)**
1640 King St. Box 1443
Alexandria, VA 22313
703/683-8183

*ASTD 2000 International Comparison Report*
1640 King St., Box 1443
Alexandria, VA 22313
703/683-8183

*ASTD Learning Circuits* Webzine
www.learningcircuits.org

*ASTD 2000 Measurement Kit*
1640 King Street Box 1443
Alexandria, VA 22313
703/683-8183

*Atlantic Monthly*
77 N. Washington Street
Boston, MA 02114
617/854-7700

**Berett-Koehler Publishers, Inc.**
155 Montgomery St.
San Francisco, CA 94104
415/288-0260

*Berkshire Record*
21 Elm Street
Great Barrington, MA 01230
413/528-5380

**Bill Communications, Inc.**
Human Performance Group
50 South Ninth Street
Minneapolis, MN 55402
612/333-0471

*BNAC Communicator*
9439 Keywest Ave.
Rockville, MD 20850
800/233-6067

*Boston Globe*
135 Morrissey Blvd.
P.O. Box 2378
Boston, MA 02107
617/929-7900

*Brainstorm Dynamics*
12 Brocster Court, Ste. 200
Phoenix, MD 21131
410/592-9156

*Brill's Content*
521 Fifth Avenue
New York, NY 10175
212/824-1900

**Broadway Books**
A Division of Random House, Inc.
1540 Broadway
New York, NY 10036
www.broadwaybooks.com

*Bulletin to Management*
Bureau of National Affairs, Inc.
1231 25th St. NW
Washington, DC 20016

**Bureau of Labor Statistics**
U.S. Department of Labor
200 Constitution Ave. NW
Washington, DC 20210
202/606-7828

**Bureau of National Affairs, Inc.**
1231 25th St. NW
Washington, DC 20037
800/233-6067

*Business 2.0*
Imagine Media Inc.
150 North Hill Drive
Brisbane, CA 94005
415/468-4684

*Business Week*
1221 Avenue of the Americas
New York, NY 10020
800/635-1200

*BYTE*
CMP Media Inc.
300 Fifth Avenue
Waltham, MA 02154
781/487-7522

**Catalyst**
120 Wall Street
New York, NY 10005
212/514-7600

**Center for Creative Leadership (CCL)**
One Leadership Place
P.O. Box 26300
Greensboro, NC 27438
336/545-2810

*Christian Science Monitor*
One Norway Street
Boston, MA 02115
617/450-2317 (fax)

**Conference Board**
845 Third Avenue
New York, NY 10022
212/339-0290

*Continental*
Pohly & Partners
27 Melcher St., 2nd Floor
Boston, MA 02210
617/451-1700

**Corporate University Xchange Inc.**
381 Park Avenue South Suite 713
New York, NY 10016
212/213-8650

*Creative Training Techniques*
*Newsletter*
Bill Communications, Inc.
50 South Ninth Street
Minneapolis, MN 55402
612/328-4329

*Cyber Law Journal*
The New York Times on the Web
www.nytimes. com

*eCompany*
Time Inc.
Time & Life Building
Rockefeller Center
New York, NY 10020
www.ecompany.com

*Daily News*
450 W. 33rd Street
New York, NY 10001
www.nydailynews.com

*Distance Education Report*
Magna Publications Inc.
2718 Dryden Drive
Madison, WI 53704
800/433-0499

*Economist*
111 West 57th St.
New York, NY 10019
212/541-5730

*Educational Technology*
720 Palisade Avenue
Englewood Ciffs, NJ 07632
201/871-4008

**Educational Technology**
**Publications**
700 Palisade Avenue
Englewood Cliffs, NJ 07632
201/871-4007

*EDUCAUSE*
4772 Walnut St., Ste 206
Boulder, CO 80301
303/449-4430

*e-learning magazine*
201 Sandpointe Ave., Ste 600
Santa Ana, CA 92707
714/513-8400

*Fast Company*
77 North Washington Street
Boston, MA 02114-1927
617/973-0300

*Financial Times*
1330 Avenue of the Americas
New York, NY 10019
212/641-6500

*Foothills Trader*
P.O. Box 665
Torrington, CT 06790
860/693-2942

*Forbes*
60 Fifth Ave.
New York, NY 10011
800/888-9896

*Forbes ASAP*
Forbes Building
60 Fifth Avenue
New York, NY 10011
212/620-2421

*Fortune*
Time & Life Building
Rockefeller Center
New York, NY 10020
800/621-8000

**The Gallup Organization**
Lincoln, NE 68501
402/489-9000

*Generation21 Learning Systems*
1536 Cole Blvd., Ste. 250
Golden, CO 80401
888/601-1300

*George*
1633 Broadway, 41st Floor
New York, NY 10019
212/767-6100

*Global Workforce*
245 Fischer Ave. B-2
Costa Mesa, CA 92626
714/751-1883

**Harper Business/HarperCollins**
10 East 53rd Street
New York, NY 10022
212/207-7000

*Harvard Business Review*
60 Harvard Way
Boston, MA 02163
617/495-6192

**Harvard Business School Press**
60 Harvard Way
Boston, MA 02163
617/495-6800

*Harvard Management Update*
60 Harvard Way
Boston, MA 02163
800/668-6705

*HRMagazine*
606 N. Washington St.
Alexandria, VA 22314
703/548-3440

*Human Resource Development*
*Quarterly*
Jossey-Bass Publishers
350 Sansome Street
San Francisco, CA 94104
415/433-1767

*Human Resource Management*
John Wiley & Sons
939 Travis Rd.
Fort Collins, CO 80524
800/225-5945

*HR News*
Society for Human Resource
Management
606 N. Washington St.
Alexandria, VA 22314
703/548-3440

*Industry Report 2000*
Lakewood Publications,
*TRAINING* Magazine
50 South Ninth St.
Minneapolis, MN 55402
612/333-0471

**International Association**
**of Conference Centers (IACC)**
243 North Lindbergh Blvd., Suite 315
St. Louis, MO 63144
314/993-8575

**International Society for**
**Performance Improvement (ISPI)**
1300 L Street, NW, Ste. 1250
Washington, DC 20005
202/408-7969

*Intranet Report*
Ragan Communications
212 West Superior Avenue
Chicago, IL 60610
800/878-5331

*Issues and Observations*
Center for Creative Leadership
One Leadership Place, PO Box 26300
Greensboro, NC 27438
910/288-7210

**John Wiley and Sons**
605 Third Avenue
New York, NY 10158
212/850-6417

**Jossey-Bass Inc., Publishers**
350 Sansome Street
San Francisco, CA 94104
415/433-1740

**Jossey-Bass Pfeiffer**
350 Sansome Street
San Francisco, CA 94104
415/422-1740

*Journal of Instruction Delivery
Systems*
50 Culpeper St.
Warrenton, VA 22186
540/347-0055

*Journal of Interactive Instruction
Development*
50 Culpeper St.
Warrenton, VA 22186
540/347-0055

*Lakewood Report on Technology
for Learning Newsletter*
Bill Communications
50 South Ninth St.
Minneapolis, MN 55402
800/328-4329

*Leadership In Action*
Center for Creative Leadership (CCL)
One Leadership Place,
P.O. Box 26300
Greensboro, NC 27438
336/545-2810

**Learning Technology Institute**
50 Culpeper Street
Warrenton, VA 20186
540/347-0055

*Legal Report*
SHRM
1800 Duke Street
Alexandria, VA 22314
703/548-3440

*Leverage*
Pegasus Communications, Inc.
One Moody St.
Waltham, MA 02453
781/398-9700

*Management Review*
American Management Assn.
International
Publications Division
Box 319, Trudeau Road
Saranac Lake, NY 12983
800/262-9699

**McGraw-Hill Companies**
1221 Avenue of the Americas
New York, NY 10020
212/512-6285

*MIT Sloan Management Review*
Room E60–100
77 Massachusetts Avenue
Cambridge, MA 02139
617/258-7485

**MIT Press**
Massachusett Institute of Technology
Cambridge, MA 02142
617/253-1000

**Mobiltape Co., Inc.**
25061 W. Ave. Stanford Ste. 70
Valencia, CA 91355
805/295-0504

*MOSAICS*
SHRM
1800 Duke St.
Alexandria, VA 22314
703/548-3440

*Ms*
20 Exchange Place
New York, NY 10005
800/234-4486

*Native Peoples*
5333 N. 7th St., Ste. C-224
Phoenix, AZ 85014
602/265-4855

**NewsScan Inc.**
P.O. Box 200549
Austin, TX 78720
512/335-2286

*Newsweek*
251 West 57th St.
New York, NY 10019
800/631-1040

*New Yorker*
20 West 43rd Street
New York, NY 10036
212/286-5400

*New York Times*
229 West 43rd St.
New York, NY 10036
212/556-1234

*New York Times Magazine*
229 West 43rd Street
New York, NY 10036
212/556-1234

*Organizational Dynamics*
American Management Assn.
nternational
1601 Broadway
New York, NY 10019
518/891-5510

*PC Magazine*
One Park Avenue
New York, NY 10016
212/503-5255

*PC World*
International Data Group
501 2nd Street #600
San Francisco, CA 94107
415/243-0500

*Performance Improvement (P&I)*
International Society for Performance
Improvement (ISPI)
1300 L Street, NW
Washington, DC 20005
202/408-7969

*Performance Improvement
Quarterly (PIQ)*
Learning Systems Institute in
cooperation with International
Society for Performance
Improvement (ISPI)
205 Dodd Hall R-19
Florida State University
Tallahassee, FL 32306
202/408-7969

*Performance In Practice*
ASTD Newsletter for Forums
1640 King Street Box 1443
Alexandria, VA 22313-2043
703/683-8135

**Pfeiffer & Company**
8517 Production Ave.
San Diego, CA 92121
619/578-5900

**Prentice Hall**
240 Frisch Court
Paramus, NJ 07652
201/909-6418

*Publishers Weekly*
245 W. 17th St.
New York, NY 10011
212/463-6758

*Quality Digest*
40 Declaration Drive Suite 100-C
Chico, CA 95973
916/893-4095

*Quality Progress*
American Society for Quality (ASQ)
P.O. Box 3005
Milwaukee, WI 53201
414/272-8575

*Ragan's Strategic Training Report*
Lawrence Ragan Communications
Inc.
316 N. Michigan Ave., Ste. 300
Chicago, IL 60601
312/960-4408

*Reflections,
The SOL Journal*
MIT Press
Five Cambridge Center
Cambridge, MA 02142

*Shoppers Guide*
35 Bridge Street
Great Barrington, MA 01230
413/528-0095

*Smart Business*
50 Beale St. 13th Floor
San Francisco, CA 94105
425/430-1663

**Society for Applied Learning Technology (SALT)**
50 Culpeper Street
Warrenton, VA 22186
540/347-0075

**Society for Human Resource Management (SHRM)**
606 North Washington St.
Alexandria, VA 22314
703/548-3440

*Soundview Executive Book Summaries*
3 Pond Lane
Middlebury VT 05753
802/453-4062

*Strategy & Business*
Booz-Allen & Hamilton
101 Park Avenue
New York, NY 10178
617/523-7047

*Systems Thinker*
Pegasus Communications
One Moody Street
Waltham, MA 02453
781/398-9700

*TechLearn TRENDS*
Online newsletter
The MASIE Center
www.techlearn.com

*Tech Trends*
Association for Educational
Communications and Technology
(AECT)
1205 Vermont Avenue NW Ste 820
Washington, DC 20005
202/347-7834

*Technical Training* (*Click.Learn*)
American Society for Training
and Development
1640 King Street Box 1443
Alexandria, VA 22313
703/683-8100

*Technology Cybertimes*
The New York Times On The Web
www.nytimes.com

*TIME*
Time & Life Building
Rockefeller Center
New York, NY 10020
212/586-1212

*Training & Development*
American Society for Training
and Development (ASTD)
1640 King St. Box 1443
Alexandria, VA 22313
703/683-8100

*Training Directors' Forum Newsletter*
Bill Communications, Inc.
50 South Ninth Street
Minneapolis, MN 55402
612/328-4329

*TRAINING Magazine*
Bill Communications, Inc.
50 South Ninth St.
Minneapolis, MN 55402
612/333-4471

*Training Research Journal,
An International Journal*
Educational Technology
Publications
700 Palisade Avenue
Englewood Cliffs, NJ 07632
800/952-BOOK

*Union Labor Report*
Bureau of National Affairs, Inc.
P.O. Box 40949
Washington, DC 20016
800/372-1033

**United States Bureau
of the Census**
U.S. Department of Commerce
14th Street, between Constitution
and Pennsylvania Aves., NW
Washington, DC 20233
301/457-2794

**United States Department of Labor**
200 Constitution Ave. NW
Washington, DC 20210
202/219-9148

**United States Government
Printing Office**
Superintendent of Documents
North Capitol and H Streets NW
Washington, DC 20401
202/512-1800

*USA Today*
99 W. Hawthorne Avenue
Valley Stream, NY 11580
516/568-9191

*U.S. News & World Report*
2400 N Street NW
Washington, DC 20037
202/955-2000

*Wall Street Journal*
Dow Jones & Company
200 Liberty St.
New York, NY 10281
800/843-0008

*Washington Post*
1150 15th Street, NW
Washington, DC 20071-9200
202/334-6000

*Weekly Standard*
News America Publishing Inc.
1211 Avenue of the Americas
New York, NY 10036
800/983-7600

**Welfare to Work Partnership**
1250 Connecticut Avenue NW
Washington, DC 20036
202/955-3005

*Workforce*
ACC Communications
245 Fischer Ave., B-2
Costa Mesa, CA 92626
714/751-1883

**Work In America Institute**
700 White Plains Road
Scarsdale, NY 10583
914/472-9600

*Workplace Visions*
SHRM
1800 Duke Street
Alexandria, VA 22314
800/283-7476

*Worth*
575 Lexington Ave.
New York, NY 10022
212/751-4550

*Yahoo! News*
ZDNet
www.zdnet.com

# 1

# TRAINING MANAGEMENT

# INTRODUCTION: TRAINING MANAGEMENT

Those responsible for managing training at the start of year 2001 are pushed in many directions by the speed of change. Businesses demand leadership, especially in all of the human resources areas as new work proliferates, work and workers are truly global, contract workers and telecommuters thrive, and everyone at work expects to continue to learn on the job. Training managers have to figure out how to efficiently and effectively provide and facilitate learning opportunities for a workforce "built to flip" and not "built to last." The biggest challenge for trainers is to set up individuals, content, equipment, and facilities so that those who need and want to learn at work and from work can do just that. Networks, teams, and communities of practice are the concepts and structures to deal with—collaboration is the word of the year.

### LEADERSHIP FOR LEARNING

American business has lived with the fallout of mergers and downsizing for nearly a decade. Those commenting on the nature of the workplace speak of transformation—restructuring of production processes, consumer-driven sales decisions, online partnering with suppliers and even competitors to shorten supply cycle times, expectation of stock options, incentives for creativity, and responsibility for self-direction in career development and in learning. In management, "bossism" is out; in training, the "sage on the stage" is slowly exiting into the wings, not to be lost forever, but rather to be on call for collaborative performances with Internet technologies.

The data are instructive. A *Business Week* column on Economic Trends suggests that the new math is "Fire 3, Add 5," meaning that for every three employees fired, five new ones are hired (March 13, 2000, p. 28). *The Wall Street Journal* of this same date cited an American Management Association study that 36 percent of nearly 2000 companies contacted reported creating new jobs at the same time they were firing, a figure up from 27 percent 12 months before. The front page article also suggested that many companies are hiring fewer but more expensive employees than the ones laid off, clearly seeking workers with Internet or e-commerce skills. The *Journal* resurrected economist Joseph Schumpeter's 1930's term, "creative destruction," by which he described the capitalist phenomenon of reinvention of economic institutions (like workplaces) as a positive engine of growth. Patrick Barta, Staff Reporter, suggests that perhaps layoff-and-hiring is management's new tool for efficiency (p. 16) ("Zero-Sum Gain" by Patrick Barta in *The Wall Street Journal*, March 13, 2000, pp. 1;16).

Training managers are challenged to develop and evaluate the skills, competencies, and performance of a newly transient and elusive workforce. *SmartBusiness.com* magazine in the July 2000 edition reported that "professional development (94%)" ranks at the top of the list of thirteen familiar perks that "smart" companies provide to keep employees happy, that 94% figure being well above the other biggies of "relocation benefits (68%)" and "paid maternity leave (53%)" (p. 92). We provide some understanding of the leadership challenges and offer help for the training manager caught in the throes of transformation in this sub-section on Leadership for Learning.

### KNOWLEDGE MANAGEMENT

Access and quality seem to be the overarching issues in the management of corporate knowledge. The morning television program, *CBS This Morning*, on July 4, 2000 reported that there are now more than 20 million American consumers online. In my own small consumer universe, this year I have seen the newspapers and magazines that I read offer discounts and actually free information for going online for news and editorial commentary, and catalogs I shop from offer bargains available only online. The March 2000 issue of *Fast Company* magazine reported that the Internet reached as many Americans in its first six years as the telephone did in its first four decades, and that 49 percent of online users believe that Internet news is actually more accurate than news from traditional news sources (p. 215).

Yet, the digital divide still grows wider between knowledge "haves" and "have nots," largely along racial and economic lines, according to a report in the April 2000 issue of *TRAINING Magazine*. The report describes a recently formed Congressional Commission on Web-based Education which has, among other charges, the challenges of reorienting Federal policy regarding Internet access and of closing this digital divide. Teacher training from elementary school through university-level faculties is high on the Commission's agenda (p. 26). Corporations also have a major job to do in assuring access to and quality of knowledge resources. Training managers are often well-positioned to fulfill major management functions to make this happen. Our sub-section on Knowledge Management gives you some background and help in sorting out the issues in managing your company's knowledge resources.

## REFOCUSING WORK FOR LEARNING

This year past has seen a marked increase in the use of the term "learning" in place of the term "training." Trainers are encouraged to think of what they do as more than just skill development or providing information; that is, trainers need to think of their jobs as facilitators of learning. We see more and more books, articles, and research studies that urge workers to be continuously vigilant learners, to be self-directed learners, and to look to their work itself as a source of new insights and skills. There is a renewed focus on experience as a source of learning, and on the exciting learning that is possible when learners become teachers as they learn. There's a renewed focus on the value of experimentation and of lessons to be learned from failure. Training managers have an important new role in restructuring and refocusing work so that it becomes an integral part of a pervasive learning culture. Building a sustainable "new economy" engine is the challenge. Many people believe that learning is this engine.

## WHAT MANAGERS NEED TO KNOW
### ABOUT E-LEARNING

During the year 2000, I have been keeping a tally of e-words that appeared in newspapers and magazines that came across my desk. This tally is many things: an indication of the breadth and growth of the dotcom universe, an inventive commentary on the flexibility of the English language, the pervasiveness of the e-vocabulary in our business communications, and perhaps an indication of the challenges of e-learning across the range of these e-nouns, e-adjectives,

e-adverbs, and e-verbs. One of the most interesting things is the frequency of new e-terms that appeared each week during year 2000. This is a new phenomenon as we enter year 2001.

Most of all, the first and now most familiar e-word, "e-mail," is now being spelled without the hyphen—"email"—and the *Wired Style* book says that's "an unmistakable cultural shift" (p. 75). In the introduction to this gem of a little book, the authors say that ". . . we write geek and we write street. We insist on accuracy and literacy, but we celebrate the colloquial." They call for writing to reflect the vernacular of the reader (*Wired Style: Principles of English Usage in the Digital Age* by Constance Hale and Jessie Scanlon, New York: Broadway Books, 1999, p. 11). Unmistakably, the content and context of our business culture is reflected in this tally of terms: These e-words provide a mirror of online enterprise and a glimpse of how much there is to learn in the e-world, and, of course, how much training managers need to be involved in it. I even found a word, "*m* e-business," defined as the *m*anagement of e-business; and, this year, we saw e-bay become a new term and a new American cultural icon too, spreading around the globe as I write this. The weary training manager, beset with change from all sides, will be tempted to pick the e-words, "e-mania," "e-stress" and "e-whatever" from my tally as you contemplate the e-learning challenge. It's geek, but it's also street.

Here's my list:

| | |
|---|---|
| e-activity | e-coaching |
| e-bay | e-collaboration |
| e-bibles | e-college |
| e-books | e-commerce |
| e-bookstores | e-company |
| e-boys | e-conomy |
| e-brand | e-courses |
| e-broker | e-date |
| e-buddies | e-delivery |
| e-bulletin | e-ecology |
| e-business | e-education |
| e-car | e-enablers |
| e-care | e-envoy |
| e-centives | e-exchange |
| e-charity | e-failures |
| e-chemicals | e-fairness |
| e-citizen | e-format |
| e-classes | e-franchise |
| e-cliner | e-funeral |

| | | | |
|---|---|---|---|
| e-gadflies | e-market | e-priorities | e-stories |
| e-gang | e-marketplace | e-procurement | e-strategy |
| e-government | e-meeting | e-productivity | e-stress |
| e-gutenberg | e-merchant | e-profits | e-tailing |
| e-health | e-minister | e-pub | e-technologies |
| e-innovation | e-news | e-publishing | e-technology |
| e-integration | e-nnovation | e-quipped | e-think |
| e-journal | e-novice | e-raider | e-time |
| e-learning | e-opportunity | e-rate | e-titles |
| e-lessons | e-orientation | e-retailing | e-toys |
| e-life | e-partner | e-service | e-trade |
| e-line | e-pay | e-slush | e-venture |
| e-listen | e-people | e-snafu | e-vents |
| e-lit | e-performance | e-sniffle | e-vote |
| e-loan | e-pinions | e-society | e-way |
| e-loyalty | e-pledge | e-solutions | e-whatever |
| email | e-politics | e-speed | e-world |
| e-mail | e-presentations | e-standards | e-zines |
| e-mania | | | |

These e-words and this new e-vocabulary may be indicative of the typical learner's exposure and sensitivity to an e-world; and to be sure, today's training manager must be thinking and communicating in this same language.

A further, and more specific, indication of the issues facing training managers is the list of "content focus" of The Masie Center's Tech-Learn + 2000 World e-Learning CONGRESS in Orlando, Florida in November 2000. This list of topics is selected from a longer list reported in the July 18 online newsletter from The Masie Center, known as *TechLearn TRENDS* :

- e-Learning: Developing a Corporate Strategy

- e-Learning: Blending e-Learning and Classroom Training

- Staffing the Learning Function in the Digital Age

- Learner Acceptance: If We Build It. . . . Will They Come?

- Marketing e-Learning

- Standards for e-Learning: Reusable and Sharable Content

- Wall Street in e-Learning "Bets."

What managers need to know about e-learning is, above all, that it is here to stay: It is part of an e-trend throughout American culture and it needs to become part of the training manager's way of doing business.

COLLABORATION: THE NEW BUZZ

The Ford Motor Company was all over the business press in year 2000 with its clean sweep ideas for collaboration with other auto makers regarding parts supply. Words like dramatic, bold plunge, transform, innovative, and consumer stimulation were frequently seen in articles about Ford's Internet strategy. In traditional Motown and elsewhere, it's called Ford's "Model E." *FORBES* magazine, July 17, 2000, describes a "B2B" (business to business) company conceived by Ford executive Alice Miles called "Covisint" which stands for collaboration, vision, and integrity (pp. 31–34). In this company, executives from Ford, GM, DaimlerChrysler, and Renault-Nissan collaborate with more than 50,000 suppliers to reap huge savings in procurement and distribution of auto parts. Even outsourced manufacturing could be in Ford's future; executives there predict that by 2010, Ford will look like Cisco (p. 31). Trainers need to be imagining what kinds of training the new Ford's employees will need, to be observing and talking with Ford visionaries, and to be ready with irresistible learning opportunities to match the excitement of Ford's new corporate directions. Ford as an e-business is nearly incomprehensible to those of us who are wedded to our red Ford F-150 pickups!

Another sort of Internet-enabled business strategy is that of the American Management

Association's *Management Review* monthly magazine. In March 2000, Editor Barbara Ettore wrote a "Farewell Address" to readers, citing that the demise of the print version of the magazine was part of AMA's internet strategy. AMA was becoming a Web-based membership organization, and the 89-year old magazine as we knew it would no longer exist. A new kind of collaborative and interactive management news and information environment was becoming the membership context of AMA. Ettore pointed out that *Management Review* was older than IBM, Yankee Stadium, and Mickey Mouse (p. 1). Trainers need to think about teaching learners about information—the "social life of information"—its features, evaluating its quality and usefulness, and the refinements of accessing and sharing it. As Ford's President of Internet Strategy says, "It's all about redistribution of assets, capital, and competitive advantage" (*FORBES, op. cit.,* p. 31).

One example from government is also instructive. As of July 1, 2000, the former Job Training Partnership Act (JTPA) was repealed. The JTPA, which so many trainers became involved with, was a welcome crutch in helping young workers and adults in transition adjust to new working schedules and values. As its name implied, JTPA was heavy on training and education, and on the partnering between educational institutions, especially community colleges, and workplaces. In its place is a new Workforce Investment Act (Public Law 105–220), key features of which are Individual Training Accounts and One-Stop Centers for information about job training, education, and employment services. The idea of a single center located in a neighborhood is an idea that capitalizes on collaboration and community: Information and people in proximity to each other, both facili-

tating the individual learner's self-direction regarding worklife.

Trainers have always been good at dealing with groups of learners, and now have a wide experience in facilitating the work of teams. As year 2001 unfolds, we can expect to see new kinds of challenges among all sectors of learners based on the foundation of collaboration—challenges in all of the familiar training functions of management, needs assessment, design, delivery, and evaluation. Overlaying all of this is the challenge of negotiating the split between "clicks" and "bricks," the new economy which we like but aren' sure of and the old ways we know that work. We need to help workers avoid the demoralizing and destructive get-rich-quick-and-get-out startup culture of entitlement that might be good for a few individuals but not good for sustaining a work ethic to support the common good.

I went to a year 2000 Independence Day Celebration in a small New England town settled in 1765. The clergyman who invoked the blessing of the Almighty on the gathering said in his prayer, "Bless our land with honorable industry, sound learning, and pure manners." Although seeming perhaps rather regional and "New England" in tone, his sentiments sum up where we are in our needs for collaborative endeavor. "The Common" is still a foundation of American life, and its strength is surely tested and stretched by new ideas and new technologies in support of collaboration. Both Presidential candidates, Al Gore and George W. Bush, articulated their visions of "the common good" in their fall 2000 campaigning.

Training managers play a pivotal role in defining the new "common" and in making learning the critical process for "the common's" continued viability.

# 1A. LEADERSHIP FOR LEARNING

## RESEARCH SUMMARY

## MANCHESTER'S SURVEY OF LEADERSHIP TRAINING

*Editor's Comment*: Manchester Inc. is a consulting company that focuses on leadership training. Their recent survey of results of approximately 200 respondents is reproduced here to introduce this sub-section on Leadership for Learning. Like many other organizations doing training surveys this year, Manchester found that leadership development was high on the list of workers' needs for training. Other "soft skills" high on everyone's list, at above the 50% response rate, were: management skills training (51%), teamwork (52%), managing change (52%), communication skills training (53%), and interpersonal skills training (59%). Leadership development was highest, at 65%. Notes with the survey results suggest that leadership development tops the list because of today's tight labor market and the difficulty of recruiting workers. The full survey report follows.

## MANCHESTER® 2000 SURVEY OF LEADERSHIP TRAINING

### ABOUT THE SURVEY

*T*he Manchester Survey of Leadership Training is a broad-based examination of the soft skills training expenditures, effectiveness measurement practices, and training needs of organizations across several industries.

Soft skills training includes areas such as leadership development, executive coaching, sales, teamwork, interpersonal skills, and public speaking. In contrast, hard skills training includes areas such as computer skills and writing skills. About 200 organizations nationwide responded to the survey.

The survey was conducted by Manchester Inc., a leading career management and management consulting firm. Manchester is a subsidiary of Modis Professional Services Inc. (NYSE: MPS), a global provider of information technology and professional business services.

### SURVEY HIGHLIGHTS

- More than half (51%) of organizations surveyed expect their training budgets to increase in 2000.

- Leadership development is the No. 1 training need of employees today, according to 65% of respondents. The other top five training needs include interpersonal skills (selected by 59%), communication skills (53%), and managing change and teamwork (both 52%).

- The features of training programs that organizations most desire are a participatory instruction method (selected by 73% of respondents), followed by advance identification of trainees' needs (71%), and a focus on current business issues (61%).

- Middle managers receive the largest portion of an organization's training budget, followed by supervisors and customer service staff. Organizations spend the least amount on training senior management, followed by support staff.

## SURVEY FINDINGS

### *Training Investment Trend*

51% of organizations expect their investment in training to increase in 2000:

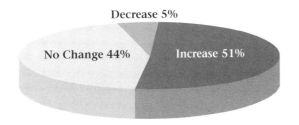

### *Soft Skills in Greatest Demand*

Soft skills in greatest demand within organizations today are:

| | |
|---|---|
| Leadership Development | 65% |
| Interpersonal Skills Training | 59% |
| Communication Skills Training | 53% |
| Managing Change | 52% |
| Teamwork | 52% |
| Management Skills Training | 51% |
| Problem-Solving | 45% |
| Customer Service | 41% |
| Retaining Employees | 40% |
| Creativity & Innovation | 36% |
| Doing More With Less | 35% |
| Executive Coaching Skills | 34% |
| Breakthrough Thinking | 33% |
| Decision-Making | 28% |
| Managing Stress | 25% |
| Time Management | 24% |
| Diversity | 21% |

*Percentage of Cases*

Leadership development is the number one training need of employees today because it is becoming more difficult to recruit people in this tight labor market.

Organizations have become more interested in developing employees they already have on board and providing them with the training they need to take on additional responsibility, such as training in interpersonal skills, communication skills, managing change, and teamwork.

### *Most Important Features of Soft Skills Training Programs*

Features found to be most important in soft skills training programs are:

| | |
|---|---|
| Highly Participatory Instruction | 73% |
| Identifying Learner Needs In Advance | 71% |
| Focus on Current Business Issues | 61% |
| Tailored Design | 53% |
| Outstanding Results | 52% |
| Low Cost | 44% |
| Method of Measuring Impact (ROI) | 42% |
| Tested, Sound Content | 36% |
| Time to Apply What Is Learned | 36% |
| Follow-up Coaching | 32% |
| Follow-up Sessions | 29% |

*Percentage of cases*

### *Organizational Levels Receiving Training*

Middle managers receive the largest portion of an organization's training budget, according to 76% of respondents, followed by supervisors (71%) and customer service (65%).

| | |
|---|---|
| **76%** | **Middle Managers** |
| **71%** | **Supervisors** |
| **65%** | **Customer Service** |
| **22%** | **Support** |
| **15%** | **Senior Management** |

# ARTICLE REPRINT

## NOT YOUR FATHER'S CTO

*Editor's Comment*: During year 2000, we heard a lot about transformation. Other similar-sounding words from the recent management past—like restructuring, or reengineering—have given way to *Transformation*, a term that carries with it something more than matrices and flowcharts, hard numbers and Wall Street. True, we've seen a lot of CEO-type terms in recent years: Chief Operating Officer or COO, Chief Information Officer or CIO, and Chief Technology Officer or CTO—all representative of the way things worked in the last decade or so. Now, a new kind of CTO or Chief Transformation Officer seems to be cropping up in corporate America, joining the ranks of Chief Knowledge Officers and Chief Learning Officers to reflect a newer kind of leadership.

## THE TRANSFORMATION OFFICER

### *by Marlene Piturro*

One describes himself as "the nerdiest engineer you would ever want to know." Another has a doctorate in organizational behavior, has been recruited into several Fortune 100 companies and is now working his magic at a multinational corporation. Yet another is a businesswoman with solid operational skills working in a small, HR-type department whose reach extends throughout a major retailing operation.

Although their actual titles vary, all three are high-ranking executives in their companies' effort to manage "transformation," working out of departments with strange-sounding names like the office of transformation, change enablement and the more mundane learning center. Their job is to radically rethink and remake either the entire organization or its business processes, corporate culture, pieces of the company that don't work well or all of the above.

This breed of executive is a relatively new addition to top management teams in U.S. companies. Transformation officers (TOs), chief transformation officers (CTOs) and similarly titled executives began to appear on the corporate scene in the early to mid-1990s as companies became determined to manage the change process itself rather than just its effects. The TO title and department are not yet widespread, but they do pop up in Fortune 500 companies and large consultancies. Nearly all of these departments are small, mingling fewer than 30 HR and operations people.

In some cases, the CTO role is occupied by the CEO or COO, in recognition of its importance to the organization. Intel CEO Andy Grove is one such person, says Edgardo Pappacena, partner in charge of the change enablement practice at Arthur Andersen Consulting, Miami, Florida. "Grove realizes that the job of transformation officer is never done," he says. "He creates the capability to change faster, to constantly revitalize the organization and to sustain the changes so that the organization is self-renewing."

Other transformation officers come from an elite group of highly skilled and highly paid outsiders brought in by recruiters to engineer a trans-

## What Makes a Transformation Officer?

Chief transformation officers are still a rare breed, so companies considering the option must look for the right mix of skills and experience.

The CTO candidate should have two major skill sets, according to Ed Mullen, national health practice leader at executive recruiter Korn Ferry International's Los Angeles office. One is a thorough understanding of strategy, including an ability to envision three or four paths to the same goal and juggle those options mentally until the right path becomes evident. The other set of skills is tactical—the operational background needed to get results quickly and decisively.

As if that weren't enough, the CTO must be a true "people" person and great communicator, someone with dazzling interpersonal skills who can calm the anxieties of those threatened by change. He should also be politically astute so as to mobilize the resources to get the job done.

"Visionary, strategist, communicator and doer, a transformation officer has to be all of the above," says Mullen. He explains that a transformation officer must achieve a huge change of high magnitude, and that takes a serious combination of skill sets to accomplish. Companies usually have to ante up an additional 10 percent to 25 percent in compensation when hiring a COO or CEO who also will serve as the CTO.

Sometimes a CEO is a de facto CTO. Edgardo Pappacena, partner in charge of the change enablement practice at Arthur Andersen Consulting, Miami, Florida, cites Intel CEO Andy Grove as one such person. "Grove realizes that the job of [the] transformation officer is never done. He creates the capability to change faster, to constantly revitalize the organization and to sustain the changes so that the organization is self-renewing," says Pappacena. The very model of a modern transformation officer.     —M.P.

formation. If they win, they have a shot at the top spot. Lose and they pick up their marbles and go elsewhere in search of transformation and a chance to become CEO. Still other CTOs are drawn to or even create the job internally, sometimes moving from a base within operations or HR to create an office of transformation.

### THE BIG PICTURE

If there's one thing CTOs have in common, it's a high tolerance for managing the uncertainties embedded in any significant organizational change. While the origins of the term *corporate transformation* are vague, the consensus is that it means enterprisewide change, as opposed to less sweeping interventions in areas such as organizational dynamics or the quality of work life.

When looking at transformation officers, what emerges is a picture of visionaries with their shirt sleeves rolled up. These are people who can see a company's Promised Land, write the road map to get there and herd the flock in the right direction.

Now two CTOs handle the complex challenge of transformation in exactly the same way, however, and they begin their interventions from different places as well. Some start from the unenviable position of the burning platform in a company so threatened by industry forces that it must either change or die. Others work with enlightened senior management, led by a CEO who sees the company as a living system that must change to stay competitive. Another group recognizes that the company's pace of change is glacial and that it needs to change, even though top management isn't sure how.

Business consultants such as Robert Miles of Corporate Transformation Resources in Boston popularized the concept of transformation officers in the mid-90s. IN 1993–94, Miles helped the Southern Co., a newly deregulated utility company headquartered in Atlanta, transform itself from an inefficient monopoly into a marketplace competitor. In *Leading Corporate Transformation* (Jossey-Bass, 1997), Miles says that in the early to mid-90s, companies such as Shell Oil, General Electric, Sears, Motorola, Xerox, Lucent, Corning and National Semiconductor bought into the notion that transformative leaders were key to the change process. They created "departments of transformation" (or similar departments named to fit their corporate culture) headed by a CTO. This person's primary job was to identify what needed to be changed, articulate why transformation was needed in a compelling vision, and generate organizational commitment to carry it through.

The ascendance of a transformation officer in a big company is a signal to shareholders that it's moving at Internet rather than industrial speed, according to Larraine Segil, a Los Angeles-based change consultant and author of *Intelligent Business Alliances* (Times Business, 1996). Calling the CTO position "an extremely hard job to fill well," Segil advises companies to look for someone who has proven skills in conflict resolution, is comfortable with a diverse workforce and has guided or been near the top of a successful turnaround or reengineering effort. The CTO must be a consensus builder who tries to create a business environment where people want to work.

## NEXT STOP

In many ways, transformation begins where reengineering, a turnaround or a merger or acquisition leaves off. While reengineering and M&As aim to maximize a company's cost-efficiencies, the transformation officer follows up on that change by asking "What's next?" and trying to take the company there.

Jerome Adams, chief learning officer at Shell Oil Co. in Woodlands, Texas [*www.shell.com*], is mentioned frequently as an exemplary chief transformation officer—"beyond wonderful," says one change management consultant. With a PhD in organizational behavior and several corporate transformations under his belt, Adams was recruited by Shell in 1995 after it had already undergone one major transformation under a CEO who then left. Although he functions as a CTO, Adams is more comfortable with the title of chief learning officer.

Before his arrival, Shell's transformation effort focused on redefining the company following a severe downturn in the early '90s when crude oil prices dropped. The company's poor financial performance was "inexcusable," according to Adams, and it went through massive downsizings in '92–93 and reengineering that made it competitive. Now, in better times, Adams' transformation role is to energize a leaner company that must mesh cultures with its international partner, Royal Dutch Oil.

Bridging the gap between Shell's organizational change goals and how they play out for each employee, Adams sees transformation as a passion, something that infects an employee and is then transmitted to others. "I want employees at every level to feel safe, that they can discuss undiscussables, set personal change agendas, be vulnerable and authentic," he says.

In addition to the massive change Shell is now coping with because of the 1998 merger of its U.S. downstream assets with those of Texaco and Saudi Aramco, Adams cites a humbler example of transformation: In this case, a small group of gas station operators and distributors were unsure of the business rationale for operating convenience stores at their stations. Pumping gas was what they knew and felt comfortable with. Milk and cappuccino sales were not.

"I first had to convince the retailers to focus on this issue as a key business activity," says Adams. "Then we learned how to track the sales of convenience store items using database technology, so that the operators could see the relationship between both parts of the business. Eventually, we got 8,000 gas station owners to understand how to see the convenience stores as a vital part of the business."

When transformation succeeds in one part of the organization, the CTO sees to it that it spreads. "Maybe we'll do a business transformation with 30 people, who become consultants/coaches to other business teams," Adams says. "We celebrate our success as it spreads from Texas to Manassas to Los Angeles." He also recommends that executives see transformation as a journey and recognize that change must be delivered on the run to ensure that a company maintains a competitive edge. In addition, create a safe space that gives people the freedom to innovate and to fail.

## THE PLATFORM OF CHANGE

When CTOs are given the resources to effect transformation, the results can be impressive. One reason is that the position is high enough up on the organizational ladder to have a broad vision of what needs to be changed and what the company must do to successfully transform itself.

Even so, transformation officers have their work cut out for them in companies with a long history and an even longer institutional memory of how things are supposed to be done. Theo Bell, director of worldwide cultural transformation at Lucent Microelectronics in Allentown, Pennsylvania [*www.lucent.com*], volunteered for the transformation assignment about two years ago. "I got tired of hearing customers say we love your products but we hate doing business with you," says the self-described "nerdy engineer."

Lucent's 120-year-old problem was AT&T's corporate culture. After AT&T spun off Bell Labs, which then became Lucent, the old culture was much harder to change than the company name. According to Bell, the blasé response to customers was tolerable when Lucent sold nearly all of its products to parent-company AT&T. But 70 percent of Lucent's business is now external, and that attitude won't do in an environment where competition reigns. Lucent was on the burning platform of change.

Although Lucent Microelectronics has a formal, companywide global transformation program, Bell eschews it in favor of microtransformation carried out by high-performance transformation teams. These teams devise ways to deliver service that will delight rather than antagonize the customer and are preauthorized to work together for 90 days.

"Generally, there are hundreds of these ad hoc transformation teams of four to seven people operating at all times. I work with them to help the change agent and the idea generators on whatever they want to do," Bell says. If the transformation team gets stuck and can't complete its work in 90 days, he assigns a coach to work with them for two more weeks. "They either effectuate the transformation or disband," he concludes.

Jane Floyd, director of transformation issues at Sears, Roebuck & Co. in Hoffman Estates, Illinois [*www.sears.com*], seems just as comfortable as Bell working with people who will commit to transformation in a company with an old culture. Sears' touchstone for transforming its retail stores is "goalsharing," a term which suggests that the route to higher revenues is for staffers to rally around the idea of good customer service.

"Goalsharing is optional and starts at the senior level, with buy-in from a regional vice president," notes Floyd. Her job, and those of the four others in the transformation department drawn from HR, market research and operations, is to tailor the goalsharing concept to each business unit and "to develop the business rationale for change."

Sears' transformation officers, spearheaded by Vice President Gary Bosak, act as business coaches by helping the units set goals, increase business literacy, sharpen communications skills, deal with employee skills and resistance, and figure out how to work on the transformation process while work continues to get done. "It's not rocket science," says Floyd, who has been doing this for more than four years. "Still, we have to be sensitive to all sorts of leadership styles and directions. A leadership style can't be mandated, and we help people accomplish their goals in ways that are comfortable to them."

Some CTOs have such a clear vision of transformation that they go to great lengths to make it real. Gary LeClair, founding partner of LeClair Ryan, a Richmond, Virginia, law firm, decided to transform the way he and like-minded lawyers practiced their profession. "In 1985, we decided to invent a new type of law firm. It wouldn't be militaristic or hierarchical. It wouldn't be driven by money, success and the fast track."

Armed with this notion, LeClair created a democratic structure in which 50 out of 90 partners (called "shareholders") would have one vote on each issue they consider. Compensation for all lawyers is set by consensus, for example. Each lawyer writes a one-page goal statement for the year that includes how many hours he or she wants to work and how much he or she needs to earn. The goal statements are made into a book for all to review, making comments if they feel someone's compensation should go up or down. Work/family balance and volunteerism are part of the mix, and compensation is adjusted to reflect these activities.

Consensus has led to some decisions the CTO marvels at, such as mandatory unscheduled drug testing for all lawyers (but not other employees) and casual dress in the office on Fridays only. "I facilitate the process and decision making, and then I have to live with it," he adds.

When asked why he chose to be the firm's CTO, LeClair says: "I like it because there's no road map. We have to constantly refine our decision-making process so that it works."

## Casebook: South Africa

Contemplating transformation from the security of a U.S. corporate office is one thing. Being propelled into transformation when political, social and economic forces are all impinging on an organization is quite another.

Even before the institution of apartheid officially ended in 1990, faculty, students and community activists at the University of Port Elizabeth in South Africa [*UPE-www.upe.ac.za*] vowed to transform the institution from a closed system to a democratic, multicultural university that would be accessible to all South Africans. UPE's chief transformation officer, Professor Andre Havenga, offers some insights into how that occurred.

UPE started its transformation effort in 1987, three years before apartheid was dismantled. "It became clear to us that the credibility of South African universities would not in the future depend exclusively on the academic standards they upheld in teaching and research. It was also going to be determined by perceptions about their social structure, organizational culture and overall commitment to redress social and regional reconstruction," says Havenga.

UPE began by developing closer relationships with the Broad Democratic Movement (BDM), which consisted of numerous political, social and nongovernmental organizations. UPE and BDM had to break down decades of apartheid to address the urgent need for change, and they placed great importance on the process design.

Havenga helped form a Joint Advisory Forum between UPE and BDM, but this entity soon failed because it did not have real negotiating power to implement changes. Havenga disbanded the forum following the campus unrest subsequent to the assassination of Chris Hani, a political dissident.

With a vacuum where the JAF had been, great tension built. In 1993, Havenga brokered the principle of a negotiated transformation of UPE. UPE and BDM set up joint working groups to address issues concerning new chancellors and deans, curriculum and admissions procedures. The process of transformation was formalized in June 1994 with the signing of an agreement between UPE, BDM and other interest groups. Three ongoing transformation working groups emerged: core values, student admissions and staff development.

The groups participate in extensive negotiations as the means of effecting institutional change. Negotiations are a prerequisite for ensuring that the process of transformation is legitimate and leads to basic compromises conducive to a democratic academic culture.

More than a decade into the transformation process, UPE is a democratic, multicultural university. "It is understood at UPE that transformation itself is not negotiable but is irreversible . . . No one should underestimate our common resolve to see the transformation process through," concludes Havenga. —*M.P.*

### NO CHEERLEADER

Despite the buzz about it, not everyone's on the transformation bandwagon. Robert "Jake" Jacobs, a management consultant at 5 Oceans Inc. of Chelsea, Michigan, and author of *Real Time Strategic Change* (Berrett-Koehler, 1998), argues that the CTO title and the department he manages are already a generation behind leading-edge thinking.

"If an organization has a transformation officer, it is already creating trouble because things appear good in the short term," he says. This systematically undermines the organization's efforts in the long term to create sustainable transformation. Jacobs cautions that the effort channeled into creating the TO office—the high energy, bold plans and focus on transformation as an organizational goal—can undermine real change because it establishes a polarity between transformation and everything else. "The organization itself, all departments, functions and work groups must embody change in their daily work, without the intervention of a transformation officer," says Jacobs.

One could reasonably argue that a company might be damaged when the competencies associated with transformation are split off from the rest of the organization. Better to ensure that such skills are transmitted enterprisewide. On the other hand, consultant Segil sees the transformation officer as a legitimate corporate position rather than a fad, as Jacobs suggests. But she acknowledges that "lots of CEOs and chairmen roll their eyes when you start talking about it."

While large corporations have been toying with the transformation officer concept in recent years, the title and the thought of creating an "office of transformation" are still too trendy, HR touchy-feely and even controversial for many CEOs and board members, according to Ed Mullen, national health practice leader at executive recruiter Korn Ferry International's Los Angeles office.

A transformation officer recruited from outside the organization rarely has that title, he says. COO and even CEO are more common. "Even if they don't have the CTO title, it doesn't mean that the organization has a hidden agenda, just that the unfamiliar title is hard to swallow," says Mullen. The TO title may also be avoided in companies that are involved in a merger or acquisition. In that environment, the transformation executive might be perceived as another hired gun who chops heads under tight deadlines rather than the harbinger of a better corporate life.

## A FAD?

Is the notion of a transformation officer just another management fad? We do get a healthy dose of jargon from TOs, but perhaps that's an indication that we accept their work and are listening. Floyd of Sears says, "Transformation is not a management fad. It plays a critical role in our organization and we are committed to it."

Indeed, transformation is large-scale, gut-wrenching change, and the need for such change will not go away in boom times or bust. Every company faces an inevitable decline after a heady period of growth, and it needs someone to infuse it with energy and help it find a new upward vector. That person, whether he's called the CEO, COO, chairman or, increasingly, CTO, provides leadership for the new century.

# ABSTRACT

## FUTURE FOCUS IN THE FACE OF "BUILT TO FLIP"

*Editor's Comment*: A major cover story on the top 50 CEOs took up most of the May 2000 issue of *Worth* magazine. The title page of the article described these CEOs as "the business leaders who are making their companies great, their shareholders rich, and the world a better place" (p. 123). Cisco Systems' CEO John Chambers, age 50 and CEO since only 1995, is credited with leading Cisco to a nearly eleven hundred thousand percent 3-year return. Worth suggests that Chambers has already created more wealth than Warren Buffet or Jack Welch, and that by year 2001, he will most likely surpass Bill Gates (p. 126). Others in the top five include #2, Timothy Koogle of Yahoo; #3, Steven Ballmer of Microsoft; #4, Scott McNealy of Sun Microsystems; and #5, James Morgan of Applied Materials. The article is worth reading in its entirety for the personal narrative included with each of the 50 featured CEOs. True stories, headaches, pet peeves, fashion statements, and passions are all explained. This is a different sort of business biography—it is lively and intimate, giving the reader a picture of today's CEOs and why they are leaders of high performing and flexible companies.

Throughout this long article, the reader will find many references to vision, passion, imagining the future, packing more information into less space, ferocious negotiation, beating archrivals, and moving with speed. At Intel, for example, Andy Grove encourages all employees to spend at least 5 percent of their time envisioning the future. They are told to work with a 5-year vision to make sure general strategy is okay, then they run a 3-year financial plan, and a 90-day organizational analysis (p. 133). These "Top 50" are the leaders with the know-how to move their companies into the future while being companies "built to flip." These CEOs reflect Silicon Valley's unwritten rule that a leader has to be a brilliant scientist or a founder of the company (p. 126).

Here's what eight of the chosen fifty said was their "most marked characteristic":

| | |
|---|---|
| Stemberg of Staples: | a sense of humor |
| Barrett of Intel: | a competitive nature |
| Ruettgers of EMC: | a militaristic style |
| Lay of Enron: | a positive attitude |
| Nicholas of Broadcom: | sheer determination |
| Koogle of Yahoo: | intuition |
| David of United Technologies: | intellect |
| Gilmartin of Merck: | a candid, forthright approach (p. 133). |

Trainers would do well to keep this article handy as you develop programs in leadership training. Training for this kind of leadership, for flexible and enduring companies, is a major challenge for managers and designers. This cleverly researched article by Robert X. Cringely can help provide a blueprint for leadership for learning.

*Source*: "The Best CEOs: Top 50" by Robert X. Cringely in *Worth*, May 2000, pp. 122–168. Robert X. Cringely is Senior Contributing Editor of *Worth* and a Silicon Valley writer and broadcaster.

# BOOK REVIEW

## COMMON KNOWLEDGE

*Editor's Comment*: This year, publications of all sorts have reflected a deeper understanding of what knowledge management means to companies and of how to do it right.

This brief but information-packed book is a must-read for all organizations looking to lower costs and increase productivity and profits. For Dixon, the key to this is sharing internal knowledge, or in other words, "knowledge that employees learn from doing the organization's task" (p. 11). Throughout the book, Dixon uses Ford Motors and Ernst & Young as examples of successful knowledge transfer. Dixon hypothesizes that organizations are becoming increasingly aware of knowledge sharing because "of the importance of knowledge to organizational success or perhaps because technology has made the sharing of knowledge more feasible" (p. 1).

Dixon explains that three myths are associated with organizational knowledge sharing. The first of which is "build it and they will come" (p. 2). In other words, the first thing that many organizations do is to construct a central electronic database, but more often than not, find that neither contributions nor retrievals occur with much enthusiasm. Instead, Dixon says that organizations need to focus more on *reusing* knowledge, not collecting and storing it (p. 3). The second myth is that technology can replace face-to-face interaction. According to the author, technology and face-to-face interaction need to be combined since they can enhance each other (p. 5). The last myth is that an organization needs to create a learning culture first. Dixon claims that the opposite is true—sharing knowledge *creates* a learning culture (p. 5).

Dixon then goes on to explain and illustrate the process behind creating common knowledge. According to the author, the key ingredient in creating common knowledge is intention (p. 18). She says that "this involves a willingness to reflect back on actions and their outcomes before moving forward (p. 18). Dixon seems to believe that this could be a problem for some organizations because most do not allow time for debriefing after concluding a project (p. 18). The following are the steps in creating common knowledge:

1. a team performs a task

2. an outcome is achieved

3. a team explores the relationship between action and outcome; and

4. common knowledge is gained (p. 19).

Next, common knowledge must be leveraged, or in other words, must be transferred across time and space (p.19). Before Dixon presents the five methods of knowledge transfer, she lists the three criteria that determine the transfer method used:

1. who the receiver is

2. nature of the task (i.e. frequency)

3. type of knowledge to be transferred (p. 22).

The author repeatedly stresses the importance of these three criteria throughout the remainder of the book. According to Dixon, it is also critical to knowledge transfer to differentiate between tacit and explicit knowledge. Explicit knowledge "can be laid out in procedures, steps, and standards" and tacit knowledge "is primarily in the heads of people" (p. 26).

The five methods of knowledge transfer are the following:

1. *Serial transfer*—knowledge that a team has gained from completing a task that can be

*Source: Common Knowledge: How Companies Thrive By Sharing What They Know* by Nancy M. Dixon. Boston: Harvard Business School Press, 2000. $29.95. Nancy M. Dixon is an associate professor of Administrative Sciences at The George Washington University. This book review was written by Katherine M. Franklin, Editorial Assistant.

used the next time the team does the same task in a different setting,

2. *Near transfer*—explicit knowledge that a team gains from doing the same task frequently that can be replicated by another team doing similar work in the same organization,

3. *Far transfer*—tacit knowledge a team acquires from doing a task that the organization thinks that other teams in different parts of the organization can use,

4. *Strategic transfer*—collective knowledge an organization needs to accomplish an infrequent but critical task, and

5. *Expert transfer*—technical knowledge needed by a team that it does not possess but is possessed by others in the organization (p. 169).

Dixon then uses all five types of knowledge transfer to explain patterns that she has noticed in how organizations are currently thinking about knowledge. The following are the three that she has observed:

- shift from thinking of experts as the primary source of knowledge to thinking of knowledge as distributed throughout the organization,

- shift from thinking of knowledge as possessed by individuals to thinking of knowledge as a group phenomena, and

- shift from thinking of knowledge as a stable commodity to thinking of knowledge as dynamic (pp.148–9).

In conclusion, Dixon points out that "the issue isn't about adding human components to a technological system but how to build an integrated system in which each element is integrated with the other elements to make the whole work as a system" (p. 162). Dixon's major point throughout this straight-forward book is that the type of knowledge needs to fit the all-important method of transfer. She is definitely advocating collaboration and teamwork in helping an organization reach its ultimate goals—reducing costs and increasing profits.

# RESEARCH SUMMARY

## THE HAY/McBER STUDY OF LEADERSHIP IMPACT

*Editor's Comment*: It seems that leaders demonstrate a different mix of skills than do ordinary managers. Many observers, including leaders themselves, have tried to analyze what these skills are and what makes them different. This short research summary pinpoints what leadership behaviors have what kind of impact on organizational climate. High impact leaders were shown to demonstrate these behaviors, some with positive effect and some with negative effect. The study included data from more than 3,700 executive leaders.

## CONSULTANT STUDIES 3,700 EXECUTIVES

Researchers from consultant Hay/McBer have observed or studied data about 3,781 executives, noting their specific behaviors and their impact on the organizational environment or "climate," according to Goleman, who wrote about the study in the March–April issue of *Harvard Business Review*.

The researchers defined an organization's climate as the flexibility workers feel they are given to innovate; their sense of responsibility to the organization; the level of standards that people set for the organization; the sense of fairness about performance feedback and rewards; the clarity people have about mission and values; and the level of commitment to a common purpose.

The research distilled leadership behavior down to six distinct leadership styles, all of which the researchers found had an impact—some positive, some negative—on organizational climate:

**Coercive.** Demands immediate compliance; best in a crisis to kick-start a turnaround; most strongly negative leadership style.

**Pacesetting.** Sets high standards to push and prod employees to accomplish tasks; can often bring about negative results.

**Authoritative.** Provides long-term direction and vision and mobilizes people toward that vision; most strongly positive leadership style.

**Affiliative.** Creates harmony and builds emotional bonds; best to heal rifts in a team or to motivate people during stressful circumstances.

**Democratic.** Forges consensus through participation and collaboration; best to build buy-in or get input.

**Coaching.** Develops people for the future; helps an employee improve performance or develop long-term strengths.

Goleman, who consults with Hay/McBer on leadership development, said leaders who used styles that positively affected the climate recorded better financial results—such as revenue growth, efficiency, and profitability—than those who did not.

The report also finds that high-impact leaders switch among the various leadership styles, depending on the situation, he said.

*Source*: "Six Degrees of Leadership: Behavioral Skills Drive Company Performance, E.I. Author Says" in *Bulletin To Management*, Workplace Policy and Practice Insights Since 1950, May 4, 2000. Reproduced with permission from Bulletin to Management (BNA Policy and Practice Series), Vol. 51, No. 18, p. 137 (May 4, 2000). Copyright 2000 by The Bureau of National Affairs, Inc. (800-372-1033) *http://www.bna.com*

# 1B. KNOWLEDGE MANAGEMENT

## ABSTRACT

## BUILDING BLOCKS OF KNOWLEDGE MANAGEMENT

*Editor's Comment*: Thoughtful people will meditate on the difference between "information processing" and "knowledge management," and will work very hard to not use the terms interchangeably. Harvard University's Chris Argyris in his new book, *Flawed Advice and the Management Trap*, (NY: Oxford University Press, 2000), calls for "theory-in-use" or "actionable" advice. Anthropologists and information science researchers at the Palo Alto Research Center (PARC) and the American Productivity & Quality Center (APQC) call for experimentation with and documentation of Communities of Practice; others note that people (not machines) own knowledge and use it in concert with each other. The building blocks of knowledge management reside in the people who use knowledge.

APQC's pre-Conference Brochure announced the call for papers for its 5th Knowledge Management Conference, to be held in December in Las Vegas. The "suggested topic areas/case studies" include the following items. They give the knowledge manager some idea of the kinds of building blocks for knowledge management that put the people first and the information systems second:

✓ Developing a knowledge management strategy: what worked and what didn't

✓ Implementing a knowledge management strategy: case studies of success

✓ Models for and approaches to measuring knowledge management

✓ Calculating the savings and return on investment of knowledge management

✓ Assessing and monitoring knowledge management initiative

✓ Identifying and selecting Communities of Practice

✓ Launching and sustaining Communities of Practice

✓ Collaborative tools for Communities of Practice

✓ The Life Cycle of Communities of Practice

✓ How to manage knowledge for existing teams

✓ Resources of knowledge management: budget, staff, and funding sources

✓ How to design and manage a knowledge management intranet portal

✓ Portal content and applications

✓ Partnering with customers for sales, service, and product development

✓ Using customer knowledge and empowering customers with useful knowledge

✓ Using external Web site for sharing knowledge

*Source:* Conference Brochure, "Taking Knowledge and Best Practices to the Bottom Line," 5th Knowledge Management Conference, American Productivity & Quality Center (APQC), Las Vegas, NV, December 7–8, 2000. Headquarters of APQC is located 123 North Post Oak Lane, 3rd Floor, Houston, TX, 77024, phone 800/776-9676, Web site *www.apqc.org*.

# REPRINT EXCERPT

## ACTION STEPS IN KNOWLEDGE MANAGEMENT

*Editor's Comment*: Most definitions of "knowledge management" include words that imply or describe action. Common definitions use the words "transaction," "usage," "support," "help," "enable," and "transfer." The previous abstract suggested some of the content building blocks of knowledge management. In this excerpt here we highlight the typical action steps in building and maintaining a knowledge system. Contact Generation21 Learning Systems in Colorado for more information: 1/888/601-1300.

## THE FUNCTIONS OF A TKM SYSTEM

With TKM, the source of sustained personal growth and organizational competitiveness comes from the following six abilities:

1. **Gathering Knowledge**—The ability to gather knowledge through ongoing learning by the people within an organization as part of an organized structure

2. **Organizing Knowledge**—The ability to organize new information so that it is tied to and integrated with related knowledge

3. **Distributing Knowledge**—The ability to distribute that knowledge to others so that the necessary people can gain quick-and-easy access and learn quickly

4. **Converting Knowledge into Action**—The ability to convert new knowledge into action to provide higher value goods and services to others

5. **Training Ourselves Continuously**—The ability to convert information into training and learning for continual growth and improvement

6. **Repeating the Cycle**—Implementing this cycle on an ongoing basis so that new information is continually added to the system, distributed where needed, applied to the solution of new problems, and then used to enhance continual learning.

This process is the essence of the value of a fully integrated total knowledge management system. A Total Knowledge Management System does the following:

- Provides a repository for the ongoing acquisition of new knowledge

- Provides the structure by which new knowledge is integrated with previously deposited related information

- Makes that knowledge available to others in a "just-in-time" fashion without extensive time lost searching for the needed information

- Provides continual training for individuals so that they can learn what they need to know on an ongoing basis

- Dynamically and continuously updates information and training so that the intelligence and skills of an organization reflect the synergistic result of the total capabilities of the organization.

TKM is the system that enables an organization to bring the power of its collective knowledge to every customer, delivered through every employee.

---

*Source:* *The 10 Things Every Training Manager Should Know About TKM* by Dale Zwart and Dr. Harold S. Resnick, research study published by Generation21 Learning Systems, January 2000. Excerpt of pages 5 and 6 are reprinted with permission of Generation21 Learning Systems. Generation21, TKM, Total Knowledge Management, and Dynamic Learning Objects are registered trademarks of Advantage Learning Systems, Inc.

# RESEARCH SUMMARY

## THE CONFERENCE BOARD'S KNOWLEDGE MANAGEMENT IMPLEMENTATION STUDY

*Editor's Comment*: Like other organizations seeking to find out how knowledge management actually works, The Conference Board sought data and information from a representative sample of companies in order to document the goals, processes, and components of knowledge management currently being implemented. The 72-page report referenced below contains the results of this inquiry. In this research summary here, we reprint three of these pages to give you an implementation overview of their findings. Included in these overview findings is a suggestion for a direction of future research, namely, in the areas of innovation, knowledge creation, and customer loyalty.

## IMPLEMENTING KNOWLEDGE MANAGEMENT AND ORGANIZATIONAL LEARNING

According to the survey, 21 percent of companies have a formally communicated knowledge-sharing strategy. Among them is a diversity of strategies and approaches. Most knowledge strategies are currently based on increasing efficiencies mainly because it is easier and more immediate to exploit what is known. Few firms have a strategy focused on innovation, knowledge creation, or customer loyalty.

### KM and Discontinuous Change

In many ways, KM initiatives are in tune with new ways of doing business and the drivers of competition in a global economy:

***Diffusion of technologies.*** The e-mail/intranet/Internet infrastructure, combined with powerful database software and groupware, has made it possible to increase the span of communication. Ideas, experiences, and problems can be shared more quickly, more often, less expensively, and more widely than ever before.

***The marketplace.*** The Internet and globalization have made discontinuous change a competitive fact. The rules guiding customer relations, competition, and the employment relationship change daily. Firms must operate as adaptive systems and anticipate change under that new set of market conditions.

***The customer.*** Sharing knowledge with customers, potential customers, suppliers, and in some cases competitors is becoming a growing

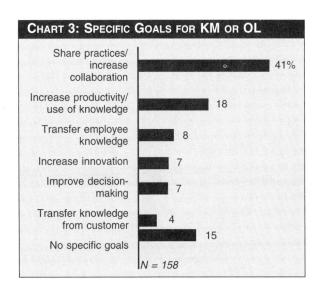

CHART 3: SPECIFIC GOALS FOR KM OR OL

- Share practices/increase collaboration — 41%
- Increase productivity/use of knowledge — 18
- Transfer employee knowledge — 8
- Increase innovation — 7
- Improve decision-making — 7
- Transfer knowledge from customer — 4
- No specific goals — 15

N = 158

---

*Source: Beyond Knowledge Management: New Ways to Work and Learn*, Research Report 1262-00-RR, pages 3, 14, and 40. The Conference Board, Inc., 2000. Excerpts reprinted with permission of The Conference Board, Inc., New York, NY. All rights reserved. Copies of the full report of 72 pages are available at a cost of $195. Telephone 212/759-0900; fax 212/980-7014; *www.conference-board.org*.

business practice. For many firms sharing knowledge with regulators, the media and the community are equally important.

***The workforce.*** Today's workers are more technology literate, more mobile in their careers, and more engaged in learning as their roles and knowledge needs change.

***The organization.*** With the spread of technology infrastructures and the move to globalization, the roles of headquarters and common workspace have been greatly reduced as the repositories of knowledge. Cross-functional teams and cross-organizational projects are an increasing part of how work gets done.

The way most people work is continuously changing. Ubiquitous and portable communications technology is a major factor in that change. People can now communicate anytime, almost anywhere, and at a relatively low cost. Work groups can capture that communication in simple-to-use but sophisticated databases. When done well, companies can mine that information so the right people can use it when they need it.

### TABLE 1 COMMUNICATION IS COMMON DENOMINATOR IN EFFECTIVE HUMAN RESOURCES INITIATIVES IN SHARING KNOWLEDGE

|  | Great | Good | Average | Poor | Very Poor | Not Used |
|---|---|---|---|---|---|---|
| 360-degree feedback | 10% | 34% | 27% | 15% | 3% | 11% |
| Open-door policy | 10 | 26 | 34 | 10 | 2 | 18 |
| Top HR management support | 8 | 32 | 23 | 11 | 7 | 19 |
| Corporate university | 7 | 24 | 20 | 9 | 5 | 35 |
| Building employee skills inventory | 6 | 18 | 37 | 20 | 7 | 12 |
| External benchmarking | 5 | 20 | 31 | 17 | 6 | 20 |
| HR staff support for KM | 4 | 23 | 28 | 16 | 8 | 21 |
| Mentoring/coaching | 4 | 20 | 41 | 17 | 7 | 11 |
| Use of teams for knowledge sharing | 3 | 26 | 32 | 17 | 4 | 19 |
| Employee involvement program | 3 | 18 | 32 | 17 | 4 | 26 |
| Internal benchmarking | 3 | 17 | 34 | 20 | 5 | 21 |
| Supporting communities of practice | 2 | 17 | 22 | 18 | 3 | 38 |
| Hiring focused on knowledge-sharing attributes | 2 | 14 | 20 | 23 | 9 | 32 |
| HR training to support KM | 2 | 12 | 24 | 25 | 9 | 29 |
| Suggestion program | 2 | 11 | 26 | 21 | 5 | 35 |
| Leveraging tacit knowledge | 2 | 10 | 36 | 21 | 9 | 23 |
| Customer involvement in KM | 2 | 4 | 20 | 22 | 12 | 40 |
| Knowledge creation/innovation | 1 | 20 | 29 | 21 | 7 | 22 |
| Communicating KM culture/goals | 1 | 8 | 26 | 24 | 8 | 33 |
| Training all employees on KM | 1 | 3 | 19 | 29 | 11 | 35 |
| Performance evaluated for knowledge sharing | 0 | 10 | 23 | 25 | 8 | 34 |
| Compensation for knowledge sharing | 0 | 2 | 17 | 23 | 13 | 45 |

Senior executives would like to see HR take more of a leadership role in KM initiatives (*Chart 7*).

### CHART 7

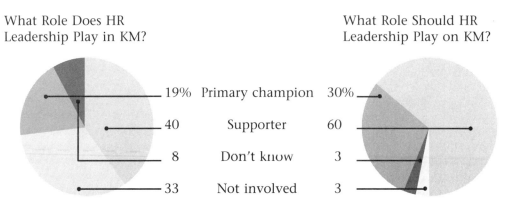

What Role Does HR
Leadership Play in KM?

19% Primary champion
40 Supporter
8 Don't know
33 Not involved

What Role Should HR
Leadership Play on KM?

30% Primary champion
60 Supporter
3 Don't know
3 Not involved

# CASE STUDY

## KNOWLEDGE MANAGEMENT (KM) INTELLIGENCE FROM IBM AND WEYERHAEUSER

*Editor's Comment*: These two case studies are included in The Conference Board's new report, *Beyond Knowledge Management: New Ways to Work and Learn*. We first reprint Weyerhauser's "Lessons," which are presented as a sort of needs analysis for making knowledge management work. We then give you IBM's concepts and definitions of knowledge management "products," a useful way to think about and grab hold of the fundamentals of creating a knowledge management system and integrating it into the business as a whole.

### LESSONS FROM WEYERHAEUSER

**General Findings**

1. Tightly link KM to a priority business objective.
2. KM entails an integrated approach to people, processes, and technology; it is not a project.
3. KM should not be a separate staff function.

**People and Culture**

1. Senior management needs to set the tone and show support. Day-to-day reinforcement and coaching must come from mid-level.
2. Learning and sharing are equally important.
3. Trust is essential: It must be built to overcome the effects of "not invented here" and "knowledge is power." You must trust your employees. Employees must trust that sharing enhances employment status and does not undermine the business's need for them.
4. Human interaction cannot be replaced. It is especially needed to transfer tacit knowledge.
5. Rewards/recognition linked specially to KM must be carefully evaluated. They can have unexpected and unintended consequences.

**Processes**

1. Key KM processes must be defined. These include: capturing, sharing, and applying knowledge; developing new knowledge; and protecting knowledge assets.
2. There is no one best process for KM. Process design must include: content, scope and speed; intended use; and expected outputs.
3. Connectivity is more effective than capture: Facilitating the connections between people is more successful than trying to capture and sort knowledge for all potential accesses. Enabling/expecting people to learn, share, refine, and apply knowledge is the key. Multiple channels of knowledge transfer must be supported.

**Technology**

1. Technology is an enabler: it is not KM.
2. Make the technology fit the work, not vice versa.
3. Technology does not eliminate the need for people to meet. It may increase the need for contact to: build trust, and freely interact in problem solving.
4. New techniques are not needed. Old methods can be just as effective, such as teamwork, process management, benchmarking continuous improvement.

*Source: : Beyond Knowledge Management: New Ways to Work and Learn*, Research Report 1262-00-RR, pages 21 and 32. The Conference Board, Inc., 2000. Excerpts reprinted with permission of The Conference Board, Inc., New York, NY. All rights reserved. Copies of the full report of 72 pages are available at a cost of $195. Telephone 212/759-0900; fax 212/980-7014; *www.conference-board.org*.

## KM PRODUCT CATEGORIES AT IBM

IBM has devised the following KM product categories by which it focuses on products and services required to integrate KM into the business. As part of an overall enterprise knowledge portal strategy, all of these applications must be accessible through the Web. However, they may not be Web-resident applications. In addition, there are essential KM services, such as developing the knowledge strategy, organizational designs, and behavioral change management, which together with various KM products yield KM solutions.

*Collaboration.* In its simplest form, collaboration is e-mail supplemented with groupware applications as well as synchronous messaging. This includes e-mail, instant messaging, e-meetings, Web conferences, and group teamrooms with calendaring and scheduling; calendaring and scheduling for the individual and tied to the team calendaring; spaces for communities of practice to congregate and transfer knowledge; and electronic messaging systems.

*Desktop and real-time conferencing.* This part of e-meetings allows IBM employees to share remotely applications on the desktop as well as engage in whiteboard activity. It also includes event-ware such as video jukebox, whereby someone can replay an event on their desktop.

*Knowledge transfer.* This is a group of applications by which e-learning is conducted and includes distributed learning applications such as LearningSpace, computer-based training, and live collaboration via electronic media. IBM provides more than 1,000 computer-based training offerings to employees directly online. Employees are electronically linked to IBM's education and training service, Global Campus, to enroll in distributed learning as well as classroom offerings.

*Business intelligence.* This set of applications includes data/text mining, information warehousing, and OLAP. IBM recently used it to look for patterns in write-in responses on its global employee survey across tens of thousands of participants.

*Knowledge discovery and mapping.* This encompasses search, classification/navigation, and document-management applications, including discovery of knowledge objects within documents.

*Expertise.* These applications include expert networks, visualization, and affinity identification, as well as yellow pages and directories.

*Source:* Fred Schoeps, IBM

# ARTICLE REPRINT

## HOW TO BECOME A CKO (CHIEF KNOWLEDGE OFFICER)

*Editor's Comment*: A recent study by the American Society for Training & Development (ASTD) of 18 global companies is the foundation for this article reprinted here. The findings of ASTD's study of what the chief knowledge officer actually does are presented as a chart on p. 1.27. Notice the title in transition: some executives are called the CIO, Chief Information Officer; the CLO, Chief Learning Officer; or CKO, Chief Knowledge Officer. The best advice for aspiring "knowledge leaders," by whatever name, seems to be to focus on learning as a business function. This article is directed at those who can see themselves in a CKO position in the near future.

## ENTER THE CHIEF KNOWLEDGE OFFICER

### by Dede Bonner

Have you ever spent weeks working for a solution, only to discover that the same problem has been solved elsewhere in your organization? Or perhaps your search for vital information is frustrated when you learn that the most expert employee on the topic left the company last year. Or maybe your HR department is searching for ways to better align their databases of employees' skills with internal job vacancies.

Those are just three examples of the wake-up call in organizations to manage their knowledge resources and knowledge workers better.

We're well into the knowledge era, in which there's an explosion of easy access to information via the Internet and elsewhere, assisted by powerful databases. As never before, senior managers are realizing that the success factors for aggressive business growth in today's highly competitive marketplace are what their employees know and how capable they are at learning the newest solutions and technologies. In this knowledge era, an organization's intangible assets—employees' collective intelligence of skills, experience, and work ethic—is crucial to business advantage and accelerated growth. Recent surveys by the Conference Board and the American Management Association show that at least one half of U.S. companies and up to 72 percent of overseas firms have some kind of knowledge management initiative planned or underway.

Knowledge management isn't new, and its basic premises are simple. Employees hold a wealth of knowledge about their companies, including the products, customers, internal processes, histories, technologies, and competitors. But that knowledge is usually scattered across people and locations. Likewise, learning usually happens at an individual level as a one-time event, without an organizational context or sense of continuity. For that reason, some pioneers in the field of knowledge management are predicting a blending of KM with organizational learning as the two areas mature. Once a firm has a grip on what knowledge it has and how to manage it, then it will be able to more effectively assess its organizational learning capabilities, maximize learning at the individual level, and use knowledge capture and sharing as ways to enhance organization-wide learning.

*Source*: "Enter the Chief Knowledge Officer" by Dede Bonner in *Training & Development*, February 2000, pp. 36–40. Dede Bonner is President of New Century Management, Leesburg, VA. Reprinted with permission of ASTD. Copyright 2000. All rights reserved. *www.astd.org*.

Knowledge doesn't happen in a vacuum. It's all about relationships and trust—people's willingness to share what they know for the greater good of a group. It takes a culture that encourages a free-flowing exchange of ideas. That makes knowledge—the stuff between people's ears—different from information and data, which are merely raw material without proven value. In order for people to be willing to capture, share, and retain their hard-earned knowledge, organizations must have environments and leadership that foster cultures of continuous learning and support the integration of internal business functions.

Enter the newest fast-track careers in the business: chief knowledge officer and chief learning officer. CKOs and CLOs, whether an official title or in duty only, are the leaders of their organizations' knowledge management and organizational learning initiatives. In many large companies and a few small ones, CEOs are creating those new senior-level positions as their strategic partners in order to initiate, drive, and integrate their firms' organizational learning and knowledge management efforts. Other positions along these lines include knowledge manager and learning architect. CKOs and CLOs are earning US$81,000 to $750,000, according to industry sources, with estimates of million-dollar figures on the horizon at the largest companies. Salaries for CKO and CLO positions are about the same, depending on the size of company, type of industry, and job complexity.

*Knowledge Management in Practice: Chief Knowledge Officers and Chief Learning Officers* (ASTD, 2000) is a series of case studies at 18 global organizations representing a wide diversity of industries, including technology, health care, consulting services, retail, financial, education, government, accounting, and insurance. The cases define initial best practices and lessons learned, and provide guidance for people aspiring to be knowledge or learning leaders.

## WHAT CKOS AND CLOS DO

Most chief knowledge officers and chief learning officers are first-generation incumbents. They typically started their jobs less than three years ago and did so without clearly defined roles, responsibilities, and daily activities. Those are a work in progress. The case studies date only from the early 1990s.

Chief knowledge officer positions are typically created to leverage knowledge into tangible business benefits. Likewise, CLO positions are designed to leverage learning. The culture of an organization, the type of knowledge and learning it wants to emphasize, and how technologically focused it is are pivotal factors in choosing one position over the other.

CKOs locate knowledge within a company and find ways to capture, distribute, and create more of it. In some of the cases, the CKO position originated from that of chief information officer, which is primarily technology-driven. But a CKO is more likely to view technology as only an enabler for an effective knowledge management system, and he or she brings the added dimensions of strategic vision and business savvy.

Nearly universally, the CKOs in the case studies and other literature on this growing profession emphasize the need for them to be relationship builders. Nick Milton, a former knowledge manager and a knowledge management pioneer for British Petroleum, says, "The fundamental issues are people, culture, roles, behaviors, and the business processes in your organization. Don't just focus on technology. It may help you manage knowledge, but knowledge is a people issue. It lives in people's heads."

Likewise, Andy Campbell, the CKO of the Central Intelligence Agency's Office of Training and Education says, "Don't get seduced by the technologists." That perspective is generally shared by the chief learning officers in the cases. Pat Cataldo, CLO for Science Applications International Corporation, adds, "People—throughout the industry in general—are often tempted to view the advantages that new technologies bring to the table as a catch-all solution. One size or one solution does not fit all training situations."

The roots for most chief learning officer positions, on the other hand, are in human resources, organization development, or sales and marketing. Most incumbent CLOs have strong backgrounds in learning strategies and a strong orientation toward setting and reaching business goals. They've been selected from such positions as director of training or vice president of sales and marketing. CLOs are committed to the strategic integration of organizational and individual learning at all levels and across all functional silos. They often have as a primary objective to change their organizations'

## WHAT THE CKO DOES

| Roles, Responsibilities, and Activities | Andersen-Knowledge Manager | BP Norway-Knowledge Manager | CIA-CKO | Clarica-Other | Entovation-CKO | Equiva-CLO | Foreign Bank-CKO | IBM (UK)-CKO/CLO | Lancaster-Other (CLO) | Luxury Retail-CKO | Mem. Hermann-CLO | Millbrook-CLO | Plante & Moran-Other | SAIC-CLO | Sedgwick-CLO | 7 Schools-Other (CLO) | StockTrade-CKO/CLO | Xerox-CLO |
|---|---|---|---|---|---|---|---|---|---|---|---|---|---|---|---|---|---|---|
| Align/Integrate diverse functions or groups | X | X | X | X | X | X | X | X | X | X | X | X |  | X | X | X |  | X |
| Best practices/benchmarking (utilized or developed) | X | X | X | X | X | X |  | X | X | X | X | X | X | X | X | X |  | X |
| Business objectives & performance (developed or supported) | X | X | X | X |  | X |  | X |  | X | X | X | X | X | X |  | X | X |
| Career planning/staff or professional development | X |  |  |  |  | X |  |  |  |  |  | X | X |  | X | X |  | X |
| Change manager role | X | X | X | X | X | X |  | X |  |  | X | X | X | X | X | X |  | X |
| Communications/build networks/use personal influence | X | X | X | X | X | X |  | X | X |  | X | X | X | X | X | X |  | X |
| Continuous and/or consistent learning systems highlighted | X | X | X | X | X | X |  | X | X |  | X | X | X | X | X | X |  | X |
| Corporate or in-house universities/learning lab | X |  |  |  |  | X |  |  |  |  | X |  |  | X | X |  |  |  |
| Create/lead expert teams | X | X | X |  |  | X |  | X | X |  | X | X |  |  | X | X |  | X |
| Culture development for learning and/or knowledge | X | X | X | X | X | X |  | X |  | X | X | X | X | X | X | X |  | X |
| Customer service orientation | X | X | X | X | X | X | X | X | X | X | X | X | X | X | X | X | X | X |
| Employee orientation program |  |  |  |  |  |  |  |  |  |  | X |  | X |  |  | X |  |  |
| Employee retention/recruitment programs |  |  |  |  |  |  | X |  | X |  |  |  | X |  |  |  |  |  |
| Executive education and/or action learning |  |  |  |  | X | X |  | X | X |  |  | X |  |  |  |  |  |  |
| Financial knowledge management |  |  |  |  |  |  |  |  |  |  |  |  |  |  |  |  | X |  |
| Identify critical areas for improvement/needs analyses | X | X | X | X | X | X | X | X | X | X | X | X | X | X | X | X | X | X |
| Knowledge-content activities (capture, share & retain) | X | X | X | X | X | X | X | X | X | X | X | X | X | X | X | X | X | X |
| Knowledge-structure (tools, manage infrastructure) | X | X | X | X | X |  |  | X |  | X | X |  |  | X |  |  | X | X |
| Leverage corporate-wide learning and/or knowledge | X | X | X | X | X | X | X | X | X | X | X | X | X | X | X | X | X | X |
| Organization of effectiveness consulting/OD activities | X | X | X |  |  | X |  |  |  |  |  | X | X | X |  |  |  |  |
| Partnerships with senior management/others | X | X | X | X | X | X |  |  | X |  | X | X | X | X | X | X | X | X |
| Project management activities |  | X |  |  | X |  |  |  |  |  | X | X |  |  |  |  |  | X |
| Sales/marketing/business development | X |  |  |  | X |  | X |  |  |  | X | X |  |  |  |  | X | X |
| Strategic planning & implementation | X | X | X | X | X | X | X |  | X |  | X | X | X | X | X | X |  | X |
| Technology for learning/knowledge (developed or supported) | X | X | X |  | X |  |  | X |  |  | X | X | X | X | X |  |  | X |
| Training & education/workshops/retreats/meeting leader |  | X | X |  |  |  |  | X | X | X | X | X | X | X | X | X |  |  |
| Visionary/champion for organizational learning and/or KM | X | X | X | X | X | X | X | X | X |  | X | X | X | X | X | X |  | X |

## *What People Are Saying*

### REASONS CITED FOR CREATING CKO ROLE (FROM THE CASE STUDIES)

#### *Internal Forces*

- ❑ CEO believes knowledge is strategic factor for business success.
- ❑ Increase skilled competence in technical jobs needed.
- ❑ Knowledge not being widely captured or shared—don't know what's there.
- ❑ Major changes in internal processes, structure, and leadership.
- ❑ Missed business because employees lacked knowledge about products and customers.
- ❑ Need for a centralized knowledge system.
- ❑ Response to reorganization.
- ❑ Solve human capital issues.
- ❑ Show position as institutionalized.

#### *External Forces*

- ❑ Competition is fierce and growing for best talent.
- ❑ Customers are increasingly informed and demanding.
- ❑ Top talent was rejecting or disinterested in our employment offers

#### *Internal and External Forces*

- ❑ Accelerating changes.
- ❑ Aggressive growth goals.
- ❑ Decreasing sales and productivity despite worldwide expansion strategy.
- ❑ People needed connections with each other (built a network).
- ❑ Employee retention issues.
- ❑ Response to downsizing mindset.
- ❑ This industry is knowledge intense, and mistakes are costly.

### REASONS CITED FOR CREATING CLO ROLE (INCLUDES "INFORMAL" CLOS)

#### *Internal Forces*

- ❑ CEO believes learning is strategic factor for business success.
- ❑ Increase skilled competence in technical jobs and business processes needed.
- ❑ Continual, faster, and better career development opportunities needed.
- ❑ Knowledge acquisition and management.
- ❑ Lack of consistency in business and learning processes.
- ❑ Limited resources or time for traditional training functions.
- ❑ Major changes in internal processes, structure, and leadership.
- ❑ Merger resulted in overlapping functions and departments.
- ❑ Need for centralized learning system.
- ❑ Quality of services were or are in a crisis.
- ❑ Realization training is often really a performance improvement issue.

#### *External Forces*

- ❑ Competition is fierce and growing for best talent.
- ❑ Customers are increasingly informed and demanding.
- ❑ Losing and gaining customers.

#### *Internal and External Forces*

- ❑ Accelerating changes.
- ❑ Aggressive growth goals.
- ❑ Must depend on a workforce with high turnover.
- ❑ People needed connections with others.
- ❑ Response to reorganizations, deregulations, and hostile takeovers.
- ❑ Severe pressure to enter new business markets.
- ❑ Solution to technical complexity and geographically dispersed locations.

## Help Wanted: Chief Knowledge Officer

Rapidly growing corporation with aggressive expansion goals seeks CKO to manage organization's intellectual assets to gain competitive advantage. Will report to CEO.

Responsibilities: Design and implement a knowledge-learning culture and a knowledge-learning infrastructure. Tie together the information in the corporation's databases, historical records, file cabinets, and intranet, as well as employees' informal knowledge that has yet to be identified or recorded in a systematic way. Draw from external information sources, such as the Internet and public databases. Align and integrate diverse groups and functions in order to leverage knowledge management strategically across the entire corporation. Use technology to support knowledge capture, sharing, and retention.

Qualifications: Successful candidate must be an evangelist for the value of knowledge sharing among employees. Must have a strong sense of vision and business strategy, and be able to partner with senior managers. Ability to conduct complex strategic needs assessments and use personal influence to IT networks.

mindsets from training (usually defined as a classroom-based delivery system) to continuous learning and human performance improvement, and to use a wider variety of delivery methods such as virtual learning options, corporate universities, and self-directed learning.

Chief learning officers aren't glorified training directors. Gary May, CLO of Millbrook Distribution Services near Atlanta, comments: "The primary success factor for being a CLO is being a businessperson first and understanding how to drive through a strategic initiative. I must be able to communicate in business-tangible results, think strategically, and talk the language of our executives." May sees his role as a strategic leader who is helping senior management translate learning into strategic business capabilities.

Due to the lack of job standards, different industries' unique knowledge and learning needs, and varying expectations, there were many differences in the incumbents' roles and responsibilities among the case studies. But what they all share is an evangelical zeal for knowledge and learning, an urgency to get their message out, and the belief that they can strategically change how their organizations use and value knowledge and learning for competitive business advantage and improved customer satisfaction.

Gary Jusela, chief learning officer at Equiva Services (a Shell and Texaco alliance), says, "The learning function is more relevant than ever in the new economy. In the future, organizations will increasingly compete on the quality of their intelligence. The landscape on this job is new. It's about bringing a lot of functions together and integrating training with organizational effectiveness."

Considering how diverse this collection of organizations and individuals is, what's most striking are the similarities in their roles, responsibilities, and daily activities—and the fact that CKOs and CLOs are considered members of the senior team.

The following activities were cited universally or nearly so by all of the CKOs and CLOs in the cases:

❏ Align and integrate diverse functions or groups.
❏ Use previous best practices or design benchmarking studies.
❏ Develop a culture of acceptance of organizational learning, continuous learning, and knowledge management.
❏ Have a customer service orientation.
❏ Identify critical areas for improvement, through needs or gap analyses.
❏ Create knowledge-content activities to contribute to or manage the capture, sharing, and retention activities.
❏ Leverage corporate-wide learning.
❏ Establish partnerships with senior managers.
❏ Conduct strategic planning and implementation.
❏ Be a visionary and champion for organizational learning and knowledge management.

Chief knowledge officer, chief learning officer, and other knowledge and learning leadership positions are likely to be created in response to severe internal and external business pressures.

## What It Takes

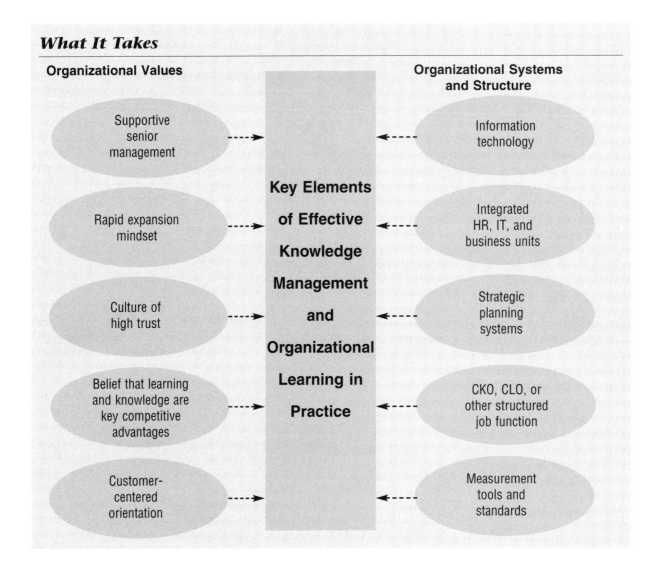

The latter include increasingly competitive markets, a changing customer base, and difficulties recruiting top talent. For example, at a foreign bank that wasn't attracting and retaining top employees, a CKO was hired to identify why applicants were rejecting employment offers. Other companies reported they'd created CLO and CKO positions in response to growing competition and more demanding customers.

There were also internal triggers, such as changes in business operations, decentralization, the perceived need to serve customers better, or a need to ensure that learning or knowledge was being leveraged across the entire firm or network. In several cases, the combination of internal and external forces resulted in senior management's decision to create CKO and CLO roles.

Chief learning officers at a major oil and gas alliance, at a global technology firm, and at a large healthcare system tell similar stories about how company mergers and acquisitions resulted in the need for a CLO who could quantify and unify the diversified learning activities, lead in the use of technology-assisted learning, and, in some cases, create a corporate university.

## A PREDICTED FUSION

An organizational profile emerged from the cases of the type of organizations most likely to support knowledge management, organizational learning, and formal CKO and CLO positions. They are companies that value learning and knowledge as critical to their business strategies, not just as nice things to do. In each case, the organization, or at least the involved individuals, had made an effort to identify what knowledge and learning were critical to operational success.

The organizational conditions for the success of CKOs and CLOs are similar, with the exception of CKOs' emphasis on knowledge and CLOs' emphasis on learning—a reflection of the need for strong organizational cultures that recognize, support, and value employees' collective intelligence. The difference also provides empirical evidence for the predicted fusion between organizational learning and knowledge management.

The characteristics of supportive organizations can be divided into two categories: 1) organizational values and 2) organizational systems and structure.

The following are characteristics of supportive organizations:

- ❏ highly supportive senior management
- ❏ an organizational mindset of rapid growth, sometimes manifested as threats from outside competitors
- ❏ a high level of internal trust among employees, which fosters open sharing of knowledge
- ❏ a belief that organizational learning and knowledge management are critical business advantages
- ❏ an exceptionally well-defined orientation to providing customer-centered products and services.

The most frequently mentioned organizational value in the cases was the need for strong, visionary senior leadership that truly values learning and knowledge. Such leaders were described as willing to "walk the talk" by investing funds and highly visible resources. The need for a strong partnership with executives was echoed across the cases if for no other reason than that the CKOs or CLOs then wouldn't have to keep selling themselves and the concept of their positions and could get on with accomplishing their missions.

Further, having direct access to the executive boardroom was seen as critical to aligning knowledge management and organizational learning efforts with an organization's overall business goals. That level of partnership keeps CKOs and CLOs thinking strategically, a must-have competency for either job.

## *Power Verbs*

One way to encapsulate the phenom of the chief knowledge officer is to parse it down to its essential verbs:

| | |
|---|---|
| ❏ align | ❏ implement |
| ❏ benchmark | ❏ integrate |
| ❏ design | ❏ leverage |
| ❏ develop | ❏ partner |
| ❏ identify | ❏ plan |

Another common organizational value that emerged from the cases is that most of the companies have aggressive growth plans and are strategically using knowledge and learning to leverage expansion. In addition, a high-trust climate is seen as a precondition to encourage knowledge flow, innovation, and intellectual curiosity leading to productivity. Another value is a belief that learning and knowledge matter on the bottom line. That sets the stage for including learning and knowledge efforts in strategic planning at the highest levels.

A last organizational value—a passion shared by every CKO and CLO in the cases—is the importance of running a customer-centered business and including customers as knowledge partners. Several of the CKOs and CLOs mentioned that their customers are developing a greater knowledge base and a greater understanding of how they want their needs met. An analogy would be a physician who must keep up with her Internet-informed patients on the newest drugs and treatments.

The second broad category of organizational systems and structure has as its first element information technology, which can be viewed either as the primary driver for knowledge management or as an enabler to maximize human interaction, knowledge sharing, and learning. Organizations must choose their own technology-people mix, based on their needs and culture.

Another element of organizational systems and structure is the integration of IT, HR, and business units to support and maximize knowledge management and learning. CKOs and CLOs almost universally view that as one of their mandates. Another element is an emphasis on high-level strategic systems, planning, and thinking. A company's strategy for knowledge management should reflect its competitive strategy and can either emphasize a codification strategy that relies on fast information systems or a personalization system that solves strategic problems by channeling individual expertise.

An additional element is the existence of formal positions such as CKO, CLO, or a variant of knowledge or learning manager to ensure that appropriate activities occur systematically and enterprisewide. A final element is the measurement and standards to ensure compliance, to support continuous quantifiable productivity of knowledge and learning efforts, and to determine their strategic outcomes.

Many CKOs and CLOs start out as management consultants, training specialists, or technology experts, although some have backgrounds in library science, engineering, geology, OD, and general management. Because these positions are new, years of experience as a former CKO or CLO isn't expected or required. The desirable skill mix for a CKO or CLO depends in large part on the expectations and needs of an organization's senior management team, its culture, and its business imperatives.

What senior managers are looking for in either position is someone with the right temperament, an ability to think strategically, and a strong sense of business imperatives. Because a CKO or CLO usually operates through persuasion and personal influence, incumbents need to have strong interpersonal skills, be energetic, be pragmatic yet highly flexible, and be tolerant of the uncertainties of their jobs. Most first-generation CKOs and CLOs enjoy the newness of the job as a plus. Kelly Bennan,

CLO at Sedgwick Claims Management Services, an insurance and risk-management firm, says that the thing she finds most appealing about her job is the "blank slate and the ability to be creative in how my group delivers learning."

Breadth of career experience, familiarity with their organizations, and an infectious enthusiasm for knowledge and learning are other characteristics of this group. Most describe themselves as "change agents"; many emphasize their design skills in the sense of designing new jobs, new knowledge or learning systems, and new solutions. They also like being on the innovative forefront of their industries. Knowledge management has been called a fusion between collection and connection, and the job qualifications reflect that.

HRD professionals, unlike any others, stand poised to help create knowledge-friendly workplaces. Knowledge and learning leaders can help organizations maximize their own unique knowledge and learning strategies; integrate the information technology, HR, and business units; and strategically link knowledge and learning to business goals and competitive advantage.

Aspiring chief learning officers can seize the moment as a unique opportunity to take training and education once and for all into the boardroom. SAIC's Cataldo advises future CKOs and CLOs to "get to know the learning resources in your company as soon as possible. Focus on learning as a business as well as a growth opportunity. Create a series of events to get your vision and message out to line managers and the learning community. Last, continually emphasize the impact learning has on achieving a company's business goals and on employees' future careers."

# ABSTRACT

## RELEVANT, RELIABLE, USEFUL:
## HELP IN FINDING GOOD INFORMATION

*Editor's Comment*: In the column "Tech Trends" in *TRAINING* Magazine, author Reid Goldsborough makes the interesting point that Web users who search for information and view the Web as a giant library need ways to organize information and help in finding relevant, reliable, and useful information. He examines issues of "the human touch" as opposed to the technology approach as information-seeking users "penctrate . . . the Web's awesome depths."

Here is a list in alphabetical order of 10 Web sites that lead users onward in information seeking— sites that are based on the fundamentally human characteristics that truly enable individuals to seek and find good information, sites that minimize the technology "wow" factor:

*www.allexperts.com*—1500 volunteers provide searching help

*www.expertcentral.com*—human assistance with search topics

*www.hotbot.com*—best all-round search site according to *PC Magazine*

*www.northernlight.com*—contains full text news reprints, with e-mail notification

*www.profusion.com*—a metasearch site that combines many search sites

*www.searchenginewatch.com*—another metasearch site

*www.searchiq.com*—another metasearch site

*www.titansearch.com*—you'll like this one if you want to advertise on the Web

*www.yourcompass.com*—tracks your interests and alerts you to new information

*www.xpertsite.com*—provides human assistance with searching

*Source:* "Untangling the Web" by Reid Goldsborough in *TRAINING Magazine*, February 2000, p. 34. Reid Goldsborough is a syndicated columnist and author of the book, *Straight Talk About the Information Superhighway*.

# 1C. REFOCUSING WORK FOR LEARNING

## ARTICLE REPRINT

## JOBS VERSUS WORK

*Editor's Comment*: This article reprint begins a set of 5 entries that deal with refocusing work for learning. The ideas contained in these 5 entries address the challenges facing training managers of viewing today's work differently—as more than a job, more than a set of skills, and of a worker as more than a labor cost. Learning has become an important context of the workplace; work and training for work, within a learning framework, presents new challenges to managers in the way they organize work processes and in the way they provide resources and support for worker-learners.

### JOBS DISAPPEAR WHEN WORK BECOMES MORE IMPORTANT

#### *by Shari Caudron*

On the surface, Koch Industries and Amazon.com don't have much in common.

Koch, based in Wichita, Kansas, employs 14,000 people worldwide and is America's second largest privately held company. It has a 60-year history in industries as diverse as chemicals, agriculture, financial services, and oil and gas. Koch employs everyone from farmers in Montana to commodities traders in London.

Amazon.com, based in Seattle, employs 5,000 people and is publicly traded. Six years ago, Amazon led the way as a standard bearer of a whole new industry—e-commerce—and employs Internet savvy business professionals.

But despite their outward differences, Koch Industries and Amazon.com are remarkably similar in one respect: They don't hire people for traditional job slots. They hire people to work.

Walk into the HR departments of these companies and you won't find a complex system of job classifications, pay grades, promotional charts and job descriptions. "We don't have any of that normal HR structure," says Paul Wheeler, vice president of HR for Koch Industries.

Neither does Amazon.com. "We focus on what needs to be done," explains Scott Pitasky, director of strategic growth—which is Amazon's word for HR. "Here, a person might be in the same 'job,' but three months later doing completely different work."

As disorganized as it may sound, these companies are actually role models for 21st century human resource practices. Why? Because their HR professionals understand that the traditional way of organizing work in which a person is hired, paid and trained to do *a specific job* is simply too rigid for today's ever-changing marketplace.

To succeed, more companies will have to follow Koch and Amazon's lead and begin to seriously rethink the way they organize and accomplish work. Simply put, jobs as we know them are fast becoming relics of a bygone era.

*Source:* "Jobs Disappear When *Work* Becomes More Important" by Shari Caudron in *Workforce*, January 2000, pp. 30–32. Shari Caudron is a contributing editor for *Workforce*. Reprinted with permission of *Workforce*, a publication of ACC Communications, Costa Mesa, CA. Copyright 2000. All rights reserved. *www.workforce.com*

While employers, employees, paychecks and careers will remain, the rigid lines we draw around work itself will be gone.

## EMPLOYEES LEAD THE CHANGE

On the surface, this sea of change in work design can seem overwhelming, especially since we've all been conditioned to think of work *as* a job. But the fact of the matter is that change is already well underway, and ironically, it's employees who are leading the effort.

After a decade of downsizing, outsourcing, restructuring and stern admonitions about the end of job security, employees appear to have gotten the message that they're responsible for their own career management. Employees get the idea there's no such thing as a steady and secure job anymore, and they're doing something about it by taking ownership of their own work situations.

Unfortunately, even though employers have been the ones telling workers not to rely on their jobs, those same employers aren't doing as much as they can to accommodate workers who are seeking more flexibility in the employment relationship. Instead, companies appear determined to fill designated job slots just as they always have.

"Clearly, there's a gap between what people actually do [in the workplace] and how organizations tend to define and organize what they do," explains David Dotlich, a Portland, Oregon-based partner of CDR International. "This isn't surprising because bureaucratic systems are always outdated and typically unwilling to change."

In fact, you have to wonder if maybe the current labor shortage wouldn't be so acute if companies were more flexible in how they organized work. For instance, a company that's having difficulty finding people to fill two full-time jobs might be able to tap into the skill sets of four people seeking part-time work, and still get the same work accomplished.

## ORGANIZE WORK WITHOUT JOBS

Since we aren't able to predict and organize work as narrowly as used to, how should companies organize the tasks that need to be done? If we don't have jobs, what do we have?

To begin to understand how to make this shift, you need to start thinking more about work and less about jobs. If you can recondition yourself to think about how to accomplish work—as opposed to how to fill jobs—you've already gone a long way toward building more elasticity into your organization.

One widely discussed approach involves using a much smaller core of payroll employees to manage the work of a much greater pool of contingent or "affinity" workers. By bringing in temporary and contract employees as project needs demand, companies can accomplish work without the drag of a bloated, job-based bureaucracy.

One way to think of this model is to think of how the Hollywood economy works. Producers, directors, actors and a huge supporting cast of business professionals come together around specific films, collaborate intensely and then disband. While the production company may oversee the entire project, the number of full-time employees who remain with that company in between films is extremely small.

Another model is the one used by Koch Industries and Amazon.com. These companies spend a lot of time hiring people who are the right fit for the company as opposed to the right fit for a job. At Amazon.com, this means recruiting people who have entrepreneurial drive and are extremely customer-centric. "We try not to be rigid around qualifications, but on the kind of people we hire and how they can apply what they know," explains Pitasky.

Beverly Goldberg, vice president of The Century Foundation in New York City, and author of "Age works" (The Free Press, 2000) is a strong advocate of this approach. "We need to begin to think about where we need what skills and how we put those packages of skills together," she explains. "We can't just look at hiring people for specific positions. We have to look at what those people bring to the company overall."

Clearly, for this kind of system to work, the organizational structure has to be pretty flexible, employees have to be exposed to different opportunities and managers have to be willing to let employees experiment and move around. "We've learned it's more important to focus on what employees want to do, what projects are available, and what skills are needed than it is to focus on the structure of the organization,"

## The Evolution of Jobs?

**W**hen you understand how jobs were developed, you can begin to see why they are no longer the most effective way to organize work in our companies.

**Farmers just worked.** Until the early 19th century, farmers, craftspeople and shop owners didn't have jobs; they did work that needed doing. They worked on shifting clusters of tasks in a variety of locations on schedules set by sunlight and the needs of the day.

But as society became more industrialized, we needed a better way to package work in the growing factories and bureaucracies—and jobs were born.

**Industrialization created jobs.** William Bridges, who was the first to identify the de-jobbing phenomenon in his book, "JobShift" (Addison Wesley, 1994), explains, "Jobs were the way we packaged work in repetitive situations in which responsibilities were narrowly defined."

In the assembly-line environment, employers could hire, train and pay people to do specific "jobs" because markets were slow moving and jobs rarely changed.

**Jobs interfere with work.** Today, however, companies, industries and work processes are changing so continually that rigid job structures actually interfere with our ability to do work. If you don't know what business your company will be involved with next year, how can you possibly know what kind of jobs will be needed? While we can rewrite an employee's job description occasionally, we can't be doing it every week.

The other problem with job-based work is that it sets up expectations on the part of employees that can impede creativity, risk taking and personal responsibility. This is because whenever the "job" dominates people's thinking, they don't work at what needs doing; they "do their jobs."

For example, if you're hired to work in a call center and your job description lists tasks to be completed via the telephone, are you likely to take the initiative to suggest a more effective approach using the Internet to service customers? Probably not.

"For a long time, HR has fooled itself into thinking that what was changing was corporate strategy, technology, market competitiveness and all of those things that are outside of the HR department," Bridges says. But in fact, what is changing is the fundamental nature of how work gets done, who does it and how it's rewarded—and it's high time that HR paid attention. —*SC*

Pitasky says. "Here, individual managers have more responsibility for organizing work than HR does."

### PERSON DESCRIPTIONS INSTEAD OF JOB DESCRIPTIONS?

Underriding both of these models is an idea proposed by Ed Lawler of the Center for Effective Organizations at the University of Southern California in Los Angeles. Lawler, who agrees that jobs are seriously outdated, believes that the work contract between employers and workers has to become more individualized.

"I believe we're seeing a fundamental shift toward HR management systems that focus on individuals and their skills and knowledge as opposed to standardized job systems," he says.

"Instead of job descriptions, we're going to start seeing 'person' descriptions that allow companies to continually match and rematch employees to specific projects."

Obviously, this is a vast departure from most current organizational models that err on the side of standardization while paying little attention to individual differences. Sure, we encourage individual contributions, but we still hire, manage and compensate employees as if they came from exactly the same mold.

In a de-jobbed world where employees are treated as individuals as opposed to cogs in a giant work machine, how can HR treat employees equitably? Hasn't the enormous job-based structure developed, in part, in response to the employees' need for fairness? Yes, but ironically, the need for fairness came about *because* we proposed to treat everybody the same.

"If employment contracts are negotiated based on business needs and individual capabilities, and everybody acknowledges that there are no standardized job slots to check equity against, then the whole notion of fairness disappears," William Bridges, author of "Jobshift" (Addison Wesley, 1994), says.

In fact, a de-jobbed world would operate very much like the world of high-profile sports and entertainment where individuals negotiate contracts based on their individual talents and contributions. "Nobody in these industries suggests there ought to be standardization," he adds.

## HOW DOES HR MAKE THE SHIFT?

Reorganizing work affects virtually everything HR does. People have to be hired based on their actual abilities and not on some subjective educational requirements. Compensation should be based on a person's individual contributions,

not on arbitrary job classifications. Job descriptions should focus on results and outcomes, not on tasks—and on and on.

Granted, these are gross generalizations about how HR needs to reinvent itself. But for HR professionals to prevent their own jobs from being outsourced, they must understand what work is required for their company to be successful, and then determine the most efficient way to accomplish that work—and jobs just don't cut it anymore.

As Roger Herman, management consultant and president of The Herman Group in Greensboro, North Carolina, explains: "We're moving into a much different world and we cannot survive tomorrow using the same approaches we used yesterday, let alone today." As we enter the 21st century, we've got to once and for all get rid of 19th century management practices. Today's workers aren't simply interchangeable parts in a machine, and we shouldn't treat them as such.

# ARTICLE REPRINT

## PARADIGM SHIFT: WORKER AS INVESTOR

*Editor's Comment*: As Thomas O. Davenport says in his opening page of this article, "A new century requires a new metaphor" (p. 30). Here, Davenport casts the knowledge worker of today as a repository of value, fueled by increasing levels of education to create more and better human capital. He sees more education resident in workers as the potential for more capital to invest and also for greater returns on investment to both the individual and the company. In short, he sees today's knowledge worker as an investor. This article elaborates on this and other interesting paradigm-shifting kinds of ideas. His kind of worker presents the training manager with unique kinds of management and training challenges.

## WORKERS ARE *NOT* ASSETS

### *by Thomas O. Davenport*

As stressful as today's workplace has become, most of us don't have to worry about being eaten alive by rats. In Upton Sinclair's 1906 muckraking novel *The Jungle*, one young boy, assigned to carry beer for other workers, sneaks too many samples and falls asleep in the corner. The next morning, his factory mates find only what the rats have left behind. Horrific as it is, this image is no more striking than many others that Sinclair created. His rendering of the danger, fear, and squalor that workers endured in turn-of-the-century meat-packing plants set the stage for widespread reform in the American food-processing industry. And of all the degradation heaped on workers by the rulers of Packingtown, which weighed heaviest? It was, in Sinclair's view, that the Beef Trust treated workers as *assets*, just like the animals they butchered:

"Jurgis [the protagonist] recollected how, when he had first come to Packingtown, he had stood and watched the hog killing, and thought how cruel and savage it was, and come away congratulating himself that he was not a hog; now his new acquaintance showed him that a hog was just what he had been—one of the packers' hogs. What they wanted from a hog was all the profits that could be got out of him; and that was what they wanted from the working man. . . . What the hog thought of it, and what he suffered, were not considered; and no more was it with labour."

"Workers are assets" has become the dominant metaphor of late 20th-century management. In some ways, it represents a worthy elevation of employees to the status they deserve. People are, after all, the chief engine of prosperity for most organizations. What other factor of production contributes so much to strategic success? In other ways, however, the asset metaphor falls short of fully expressing the value that people bring to the workplace and the control they exercise over its investment. I believe we have a better metaphor at our disposal.

## IF WORKERS ARE ASSETS, WHAT DOES THAT MAKE MANAGERS?

Why spend time contemplating this common managerial expression? The reason, simply put, is that language matters. Indeed, some sociologists believe that the essence of management is skillful use of language to create meaning. Confucius, when asked what he would do if he ruled a country, said that his first act would be to fix the language. Given the potential power of metaphors, it is easy to see why managers become enamored with their use. To leaders, they represent a tool not merely to describe reality but also to create it. To observers, they provide a window onto the managerial landscape. The asset metaphor exemplifies the evolution of a figure of speech—and of the underlying attitude toward workers—over the better part of a decade. In the late 1980s and early 1990s, workers had not yet ascended to asset status in the minds of most senior managers. As the downsizing trend of that period suggests, managers viewed workers as costs to be cut back whenever economic pressures forced an expense reduction.

Things turned around over the next several years, however, and we entered the Age of the Employee as Asset. Although job cuts continued at high levels, they nevertheless decreased from the 56 percent of 1990-91 to the mid-40s for the next several years. "Employees are our most important assets" became the mantra for annual reports and press releases. But the phrase often had a hollow ring. In its *People Strategy Benchmark Awareness and Attitude Study*, for example, Towers Perrin consultants noted: "An overwhelming majority of corporate executives seem to be giving lip service to the notion of people as strategic assets." The study went on to say, "Although 90 percent of the 300 executives interviewed said their employees are the most important variable in their company's success, they ranked specific people-related issues far below other business priorities." When asked to rank strategic business priorities, respondents placed investing in people behind customer satisfaction, financial performance, competitiveness, and quality of products and services. If companies truly treated people as valuable strategic assets, managers would quickly see that a competent, ded-

icated workforce is a prerequisite for success in any of these other areas. Investing in people would surely take on a higher priority.

A manager who likens a worker to an asset has evoked two related but distinct ideas. On the one hand, the metaphor ennobles workerhood by emphasizing the tangible value that people contribute to the enterprises in which they toil. In this sense, the asset idea helps underscore that workers represent more than grist for industrial mills. People bring ingenuity, creativity, and initiative to their companies; they deserve more respect than the average drill press. When considered from this angle, the asset metaphor represents a clear improvement over the worker-as-cost idea that lay at the heart of widespread downsizing.

On the other hand, the asset metaphor shortchanges workers by placing them in the same class as those very drill presses. Think back to Accounting 101, where your professor defined an asset as an object or a legal right that meets three criteria: It can produce future service value, can be owned or controlled, and can be valued in monetary terms. Obviously, people do perform services that create financial value; to that point, the metaphor holds. Apart from representing value in a general way, however, workers bear little resemblance to assets. Consider that:

- With a decline in loyalty between worker and organization, the notion that a company enjoys ownership—even abstract or emotional—of employee assets has long since become passé.

- Assets are passive—bought, sold, and replaced at the whim of their owners; workers, in contrast, take increasingly active control over their working lives.

- Despite the best efforts of accountants, methods for attaching financial value to human resources have proved elusive and flawed; moreover, the effort to denominate all value in dollar terms obscures other value sources and metrics.

And consider this question: If workers are assets, what does that make managers? Buses are assets, and they have drivers. Airplanes show up on the asset side of the balance sheet, and they have pilots. Soldiers consider tanks assets, and tanks have commanders. If people are assets, then managers are clearly in the driver's seat.

The asset metaphor perpetuates the gulf between the brawn and the brains, the doers and the thinkers, the hogs and the packers. In the words of management accounting expert Eric Flamholtz, "To treat people as an asset is to confuse the agent that provides services with the asset itself (the expected services)."

Casual users of the employee-as-asset metaphor would protest this assessment. They would declare that they mean people have value to companies, not that the companies actually own their people. One might respond that casual users should choose their words more carefully. As Mark Twain wrote, "The difference between the *almost*-right word and the *right* word is really a large matter—it's the difference between the lightning bug and the lightning." It's time to take the asset metaphor to a new level, to think of workers not as human capital but, rather, as human-capital owners and investors. Two important ideas underlie the work-as-investor metaphor: ownership and return on investment.

**Human-capital ownership and control:** Like the asset notion, the investor metaphor emphasizes value. Investorship, however, also evokes active ideas like building human capital, contributing it to organizations, and controlling its investment. People possess innate abilities, behaviors, personal energy, and time. These elements make up human capital—the currency people bring to invest in their jobs. Workers, not organizations, own this human capital. Workers, not organizations, decide when, how, and where they will contribute it. Like financial investors, some human-capital investors are more active than others. The point is that, as the owners of their capital, they can make choices. Control differentiates asset owners from assets, investors from the currency they invest.

**Return on human-capital investment:** A worker who acts like a human-capital investor will place his investable capital where it can earn the highest return. Thinking of workers as investors underscores a fundamental reality: Investment and return make up a two-way flow. Training provides a good example. Thoughtful managers understand that increasing worker knowledge improves productivity—by as much as 16 percent, according to a study cited in a

National Bureau of Economic Research working paper. Training therefore looks like an excellent investment in worker assets. Increased training investment was one milepost on the road between employees-as-costs and employees-as-assets.

Training also contributes to improved return on people's investment in work, however. In a knowledge-intensive workplace, people believe that learning new skills will help them in finding and keeping a satisfying job—a job that pays a high return on their human-capital investment. Moreover, the gratification that comes from learning is itself a return on the human capital that a worker puts into the job.

Conceiving of workers as investors rather than assets emphasizes that the link between employee and company depends not on ownership, paternalism, or blind loyalty. Instead, the cord binding organizations and people derives from the ability and willingness of each to provide benefits to the other. The relationship assumes mutual benefit, with neither party elevated at the expense of the other. If I want to energize my workforce, I will tell them what I expect them to invest and how I intend to earn their investment. I will not liken them to forklifts or other line items on my balance sheet.

## THE WELL-ENDOWED WORKER RULES

If the investor metaphor has legitimacy, then it must faithfully reflect the reality it is intended to express. Let us see if worker-as-investor passes muster.

**Who they are:** Investorship emphasizes the primacy of personal resources, the (chiefly) mental powers that workers bring to their jobs and their organizations. These powers carry increasing importance in today's and tomorrow's workplace.

The term *knowledge worker* flows easily off the tongues of managers these days. It borders on cliché status; still, it is too important to dismiss just because people use it loosely. Economy-wide employment trends illustrate the growing importance of work whose value comes from what people know instead of what they produce with their physical powers.

Even if downsizing has subsided, human-capital market shifts have not. In the year ending mid-1997, for instance, hourly jobs represented the largest class of new jobs added, and the biggest focus for job elimination as well. Among professional and technical workers (the core of the knowledge-worker class), things looked rosy. This category had the second-highest job-creation percentage in each of the previous three years; companies have consistently created more technical and professional jobs than they have eliminated. The opposite is true for supervisory and middle-management jobs. These groups showed the most anemic job growth and elimination percentages far above creation percentages over the whole three years.

Moreover, changes in the substance of the managerial job give further evidence of how human-capital requirements continue to evolve. Two things seem to be happening at once. On the one hand, a broad spectrum of workers have taken on what used to be considered managerial tasks. As the same time, people with manager titles do not necessarily (or solely) oversee people. They may also act as analysts, coordinators, and problem-solvers; they make decisions, oversee outsourced functions, and call on clients.

Looking ahead to the future state of flat organizations, management guru Charles Handy says that eventually, "Everyone will increasingly be expected not only to be good at something, to have their own professional or technical expertise, but will also very rapidly acquire responsibility for money, people, or projects, or all three, a managerial task in other words." Everyone will manage something, but nobody will only manage, and we will all need to know things to succeed.

**What they have to invest:** Education builds human capital the way fertilizer grows plants. In 1960, among all Americans 25 years or older, 7.7 percent had completed four years of college or more. By 1990, the percentage had almost tripled to 21.3 percent; it increased to 23 percent in 1995. Almost 1.2 million people received bachelor's degrees in 1993, a 19 percent gain over the 1985 total. Colleges and universities awarded 411,717 master's degrees and doctorates in 1993, 29 percent more than the 1985 total.

More education means more capital to invest and potentially greater returns on investment. Analysis by the Bureau of Labor Statistics shows that a college degree provides particularly significant leverage when combined with later job training. The extra time and effort required to

finish college no doubt imparts some valuable knowledge that translates into earning power. Getting the degree also bespeaks initiative that doubtless contributes to greater productivity and higher compensation. Whatever the source of the effect, the BLS analysis lends credence to the investor metaphor—more human capital to invest means greater investment returns.

Having more human capital also means more job opportunities. These days, well-endowed worker-investors sit in the driver's seat when it comes to finding work. Consider that while the nationwide unemployment rate hovered a little under 5 percent, the unemployment rate in Silicon Valley fell to a microscopic 2.3 percent at the end of 1997. In this cradle of high-tech civilization, technically oriented human capital means a multitude of job opportunities. The only people unemployed are those who prefer surfing the waves in Santa Cruz to surfing the Net in Santa Clara.

**How much investment flexibility they have:** Knowledge workers have ascended; education has built human capital. By themselves, do these facts support the investor metaphor? Yes, but not much more strongly than the asset metaphor. The tiebreaker is flexibility. Financial investors move their capital when they think they can find higher returns elsewhere. This is the essence of free-market investing—taking action (or choosing not to) in response to return-on-investment results. The keys are choice and flexibility. Do human-capital investors have them? Increasingly, it seems they do. In the late 1980s and early 1990s, declining job duration reflected widespread downsizing. However, the continuing trend toward shorter employment tenures must reflect something more than unilateral company cuts. More likely, the trend suggests growing worker confidence in the availability of other jobs. In a 1997 *Inc.* magazine survey, 42 percent of respondents said they expected to stay with their current employers for the next 10 years. Almost as many, however, said they will probably change jobs voluntarily during that period. Only 4 percent expect to be forced out by job termination.

Although labor-market mobility may frustrate employers, a certain amount contributes to economic health. Human capital needs to move as freely as does any other capital form, finding the highest yields on its investment. The increasing velocity of human-capital flows carries a wake-up call for employers. Employees' freedom to leave, to transfer this investable currency, is what makes people investors in a world where assets wait passively to be deployed.

## A RETURN TO THE BAD OLD DAYS?

Viewing workers as investors underscores an essential fact of workplace life—work is a two-way exchange of value, not a one-way exploitation of an asset by its owner. At this point, a thoughtful reader will ask the following questions: Does this point of view have staying power? Will some new metaphor take its place in half a decade, the way other metaphors have been displaced before it? Will the next shift in our economic fortunes mean a return to the bad old days of viewing workers as costs?

My crystal ball is no clearer than anyone else's. Unemployment may well fluctuate from lower-than-a-snail's-basement numbers to buddy-can-you-spare-a-dime levels. Buyer's markets become seller's markets, and on we go.

Although the workplace will surely continue to transmogrify, I believe, substantial time will pass before economic factors undercut the value of human capital. In good times, companies need to attract the owners of valuable human capital, make a deal with them, and provide the highest possible return on investment commensurate with sound fiscal management. In cost-conscious periods, companies still need to hold on to key people, keep them engaged in their jobs despite a risky and threatening environment, and cast an even more watchful eye on the costs associated with rewarding individual contribution. The two situations call for fundamentally the same human-capital management skills, applied in different ways.

Moreover, regardless of what happens in the economy at large, technological evolution will continue to support human-capital creation and flow in three ways. First, technology feeds on human-capital creation, increasing the demand for people who have the knowledge, skill, and talent to create the hard and soft components of information systems. Want a career with a future? Try computer sciences. Of the five occupations expected to grow fastest as the United States moves toward the year 2005, two require computer know-how (computer engineers and systems analysts).

Second, technology-based information networks enhance the marketplace for human-capital exchange; witness the rise of Internet sites that reduce the time and cost required to change jobs. Third, technology spurs the speed-of-light creation and transfer of knowledge, further fueling the growth of human capital and making it harder for companies to corral.

What does all this mean for individual worker-investors? Simply this—they must deal with a constantly evolving context for human-capital investment. The workplace is its own micro-climate; wait a minute and the weather will change. The predictability that once characterized the employment relationship is a fossil left behind by organizational evolution.

What does it mean for companies? Instead of worrying about calculating the worth of human assets, companies should concern themselves with defining what human-capital owners get out of their association with a business. In other words, they should focus less on the value of the individual to the organization, and more on the value of the organization to the individual. This is the true value that deserves attention from managers who hope to create lasting success.

Companies that care enough to measure the value of the organization to the employee will attract people looking for the best place to put their human capital. These organizations position themselves to increase other forms of value—tangible, intangible, and financial. Such companies will prosper, at the expense of competitors and headhunters.

# CASE STUDY

## RESTRUCTURING FOR PERFORMANCE

*Editor's Comment*: This long article in *Sloan Management Review* is a detailed case study of Xerox Corporation's experiment with the intentional creation and development of a "strategic community" built upon the challenges of responsible and independent action that faced a pivotal information technology group within the larger organization. Xerox called this the Technology Strategy Infrastructure Group, and its mission clearly was strategic action. We reprint here an introductory paragraph about the project, and give you two tables that succinctly capture the principles and action directions of the new "community." Training managers who need a model for refocusing work to encourage and enable individual and organizational learning, take notice! It is well worth reading the entire article in the Winter 2000 edition of *Sloan Management Review*. Phone 617/253-7170; ask for Reprint #4125.

Xerox Corporation, in making the transition from a proprietary information technology (IT) infrastructure to an industry standard, took a third approach: the purposeful development of a *strategic community* consisting of a large group of IT professionals working at corporate headquarters and in the business units (see "More about the Transition Alliance"). We believe that this structure is a new, important organizational phenomenon, of great use in a world of increasingly dispersed human resources where firms need to wisely leverage their intellectual capital. For Xerox, this approach produced a variety of benefits. First, the strategic community provided a means for IT professionals to manage their complex infrastructure more effectively. They were better able to provide high-quality, validated solutions to issues; to handle unstructured problems; and to deal with the never-ending new developments in hardware and software. Second, the group operated as an efficient mechanism for knowledge sharing, which filters into the business units. In either of the more traditional matrix structures, knowledge sharing may occur, but that knowledge frequently remains *unused*. Finally, motivation for learning and developing at an individual level seemed greater in this community structure than in other organizational forms, which has important implications for the longer-term performance of these individuals at Xerox.

## STRATEGIC COMMUNITY: ADDING VALUE TO THE ORGANIZATION

| Nature of Added Value | Attributes that Create Value |
|---|---|
| Higher quality knowledge creation | • Diversity in membership and less emphasis on hierarchical status reduce the probability of group-think.<br>• Limited requirement for format reporting allows people to engage in riskier brainstorming.<br>• Reflection process that occurs at the end of a meeting consolidates learning. |
| Fewer surprises and revisions in plans | • Broad participation diffuses knowledge across business units.<br>• Openness of interaction format results in effective conflict resolution. |
| Greater capacity to deal with unstructured problems | • Work occurs under a set of superordinate goals rather than task goals.<br>• Self-modification of the community role is acceptable to the sponsoring organization.<br>• Knowledge leaders are allowed to emerge on the basis of issues rather than by assignment to a team or roles within a team. |
| More effective knowledge sharing among business units and corporate staff units | • Voluntary participation implies higher motivation that in turn leads to faster, deeper internalization of learning.<br>• Indeterminate life span and long-term relationships increase trust. |
| Improved likelihood of implementing joint goal | • The community yields greater external validity because the community exists outside of the formal organizational structure.<br>• The community has more influence than a single individual, particularly given the organizational level of the community members. |
| More effective individual development and learning | • Learning as part of a group is more effective than learning alone.<br>• The opportunity to learn by engaging in practice is embodied in processes that the community developed. |

## KEY PRINCIPLES SUPPORTING STRATEGIC COMMUNITIES

| Community Characteristic | Actions |
|---|---|
| Interaction format | • Organize regular face-to-face meetings.<br>• Stimulate candid dialogue.<br>• Structure for serendipity. |
| Organizational culture | • Leverage common training, experience, and vocabulary<br>• Facilitate working around constraints. |
| Mutual interest | • Build commitment by demonstrating visible progress toward a common goal.<br>• Promote continuous improvement of the community's processes. |
| Individual and collective learning | • Recognize and reward teaching others and learning from others.<br>• Leverage knowledge and experience of respected peers.<br>• Provide an environment in which reflection about learning occurs. |
| Knowledge sharing | • Embed knowledge sharing into work practices.<br>• Reinforce its value with immediate feedback. |
| Community processes and norms | • Permit establishment of a "zone of safety" that builds trust and community identity.<br>• Minimize linkage to the formal control structure.<br>• Motivate the community to establish its own governance processes. |

# EXCERPT

## NEW TOOLS FOR FACILITATION AND SHARING

*Editor's Comment*: These pages from the larger Conference Board report, *Beyond Knowledge Management: New Ways to Work and Learn*, give descriptions of Common Tactics in practice and Common Tools in use in various companies and organizations (Xerox, Shell Oil, IBM, U.S. Army, Alcoa, Nortel, Nickleodeon, Steelcase, NBC, and others). Useful tips on turning knowledge into action are reprinted here.

## COMMON TACTICS

### *Communities of Practice*

The notion of a community of practice came from research at the Institute for Research on Learning and Xerox PARC in Palo Alto, California. The research discovered that learning takes place in and around communities of practice.[6] As people find a reason to work together, they share stories and lessons learned. In short, they teach each other the practice.

Communities of practice have proven to be one of the most valuable forms of knowledge sharing, yet they:

- lack a formal structure, although they can fit within an existing organizational structure or may be converted to a formal structure at some point;

- are not standardized, although they can choose to set and follow standards for themselves;

- are hard to locate and define, but organizational ethnography and anthropology can help find them;

- have an exclusive membership defined by the community; and

- are early warning systems and drivers of changes in the organizational "ecosystem" if properly cultivated, not managed."[7]

Rather, a community of practice is a group of people who share a particular practice, interest, or discipline and who share information and tacit knowledge. They may be HTML programmers, service technicians, a sales team, etc. Scott Beaty of Shell Oil Company communicates this notion to Shell employees as "like people doing like work." Other firms use the term networks to describe communities of practice, in order to avoid jargon.

[6]J.S. Brown and P. Duguid, "Organizational Learning and Communities of Practice: Toward a Unified View of Working, Learning and Innovation," *Organization Science*, Vol. 2, No. 1, 1991, pp. 40–57. See also Etienne Wegner, *Communities of Practice: Learning, Meaning and Identity* (Cambridge, United Kingdom: Cambridge University Press, 1998).

[7]Adapted, with comments by Arian Ward, from Robert H. Stambaugh, "The Death and Life of HRIS: How Engineering and ERPs are Suffocating HR Innovation and Knowledge Creation in the Modern Corporation," *IHRIM Journal*, December 1998, pp. 23–32.

*Source: : Beyond Knowledge Management: New Ways to Work and Learn*, Research Report 1262-00-RR, pages 25–31. The Conference Board, Inc., 2000. Excerpts reprinted with permission of The Conference Board, Inc., New York, NY. All rights reserved. Copies of the full report of 72 pages are available at a cost of $195. Telephone 212/759-0900; fax 212/980-7014; *www.conference-board.org*.

But not everyone agrees that a community of practice cannot be defined. IBM's Fred Schoeps says:

We invest very systematically in communities of practice. Each has a competency leader and a core team of practitioners. We manage intellectual capital and organizational knowledge through these communities. Membership in the community includes both trained practitioners who have access to methodologies and extended members. Decisions about training requirements, certification, methodologies, community tools, and management of the communities' intellectual capital are within the purview of the competency leader and the core team. Furthermore, communities are moving onto the intranet, using a suite of Web and Lotus applications to support the members of the community.

As part of a systematic learning effort, companies can provide resources, such as free time and meeting spaces, to support communities of practice. They can also provide opportunities for bridging across communities or even to customers or suppliers. This is done face-to-face and is supplemented with intranets, e-mail, or video conferencing.

The value of communities of practice can go unrecognized by senior and middle management. One key role for executives is to foster such communities and explain their value, but avoid getting in their way. One example is to give the manufacturing team access to the sales forecasting information. By taking that step, the company is doing more than shortening time-to-market; it is creating a new bridge across communities.

Other ways of aiding communities of practice include:

- recognizing, acknowledging, and training the key support roles, such as facilitators, knowledge stewards, and knowledge/relationship brokers;

- helping identify communities of practice that do or could exist in the organization and supporting their attempts to cultivate an effective group with visible commitment and extra resources;

- building the cultivation and nurturing of these communities into business strategies;

- leading the cultivation and nurturing of external communities, including customers, suppliers, and the investment community;

- tapping the knowledge and potential for key projects; and

- leveraging the power of communities for driving organizational change efforts.

## After Action Reviews

The U.S. Army defines After Action Reviews (AARs) as a professional discussion of an event, focused on performance standards, that enables participants to discover what happened, why it happened, and how to sustain strengths and improve on weaknesses. AARs integrate learning and action to collectively analyze decisions made at all levels. They combine use of information with careful facilitation to create a non-hierarchical environment for inquiry and team learning. Formal AARs are scheduled after each mission and can last a few hours; informal AARs are run consistently after other events, even if it is a five-minute review to build on lessons learned. The ability to lead an AAR is critical for Army leaders. The process entails asking three consecutive questions: What happened? Why did it happen? What should we do about it? Clear ground rules encourage candor, total involvement, and focus on objectives.

## Learning Histories

A learning history is a retrospective history of significant events in a company's recent past, described in the voices of people who took part in them. Researched through reflective interviews and quote-checked scrupulously, the learning history uses story-telling to help a company evaluate and accelerate its progress in learning.

Managers, hourly workers, union leaders, senior executives, suppliers, consultants, and customers are all included in the circle—identified only by position, as anonymously as possible. In this way, the document creates a record that allows people to recognize their own blinders and to see their own point of view in the context of a larger, shared understanding.

The value of the learning history comes not so much from the document itself, but from the consultation process that is built around it—the conversations in which people create shared meaning, deepen their understandings, and talk through possibilities for more effective action.

## *Making Conferences More Productive*

Currently on trial at one working group company is an innovative conferencing system aimed at filling the gap between existing audio and video conferencing services. It uses the PC on people's desks to enhance audio conferences through the use of a virtual meeting room displayed on the screen. This supports:

- Graphical display of the other participants;

- Microphone and speaker muting;

- Optional floor control by a chairperson;

- Whiteboarding, application sharing, file transfer, and chat facilities;

- Invitation of additional participants (including audio-only participants); and

- Single-click joining of conferences

Conferences are more productive: They empower the users to tackle a range of business activities with the consequent savings of time and money. Examples of likely applications are:

- Meetings. The whiteboard or a shared word processor can be used to capture issues, brainstorm, or take minutes and make them visible to all.

- Team briefings. Slide presentations can be imported into the whiteboarding tool and shown to all during a briefing. Annotations can be added during the presentation.

- Collaborative working by sharing a word processor or spreadsheet. Members of a distributed team can work together on a document or set of figures without meeting face to face.

### *Knowledge Fairs*

Knowledge fairs are forums where various company units congregate to demonstrate their knowledge-sharing efforts and learn from each other. This can be done face-to-face or online through knowledge Web pages.

### *Talk Rooms and Work Villages*

Many firms are using physical workspaces specifically designed to foster reflection, interaction, and collaboration. They generally provide open space for people to run into each other. Whiteboards and other tools for sharing and recording ideas are available. Alcoa, Nickelodeon, Nortel, and Steelcase are examples of companies with these types of workspaces in some of their offices. However, they are generally present at headquarter locations and less often utilized at regional or manufacturing locations.

### *Collaborative Conversations*

These facilitated conversations revolve around questions that matter to the organization. This involves making conversations a core business process. One type of collaborative conversation is strategic conversations that serve as the plat-

form for developing a future-oriented mindset and direction for the organization. Open-space meetings are one approach to this.

### *Futurizing*

Futurizing, or future search conferences, is an approach to large-scale involvement that starts with a focus on the past (who we are and how we got here). Individuals analyze their history, identifying and interpreting patterns and themes in their organization. Next, the group brainstorms an ideal community of the future in which they would like to live and work. Then they are facilitated in a large group to produce a mindmap of the present system and vote on the trends they think are most important. Finally, they prepare a consensus list of elements they think ought to be in the future vision.

### *Action Learning*

There are a host of different tools and approaches to this. The value of most action learning initiatives is the common language and common sense of purpose that results from such methods. Coaching and mentoring are key tools for facilitating action learning.

### *Workplace Digital Storytelling*

Storytelling has always been the means for passing on the lessons learned. The use of video, digital recording, and other technologies includes methods of telling and transferring stories that, in turn, transfer lessons learned and offer key insights and cultural understanding.

### *Organizational Ethnography and Archaeology*

Included in this approach are tools and techniques for gathering knowledge about an organization by observing its knowledge behaviors and by studying the knowledge artifacts utilized and produced.

### *Research Outposts*

A research outpost is the establishment of an R&D facility in a hotbed of innovation such as Silicon Valley, Silicon Alley, or in a key market. The purpose is to gather knowledge of either hot new emergent ideas or technologies or of customers living and working in the area where the knowledge resides or is being created.

### *Suggestion Programs*

Suggestion programs have always been at the essence of knowledge sharing. However, it is rare to see them cited as examples of knowledge management. The notion that every employee can contribute their unique ideas, experiences, and abilities to improve how work gets done and innovate has been discounted by the current KM movement. Much can be learned by looking at Toyota, Dana, and other firms that make suggestion programs work.

## COMMON TOOLS

### *Electronic Mail and Messaging, Group Calendaring, and Scheduling*

The fundamental tool kit for KM is increasingly built upon the corporate infrastructure for normal computing. It includes messaging infrastructures and combining e-mail utilities with products for calendar, meeting, and resource coordination. As corporations have moved to a single standard for computer networks with a common desktop deployed to employees, the ability to move text, images, and data has been multiplied. The tools for rapid exchange of knowledge based on common document formats and directories have removed many of the technical barriers to sharing knowledge and have increased the likelihood that a significant exchange of ideas can take place.

### *Skills Inventories, Yellow Pages, and Subject Experts*

These online databases contain information on "who's who" and "who knows what"—a vehicle to find expertise from people throughout the firm who might otherwise never learn what each other knows. As with the best practices databases, expert databases or corporate yellow pages can be extremely useful if designed and managed correctly. Generally, large databases created centrally are underutilized. However, databases of expertise developed locally and then expanded tend to have more success. The information is more relevant and more current, and there is a higher level of connectedness between participants.

### *Electronic Meeting Systems*

These products support small groups of people usually working in the same room at the same time (although distributed and any-time access are also supported), each with a PC. The groups use the software to brainstorm on issues, categorize responses, and create instant surveys and vote. Input can be offered anonymously and a facilitator generally assists these sessions.

Software for virtual meetings on the Internet or intranet allows multiple structured, focused, online discussions and meetings for everything from employee forums to process improvement teams to corporate conferences. It can also be used for focus groups or customer surveys. Sessions can be real-time or ongoing, and groups can make use of different tools (brainstorming, organizing, voting, surveying, or chat.)

Increasing use is being made of tools for conferencing: "Net Meetings Desktop" and real-time data sharing connected with common intranet and telephony are becoming affordable as part of the common desktop and shared network. Products in this category store documents and/or allow others to see and work on documents simultaneously, on each other's screen, or on a whiteboard. The products are often linked by audio and sometimes by video. Using a PC and the Internet/intranet, people can now hold conversations—a "Net meeting" with others who can link into it from wherever they can connect to the Internet/intranet. The meeting can be enhanced by adding a camera to the PC or by using audio sound cards to hold an audio conference. Failing this, employees can just connect by a telephone audio conference and then use the screen multi-point data conferencing features, which let them collaborate with a group of people in real time.

Non-real-time conferencing or asynchronous conferencing is most like a bulletin board, where a group of people with a similar interest carry on a conversation, leaving and responding to messages over time. This is known as "threaded" messaging. These messages can be public (as in a bulletin board system) or private (as in a groupware discussion database).

### Virtual Communities

Virtual communities are being supported with a package of capabilities including highly evolved bulletin boards, chat capabilities, and computer conferencing. This is an important concept for connecting to the marketplace; more and more companies are creating an Internet environment that facilitates connection to and interaction with their current and potential customers and suppliers. An important aspect of connecting to a virtual community is the providing of knowledge to the community regarding their products and services and how to effectively use them, and the gathering of knowledge from the community about their needs and behaviors. Ad Hoc Community Creation allows people to find documents in a chosen area as well as connect with other people who have produced or read documents in the same area of interest.

One variation on conferencing is Event-Ware—a class of products that allows people to participate in virtual conferences where a remote speaker gives a talk and shows slides; both media are accessed via the participant's Web browser. They can type comments on slides or ask questions either by typing or by audio connection.

### Document Management and Creation/Workflow

Documents are the most common repository of explicit knowledge. There is a wide range of software that aids in the capturing, storing, retrieving, and filtering of knowledge stored in documents. Increasingly, these tools are being used as shared repositories of enterprise information or for special work groups.

Basic tools have been in place for nearly 20 years to route documents and data from one in-basket to the next. They are becoming increasingly sophisticated in all areas of content creation and distribution, and their use has grown exponentially in Web-based publishing applications.

Workflow tools include process diagramming and analysis tools, workflow enactment engines, and electronic forms routing products. Coupled with document management technologies, they are becoming the engines for corporate-wide content management, where more and more encyclopedic information is becoming available.

### Workgroup Utilities and Groupware Development Tools

These development tools include utilities to support group working and remote access to someone else's computer, and specific tools for workgroup applications development. These provided the initial foundation for many KM applications. Systems based in Lotus Notes, for example, have been widely used for nearly a decade in multinational accounting firms and elsewhere with considerable success. Their advantages include the ability to design very rich functionality and targeting of special information needs of particular work groups, and to create knowledge maps of the enterprise. Although they entail high initial learning and development costs, they are gaining new momentum once coupled with intranet applications. Many more generic Web authoring and look-up tools are becoming the backbone of some of the most advanced KM systems. Collaborative functions are moving to the Internet using Internet browsers as the input and output connections while still using traditional groupware on the LAN.

While most corporate intranets are still primarily used as top-down controlled media for corporate information distribution, some firms are dedicating the same resources to foster collaboration. For example, the NBC Corporate Communications Web site intranet is run by "Franchise Holders" in different divisions, with "information providers" shaping the material for Web publication that has been provided by "content providers."

### *Information Distribution and Push Products*

These products search for and place up-to-date information on a Web browser according to pre-determined categories or categories determined with a growing knowledge of the user's interest as determined by prior searches on the Internet or intranet. They are increasingly integrated with content management systems. Intelligent software agents for Internet/intranet users:

- know and represent a user's interests in his or her profile;

- modify a user's profile based on what he or she looks at on the Internet;

- search the Internet to find information of interest to their users;

- automatically communicate with other users to share information;

- summarize information for local storage; and

- extract key words for indexing and later retrieval of information.

### *Intelligent Search Engines and Taxonomies*

These IT-based tools connect to concepts around word and phrase searches. They can:

- track competitors;

- develop strategic plans based on relevant data and insights;

- reveal insights about one's industry;

- tap into employees' knowledge about the market, products, competitors, etc;

- share information with key stakeholders; and

- develop a knowledge base of people, documents, Web sites, and contacts in an easily accessible visual format.

### *Data Visualization and Knowledge Mapping*

Data visualization is used to display a graphic view of concepts related to a user query. By delivering information graphically, the software allows users to view query results in context and find relevant data quickly and easily. When a collection of information changes, the software dynamically reflects the change in its concept map.

# ABSTRACT

## 6 EXAMPLES OF MORE THAN SKILLS

*Editor's Comment*: This abstract brings together six examples of restructuring work for learning. These examples come from disparate sources, yet each illustrates the management challenge to reorder the context of learning by creating more than the typical skill base that training managers are used to doing. In this abstract, we focus on three companies—Lucent Technologies, Bell Atlantic, and Visteon, and on three issues—the issue of 'creative abrasion' and learning from failure, the issue of diversity as a business opportunity, and the issue of training for free agent workers. Together, these six suggest some of the new ways in which training managers must think in order to build and maintain a learning company.

## 1. LUCENT TECHNOLOGIES

At Lucent, ten teams of "Innovation Masters" have formed grass-roots groups whose responsibilities include taking personal, individual action to help create a high performance operating environment. About 800 individuals are involved in the effort to embrace what Lucent calls a "knowledge ethic." The Innovation Masters teams search out and implement ways to share, capture, distill, and generally make sense of the immense *personal* knowledge resident in the "heads, file cabinets, and hard drives" of employees. Contact Lucent VP Ben Verwaayen or General Counsel Rich Rawson for more information, or *www.lucent.com*.

## 2. BELL ATLANTIC

Bell Atlantic's recent merger with NYNEX was the trigger for a "more than training" approach to getting employees working smoothly together. What Bell Atlantic needed was a "big picture way" to get the multiple cultures, outdated job descriptions, and catch-as-catch-can skill development into some meaningful systemic approach to learning and growth. Bell Atlantic's human resources leaders took a team approach, bringing together representatives from the training and quality operations to meet with subject experts to identify critical skills needed for the company's move into its new culture. The teams worked on skills in three areas: leadership, job skills, and skills needed to demonstrate the new company's core values. The teams used Minneapolis-based Lominger Ltd.'s "Career Architect" software, and focused on the individual skills and competencies needed to demonstrate the team-developed desired performance. "Ownership" and "empowerment" were the result of this experiment. Contact Thom Long, Bell Atlantic Directory Group, or Lominger Ltd. for more information.

## 3. & 4. "CREATIVE ABRASION" AND DIVERSITY

"Creative Abrasion" is a concept developed by Harvard Business School professor Dorothy Leonard in which learning from failure is the goal. Her approach is to gather together a team of diverse individuals to intentionally analyze the failure from different points of view. She

---

*Sources*: "Future Perfect" by Suzanne Sidhu in *Lucent Magazine*, February 2000, pp. 8–9; "HR Shop Talk" in *Bulletin to Management*, Bureau of National Affairs, 4/13/00, p.118; "How to Encourage 'Failing Forward' " in *Harvard Management Update*, April 2000, p. 8; "Diversity Q&A" in *Mosaics*, a SHRM newsletter, May/June 2000, p. 5; *Visteon* shareholder report, Ford Motor Company, June 5, 2000, p. 7; "A Look Ahead: Free Agents and the Human Resource Profession" in *Workplace Visions* n.2-2000, SHRM, 2000, pp. 2–3.

looks for these differences in the makeup of the team: expertise, training, education, background, learning style, cognitive preference, and others. Her point is that the constructive, creative abrasion of ideas about the failure will frame the failure in ways that lead to learning. Trainers can certainly help facilitate the process of team building and project analysis to enable the concept of creative abrasion to yield positive learning results.

This concept is part "errors are your friends" left over from the quality movement of the last two decades, and part evolution of the diversity movement of the last few years. The bottom line cry now is for "differences" to be seen as a business opportunity; for diversity to be "leveraged" by management for the positive influences it can have on both individuals and the organization. Professor Leonard's concept of creative abrasion takes it one step further and casts it in a learning context. Find her at Harvard Business School, Cambridge, MA.

## 5. VISTEON

The Ford Motor Company made news this year with its headlong plunge into e-business, partnering online with suppliers and competitors, and announcing an unprecedented 16 consecutive quarters of earnings that exceeded the previous quarter. In various reports and letters to shareholders during year 2000, Ford officers focused on its strong commitment to being "customer-focused" and "shareholder-driven." One of the organizations created from Ford is Visteon, a supplier of electronics integration in automotive systems, now an independent corporation to be traded on the New York Stock Exchange. The summer brochure describing Visteon and announcing its independence from Ford Motor Company contained these words: "Visteon teamed with high-tech companies like Intel, Microsoft, Nintendo, Palm, and Texas Instruments, to integrate consumer electronics into the harsh vehicle environment. It's these kinds of relationships that create innovative and award-winning products." Ford notes that the electronic content in new vehicles accounts for a large percentage of vehicle value, and that Ford's global customers expect this kind of innovation. Technical trainers for America's heartland industries, like Ford, in past years would never have imagined that they'd be soulmates with Nintendo and Palm. Today's technical trainers require whole new sensitivities to the critical new business partnerships and changing consumer expectations associated with companies like Visteon and the new Ford Motor Company. Peter J. Pestillo is Chairman, President, and CEO of Visteon in Dearborn, MI.

## 6. FREE AGENTS

The ever-growing phenomenon of free agents providing services and making products, doing research, and even managing companies seems to be a fact of working culture now and into the foreseeable future. Predictions of a growing trend abound: by 2004, there will be 11 million more free agents; by 2020 the workforce will be made up of 50 percent free agents; and by 2050, free agents will comprise two-thirds of the workforce (SHRM *Workplace Visions*, referenced below). The idea that the locus of work rests with individual talent and skills and not at the workplace is a novel but not surprising view, and for sure it is a challenge to traditional training managers. These are some of the companies that currently specialize in supporting free agents:

Working Solo, New Paltz , NY
Working Today, New York, NY
Trattner Network, Los Angeles, CA
Opus 360 Corporation, New York, NY
Guru.com, San Francisco, CA
Aquent, Boston, MA
IMCOR, Stamford, CT

# 1D. WHAT MANAGERS NEED TO KNOW ABOUT E-LEARNING

## CASE STUDY

## 9 RULES FOR GETTING STARTED WITH E-LEARNING

*Editor's Comment*: Scan through any training conference brochure these days and you'll find a host of seminars and workshops, breakout sessions and pre-conference training on e-learning. For example, the popular Training Directors' Forum in year 2000 brochure advertised these kinds of sessions: "Get Real: Deliver Online Learning That Counts!"; "Why Online Learners Drop Out"; "Realizing the Impact of Online Learning Through Distributed Learning Solutions"; "Fulfilling the Promise of Online Learning," and others with similar titles. Companies of all sizes have had some experience with e-learning, and are now flooding conferences and public seminar providers with advice.

These kinds of listings provide a litmus test of the field of e-learning right now, and tend to show that many companies are truly interested in getting started with e-learning. The article we've reprinted for you here is a case study of Dell Computer Corporation's experience in getting started.

### GETTING STARTED WITH E-LEARNING, AN INTERVIEW WITH JOHN CONÉ

*by Patricia A. Galagan*

You work in a fast-moving computer company. Your CEO has written a popular book on doing business in cyberspace. Getting started in e-learning should be a cinch, right? Wrong, says John Coné, vice president of Dell Learning at Dell Computer Corporation. Coné realized he had some lessons to learn about e-learning.

"The good news is that the hardest part is already over," says Coné of Dell's progress toward making the transition from traditional to online learning. "We don't have to convince anyone that this is not just a fad. Our conversations today are not about 'Shall we do this?'

They're about 'How shall we do it?' We know that we want to move online to make learning more scalable, flexible, and focused on learners' needs. Now, the question is, How do we reap those benefits?"

### START SMALL, BE TALL

Coné offers 9 rules of thumb for bringing e-learning into an organization.

**Rule 1: Engage the learner.** No transition to technology-enabled learning will succeed unless all learners embrace the change, but that doesn't happen automatically. Dell discovered many ways to help get learners on board. One of the most important was to make the use of technology-enabled learning as similar to traditional learning as possible. Here's what that meant:

❏ Help people evaluate their e-learning options and judge the credentials of a course. Make them comfortable about their readiness to learn online and how to calculate the time it will take to complete an online course.

❏ Give permission to learn. Though the most important benefit of tech-based learning is the ability to learn at any time, anywhere, people are used to having a set time and place for learning and permission to be there then. We had to give people the sense that they have permission to take the time to learn.

❏ Get people signed up. With asynchronous online learning, you don't have to register until you show up for a class. There's no implied contract and, therefore, no sense of commitment to do the learning. We rediscovered the benefits of registration and schedules.

❏ Assure new online learners they don't need school supplies. Most technology-enabled learning programs include all of the resources you need.

❏ Re-create some of the benefits of classroom learning: getting away from your familiar workspace, meeting the instructor and other participants, taking breaks, and influencing the learning event.

❏ Let learners graduate. Learning online can be a series of private successes, but people crave acknowledgement just the same. Try to create a sense of official completion and shared success among e-learners.

**Rule 2: Have a strategy that links e-learning to your business goals.**

**Rule 3: Develop standards for working with the IT department.**

**Rule 4: Know your baseline technologies.**

**Rule 5: Be prepared.** You need to change your systems and processes for such functions as registration, scheduling, and tracking and reporting progress.

**Rule 6: Rethink your metrics.** Companies tend to count hours of training and dollars invested as a way to show their commitment. But if technology is supposed to provide training in less time at lower cost, there goes our argument. If we're providing more hours of training, is that good or bad?

There is no well-understood alternative metric to an hour of training. At Dell, we've been experimenting with the concept of the learning incident as a unit of measure. A learning incident could be five minutes spent online. It could be learning that occurs when you use a tool. It could even be a hallway exchange. We're still trying to figure out how to make that meaningful without inventing a whole new language. In the meantime, we're artificially converting learning incidents into equivalent hours.

What's a learning solution? Right now, it's anything that we intentionally set out to make a learning solution. But, eventually, we'll be unsatisfied with that. At the same time, people are coming forward with tools they've created and asking, "Is this a learning solution? It works the same way yours does. Can we put it in the system?"

We also measure the average duration of various learning solutions and the average cost. Once you know the average, you can begin to drive it down.

**Rule 7: Make alternatives available.** If you're going to meet your goals for making the transition to online learning, you have to change behavior. I did that by pulling the big lever. I said that in the first year, 25 percent of all new learning solutions must be technology-enabled and not classroom-based. The second year's goal was 40 percent, and the year after that it was 60 percent. In 2000, 90 percent of all learning solutions at Dell will be either totally or partially technology-enabled.

We know that the use of technology-enabled learning lags the amount that's available. But that's not a surprise because we're pursuing an overtaking strategy, not a replacement strategy. We're controlling availability and creating technology-enabled alternatives to traditional learning.

For example, managers are required to attend legal briefings on hiring, termination, and preventing sexual harassment. Last year, managers who had already been through a briefing could take a refresher course online. This year, some of the briefings are available only online.

**Rule 8: Prepare training staff for learners taking control.** Technology-enabled learning fundamentally changes the locus of control from the trainer to the learner. That's more than a major philosophical change. It has tremendous practical implications. If the people running HR and training can't give up control of the learning process, then technology is just a way to shove the same old thing through new channels.

It's a mistake to approach e-learning as just a way to reduce costs and gain efficiencies. That traps people into using technology to do things differently when we really should be doing different things.

I've been preaching the gospel of learner control for more than five years. It's an inevitable byproduct of using the Internet. If you don't give people the ability to control the terms of their own learning, they will go outside the company. They can already go to a public portal for many kinds of learning.

That doesn't mean that people in corporate education will lose their value when learners are in control. But we will be disintermediated as the providers and creators of knowledge. When anyone can sit down at a computer and publish a course with the help of an authoring tool and a public portal, we have to find new roles.

Many trainers have a museum mentality. We collect and codify learning in the equivalent of the rooms in a museum: Impressionists over here, Postmodernists over there. A more appropriate metaphor is to imagine that you have just been appointed to run the National Park Service. You're not going to put all of the waterfalls in upstate New York and all of the palm trees in California. But you have two important new jobs: telling everyone where the parks are and what's in them and improving access to them in any way that you can.

**Rule 9: Think short-term and disposable.** It can be tempting to make a full-scale assault on technology-enabled learning and to want to arm oneself with server farms and networks and other gear. But it's more important to forget about so-called complete solutions and just go for some small steps. We're not building for the ages. Anything you buy today—any infrastructure, any application—will make you unhappy 18 months from now.

That's not to say that you won't end up making investments in technology. You will. And, over time, some will be pretty big and very important. But don't try to build the bridge from both shores and the middle of the river all at once—especially when it comes to the learning solutions themselves. Invest in technology as if you're going to throw it away. If you don't, you'll get into an endless discussion loop with your IT department.

I say start small and be tall.

## ARTICLE REPRINT

### MANAGING E-LEARNING

*Editor's Comment*: Like the companies featured in this article, many other companies are forging ahead with speedy plans to move to e-learning within a year or two, or to at least supplement classroom training with online courses and content of various sorts. This article examines the management issues involved in moving to some kind of balance between learning in traditional classrooms and learning online.

### WHO'S IN CHARGE OF E-LEARNING?

*by Kevin Dobbs*

Alex Pass, project manager for Motorola's education-assistance program, has spent a lot of time lately researching online-training providers. He's facing a strict corporate mandate: Within a year, 35 percent of the company's education and training must be done via "alternative means"—namely the Internet. By 2002, that figure jumps to 50 percent. For a company that largely relies on classroom training—it has garnered much acclaim for the traditional instruction conducted at Motorola University— this represents a daunting challenge.

Like every company trying to gain competitive advantage in the New Economy, the wireless communications giant, headquartered in Schaumburg, IL, is bombarded with pleas from both clients and employees thirsty for new technology and information. It's not surprising that Motorola is coming to terms with what it calls the evolution of workplace education. Pass puts it this way: "There's a need for training in the moment—you have to deliver content to someone who can apply it immediately. That's the overriding need. The model is changing, and we have to keep up with it. It's all about e-learning and that means completely altering the way education is delivered, valued and measured."

That's why Pass and his colleagues, still in the early stages of creating a systemwide e-learning strategy, find themselves closely examining Web-based training and what it has done for other companies. They've seen the likes of Ford Motor Co. and software maker Adobe Systems establish significant training initiatives on the Web. Ford took its dealership certification program online, replacing 12 instructor-led courses. Adobe uses the Web to teach its 750-person sales force about new technologies and products.

Then there's Genzyme Corp. Only 10 months ago, the Cambridge, MA, maker of health care products found itself facing a challenge similar to Motorola's. With a growing work force of 3,200 scattered across 25 U.S. locations, it was struggling not only to develop training programs but to find the time to bring people to corporate headquarters for formal classroom sessions.

"Things are changing too fast," says Russ Campanello, Genzyme's vice president of human resources. "We had to schedule everybody months in advance in order to coordinate everything for people to come to Cambridge. But by the time they got here, their training needs had changed."

So the company started putting internally developed courses on its intranet and also encouraged employees to register for online classes offered by outside providers. Within six months more than 400 Genzyme workers had logged on for Web-based courses. Campanello says it's too early to calculate savings in terms of time and money, but with interest growing, he sees the Web as a way to deliver the "just-in-time development" employees are clamoring for.

Perhaps the best example of this mass movement to the Web is KPMG. Doug Stefanko, director of e-learning for the international accounting consultancy, recalls the perils of conducting 90 percent of his company's formal training in classrooms. Introducing some 8,000 employees to new technology and financial legalities each year translated into colossal travel expenses and countless hours of lost office time while workers made their way to myriad locales for face-to-face instruction. KPMG is headquartered in New Jersey but has offices throughout the world. "The costs were tremendous," he says, "but there was a time when we just had to live with it."

That was just three years ago, but to Stefanko it seems like a distant memory. He credits one innovation: the Web. Today, KPMG addresses 70 percent of its training needs via computers—the majority of that online. The company contends that it—and any other outfit wishing to keep pace with fast-changing New Economy businesses and a free agent labor force—has to train its people quickly and continually. And that means making the most of their time.

Case in point: KPMG recently used the Web to unveil a companywide training initiative about the Web. Its "Internet 101" course was designed in five weeks and deployed to all 8,500 of its U.S. employees in 90 days. The course covered the Net's impact on the economy, intellectual property, new software developments and e-commerce principles. Nobody had to leave his desk or accrue travel costs to attend.

Stefanko insists it would have taken classroom instructors "years and a heck of a lot more money" to cover that kind of ground. Overall, he estimates that KPMG's Web-based learning programs cost 70 percent less than traditional training and are regularly completed in a frac-

tion of the time. "It's a tremendous movement," he says, "and the trend will only continue."

## ANY TOM, DICK OR HARRY?

Indeed, the Internet has redefined the way training gets done. From accounting firms to software developers to hotel chains, employees are training at their desks and on their own schedules, logging on between meetings or at home. "It's getting to the point where you have to justify why in the world you'd send people to a classroom," Stefanko says.

Studies by analysts at U.S. Bancorp, Piper Jaffray in Minneapolis and WR Hambrecht & Co. in San Francisco suggest that the e-learning market will more than quadruple in size over the next five years, eventually accounting for the majority of all the training conducted by most major corporations.

Helping to drive this radical shift is a mushrooming field of so-called "learning portals." The label is seized upon by everyone from course aggregators to suppliers of the training management platforms that enable companies to deliver and administrate major online initiatives of their own. In the interest of coherence, however, *TRAINING Magazine* defines portals as Web sites that sell courses from a variety of vendors, provide access to online classes, and allow for e-commerce transactions (for a sample of such sites, see "E-Commerce Meets E-Service," page 42). Any Tom, Dick or Harry with a credit card can buy training programs directly from these sites.

## THE RUSH TO GET ONLINE

The seemingly universal urge to do everything on the Web accounts for some of the stampede to online learning, but users and providers say the real impetus comes from the "just-in-time" demands of an information-driven economy. "It's all out of necessity," says Steve Zahn, vice president of operations for DigitalThink, the San Francisco company that developed KPMG's Internet 101 course. Employees and managers alike recognize that the only way to stay abreast of constant workplace transformation is through continual training.

Technology changes in the blink of an eye, which, in turn, changes job descriptions week to week. And while many training needs might be addressed more thoroughly in a classroom, workers simply do not have time to wait for formal training sessions to be designed and scheduled, much less block out days on end for travel and classes.

Moreover, as markets rapidly expand and contract—and corporations adjust to changing conditions through mergers and acquisitions—work force downsizing is as much a reality as the creation of new jobs. Rather than depending on a specific company and a traditional career ladder, workers have learned to seek security in the options they might have with any number of employers. This reality, coupled with record low unemployment that has upped the demand for skilled workers, has created a transient labor force. These people are anxious to learn new skills that will benefit their current employer—or the outfit down the street.

All of which bolsters the significance of online learning: Employers can train their people in brief increments and get them up to speed in a hurry so that they start adding value almost immediately. That way if they leave after a few months, the company still gets some of its money's worth. At the same time, training online gives workers a faster way to update and customize their portfolios, supplying the ammunition they need to go after better jobs—or at least maintain their marketability should they find themselves casualties of a round of layoffs.

"People want to be in control of their own destiny. They hear about the job market every day, and they see that they have to advance at their own pace, not the organization's," says Chris Moore, chief technology officer for Baltimore-based TrainingServer, one of many online-training providers working to capitalize on the changing business climate.

## BYE-BYE TRAINING DEPARTMENT?

Not surprisingly, instant access to online-learning providers is changing the role of corporate training departments. Traditionally, a line manager would document a particular need for staff development, then submit a request to the training department. Trainers would evaluate the need and decide how it could best be addressed. They would then design a course and later schedule classroom sessions to teach it.

While that process is far from obsolete, it is no longer *the* process—especially at burgeoning

start-ups and large organizations. Employees are evaluating their own needs (and wants), and going through their bosses for approval. And if individuals aren't taking charge of their own development, line managers eager for immediate results are doing it for them. Either way, a lot of people are online and studying long before a trainer would have the chance to evaluate and address their requests through traditional means.

At first glance it may appear that this decentralization of decision-making power spells doom for the training department. If individual employees and their bosses can make their own training choices, who needs trainers? Neither Web-based training providers nor trainers we talked to see it that way. Rather, they say, the role of in-house training specialists is simply evolving with the times.

Instead of design and instruction, their primary focus is shifting to quality and career-development assurance. Trainers may not create or choose specific courses for employees, but they will select which online providers and programs meet their companies' goals and standards.

"It's absolutely essential that you have trainers in the decision-making loop," says Rob Chipman, CEO of Salt Lake City training firm TrainSeek.com. "They are the ones with the expertise. They can differentiate between substantive education and people going off all willy-nilly in various directions for personal reasons. You need someone who knows learning to manage learning."

An important aspect of this new management role involves the trainer as adviser. If companies concede responsibility for training to individual workers, then the training department not only must provide quality sources for that education, it should help employees create a long-term plan for their development. If a worker is building a portfolio of skills by taking online courses from a variety of sources, he needs someone to attest to the relevance and quality of those courses as a whole.

"When it comes time for promotion or a new job, you need to have a neat way of showing on your résumé that you have more than just some fragmented list of courses," says David Martin, vice president of Saba Inc., a Redwood Shores, CA, online-training firm. "You need to show that your training was part of a development plan, that you were working on a program that meant something. Learning portals can't do that, but trainers can."

And note that all of this addresses only the training specialists' role in helping the organization shop for "off-the-shelf" courseware. Online learning in the corporate world involves a great deal more than downloading generic courses from the Internet. KPMG and Genzyme are typical in that their online initiatives rely heavily on custom courseware designed specifically for them. Whether such courses are created by in-house trainers or farmed out to commercial design shops, training specialists obviously will have to manage the projects. Even in a world where classroom training ceased to exist (a very unlikely prospect), there would be plenty of hands-on work for learning experts to do.

## PITFALLS AND ROADBLOCKS

There are other challenges to contend with as well. Slow Internet connections and high online student dropout rates are among the most pressing.

Broad bandwidth and high-speed Web service remain a luxury, meaning many online-training programs cannot be used to their full potential. Until that technology becomes the norm, trainers have to find ways to complement their Net-based initiatives. For example, auto manufacturer DaimlerChrysler established a series of courses on its corporate training Web site, but employees couldn't download the graphics, color and sound found on most Web pages because their standard dial-up connections were too slow. Instead of abandoning the plan, however, DaimlerChrysler simply distributed much of the material on CD-ROM, and the courses became a hybrid of Web- and PC-based training.

As for problems such as high dropout rates, it's often a matter of common sense. You just need someone to think it through, trainers say. KPMG, for one, convinced all its U.S. employees to complete its Internet competency course in three months by making it a prerequisite for raises and promotions. "If it's important enough to take the course to thousands of employees, it's important enough to find a way for them to finish it," Stefanko says.

Of course, for some training, all this worry about the Internet is irrelevant. Some instruction will always be done face-to-face. Even companies like KPMG that have embraced the online movement aren't abandoning the classroom altogether. KPMG's new-employee orientation programs are still conducted with live instructors because much of that process is about networking, meeting people, and getting personalized accounts of the ins and outs of the office.

But even orientation depends on the Web. In the past KPMG would devote a portion of the formal orientation session to a lecture on company history and financial conditions. Today, all that information is delivered via computer before the new recruit ever sets foot in the classroom. "It's all about time," Stefanko says. "You make the most of people's time."

That leaves organizations like Motorola scrambling to get training online, even setting "alternative means" mandates. But for Motorola's Alex Pass, this great push to get things done on Internet time raises an interesting question. "Today, getting on the Net is *the* alternative means for training. But in two years, who knows?"

# CASE STUDY

## DIFFUSION OF E-LEARNING AT IBM

*Editor's Comment*: This article tells the story of how IBM Management Development (IBM MD) looked back to the classic studies of "diffusion of innovation" for guiding principles in implementing an e-learning program for management training. Program developers were not afraid to challenge newer assumptions about learners and learning, and, instead, saw the e-learning experiment as a "diffusion of innovation" challenge.

## THE FIVE ATTRIBUTES OF INNOVATIVE E-LEARNING

### *by Nancy J. Lewis and Peter Orton*

❏ *Different learners have different learning styles.*
❏ *Let learners tell you how to design your interventions.*
❏ *Give your customers what they want.*

We hear it frequently: "If you want learners to embrace training, offer choices and let *them* decide how they learn." We're told that focusing on learner preference is the key to more effective interventions and that it's the answer to deploying new technology-enhanced learning successfully.

Moreover, it sounds plausible for online learning: The unique power of multimedia is that it gives designers and learners choices of different media. Ergo, it's a no-brainer. Just ask learners what they want and then design e-learning accordingly.

Unfortunately, that approach may not produce effective e-learning.

In an ideal training world, a wide range of viable options would be available to learners, and they would have a deep understanding of their relative strengths, weaknesses, and attributes. Choosing among the options would be similar to leasing an automobile. Do you need a four-wheel drive for rugged mountain terrain, or do you need touring comfort for a long trip on the Autobahn? Do you want factory air-conditioning for the Sahara or a powerful heater for the high Alps? A range of alternatives allows a customer to choose the transportation best suited for him- or herself and the destination. Isn't that also true for corporate learning?

In a word, no. Knowing learner preferences can inform instructional design, but only if learners understand all of the variables and features. The current problem with learning interventions is that not all choices are salient to learners, and, especially with online learning, not all attributes are understood.

Suppose that Emma Employee needs to improve her leadership skills. Her choices may include online offerings and in-class workshops. Like most of us, Emma has experienced a lot of classroom presenters—some of whom are accomplished and exciting and others who could cure insomnia. But because the online instructional field is so young, Emma hasn't experienced many engaging programs.

*Source:* "The Five Attributes of Innovative E-Learning" by Nancy J. Lewis and Peter Orton in *Training & Development*, June 2000, pp. 47–51. Nancy J. Lewis is Director, IBM Management Development; Peter Orton is Program Director, Global Learning Technologies for IBM Management Development. Article reprinted with permission of the American Society for Training and Development, ASTD. Copyright 2000. All rights reserved. *www.astd.org*

Deployment of effective online interventions for so-called soft-skills learning is still in its infancy. With due respect to colleagues in soft-skills development, few online interventions hook learners and deliver them to new insights and behaviors. In fact, many users' experiences with online learning have been fraught with long download waits, choppy video, confusing navigation, and endless text screens. For some people, just having to install a plug-in can roadblock any sampling of online instruction. Many, if not most, learners have scant knowledge of what a dynamic, engaging online learning experience can be.

So, given Emma's limited experience with online learning, she opts instead for a live presenter for her instruction in leadership skills. At least if the presenter is atrocious, she can commiserate with like-minded peers.

## REMEMBER THE NEW COKE?

In market research—whether it's for cars, beverages, or new packaging—consumer responses must be based on a clear understanding of the items' qualities and potential benefits and downside. For instance, they may be asked to compare the taste of Sprite with the taste of 7-Up. They're never asked to compare a twist-off cap with a framistan because no one knows the relative attributes of a framistan in order to make an informed comparison.

What happens when market researchers try to measure user preferences when important attributes aren't salient? Recall the New Coke travesty: Coca-Cola's market researchers believed that with New Coke, the only attributes they manipulated were name, scent, and taste. In double-blind taste tests, New Coke consistently scored higher than Classic Coke, as it's now called. Market researchers were convinced that New Coke would be a huge hit. But neither the researchers nor subjects identified a product attribute that transcended name and taste: sentimental value. Generations had grown up drinking Coke and associated their youth with something more than its taste or scent. When expected to replace it with New Coke, they demurred in droves.

The problem with asking learners about their preferences regarding online learning versus other modalities of learning isn't unlike the New Coke situation. Not all product attributes

are salient. Learners often don't have a deep enough understanding about online learning to assess such preferences. Nor do researchers yet fully realize Web-based learning's attributes, power, and intellectual or visceral appeal.

IBM Management Development discovered exactly that dilemma when rolling out a new learning intervention, Basic Blue for Managers, which incorporates a five-day classroom experience into 50 weeks of online learning. Using an initial questionnaire administered to a randomly selected sample of 63 new IBM managers, professor Youngme Moon of Harvard Business School assessed general preferences for different learning modalities. Moon found that, although IBM is a technology company, new IBM managers consistently reported a preference for classroom learning over online learning.

When Moon later conducted post-program interviews for specific reactions to the Basic Blue components, she found that respondents universally extolled both learning modalities—classroom and online—with equal enthusiasm. Most telling was that all respondents answered that they preferred learning the informational material (the cognitive-based development) online from their home or office rather than in a classroom setting.

Says one manager, "Because the information was the type of stuff I could learn on my own, there was really no reason for it to be communicated in a classroom. I think I would've been resentful if it had been dumped on me in a classroom. We're no dummies. We can learn this kind of stuff on our own."

Another: "It's too much information to be taught in a classroom format. You need to be able to sift through the stuff from the comfort of your home, at your own pace."

Another: "There's no question that the ability to work at home or in my office made some material easier. That was a huge advantage."

Conversely, the managers preferred learning the behavioral-skills material in a classroom environment rather than in an online setting:

"Just as the informational material wouldn't have worked in the classroom, the skills stuff wouldn't have worked online or in any other setting. It was absolutely essential that we all sit in a classroom together for the skills part."

Another: "Skills built on the information. With the online learning, we were all just absorbing standard material and learning a new vocabulary for being a manager. That laid the groundwork for the stuff we accomplished in the classroom, which involved taking the groundwork and building on it."

Moon cited the difficulty for respondents to express accurately their preference for any particular learning modality in the abstract. She says, "With the online learning modality, the problem is compounded by not only a specific lack of personal familiarity, but also a general lack of understanding about the full potential of this particular medium."

After being given the opportunity to experience online learning, respondents indicated that they preferred a learning modality that was best suited to the content. They cited such factors as the amount and type of material presented and the time available to review it. Participants recognized that when implemented appropriately, learning modalities don't have to compete:

"The key was the hybrid model. Rather than adopting a totally online program or totally classroom program, they decided to take a best-of-both-worlds approach, and it really worked."

Asking the managers general questions about their learner preferences clearly would not have informed IBM about an optimal distance-learning design. So, what exactly did IBM do to design and deploy its Basic Blue for Managers program?

IBM Management Development took the approach that online learning is a technological innovation—a paradigm shift. Because innovations break the mold, moving users over to them requires a strategy beyond just understanding learner preferences and understanding specific factors that change behavior.

## Diffusion of Innovations

For five decades, scholars have studied how and why innovations in technology, agriculture, health care, transportation, education, and almost every walk of life are adopted or rejected by their target audiences. Everett M. Rogers, professor at the University of New Mexico, has spent 30 years studying that phenomenon. In *Diffusion of Innovations*, Rogers writes that an innovation "presents an individual or organization with a new alternative, with new means of solving problems. But the probabilities of the new alternative being superior to previous practice are not exactly known by the individual problem solvers."

Given the uncertainty about an innovative technology, how can advocates for an innovation target and promote it to the appropriate audience?

The innovation process typically begins with recognition of a problem or need, which stimulates the creation of an innovation. In leadership training for IBM managers, the problems included high classroom training and travel costs, managers' scarce time, and a lot of material to be covered.

Other concerns about innovation can outweigh whether it will be embraced. The half-century of diffusion research suggests that five distinct attributes are strong predictors of an innovation's acceptance. It's those attributes and not learner preference for one modality over another (or even the perceived need for change) that training organizations must assess and use to inform an online intervention. They are the innovation's

- ❏ relative advantage
- ❏ compatibility
- ❏ complexity
- ❏ trialability
- ❏ observability.

According to Rogers, though all of those attributes may not be equally important for all respondents, they are common enough that innovation promoters should keep them in mind.

**Relative advantage.** This is the degree to which the proposed innovation is perceived as better than existing alternatives. The advantage may be viewed in terms of profitability, speed, social prestige, effectiveness, or any of many other potential positive outcomes. In the case of online learning, that may be just-in-time access (getting information immediately when the need arises) or the advantage of being able to focus on precise skills development for a specific need instead of having to sit through an entire class covering a broader set of skills.

**Compatibility.** This is the degree to which an innovation is viewed as consistent with the existing values, past experiences, or needs of potential adopters. a compatible idea or process will fit more closely with a learner's life situation, requiring less adjustment. Compatibility with previously introduced processes, values, or ideas helps learners regard the innovation as "familiar." If online usability is consistent with already familiar interfaces and navigation, then the learners will likely feel more comfortable with the new learning technology.

**Simplicity.** The degree to which an innovation is perceived as relatively easy to understand and use. The perceived complexity of installing a plug-in is just one example of an impediment to the adoption of online learning.

**Trialability.** The degree to which an innovation may be experimented with on a limited basis. The opportunity to try an innovation—with no requirements or expectation for continued use—gives users a chance to see how it works under their own situations and conditions, and helps to dispel uncertainty about the new practice. Much like stores that provide display computers allowing people to try new software, training organizations can provide mini programs and other opportunities, without obligation, to introduce new learning technologies. Trialability is especially critical for early adopters who have no precedent, unlike later adopters who may have peers with whom they can experience vicarious trialability.

**Observability.** The degree to which the results of an innovation are visible to others. In the case of online learning, some effects are more immediate and easier to acknowledge. For example, online instruction that teaches how to use a specific piece of software will likely be more visible and the results more quickly observed than with leadership skills, which typically have long-term accrued effects. That important attribute should help inform the staging and rollout of different skills applications: Easily and quickly demonstrable skills ought to be available first so that their short-term, visible effects can help promote continued adoption of the longer-term goals of the innovation.

## THE BIG BLUE WAY

To ensure success in its endeavor to build the leadership and people-management skills of 30,000 managers worldwide, IBM MD uses Rogers's Diffusion of Innovations attributes to inform the design and deployment of online offerings.

**Relative advantage.** IBM managers are pressed for time. Most work 10- to 12-hour days, some longer. To maximize the efficiency of online information, IBM MD designed a Manager QuickViews Web site to provide instant access to the best thinking about leadership and people management. Each of the 40-plus topics

is concise and practical, and all pictorial images are small-file illustrations for fast downloading.

Easy-to-access, just-in-time online Web tools are the building blocks that permit face-to-face classroom activities to move beyond information exchange. Classroom facilitators no longer need to impart information; that's now done in the online modules. Instead, precious classroom time in the Learning Lab focuses entirely on rich-skills development, collaborative exercises, and in-person interaction, building on the information from the Web material.

For instance, an important leadership skill is coaching. At IBM, managers learn the basics of the IBM coaching model via an online Quick-View. Then, they practice using the basic skills via an online coaching simulator. In class, managers can build upon the simulator by role playing a coaching exercise on real issues they bring to the session. That develops higher-level skills. Hence, technology-enhanced learning maximizes the effectiveness of class time, which is spent on experiential learning, case studies, and peer discussion. The class exists only because the foundation content was mastered through e-learning.

**Compatibility.** All 307,000 IBMers communicate internally via Lotus *Notes* and work in virtual e-spaces using the same Lotus interface. Thus, all IBM MD Web sites are designed to replicate the Lotus *Notes* look and navigation. All IBM MD e-learning tools use the same Lotus interface. Therefore, navigating any IBM MD Web-based learning Web site, simulation, collaborative workspace, or remote-learning module is familiar to users. As the number of sites grows, each additional topic site is new and different only in content, not in look and feel.

One IBM manager describes it this way: "I don't have the time or patience to learn new software. When I need information, I need it now. I want to be able to go to the site, find what I need, and get going. I like these products because they work just like *Notes*."

That compatibility has been likened to shopping at a grocery store where you know where everything is.

In addition to technical compatibility, IBM's e-learning emphasizes organizational compatibility. The terminology, conceptual models, and survey instruments are coordinated with other educational and organizational development departments within IBM. Everyone speaks the same language. For instance, the coaching simulator contains executive and managerial case studies, and its model has been adopted by IBM's consulting division and by IBM Global Organizational and Executive Development, as well as IBM MD.

**Simplicity.** Prior to deployment, repeated user-testing and a lengthy formative-evaluation stage diffused the complexity from the beta versions of every online deliverable. Process evaluation is a continual task, using focus groups specifically to simplify usability and navigation. About 4,000 new managers using Lotus *LearningSpace* as their "classrooms" are solicited for feedback continuously to refine and improve the ease of use of each database.

Setup requirements by a user are minimized or, ideally, eliminated. For example, no plug-ins are required to use any of IBM MD's 70-plus e-spaces, Web sites, and Lotus *Notes* databases. For all sites, simulations, assessments, and tools, users just point and click.

Simplicity in authoring and updating instructional Web sites is paramount. Using Lotus *Domino*, people without any programming expertise can build and update a Web site by typing in text, with no coding necessary. In one instance, a Web author had used language that was construed incorrectly by overseas managers. When they began questioning the material via the site's feedback tool, the developers immediately reworked the content. A clear, acceptable, revised version was on the IBM intranet within an hour. By reducing complexity for designers as well, the Web accelerates deployment and enhancement of programs globally, further speeding adoption.

In addition to technical and navigational simplicity, IBM MD developers focused on content simplicity via modular content chunking. Advanced tools are separated such that learners can concentrate first on the basics and subsequently go deeper into the Web site for advanced instruction.

**Trialability.** When IBM MD began building the first of 22 online interactive simulation modules, the received wisdom was to track users' mistakes. "It would be a huge value-add," IBM MD was told, "in order to focus on our learners' weaknesses." We were advised that tracking errors had become a standard feature for online simulations.

The importance of trialability, however, argued strongly against tracking. IBM MD wanted learners to feel safe to try the simulations without thinking their errors would be recorded. Good learning requires that learners feel comfortable about making mistakes. IBM MD intentionally allows free access to all online simulations, QuickViews, team assessments, and so forth with no personal tracking.

Additionally, the IBM MD Web site asks for no passwords or entry requirements. Although the site is designed for IBM managers, it's also open to the 277,000 IBM nonmanagers who want to develop leadership skills.

In its first five months, the IBM Coaching Simulator had more than 1 million page requests, and the numbers per month are steadily increasing.

**Observability.** This critical determinant of an innovation's success is the opportunity for users to perceive its immediate impact. That has been a challenge for IBM MD. Its focus on developing leaders is hardly a quick fix but an incremental, long-term commitment to people-skills improvement.

IBM MD's first online innovations emphasized visible short-term wins—immediate results that are clear and observable. The Manager QuickViews, with its emphasis on practical insights and information, was rolled out first and heralded immediately by managers as a valuable, on-the-job performance-support tool. With a few clicks, users can review the key practical tips for running a meeting, conducting an interview, or any of nearly 40 other day-to-day people-management tasks. That initial focus on everyday, practical skills was critical to observability.

Another online offering includes the requirement of review by a learner's manager, who is given a set of questions to guide the discussion. The questions aim to elicit the learner's observations of how well the application of the material works for him or her. It's sometimes not enough to assume that people will realize the impact of an innovation. Asking them to reflect on and describe the impact can increase their awareness and observability.

IBM's results shouldn't imply that a change to e-learning is easy. Continued evaluation, fine-tuning, and enhancement are crucial to development. IBM MD's perception of e-learning is that it's fundamentally an innovation: All e-learning design and launches have been—and continue to be—guided by the Diffusion of Innovations principles. While learner preferences are always part of the formula, the innovations guidelines have provided the critical foundation for success.

# RESEARCH SUMMARY

## BUILDING AN E-LEARNING SYSTEM

*Editor's Comment*: The February issue of *Technology for Learning*, Lakewood Publications' newsletter now published by Bill Communications and edited by Brandon Hall, announced a benchmarking study "to locate and learn from world-class practices of e-learning." What is particularly interesting at this "call for papers" announcement is the three major areas of focus for the study: quality, quantity, and business impact. A potential respondent base of 5,000 persons formed the study's pool. Training managers who are either designing or evaluating an e-learning program can adapt these indicators as guidelines for building an e-learning system.

**Quality, including:**

- Degree of collaboration among learners
- Use of online expert mentoring
- Use of online assessment
- Use of streaming audio and video
- Live, real-time instruction online
- Virtual environments for workplace simulation
- Online competency management
- Sophisticated blending of instructor-led and online instruction

**Quantity, including**:

- Percentage of total course online
- Percentage of training dollars spend for online training

**Business impact, including**:

- Return on investment
- Measures of effectiveness of e-learning
- Learning management systems
- Tools for creating, delivering, and tracking e-learning.

---

**ARTICLE RERINT**

## STRATEGIC JUSTIFICATION FOR WEB-BASED TRAINING

*Editor's Comment*: This succinct article presents six good reasons for reexamining the "justification" rules for Web-based training. Like many other authors, Margaret Driscoll urges training managers to think strategically when approaching any major change.

### "WEB-BASED TRAINING: IT'S JUST NOT THE SAME"

#### by Margaret Driscoll

Web-based training is a tool to which the old rules don't apply.

In so many ways, WBT differs from traditional instructor-led or self-paced training. The design, development, delivery, and maintenance of WBT differentiates it from traditional training methods.

Making the most of this new medium requires trainers to think differently if they want to take advantage of WBT's interactive possibilities.

Here are six reasons why the old rules no longer apply, and how training professionals might define the new rules to do business in this environment.

**1. Web-based training is interactive,** not just another form of mass media. If you surf the Web and try out training programs, you will quickly notice many use the old rules. It seems everyone is trying to turn the Web into a better form of television, slideshow, or an online book. Why? Presumably because that's the paradigm most people understand best. They see the Internet as a mass medium that can sell anything, just like television. But the Internet is more than a sales=delivery tool or an educational video. It is a new form of two-way communication.

Take advantage of its full capabilities. Look for tools that will help you deliver custom Web pages on the fly based on learners' preferences. Create a unique training experience: Set up a database of user profiles. Link users through their profiles to other databases offering training modules, plans, products and services.

**2. WBT is alive.** It needs a visit every day, and regular updates. The old rules allowed outdated manuals, videotapes, and flipcharts to gather dust on a shelf until the next offering of the course.

Training materials by their nature become outdated quickly. Because products change, programs must change. This means you must adjust goals to accommodate new audiences and outcomes.

Keeping training materials up to date is a full-time job in any format, and it is daunting in the Web-based training environment as well. What you design and release today will look very old in 60 days. Allow for adjustments in look, feel and capabilities. Budget the time and money needed to keep WBT programs alive.

*Source*: "Web-based Training: It's just not the same" by Margaret Driscoll in *Technology for Learning* newsletter, January 2000, pp.4–5. Margaret Driscoll was an instructor in Instructional Design at University of Massachusetts, Boston, and a frequent contributor to *Technology for Learning* newsletter. She now works at IBM. Article reprinted with permission of Margaret Driscoll. Copyright 2000. All rights reserved.

**3. WBT is best suited for teaching cognitive skills.** You can't teach everything on the Web. There are limits to what any medium can deliver effectively. It may be possible to teach someone to swim via WBT, but it wouldn't be an efficient or effective use of the technology. Match the tool to the task. Select WBT only when it makes sense for your content. Web-based training is best suited to teach cognitive skills.

**4. WBT is justified in terms of strategic goals** and doesn't need justification in terms of return on investment (ROI). Under the old rules, training professionals devoted hours to cost-justification calculations demonstrating the value of investing in a training intervention.

Many organizations now realize that ROI calculations on the Web don't make sense. The Web economy can be deceiving. Payback isn't clear-cut.

WBT costs for development maintenance can be significant. Avoid the trap of seeing WBT as a replacement for the costs associated with instructor-led training. Well-designed WBT will eliminate some travel and lodging outlays, but your development costs may offset any savings. And don't forget to factor in maintenance costs for the site. Focus on establishing how WBT is related to the organization's strategic goals.

**5. WBT requires new learning skills.** The Internet has changed the way a company does business. The same is true for learning. WBT will change the way people learn.

Playing by the old rules, employees came to the workplace with the skills needed to learn in traditional instructor-led classrooms. Participants were familiar with how to use workbooks, take notes, respond to questions, and participate in group activities. The new rules require learners to play a greater role in initiating, managing, and assessing their own learning.

In WBT, learners must use self-directed learning, discovery learning, guided practice, learning communities, and referenced-based learning strategies. Training arrives in short units accessible on the spot, when the learner needs instruction—rather than in larger chunks of content that learners *may* need to know, sometime.

The new rules require training organizations to help employees gain the skills they need to learn in this way. Companies must also adjust their hiring profiles to attract employees who have the learning skills needed to thrive in the new initiative-taking learning environment.

**6. Content is the motivating factor** in WBT. The practice of motivating learners to attend training courses has a checkered past bristling with both sticks and carrots. Most people can recall a mandatory training course they endured politely to earn a promotion, take a certification exam, or gain access to an e-mail account. Learners have used training as an opportunity to socialize, as a form of recognition, and as opportunity to escape the office.

Carrots and sticks are fewer in Web-based training. Content is paramount. Whether it's new software or understanding human-resource policies, content must have value for the learner or the learner will not engage.

Under the new rules, learner-centered instruction takes on new meaning. Learner-centered programs must focus on what the learner needs to know. Such programs must present content in a meaningful context, or learners will ignore it.

First, conduct a needs-assessment study to define what learners need to know. This has never been more important. Then, use the resulting data to determine what content best meets the needs of the learner—and will therefore motivate learners to participate.

# 1E. COLLABORATION: THE NEW BUZZ

## BOOK REVIEW

## THE SOCIAL LIFE OF INFORMATION

*Editor's Comment*: As its title suggests, this book is a case for human and social processes that define our search for meaning (in life and in work). It is a book that does not worship the Web as the ultimate icon of the information age. Brown and Duguid's new book explores information, knowledge, and learning from a foundation and frame of community and context. Training managers who still believe strongly in the value of learning face-to-face with flesh-and-blood human beings will appreciate this work.

The first 100 pages of the book slowly build the case for the necessity of human processes in building knowledge. The authors define some of these typically human ways of doing things— negotiating, choosing, interpreting, making judgments, narrating, improvising, discerning—and contrast them with the technological point-and-click kind of process of accessing information online. They state their opinion that "... the Web is a vast, disorderly, and very fast-changing information repository ... and all its catalogues are incomplete and out of date...." (p. 44). They suggest that the really tough jobs today require "sense-making," and that the only way to do this is to collaborate with peers and fellow-seekers in physical proximity to each other (pp. 54; 96; 102). Information is easy to detach from people; knowledge is rooted in the complementarity of social interaction and therefore impossible to detach from people (p. 123).

The authors point out that the "D" words often associated with the information technology "future" are words that force our thinking backward into units instead of composites, individuals instead of groups, and ubiquitous information instead of personal knowledge. Some of these familiar words are: demassification, decentralization, denationalization, despacialization, disintermediation, and disaggregation (p. 22). They challenge corporate leaders who would be knowledge managers to always focus on the acquisition of knowledge, perhaps the most human of processes, which they define as learning (p. 124). They encourage learners to "talk and walk," "walk and talk" (p. 126); they advocate participating in a "community of practice" in order to produce "actionable knowledge" (p. 135). They suggest that it is along networks of practice that knowledge travels, multiplies, and "leaks" (p. 158).

Throughout the book, and especially in the last half of the book, Brown and Duguid draw comparisons between learning about and learning to be, and that one is not the other. They suggest finding ways to use the great information resources of the Internet in a complementary way to "cohorts of learning" and "communities of interpretation" (p. 222). Perhaps their bottom-line message of the book is found on page 227, and is stated as a caution to those planning or facilitating workplace learning: "Online learners need access to peers, communities of practice, and social resources in order to thrive." The wide experience of John Seely Brown in the structure, function, and meaning of documents and that of Paul Duguid in research on culture and education work together here to provide the reader with a book that recognizes both the value and the de-value of blind acceptance and rush into an information society.

*Source: The Social Life of Information* by John Seely Brown and Paul Duguid. Boston, MA: Harvard Business School Press, 2000. $25.95. John Seely Brown is Chief Scientist at Xerox Corporation and Director of the Xerox Palo Alto Research Center (PARC). Paul Duguid is a Research Specialist in Social and Cultural Studies in Education at the University of California at Berkeley.

# ARTICLE REPRINT

## TEXT, MEDIA, AND ONLINE MENTORS

*Editor's Comment*: This short article is for the training manager who is considering hiring a training service provider or consultant to design and possibly manage IT (information technology) training as distance learning or Web-based courses. It addresses the issue of the need to blend text, media, and persons to deliver the training. It is an example of the kind of thinking training managers need to exercise in order to provide the best possible "mixed media" blend of management, design, and delivery of training.

## ONLINE MENTORING GIVES E-LEARNING A BOOST

### by Vince Rowe

Just a few years ago a classroom setting was the norm for employees honing their computer skills. Web-based training came along and offered the promise of 24 × 7 access to course materials via the Internet. There were other variations, such as training courses on CD-ROM and combinations of live classroom training and online testing, all offering return on investment (ROI) in some fashion or another to fiscal and business aspects, but never the learner.

Training methods, especially for those in the information technology industry, have evolved rapidly from text-only presentations to media-rich courses that include student interaction and collaboration that steps the traditional classroom learner through the process of shifting knowledge transfer modalities.

The hottest learning trend, especially when it comes to information technology (IT) training, is the online course coupled with a live mentor. This type of experience is extended even further when those mentors are trained to mentor in a teaching style that correlates to individual learning styles and are backed up by a robust test prep and frequently asked ques-

tion (FAQ) function. Such self-paced courses will dominate instruction in the future.

Eric Parks, president and CEO of ASK International, includes in his *Distance Learners' Bill of Rights*: "Provide me with access to a real 'live' person of whom I can ask questions."

It seems like a simple request, but not many e-learning providers have developed on-demand tutors as an integral part of their instruction offerings, and the situation gets even worse when a method of instruction is applied that is not conducive to the individual's preferred learning method.

When considering an online training service there are several features that users should look for so they can be assured of the best and most productive e-learning experience that covers as many learning styles possible.

Seek providers that include a combination of the best of online and instructor-led learning experiences, such as online group exercises, online post-tests, and ongoing discussion forums.

Collaboration is becoming a key feature for online learning. Online courses must include discussion forums, online mentors and chat to be sufficiently stimulating. Communication

*Source:* "Online mentoring gives e-learning a boost" by Vince Rowe in *e-Learning*, May 2000, pp. 42–43. Vince Rowe is VP of KnowledgePool Inc., Dallas, TX. Editorial Assistant Elsa Schellin also contributed to this article. Reprinted with permission of *e-Learning* published by Advanstar Communications Inc., Duluth, MN. Copyright 2000. All rights reserved.

between mentor and student can occur through many channels:

■ **Live interactive chat/online mentoring**—The live chat area is visible to all registered users, letting them communicate with online mentors and classmates. The most sophisticated providers of this type of training have mentors located at global support centers to provide real-time answers to questions, 24 × 7.

These mentors should provide support during their regular working hours. This type of support is much more effective than support from people who have already put in time at a day job and are making extra money in the evenings.

Students should get support from mentors who are in the same geographical location as they are, which translates into more personal help. The needs and questions of students in Tokyo, for example, are often far different than those in the United Kingdom.

■ **E-mail**—If students don't want to ask questions publicly, they can e-mail their mentors. The best providers guarantee a response within four to six hours.

■ **FAQs**—Data collection from instructor-led courses and online mentoring has created libraries of frequently asked questions. Students can search by topic; information in the libraries is continuously updated.

■ **Message boards**—Message boards are a general area for the mentors or students to post information relating to the course. Messages can include useful links to additional information sources, book titles for additional reading, exam tips, and other resources.

■ **Assignments/assessment tests**—Assignments let students gauge their levels of learn-ing. The student maintains control of when to take the assignment. When completed, the mentor grades and returns the assignment to the student in real-time.

These services ensure motivation through teacher-student interaction while retaining the cost-effectiveness and geographic independence associated with Web-based and CD-ROM training.

**Key benefits for students include:**
■ The ability to manage and schedule a self-paced learning timetable;
■ Mentors to answer questions 24 × 7;
■ The motivation and discipline of instructor-led training;
■ The use of online training to consolidate knowledge prior to taking exams or as a prerequisite to an instructor-led course; and
■ Training that is tailored to meet individual learning styles vs. a one-size fits all approach.

**Key benefits for employers include:**
■ A consistent global training program while enjoying significant cost-savings on course prices and associated training expenses;
■ Maximum ROI with minimum disruption to the workforce;
■ Employees can study when and where they please; and
■ Studies have proven that after training, employees are more productive and committed to job excellence.

Online training with human interaction anytime, anywhere has brought flexibility, lower cost and higher success to the learning business.

## INFORMAL TRAINING: LEARNING FROM EACH OTHER

*Editor's Comment*: Amidst this year's proliferation of information and points of view on technology-driven training and how to blend it with more traditional face-to-face training, this article considers the most basic kind of collaboration for learning, that of the informal one-to-one training that goes on throughout workplaces. Training managers need to be watchful for this kind of "just-in-time" and person-to-person training and to create working environments that encourage this kind of simple collaboration.

## SIMPLE MOMENTS OF LEARNING

### *by Kevin Dobbs*

The young man taking orders at the McDonald's drive-up window is struggling to keep up, what with anxious lunchtime customers streaming in and a computer rejecting his requests for a Big Mac with no lettuce or sauce.

He starts sweating. It's his first week on the job. "What do I do? This guy wants no sauce and the computer won't take the order?"

"Don't worry," a co-worker says. "You just need to enter your order differently." She leaves her post at the soda dispenser and instructs him. Within seconds, the problem is solved.

Such brief episodes of informal training are commonplace at the fast-food chain's 12,500 U.S. restaurants. On a typical shift, much of the crew is comprised of high school students who are new to the work force (on average, 40 percent are under age 22). And with an annual turnover rate of 120 percent, acclimating new employees is part of the daily routine, says Tony Chiappetta, a manager at this particular McDonald's restaurant in Maplewood, MN.

"Turnover is an ongoing issue—something we deal with every day. It's just part of the job," he says. "We're always training new people."

Such has long been the case in the fast-food industry. McDonald's has tweaked and refined its training processes for decades, and its formal training programs are renowned for the speed and effectiveness with which they teach new hires to do their jobs. But these days, workers are exceptionally tough to find and to keep. With unemployment virtually nonexistent, managers like Chiappetta are in constant competition with everyone from Burger King to the Gap—"anyone paying minimum wage to eight bucks an hour," says Rogercarol Rogers, director of McDonald Corp.'s Human Resources Design Center in Oak Brook, IL. That means it's difficult just to keep crews fully staffed, not to mention adequately trained.

So, hoping to foster the simple moments of learning that take place between crew members, McDonald's is taking a closer look at informal training. The hamburger giant has enlisted the services of Education Development Center Inc. (EDC), a Newton, MA, research organization. In 1997 EDC released findings from a two-year study of corporate cultures across the country (see "Learning Ecologies," *TRAINING*, January 1998). One of those findings echoes estimates

*Source:* "Simple Moments of Learning" by Kevin Dobbs in *TRAINING Magazine*, January 2000, pp. 52–58. Kevin Dobbs in an Associate Editor of *TRAINING Magazine*. Reprinted with permission from the January 2000 issue of *TRAINING Magazine*. Copyright 2000. Bill Communications, Minneapolis, MN. All rights reserved. Not for resale.

from other studies that have attempted to quantify formal training's contribution to over-all job knowledge: 70 percent of what people know about their jobs, they learn informally from the people they work with.

EDC director Sue Grolnic is now in the midst of a six-month research project at McDonald's that has involved observation and interviews at restaurants as well as an examination of Hamburger University, the company's corporate training center for managers. She's trying to find ways to mesh daily, informal learning with the staff-development skills managers learn at Hamburger U. She hopes the results will help the company curtail turnover rates, enhance career-development opportunities, and alter an unfavorable public perception of what it's like to work on the restaurant chain's front lines.

Grolnic sees McDonald's as the ideal place for continuing EDC's research because the fast-food industry is the initial training ground for much of the country's work force. "Fast food is where America learns to work," she says. "It's where so many people learn the basic skills that they take to future jobs."

## THE INFORMAL LEARNING ORGANIZATION

EDC's research suggests that even companies with top-notch formal training programs may be failing to encourage the greatest learning opportunities their employees have. In their two-year study of seven manufacturing firms, Grolnic and her colleagues found that *informal* training was continuous, usually taking place during chats at the watercooler or during impromptu hallway meetings. Often viewed by management as drains on productivity, such encounters actually proved good for business.

"You see some workers walking around and chatting, and you immediately think there is no way that's productive. But that's not the case," says Lisa Casey, employee-development man-ager at Reflexite North America, an Avon, CT, manufacturer of reflective materials. "People learn an awful lot just by asking each other questions and having brief conversations."

Five years ago, Reflexite's New Britain, CT, plant was arranged like many other manufac-turing facilities. Each worker focused on a cer-tain step in the production process. Every few

hours they rotated jobs, but nobody ever saw a product go from start to completion. Conse-quently, Casey says, employees weren't able to learn how the company functioned as a whole or how their individual roles contributed to the company's financial performance.

Starting in 1995, Reflexite rearranged its plant into work centers. Employees now work on only one product line, seeing the product from the customer order to the final inspection. Workers function in small teams and infor-mally cross-train each other in their tasks.

Reflexite also moved its customer service department down to the shop floor, then cre-ated 10-minute overlaps from shift to shift. Supervisors encourage their people to mingle with others from different shifts or departments. The theory is that if workers get to know each other personally, they're more likely to take an interest in one another's work. When that hap-pens, conversations veer toward work-related matters—and learning inevitably takes place.

When EDC evaluated the Reflexite plant, it determined that about 80 percent of all learn-ing at the company was informal. "It seems like a high number at first," if you're used to think-ing of learning as a synonym for formal train-ing, Casey says. "But when you really look at it, it makes sense."

And informal learning can make sense for just about any company in any industry, including fast-food outfits like McDonald's, EDC researchers and others say. But first they have to recognize its prevalence.

## HOLD THE EXPERTS

The flood of computers into the workplace has upped the demand for continual learning. The knowledge economy dictates that most workers, even the drive-up cashier at McDonald's, keep pace with constant changes in technology. Often the only way to do that is to ask a co-worker or learn it on your own. Today's workplaces are leanly staffed and typically fast-paced, meaning there often isn't time for a formal training ses-sion, says Nancy Dixon, an author and professor of administrative sciences at George Washington University in Washington, DC.

"Our unshakable trust in experts led us to act as if knowledge only resides in a few small pock-ets of an organization. But I think that view is changing," says Dixon, whose latest book, *Common Knowledge: How Companies Thrive By Sharing What They Know* (Harvard Business School Press) was published in March. "The change is from thinking of knowledge as limited to thinking of it as abundant and distributed. There is a growing recognition that a great deal of learning goes on outside the classroom. It has to."

In fact, that recognition has been hard to ignore since Peter Senge popularized the concept of the learning organization in 1990 with the publication of *The Fifth Discipline*. For a decade, Senge has taken pains to point out that formal training accounts for only a fraction of the learning that goes on in companies (see "Why Organizations Still Aren't Learning," *TRAINING Magazine*, September).

Acknowledging that a lot of learning stretches beyond the training department's walls is only a first step toward understanding just how informal learning works or fostering it. Companies that want to capitalize on informal learning have to find out where it takes place and then how to bolster it, says EDC's Grolnic. Such initiatives are typically rooted in the concepts of mentoring and teaming, or "communities of practice." In these approaches, management sets the goals, but workers help decide the team's methods. Reflexite's tactic of creating small teams with a specialized focus on one product is a good example. The move encouraged workers to plan their own work and informally teach each other various tasks on the job.

Honeywell Data Instruments, an electronics manufacturer in Acton, MA, is another case in point, if on a smaller scale. Workers there are often grouped into small teams and encouraged to break from their routines for team discussions. It is not uncommon to see a small group standing around talking on the shop floor. Sometimes these meetings consist merely of social chatter, but often work finds its way into the banter because it is the group's common interest, says Bruce MacDonald, HDI's human resources director.

MacDonald says these informal meetings are encouraged out of necessity. With an annual turnover rate of 20 percent, a fifth of the company's line workers are always in their first year on the job. Since assembly lines have to keep moving at full speed, formal training can't carry the whole learning load for each employee; there's not enough time. HDI estimates that two-thirds of all its training is accomplished informally between co-workers.

"The key is to eliminate barriers to communication and give employees the authority to take training upon themselves," MacDonald says. "It saves valuable time."

## CLEARING A PATH

Sometimes tearing down those barriers literally means removing office walls—much as Reflexite did when it moved its customer service office near the production floor.

Chris Turner, a former line manager at Xerox Business Services, based in New York, spent years searching for the right mix of on-the-job and formal training. But it wasn't until her department physically changed the layout of its office that the company really took notice of informal learning. Turner condensed office spaces to make room for an open gathering area, where lingering coffee breaks and idle chatter were encouraged. Xerox soon found workers in casual discussion groups, taking an interest in each other's projects. Questions were asked and ideas were shared. Turner says her department's productivity and creativity increased as a result.

"People are learning all the time. We make a big mistake when we assume that knowledge comes only from certain positions in the corporate hierarchy. We are all learners and teachers," says Turner, author of *All Hat and No Cattle* (Perseus, 1999), in which she draws upon her 16 years at Xerox to examine workplace learning.

Turner argues in her book that focusing on informal learning means departing from what she calls the basic premise of training: *Tell them and they will know*. She writes, "There is some deep belief that knowledge is a substance that can be packaged and placed in people's hands. It ain't." Too often, she contends, companies approach training with a "checklist" mentality. After watching a video, for example, trainers may simply ask participants to sign a form certifying that they have been trained. The true learning opportunities, however, lie in the conversations following the video. "That's when people construct meaning out of information," she says.

Some of the country's biggest names apparently heed such advice. IBM, for one, gets its best sales-training results when it matches beginners with seasoned veterans so that they can learn from casual interaction as well as explicit teaching. Boeing Commercial Airplane Group in Seattle takes a similar approach with its maintenance trainees, putting them on the job at airports and incorporating hands-on practice with formal training.

"It's all part of the training organization getting out of the classroom and helping learning to take place as a normal part of the business process," says John Panattoni, a training and development manager at Boeing. "But that's still alien thinking for a lot of people, especially trainers, because that's not what we're used to doing."

## THE BIG PICTURE

None of this suggests that formal training has lost its place. McDonald's, for instance, has no plans to cut back its structured training programs for restaurant workers.

The challenge here for McDonald's and others is to incorporate informal learning into the greater picture of organizational development—to make it a recognized function within the company. To do this you have to look at everything that affects informal learning, says EDC's Grolnic. "What are the cultural factors that contribute: company policies, schedules, work groups, physical layout of the office? These are the things you have to identify first."

Then it's a matter of giving a name to informal learning strategies and putting them to use.

The U.S. Army has done this for years. After any formal military action, a combat unit holds an "After-Action Review," in which soldiers and officers reflect informally on that day's work. They speak openly, questioning policies and suggesting changes—regardless of rank.

"It works because they are doing it for themselves, not to satisfy someone higher up in the chain of command," says Dixon, the George Washington professor. "They are acknowledging that everyone has a part in making sense of what has happened and that everyone has the capability to do that. . . . And they are tapping into a wealth of information that a lot of companies overlook."

For McDonald's and its store managers, this means taking a closer look at the problem-solving and interpersonal skills employees rely on to serve hoards of customers every day—everything from trouble-shooting at the drive-up window to taking orders from customers who don't speak English. "We're hoping to shine a light on all the little things that add up to a great deal of learning," says Grolnic.

"We think finding the right combination of informal and formal training will help us leverage something that's already going on," says Rogers of McDonald's human resources department. "There are a lot of people coming into the work force, a lot of people to constantly train. If this is already going on—and we know it is—why not take advantage of it?"

# RESEARCH SUMMARY

## NEW COMMISSION ON TECHNOLOGY AND ADULT LEARNING REPORT DUE 1ST QUARTER 2001

*Editor's Comment*: Access to knowledge and the process of learning are among the important issues driving the creation of a government commission of Technology and Adult Learning, a joint project of the American Society for Training and Development, (ASTD) and the National Governors' Association (NGA). The first public report of the Commission is expected to address numerous policy issues surrounding the adult as continuous learner and as learning consumer. Of particular interest is the many references within this article reprinted here to building relationships, systems development, and collaboration within public policy development. Training managers who are pivotal in positioning their organizations within a new learning economy will find this summary of public policy research of great interest.

## THE COMMISSION ON TECHNOLOGY AND ADULT LEARNING

*A Joint Project of the American Society for Training & Development (ASTD)*

*and the National Governors' Association (NGA)*

## THE COMMISSION

The American Society for Training & Development (ASTD) and the National Governors' Association Center for Best Practices (NGA) will establish a Commission on Technology and Adult Learning to clarify the most critical public policy issues raised by increasing the use of technology for adult learning. The commission will consist of leaders from business, government, and postsecondary education. By combining the perspectives of chief learning officers, senior state and federal government officials, and leaders in the field of technology and learning, the commission will bring together information and expert testimony to identify critical trends and best practices and will make recommendations for public policy and private sector action.

## THE NEW CONTEXT FOR LEARNING

The "New Economy" (whether described as the information economy, digital economy, or knowledge economy (is characterized by structural changes that have profound implications for the public policies that frame lifelong learning. These structural changes include industrial and occupational change, globalization, the changing nature of competition, and the progress of the information technology revolution.

In order to develop new systems for adult education and training that will support the skills needed in the 21st century, we must understand the implications for radical change in the nation's traditional context for learning driven by information technology.

Information technology is changing the access to knowledge, the process of learning, and the delivery of education and training. Teaching and learning can now take place outside the traditional education and training venues. Within this new context, the adult who has been an occasional "student" becomes a continuous "consumer" of knowledge that is available anytime, anywhere. As employees increasingly gain control over their own learning and career development, employers face difficult challenges in training and retaining their workforce.

The speed with which technology changes work occurs in many ways, including: the relentless unending demand for new skills created by the use of information technology has reinforced the demand for education and training that is effective (improves performance) and measurable (increases return-on-investment). In response, a dynamic market of for-profit providers is developing parallel to the existing public education and private sector training systems.

## FRAMEWORK FOR THE POLICY DISCUSSION

Online learning and education and training via other technology-based methods are growing rapidly. The implications for traditional postsecondary and workforce development systems are formidable. Consumers and entrepreneurs are driving much of this new system of learning outside the domain of traditional state, regional, and national oversight authorities. Furthermore, employee mobility and a greater range of choices for education and training are changing the traditional roles and interactions between public and private sector education and training systems. Policy issues are emerging in the following areas:

**1. Equitable access:** There is a need to ensure access to computers and the Internet for all socioeconomic groups, overcome barriers that affect how well adults learn using technology, and develop and implement common technology standards, such as interfaces, objects, and platforms that will enable reuse, communication, and the overall capability to access and use existing online or technology-based education and training resources.

**2. Accreditation and licensure:** Issues here concern the need to revise existing systems for ensuring quality and excellence of curricula,

developers, trainers, and educators. Current systems are not easily applied to the methods, content, and flexibility of online learning.

**3. Assessment, certification, and credentials:** The need is to define and establish appropriate systems and processes for assessing competency and knowledge and for formal assurance of the acquisition of knowledge that takes place outside of a traditional institutional structure or curriculum format. Individuals must be able to rely on credentials that are portable and recognized in relevant professional or academic environments.

**4. Lifelong Learning:** There is growing realization that we can no longer define education and training in terms of traditional "blocks" and "silos." We need to move instead to a lifelong learning "pipeline" and to consider the role that online and other technology-based learning can play in an interdependent system that begins with pre-school and carries forward through workforce development and adult learning

**5. Funding sources and models:** Funding for adult education and training has been related primarily to institutions-postsecondary education institutions, private companies that provide training, and organizations. Individual student aid is frequently restricted to a particular number of hours or courses. We need to examine the processes and structures for funding to ensure they address online education and training.

**6. State investments for economic development:** The practical appeal of online learning has implications for state policies governing investments in education and training infrastructure needed to attract business and create jobs. The increasing importance of a workforce for the information technology and engineering sectors, as well as the necessity for all workers to use technology, requires the availability of online resources for skill development and retraining.

**7. Intellectual property:** "Ownership" of content becomes more complex as open access to information expands. Traditional processes of copyright and "fair use" do not address online "learning objects" or the new ways content will be recombined and reused by teachers, trainers, and learners. As organizations develop new business models to support learning anytime, anywhere, we need to take a new look at "rights management" for creators, authors, and publishers.

**8. Tax and regulatory policies:** Tax and regulatory policies governing not-for-profit and for-profit education and training providers may no longer be appropriate or optimal, as the process of learning "anytime, anywhere" blurs state and national boundaries with respect to location of providers and adult learners.

### *Expected Outcomes of the Commission*

Over the next eighteen months, the Commission will

- Frame the questions and implications for the public and private sectors about adult learning and information technology;

- Identify critical trends and best practices in the public and private sectors for promoting access to and the effective use of information technology for adult learning;

- Describe the appropriate public and private sector roles and responsibilities that will facilitate the use of information technology for lifelong learning;

- Connect this work to similar activity focused on K–12 education; and

- Make recommendations for state and national public policy to facilitate the nation's transition to an information economy.

## IMPACT AND DISSEMINATION ACTIVITIES

ASTD and the NGA will publish an interactive, electronic report, to be released early in 2001. High visibility public meetings to discuss the report's findings and recommendations will be held in Washington, D.C., and in other locations, hosted by commission members. A Web site, established at the inception of the project, will incorporate the ongoing dissemination activities and discussion of the findings and highlight opportunities to get involved in priority issues.

ASTD and NGA will create opportunities for business, government, education, and labor to come together on national, state, and local levels to develop and create useful initiatives that use technology to enhance lifelong learning.

# CASE STUDY

## WORKFORCE INVESTMENT ACT CONSOLIDATIONS

*Editor's Comment*: *The Workforce Investment Act (WIA)*, passed in 1998 and funded through Federal fiscal year 2003, requires the phaseout of the old workhorse *Job Training Partnership Act (JTPA)* as of July 1, 2000. Trainers familiar with public sector training under *JTPA* are now under a new kind of government umbrella, requiring new thinking about collaborative enterprises of all sorts. A major challenge of *WIA* is for states to enact legislation to codify structural changes to workforce systems. The concept in this legislation is that of personal responsibility for career development through "One Stop" neighborhood centers. The worker/learner as consumer underlies the policy in *WIA*.

Behind the new implementation plans lurks the problem in year 2001 of the economic divide in American worklife. According to a report in the February 2000 issue of *TRAINING* magazine (p. 50), more than two-thirds of today's labor force does not work in the "New Economy." Credit card debt is on the rise; retail, service, education, and even manufacturing sectors are falling behind in terms of wage rates. The concept of "a living wage" permeates policy discussions. From a minimum wage rate of $5.15 per hour in most places to a "living wage" of $10.75 per hour in San Jose, California or $9.00 per hour in Tuscon, Arizona (SHRM, *HR News*, February 2000, p. 18), workers are faced with discrepancies and unequal opportunities at the good life. Policy trends and innovative government support programs are of concern to training managers, especially as we seek as a society to move forward with economic well-being for all of our workers.

We reprint several introductory pages from the DoL public information about PL 105–220.

## THE WORKFORCE INVESTMENT ACT OF 1998, PL 105-220

### EMPOWERING THE NATION'S JOBSEEKERS

The **Workforce Investment Act of 1998** provides the framework for a unique national workforce preparation and employment system designed to meet both the needs of the nation's businesses *and* the needs of job seekers and those who want to further their careers. Title I of the legislation is based on the following elements:

- Training and employment programs must be designed and managed at the local level—where the needs of businesses and individuals are best understood.

- Customers must be able to conveniently access the employment, education, training, and information services they need at a single location in their neighborhoods.

- Customers should have choices in deciding the training program that best fits their

*Source: Workforce Investment Act (WIA) of 1998, Public Law 105-220*, U.S. Department of Labor, Washington, DC. Alexis M. Herman, Secretary of Labor; Ray Bramucci, Assistant Secretary for Employment and Training Administration; Gerald F. Fiala, Administrator, Office of Policy Research. Follow its implementation on the Web site of the Society for Human Resource Management, SHRM, at *www/shrm.org/government*.

needs and the organizations that will provide that service. They should have control over their own career development.

- Customers have a right to information about how well training providers succeed in preparing people for jobs. Training providers will provide information on their success rates.

- Businesses will provide information, leadership, and play an active role in ensuring that the system prepares people for current and future jobs.

## A CUSTOMER-FOCUSED SYSTEM

The most important aspect of the Act is its focus on meeting the needs of businesses for skilled workers *and* the training, education, and employment needs of individuals. Key components of the Act will enable customers to easily access the information and services they need through the "One-Stop" system; empower adults to obtain the training they find most appropriate through Individual Training Accounts, and ensure that all State and local programs meet customer expectations.

### *"One-Stop" Approach*

The new system will be based on the "One-Stop" concept where information about and access to a wide array of job training, education, and employment services is available for customers at a single neighborhood location. Customers will be able to easily:

- Receive a preliminary assessment of their skill levels, aptitudes, abilities, and support service needs.

- Obtain information on a full array of employment-related services, including information about local education and training service providers.

- Receive help filing claims for unemployment insurance and evaluating eligibility for job training and education programs or student financial aid.

- Obtain job search and placement assistance, and receive career counseling.

- Have access to up-to-date labor market information which identifies job vacancies, skills necessary for in-demand jobs, and provides information about local, regional and national employment trends.

Through the "One-Stop," employers will have a single point of contact to provide information about current and future skills needed by their workers and to list job openings. They will benefit from a single system for finding job-ready skilled workers who meet their needs.

To date, over 95 percent of the States are building these Centers, and over 800 Centers are operating across the country. Each local area will establish a "One-Stop" delivery system through which core services are provided and through which access is provided to other employment and training services funded under the Act and other Federal programs. There will be at least one Center in each local area, which may be supplemented by networks of affiliated sites. The operators of "One-Stop" Centers are to be selected by the local workforce investment boards through a competitive process or designation of a consortia that includes at least three of the Federal programs providing services at the "One-Stop."

### *Empowerment Through Training Accounts*

Provisions of the Act promote individual responsibility and personal decision-making through the use of "Individual Training Accounts" which allow adult customers to "purchase" the training they determine best for them. This market-driven system will enable customers to get the skills and credentials they need to succeed in their local labor markets.

Good customer choice requires quality information. The "One-Stop" system will provide customers with a list of eligible training providers and information about how well those providers perform. Payment for services will be arranged through the Individual Training Accounts. Only in exceptional cases may training be provided through a contract for services between the "One-Stop" Center and organizations providing the training.

# RESEARCH SUMMARY

## *TRAINING* INDUSTRY SURVEY 2000

*Editor's Comment*: The "Industry Report" published in *TRAINING Magazine* near the end of each calendar year has come to be known as the most complete snapshot of the training industry in America. The year 2000 report is based on an online survey conducted for *TRAINING Magazine* by Custom Research Inc (CRI), a market research firm in Minneapolis, MN. This year's Industry Report covers approximately 50 pages of the magazine; we reprint 6 pages from this Report here. The full *Industry Report 2000* is available for $38.00 from *TRAINING Magazine* by phoning 800/328-4329.

The population of organizations in this large and comprehensive survey of the field is 152,124 organizations employing 100 or more employees. Only organizations with formal training operations are included. This is about 10,000 more organizations than formed the population for last year's study. To begin the survey, CRI conducted telephone interviews in May 2000 to qualify respondents who were then directed to an online questionnaire. This qualification procedure resulted in a remarkable 44.5 percent usable response rate or 1,347 usable responses from a sample pool of 3,026 qualified candidates. Categories in this year's Industry Report include:

- The Money
- The Methods
- The People
- The Delivery
- The Tech Emergence

The "2000 Highlights at a Glance" chart indicates some of the trends as the new Millennium unfolds. There's much good news as we enter year 2001. Total dollars budgeted for formal training in the immediate year past is $54 billion. This figure does not include training hardware or facilities and overhead, reflecting increasing use of desktop computers, company intranets, and the Internet for training throughout organizations—hardware and facilities that tend to be budgeted in organizations other than training. As in the recent past, managers and professionals get the lion's share of training, and in-house staff share design and delivery with outside trainers and consultants. As in the recent past, the classroom is still a huge favorite for delivery of instructional programs, including information technology (IT) instruction, with a full 80 percent of organizations using classrooms with live instructors. We still have a strong commitment to the preservation of "high touch" in an environment of "high tech" in our workplace learning.

## 2000 Highlights At A Glance

Total dollars budgeted for formal training this year by U.S. organizations: **$54 billion**

Of that sum, amount that will go to outside providers of training products and services: **$19.3 billion**

Percentage of U.S. organizations that teach employees to use computer applications: **99%**

Percentage that pay to teach some employees remedial math/arithmetic: **35%**

Percentage that will send some employees to an outdoor experiential program: **12%**

Of all formal training, percentage currently delivered by an instructor via remote location: **6%**

Of all training delivered online, percentage in which the student interacts online with other humans: **29%**

Of all computer-delivered training, percentage devoted to teaching computer skills: **55%**

Of all computer-skills training, percentage delivered in a classroom, by live instructors: **72%**

*All figures refer to formal training by U.S. organizations with 100 or more employees.*

## About The Survey: Respondents By Region

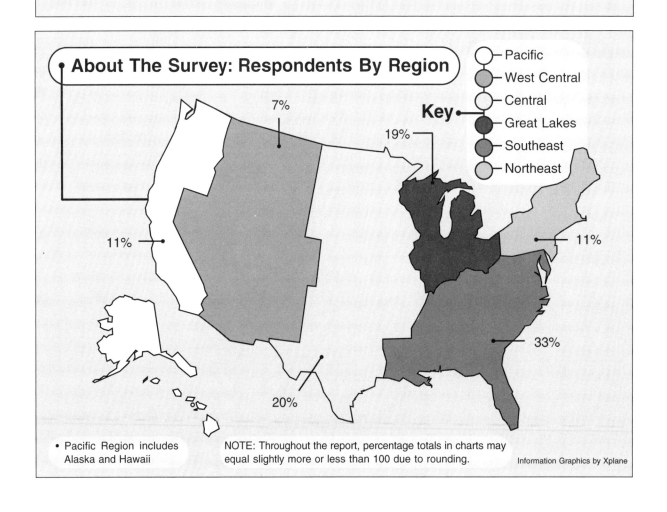

Key
- Pacific
- West Central
- Central
- Great Lakes
- Southeast
- Northeast

7%
19%
11%
11%
20%
33%

- Pacific Region includes Alaska and Hawaii

NOTE: Throughout the report, percentage totals in charts may equal slightly more or less than 100 due to rounding.

Information Graphics by Xplane

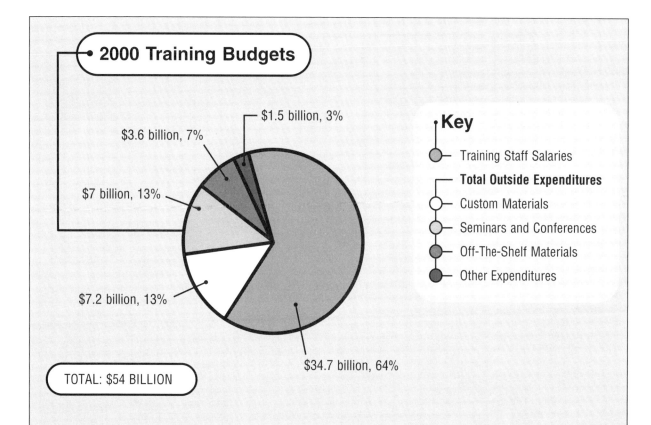

**2000 Training Budgets**

$1.5 billion, 3%

$3.6 billion, 7%

$7 billion, 13%

$7.2 billion, 13%

$34.7 billion, 64%

**Key**

○— Training Staff Salaries

— **Total Outside Expenditures**

○— Custom Materials

○— Seminars and Conferences

●— Off-The-Shelf Materials

●— Other Expenditures

TOTAL: $54 BILLION

**DEFINITIONS:**

**TRAINING STAFF SALARIES:** Salaries paid to internal trainers and administrative support staff in the training department.

**TOTAL OUTSIDE EXPENDITURES:** Dollars budgeted for the following categories:

CUSTOM MATERIALS: Materials tailored/designed by outside suppliers specifically for an organization. For example: A/V, video, film, classroom programs, computer courseware, etc.

SEMINARS/CONFERENCES: Training by outside providers/contractors either at an organization's location or off-site, including public seminars, but not trainee travel and per diem costs.

OFF-THE-SHELF MATERIALS: Prepackaged materials purchased from outside suppliers. For example: computer courseware, books, videos, classroom programs, etc.

OTHER EXPENDITURES: Other training products or services from outside suppliers.

**U.S. employers will spend $54 billion on formal training this year in the categories shown.**

Most of the money pays the salaries of in-house training specialists, but more than $19 billion will flow into the outside market for materials, courses and services. Beneficiaries include everyone from book publishers, video producers and computer-courseware suppliers to consultants, community colleges, and the sponsors of public seminars and conferences.

Note: These figures do not compare directly with those we have reported in previous years (see introduction, page 46). For one thing, our 2000 survey did not ask respondents about dollars spent for hardware used in training or about expenses for facilities and overhead; both of those spending categories were included in the past. Also, significant changes in our survey methodology this year preclude direct comparisons with previous years' findings. We believe the new methodology is superior and provides a more accurate gauge of spending and other training activity.

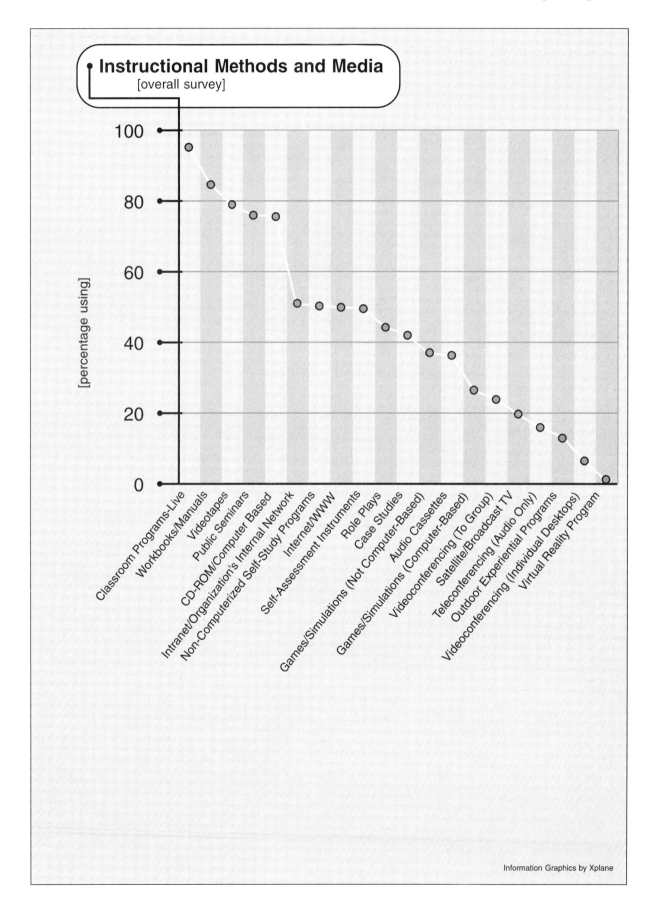

## Instructional Methods and Media
[overall survey]

[percentage using]

Classroom Programs-Live
Workbooks/Manuals
Videotapes
Public Seminars
CD-ROM/Computer Based
Intranet/Organization's Internal Network
Non-Computerized Self-Study Programs
Internet/WWW
Self-Assessment Instruments
Role Plays
Case Studies
Games/Simulations (Not Computer-Based)
Audio Cassettes
Games/Simulations (Computer-Based)
Videoconferencing (To Group)
Satellite/Broadcast TV
Teleconferencing (Audio Only)
Outdoor Experiential Programs
Videoconferencing (Individual Desktops)
Virtual Reality Program

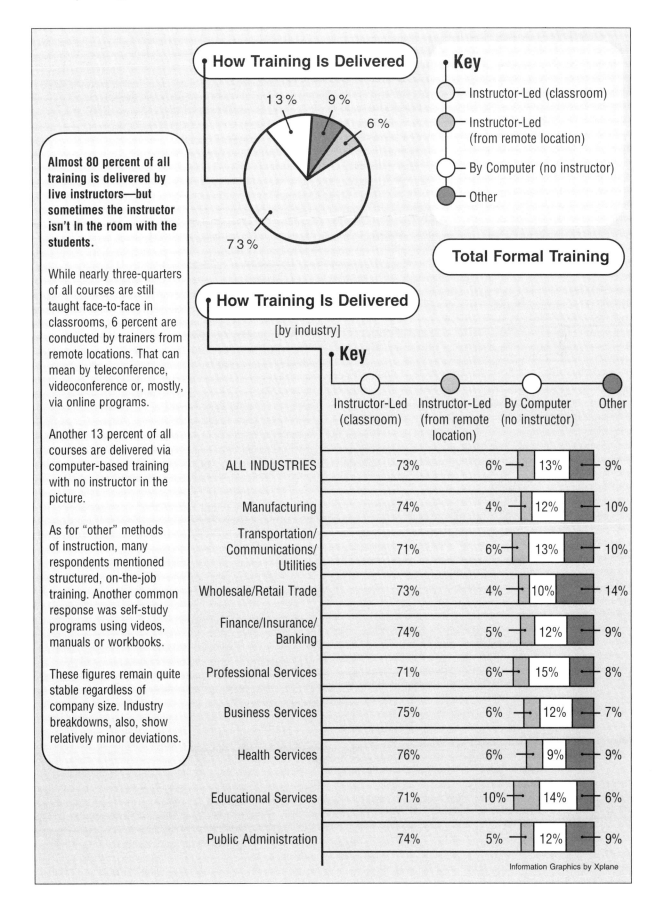

# How Training Is Delivered

13% 9% 6%

73%

## Key

- Instructor-Led (classroom)
- Instructor-Led (from remote location)
- By Computer (no instructor)
- Other

## Total Formal Training

**Almost 80 percent of all training is delivered by live instructors—but sometimes the instructor isn't In the room with the students.**

While nearly three-quarters of all courses are still taught face-to-face in classrooms, 6 percent are conducted by trainers from remote locations. That can mean by teleconference, videoconference or, mostly, via online programs.

Another 13 percent of all courses are delivered via computer-based training with no instructor in the picture.

As for "other" methods of instruction, many respondents mentioned structured, on-the-job training. Another common response was self-study programs using videos, manuals or workbooks.

These figures remain quite stable regardless of company size. Industry breakdowns, also, show relatively minor deviations.

## How Training Is Delivered

[by industry]

### Key

| Industry | Instructor-Led (classroom) | Instructor-Led (from remote location) | By Computer (no instructor) | Other |
|---|---|---|---|---|
| ALL INDUSTRIES | 73% | 6% | 13% | 9% |
| Manufacturing | 74% | 4% | 12% | 10% |
| Transportation/ Communications/ Utilities | 71% | 6% | 13% | 10% |
| Wholesale/Retail Trade | 73% | 4% | 10% | 14% |
| Finance/Insurance/ Banking | 74% | 5% | 12% | 9% |
| Professional Services | 71% | 6% | 15% | 8% |
| Business Services | 75% | 6% | 12% | 7% |
| Health Services | 76% | 6% | 9% | 9% |
| Educational Services | 71% | 10% | 14% | 6% |
| Public Administration | 74% | 5% | 12% | 9% |

Information Graphics by Xplane

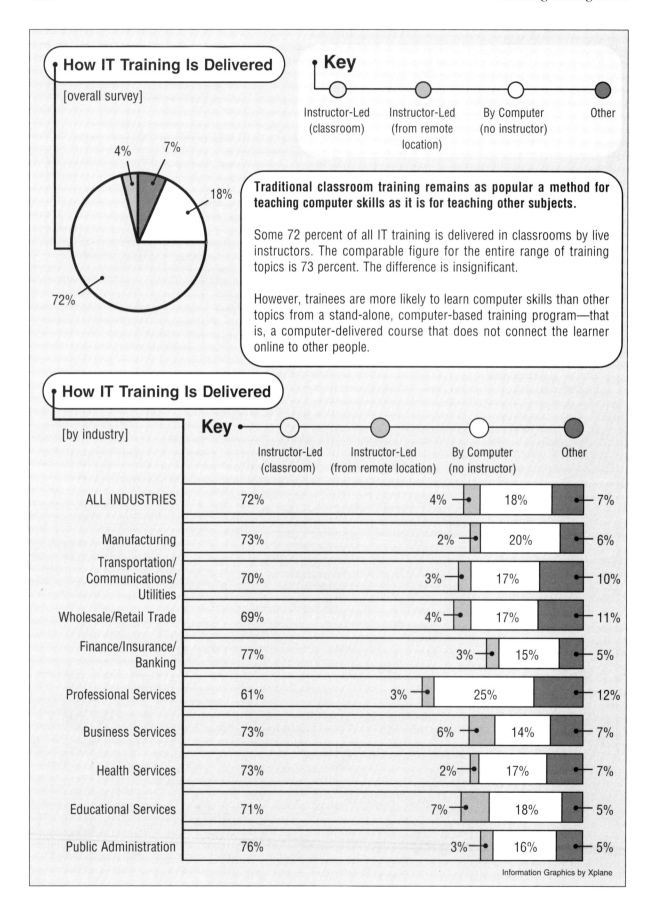

**How IT Training Is Delivered**

[overall survey]

**Key**
- Instructor-Led (classroom)
- Instructor-Led (from remote location)
- By Computer (no instructor)
- Other

4% · 7% · 18% · 72%

**Traditional classroom training remains as popular a method for teaching computer skills as it is for teaching other subjects.**

Some 72 percent of all IT training is delivered in classrooms by live instructors. The comparable figure for the entire range of training topics is 73 percent. The difference is insignificant.

However, trainees are more likely to learn computer skills than other topics from a stand-alone, computer-based training program—that is, a computer-delivered course that does not connect the learner online to other people.

**How IT Training Is Delivered**

[by industry]

**Key**
- Instructor-Led (classroom)
- Instructor-Led (from remote location)
- By Computer (no instructor)
- Other

| Industry | Classroom | Remote | Computer | Other |
|---|---|---|---|---|
| ALL INDUSTRIES | 72% | 4% | 18% | 7% |
| Manufacturing | 73% | 2% | 20% | 6% |
| Transportation/Communications/Utilities | 70% | 3% | 17% | 10% |
| Wholesale/Retail Trade | 69% | 4% | 17% | 11% |
| Finance/Insurance/Banking | 77% | 3% | 15% | 5% |
| Professional Services | 61% | 3% | 25% | 12% |
| Business Services | 73% | 6% | 14% | 7% |
| Health Services | 73% | 2% | 17% | 7% |
| Educational Services | 71% | 7% | 18% | 5% |
| Public Administration | 76% | 3% | 16% | 5% |

Information Graphics by Xplane

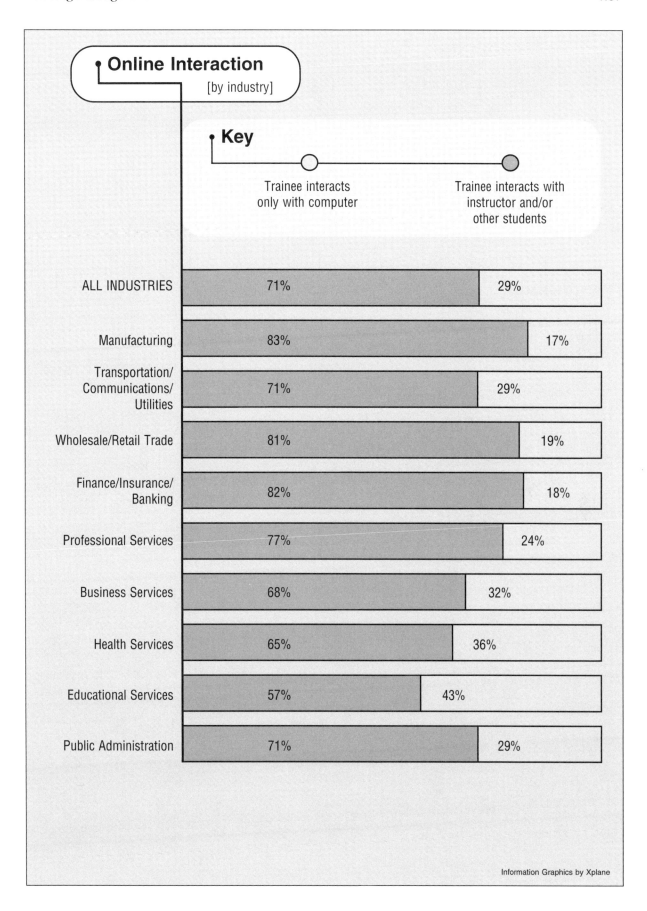

Online Interaction
[by industry]

Key

Trainee interacts
only with computer

Trainee interacts with
instructor and/or
other students

| Industry | Computer only | Instructor/students |
|---|---|---|
| ALL INDUSTRIES | 71% | 29% |
| Manufacturing | 83% | 17% |
| Transportation/Communications/Utilities | 71% | 29% |
| Wholesale/Retail Trade | 81% | 19% |
| Finance/Insurance/Banking | 82% | 18% |
| Professional Services | 77% | 24% |
| Business Services | 68% | 32% |
| Health Services | 65% | 36% |
| Educational Services | 57% | 43% |
| Public Administration | 71% | 29% |

# SECTION

# 2

# NEEDS OF LEARNERS

## INTRODUCTION TO NEEDS
## OF LEARNERS: SECTION 2

Perhaps the most basic underpinning of today's workplace learners is the notion of "24/7"—work is 24 hours per day and 7 days per week. Behind this, of course, is the information technology revolution that has connected people around the globe and has provided good jobs for millions of workers, and America's booming economy that encourages and funds entrepreneurs and innovators. America's hero-of-the-day is Alan Greenspan, Chairman of the Federal Reserve, whose body language and every phrase set the stock markets dancing, the dotcoms shaking, and workers scrambling to strategize their next career moves.

In this section on Needs of Learners in this culture of hard work, connectivity, and movement, we focus on three major topics of particular relevance at the start of year 2001: what kinds of soft skills workers need to maximize their effectiveness; the needs of learners for stability and growth; and the needs of learners for government support, particularly in areas of equal opportunity and fair employment practice. Today's workplace and workers have special kinds of needs for learning in order to thrive, and sometimes, even to survive. George B. Weatherby, President and CEO of the American Management Association, said in the Commentary column in the February 2000 issue of *Management Review*, ". . . the speed, quality and cost of *learning* are as significant in determining financial success as are the speed, quality and cost of production" (p. 6). In this section of *Training & Development Yearbook 2001*, we suggest some of the major requirements for learning and needs of learners in this work environment that is increasingly being built, and judged, on its capacity to support learning. We'll help you make sense of these learning requirements for speed, quality, and cost. We'll help you analyze learning needs of your organizations and of the people in them.

NEEDS OF LEARNERS FOR NEW KINDS
OF SOFT SKILLS

In spring and early summer, many corporate annual reports and letters to shareholders come across my desk. One, that of IVAX, a pharmaceutical research organization, had a cover with three pictures on it: a sumo wrestler, a seal balancing a globe, and a magnificent tree in full green of summer. Inside, the text explained that IVAX was guided by the three principles of strength, balance, and growth as the company moves into year 2001. These three words, "strength, balance, and growth" contain the semantic charge that defines the soft skills challenge for trainers.

For several years, we have been trying out new ideas and programs to help workers balance their work demands and the demands of living. Managers and dotcom entrepreneurs seem to be working longer and longer days; more working mothers are working more hours. Global opportunities make computers and Internet connections hum all the time—24/7. The emotional requirements in such job behavior are enormous; emotional intelligence, its assessment and development, has become a very important framework of soft skills for maintaining balance.

The online work environment also has its own peculiar challenges in the soft skills area. The June 2000 issue of *SMARTBUSINESSMAG.com* has a major feature article, "The New Business Ethics: Cheating (Technology Makes It Easy), Lying (Get Used to It), Stealing," which is full of examples and charts illustrating how pervasive the ethical issues and abuses are at work, and how the Internet has been the catalyst for workers and companies to behave badly. One of the big issues that has gotten a lot of press this year is the issue of personal use of company resources, especially time, and especially e-mail and Web browsing. Many put the percentage of employees who conduct personal business on company time at more than 60 percent (Ziff Davis *SMARTBUSINESSMAG*.com reader survey, p. 90). In the June 12, 2000 issue of *Business Week*, studies by Info Worldwide, the American Management Association, and Vault.com put the number at 70 percent for employees who admitted to viewing or sending adult-oriented personal e-mail at work, 64 percent who sent politically incorrect or offensive personal messages on work time, and 37 percent who say they constantly surf the Web for personal reasons on company time. Visiting porn sites, shopping, and day-trading are all favorite non-work activities going on daily at work (p. 106). Many employers are worried about not only the loss of productivity that these numbers imply, but also about legal action of all sorts due to the loss of privacy that Internet communication all too often means. Hackers cracking privacy codes and web address piracy have been all too common this year. Net copyright issues are hot; privacy (4th amendment) versus access (1st amendment) complicates the workplace behavior of net entrepreneurs and their managers.

Learners from executive suite to mail room need to learn new kinds of communications skills and be reminded of the values of a capitalist democracy in a 'net-mediated world. The old communications skills training that focused on listening, giving and receiving feedback, writing literate sentences, making eye contact, and facilitating groups seems quite quaint and out of date for today's workplace. Training managers need to take a look at communication issues in today's workplace, and design and facilitate training to match the new knowledge and skills required.

### NEEDS OF LEARNERS FOR STABILITY AND GROWTH

During the spring of 2000, we began to see stories in the business press about Internet companies that were failing and about venture capital that was drying up. We heard about executives and researchers out of jobs, and about others ready to take their places with new ideas and new enthusiasm. We heard about the lessons to be learned in failure, and how a resume with a different job in a new company every year wasn't such a bad thing these days. *TRAINING Magazine* in July 2000, had a cover article called "Who Will Replace Those Vanishing Execs?" and highlighted another article called "Dot-Com Management Grows Up." Churn at the top, especially in young, technology-based companies, is obvious throughout the workplace. Those caught up in it need to learn skills to remain personally stable and professionally grounded during change. These skills are for those who stay as well as those who leave. Workplace stress is on the rise.

We heard a lot about finding colleagues who were compatible, and about the value in experimentation. "Built to Flip—The Battle for the Soul of the New Economy" was the cover article in *Fast Company* magazine in March 2000. *Fortune* magazine, March 6, 2000 also used the word "soul" several times in Brent Schlender's article on Yahoo! founders David Filo and Jerry Yang. Yang was quoted as saying that they chose their Venture Capitalist because he "seemed to have more soul," and he shared the Yahoo! Founders' "values." Gut decisions, intuition, vision, and believing in both the art and the science of building a company were important to Filo and Yang. While they got rich like so many other young Internet-based company founders, they also had or learned the values and the soft skills for building a company to last (p. f-82). These kinds of workers, too, need to learn skills for stability and growth.

Finally, the other important learning challenge around the issues of stability and growth is the challenge of keeping the workforce stable and growing in depth as well as breadth of knowledge. Perhaps because of the year 2000 Census, as well as the record number of new jobs created, Americans were sensitized this year to various segments of workers, categorized by age range. Political discussions on the long-term viability of Social Security perhaps also raised our collective consciousness about older workers especially. By mid-summer, there were many reports touting the benefits to all concerned of keeping workers at work well past the current typical retirement age of 65. Our love of job sharing, working at home, and making a living as a contingent worker highlighted the value of keeping skills sharp and current. TV and magazine advertisements showed young moms and dads with toddlers at home/at work telecommuting; brochures aimed at stay-at-home workers advertised online college degrees and Web-based professional courses of all sorts to serve the learning needs of workers who are not based in an office. Generation-based training and investment in learning in order to leverage assets are new ideas in helping individuals and companies grow and prosper. Worldwide, as the new century marches on, industrialized and computerized nations will continue to age. Nurturing, building, and keeping talent across the wide spectrum of working ages will challenge trainers as business leaders work together to keep their companies stable and growing.

NEEDS OF LEARNERS FOR GOVERNMENT SUPPORT:
EQUAL OPPORTUNITY GUARANTEES
AND FAIR EMPLOYMENT PRACTICES

In this sub-section, we consider current trends in government involvement in workplace learning, especially in the areas of equal opportunity guarantees and fair employment practices. As year 2000 ends and 2001 begins, the most visible government involvement in corporate life is the Microsoft anti-trust case, in which a federal judge ordered the company split in order to avoid continued violations. Microsoft appeals are expected to last well into year 2001. Press consensus was that, in addition to breaking the law, Microsoft leaders irritated the judge and were arrogant. During the litigation, other information technology companies—Cisco Systems, AT&T, Yahoo!, Disney, Viacom, to name just a few big ones—wondered whether they were next. An article in the January 24 *Business Week*, "So Who's Next?" identified the three major areas of content, Web portal, and distribution as the key areas onto which the future was pegged, and areas in which competitive behavior was being watched. Mega-dealmakers AOL and Time-Warner made the business world stand up and take notice of old-style conglomeration based on ownership, not the new-style partnership. Training managers need to ask themselves, what do the men and women at the tops of these companies need to know about today's fair competition, and how can trainers help structure workplace learning so that clear paths of fair, legal action can be taken. And, of course, throughout merged or divided companies, employees, like their leaders, need to gain knowledge about new definitions of fair practice and need to know how to behave at work in a environment of personal and corporate fairness.

Another kind of government involvement in workplace fair practice is the kind of regulatory involvement that facilitates the hiring of adequately trained high-technology workers which have been in short supply during the last several years. The continuing tinkering with the H-1B Visa allotments illustrates a complicated and political problem of whether or not government regulation is helping or hurting business. Regardless of what the magic number of visas allowed, trainers have a job to do in assessing the learning needs of holders of H-1Bs as well as those who work side by side with them. Expect to see more of the H-1B Visa issue in 2001.

While these two examples of government involvement in fair practice were highly visible this year, the other and ongoing way in which government supports workers is its involvement in equal employment opportunity guarantees. We share with you several articles on current EEO concerns: the persistent gender gap in wages and promotions, some thoughts on affirmative action and race, commentary on the stubbornness of poverty and current effects of efforts at Welfare reform, a new challenge in sexual harassment of *non*employees, and new ways to look at equal opportunity for contingent workers. American companies are being shaped by economic forces from society in general, and the nature of working is changing. Trainers have an opportunity to shape the learning quality of the workplace by astute analysis of learner needs. The challenges today are enormous and exciting.

# 2A. NEEDS OF LEARNERS FOR NEW KINDS OF SOFT SKILLS

## RESEARCH SUMMARY

### WORK/LIFE BALANCE STUDY

*Editor's Comment:* "Holding a Job, Having a Life: Making Them Both Possible" is the title of an extensive research study currently being conducted by the Work in America Institute of Scarsdale, New York. Jill Casner-Lotto and Jack Hickey, principals of the organization, can be contacted for more information at 914/472-9600. The news release that follows was issued by Work in America Institute in March 2000. A key component of the project was a site vist to Merck & Company, Whitehouse Station, New Jersey, and case studies from Hewlett-Packard/Agilent and other companies will become part of the finished report. All together, nine case studies will be included. Of particular interest to the Institute are the issues of evaluation methods for work/life initiatives and partnerships between labor and management in implementing work/life actions. The Ford Foundation provided initial funding for the project.

### STRATEGIES LINKING WORK REDESIGN AND WORK/LIFE BALANCE IMPROVE BUSINESS AND EMPLOYEES' LIVES: WORK IN AMERICA INSTITUTE STUDY

A growing number of America's leading companies find that it is good for business *and* employees to make work/life effectiveness integral to organizational change and work redesign strategies, reports Work in America Institute.

**"Holding a Job, Having a Life: Making Them Both Possible,"** a current research project of the national not-for-profit research organization, is studying companies that are breaking new ground in the work/life field with a focus on changing work cultures and practices. Such companies as **Merck & Company, Hewlett-Packard/Agilent, Bank of America, Fleet Financial Group, and Ernst & Young** have developed strategies that enhance business performance and help employees achieve a better balance between work and personal life. In most cases, employees themselves participate in developing the strategies through their observations and input, with important benefits for both businesses and employees.

Businesses have improved productivity, quality, and customer service; reduced turnover and absenteeism; and enhanced recruitment. The new model of work redesign has increased employees' satisfaction and empowerment, given them more flexibility and control over how and where work is performed; reduced overtime and stress levels, and allowed more time for family and leisure activities.

"These work redesign and other change initiatives differ radically from management-driven, top-down reengineering, which is focused solely on work processes and organizational needs," says Jill Casner-Lotto, Vice President for Policy

*Source:* "Strategies Linking Work Redesign and Work/Life Balance Improve Business and Employees' Lives: Work in America Institute Study" news release by Jill Casner-Lotto, Work in America Institute, Scarsdale, NY, March 16, 2000. Reprinted with permission of Work in America Institute.

Studies and director of the project. "Instead, the redesigns that we are studying are marked by strong employee involvement in changing the way work is done, and they address employees' personal priorities as well as strategic business needs. Addressing both dimensions creates a synergy that strengthens employees' lives and accelerates and sustains the change process."

As part of this project, the Institute has studied various strategic approaches to work/life effectiveness and business success at such companies as Baxter Healthcare, Statistics Canada, Eli Lilly & Company, Kraft Foods, and First Tennessee Bank, as well as at the companies listed previously.

This research project was initiated by a lead grant from The Ford Foundation and is now being supported by several major corporations and labor unions, including Bell Atlantic, Capital One, Chase Manhattan, Cinergy Corporation, Corning, Federal Express, GTE, Household International, Kraft Foods, Merck & Co., Inc., Miller Brewing, Philip Morris, State Farm Insurance, Service Employees International Union (SEIU) and Union of Needle Trades, Industrial and Textile Employees (UNITE).

## BEYOND "FAMILY FRIENDLY"

Work in America's project looks beyond traditional, stand-alone "family friendly" programs—such as child care, maternity or paternity leave, and flexible work schedules. Instead, it is studying underlying factors of organizational culture and work environment that either encourage or discourage employees' use of these programs. It focuses on approaches that address work/life issues strategically and systemically through:

- work redesign
- linkage with other business processes and goals (for example, quality, teamwork, leadership development)
- organizational changes in workplace culture
- integration of work/life factors in human resource systems
- partnerships (labor-management, public-private, and multiple employers)

A key component of the project is the National Advisory Council, a diverse group of experts on work/life issues representing business, unions, academia, and government. Back-

ground papers and best practices and key lessons drawn from the case studies have been discussed at NAC semiannual meetings since the start of the project in 1997.

The Institute is currently reviewing these change initiatives with a view to spotlighting their successes and encouraging other firms to apply some of the practices. The goal is to provide business leaders and managers with state-of-the-art resources, case study models, and practical tools to help them repeat the successes achieved by these pacesetting companies.

With the first phase of the study nearing completion, work is currently in progress on a volume that will include a final report, nine case studies, and background papers that examine (1) state-of-the-art methods of evaluating work/life initiatives; (2) the role of unions in initiating collective bargaining solutions to reduce work/family conflicts and improve customer service, such as the recent labor contracts between the Communications Workers of America and several telecommunications employers to limit mandatory overtime; and (3) seven joint labor-management partnerships around work/family issues such as the Harvard Union of Clerical and Technical Workers and Harvard University and Hotel Employees and Restaurant Employees International Union Local 2 and San Francisco Multi-Employer Group.

## EXAMPLES OF WORK REDESIGNS: HEWLETT-PACKARD/AGILENT AND MERCK & CO., INC.

Two case studies to be included in the report and featured at upcoming Work in America Institute events are change initiatives underway at Hewlett-Packard/Agilent and Merck & Co. The Hewlett-Packard/Agilent case, to be presented at Work in America's Roundtable conference in Scottsdale, Arizona on May 3, highlights a breakthrough in work/life activities with an emphasis on changing work processes and cultural norms. The focus is on how Hewlett-Packard and Agilent Technologies (a recent spin-off of HP) have partnered with Artemis Management Consultants to introduce a process called "Reinventing Work," which helps organizations analyze the interdependencies in the world of work and the world outside of work. Managers and their teams learn how to challenge traditional cultural assumptions and how to redesign their habitual work practices and cultures so that business results are improved and customer satisfaction further increases along with employee satisfaction.

The objective is to provide insights on how Reinventing Work concepts can be applied to other organizations to help them more effectively meet their business and work/life objectives. Included are examples of how HP/Agilent business organizations have:

- Realigned work schedules to more cost effectively meet customer requirements seven days a week, 24 hours a day in a customer engineering organizations *and* ensure that employees can juggle work and personal life responsibilities.

- Established processes (such as development plans for time off) in a sales organization that have helped increase retention *and* meet sales quota goals.

- Worked on restructuring a finance department within a high-growth business to more effectively meet customers' changing demands *and* maintain flexibility tools such as part-time schedules and telecommuting.

**The Merck case was featured as a Site Visit on May 23 in Whitehouse Station, New Jersey**, describing the Work Group Action Planning Process (WGAPP—pronounced "We-gap"), a work redesign process that is helping work groups evaluate the effectiveness of their current work environment and identify ways to improve it. Managers use tools and training to help their employees handle work and life demands and increase productivity.

Merck is using WGAPP throughout the company, particularly in its manufacturing and sales divisions. For example, in the payroll department, where morale was low and excessive workloads and overtime made work/life balance impossible, employee groups identified the underlying issues contributing to inefficiencies and redundancies in the work flow. Working together, they identified job elements that could be dropped, delegated to a lower level, or done at home just as easily as at the office. They discovered that some apparent deadlines were actually quite flexible.

Employees were also asked, for the first time, to identify issues in their personal lives that affected their lives at work, a process that energizes employees by giving them the opportunity to talk about sensitive issues in a safe environment with both their peers and managers and come up with creative solutions.

One year after WGAPP began, productivity is up in the payroll department, overtime has been cut in half, and the number of employees on flexible schedules such as telecommuting or compressed work weeks has doubled. A key element in WGAPP's success is that, rather than being a "stand-alone" program, it is anchored in two broader long-term corporate commitments—Merck's Strategy for Growth, which outlines the company's financial and operating priorities; and The Leadership Model, which is the centerpiece of Merck's HR strategy and which the company communicates throughout the organization on an ongoing basis.

## BEST PRACTICES, KEY LESSONS

Each of the companies studied by the Institute has tailored work/life effectiveness initiatives to its own needs. However, analysis of the case studies reveals certain key features that have contributed to their success, such as:

- *Senior leadership support is critical.* It is exhibited in various ways: by modeling desired behaviors and providing resources for pilots and prototypes that are experimenting with new ways to integrate work and life.

- *Successful initiatives are collaborative change efforts.* They combine top-level support and commitment with mid-level managerial training and support and grass-roots employee involvement.

- *The focus is on the group.* In contrast to programmatic responses, which tend to focus on individuals' work/life needs, the cited change initiatives are focused on work groups or teams, on collective rather than individual action plans, and on the structure and organization of work systems.

- *Managers are held accountable* for implementing action plans that meet both business and personal goals. Increasingly, support for work/life balance is a factor in managers' performance reviews, in promotion decisions, and pay.

- *Employers sustain and diffuse work/life change initiatives.* They keep the initiatives going over the long-term and diffuse the lessons learned to other parts of the organization. For example, they use such methods as highly accessible electronic "tool kits" or databases that capture and disseminate best practices and the development of work/life "champions," or change agents, throughout the company.

- *Evaluation is ongoing and collaborative.* Assessment of the change initiative is done on a continuing basis in order to monitor progress over time, and the mea-

sures used are designed in collaboration with the employees who took part in the pilot design and implementation.

## NEXT STEPS: REPORT, SITE VISIT, ROUNDTABLE

The report, published in mid-2000 and distributed nationally, captures the learnings, best practices, and key findings of the project. It includes 10 case studies and three background papers on specific issues or challenges in the area of work/life plus an overview and analysis highlighting practical lessons.

## ABSTRACT

### NEW INCENTIVES, OR MONEY CAN'T BUY YOU LOVE

*Editor's Comment*: For several years, we have been hearing about the death of loyalty and the demise of authoritarianism in our workplaces. Downsizings and layoffs have turned employees sour on devoting their working lives to single employers, and many people will admit these days that they're in it only for the money. And there appears to be plenty of money available in the "sellers' market" that seems to be American business right now. *The New York Times Magazine* on March 5, 2000 showed a photo of a harried man in a suit running with clenched jaw across the page, with the issue title, "The Liberated, Exploited, Pampered, Frazzled, Uneasy, New American Worker." The entire issue of the magazine is devoted to the topic of the characteristics and needs of today's workers, and is well worth keeping in your business library. The title conveys the mixed message of freedom and servitude, and sensitizes our thinking to just exactly how workplaces can attract and keep workers. The bottom line is that money can't do it alone: New incentives are needed for workers to sign on to jobs and to keep growing in them.

The particularly insightful article by Michael Lewis, "The Artist in the Gray Flannel Pajamas," in *The New York Times Magazine* cited below makes the observation that today's workplace is infused with a "new spirit of nonconformity" (p. 48), and that managers everywhere are using the term "outside the box" to describe work as a creative endeavor—and perhaps an endeavor that depends on learning, and not pay, as the engine that drives enterprise. An article following this by Nina Mink knocks the hype about the free-agent, liberated worker, and suggests that the freedom is actually freedom from benefits and vacations too (p. 50). We have seen plenty of business press this year about outrageous incentives to attract and keep full-time workers on the job—free

*Sources:* "The Artist in the Gray Flannel Pajamas" by Michael Lewis in *The New York Times Magazine*, March 5, 2000, pp. 45–48; "Canadian Unions Expand Organizing in 'New' Economy" in *Union Labor Report*, March 9, 2000, The Bureau of National Affairs, Inc., Washington, DC; "The Demographic Trend: America Is Aging" in *Workplace Visions*, Society for Human Resource Management (SHRM), No. 1, 2000, pp. 2–9; and help wanted/employment opportunities advertisements in local newspapers: *The Shopper's Guide*, Great Barrington, MA, July 13, 2000, p. 36, and *The Foothills Trader*, Torrington, CT, July 17, 2000, pp. 31G–33G.

vacation houses, trips to romantic islands and beaches, Mercedes and BMW cars, and multi-hundred-thousand-dollar signing bonuses. Today's incentives make yesterday's fitness centers and walking tracks look pale in comparison.

The Bureau of National Affairs' *Union Labor Report*, March 9, 2000, noted that unions in Canada are offering tax planning and financial advice, career counseling and retraining, discount loans, insurance and credit cards in hopes of increasing membership. The Conference Board of Canada is quoted in the article as saying that the emphasis today is on "knowledge, information and service," industries that are traditionally characterized by low unionization rates, and that unionizing today requires different strategies and needs to target industries such as retail trade, finance, and hospitality (p. 80). A different kind of training is apparently in the union future, and learning to deal in the information economy is essential.

A major challenge facing American workplaces is the challenge of keeping older workers employed and productive. We've seen numerous articles and books on the topic this year especially. The statistics are carved up many different ways: The essence of the data, however, is that the American worker pool is growing older and that individuals and companies need this older worker to remain in the workforce and to remain productive in a strategic way. SHRM's newsletter, *Workplace Visions,* No. 1, 2000, contains 8 pages devoted to various issues in dealing with the needs of the workplace and how older workers can fill these needs. A recent survey by Civic Ventures in California is quoted as finding that 40 percent of Americans are working in retirement; yet, there are conflicting reports about employers' perceptions of the capabilities of workers 55 and over. The best thing that has been said is that the typical 20–30 years of business savvy and interpersonal skills that the long-term older worker amasses cannot be quickly taught to a younger worker (National Council on Aging Survey of 240 U.S. employers). Other studies point to deficiencies in "fluid intelligence" that come with aging, and numerous studies report blatant age discrimination among all kinds of employers (p. 4).

Challenges are many, in terms of facilitating work for the older worker and of providing incentives to keep the 55+ worker on the job instead of in retirement. Some of these include:

flexible work schedules, the chance to move to jobs with reduced pay or reduced responsibilities, phased retirement programs, bridge jobs, training to maintain and upgrade technical, particularly computer, skills (p. 4). Public policy initiatives in the next year can be expected to become more visible and more contentious as Social Security and health benefits providers change to accommodate the aging population. No matter what happens, training and workplace learning will play an important role in providing opportunities to and responsibilities for work for older Americans. The issue of *Workplace Visions* cited here includes these Website resources culled from a longer list (p. 7):

| | |
|---|---|
| *www.aoa.dhhs.gov/aoa* | Administration on Aging |
| *www.aarp.org* | American Assn. of Retired Persons |
| *www.asaging.org* | American Society on Aging |
| *www.ebri.org* | Employee Benefits Research Institute |
| *www.ezsis.org/portal/ Oworkers.htm* | Employment of Older Workers |
| *www.50andoverboard .com* | 50 And Overboard |
| *www.maturityworks.org* | Maturity Works! |
| *www.ncoa.gov* | National Council on Aging |

And finally, a word or two must be said about low-end jobs and entry-level workers. Throughout this year especially, we have been aware of the difficulty of many businesses to attract and hold entry-level workers. For some intelligence on this, we look to the "Help Wanted" sections of two local, small community newspapers, *The Foothills Trader*, Torrington, CT and *The Shoppers' Guide*, Great Barrington, MA. In both of these papers, the ads for workers are full of enticing offers for benefits, whereas in the recent past, such ads would have listed only a brief listing of job requirements. Many ads advertise idealistic or psychological benefits of the jobs; clearly, money only is not the thing that employers expect will bring workers running to sign up.

Here are some examples from *The Foothills Trader*:

"*Child Care*: Make a difference in the life of a child. Work at home as a therapeutic parent for a young child."

*"Caregivers*: Know the satisfaction of making a difference in the quality of life at home. Unlimited homecare needs."

*"The Sarah Pierce* an elegant assisted living community is offering career opportunities for professional and qualified CNAs and HHAs."

*"Housecleaners Wanted*: Great for Moms. Make your own consistent hours."

*"Now Hiring*: Companies desperately need employees to assemble products at home. No selling. Any Hours."

And from the *Shopper's Guide* (oversize ads outlined in bold black lines*)*:

*"PepperMill, A Family Style Restaurant and Lounge*: Work part-time hours and take home full-time pay. We need waitstaff and buspeople. Willing to train."

*"The Red Lion Inn*: Our Housekeeping Department needs dedicated and detail oriented Individuals for Year Round Room Attendants full and part time, Weekend Room Attendants, Turndown Attendants (5:00–9:00 p.m.). *Benefits*

*include: Health Insurance, 401K, Profit Sharing, Child Care Cost Reimbursement, Free Lunches, Vacation, and much more" (Italicized in the ad).*

*"Woodworking Positions Available*" Full or part time: If you are tired of working at jobs where you are just a number on a time card, give us a try . . . having a desire to learn and increase your woodworking knowledge is more important than experience."

*"Assistant Branch Manager:* Promote the image of the Bank in the community."

Clearly, these ads are advertising benefits that exceed just pay. The companies placing the ads are trying everything they can think of to make some potential employee come forth, grabbed by a need to serve, by the perception of a job with a higher purpose, or by outstanding benefits. Training managers will play a strategic role in skill development of all sorts for employees, but need to be aware especially of the newly important issue of the soft skills implied in these sample want ads.

# RESEARCH SUMMARY

## UPDATE ON EMOTIONAL INTELLIGENCE

*Editor's Comment*: This lengthy article by Daniel Goleman in the March–April 2000 *Harvard Business Review* is based on an extensive study by the consulting firm, Hay-McBer. In this recent study, a sample of 3,871 respondents was drawn from a worldwide database of more than 20,000 executives. The research focused on how the best leaders get results— business results—and on defining the leadership styles that most facilitate leadership accomplishment.

Researchers found that there are six distinct leaderships styles. The *HBR* article provides numerous examples, case studies, and charts describing the findings. These are the six leadership styles exhibited some or all of the time by leaders in the study (p. 2.12):

1. Coercive, demanding immediate compliance,
2. Authoritative, mobilizing people toward a vision,
3. Afiiliative, creating emotional bonds and harmony,
4. Democratic, building consensus through participation,
5. Pacesetting, expecting excellence and self-direction, and
6. Coaching, developing people for the future.

In addition to the performance and business results focus, the study included carefully designed correlation studies that focused on organizational climate and leadership style. Among the conclusions of the study is that leaders who had demonstrated mastery of four or more of these six styles, had the best performance and climate; and of these four, the most important were authoritative, democratic, affiliative, and coaching (p. 87).

Training managers who are developing leadership programs will find this article an important one for reference. As a reminder, for those who might have forgotten Daniel Goleman's earlier work, we reprint here for you his "Primer" on Emotional Intelligence from page 80 of the article cited here:

*Source:* "Leadership That Gets Results" by Daniel Goleman in *Harvard Business Review*, March–April 2000, pp. 78–90. Daniel Goleman consults with Hay-McBer on leadership and is Co-Chair of the Consortium for Research on Emotional Intelligence in Organizations based at Rutgers University's Graduate School of Applied Psychology, Piscataway, NJ. He is author of the trend-setting book, *Emotional Intelligence*, Bantam, 1995. The complete article is available as HBR Reprint Number ROO204, $5.50 each, 617/783-7500. The chart on page 2.12 is reprinted by permission of *Harvard Business Review* from "Leadership That Gets Results" by Daniel Goleman, March–April 2000. Copyright 2000 by the President and Fellows of Harvard College. All rights reserved.

## EMOTIONAL INTELLIGENCE: A PRIMER

Emotional intelligence—the ability to manage ourselves and our relationships effectively—consists of four fundamental capabilities: self-awareness, self-management, social awareness, and social skill. Each capability, in turn, is composed of specific sets of competencies. Below is a list of the capabilities and their corresponding traits.

**Self-Awareness**
- *Emotional self-awareness:* the ability to read and understand your emotions as well as recognize their impact on work performance, relationships, and the like.
- *Accurate self-assessment:* a realistic evaluation of your strengths and limitations.
- *Self-confidence:* a strong and positive sense of self-worth.

**Self-Management**
- *Self-control:* the ability to keep disruptive emotions and impulses under control.
- *Trustworthiness:* a consistent display of honesty and integrity.
- *Conscientiousness:* the ability to manage yourself and your responsibilities.
- *Adaptability:* skill at adjusting to changing situations and overcoming obstacles.
- *Achievement orientation:* the drive to meet an internal standard of excellence.
- *Initiative:* a readiness to seize opportunities.

**Social Awareness**
- *Empathy:* skill at sensing other people's emotions, understanding their perspective, and taking an active interest in their concerns.
- *Organizational awareness:* the ability to read the currents of organizational life, build decision networks, and navigate politics.
- *Service orientation:* the ability to recognize and meet customers' needs.

**Social Skill**
- *Visionary leadership:* the ability to take charge and inspire with a compelling vision.
- *Influence:* the ability to wield a range of persuasive tactics.
- *Developing others:* the propensity to bolster the abilities of others through feedback and guidance.
- *Communication:* skill at listening and at sending clear, convincing, and well-tuned messages.
- *Change catalyst:* proficiency in initiating new ideas and leading people in a new direction.
- *Conflict management:* the ability to de-escalate disagreements and orchestrate resolutions.
- *Building bonds:* proficiency at cultivating and maintaining a web of relationships.
- *Teamwork and collaboration:* competence at promoting cooperation and building teams.

# ARTICLE REPRINT

## COMPANIES AT THE BRINK, AND BACK

*Editor's Comment*: This article on the emotional needs of the entire workforce is a complement to the previous article on executive leadership and emotional intelligence. Here, we address the costs to companies of employees who are emotionally out of balance because of long hours, productivity expectations, and imbalance in work and personal life. By all accounts, stress is on the rise. This article contains numerous references to real people and companies who have been to the emotional brink of breakdown and loss, and have figured out ways to learn to balance the demands on them and move on to success and well-being.

## THE EMOTIONAL TIGHTROPE

### *by Louise Wah*

You're having difficulty making decisions. You're forgetful. You miss appointments, lose your temper easily and mistrust others. Plus, you feel excessively worried about things. If you're experiencing all or most of these symptoms, you are definitely stressed out and emotionally out of balance.

You're not alone, by any means. The number of Americans suffering from burnout has almost doubled in the past three years. And the proportion of employees suffering from stress and negative spillover from work is staggering. According to a Families and work Institute survey of 3,000 salaried workers in 1997, 36 percent often or very often felt used up at the end of the workday, 28 percent often did not have the energy to do things with their families or others, 26 percent often felt emotionally drained by their work, and nearly one-fourth often felt nervous or stressed.

The growth of emotional stress may not be surprising when you consider the causes: restructurings and consolidations, longer working hours, increasing demands to focus on bottom-line results, the quickening pace of technological and market changes, and shorter product cycles. But the victims of stress aren't limited to the busy executives themselves. Their employers also suffer from a decline in the bottom line, and that means they cannot view the need to regain balance as employees' own business.

## IMBALANCED BOTTOM LINE

From a collective standpoint, businesses aren't necessarily becoming more productive by having employees work longer and harder. The latest International Labor Organization study found that Americans put in an average of 1,966 hours at work in 1997, 83 hours more than the average recorded in 1980—and the longest among all industrialized nations. But the increase in U.S. productivity during the same period lagged behind nations whose workers put in far fewer hours of work.

Looking at a company's balance sheet, the detrimental effects of emotional stress are even more daunting. Recent estimates show that job stress costs employers more than $200 billion a year in absenteeism, tardiness, lower productivity, and high turnover. Jim Osterhaus, an expert on stress and emotional balance at The Armstrong Group, a management consulting firm in Fairfax, Virginia, has seen the following effects of emotional imbalance in companies:

- Eighteen percent of employees aren't working to their full potential.
- The average company spends 25 percent of after-tax profits on medical bills.
- Fifteen percent of employees abuse alcohol and drugs.
- Morale tends to plummet, commitment decreases, work quality diminishes, turnover increases, productivity suffers and profit edges downward.

"If you don't attend to emotional health, instead of going up, your bottom line is going to go down," Osterhaus says. "You need to see this as a priority, not as a luxury anymore."

In fact, the younger-generation in the workforce expects companies to attend to their emotional balance as a matter of course. "They are sophisticated about themselves; they are not going to tolerate companies that use or abuse them," says Osterhaus. "They're going to say, 'Nuts off, I'm going to go somewhere else.' "

If employees are not heading out, they are taking unscheduled days off as a form of protest. A survey of HR managers at 305 U.S. companies by CCH found that stress as a reason for unscheduled absences has tripled over the past five years, from 6 percent of employees in 1995 to 19 percent in 1999. In dollar terms, unscheduled absences mean a loss of an average of $602 a year per employee, according to the Riverwoods, Illinois, provider of business law and information for professionals.

Nancy Kaylor, human resources analyst at CCH and director of the study, says that five years ago, people called in sick because they were indeed sick. Now the main reason employees call in sick is because they are tired, stressed out or have personal needs to attend to. Equally common is the "entitlement mentality." "When employees are stressed out and overworked, what we hear is that, 'I've had it, and you owe me the time. I'm not coming in tomorrow.' Or, 'I've been giving 120 percent, what about me?'," Kaylor says.

She notes that last-minute absences can affect many areas of a business, including customer service, deadlines and order fulfillment. In a competitive environment, these failures can drive customers away. "This should send a wake-up call to managers and supervisors," Kaylor says.

## WHAT SMART COMPANIES DO

Indeed, the message is loud and clear. And wise companies have begun to do something to address the imbalance faced by many employees. "The tide is coming in and people are being maxed out. Employers can only push workers so far. We are probably seeing some course correction now," says Kaylor, who has seen throughout the nine-year history of the CCH survey that smart managers are beginning to remove many of the barriers that crop up when people are overworked.

The 1999 annual benefits survey by the Society for Human Resource Management showed an increase in company programs to help employees reduce stress and stay healthy. Nearly two-thirds provide EAP programs, 56 percent have wellness programs, and 21 percent provide stress reduction programs. According to Kaylor, EAPs are one of the most effective programs, but their use could be much higher if managers continually promoted them. In fact, she says, increased utilization won't drive costs up. Just the opposite.

In addition to these programs, companies also offer flexible work schedules and part-time telecommuting, and some use an absence-control program to give employees personal flexibility, Kaylor says. With these programs, employees can draw days off from a "paid-leave bank" and use them for any reason without having to call in sick. "When they feel a 'mental health' day coming on, they will plan ahead without leaving other people in a lurch so coverage can be planned," she says.

Other companies, like clothing retailer Eddie Bauer, now offer employees "balance days" to help them juggle work and personal demands, says Kaylor. Sabbaticals can also help employees regain a sense of balance amid the craziness of their lives. Arrow Electronics Inc. [*www.arrow.com*], Melville, New York, runs a unique sabbat-

PERSONAL STORY

## MAX CAREY

Founder and chairman of CRD, Atlanta, Georgia
Author of *The Superman Complex* (Longstreet, 1999)

**Emotional Crisis:** The company was growing and becoming more and more complex. My children were growing. I thought I was in control of everything, of every employee and my family. But my body and my mind couldn't handle the burden anymore. One Saturday morning, I was at home opening up a paper and my eyes were in tears. A week later it happened again, this time in a business meeting. Tears just started flowing down my cheeks, an enormous well of sadness filled my stomach. One day in church I burst into tears with such velocity that the tears shot out of my eyes at another person.

**Watershed:** I talked to a college classmate who's a psychologist. I asked him if I was losing my mind. But he said I was about to reclaim what I had lost. What was happening was, when we build a façade for ourselves, we build a wall between who we really are and who we want to become. The disparity between the two gets bigger, the wall can no longer hold them apart. I finally said to myself, "You can't be this contradiction anymore."

**Resolve:** A catharsis started taking place ever since I decided to be myself and abandon my "superman complex," which is an addiction to achievement followed by depression and sadness. Rather than wanting to have control over everything, I've adopted the philosophy of weakness management—to reveal my weakness first and then enlist others to help me become more successful.

*—L.W.*

ical program, overseen by a sabbatical director, that allows employees with a seven-year tenure or more to take a 10-week paid sabbatical to do whatever they want. Since the program started in 1994, as many as 1,400 out of the 6,800 North American employees have gone on sabbaticals.

According to Jean Sheng, vice president of human resources for North America, the program has had a positive effect on employee morale. "It's been a very motivating program," she says. "They come back all renewed, energized." Sheng says these people usually reassess their life goals during their time off and often find that they appreciate their jobs more. "People come back and don't feel tired anymore," she says, adding that this has a positive effect on the morale and productivity of their work teams.

Carol Orsborn, author of *Inner Excellence at Work* (AMACOM, 1999), says some companies set aside a spare room for employees to meditate or provide stress management programs. But one thing management often neglects to do is to get personal with employees' needs. "People at the top of the organization need to do some soul searching and think about whether they have expressed an interest in

what employees do outside of work," she says. "If the managers have resistance [to doing that], they have to see if they are contributing to the burnout situation. If we're not genuinely interested in people's outside life, we are paying a price to hire someone else."

## WHAT ABOUT MANAGERS?

While managers are expected to care for their employees, they themselves are not immune to emotional stress. People in supervisory positions are in fact more vulnerable to emotional stress because employees often look to them for solutions and comfort.

Peter Frost, professor of organizational behavior at the University of British Columbia in Vancouver, Canada, studied 70 managers in the United States, Canada and Europe who take on the role of "toxic handlers" in their organizations. These emotional healers usually volunteer to shoulder the sadness, frustration, bitterness and anger in the organization, but the toll on their physical and emotional well-being is enormous. Many of them experience burnout and, in some extreme cases, strokes and heart attacks.

## PETE BEAUDRAULT

CEO of Hard Rock Café International, Orlando, Florida

**Emotional Crisis:** In February 1995, I had a heart attack [when employed at another restaurant]. At that time I lived in Philadelphia and commuted to Boston every week. Balance at home was nonexistent. My priority was first and foremost the job. I sacrificed my personal life in the name of my profession, and that's going backwards. Everyday for 40 years you feel like you are bulletproof. But in February '95, I woke up. I decided to leave.
**Watershed:** Ironically, at the same time, Hard Rock was recruiting me. It gave me an opportunity to start over. Prior to this, Hard Rock had an awful lot of focus on taking care of people. The piece that was missing is taking care of people's personal and professional balance. The single greatest thing that I brought about was I introduced Stephen Covey's seven habits of highly effective people at every level of the organization. We created the understanding of the foundation of balance.
**Results:** We have one of the lowest management turnover rates in the industry: 20 percent in management and 60 percent in hourly workers. (Industry average: 70 percent in management and 120 percent hourly.) Our culture of 28 years, both proactive and reactive, is the No. 1 reason for our success today, because it's all about people.                              —*L.W.*

The problem with toxic handlers, Frost says, is that they are not equipped to handle other people's emotional stress and manage their pain. But because this role is necessary in any organization, he says the ideal solution would be to put a counselor in place—much like Counselor Troi on board the USS Enterprise in *Star Trek*. "In society we have psychiatrists and therapists, and in religion we have priests [for emotional caretaking]. Why not have that in an organization?"

Until companies appoint a Counselor Troi in lieu of ad hoc emotional healers, they need to recognize the important role toxic handlers play and support them in a systematic way, Frost says. For example, they can train managers in the necessary skills, such as better listening and communications. They should also include the managers' efforts to heal others in their performance assessments. Recognition will make toxic handlers feel much more supported and reduce the chances that they will get hurt by absorbing too much pain. At the same time, employees who are helped will benefit greatly as their emotional stress gets channeled properly. They will then be able to go back to work in a more productive way.

"Many companies haven't seen the connection between emotional well-being and the bottom line," Frost notes. "I think it's there. It's very clear it's there."

Companies that recognize this connection and regard emotional well-being as a strategic issue find that their workers are more productive and creative. These companies institutionalize their concern and create positions that take care of employees' balance. The chief medical officer or chief medical advisor is one such post. Although the title conjures up the image of someone in a white coat and stethoscope, the role has little to do with treatment programs. Rather, it is there for preventative purposes.

Burmah Castrol plc [*www.burmah–castrol.com*], a multinational business-to-business lubricant and specialty chemical distributor based in Wiltshire, UK, has had a chief medical advisor position for more than 20 years. Tony Yardley-Jones, the holder of that title and head of occupational health for 12 years, says his role is to provide strategic vision and advice on occupational health issues. His work is focused on, but not limited to, senior managers because when they are burnt out, they lose the clarity of vision that's crucial for innovation and strategic planning.

"The clarity of thought is strategic," he says. "It is fundamental for senior executives to have that. If you get the senior cadre of people in the company ticking, the rest of the corporation should follow."

Yardley-Jones says his company genuinely believes that a healthy and balanced workforce is

## CYNTHIA GUIANG

Vice president of Townsend Agency, San Diego, California

**Imbalance Signals:** I helped co-found this agency six years ago. I poured my heart and soul into it. . . . It was tough on my husband, who was incredibly supportive, but we couldn't spend a lot of quality time. About a year and a half later, I had my first child. Things started to change. About a year and a half to two years later, my husband decided to start his own optometry practice, so I helped him get financing and funding. Then I gave birth to my second child, so I basically have two jobs and two young children.

My husband really felt for them and for himself that he wanted to see more balance. At the same time, the agency has started to grow, from two partners to 16 employees now. I said to myself, "How do I keep balance and how can I be fair to both my agency and my family and how can I still get fulfillment out of everything?"

**Watershed:** I found the WayFinding program. I've learned to say, "That's enough for the day. There's only physically so much time you can do things in a day." So when I go home, I leave my work behind and completely focus on the family. Some people bring work home, but it might make things worse if you bring your problems home.

**Results:** I realized that my purpose is beyond just family, but to help people grow and have harmony and balance in their lives. That's why I spend so much time with my people. Part of the reason they work here is they know we are willing to work with them to find balance. . . . Several years back, in times of stress, I was in a bad temper, and everybody described me as Hitler. I think if you would speak to them now, they would tell how different I am.     —*L.W.*

good for business. "I think emotional, physical and mental balance is very important, because human beings function much better in balance," he says. "When you are out of balance, you get discord and lack of clarity."

Burmah Castrol has medical facilities in its larger sites where the staff can detect early symptoms of imbalance and take steps to address them. Because the medical professionals understand the business and its commercial aspects, he says, they can detect symptoms of stress or imbalance at an early stage. For example, when Yardley-Jones saw the stress being caused by information overload, shrunken time-to-market schedules and other phenomena, he began to explore ways to help employees regain balance and better mange their work performance. One of the programs he introduced is a one-day workshop from the Institute of HeartMath, a nonprofit educational think tank in Boulder Creek, California, that has pioneered a biomedical approach to human performance and organizational effectiveness.

In the workshop, HeartMath consultants explained the physiology behind stress responses and how they affect the body's adrenaline and hormonal systems. By measuring the length of intervals between the employees' heartbeats and tracking their variability, the consultants were able to tell participants how stressed they were. The lesser the variability, the more synchronized the heart and the body are, which translates into clearer neurological states for the brain and better cardiological performance for the heart.

When the variability was high, employees could do an exercise to bring the hormonal system back in balance, thus releasing the brain's capacity for clarity and creativity. The effects of this exercise were measured through psychometric data such as the feelings of stress, motivation, mental clarity and balance, according to Yardley-Jones. He says the participants felt significant beneficial effects six weeks after the session, and the effects can last for as long as 12 months.

## HUMANE SOCIETY

Not every company uses such a scientific approach to helping employees achieve balance. Sometimes it just takes natural emotions—

compassion and understanding—to create a humane work environment.

At Hard Rock Café International *[www. hardrock.com]*, for example, balance is one of the most important issues on management's agenda and a part of all performance evaluations. CEO Pete Beaudrault says that if an employee is out of balance, managers will offer help in whatever ways suit him or her. "As leaders, it's our job to say, 'You think you're okay, but you're not. You're burnt out. I'm going to hire a trainer or pay for your gym membership,' " he says.

One example: On the opening night of the company's restaurant in San Diego, a general manager's wife went into labor. Instead of making him stay for the important event, Beaudrault and other senior executives urged him to leave immediately to join his wife. "There are a million kinds of those stories, and they happen at all levels of the organization," he says. Because Hard Rock Café believes its No. 1 asset is its people, Beaudrault explains, this proactive, case-by-case approach to helping employees regain balance is practiced by managers right down to the staff level.

A one-on-one approach to addressing employees' emotional balance issues is also used by Cynthia Guiang, vice president of Townsend Agency, an advertising and PR agency in San Diego, California. When the company goes through a stressful period, she calls individuals into her office to ask them how they are doing and feeling. "I let them feel supported," she says. "Then, based on their individual situation, find out how they can deal with the situation and how I can find them additional support." She actually reassures employees to feel okay about not having completed everything when they go home at night.

Guiang has created such a supportive environment for people who need to regain balance that her employees have been working at peak performance. Townsend Agency's revenues grew 60 percent last year to $5 million and are expected to reach $8 million this year. "I don't believe you can have people continuously work at their peak unless they are in balance."

## DIGGING TO THE ROOTS

While executives like Guiang understand the importance of deeper personal issues in achieving balance, most people tend to deal with their imbalance on a surface level. They may use time-management methods, for example, but fail to realize that achieving balance also means aligning your work with your personal identity and beliefs, according to Randall J. Alford, vice president of ARC International Ltd., an employee development and consulting firm, Aspen, Colorado.

When an individual's identity and beliefs are out of sync with the bigger environment, he says, it produces emotional stress. "Choosing to do something that's contrary to your nature and something that's unrealistic—this creates acute imbalance," Alford says. Hence, finding meaning in the bigger context is paramount to regaining balance.

At the individual level, employees can ask themselves these fundamental questions: "Who am I" and "What do I believe in?" According to Alford, only when you are aware of your beliefs, aspirations and needs, and understand how they align with business dynamics and the larger market environment, can you resolve the internal incongruence that results in emotional imbalance.

One company that helps executives engage in such soul-searching is eLuminate Inc., based in Vista, California. Its two-day training program, called the "WayFinding Journey," helps participants identify their ultimate life purposes and see if they can align their personal goals with the company's goals. "When a purpose has been clearly defined by individuals, they are highly productive and their loyalty goes up," says Greg Voisen, founder and chief eLumination officer.

Equally important is that a company's leaders articulate the values and purposes of the business. As Alford says, the emotional imbalance of individuals may very well be a microcosm of the larger organization's lack of purpose and values. "The stresses within the business system will ultimately show up in individual experience as emotional imbalance." Fortunately, "more and more leaders are aware that it is in fact one of their key roles to set the context of meaning, rather than maintaining illusions of control," he says.

In addition to finding their purpose, executives need to adjust their expectations of themselves and those the company has of them. Osterhaus says some people become so driven at work that nothing they do seems to be enough. Consequently, they lose touch with outside activities and relationships that would help them remain healthy. A company's focus on driving the bottom line can intensify already high self-expectations. "What I expect for myself and what the company expects of me, that can become a real toxic mix for me if I'm not careful," he warns.

## WHAT'S NOT ENOUGH

Though more and more companies are trying to handle employee stress with flextime, recognition and wellness programs, it is not enough to simply offer up such programs without reflecting on the company's culture. In a culture where employees feel pressured to work ever harder, they can't really take the mental break they need to restore balance. As Osterhaus puts it, "These things are helping me but killing me at the same time."

Companies that offer wellness and fitness programs, for example, need to see if they provide the catalysts for people to use them. Those that offer stress management courses shouldn't ask people to attend them after-hours, says

author Orsborn. Instead, they should do it during work hours and make sure they have assistance to cover for them.

Coverage is an important mechanism but one that most companies neglect. But Orsborn says employing or deploying more "high-quality floaters" to cover for employees on break is the only way to give them a real break. "If it's not built into the position, nobody gets a break or vacation."

*Ultimately, individuals and organizations* need to step back and expand their perspective so that they can connect their work with their purposes in life.

To organizations, Yardley-Jones offers this caution: "Companies that always focus on the bottom line, drive their workforce too hard, set unreasonable objectives and time scales—I don't believe that is a recipe for a successful company, certainly not for the medium to long term."

To the individual, here's a word of advice from Orsborn: "If you pin all of your hope on the idea that only when you make your great success, then you'll be happy and give back to the community, you may find that a good chunk of your life has passed you by and you may be back to square one."

# ABSTRACT

## BEHAVIOR FOR NET COMMUNICATIONS

*Editor's Comment*: One of the biggest concerns for all companies, Internet-based companies as well as traditional companies, is the concern about Net communications. To put it simply, the rules have not yet been written that govern how people relate to each other on the Internet. Personal behavior on the Internet is still in the "Wild West" stage, uncodified by written or common law. The articles referenced below provide some background on the issues; training managers who need to design and deliver training for Internet communications must begin to translate the needs implied into learning opportunities and behavioral skills for today's and tomorrow's workers.

The "Leaders" column in *The Economist*, (February 26, 2000) after considering the plusses and minuses of Internet use at work, sums it up clearly by saying, ". . . business needs to be redesigned around the cost-saving, communication-easing properties of the net" (p. 24). They cite various studies that illustrate the wide use of the Internet as a "source of information," not necessarily as a profit-generating engine of commerce. *The Economist* points out, for example, that last year only 3 percent of new car sales were made over the Web, but that about 40 percent of car buyers last year used the Web for information—mainly for price comparisons. They also point out that about 80 percent of last year's $150 billion of e-commerce business was B2B, or transactions between businesses, that is, not *consumer* to provider of goods and services. Trainers need to develop programs that help workers efficiently and effectively find and use the Internet for information to speed business decisions and remain competitive.

Mid-February 2000's gigantic hacker attack on U.S. businesses brought a White House roundtable discussion of the problem, a Presidential proposal to create a Cyber Corps program to recruit government security specialists, and the creation of an Institute for Information Infrastructure Protection (*The Wall Street Journal*, February 17, 2000). Mike McConnell, a former director of the National Security Agency, wrote a commentary on the *Journal*'s editorial page in which he suggests that "hygienic habits of online security" should become a part of every Internet user's daily behavior. McConnell says that we need a "new security culture" that pervades all Internet use, the hallmarks of which are personal responsibility and accountability. Above all, he urges the Internet user to resist the "hacker ethic" that glorifies destructiveness in the guise of inquisitiveness. He calls for collaboration among agencies, corporations, and individuals, and above all, for the introduction of the element of trust into Internet communications (p. A16).

Some of the personal "health habits" McConnell advocates are these:

- change passwords from time to time,
- disconnect from the Internet when you are not using it,
- run anti-virus software daily,
- change the default password whenever you buy a new computer,
- sign up with a company that provides personal encryption services.

This list, expanded, could provide the basis for training in "Habits of Cyber Health." Training managers need to think in such dimensions.

*Source:* "Dotty About dot.commerce?" column on Leadership in *The Economist*, February 26, 2000, p. 24; "Get Serious About Cyber-Crime" by Mike McConnell in *The Wall Street Journal*, February 17, 2000, p. A16; "Workers, Surf at Your Own Risk" by Michelle Collins in *Business Week*, June 12, 2000; and "Norwegian Teenager Appears at Hacker Trial He Sparked" by Carl S. Kaplan in *Cyber Law Journal* in *The New York Times on the Web*, July 21, 2000.

Supervisors everywhere are beginning to worry about declining productivity as a result of employee misuse of Internet connections. The *Business Week* article referenced below points out that an American Management Association survey discovered that 57 percent of Internet users said that Web surfing decreases their productivity, and that 37 percent admitted that they "constantly" surfed the Web at work (p. 106). Reporter Michelle Conlin writes that while more than a third of employees are whiling away their boss's time, companies are having a hard time figuring out what the right balance should be between work-related and private use of the Internet. She further suggests that the situation regarding balance and communication will only get worse in the immediate future with the advent of hand-held devices and ever more powerful cell phones. She even suggests that the costs of these "improved" devices could in fact outweigh the benefits. Perhaps convenience of access and ubiquity are not so wonderful after all. Trainers need to be aware of the balance between techie-skills development for using the Internet and the soft skills development of ethical decision making and business-wise choice. Because it's there doesn't mean you should go find it. Managers are going to need help in structuring workplaces that facilitate profitable and productive communication; trainers should have an important role to play.

The *Cyber Law Journal* article, referenced below, on the Norwegian teenage hacker and his two friends tells an all-too-frequent story of computer-savvy teens whose escapades into online security jeopardize the profitability of honest companies and cause havoc among competitors to those companies and drive lawyers, judges, and company executives and stockholders crazy.

This article is about some kids who figured out how to decode the encryption software on Digital Video Disks (DVDs), allowing users to copy movies onto their hard drives for viewing whenever they wanted to. The article says that this particular hacking "has Hollywood in a tizzy." About 30,000 people have downloaded the code. That said, another important undercurrent in the *Cyber Law Journal*'s report is that of the diffusion of information about the decoding program and the violation of the new U.S. Digital Millennium Copyright Act. The article reports that eight major Hollywood studios are suing a Long Island, NY publisher of a hacker magazine and Web site for making the code available online around the world. First amendment rights are all wound up with protection of legitimate business. As of this writing (July 21, 2000), the Norwegian financial crimes police unit officers are in charge of the investigation and have seized the teenager's computer and other electronic devices, and he and his father are subject to fines and jail time. He is, of course, a celebrity in the Oslo area, has won several prestigious academic prizes, and has had job offers from computer firms.

This one case is just the tip of a communications iceberg that rests on a foundation of copyright and free speech. It suggests the new dimensions in both these areas, and challenges training managers to keep abreast of the latest legislation and litigation on Net communications, worldwide, and to devise workplace learning to meet these considerable challenges.

# 2B. NEEDS OF LEARNERS FOR STABILITY AND GROWTH

## ARTICLE REPRINT

## EXECUTIVE LEADERSHIP

*Editor's Comment*: With this article reprint, we begin a sub-section on the needs of learners for stability and growth. Here, we focus on the needs of executives, whose ranks seem to be particularly prone to change and churn these days. This particular article is a strong challenge to trainers to help focus organizations and the executives who lead them toward a business analysis that can indeed help create stability and personal and organizational growth.

## FIVE STEPS TO LEADERSHIP COMPETENCIES

### *by Robert Barner*

It's no secret that we are entering a time of incredible competition for executive talent. A recent McKinsey Company study involving 77 large U.S. companies, 400 corporate officers, and 6,000 executives concluded that "companies are about to be engaged in a war for senior executive talent that will remain a defining characteristic of their competitive landscape for decades to come. Yet, most are ill prepared, and even the best are vulnerable."

As the war for top-level talent continues to escalate, those of us who manage training, OD, and HR functions can expect to find ourselves placed under increased pressure to formulate the executive resource strategies that can help our companies attract, select, develop, and retain exemplary leaders.

Sounds good, but given that the job of building an executive talent base can be monumental, the question we face is, "Where do we start?" That's what I inquire of colleagues when I ask them to walk me through the first steps they usually take in designing an executive resource strategy. They often start describing how they go about creating leadership competency models or executive staffing or development systems. Though those elements are important, they miss a crucial point: We can't begin to talk about executive staffing requirements until we first clearly articulate our organization's business requirements. It makes no sense to try to identify essential leadership capabilities unless one knows the business context in which the leaders will be expected to excel.

Leadership competency assessments must be designed around a clear understanding of the current and future needs of an organization. If people don't understand the problems that their company is likely to encounter as it shifts 30 percent of its market base overseas during the next five years, how can they anticipate the types of international leadership skills that will be needed to support that effort? If an HR executive with a public service agency isn't aware of the types of customer complaints driving the overhaul of the service delivery process, how can he or she deter-

*Source:* "Five Steps to Leadership Competencies" by Robert Barner in *Training & Development*, March 2000, pp. 47–51. Robert Barner is VP of Organizational Development and Learning at Choice Hotels International, Silver Spring, MD. Reprinted with permission of ASTD. Copyright 2000. All rights reserved. *www.astd.org.*

mine whether the needed leadership skills are in place to tackle that challenge?

Al Vicere, management consultant and co-author of *Leadership by Design*, says, "A lot of companies are basing their leadership development up-front on the design of competency models. The problem is that they've designed those models strictly in terms of behavioral models that are disconnected from their business strategies. It shouldn't be the competency model that's the driver; it should be the business strategy. That means answering such questions such as, Where we are we going? Where are our technology and IT strategy going? What skill sets do we need to prepare for the future?

University of Michigan business professor Dave Ulrich suggests that HR planning approaches can be arrayed on a continuum. At one end lie add-on HR plans that are, Ulrich says, created as an afterthought to business planning and are "no more than a postscript to the business planning process." At the other end lies the isolated HR approach, in which HR attempts to carry out HR strategy with little or no input from line management. Ulrich argues that the most effective HR strategies are located midpoint on the continuum and have as their intended outcome "an architecture or framework for incorporating HR practices into business decisions to ensure results."

Ulrich points to the HR team at Frontier Communications, which forced the company to review critical HR issues before acting on an acquisition—such as the value to Frontier of an acquired firm's talent and the consistency of an acquired firm's management style and culture with Frontier's.

In short, the first step in articulating an executive resource strategy is to step back and take a big-picture view of the long- and short-term business requirements that determine the need for certain types of leadership competencies. Understanding those requirements provides the necessary linchpin for connecting your company's business strategy to its capabilities.

## STEPPING UP TO THE PLATE

The operating principle is that we, as training and HRD leaders, need to move to the forefront of our corporate business initiatives if we want to be in a position to help senior managers anticipate the potential implications of execu-

tive resource issues. One way to do that is by applying the technique of business analysis, which has a variety of connotations depending on the business context in which it's applied. Here, it refers to having each executive in an organization generate a one- to two-page assessment of

- the business challenges they anticipate their particular functions to encounter next year,
- the leadership competencies their teams will need to meet those challenges,
- how significant competency gaps may affect organizational performance.

When the analyses have been consolidated into an organizational overview, they yield two valuable applications: the front-end application and the backend application.

**Front-end application.** You can use the organizational overview to help build your model by identifying the leadership competencies that will take on particular significance in the coming year. Examples include competencies required to forge supply-chain relationships, launch e-commerce, or manage international distribution channels. Performing a business analysis prior to creating the competency model helps ensure that the model will be based on all data that accurately represents the leadership structure of your continually evolving organization. If the organizational overview indicates that over the next year your company will be opening new field offices or launching a new international sales group, you should design the competency model to break out the separate leadership needs of the different groups.

**Backend application.** The business analysis can also be used to evaluate your organization's readiness to successfully execute its business strategy. Once your organization has designed a competency model and identified the key leadership competencies, a business analysis can identify any competency gaps that might prevent moving forward in meeting planned business objectives.

A business analysis serves as a connecting link between a company's business strategy and the continual evolution of its leadership competency requirements. If your company has never performed a business analysis, you may find it useful to schedule a series of interviews and to walk executives and managers through each of the five steps. It's best to begin the interviews at the highest level of management and work your way down. That information should be updated yearly by making a written business analysis a formal part of annual executive talent reviews. Once the management team has had experience in formulating business analyses and observing the benefits, they can participate in an analysis through e-mail.

**Step 1: Summarize business objectives and accountabilities.** Begin the interview process by asking executives to summarize their major business objectives and accountabilities for the coming year and to pay particular attention to the areas that represent significant changes in the scope of their current work responsibilities or that represent entirely new responsibilities. It's important to highlight objectives that are expected to exert a substantial impact on the company's overall performance.

**Step 2: Identify anticipated challenges.** Next, ask the executives to list the major challenges they anticipate in attempting to meet their objectives. Such challenges might involve changes in organizational structures or reporting responsibilities that will require them to take on new leadership roles, new untested work systems or processes, shortfalls in technical or leadership skills, or expansion into new markets.

The anticipated challenges establish the "demand features" for your company's leadership positions and provide a clear context for understanding the difficulties that work functions and leaders will face in trying to achieve new goals.

**Step 3: Specify assumptions.** The next step involves specifying all assumptions on which your business analysis is based. Though assumptions are always built into business plans, they're seldom stated explicitly. By highlighting the assumptions, we make certain that we've realistically assessed the likelihood that the anticipated business events will occur during the next 12 months, and that we've assessed the potential impact correctly. The point is to encourage leaders to be sensitive to uncertainties that can shape their evaluation of the feasibility of their business objectives and the degree of difficulty in the business challenges they've identified.

---

**QUESTIONS TO ASK WHEN ASSESSING THE IMPLICATIONS OF A BUSINESS ANALYSIS**

❏ Will there be shifts in responsibilities?
❏ Will certain leaders be expected to take over work functions now performed by other departments?
❏ Are we increasing the span of control of selected work units?
❏ Are we planning to take on any new responsibilities or objectives that will require the application of completely new technical skills?
❏ Are we making any changes to our work structure that will make selected work functions more complicated or difficult?
❏ Are there objectives or accountabilities that will raise the performance bar significantly over the next year?
❏ Within the array of objectives and accountabilities are there any responsibilities that could significantly affect the overall performance of the company?
❏ Will certain executives be required to assume greater responsibility for managing such external stakeholders as key accounts, customers, board members, and vendors?
❏ What's the worse-case scenario should we not have the technical and leadership competencies necessary to meet objectives?

---

Assumptions frequently cited in a business analysis are

- resource constraints
- speed of new products or services to market
- type of staffing structures needed to support new work initiatives
- effect of outsourcing on current work processes and staffing levels
- reaction of customers to changes in the service delivery system
- types of challenges likely to be imposed by a new IT network
- projected growth of new markets.

**Step 4: Determine implications.** This step involves helping executives assess the perfor-

## A BUSINESS ANALSIS BY AN HR DEPARTMENT

During 2000, our organization took the first steps in making the transition from a domestic sales firm to an international one, by bringing on board plant sites in Canada and Mexico City.

Our 2001 sales plan calls for continued expansion with launch teams into Costa Rica and the Caribbean. That expansion will involve a total of five separate sales teams, each led by a senior director of international sales. To meet that objective, the HR department will need to finalize our international compensation guidelines by the first quarter of 2000. In addition, to ensure that the sales department meets its goal of having teams fully staffed by April 1, 2001, we will need to shift from part-time use of a domestic HR recruiting director to full-time placement of a director of international recruiting and compensation.

In support of the international team, we need to bring on board local HR managers in Toronto and Mexico City who can manage HR policies and (in Canada) collective bargaining activities. Those areas are currently being managed only sporadically through help from an external HR consulting service, resulting in poor service support and high turnover at the Toronto plant. The absence of a full-time HR manager also increases the risk of regulatory violations.

Another major change that will affect the HR function is the planned extension of the IT platform across all sites, concurrent with the integration of field and headquarters IT groups, and supported by the newly created position of CIO. A recent benchmark study has suggested that our IT executives and managers are currently being compensated well below market value for comparative industries. Exit interviews suggest that if the problem isn't solved, the recent exodus of IT staff (18 percent turnover) could worsen, with key defections going to competitors. Should that occur, it would hamper the achievement of 2000 IT goals. Accordingly, the HR department has set the goal to create an IT retention plan that calls for identifying at-risk IT executives in key positions, appropriate salary adjustments, and a complete review of the IT objective bonus plan.

The third major business objective expected to affect the HR function is a plan for placing high-performance work teams at three production sites (Chicago, Cincinnati, and Atlanta), over the next two years. That will represent a completely new organizational design. Though the initial design of team structure has been completed through an external consultant, the Team Readiness Study done in March recommends strongly that we provide substantial training support for team members and their supervisors, who will be required to make the transition to the new role of team advisor. The delivery of the training, along with the need for supplemental coaching, require the company to add an HR director next year.

mance implications of their business analyses, by encouraging them to address these questions:

- *Given my business objectives for the upcoming year and the challenges I expect to encounter in meeting those objectives, what kind of executive leadership do I need to have in place?*
- *What kinds of leadership talent do I currently have in place?*
- *What are the implications of any competency gaps for our readiness to successfully execute key business objectives?*
- *To what degree are we prepared to move forward?*

If your company hasn't developed a leadership competency model, the executives may not be able to give complete answers to those questions. On the other hand, even without access to a competency model, the interview process will help the leadership team sketch a rough outline of executive resource requirements.

**Step 5. Troubleshoot your analysis.** In this step, encourage the executives to review their business analyses with their managers or someone who can provide an impartial critique and point out the weak spots. The troubleshooter's role is to help the executives examine their

## ASSESSING LEADERSHIP COMPETENCY GAPS FOR THE HR LEADERSHIP TEAM

| Leadership Competencies | | 1<br>(low) | 2 | 3 | 4 | 5<br>(high) |
|---|---|---|---|---|---|---|
| Customer focus | I | | | | | |
| | C | | | | | |
| Decision making | I | | | | | |
| | C | | | | | |
| Interpersonal skills | I | | | | | |
| | C | | | | | |
| Adaptability | I | | | | | |
| | C | | | | | |
| Financial analysis | I | | | | | |
| | C | | | | | |

I = importance
C = capability

assumptions critically and provide them with alternative ways to interpret the leadership resource implications.

## PUTTING IT ALL TOGETHER

Note that the business analysis in the box shows a firm link between current and anticipated business changes, and explains how those changes will affect the need for related HR staffing and management activities. Consequently, the anticipated changes in the IT function over the next year aren't likely to succeed if retention in the HR department becomes a significant problem. The retention issue, in turn, is directly related to inadequate compensation for the company's IT professionals.

The competency implications are obvious: The vice president of HR needs to have on board an HR leader who is experienced in countering retention problems. If that competency doesn't exist within the organization, the VP will need to acquire it.

In addition, the lack of a full-time director of international HR recruiting and compensation could impede the company's plans for international growth. Though a new director would need to have technical competencies in recruitment and compensation to work effectively with a diverse international team, he or she would also need such basic leadership competencies as adaptability, effective interpersonal communication, and good decision making.

The relative importance of those competencies to a successful placement can be confirmed through executive interviews and benchmark studies of other international HR functions.

So far, we've considered how leadership resource requirements can be assessed informally through a business analysis. For leadership competencies, a more formal assessment is necessary through the use of the comparative rating technique.

The box shows how the VP of HR rated the importance of five leadership competencies in meeting her company's business goals in the area of international marketing and sales. At the same time, she rated her team's overall capability on the five competencies. A comparison of the two ratings shows significant competency shortfalls in adaptability, customer focus, and interpersonal skills—deficiencies that could hamstring her organization's future business performance.

As the clamor for executive talent increases, training and HRD professionals will be called upon to select, assess, develop, and retain exceptional leaders. They will help determine whether an organization has on board the leadership talent needed to meet tough objectives and move ahead of the competition. One way to bridge the gap between business strategy and leadership assessment and development is through the use of the business analysis. By helping senior managers target competency gaps that can sabotage performance, the training function can provide a valuable service for evaluating an organization's overall performance capability.

# ARTICLE REPRINT

## THE SPECIAL NEEDS OF MANAGERS

*Editor's Comment*: This article is built on the premise that the knowledge economy creates particular challenges for managers to define jobs that are hard to define, and to help employees understand the work that must be done. This is a little different from yesterday's managers, who supervised employees who pretty much knew what was expected of them because their job descriptions were specific and contained skill requirements and clear job responsibilities. Shari Caudron's point is that managers are needed more than ever these days. Her article focuses on the issues surrounding the needs of managers and supervisors for training that's effective in addressing the special needs for working in the knowledge economy.

## BUILDING BETTER BOSSES

### *by Shari Caudron*

Suzanne Larsen has been a manager at US WEST in Richfield, Utah, for eight years. Currently, she oversees a team of 19 network technicians. These are the people with hefty tool belts who install residential and commercial phone service. Ask Larsen about the toughest part of her job and without hesitation she'll tell you: "I think the hardest thing for managers is getting the job done while dealing with different personalities. Some days I feel like I'm babysitting." But ask Larsen about the most rewarding part of her work and first you'll hear nothing but a long pause. Then she'll laugh. Then she'll ask for time to think about it. Then she'll tell you that management isn't what it's cracked up to be. "Some days I don't feel I accomplish anything," she says. "Can I have more time to think about this question?" Ten minutes later, Larsen is still thinking about the rewards of managing others.

Larsen, who is animated and easygoing and absolutely hates conflict, desperately wants to say something nice about being a manager. But for her and scores of others in the workplace today, management is a tough and often thankless job.

But let's face it: It isn't easy being managed, either. "So much [of your job satisfaction] depends on who you work for," explains an IBM employee on a Vault.com message board, "Some managers . . . are open, receptive, collaborative—their divisions and their results speak to the working environment they create. Then there are the my-way-or-the-highway types, the holdovers from long ago. God help you if you get on their bad side."

A colleague agrees, adding: "I cannot enumerate the number of times I or my co-workers have been completely neglected or downright disrespected by management . . . no wonder we have the pitiful retention rates we have. No wonder we have such poor loyalty. Who is there to be loyal to?"

Combine the scorn of employees with the lack of intrinsic rewards, and you have to ask yourself why anyone in their right mind would want to become a manager. Dig a little deeper, and you begin to realize that managers do their jobs for the simple reason that they're *needed*— "I get satisfaction knowing people depend on me," Larsen finally admits—and they're needed now more than ever before.

In a knowledge-intensive economy where jobs aren't clearly defined, manager are the ones who help employees understand the work that must be done. Managers also are responsible for motivating workers, developing potential, increasing productivity, mediating disputes, maintaining work/life balance, and boosting retention rates. No wonder managers have a hard time; there's a lot riding on their shoulders.

Confirming this is research by the Gallup Organization, which reveals that employee loyalty, job satisfaction, and productivity are all determined to a great extent by employees' relationships with their immediate supervisors. Sure, people may join companies because of pay, benefits, promotions, and training. But how long those employees stay and their level of productivity are determined by the relationship they have with the boss.

Given the tremendous importance of managers and the enormous challenges they face, you'd think companies would be doing all they can to develop and support their management employees. Unfortunately, you'd be wrong.

Despite the vital need for management development, companies spend on average only 11 percent of their training budgets on managerial and supervisory skills training, according to the 2000 State of the Industry Report published by the American Society for Training and Development, based in Alexandria, Virginia. Information technology and technical processes receive the lion's share of training dollars.

Furthermore, in 1997—the last year figures are available—less than half of all employees with supervisory, management, or executive responsibilities participated in some type of formal leadership training or development.

Worse yet, even companies that do invest in management training may be going about it all wrong. Well, maybe not *all* wrong, but they're not being as effective as they could be.

Why? Because companies tend to provide one-shot training programs for groups of managers instead of the ongoing and individualized support that many managers need. One manager may have a problem with delegation, for example. Another may have difficulty handling conflict. Put them together in a course on motivating employees, and neither one gets what is needed to be effective.

Clearly, it's time for a change. In a tight labor market where every company must get the best from every worker, employers must begin to pay attention to the biggest contributor to employee productivity: their supervisors.

## WHAT'S THE PROBLEM WITH MANAGEMENT TRAINING TODAY?

To understand how to improve management training, it may help to understand what's currently wrong with it. For starters, there's just not enough training being done.

"Many people move into management positions without ever taking a single management course," explains Gerry Faust, president and CEO of Faust Management Corp. and co-author of *Responsible Managers Get Results* (AMACOM Books, 1998). Indeed, Larsen managed people at US WEST for eight years before she received any type of comprehensive management training. "I think it's a good idea to have people learning how to manage and work well with others throughout their careers, not just when they get promoted," Faust says.

While companies are starting to recognize the importance of ongoing leadership development, those activities are still directed mainly toward top executives, senior managers, and high potentials, according to a 1999 Conference Board Report. The rank-and-file managers who are the majority of bosses in companies today appear to be neglected.

The second problem is that training often doesn't take into account individual needs and differences. Horror stories abound of newly minted MBAs being put in charge of people without a clue how to manage them, of uncommunicative high-tech workers being promoted to supervisory positions without any support, of blue-collar workers being put in the uncomfortable position of directing their former peers, Each of these managers has special needs that one-size-fits-all training can't possibly cover.

Third, management training is frequently just plain ineffective. "Companies tend to 'mass' their training," Faust says. That is, they take groups of managers away from their jobs, herd them into a classroom for several days or weeks, dump a bunch of management theory on them, and expect them to waltz back to work with heightened abilities. Unfortunately, adults don't learn that way.

"Putting people into mass training sessions is like force-feeding them for a weekend and then telling them they'll get no food for the rest of the year," Faust says. This is because people

## IT WASN'T WHAT I WANTED TO HEAR, BUT . . .

*A journalist discovers why individual assessment is so important to management development.*

The first clue that I might not be totally thrilled with the results of my Kinsel-Hartman profile hit me as I read this assessment of my approach to problem-solving: "It is very common for this pattern to signal either high intelligence or attention deficit disorder."

Staring at the report, I hoped the first part of that description was true and that . . . I'm sorry . . . what were we talking about?

Oh, yeah . . . the Kinsel-Hartman profile. The profile, developed by Dr. Robert Smith of Kinsel Enterprises in Dallas, uses a science called formal axiology to measure and describe how people think, make decisions, and evaluate themselves and others. Smith believes that managers—or any other thinking people, for that matter—can't improve their effectiveness unless they understand the biases and patterns that influence their thoughts and interactions with other people.

Intrigued by the thought of learning about my own strengths—never mind my weaknesses—I signed up to complete the online profile. It was surprisingly simple, taking less than 15 minutes to work through a series of screens in which I had to rank-order words like "nuclear war" and "parking ticket" from best to worst according to my own interpretation.

Because I had no idea what the profile was measuring, there was no way for me to cheat—not that I would anyway, but, well, that's another matter. After completing the form, I returned it online, and at 8:30 the next morning I downloaded my very own 60-page personal profile.

Eager to know the real me, I printed the report and began reading. The first few pages detailed my strengths. I scanned it, happily reading phrases like "naturally optimistic," "intuitive," "concerned about people," and "very good ability to empathize." This is amazingly accurate, I thought to myself. What a phenomenal tool this is.

Then, a third of the way into the report, my weaknesses began to show. "Moderate-to-low attention to rules, order, and agendas," it said, followed by adjectives such as "impatient" and "unconventional." All right, already. The words pinched, but on some level, I know this stuff is true. After all, normal people who like structure don't freelance for a living.

By about page 40, I started reading characteristics that clearly belonged to someone else: "excessive self-judging," "crippling fear of failure," and "a perfectionist who thinks good enough is rarely good enough." Suddenly, the profile was so obviously *not* about me that I started flipping through the pages to make sure I didn't accidentally get my mother's report. Seeking validation, I showed the results to my best friend, Angela. "This is incredible," she exclaimed. "They have you nailed!"

I stared at her slack-jawed. Something had happened to this friend I'd trusted for years for advice and support. Maybe she was feverish. There was that spring flu going around. In fact, she seemed a little vicious. Maybe she had rabies. As I headed to the phone book to find Angela a doctor, it began to dawn on me that maybe, just maybe, the profile was mine after all.

I seemed to recall Smith saying how hard it is for people to see themselves objectively and that is why individualized assessments are so important to the development process. "Without an understanding of your own particular biases, the likelihood of making any lasting change is slim to none," he said.

Putting down the phone book and smiling sheepishly at Angela, I started to see why individual assessment and attention matter so much to management training. A class in which everyone is treated the same would not address my "special needs." In fact, a highly structured class probably wouldn't work for me at all. Nor would it take into account the two or three strengths I do have.

For instance, I don't need to learn how to *empathize*; I need to learn how to organize. I don't need to learn how to reward *others*; I need to be better about congratulating *myself*.

If you're talking about training one or two managers at a time, such differences may appear minor. But multiply these idiosyncrasies across the entire management team and you begin to see how much money and time companies stand to waste by providing one-size-fits-all training courses. So when you think about management training, don't think group, think individual. And don't think training before you think assessment.

As Thomas Mann once said: "No man remains quite what he was when he recognizes himself."

don't tend to remember large amounts of information. In fact, research on the typical "forgetting curve" shows that 30 minutes after adults hear new information, they will remember only about 8 percent of it. A day or two later, their recall drops to 2 percent. However, if people learn a little bit of information and practice it right away, retention swells to 90 percent immediately and drops to 50 to 60 percent over time.

"What this tells us is that if we want management training to work, we need to train in smaller chunks of time and allow people to practice on the job," Faust explains.

Another problem with the force-feeding approach is that it doesn't acknowledge the fact that adults learn best when they have control over what and how they are learning. Unlike children, who are used to being talked to, adults want to interact in their educational process and are more motivated to learn when they get to pick the topics *and* the method of delivery. One person may learn best with the help of a mentor, another may turn to books for new information, and still another might prefer role-playing or classroom discussion. Because of these variations, it's often demotivating for adults to be told what skills to learn and how to learn them.

## CREATE BETTER TRAINING

So what should companies do to create more effective management training and thus more effective managers? Three things. One, individualize the training; two, give managers more control over their learning process; and three, provide ongoing, on-the-job support. Let's look at each of these in more detail.

**Individualized training:** Every manager comes to the job with certain strengths and weaknesses that more than likely differ from the strengths and weaknesses of his or her colleagues. Because of this, companies should base their training efforts on the trainee's actual developmental needs. After all, it doesn't make sense to waste time and money training a manager to be a more effective communicator if that person already excels at interpersonal communication.

How do you discover these individual needs? Through assessments. "People are hard-wired with different skill sets, strengths, limitations, and biases," explains Dr. Robert Smith, chair-

> ## WHAT SKILLS ARE NEEDED BY TODAY'S MANAGERS?
>
> An increasingly competitive and changing work environment has ratcheted up the skills and competencies needed by managers. Today, the most effective managers are people who:
>
> - Can create and communicate an inspiring vision
> - Know how to attract and develop talent
> - Communicate well in both individual and group settings
> - Create opportunities for employees to demonstrate their abilities
> - Solicit questions and guide subordinates in expanded thinking
> - Help people, on an individualized basis, gain confidence in themselves through demonstration of their skills and abilities
> - Help employees understand their career paths and developmental needs
> - Surround themselves with effective advisors

man of Kinsel Enterprises, a management consulting and industrial psychology firm based in Dallas. "If you don't take these differences seriously, your training won't be effective."

Smith, who provides personalized management coaching, has developed something he calls the Kinsel-Hartman profile to determine differences in thinking patterns that influence management ability. (See "It Wasn't What I Wanted to Hear, But . . ." on page 2.29.) He uses this assessment tool prior to doing any development work because, he says, "all training has to be done in context."

Another popular way of assessing a manager's abilities is the 360-degree evaluation. This instrument uses feedback from a manager's peers, subordinates, and supervisors as a way of assessing that individual's strengths and weaknesses.

Last November, Larsen attended a six-day supervisor-training program at US WEST that began with a review of her 360-degree assessment results. "The assessment showed me what skill areas needed the most attention," she says. One of her weaknesses, for example, is a tendency to avoid confrontation. Knowing this, Larsen was able to focus her attention on the training discussions and role-plays that would help her become more comfortable with confrontation. Furthermore, she left the training with an individualized list of skill-improvement activities.

In addition to helping trainees understand their unique needs, assessments can also provide the motivation to change. Susan H. Gebelein, executive vice president of Personnel Decisions International, based in Minneapolis, explains that motivation is a key component of the management development process, for without it, lasting change is virtually impossible. "People are more likely to be personally motivated to improve their skills once they understand why it's important for them to do so," she says.

**Control:** Let's be honest: Most grownups are control freaks. We want to be in charge of our own lives, careers, professional development, you name it. Because adults learn best when they can make decisions for themselves, some of the best management development programs are ones that offer choices to managers as to how and what they learn.

Instead of requiring managers to attend workshops—which may not be the most effective style of instruction for some people—organizations can often get a bigger bang for their buck by offering managers a menu of options. This might include seminars, reading groups, online training, self-paced computer-based instruction, college courses, individual mentoring, discussion groups, and management support networks.

At Aetna Financial Services in Hartford, Connecticut, Ginette Purcell, education director, has put together a very practical, inexpensive, and effective lineup of management development efforts. "We used to have the Aetna Institute for Corporate Education, which was housed in its own building and offered mandated management education," she explains. At the time, there were something like 130 educators and support staff who made up the training department.

But the program was expensive, and with corporate cost-cutting, Purcell and her team had to find out how to deliver management training in a more efficient, cost-effective way. So they put together a menu of training efforts that allows managers to pick and choose not only the topics that matter most to them but also how they want to participate in training.

Among the list of developmental opportunities are 1) mini-case studies focusing on a specific workplace issue—e.g., employee hygiene—that are e-mailed to managers and then discussed in conference calls; 2) leadership reading groups in which managers discuss articles on relevant topics—e.g., managing generation X; 3) hour-long programs focused specifically on HR issues such as compensation and workplace flexibility; 4) handbooks on such things as performance management; 5) half-day workshops on traditional supervisory topics such as motivating and delegating; and 6) a supervisory network program that meets for 40 hours over the course of a year. In addition, much of the content covered in these modules is also being made available on the company intranet so that managers with specific issues can immediately find resources online.

Not only are these programs less expensive than those previously offered at Aetna Institute—they're managed by 8 educators versus 130 staff members—but Purcell also believes they are much more effective. "We're working with practical, day-to-day management issues," she says. "We're giving managers tools they need when they need them."

**Ongoing support:** In addition to providing managers with insight into their individual needs through assessments and giving them control over what and how they learn, a key component of management development is ongoing support. Why? Because as anyone who's been there can tell you, it's lonely at the top. Managers vitally need people with whom they can confidentially discuss difficult personnel issues. Support can be provided in a number of ways, including external coaching, mentoring from a higher-up elsewhere in the organization, and management support networks.

Polaris International North American Network is an association of 75 independently owned accounting firms. The association provides member firms with leadership training to help develop the skills and abilities of their partners and senior managers. "Our thrust is developing managers so that they know how to motivate the next-generation workforce," explains Daniel Shogren, director of human resources and training.

Polaris has designed a management development program that begins with a 360-degree assessment of each manager's skills. Then managers are brought together a total of four times over an 18-month period for three days each. The three-day sessions cover various topics related to management, including strategic planning, communication, motivation, and the changing accounting environment. The sessions are spread out over a year and a half in order to give participants time to digest the information presented before learning new information. Remember the forgetting curve?

But, content aside, the most powerful elements of the program are these: 1) each manager receives one-on-one coaching and developmental planning during every three-day session; 2) participants develop an external support network consisting of their peers in other member firms; and 3) trainees are assigned mentors in their own firms to talk with about the course material and get ongoing feedback on their own abilities.

Shogren believes that the individualized and ongoing support is what has made the program so successful. "People tend to have an easier time working through specific issues one-on-one with a counselor or a peer than they do speaking up in group situations," he says.

## IT'S NOT ROCKET SCIENCE

When you look at the elements necessary for management training to be effective—assessment, control, and support—you may be struck by the fact that there's nothing very revolutionary about these ideas. "We've been talking about this stuff for 2,000 years," says Rex Gatto of Gatto Training Associates, in Pittsburgh, Pennsylvania. "We know what it takes for people to be more successful in their jobs. The trick is giving managers the tools and opportunity to practice what it takes to be successful."

And that's exactly what some companies appear to be missing. Managers don't automatically know how to manage, what they need to know, how to talk through their issues, and why they may—or may not—be successful on the job. But they can learn. And in a tight labor market where good bosses are the key to employee productivity and retention, doesn't it make sense to take the time to teach them?

## ARTICLE REPRINT

## TRAINING NEEDS OF "THE NET KIDS"

*Editor's Comment*: Bill Gates, Michael Dell, and Tiger Woods—these are the role models for "the Net Kids," according to writer Charlene Marmer Solomon, whose insightful article on the personal characteristics and workplace needs of the age cohort born between 1977 and 1997 we include here. She uses words like "curious, contrarian, and flexible" to quickly describe them; and through her analysis, we can begin to see their needs for workplace stability and growth—and perhaps what role training can play in their contributions to a vibrant workplace.

## READY OR NOT, HERE COME THE NET KIDS

### *by Charlene Marmer Solomon*

Michael Furdyk and Michael Hayman have made all the right moves.

The company they co-founded, Buy-Buddy.com, an online computer and software comparison shopping service, has been on the fast track since it was launched in March of 1999.

They doubled staffing after securing venture capital in October and are planning a move into larger quarters that will replace the open space where employees are free to shape the work environment to their own tastes and where desks are strictly optional. Sofas, pillows and throw rugs are the furnishings of this close-knit corporate culture of people who are highly motivated, hardworking, self-directed and creative.

It's no wonder, then, that Furdyk and Hayman are confident about their management style, their training, and their business objectives. Their flexibility, trust, and a hands-off management philosophy work very well in this environment, which should be no surprise because this is the second company they've founded (they sold their first, mydesktop.com, for an amount reported to be seven figures).

What is astonishing, though, is the fact that Michael Furdyk is 17 years old, Michael Hayman is 19, and most of their employees are in their late teens and early 20s!

Welcome to the Net Generation, whose ranks include young, *very* young, people who are already entering the workforce and are reshaping the nature of work in the very same way their Baby Boomer parents reinvented a very different world.

Leave behind your quips about "uppity children" and your prejudices about the Backstreet Boys and Britney Spears, and take a long, close look at these "kids." They're the ones who teach you how to use your computer; they're the ones whose role models are Bill Gates, Michael Dell, and Tiger Woods.

### WHO *ARE* THESE PEOPLE?

They are the 81 million children born between 1977 and 1997. "This is the first generation to be raised with the Internet," says Don Tapscott, author of *Growing Up Digital: The Rise of the Net Generation* (McGraw-Hill, 1998). "The Internet, computers, and interactive technology are changing every institution in our society. And, this is the first time in human history when children are an authority on something really important. These kids are a part of a big revolution that is changing everything. When they enter the workforce, they bring a very different culture with them and a very different view of authority, of work, and of innovation."

Talk to researchers, psychologists, and marketing specialists about this group, and you'll discover they attribute overall positive traits to these youngsters. The Net Generation is known to be initiators and doers, not passive observers. They're creators, not recipients. And they are curious, contrarian, flexible, collaborative and high in self-esteem.

Because of the Internet, they read, write, collaborate and develop strategies while online. And they've been raised with a global vision and an intuitive understanding of today's technology. Critically important to business, they understand the idea of knowledge sharing on a visceral level, and they believe in creating wealth. Remember, they share stories with their friends about students who've sold dot-com businesses for millions.

Says Tapscott, this leads to huge pressures for radical changes in existing companies. In other words, we're in the midst of profound change. For example, Netters search for information and develop thinking and investigating skills; they also question the implicit values contained in information. In fact, Tapscott points out, the knowledge hierarchy is flipped on its head.

"In the past" he says, "parents have always been the authorities on everything (with the exception of children of immigrants). But now, children know more than the adults in the major communications device of our time."

Contrary to popular opinion, the Net Generation is the most well educated group in the United States in the last century, according to U.S. Department of Education statistics. They're also among the most privileged, coming of age at a time of continuing prosperity.

The vast majority of them expect both parents to work. According to Denver-based Claire Raines, co-author of *Generations at Work* (AMACOM, 2000), their boomer parents see themselves as devoted, and will do whatever it takes to be good parents: weekly soccer matches,

dance and karate classes, computer camps, and so on.

Indeed, according to the Roper Youth Report, published by New York City-based Roper Starch Worldwide, 82 percent of kids 8 to 17 feel that they are very or somewhat likely to have a better life than their parents. In fact, 37 percent of 17-year-olds say they are very likely to have a better life than their parents.

"This is a reflection that many of these kids, like their parents, are receiving an almost constant avalanche of good economic news," says Peter Silsbee, vice president at Roper Starch. "And one of the tributaries of that river to the waterfall of economic news is news about young people—20-year-olds—who are benefiting from the Internet economy. Kids experience a gold rush mentality regarding the Internet."

## WHAT ARE THE CHALLENGES THEY PRESENT TO HR?

Given the role models of this generation, the number of dot-com millionaires under 25 years old, and the world view of this group, they present an interesting array of issues to HR. Add to that the fact that a large percentage of these people were raised as latchkey kids who learned to take care of themselves early on.

"These kids have extraordinarily high expectations," says Silsbee. "They are going to have some trouble with long, drawn-out apprentice periods."

Interestingly, Silsbee sees the abandonment of authoritarian structures at home. "More and more within the family unit, they've been given a voice. Parents give kids more freedom and autonomy; they have more and more influence over family purchases; they have real responsibilities." In other words, they will be impatient and expect more than menial jobs.

At the same time, the kind of after-school part-time job that was commonplace just a decade ago is also changing. Carol Hickman, senior manager of benefits and HRMS for Ben & Jerry's Homemade in South Burlington, Vermont, thinks that the current affluence in the United States is reflected in kids' being able to choose extracurricular activities over part-time retail jobs.

"It's my gut feeling that you're going to see these kids go into college and very quickly rise

---

## BUT HOW CAN WE ALL GET ALONG?

Ron Zemke, Claire Raines, and Bob Filipczak, authors of *Generations at Work: Managing the Clash of Veterans, Boomers, Xers, and Nexters in Your Workplace* (AMACOM, 2000), have come up with a five-point guide based on their work to help HR encourage cross-generational participation and effectiveness. Here's a brief description of the steps.

1. **Accommodate employee differences.**
   Learn about employees as you would about your customers; make real efforts to accommodate personal needs.

2. **Create workplace choices.**
   Shape the workplace around the work being accomplished, the customers' needs, and the employees.

3. **Operate from a sophisticated management style.**
   Monitor and alter supervisory styles based on the individual employee. Create a sit-uationally varied leadership style where some decisions are made by the manager (with input) and others are consensus-driven. Create a place where positional power is less important than personal power. Know how and when to make exceptions. Be thoughtful when forming teams and giving individuals assignments. Balance concern for tasks with concern for people. Create elements of trust, and work for it in your environment.

4. **Respect competence and initiative.**
   Hire carefully, and assume the best of your people, young and old.

5. **Nourish retention.**
   Make your workplace a magnet for excellence by encouraging lateral movement, with broad job assignments. Offer lots of training (from mentoring to computer-based to classroom), and continue to market internally to your employees.
   —*CMS*

---

through organizations," says Hickman. "I think this is going to be a generation where a lot of them are starting their own businesses and are making a lot of money. They aren't going to be satisfied sitting behind a desk and pushing paper. In fact, companies that don't get technically savvy are probably not going to get the employees to work for them. Computers are second nature to them, and I see them getting very bored if they don't have technology at their fingertips to use when they need it. Whatever they do, they do it very quickly."

Of course, this is only one segment of the population. There is, of course, a less-privileged group of individuals who may not have had the same access to technology, nor the same chances to learn from it. It may not be based on affluence either, but on availability and the chances to use the technologies to full advantage.

Even students who graduate from high school don't have equal opportunity on the Internet. The National Center for Education Statistics states that 58 percent of schools where more than one-third of students are eligible for government assistance for school meals are connected to the Internet. In more affluent areas where only 10 percent of students receive aid, 78 percent are connected.

Furthermore, according to the Toronto-based Alliance for Converging Technologies, the ratio of U.S. public school students who have access to the Internet is 33 to 1, even though the ratio of students to computers is 9 to 1.

Beyond that, it is wise to remember that this is a generation that has seen more violence directed at their peers than previous generations. Elementary and high school crimes are commonplace problems. Certainly, school shootings also make traumatic impressions. How those will affect this generation, however, is still unclear.

## HOW WILL MANAGERS HAVE TO TREAT THEM DIFFERENTLY?

Trust in their capabilities and their commitment; communicate with them; create opportunities for teamwork and entrepreneurship; and approach situations with mutuality. Those will be the defining characteristics of a good working relationship between Net Generation workers and their older managers. Obviously, it requires some realigning of ideas.

Vicki Saunders, chief innovation architect at the Toronto-based NRG Group, knows what it's all about. As close to the workplace of the future as you can get, her company focuses on taking techno-savvy youth between the ages of 14 and 24, and creating effective technology teams that are structured to be strongly entre-preneurial. The group might be young, but they work on real-life projects for organizations such as Xerox, Air Canada, and Visa that want fresh approaches for new products and services.

Saunders started with a team of 50 young people to work on 10 projects. It was manage-ment by teams, not by Saunders. When the group started, 35-year-old Saunders and her senior management team listed the 10 current projects on sheets of paper on the wall. They described each one and what kind of team members were needed (two designers, one content person, one marketing person, etc.). Then, Saunders and the senior team left the room with instructions for the youngsters to create the teams themselves. When they returned, of course, there were 16 people in one group and 2 in another. The kids complained that they couldn't decide.

Saunders explained that in self-directed teams, everyone must work on the problem; it is not her responsibility to decide.

This was the first lesson. It was the beginning of taking "the wisdom of inexperience" and adding "the wisdom of experience" to find what Saunders calls "the sweet spot in the middle." She says that the wisdom of inexperience—the passion—is very powerful if you don't try to con-trol it, if you can set it free. "We believe the key mindset to drive success is [one in which] they believe possibilities are limitless—keeping them in dreamscape—while at the same time develop-ing team skills."

These individual employees are incredibly demanding, really fast, totally media savvy, and always pushing the limits. And this offers tremen-dous advantages to clients—if managers can learn to effectively harness the energy and stay open during the process. The results are impressive.

One group worked on a project for Visa. The team of youngsters interviewed the department heads to find out about marketing the card. All that the adults talked about were different fea-tures of the card, such as travel insurance and lost-card insurance. The company's marketing focused on these benefits.

All that the kids wanted to know was, "What's my limit?" That was all. They didn't care about anything else. They clearly explained that to the senior people who were marketing benefits that were meaningless to teens.

Xerox hired a group to create a mission state-ment for the learning environment of the future. Four young people, ages 16 to 22, sat in a room for four days poring over boxes of mate-rial the company gave them about the ultimate learning environment.

Then the kids asked one of their first ques-tions. "What is a mission statement?" The Xerox managers described it, saying the team was creating a statement that would engage people in learning.

"The [team] just looked at them," says Saun-ders. "They were stunned, and asked, 'How can a statement get you excited? It is just a state-ment. There's no call to action.' "

They dug deep and struggled, and had conver-sations all week, and realized in the end that it had to be a question. It had to be several ques-tions. Only questions open you up to inquire.

Ultimately, they came up with five ques-tions: What do you want? What do you have? What do you need? How are you going to get it? What are you going to do with it?

Says Saunders, those five questions served as one of the most powerful tools for The NRG Group, as well as Xerox. Whenever someone would get stuck on a project, they would ask themselves what they want, then they would strategize about how to get it. Finally, they would ask the question at the end, which is the feedback question: What are you going to do with it? Is there a point to what you want?

The managers at Xerox were elated when the group made the presentation about the learn-ing center. Before they even got to the final questions, the team of Netters took the Xerox team through a 45-minute presentation.

In fact, Xerox said, the group had created the actual learning environment of the future in their process to create the mission statement. The lead manager printed the five questions on the back of his business cards after that, and handed them out to all of his clients.

Again, says Saunders, it's their fresh perspective that's so valuable. It's that ability to help them to harness it within a structured organization.

However, with this energy and innovative talent comes impatience and some overconfidence. Saunders has to handle requests for doubling salary after two weeks because the youngsters believe they're doing so much more than they thought they would have to do in the beginning. The group challenges Saunders to tell them why there should even be a salary scale. Then they ask her to explain how she adds value to the process. In other words, they can be exasperating.

How will they work within a corporate structure? Saunders think that will be the test. In her situation, they actually set up centers within the corporations to manage intergenerational teams. Bank of Canada was trying to mix generations and corporate cultures at the same time. Both young and more mature members of the team would undergo training.

When a young person would ask how to do something, the response might be, "You can't do that." And the youngster's first reaction would be, "Of course I can do it. I just did it."

They also would get frustrated by people in bureaucracies going through channels. Much of Saunders' coaching of the teens centered on these issues: dealing with difficult personalities, helping them focus on the outcome and the bigger picture of the project rather than the small frustrations along the way.

## HOW WILL TRAINING NEED TO BE DIFFERENT?

How do these individuals learn? Forget the idea of a classroom setting. Lifelong learning is a given with this group. Michael Furdyk has an educational coach because he's too busy running a successful firm to finish high school in the traditional way. Anyway, why should learning be separated from work?

Every age group may know you have to keep your skills current today, but Netters knows firsthand the nanosecond longevity of information on the Internet. Their recreation includes learning.

"We're going to have to look at training in different ways," says Hickman. "Some won't be happy sitting in a classroom setting; others won't be able to learn as well online. Companies are going to have to look at the target audience and offer a variety of ways to handle the teaching." No matter what they do, information will have to be presented in an engaging, exciting way. It will have to be relevant to the learner and available whenever the employee needs it.

You might ask Michael Furdyk, and he'll tell you that competitive pay, stock options, and generous performance bonuses are just starting points of the deal for this group. Flexibility, trust and incentives are key values in the culture, and the ability to share in the information and in the creation of the wealth is a must.

This group of young people is just starting to make their presence felt in the workforce. Expect flexibility; they've been raised in households of single parents or dual careers, and they know firsthand what work/life balance is all about. They want the opportunity to be taken seriously from the beginning, to prove themselves on the basis of talent and skills, and not be dismissed because of age.

They are a demanding bunch, but they respect the society that has given them such affluence, and they respect their elders who have created the culture in which they are now going to participate. They want the chance to make a difference and begin to launch the 21st century.

# BOOK REVIEW

## THE REALITY OF SILICON VALLEY: *THE MONK AND THE RIDDLE*

*Editor's Comment*: *The Monk and the Riddle* is rich in metaphor that helps to define the "Silicon Valley" worker's life/work needs.

This entertaining yet informative book is not your typical business book. Instead of telling you how your business can increase its profits or lower production costs, Kosimar gives us an insider's guide to what it is like to work, live, and find success in the bustling world that is Silicon Valley, California. In order to give the reader a little background on what Silicon Valley is really like, Kosimar has this to say: "everything in this Valley turns on risk" and "the biggest risk of all in Silicon Valley is the risk of mediocrity" (p. 150).

*The Monk and the Riddle* centers around an ongoing conversation that Kosimar has with two entrepreneurs, Lenny and Allison. Lenny and Allison seek funding from Kosimar's company in order to launch their startup Web site, *funerals.com*. Through Kosimar's "coaching" of Lenny and Allison, the author gives the reader a first-hand account of just how much time and effort go into preparing and presenting a startup idea.

Kosimar also gives the reader a taste of what venture capitalists (referred to as VC's in the book) are really like during a startup presentation. For example, one VC will be the "good cop" and another will be the "bad cop," and ask the presenters difficult questions (p. 117). The author also gives you a feel for what happens as a startup is prepared to be launched. Kosimar has this advice for startups: "stay small and remain flexible" for awhile until your business has its feet on the ground (p.52). Kosimar points out that there are two types of startups: "Better-Faster-Cheaper" and "Brave New World." Kosimar describes the "Brave New World" model as having "no existing market, no incumbent competitors, and no economic model, you're literally inventing the business as you go along" (p. 37).

Kosimar talks in depth about the Deferred Life Plan, something that seems to dominate Silicon Valley (p.65). He has this to say about the Deferred Life Plan: "for the promise of full coverage under the plan, you must divide your life into two distinct parts:

- Step One: Do what you have to do; then eventually . . .
- Step Two: Do what you want to do" (p. 65).

The author goes on to explain that "in the Deferred Life Plan, the second step, the life we defer, cannot exist, does not deserve to exist, without first doing something unsatisfying" (p. 83).

Kosimar's ongoing dialogue with Lenny and Allison leads him to the main point of this book: you cannot allow yourself to get so wrapped up in the success of your company that you forget your own definition of success. For Kosimar, this is truly the "bottom line": "Only the Whole Life Plan leads to personal success. It has the greatest chance of providing satisfaction and contentment that one can take to the grave tomorrow. In the Deferred Life Plan, there will always be another prize to covet, another distraction, a new hunger to sate. You will forever come up short. Work hard work passionately, but apply your most precious asset—time—to what is most meaningful to you" (pp.155–156).

In conclusion, this book intends to *teach* the reader through dialogue and stories of how a startup is launched in Silicon Valley. Kosimar uses his own career growth to show that there is nothing wrong with numerous career changes

*Source*: *The Monk and the Riddle: The Education of a Silicon Valley Entrepreneur* by Randy Kosimar with Kent Lineback. Boston: Harvard Business School Press, 2000. $22.50. Randy Kosimar is a virtual CEO who has worked with companies such as WebTV and TiVo. He was CEO of LucasArts Entertainment and Crystal Dynamics, CFO of GO Corporation, and one of the founders of Claris Corporation. This book review was written by Katherine M. Franklin, Editorial Assistant.

throughout your lifetime, especially if it adds to your personal success and happiness. Mainly, Kosimar is trying to convey to Lenny and Allison, as well as to the reader, that your individual fulfillment and success is what truly matters in the tipsy-topsy world that is business.

# ARTICLE REPRINT

## GENERATION-BASED TRAINING?

*Editor's Comment*: Just when you think you knew what the adult learner was all about, the workplace changed and learners on the job looked very different from one another. This lively article by Jennifer Salopek, self-described "member of Generation X" and "vibes" editor of *Training & Development* magazine, suggests a radical approach to the learning needs of today's workforce: generation-based training.

## THE YOUNG AND THE REST OF US

### *by Jennifer J. Salopek*

At Compass Foods in Rye Brook, New York, Joe Machicote and Ron Tremper teach employees as young as 16 the finer points of contract food service through a program called Compass in the Community. For many of those young workers, it's their first job.

In New York City, Steve Hochberg is responsible for training 26,000 temporary employees to handle clerical and administrative tasks during the city's twice-yearly elections. A majority of the employees are retired; several of Hochberg's workers are well into their eighties.

Recently, many books and articles have been published about cross-generational conflict, work, and management. Why this, why now? We asked Bradley Richardson, principal and founder of JobSmarts, a consulting firm in Dallas that specializes in teaching companies how to relate to their Generation X employees.

"People have been entering the workforce forever," Richardson concedes. But, he explains, there just aren't enough bodies to go around.

The baby boomer generation, of which virtually every member is currently of working age, numbers 78 million. By contrast, Generation X has only 48 million members. "That 'birth dearth' means that there are almost 50 percent fewer Gen X workers out there than baby boomers. Demographics lead to demands, so employers are doing the scramble to recruit, train, and retain young talent."

Can and should the trainers at Compass Foods and the New York Board of Elections—and at your organization—adapt their approaches to suit the age of trainees? Our research reveals clearly that yes, they can, and yes, they should.

### YOU'RE FROM MARS, THEY'RE FROM VENUS

"Trainers should adapt their approaches for younger learners," says Richardson. Although people will still have individual learning styles,

| GENERATIONS AT A GLANCE | | | |
|---|---|---|---|
| **Generation** | **Age** | **Influences** | **Traits** |
| Millennium | 0–late teens | ❑ Fall of the Berlin Wall<br>❑ Expansion of technology<br>❑ Mixed economy<br>❑ Natural disasters<br>❑ Violence<br>❑ Drugs and gangs | ❑ Independent spenders<br>❑ Globally concerned<br>❑ Health conscious<br>❑ Cyber literate |
| Generation X | Early 20s–Mid 30s | ❑ *Sesame Street*, MTV<br>❑ End of Cold War<br>❑ Rise of personal computing<br>❑ Divorce<br>❑ AIDS, crack cocaine<br>❑ Missing children on milk cartons and missing parents at home | ❑ Technosavvy<br>❑ Diverse<br>❑ Independent<br>❑ Skeptical<br>❑ Entrepreneurial |
| Baby boomers | Late 30s–Early 50s | ❑ Booming birthrate<br>❑ Economic prosperity<br>❑ Expansion of suburbia<br>❑ Vietnam, Watergate<br>❑ Human rights movement<br>❑ Sex, drugs, rock 'n roll | ❑ Idealistic<br>❑ Competitive<br>❑ Question authority<br>❑ "Me" generation |
| Traditionalists | Mid 50s–Early 70s | ❑ The Great Depression<br>❑ The New Deal<br>❑ World War II<br>❑ The G.I. Bill | ❑ Patriotic<br>❑ Loyal<br>❑ Fiscally conservative<br>❑ Faith in institutions |

Courtesy of BridgeWorks, 888.519.1187; www.generations.com.

Richardson says we can count on the fact that Gen X workers will process information differently.

"We need training now more than ever," says Machicote, director of relations development for the Compass Group. "We're tapping sources we normally wouldn't have gone after, due to the low unemployment that's been facing the food industry for several years."

Compass in the Community was developed because the company recognized a need to change the image of its industry. "When you say *hospitality*, people think hotels," says Machicote. "If you say *food service*, they think *cafeteria lady*." To combat those narrow stereotypes and entice younger workers into its contract food-service business, Compass decided that it needed to take its knowledge and business into local high schools. "If students can learn about us ahead of time, we can change the impression of our industry," continues Machicote.

The program is structured as a set of 6-to-14-week internships offered twice a year, in fall and spring. At Compass's New York location, about 20 students enter the internship program during each enrollment period. Interns are selected through an application and interview; at the end of the internship, the employee receives a certificate of completion and a stipend of about US$1,000. Compass also sponsors exceptional interns to the Culinary Institute of America and supports them with letters of recommendation.

Each internship period begins with an Orientation Forum on the first day, in which trainers cover such basics as

- sanitation and hygiene
- conduct
- safety
- customer service
- sexual harassment and violence prevention
- diversity and respect.

Those are all good, basic topics every food-service employee should know, but how do you make them and other mandatory training interesting to young workers?

**Make it make sense.** David Stillman and Lynne Lancaster, principals of the generational consulting firm BridgeWorks, advise you to spend extra time on background when training Gen Xers. They recommend that you explain why you're doing the training, how it fits in with corporate culture, and what it will do for trainees' careers.

**Make it fun.** "We designed our program to be fun," says Machicote. Interns work in small groups and are encouraged to be creative. They can play around in the kitchen, write their own menus, and experiment with recipes. Compass serves such clients as health-care facilities, corporate cafeterias, schools and colleges, and prisons. Everything is made fresh and from scratch, so interns can work with the chefs to create their own ideas for salads or specials, or whatever.

**Make it personal.** Every Compass intern is linked with the manager of the unit, who serves as a mentor. He or she offers one-on-one guidance, helping the intern work through the training manual and demonstrate mastery of skills such as knife handling. Managers receive special training in mentoring and working with young people.

Andrea Nierenberg, a management consultant based in New York, offers these suggestions for making your training more personal:

- Provide many opportunities for trainees to ask questions.
- Ask them whether the information pertains to them.
- Adapt your information to the scenarios they give you.

But, while making your training personal, says Nierenberg, don't take things personally. "Younger people tend to challenge you. Trainers need to be prepared for that and shouldn't get offended. Sometimes, [those young] trainees will look at you as if you're from Mars."

**Make it fast-paced.** Nierenberg advises, "You must go faster than you even thought possible."

Says Richardson, "Gen Xers have been bombarded with messages while growing up." Therefore, they process information more quickly. Often, he says, older people interpret that propensity as a short attention span, but it's not. "It just appears that way."

**Make it involving.** "On television, you have a change of scenery every 20 seconds," Richardson says. "Trainers need to change their deliv-

---

> **OVERCOMING RESISTANCE: TRAINING THAT COUNTS**
>
> Before introducing a new training program, make sure that you can answer *yes* to all of these questions:
>
> ❏ Has the need for the new system been explained in terms of the organization's business strategy and future goals?
> ❏ Has the workload of employees involved in skills training been adjusted to allow for training time?
> ❏ Do training schedules take concurrent initiatives into account?
> ❏ Is the training tailored to different learning styles, or does one size fit all?
> ❏ Is the relationship clear between the training curriculum and trainees' jobs?
> ❏ Is the equipment used in technology training ergonomic?
>
> From *Age Works: What Corporate America Must Do to Survive the Graying of the Workforce*, by Beverly Goldberg (The Free Press, 2000).

---

ery, message, or activity every 8, 10, or 15 minutes—maximum."

**Make it chunky.** Richardson recommends chunking information into small bits, as the average Gen Xer reportedly processes a message in just 20 seconds.

**Make it safe to participate.** "No one wants to be first," says Richardson, noting that Gen Xers are reluctant to participate. He recommends that instead of calling on people, you structure discussions so that trainees pick each other by passing around a talking stick or ball.

**Make it yours.** Keep learners involved while still holding the reins, cautions Richardson, or your training session could turn into a social activity. He recommends setting ground rules and expectations clearly at the beginning of the session. Stillman and Lancaster suggest setting more ground rules than you would for other age groups.

**Make it theirs.** Richardson also recommends letting learners themselves discover the aha! moments. "Young talent typically views internal people with some skepticism." Nierenberg adds that trainers of the baby boom generation shouldn't try to identify with Gen X trainees too much: "Don't try to be their age. Be accepting, and ask for their help in keeping the session on track and relevant."

Stillman points out the increasing reliance on CBT, WBT, and self-paced learning for younger workers, which suits their learning style well. However, he cautions, "Be careful that Xers' love of technology doesn't cause you to overlook the interaction and collaboration that everyone needs in order to learn."

## AULD LANG SYNE

Twice a year, the New York City Board of Elections employs 26,000 temporary workers at 1,300 voting sites. Many of those workers are retirees. Due to frequent changes in rules and regulations, Hochberg and his staff retrain the temps for each election regardless of whether they have operated a voting site before. Workers for the six positions at each site attend a three-hour course that covers such subjects as

- an overview of the electoral process,
- how to interact with candidates and poll watchers,
- communication and customer service skills
- electoral and assembly districts,
- legalities,
- logistics,
- the steps in servicing a voter.

Hochberg characterizes his mostly older employees as dedicated and concerned about getting things right. He also notes that they take their political affiliation and the electoral process very seriously. So, what do he and other experts recommend for training older workers?

**Make it learner-centered.** Hochberg conducts much of his training through role plays, demonstrations, and hands-on activities. He says, "Trainees must get involved or they become remote." Nierenberg, who works with all age groups, finds that her older trainees prefer interaction and discussion. "Don't play games," she cautions. "Older people typically don't like being put on the spot."

**Make it positive.** Nierenberg says that you can counter the change-averse attitude found among some older workers if you emphasize the positive and explain the benefits of the change.

**Make it matter.** Lancaster says, "Trainers need to get away from the mindset that training for older workers is remedial. It seems we're always playing catch-up. Instead, training should be strategic and proactive." Retaining older workers (and by this we mean anyone on the far side of the baby boom) is becoming more important as the birth dearth is felt in the workplace. Companies need to keep more experienced employees from retiring and can do that, Lancaster explains, through "careering."

"Assuming a company can identify who it wants to keep," she says, "it needs to determine what kind of training it has to provide so that employees can keep recareering within the company." In that scenario, the purpose of training is to stimulate and educate.

Stillman concurs: "Remedial training assumes that an employee wants to keep doing the same job. Maybe there's a completely different role for that person. There's no magic age at which you stop talking about a person's career path."

**Make it comfortable.** Nierenberg recommends calling participants in advance if possible. "I introduce myself, briefly explain what I'll be doing in the session, and invite them to call me if they have any questions or suggestions." Even if you can't call all of the trainees in advance, call at least a few. Those early contacts can also make the training more comfortable for the trainer.

Physical comfort is also important, points out Beverly Goldberg, author of *Age Works: What Corporate America Must Do to Survive the Graying of the Workforce* (The Free Press, 2000). Her suggestions:

- Make sure that the seating is comfortable.
- Allow trainees to adjust the distance of the chairs from the computer monitors.
- Check the lighting. Too much dimness or too much glare can be hard on older eyes.

Goldberg also suggests that training for older workers is best done "on the floor"—that is, informally *before* a formal classroom session. Let trainees have a half hour or so before a technology session to get acquainted with the equipment.

**Make testing less stressful.** Trainers need to remember that older workers may have been out of a classroom for a long time, says Goldberg, and can be uncomfortable with tests and grades. Although Hochberg's trainees must pass a certification quiz, it's open-book.

**Make trainees' experience count.** Nierenberg notes that some older workers can suffer from "know-it-all syndrome," which is really collective wisdom and experience. Ask older trainees to contribute their anecdotes and success stories. "You're there to enhance skills they already have," she says. "Don't tell them what to do." Lancaster also recommends teaching techniques that evolve from what trainees already know. "Be respectful of their credentials," she says.

Many senior employees fear looking dumb or outdated, especially when an executive is sitting in on the session. Lancaster suggests that you can draw out their sense of pride by asking them to tell stories about when they did something well or solved a problem. If an executive *is* sitting in, Lancaster suggests coaching him or her in advance about creating a safe environment and praising people for dissent.

**Make it safe to disagree.** Goldberg urges us not to forget downsizing, the quality movement, and many other management fads that have "tiptoed away quietly," as she puts it.

"Trainees are going to be skeptical. Let them express that skepticism, listen, and then show where the differences are between past efforts and what you're trying to do now."

Lancaster recommends creating exercises in which you give permission for trainees to dissent and that you reward them. She notes that it can work especially well if you group trainees in pairs and let them rehearse before reporting to the class.

Although you may feel as if you're trying to be all things to all people, take heart. Nierenberg says, "People are people. Trainees of any age will respond well if you're gracious and open."

Or you can do as Lancaster and Stillman recommend: Mix trainees of all age groups. "Although that's harder for the trainer," admits Lancaster, "the richness of that interaction can be wonderful." She thinks that organizations are already too stratified by age and recommends that companies encourage employees from different cohorts to talk together about how they view the world.

"That causes people to learn from each other," she concludes, "and that's great for the company."

# ABSTRACT

## KEEPING TALENT

*Editor's Comment:* The business press was full this year of articles about hiring smart and keeping the talent inside your company once you found it. Ideas for incentives and motivation were all over the news. Headhunters seemed to have no scruples, accused everywhere of invading good companies to steal away top performers. Employees seemed to have no loyalty. Stability is a problem. Providing opportunities for personal growth in the job looks like the answer. Training, education, learning—whatever name you give it—is a strategic function of the company in times like these.

One of the clues to providing real opportunities to learn at work in our computer-mediated workplace is Andrea DiSessa's idea that computers might actually extend our intelligence, and that "computational literacy" (in the sense of computer-enabled literacy) is some kind of new foundation of cognition. DiSessa's focus is on teaching learners to be active creators, not passive consumers, and to design learning opportunities that recognize the complex set of technical competencies that is computer literacy in what could be its second growth phase. His book, *Changing Minds: Computers, Learning, and Literacy* (MIT Press, 2000) suggests that computers can change the way we think, not only the way we learn. Perhaps training managers need to engage, with DiSessa, in dialogues about the next wave of cognitive theory and the role computers can play in stretching our brainpower. That would be real opportunity for growth, and may be the kind of effort that it takes to keep top performers on the job in your company.

*Fortune* magazine has not exactly been known as a publication that focused with any depth on training and workplace learning. The magazine's traditional bottom-line, financial slant has all but excluded training as a favorite topic. This, of course, is not *Fortune*'s "fault," but rather, training's stubborn refusal to think of itself as a strategic or bottom-line kind of function. It was a surprise, then, to find two examples of the strategic value of training in Nicholas Stein's article, "Winning the War to Keep Talent" in the May 29, 2000 issue of *Fortune*. In this article, Stein fea-

tures ten companies that have managed to keep talent; of these, General Electric (p. 134) and Cisco Systems (p. 138) report creative and strategic approaches to training for the purpose of keeping talent within company walls.

General Electric, Fairfield, CT, (340,000 employees) says upfront that it identifies the best people already in the company and then invests heavily in training and mentoring them in order to keep its talent intact and growing. At GE, managers who want to move up create internal resumes listing their accomplishments at GE, their strengths, and their ideal next moves; CEO Jack Welch himself and his head of Human Resources look through the resumes and, with unit leaders, choose 360 to go through the top-level management training at Crotonville, NY. Other executive development programs, specialized for would-be officers or general managers, are organized around business problems or the big issues facing GE, and feature student presentations at GE's executive council meetings or at the annual officers' meeting. GE boasts only an 8 percent talent attrition rate; Welch and group attribute at least some of this to a strategic approach to training—training for stability and for growth.

Cisco Systems, San Jose, CA, (30,589 employees) takes a very proactive approach at the front-end of the hiring and placement process. Cisco shepherds each new employee through a "honeymoon" period of getting to know the company and the company getting to know the new hire. This is orientation training, but with

*Source:* "Changing Minds" book review in *Publishers Weekly*. May 1, 2000, p. 66; and "Winning the War to Keep Talent" by Nicholas Stein in *Fortune*, May 29, 2000, pp. 132–138; and "They're Coming to Take You Away" by Devin Leonard in *Fortune*, May 29, 2000, pp. 89–93.

a mission to enable the individual to succeed in the company culture. Cisco's secret weapon is a transition team assigned to each new hire with a personal sponsor—a colleague not a boss—for each new employee. Cisco focuses on skills for negotiating the culture, in hopes that feeling welcome will quickly translate into being productive. A more than 900 percent increase in share price over the last three years says that Cisco must be doing something right.

Finally, an indication of the problem of stability and growth is what *Fortune*'s Devin Leonard in his article on the body snatchers calls "an all-out war" to get skilled employees (p. 91). On the frontlines of this war, of course are the recruiters, whose ranks have increased 45 percent over the past three years. It is estimated that there are about 9,500 headhunters on the prowl as the unemployment in the U.S. has dipped to under 4 percent—the lowest in 30 years—at the same time as nearly 2 million new information technology jobs are projected to be created by the end of year 2001. Leonard comments that we have capital, venture capital, and customer spending to fuel our booming economy; what we don't have is talent. Training managers need to see that this is at least partially training's problem; and hopefully, with some innovative and strategic thinking, the talent crisis can be addressed with training as part of the solution.

# ARTICLE REPRINT

## OLDER WORKERS: YOUR BEST ASSET LEVERAGE

*Editor's Comment:* Finally, in this sub-section on stability and growth, we give you this systems-focused article from Pegasus Communications' *The Systems Thinker* newsletter. This comprehensive review of issues surrounding the employment of workers age 55 and above is more than a research summary; it is a presentation of practical ideas for "working wisely" with older workers. The list of eight "Steps for Leveraging the Older Worker" near the end of the article is especially helpful.

### LEVERAGING THE ASSETS OF OLDER WORKERS

*by Barry Dym, Michael Sales, and Elaine Millam*

There's a tempest brewing in the American workplace. The graying of the vast baby-boomer generation, cultural misconceptions about aging, and an impoverished sense of how to improve the situation have created the prospect of a head-on collision between a group of people who want to work and organizations that have no satisfying place for them. This issue is particularly relevant now, when the robust economy and historically low unemployment rate have left many organizations scrambling to hire and retain qualified workers. Unless we act wisely and view this issue as a systemic—rather than an individual or a group—problem, the failure to better utilize and integrate older workers into our companies may seriously damage productivity and organizational effectiveness throughout the corporate world.

*Source:* "Leveraging the Assets of Older Workers" by Barry Dym, Michael Sales, and Elaine Millam in *The Systems Thinker*, May 2000, pp. 1–5. Barry Dym and Elaine Millam are principals in the consulting firm, WorkWise; Michael Sales is a partner in New Context Consulting. The article is reprinted with permission of Pegasus Communications, Inc., Waltham, MA. Copyright 2000. All rights reserved.

# THE BABY BOOMERANG?

According to the most recent U.S. Census, the 76 million children born between 1946 and 1964—the so called "baby boomers"—are turning 50 at the rate of one person every eight seconds. The boomers now make up slightly more than half of the working population. Because of the sheer size of this demographic group, the average employee age is rapidly rising to about 40.

As the first wave of this generation begins reaching 55 in 2001 and heads toward retirement, the workforce could lose substantial numbers of experienced workers from all walks of life. But most boomers have neither the inclination nor the financial means for early retirement. According to a recent study, 80 percent of those born between 1948 and 1965 expect to work past age 65. Compare that with the roughly 10 percent of the over-65 group who held jobs in 1998.

The declining value of Social Security and pensions lends fuel to many boomers' anxious decision to keep on working. The U.S. Social Security Administration estimates that only 2 percent of the population will be financially self-sufficient when it retires, making work a necessity for most. And if Social Security runs out of money by 2030, as currently predicted, employment after 65 will become a necessity for a large number of people.

However, ample evidence exists that, over the last couple of decades, business has given up on many older workers—that is, those over 50, although in some industries, the "cut-off point" is even earlier. In spite of legal efforts to the contrary (culminating in the Age Discrimination and Employment Act), companies are inclined to let older employees go. Why? Because these organizations believe that their graying workforce is responsible for high salaries and medical costs, declining productivity, stagnating career pipelines, and morale problems. Even when older workers are kept on the payroll, they seldom have the chance to sharpen their skills through additional training. Organizations seem inclined to let many older workers drift into boredom and stagnation.

We have found that many senior employees in high-tech firms, newspapers, and insurance companies feel like "has beens." But because they must work to pay their mortgages and send their children to college, many seasoned workers respond to the lack of opportunity for continued personal and professional growth by "retiring on the job"—they no longer approach their work with enthusiasm or commitment. Thus, they end up fulfilling the low expectations that their managers have for them.

For example, in some news organizations, editors routinely favor younger reporters over more senior journalists, who are said to "lose their legs at 40." As editors increasingly assign stories to younger reporters, the older reporters drift into unproductive marginality or frustrated opposition to their "arrogant and misguided" superiors (R2 in "From Perception to Reality," p. 2.47). This behavior further confirms the editors' belief that the older reporters are "over the hill." Over time, the individuals involved become stereotypes—the angry, ineffectual older reporter and the shallow young editor—playing out the roles that they had struggled to avoid. The caricatures seem so real that some editors refer stories to 23-year-old reporters when a savvy, prize-winning, 55-year-old journalist, who has covered the field for 30 years, sits just 10 feet away.

Companies lose, too, when they fail to capitalize on the knowledge and potential of their aging workforce. Older workers frequently have a level of experience, business acumen, and personal maturity that makes for conscientious effort, excellent customer and client service, and better decision-making ability than their younger peers. In many organizations, older workers know the customers and suppliers. They know the internal operating systems and the influence networks, as well as the strengths and weaknesses of the product line. Finally, they know the firm's strategy, and they know how to get the job done. In short, they are the "institutional memory."

In an era when knowledge management is a buzzword in every MBA program, the older worker is a knowledge holder and a wisdom maker. Getting rid of senior employees means the loss of insights and can lead to unproductive chaos. But companies overlook many possibilities for mobilizing the productivity of mature employees because of the pervasive myths about over-50 workers (see "Older Workers: Myths and Realities," p. 2.49). And, without an understanding of the dynamics that create—and perpetuate—these stereotypes, both older workers and those who manage them are destined to fall into them.

## FROM PERCEPTION TO REALITY

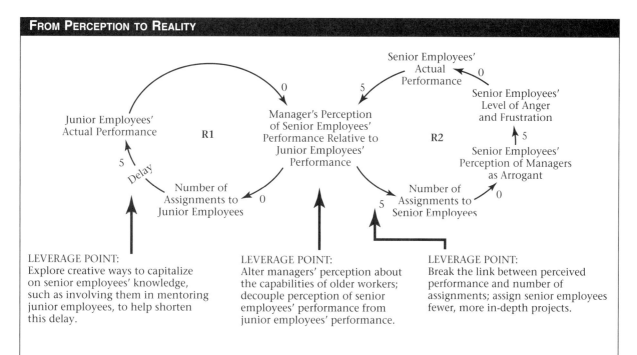

In certain professions, managers routinely favor younger workers over more senior ones (R1). In response, the older employees drift into frustrated opposition to their "arrogant" superiors, and their actual performance declines (R2). This behavior further confirms the managers' belief that the older workers are "over the hill." Leverage points for changing this dynamic include altering managers' perceptions of seasoned employees' capabilities, involving older workers in mentoring, and assigning senior employees fewer, more in-depth projects.

## THE MISMEASURE OF AGE

People commonly joke about their lapses in memory by saying that they have "early Alzheimer's" or that they have "creaky old bones." But it's no laughing matter when employers start to marginalize older workers because they are convinced that the post-50 crowd can no longer perform effectively. Research is beginning to demonstrate that mature workers are much more capable of all sorts of exertion than is commonly believed. Those who continue to work are the healthiest of all.

One study tells us that workers between 55 and 65 are as physically healthy as those between 45 and 55. They report to work as reliably as younger employees, and they perform virtually all but the most demanding physical tasks with comparable ability. A review of 185 research papers also found that older people may actually have higher motivation and job satisfaction than younger workers.

What about the idea that people slow down mentally? Longitudinal studies show that, unless a person has suffered a serious health problem such as a stroke or head injury, most of us sustain our intellectual functioning well into our 70s and beyond. Additionally, advances in medical and genetic technology promise to enhance the longevity and quality of life for many people who would have been forced into full retirement a decade ago. Taking the desire to work and the ability to work together, many people well past 65 are more than qualified for continued employment of all sorts.

So, why do so many companies routinely devalue the qualities that senior employees have to offer? Part of the problem may be that managers tend to compare older workers to younger ones. The flaw in this approach was dramatically pointed out by feminist researcher Carol Gilligan, when she challenged traditional theories of human development in her book *In a Different Voice* (Harvard University Press, 1982). She contended that Freud, Erikson, and

Kohlberg, the gurus of developmental psychology, did not produce theories of *human* development but rather of *male* development. They neglected to take into consideration that men and women mature differently.

Likewise, in the workplace, older people are generally measured by standards that make them look less adequate than their younger peers, primarily by emphasizing mental quickness over depth of experience and physical stamina. This bias is reflected in the career development literature, which caps at about the age of 40, as though people and their careers could not develop further.

To counter this tendency to devalue the contributions that mature workers can make, we need to measure their capabilities and preferences on the basis of their distinctive qualities. We must view them as different but hardly less than youth. Measures should include older workers' experience, personal and political savvy, and wisdom. Managers must take into account—and capitalize on—senior employees' capacity to take the long view, and to keep small setbacks and slights in perspective. Organizations should place greater value on seasoned workers' ability and inclination to nurture younger workers, and avoid placing them in direct competition with their youthful colleagues. Undoubtedly, there are many other capacities and mental attitudes that older workers possess that we have not yet associated with corporate productivity.

One way to deepen our knowledge of what workers in different age brackets have to offer is to learn about the stages of professional and human development. Students of the life cycle like Dan Levinson, an eminent authority in the field of adult psychological development, report that people in their 20s, 30s, and 40s focus on acting with autonomy, pursuing ambitions, and demonstrating competence. Those in their 50s, 60s, and 70s have a different set of requirements, involving the desire to appreciate their achievements, accept their limitations, and leave their mark on their families and communities. Older workers tend to focus on fine-tuning systems, procedures, policies, and methods so that they will stand up to the test of time. Their ambitions are likely to be consistent with what they know to be their strengths and competencies, so managers can generally rely on them to follow through on their commitments.

Based on these interests and needs, many in the post-50 age bracket may no longer want to work the same job that they have been working and they may not want to put in as many hours. However, there are many roles that they would very much like to—and can—take on. To get the best out of mature workers, organizations need a strategy and structure that leverages the talents and responds to the developmental conditions and needs of this growing segment of the workforce.

## NEW CONCEPTS OF CORPORATE STRUCTURE AND WORK

Once organizations see the value in retaining older workers, how can they take actions to keep these employees—and all of their insights and skills—involved in work? How can mature workers participate in a new sort of way, but still remain immersed in the systems that they know so thoroughly? It is admittedly hard to think of what to do with nontraditional workers within the standard corporate "pyramid." From the traditional perspective, each employee climbs a ladder, peaks, plateaus, then declines. For example, journalists, dentists, and nurses are generally considered "to go downhill" around 40. The question remains: What can we do with these professionals for the remaining 25 years of their careers?

Management theorist Charles Handy's conception of the new corporation opens the way to rethinking the place of older workers. Handy's framework affords businesses the possibility of increased flexibility and cost savings by identifying three kinds of employees:

**1. A core group of managers and skilled workers.** These people lead the organization and provide its stability and continuity. They tend to be ambitious, totally immersed in their work and their organization, and very well paid for their efforts.

**2. Key external resources hired on a contractual basis.** These individuals and groups might provide outsourced accounting or legal services.

**3. A project-based employee pool.** These workers are loosely connected to the organization on a job-by-job basis, allowing the organization to expand, contract, and change shape, according to the demands of the market.

| OLDER WORKERS: MYTHS AND REALITIES | |
|---|---|
| **Myth** | **Reality** |
| As people age, they grow less capable | As people age, more is gained than lost |
| Mature workers cost more because of higher absenteeism and accidents | Mature workers have better attendance and accident records than younger workers |
| Older people don't want to work | Older people want to work differently |
| Corporations save by getting rid of older workers | Corporations gain by retaining, redeploying, retraining, and revitalizing senior employees |

It is easy to imagine older workers in each of these three groups. The traditional core is generally filled by the most skilled, powerful senior managers. Many of those who "retire" return to their long-time employers as consultants and contractors, which offers them greater control over their time. The project-based employee pool provides even greater flexibility for employees who, later in their careers, may wish to labor intensely and then take prolonged vacations, or to work from their home offices instead of being burdened by demands for "face time." The second and third functions also offer alternative career paths for parents of young children, children of aging parents, and individuals with health problems.

A basic ingredient of this approach is what Professor Lotte Bailyn of MIT refers to as the "disaggregation of work." Our assumptions about what constitutes "working" are largely based on a model constructed during the industrial era. According to this view, work happens:

- in a particular place (in an office or factory),
- during a certain time frame (usually 9 to 5),
- for a certain amount of time (8 hours),
- in the context of certain social relations (i.e., with a particular group of people),
- with the use of pre-identified technologies (i.e., technologies that are owned and approved of by the organization),
- to accomplish a specialized function or goal.

Bailyn and those on the leading edge of career development theory and practice recommend unpacking this cluster of assumptions about the nature of work for all employees.

Many private-sector companies and other organizations are already experimenting with these elements, separately and in combination, through flextime arrangements, telecommuting, intranet- and Internet-facilitated group work, rotating work groups, and so on. Sources such as *Fortune* magazine's annual listing of the "100 Best Companies to Work for in America" often include "best practices" that offer alternatives to the standard eight-hour in-office work day. These policies can easily be refashioned to address the needs and wants of older workers.

## WORKING WISELY WITH OLDER WORKERS

How can decision-makers help their organizations to break free from the negative stereotypes about older workers that inevitably become self-fulfilling prophesies? How can companies find ways to better utilize the knowledge and experience that this group possesses? We suggest the following steps (see "Steps for Leveraging the Older Workforce," p. 2.50):

**1. Identify warning signs.**
Through informal conversation and interviews, determine:

- if a significant portion of the older workforce seems less than optimally productive,
- if there is considerable misunderstanding, miscommunication, and conflict between generations,
- if there is difficulty retaining skilled workers and experienced managers,
- if these problems are contributing to low morale in your corporation.

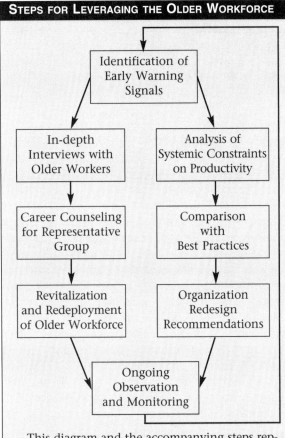

## STEPS FOR LEVERAGING THE OLDER WORKFORCE

Identification of
Early Warning
Signals

In-depth
Interviews with
Older Workers

Analysis of
Systemic Constraints
on Productivity

Career Counseling
for Representative
Group

Comparison
with
Best Practices

Revitalization
and Redeployment
of Older Workforce

Organization
Redesign
Recommendations

Ongoing
Observation
and Monitoring

This diagram and the accompanying steps represent a two-pronged approach to better utilizing the knowledge and experience of older workers. The left-hand side of the figure shows how an organization can work with individuals to revitalize their careers within the company. The right-hand side depicts the deeper and more complex processes of organizational change that a company must undertake to create a lasting solution to the problem of disaffected and underutilized senior employees.

*If the warning signs are present, take actions to address both individual and organizational issues, as follows:*

## 2. Conduct in-depth interviews with older workers.

These interviews should focus on people who can be helped by organizational improvements, rather than on chronic poor performers or entrepreneurial self-starters.

- Explore workers' present and past interests; their experiences of being underutilized, pressured, ignored, or marginalized; their emotions about their treatment within the organization; and their ambitions.

## 3. Explore systemic causes of the problem.

- Analyze underlying constraints on productivity and job satisfaction. For example, management may not keep up with the particular abilities and interests of older workers or may let them languish in boring and unchallenging positions. This analysis should derive from a combination of key informant interviews, conducted with a diagonal slice of the organization, focus groups, and a broad-based questionnaire. The tools of systems thinking—such as causal loop diagrams—can be useful here as well.

- Determine which formal and informal systems, cultural values, and organizational dynamics constrain and which enhance productivity and job satisfaction for mature workers and for workers in general.

## 4. Provide career counseling where needed.

- Offer counseling for older employees to determine how to redeploy or restrain them to revitalize their careers.

## 5. Compare the present situation with "best practices."

- Identify best practices from other organizations that might work for you.

- Look for examples of excellence within your business that might be brought into service elsewhere in the company.

## 6. Design programs for senior workers to:

- Continue to upgrade their skills,

- Shift them into lines of work that capitalize on their old competencies but also demand new understandings,

- Use their experience through teaching, mentoring, or leading cross-departmental initiatives.

## 7. Develop organizational change strategies for implementing the recommended programs.

- Evaluate the organization's core beliefs and culture to ensure that any new policies complement current management practices.

## 8. Once you've implemented the new programs, observe whether the corporate culture supports these changes over time.

- Determine if organizational and individual efforts have significantly increased the productivity and job satisfaction of older workers, as well as the productivity and morale of the entire corporation. You should continually be alert for the warning signs listed in step 1 and be willing to cycle through the steps again as needed.

## OVERCOMING THE "PYGMALION EFFECT"

We are all prone to think that what we see is true. Yet everyone knows that we each change according the context we are in: home or work; friendly or unfriendly; familiar or unfamiliar; supportive or unsupportive; challenging or accepting. Like anyone else, older workers are more or less productive in different environments. The same people who look bored, uncommitted, or incompetent in contexts not geared to bring out their best can be excited, engaged, and extraordinarily skilled in settings that expect, require, and facilitate their performance.

In a well-known research project by Robert Rosenthal and Lenore Jacobson, published as *Pygmalion in the Classroom: Teacher Expectation and Pupils' Intellectual Development* (Irvington Publishers, 1989), two teachers were presented with two groups of students of equal ability. One was told that the members of her class were very intelligent and talented. The other teacher was told that her class was mediocre at best. During the course of the year, the first group did well, and the other did badly. The power of expectations on people's performance is almost impossible to believe, until you see the outcomes of studies like this one. Only by being vigilant and by creating structures that accommodate people's differences can we overcome this tendency for perceptions to become realities.

So it is with older workers. Raise expectations, provide flexible working conditions, manage them according to their experience, skills, inclinations—and wisdom—and they will produce far,

| NEXT STEPS |
| --- |
| • Evaluate whether your organization or department exhibits any of the warning signs that older workers are being marginalized or underutilized. |
| • Find creative ways for junior and senior workers to mentor each other on-the-job. For instance, pair a younger employee with experience using the Web with a more established contributor who knows the ins and outs of project management. |
| • Familiarize yourself with the dangers of perception, as illustrated in "Older Workers: Myths and Realities" and described in *Pygmalion in the Classroom*. How can managers avoid falling prey to stereotypes about certain groups of workers? |

far more than the stereotyped senior employee so prevalent in our imaginations. The public at large has a real stake in the success of initiatives that keep older workers at a high level of capacity. Even a 20 percent rise in productivity in the healthcare industry, which has a high percentage of workers over 50, would result in nearly a billion-dollar increase in revenues, efficiencies, and savings. This figure doesn't include benefits in the form of innovations and quality initiatives.

Imagine the productivity increases that the corporate world would experience by making the best use of the hundreds of thousands of aging boomers on the payrolls. And also consider the society-wide toll that failing to provide meaningful opportunities for seasoned employees to continue contributing and supporting themselves financially may take. Fortunately, by retaining, revitalizing, and retraining the most skilled, savvy workers in the workforce, we can improve productivity—and people's lives—well into the future.

# 2C. NEEDS OF LEARNERS FOR GOVERNMENT SUPPORT: EQUAL OPPORTUNITY GUARANTEES AND FAIR EMPLOYMENT PRACTICES

## ARTICLE REPRINT

### THE PERSISTENT GENDER GAP

*Editor's Comment:* This article about "sex segregation" and "discrimination" is the first in a group of entries that outline the needs of learners for government support. A major point of this piece by Ellen Bravo is that employers need to be aware of political agendas from the right and the left, and should be careful about which statistics they use. Equal pay for equal work, gender-based, is a problem that seems not to be going away. It continues to be one of our most sensitive equal opportunity and fair practices challenges.

## GO FIGURE

### *by Ellen Bravo*

Oh, the thorny problem of the wage gap— what's the right wing to do? They used to say that women didn't deserve as much money as men. But hey, it's the dawn of the twenty-first century; you can't stand by that outdated notion anymore. So in the name of progress, the right has decided to prove that the gap simply doesn't exist. Select a few statistics here, throw in some rosy predictions there, pin any disparity on the choices women themselves have made, and voilà!—the wage gap disappears.

The arguments against the gap are all set out in *Women's Figures: An Illustrated Guide to the Economic Progress of Women in America*, by Diane Furchtgott-Roth and Christine Stolba, published by the conservative American Enterprise Institute.

The authors maintain that young women without children make almost the same amount as men in their fields. Therefore, wherever women earn less than men, factors other than discrimination are at play. Women "choose" lower-paying jobs because these positions offer "much-needed flexibility." Women earn less because they work fewer hours and take more breaks from work to spend time with their children. And women just haven't been in the workforce long enough to gain the experience necessary to rise to the top. Given the growing array of flexible options at work, the greater number of women in jobs previously dominated by men, and the simple passage of time, those women who want to reach the top will be able to do so. Or so say the wage-gap vaporizers.

First off, let's admit it: there's a tiny bit of truth in their argument. Young women who don't have any children and who are just entering the workforce do earn roughly the same salaries as men in their fields. *Women's Figures* would have you believe that those equal paychecks will last. If only it were so. Wait five or ten years. Even if she doesn't take time off to have a family, and puts in the same amount of "face time," the woman who started out on a par with the guy next to her will have gotten fewer raises, smaller bonuses, and less frequent promotions. It's certainly not because she's less competent. This truth was brought home to professors and administrators at the Massachusetts Institute of Technology recently. The university conducted a pay-equity study that confirmed women professors' gut feeling that they weren't faring as well as their male colleagues. It wasn't that the university offered unequal pay—at least not at first. But over the years, men were offered research grants more often than women, given better teaching assignments, nominated for awards more often. And all of that led to higher salaries. MIT is doing something about the problem, thanks to the establishment of a committee on women faculty. Yet Furchtgott-Roth and Stolba want us to think there's no problem, so why remedy the situation?

And what about jobs that aren't quite equal, although the work is at least comparable by anyone's standards? Why do maintenance workers make more than cleaning women? The authors of *Women's Figures* don't have an answer to that, since it's a fact that in *any* job or profession where women concentrate, the salaries are lower than in those where men predominate—even when they're doing virtually the same work.

**Despite the figures in *Women's Figures*, it's hard to find jobs in which women make what men do.**

- The Web is one of the newest industries around. But female Internet technology professionals pull in only 88 percent of what men in the field make. Same job, equal seniority, but the paychecks don't match.

- Women in executive, administrative, and managerial positions earn 68 percent of what their male counterparts bring home.

- Female general surgeons take home 77 percent of the average male general surgeon's salary.

- Overall, women still earn only 76 cents for every dollar a man earns. Part of the reason is the poverty wages many women earn. Twelve percent of women in year-round, full-time jobs earned less than $12,500 in 1998. The figures for women of color are even worse—16 percent of

African American women and 24 percent of Latinas had such low earnings. Nevertheless, the wage gap between men and women in the U.S. has decreased—it was 59 cents to a dollar in 1961, when the Census Bureau first began looking at pay equity. But the improvement isn't just because women's wages have gone up; it's also because of a drop in men's earnings. Downsizing and the closing of manufacturing plants have forced men to take lower-paying jobs. Men of color have been particularly hard hit by declining pay.

### What about Furchtgott-Roth and Stolba's other arguments?

- Women choose lower-paying jobs because they offer more flexibility. That's really playing fast and loose with statistics and with logic. Women may cheerfully choose to be child care workers, but they hardly choose to live in poverty as a result. And forget about flexibility. Most women can't get time off to care for their families. Half of the workforce—mostly the low-paid half—isn't covered by the Family and Medical Leave Act. And many of those who are covered can't afford time off because it's unpaid. Meanwhile, 80 percent of working-poor mothers have less than one week of sick leave, which they have to use to care for family members as well as themselves.

- Women work fewer hours and take more time off than men. Furchtgott-Roth and Stolba are right about women making sacrifices to care for their families. The question is, should there be a penalty for that? And if so, how long should it last? One study of professional women showed that years after they had taken an average of only 8.8 months of family leave, they still earned 17 percent less than women who had not taken leave. For lower-wage women, taking time off can have even worse repercussions. It may mean losing a job altogether.

- Women haven't been in the workforce long enough to earn what men do. Forget it. We've already seen that women make less compared to men as time goes on, not more.

There are other ways *Women's Figures* flouts both statistics and logic. It argues that the reason

| Job | Women's Median Weekly Earnings | Men's Median Weekly Earnings | Women's Salaries as a Percentage of Men's |
|---|---|---|---|
| Accountants and Auditors | $618 | $821 | 75.3% |
| Bookkeepers, Accounting, and Auditing Clerks | $426 | $455 | 93.6% |
| Cashiers | $259 | $302 | 85.8% |
| College and University Professors | $769 | $998 | 71.1% |
| Computer Programmers | $715 | $884 | 80.9% |
| Computer Systems Analysts and Scientists | $890 | $996 | 89.4% |
| Construction Workers | $408 | $545 | 74.9% |
| Editors and Reporters | $616 | $812 | 75.9% |
| Elementary School Teachers | $677 | $749 | 90.4% |
| Engineers | $831 | $1,011 | 82.2% |
| Executive and Administrative Positions | $626 | $915 | 68.4% |
| Farmworkers | $262 | $285 | 91.9% |
| Financial Managers | $703 | $1,017 | 69.1% |
| Food Preparation Service Workers | $271 | $303 | 89.4% |
| Health Technologists and Technicians | $486 | $588 | 82.7% |
| Lawyers | $951 | $1,350 | 70.4% |
| Legal Assistants | $581 | $561 | 103.6% |
| Pharmacists | $985 | $1,146 | 86% |
| Physicians | $966 | $1,255 | 77% |
| Psychologists | $621 | $740 | 83.9% |
| Real Estate Sales Agents | $575 | $763 | 75.4% |
| Registered Nurses | $734 | $774 | 94.8% |
| Secretaries, Stenographers, and Typists | $436 | $484 | 90.1% |
| Social Workers | $568 | $609 | 93.3% |
| Textile, Apparel, and Furnishing Machine Operators | $285 | $318 | 89.6% |
| Truck Drivers | $371 | $520 | 71.3% |
| Waiters | $282 | $343 | 82.2% |

*Source:* U.S. Dept. of Labor, Women's Bureau, 1998

women are so underrepresented in many occupations is that those jobs require physical strength and involve great hazards. Yet this hardly explains why women make up a scant 3.4 percent of airline pilots or navigators, 10 percent of engineers, and 27 percent of physicians. Nor does it explain the discrepancy between the wage and the inherent worth of work traditionally done by women. Why do accountants make more than kindergarten teachers when both jobs require equal levels of training?

**The truth is, women's earnings are still much lower than men's—and so low period—for complex reasons, most of which come down to the persistence of sex segregation and the legacy of discrimination.**

- **Sex Segregation** While there has been growing opportunity in jobs formerly closed to women, most women do the same jobs they've always done, and those jobs pay less than comparable jobs done by men. Even within certain occupations, such as sales, women are clustered in the lower-paying jobs. For instance, women constitute 82 percent of employees in gift and novelty shops but only 19 percent of those in higher-paying car dealerships. Women of color are concentrated in the lowest-paying jobs, including domestic workers, nurse's aides, and sewing machine operators.

- **Discrimination** The continuation of discrimination holds women back—whether it is the traditional "We don't want a woman doing that job" or something more subtle, such as when women are left out of informal gatherings where people pass on skills, connections, and workplace savvy. Because of the expense and often the humiliation involved, women who experience this type of discrimination tend to leave jobs in higher numbers than those who don't. This affects their earnings as well as their opportunities for advancement.

We know how to end both the wage gap and poverty wages. We need to lobby for comparable pay standards that guarantee that the jobs done by women are valued as much as those done by men. We need to continue to push for women to enter traditionally male fields, like construction and engineering. We need to expand equal-pay protection to part-time workers. And certainly not least, we need to organize—to join unions and to become activists.

By masking the wage gap, the right hopes to eliminate the fight for these solutions: you don't need better pay, honey, you just need to embrace the choices you've made, or make different ones.

Why do they think women will buy this lie? Go figure.

# ARTICLE REPRINT

## A CRITIQUE OF AFFIRMATIVE ACTION IN TRANSITION

*Editor's Comment:* In April of year 1999, the Coca-Cola Company of Atlanta, GA was sued by a group of its African-American executives in allegations that indicated Coke top management was insensitive to and lacking in support of black managers and executives. The high profile suit said that Coke created a perception that Coca-Cola Company was a "high-risk environment for high-potential and aggressive African-Americans" (*The Wall Street Journal*, February 10, 2000, p. A11D). The February 2000 article in *The Wall Street Journal* ten months later said that Coca-Cola was just now admitting that its diversity efforts were slow, and that it would do better in the future.

A brief article in *USA Today* newspaper on February 14, 2000, p. 6 on recently released U.S. Census data indicated that the black population is getting younger (33 percent under age 19) in recent years compared to the white population (24 percent under age 19), and that blacks continue to be less well-educated than whites (15 percent black college graduates versus 28 percent white college graduates. In a knowledge economy that spins out good jobs at the high end but not necessarily at the low end, this is not good news for equal employment opportunity.

And on July 16, 2000, *The New York Times Magazine* devoted its cover and much of its content to the topic, "Talking About Race." The magazine was different because of its pictorial way of presenting statistics about how race is currently lived in America. For example, pages 38 and 39 contained side-by-side photographs of a "White Living Room" and a "Black Living Room," with numerous measures of the way people live, so that readers can easily see comparisons and contrasts. In many areas, the statis-

tics are very close together. In other areas, however, they are far apart. For example, only 42 percent of children in black households have two parents, contrasted with 76 percent in white households; 39 percent of black households subscribe to at least one magazine, contrasted with 63 percent of white households; 58 percent of blacks have a checking account, contrasted with 82 percent of whites having a checking account. The median family income for blacks is $20,000; for whites it is $35,750. Black home ownership stands at only 45 percent, contrasted with white home ownership at 73 percent. These contrasts suggest some of the areas of our cultural life that still need attention from an "affirmative action" standpoint. That is, the spirit of affirmative action in its original political intent of targeting business and public education still needs to be at work in society as a whole.

The article that follows here is written by 75-year-old Arthur A. Fletcher, an observant and articulate critic of where we are as a nation on affirmative action.

# BUSINESS AND RACE: ONLY HALFWAY THERE

*by Arthur A. Fletcher*

Arthur A. Fletcher, 75, may just be the father of affirmative action. A World War II veteran (he served under Patton) and former professional football player (for the Los Angeles Rams and the Baltimore Colts), he joined the Republican Party in the 1940s. Later, as Assistant Secretary of Labor under President Richard Nixon, he helped craft rules that made the original affirmative-action legislation more enforceable.

Before Fletcher came along, affirmative action was a relatively feeble notion because laws outlined in the Civil Rights Act of 1964—which, among other provisions, barred discrimination in the workplace—did not force employers to keep track of the number of minorities and women they hired. Fletcher gave the program teeth by aligning affirmative action with procurement laws governing hiring policies in the public sector. Fletcher's ideas, spelled out in a document called the Revised Philadelphia Plan, are still the basis for affirmative-action enforcement. Fletcher remains a passionate advocate for affirmative action, speaking regularly to business audiences and advising managers and executives on diversity. He spoke recently with *Fortune* writer Eryn Brown.

I'm proud to be able to say I set the stage for today's workplace and work force diversity efforts. Affirmative action changed the American workplace for the better, forever. And despite the efforts by opportunists like [anti-affirmative-action leader] Ward Connerly to undermine the rules and spirit of affirmative action, it should remain in place indefinitely.

Over the past 30 years, affirmative action has made pursuing economic equity a rational, reasonable, and achievable goal for all American taxpayers. Yet as we move into a new millennium, the sad truth is we are only halfway home, with a very long way to go. How long? At least another 50 years, if not a full century.

A lot of people—including too many corporate executives—still believe many professions are too difficult and complex for anyone but white men. But there's not a single industry in which you will not find women, African Americans, Asians, or Hispanics performing at almost every level, including management. The change is real. It is permanent. And I consider myself blessed to have lived to see it happen.

I know I'm closer to the end of the journey, but I hardly think my work is done. I still lecture corporate executives all across the nation, as often as 30 or 40 times a year, explaining my vision of equal opportunity. I'm the keeper of the flame. I have to be. Affirmative action's opponents have been at war with us for 30 years. But despite a few defeats regarding set-aside programs, the courts have largely remained on our side. We've seen people use isolated cases where affirmative action may not be working to get anti-affirmative-action referendums on the ballots. Then they lie to voters to sway public opinion. But laws aren't made from anecdotes. I won't be concerned about the Supreme Court, the U.S. Congress, or the state legislatures ending affirmative action until someone comes up with a study proving white males have really been discriminated against in the workplace.

But legislation alone is not enough to keep affirmative action alive. In fact, I don't need any more public policy. I need corporate America to do what it alleges it can do—make it work. For years business leaders screamed for less government: "Get out of our way. Let us show you how to get things done." So Congress redirected money from Washington to cities, to states, and to the private sector. Okay, corporate America, the ball's in your court, the reins are in your hands.

One thing's for sure: Companies that ignore diversity will struggle to flourish in the global marketplace during the 21st century. According to Department of Labor statistics, the pool of talent that will supply the next generation of employees, managers, and executives will soon be dominated by women and ethnic minorities. They will be hard to ignore.

Look at what's already happening as a result of the growing Hispanic population in the U.S. Back when NAFTA passed in 1993, American companies started rewriting their strategic plans to take advantage of new business opportunities in Mexico. As they did this, they began asking some new questions regarding Latinos in the

U.S.: How many are there? Where do they live? What is their education level? What is their income level? What radio stations do they listen to? What TV do they watch? And the like.

Soon the book on Hispanics was rewritten. Now many companies have specific initiatives not only to reach Hispanics as consumers but as potential employees. Why? Certainly not because of any lofty social agenda. Hell, no. It's because of need. Smart corporate executives are saying, "If these people have skills and can keep me productive, I want them." It's as simple as that.

I would say that somewhere between now and 2015, Hispanics (and anyone who can speak Spanish, whether they're Hispanic or not) will become invaluable human capital. I see them moving quickly in the workplace, in fast and giant leaps. All because of concrete business needs.

The benefits should extend to all minorities, but companies can't simply wait for minorities to flood the workplace. If corporations don't invest in educating today's underprivileged minorities, then those citizens won't be prepared to be tomorrow's productive workers and future leaders. In the past, a blue-collar worker could make a middle-class living without higher education. All he had to do was pass a high-school equivalency test. But technology has changed everything. Today if you can't write, calculate, communicate, think, reason, and use sound judgment, you're in a world of trouble.

The public education system isn't getting the job done right now. Not at any level. So more and more businesses—especially technology businesses—will have to do it themselves. Some have already started to impact the education process by creating onsite training centers, for instance, that utilize current employees and managers as teachers. That should be a growing trend.

But there should be another movement in the area of education: You always hear people asking what America can do to improve math and science scores in our schools. I think businesses should concentrate on literacy. For most people in the work force, being educated means proving that you can continue to learn. It's a self-development thing. But you can't take advantage of programs like distance learning or onsite training if you don't know how to read.

Now, this might sound like a stretch, but I truly believe we as a nation will struggle to remain a superpower if we don't do everything we can to provide all people with the resources to build their skills and become productive participants in the economy. Back in 1989, I wrote a letter to then-President George Bush, putting him on notice that if we dropped programs like affirmative action, America would lose opportunities to develop willing and able workers. To me, that's a national security issue.

Make no mistake about it: In a world that is as treacherous, unpredictable, and dangerous as the competitive global market is turning out to be, maintaining anything less than superpower status will be unacceptable. For America, this won't be possible without prized human capital. So the country will need to create workplaces where individuals—male, female, brown, black, you name it—can perform at their best. In other words, we need workplaces without harassment, without gender bashing, and without racism.

Management will have to lead the way. Executives do not have the luxury of staying out of the battle. If they are going to create workplaces that are conducive to top performance from all their employees, then they have to make their attitudes known. They have to make their presence felt on diversity.

Yes, I think there's hope. I see a growing number of young whites who are not shocked when they meet a person like me, a black person, with skills. They're not caught off guard when they walk into a courtroom and see a black judge. Or have a black boss. Well, some of them may still faint at the sight of a black person in the corner office. But compared with the way it was in the '50s, when I finished school, the progress is really overwhelming.

Let me say this: I worry that African Americans are falling behind other minority groups. I worry, as the disparities between ethnic groups become more apparent, that one group will turn against another. That will hurt us all. It will diminish America's strength, security, stability, and prosperity, and our promising future. Some folks believe that when the economy is good, racial animosities disappear. Well, the economy is at an all-time high, and it promises to remain there for a while. But ask anyone to give you the top ten items on the national public policy agenda, and race will be up there. It shouldn't even be in the top 20.

Believe it or not, American business can play a role in the national agenda to improve race relations. How? By supporting sensible, economically driven government programs like the Community Reinvestment Act, which prods banks to make loans in low-income neighborhoods. Look, every minority individual will not reach the executive suite or even thrive in a corporate environment. But the CRA provides entrepreneurial-minded residents in poor areas an opportunity to join the mainstream economy by being upfront, out-front, participants in the economic revival of their own neighborhoods.

In my view, it will be at least another decade before we're taking full advantage of programs like the CRA, or truly embracing more minorities in the corporate world. And that'll happen only if we treat diversity like a two-minute drill, as we'd call it in football. That's if we work day and night.

It's amazing, but when you consider how fast—and how much—America's economy is changing, we're still practically a developing country. Clearly, we've got a long, long way to go.

# ARTICLE REPRINT

## STUBBORN POVERTY AMIDST PLENTY

*Editor's Comment:* It has been four year since President Clinton signed welfare reform into law, and most observers agree that the success of the reforms in getting people off welfare and into work has been outstanding. Companies have joined the Welfare to Work Partnership organization, pledging to hire persons off welfare. Partnership companies alone have place 650,000 former welfare recipients into jobs over these recent years (SHRM *HR News*, April 2000, p. 1). Yet, problems remain.

Low-productivity jobs have expanded, as have low-wage jobs in retail and service sectors. Labor economists report that the minimum wage today of $5.15 per hour is in real wage terms significantly lower than an equivalent minimum wage thirty years ago (*The Wall Street Journal*, June 29, 2000, p. A12). Even at the professional level, young lawyers just starting out are paid four times as much as young teachers just starting out; the bottom fifth of U.S. households receives less than 4 percent of the income distribution, while the top fifth of U.S. households receives more than 49 percent of income distribution (*US News & World Report*, February 21, 2000, p. 43). The wage gap is real and pervasive. It is an area in which government has tried to help, but not all observers believe that those efforts have been helpful. Robert Kuttner's commentary which follows analyzes the possibilities, promise, and problems of welfare reform, suggesting several roles for education and training.

# THE STATES ARE ENDING WELFARE
# AS WE KNOW IT—BUT NOT POVERTY

*by Robert Kuttner*

In 1996, President Clinton and the Republican Congress carried out Clinton's campaign pledge to end welfare as we knew it. But Clinton, in his 1992 campaign manifesto, "Putting People First," made another famous pledge: People who worked hard and played by the rules should not live in poverty.

Thanks to the fortuitous rendezvous of welfare reform and a full-employment economy, redemption of this pledge is possible. Industry is now eager, and in some cases desperate, for more and better workers. The public-policy tools are available, and in some states are actually being used, not just to end welfare as we know it but to end poverty as we know it.

The welfare rolls have declined by 43% since 1996. That has freed billions of dollars in funds under the federal welfare-reform program, Temporary Assistance to Needy Families (TANF). This program mandates time limits on welfare checks but also allows states to reprogram money saved from unspent welfare outlays into expenditures necessary to help former recipients succeed as workers. These include tuition reimbursements, wage supplements, and, above all, child care.

**"LADDERS."** In the most imaginative states, such as Washington, governors have risen to the occasion and worked with business leaders and educators to convert TANF into a program not just to purge the welfare rolls but also to help all of the working poor rise out of poverty. Governor Gary Locke, the son of Chinese immigrants, devised such a comprehensive program. This year, some $129 million was reprogrammed to job training. Unlike many states, where former welfare recipients are simply pushed into low-wage work and punished if they choose instead to go to school, Washington gives free tuition to people who sign up for a "career ladders" program at community colleges that combines work and learning.

Unhappily, states like Washington remain the exception. In neighboring Idaho, the policy is just to clear the rolls. Idaho leads the nation, so to speak, with an 89 percent drop in its welfare caseload. But Idaho has spent just $12 million of its $55 million TANF savings on such services as training and child care. Collectively, the states have stashed away fully $7 billion in TANF funds, rather than spending the money to help former welfare recipients succeed as workers. This money is now a tempting target for hardliners in Congress, who want to reduce outlays on the grounds that they are not needed.

A recent national conference on low-wage workers in the New Economy convened by Jobs for the Future and co-sponsored by the AFL-CIO, the National Association of Manufacturers, and others, made clear that there is a better path. Even hard-line sponsors of the 1996 law recognized that former welfare recipients needed support. This included child care, health insurance, training, and what manpower jargon calls "income disregards." The latter term means that new workers, mostly women with children, should not lose a dollar of welfare benefits for every dollar in their paychecks, because this would kill their incentive to work. Three long-term experiments, recently evaluated by the Manpower Demonstration Research Corp., found that more generous income-disregard formulas make dramatic improvements—in success at work, the well-being of children, and even marriages.

Unfortunately, in their zeal to purge the rolls, most states are taking the opposite path. Welfare offices, rather than serving as bridges to successful employment, are programmed to be obstacle courses. Applicants for welfare benefits, or work-transition benefits, must run a gauntlet of multiple appointments and are "sanctioned"—purged from the rolls—for missing appointments because of innocent mistakes or sick children. As a result, a great many people are diligently working but even worse off economically.

This is a needless tragedy, both for the people themselves and for industry, which desperately needs the workers. Ironically, the Federal Reserve is braking the recovery because labor markets seem too tight. But if every potential worker could be helped to succeed, the labor force would expand by millions.

All of the elements are now present for a national commitment to end poverty as we know it by making work pay. These include a full-employment economy, a generous Earned Income Tax Credit, a flexible post-welfare system that supports work, higher minimum wages, and a resurgence of union organizing in the low-wage service sector. But wages at the bottom have only just begun to rise. Unless creative national policy connects the dots we will have traded an inadequate welfare system for one that demands that everyone work—but leaves millions in poverty.

# ARTICLE REPRINT

## NONEMPLOYEE HARASSMENT

*Editor's Comment:* The number of civil rights lawsuits against employers has nearly doubled in the decade 1990–2000, with plaintiffs winning a greater percentage of them at the end of the decade than at the beginning (23.8 percent in 1990; 35.5 percent in 1998, the last year for which figures are available). These figures were reported in the Society for Human Resource Management's newsletter, *Legal Report*, in May–June 2000, p. 1. They should be a wake-up call to employers—and to training managers who train employees in matters of the law, civil rights and employment law—to constantly update the information in employee orientation packages and training. Case law changes as the workplace changes, and managers must keep abreast of the latest legal decisions and trends. This article reprinted here represents one of these "latest trends" in civil rights law, that of the rights of persons who are not employees, but rather, are others legally involved with an employer. Persons such as contractors, consultants, contingent workers of all sorts, and even customers. All employees as well as all persons in contract of any sort with an employer need to know the law as it currently is being interpreted and enforced. Action at the Supreme Court level is important to watch as the Administration changes in Washington and as deliberations and decisions are made by the Court in civil rights cases. Trainers need to teach more than the original legislation; you need to also pay attention to current developments in the courts and design training accordingly.

## NONEMPLOYEE HARASSMENT

### *by Adam Jack Morell, Esq.*

Sexual harassment is one of the fastest-growing areas of employment litigation and is also a controversial and much-discussed topic. The two landmark cases the Supreme Court decided in 1998, *Burlington Industries v. Ellerth* and *Faragher v. City of Boca Raton*, made clear the obligation that employers now shoulder in protecting themselves. But even if an employer has a written policy and conducts ongoing employee training it still may not be complying with the law. Many training courses and company policies do not address the following question: What happens if an organization's employees conduct themselves professionally, but nonemployees, with whom the employees interact in the course of their jobs, get out of hand?

For example, what are the consequences if an independent contractor, whom an employer retains to administer pre-employment lie detector tests, touches the female job applicants inappropriately and asks them non-related job questions of a sexual nature? Or what happens if a customer stares at and verbally abuses an employee by making explicitly vulgar comments about her anatomy? Or what about the consultant who is hired to talk to employees about workplace safety, but who engages in unwelcome sexual commentary with one of the employees?

In the above examples, all of which are taken from actual cases, none of the alleged harassers were employees of the organization. Are the employers still responsible for the conduct of those nonemployees?

In a word, yes. EEOC regulations specifically provide that an employer may be responsible for the acts of nonemployees, with respect to sexual harassment of employees in the workplace, where the employer (or its agents or supervisory employees) knows or should have known of the conduct and fails to take immediate and appropriate corrective action.

There are many cases that have dealt with this issue. Many federal district courts have held that an employee has a cause of action against his or her employer when a nonemployee sexually harasses the employee. Further, the types of employees and nonemployees involved in these cases have run the gamut from casino workers to aldermen.

## THE STANDARD

The decisions handed down by the federal courts have recognized that employers can be liable for nonemployee sexual harassment when these two things occur:

(1) The employer knows or should have known of sexual harassment by nonemployees, and fails to take reasonable steps to stop the harassing behavior.

This part of the standard is not as strict as the standard created by *Ellerth* and *Faragher* for harassment committed by a supervisor, but rather is identical for harassment committed by co-workers. Under those two cases, if a supervisor is committing the harassment, the employer is deemed to have known about it, even if the targeted employee does not report it to manage-

ment. If it is a co-worker, rather than a supervisor committing the harassment, the employer is only liable if it knew about, or should have known about the harassing behavior.

(2) The second point of the standard, however, is different from the standard that is used when the harassment is coming from co-workers. In cases of harassment committed by employees, employers are expected to stop the harassment. When the harasser is a nonemployee, employers are expected to take "reasonable steps" to stop the harassment. Nevertheless, the bottom line is that employers may be liable if they fail to remedy or prevent harassment of employees by nonemployees.

## EMPLOYER'S DUTY TO RESPOND

A recent case that dealt with an employer's duty to respond to sexual harassment committed by a nonemployee was *Lockard v. Pizza Hut, et. al.* In this case, an Oklahoma court ordered an Oklahoma Pizza Hut franchisee to pay $200,000 in compensatory damages for allowing a hostile work environment created by two customers who harassed a waitress. *Lockard* involved a manager who disregarded his employee's complaint that she was being sexually harassed.

The plaintiff complained that she was subjected to hostile environment sexual harassment when two regular customers of the Pizza Hut restaurant where she was employed made lewd comments to her on several occasions and, on at least one occasion, grabbed her breast. Although the employee notified her manager of the incidents, and clearly communicated her desire not to wait on these customers anymore, nothing was done. In fact, when the offensive customers came in again after she had informed her manager of the past harassment, the plaintiff's manager insisted that she wait on them. When she went to the table to take their order, the customers pulled her hair. Nonetheless, the manager still told her to continue to wait on the patrons.

The court in that case said that an employer who condones or tolerates such an environment should be held liable regardless of whether the hostile environment was created by a co-employee or a nonemployee, since the employer ultimately controls the conditions of the work environment.

So how did the standard apply in this case? The *Lockard* court said that in cases involving the actions of customers, an employer could be liable if it knows or should have known about the harassment and does not take reasonable steps to stop the harassment. Interestingly, Pizza Hut had a manual on sexual harassment that specifically outlined the options for a manager in situations like this one. According to the manual, the manager could have directed a male waiter to serve the men, served them himself, or asked them to leave the restaurant. The existence of the manual (just like the existence of the policy in *Faragher v. City of Boca Raton*) was not enough, however, to shield the employer from liability. Once the waitress notified the manager of the harassment, the employer was deemed to have known about it. Because the manager (and thus, the employer) failed to take reasonable steps to remedy or prevent the hostile environment, the employer was held accountable for its manager's failure to act.

## THE WRONG APPROACH

Even worse than the employer that does nothing in response to sexual harassment committed by a nonemployee is the employer that encourages the conduct which leads to the sexual harassment. In *Rodriguez-Hernandez v. Miranda-Velez*, a female employee sued her employer under Title VII alleging that she was discharged from her job after complaining to her employer about the sexual advances made by a high-level executive of one of her employer's most important clients. The First Circuit upheld the jury's verdict for the plaintiff on the customer's harassing behavior, stating that "employers can be held liable for a customer's unwanted sexual advances, if the employer ratifies or acquiesces in the customer's demands." The court concluded the employer in that case "not only acquiesced in the customer's demands, but explicitly told her to give in to those demands and satisfy the customer."

The facts of this case reveal a truly reckless disregard for the plaintiff's circumstances and a blatant ignorance of sexual harassment law. Sandra Rodriguez-Hernandez worked for the defendant company, Occidental. Omar Chavez was Occidental's president and sole shareholder. Occidental had a very profitable client, Puerto Rico Electric Power Authority (PREPA). The president of PREPA was Edwin Miranda-Velez. Chavez introduced Rodriguez to Miranda, and told her that Miranda was very important for Occidental's business and that she and the other employees should be nice to him and "keep him satisfied." In December 1990, Chavez threw a party for PREPA officials at a local hotel. Chavez instructed many female employees to attend the event unaccompanied, so they would be available to dance with the PREPA executives. The night's entertainment at that party included a dancing show performed by scantily clad women.

Miranda began to make unwelcome approaches and suggestive comments to Rodriguez. He invited her out to dinner. He asked her to visit his office after hours and on Friday evenings. He anonymously sent her flowers for her birthday and included a sexually explicit card. Rodriguez complained to Chavez about this behavior. Chavez responded by stressing that Miranda was an important client, but assured her that he would deal with the problem.

He did not deal with the problem. The culmination of Miranda's advances came when he called Rodriguez and told her he would come pick her up to take her to a motel. Rodriguez, upset by Miranda's latest advance, called Chavez to complain about Miranda's call. Chavez responded by defending Miranda, and saying that Rodriguez should respond to Miranda "as a woman."

She refused to do so, and within two months was fired for what Occidental claimed was "an unexplained imbalance of money in petty cash funds." The appellate court ruled that the jury could have found that the reason given for her firing was pretextual and a cover up for the retaliation that Occidental inflicted upon Rodriguez for complaining about the harassment that she suffered at the hands of Miranda, a nonemployee.

Several things can be learned by the mistakes that Occidental made in this case. The most blatant error in judgment on Occidental's part was, of course, the ignorance of Ms. Rodriguez's initial complaint, and the encouragement of her to "react like a woman" and "keep him satisfied." This flies in the face of the EEOC's guidance, which specifically recommends "immediate and appropriate corrective action" in such circumstances.

In addition to possibly being illegal, such disregard for employees' rights can also poison a workplace with anger, jealousy and lack of esteem. Employees should enjoy a positive, supportive work environment. Achieving this goal requires, among other things, a clear understanding on the part of all employees of what is inappropriate conduct in the workplace. The conduct of both Miranda, the customer, and Chavez, the employer, was wholly inappropriate.

Another lesson to be learned from this scenario revolves around the holiday party. Many employers that conduct training fail to mention that a company-sponsored party, like the one in this case, is the workplace, despite the fact that it may be held off-site. This applies to luncheons, softball games and business trips. In general, if your employer sends you to a destination (meeting, party, convention, etc.), then you are in the workplace. This creates issues related to nonemployees because an employee is bound to interact with guests of employees at company parties as well as service people, delivery people, consultants, vendors, etc. in the course of doing his or her job. These people can subject an employer to liability, just like employees can.

Another important point one can glean from this case is the caution an employer must exercise if it decides to fire someone shortly after he or she reports (what could be) illegal activity. An employer in this situation is susceptible to a claim of retaliation if it does so. Many claims that employees file that have both sexual harassment and retaliation included in the allegations fail on the merits of the harassment, but the court still rules for the plaintiff on the count of retaliation. A baseless harassment claim may not preclude a successful allegation of retaliation based on treatment given after the claim is filed.

In the larger picture, it always makes sense to keep good records of employee conversations and employment actions. If circumstances arise in which an employer absolutely does have to fire someone for performance reasons who has also coincidentally filed a grievance or complaint (either internally or in court), that employer should ascertain that it can show that the termination is totally separate and apart from the grievance or complaint.

## THE RIGHT APPROACH

Employers may wonder what they can do to protect themselves. The case of *Dornhecker v. Malibu Grand Prix* illustrates the effectiveness of a prompt response to an employee's complaints. The facts start out similar to the *Rodriguez* and *Lockard* cases. Dornhecker, a new employee, was on a business trip, traveling with a consultant with whom the employer had a longer relationship. During the trip, the consultant did many inappropriate things, including putting his hands on the plaintiff's hips in an airport ticket line, dropping his pants in front of the passengers while waiting to board the plane, touching her breasts and "playfully" choking her when she complained.

Dornhecker responded with appropriate promptness; she confronted her immediate supervisor and told her about the behavior. In response, the president of the company personally reassured Dornhecker that she would not again have to work with the offending consultant. Nevertheless, despite the employer's assurances, Dornhecker resigned immediately and sued her employer.

The court upheld the employer's defense that it had taken prompt corrective action to remedy the harassment by responding to the reported harassment in a prompt and decisive manner, thus shielding it from liability.

Note that the court did not expect the company to sever all ties with the consultant—the separation of the consultant from the employee was viewed by the court as "reasonable steps" that would stop the harassing behavior.

What is truly impressive was the quick turnaround time from notification to response; the company president's reassurance to Dornhecker occurred approximately 12 hours after she had tearfully confronted her immediate supervisor and first acquainted her with the consultant's behavior.

## GUIDELINES FOR PROTECTION

As the court in this case made clear, an employer need not be heroic in its attempts to prevent and/or redress nonemployee sexual harassment. It need only take reasonable steps to stop the harassing behavior.

If an employer does receive a report of harassment committed by a nonemployee, it should treat that claim the same way it would treat any complaint—by investigating it promptly and thoroughly, ensuring confidentiality, and when evidence of harassment exists, take steps to stop the behavior. As a practical matter, this often means a senior manager from the target's employer contacts a senior manager for the contractor or client company (whose employee allegedly committed the harassment) to report the behavior and request assistance in resolving the matter.

Finally, employers should be training all managers and employees in sexual harassment prevention (as discussed at the outset). In assessing a training program, an employer needs to make sure that the curriculum is both accurate *and* complete. In this case, ensure that the program includes instruction on sexual harassment by nonemployees—vendors, independent contractors, customers, volunteers, consultants, etc.

## CONCLUSION

While the appropriate response to these situations will largely depend on the unique facts of each individual case, employers need to keep in mind that they could be liable if they do not respond to an employee's claims of sexual harassment committed by nonemployees. While there is no specific universal response that will give employers total insulation from liability, courts are less likely to impose liability on employers that take prompt and reasonable steps to end the harassment.

## ABSTRACT

## REGULATION OF CONTINGENT AND PART-TIME WORKERS?

*Editor's Comment:* Contingent workers are here to stay. The questions for employers, and for training managers particularly, are focused at this time on the issues of pay/benefit balance and of who's responsible for work done at home and its environment. During 2000, Secretary Alexis Herman's decision and then rescission of a Labor Department regulation regarding home-based workers created a furor among employers and a collective sigh of relief when the ruling was reversed. This was surely an indication of things to come, in that federal laws governing equal employment guarantees and fair labor practices will continue to be interpreted to serve whatever workforce we have. Trainers need to be aware of what's happening on these legal fronts as workers of all stripes need to be informed and trained in knowing the law.

SHRM's *HR News*, January 2000, deals with the issue of balance between employer and worker. It is SHRM's position that employers should have the upper hand when it comes to hiring, paying, and making work assignments for contingent workers. SHRM clearly states that "contingent employment is a legitimate staffing strategy," and the organization "opposes legislation that attempts to regulate, restrict, or interfere in any way with an employer's legitimate use of contingent labor." SHRM believes that the worker's choice regarding working arrangements needs to be balanced against the employer's needs. Such choices include need for supplementary income, career exploration, lifestyle, flexibility, and financial considerations. SHRM's statement is that employers should be protected against "frivolous challenges" as long as the employer undertakes practices that are based on sound business judgment and do not infringe on individual rights (p. 44).

Another issue that faces training managers is that of e-learning time. The Masie Center, Saratoga Springs, NY, is currently collecting information about how to count e-learning time, and who pays for it. At issue, especially, is whether or not the time a contingent worker spends learning online at home counts as billable hours or work time. The June 30, 2000 issue of The Masie Center's online newsletter, *TechLearnTRENDS*, calls on readers to send in case material if they've had experience with either the issue of pay for on-the-job e-learning at home, with workman's compensation for home-based work hours, or for any other legal issue of home-based workers. Training managers can expect to see more of this kind of dialogue in year 2001.

*Sources: TechLearn TRENDS* online newsletter of The Masie Center, June 30, 2000, p. 2; and "SHRM Board Adopts Positions on Contingent and Part-time Workers" in *HR News*, newsletter of the Society for Human Resource Management (SHRM), January 2000, p.44.

## ARTICLE REPRINT

## IS CONGRESS THE ANSWER FOR HIGH-TECH WORKERS?

*Editor's Comment:* The most visible legislative issue regarding information technology (IT) workers has been the H-1B Visa, which allows employers to hire IT workers from other countries to fill the need for workers in the U.S. With so many IT jobs going begging here in our current economy, employers are lobbying heavily in Congress for the numbers of visas to be raised and for the current 7 percent cap from any one country to also be raised. Employers contend that they should be allowed, legislatively, to hire the best and brightest worker from anywhere in the world. Workers from India and China, highly sought after by U.S. firms, currently have to wait several years for H-1B visas under current laws (*The New York Times Magazine*, May 24, 2000, p. 37).

There are other employment issues too, which Congress is wresting with over the regulation of information technology workers. One important one is the issue of teenage workers and their protection under current law. Another is the issue of training and incentives for the preparation of information technology workers in U.S. schools and colleges. Training managers will get involved in these and other issues regarding how to close the worker gap in the information technology industry. The article reprinted here is chock-full of ideas and issues, perhaps the most important of which is just exactly how and how much should Congress get involved in a specialized way on behalf of this industry and these particular kinds of workers.

## LEGISLATING AN IT FIX

### *by Paul Gilster*

Oh, to be young and in IT again! Information technology professionals are in demand as never before. In fact, our colleges and universities are not producing enough of them to meet the need, leading to a continuing reliance on IT talent from overseas. Whether it's a shortage or a crisis depends on your point of view, but evidence both statistical and anecdotal says that an Internet-hungry economy has outrun the available workforce.

What to do? A variety of bills in Congress address the issue. Some are emphatically short-term in their approach, such as attempts to raise the cap on visas for foreign IT workers so that companies can complete planned projects. Others, like the Information Technology Act of 2000, are broader attempts to stimulate American IT training through the use of matching federal funds to back training partnerships. And one bill, SR.456, seeks to give business a lift by offering tax credits for IT training expenses.

These measures have two things in common. They are being considered in the charged atmosphere of an election year, and they address a need that, although debated in its particulars, is felt by HR professionals in businesses in and out of the computer industry. The economy's reliance on information technology has never been greater, and the definition of IT seems to be broadening.

"Information technology has a core: systems analysts, computer scientists, engineers, and programmers," said Marjorie Bynum, vice president for workforce development for the Information Technology Association of America (ITAA). "The Bureau of Labor Statistics only tracks those kinds of jobs. But in today's information economy, support jobs like network administrators, Web developers, and technical support people are also critical to business."

Which is why, when the ITAA released a new study called "Bridging the Gap: Information Technology Skills for a New Millennium," it worked with a broad brush. ITAA found heavy demand for workers with Web-related skills involving electronic commerce and interactive media, and discovered that 50 percent of all IT jobs are in technical support—hardware and software installation, customer service, systems monitoring—and network administration. The spread of technology through the economy means that these jobs are in demand not just at traditional IT firms, but also at any companies that deploy IT resources in their operations.

And here is the heart of the matter: the IT workforce under this broader definition has reached the 10 million mark. Employers will try to fill 1.6 million new IT jobs in 2000. Fully half of those jobs—some 840,000—are likely to go unfilled. That's one job in every 12.

The Computing Technology Industry Association backs up the urgency of the IT demand. In its "Workforce Study for IT Service and Support," released in October, the organization finds that nearly 10 percent of IT service and support positions are unfilled. The Department of Labor finds an additional 350,000 unfilled jobs among programmers, systems analysts, and computer scientists. It's a situation that cries out for long-term solutions.

The Information Technology Act of 2000 (S.R. 2347) is one move in that direction. Introduced in April by Sens. Harry Reid (D-Nev.) and Kent Conrad (D-N.D.), the bill provides $100 million in matching federal grants for partnerships between the private sector and universities or training providers that offer IT training programs. The bill targets a part of the workforce that is underrepresented in IT: women, older people, veterans, Native Americans, dislocated workers, and students who have not completed their high-school education.

An early proponent of S.R. 2347 has been the American Society for Training & Development (ASTD). The organization's recent "State of the Industry Report for 2000" found that training expenses increased eleven percent between 1997 and 1998, and the rise from 1998 to 1999 is projected to come in at 14 percent. The survey, which collected information from 500 organizations around the country, found that the greatest percentage of this additional training was being directed at technical processes involving information technology skills. ASTD sees this as evidence of the importance of IT training.

"The new economy has created a huge demand for individuals with technical skills," said Cynthia Pantazis, director of policy and public leadership at ASTD. "We back the Information Technology Act of 2000 because it acknowledges the importance of building the IT workforce and provides seed money for this critical enterprise."

While S.R. 2347 authorizes $100 million of fiscal year 2001 funds to be administered through the Departments of Education and Labor, it also provides an additional incentive to educators: a $5,000 bonus for teachers who become certified in one or more information technology skills. An additional $100 million would be authorized for this program annually over a five-year period beginning in 2001. On the Senate floor, Conrad cited a study by the National Center for Education Statistics, which found that only 20 percent of public school teachers believe they are well prepared to use technology in the classroom.

At press time, S.R. 2347 had been referred to the Committee on Health, Education, Labor and Pensions. In the House of Representatives, companion bill H.R. 4176 is also in committee. Meanwhile, an older bill, S.R. 456, remains under consideration by the Senate's Committee on Finance. Introduced by Conrad, the bill would create an income tax credit for employers for IT training expenses. Under the provisions of S.R. 456, companies would receive tax credits for 20 percent of their IT training program expenses per year, with additional incentives for programs operating in disadvantaged areas. Companion bill H.R. 838 is now in the House Committee on Ways and Means.

While his organization takes no position on either bill, Robert Loller, who is vice chairman of the board of directors for the International Association for Human Resource Information Management (IHRIM), says that education in IT is crucial. One big reason is the nature of a changing technology, which has brought functions into human resource management that would traditionally have been handled by IT departments. "Fifteen years ago, HR didn't do reports; IT people did reports," said Loller. "Today HR is doing almost anything, including building front ends for programs. We need to deliver education that points up the use of new tools for HR as this process continues."

William Aspray, executive director of the Computing Research Association, takes no position on S.R. 456, but thinks tax incentives are a good idea if they're carefully deployed. The author of *The Supply of Information Technology Workers in the United States*, Aspray is cautious about the IT shortage, noting that its size is hard to measure, although he believes it to be real. And he notes the rapid growth in nontraditional training. "Corporate, for-profit education leads to a caveat emptor. The lack of standards is a problem here. The government can't get into the certification business, but we need rules about what kind of training programs are allowable for tax credits."

While such training and tax-credit issues are debated in Washington, the influx of foreign professionals continues. But tapping talent in India or Ireland—two of the rare countries that actually have a surplus of IT workers—creates its own problems. For one thing, it fills jobs that American workers could occupy, a fact noted by some labor unions as well as organizations like the Institute of Electrical and Electronics Engineers (IEEE). While IEEE-USA supports S.R. 456, it has proposed reforming the H-1B visa program rather than simply increasing the existing cap on foreign workers.

Under existing law, 115,000 visas for such workers can be issued by the Immigration and Naturalization Service (INS) each year, using rules adopted by Congress in 1998. H-1B visas allow workers to remain in the United States for up to six years. So heavy has the demand been for foreign IT skills that the INS announced in March that it would accept no more petitions for fiscal year 2000, which ends September 30. This has led to calls for Congress to raise the H-1B ceiling. The Senate Judiciary Committee, for example, approved a bill, S.R. 2045, that would raise the cap to 195,000 visas for each of the next three fiscal years.

Other bills have been proposed, offering a variety of solutions but generally raising caps close to 200,000. As Congress weighs these issues, even supporters of a raised visa cap see an increase as nothing more than a short-term solution to the IT labor problem. Deron Zeppelin, director of

governmental affairs for the Society for Human Resources Management (SHRM), likens the situation to that of a baseball team that needs to find new talent. "We simply have no minor league system for this type of worker," Zeppelin said. "Our farm club is now made up of people who need visas. This is a situation we have to reverse. We believe the visa cap must be raised, but in the long run, we have to go to work in our schools to encourage students to get into math and science so they can fill these jobs."

Longer-term solutions to encourage training and IT education are much on the minds of a group known as the Technology Workforce Coalition. More than 100 companies have joined this effort to address the IT labor shortage at both the federal and state level. The coalition advocates a higher H-1B ceiling, but it is also an active supporter of S.R. 456, and it directs lobbying efforts on a state-by-state basis. In April, the first state-level IT training tax credit bill was passed in Arizona, and efforts to pass similar legislation are under way in North Carolina, Maryland, California, Washington, Pennsylvania, and Texas.

"Government alone cannot solve this shortage," said coalition manager Grant Mydland. "With the workforce changing so rapidly, the people with the best opportunity to affect the pipeline of workers are in the private sector. They know the who, what and where of their situation better than anyone else. So if we can provide a 20 percent tax credit through a public/private partnership, that leaves 80 percent still paid for by the private sector. It's still in their hands, but the result of the credit is to provide incentive to increase IT training."

While action on the IT labor issue has been slower than some would have wished, the odds on passage of both bills may be improved by the upcoming election. Stephen Rohleder, managing partner USA government for Anderson Consulting, notes that the demand for IT workers is becoming obvious at both the state and federal levels. Universities in particular are hard hit because they must compete with the commercial sector, now dominated by dot.com start-ups paying salaries the schools can't match.

But Rohleder expects action on these issues this year. "Information technology—training, attracting jobs, and growing our GDP around technology—is a bipartisan issue. Nobody in the administration or on Capitol Hill opposes the expansion of our IT workforce. By the time the year is over, legislators will be pushing to see who can take credit for passing these bills the fastest."

If Rohleder is right, the latter half of 2000 should have seen significant progress on this issue. Readers eager to track the progress of these bills can do so on the Internet at thomas. loc.gov/home/c106query.html, which provides search facilities for pending legislation. And the main Thomas server (thomas.loc.gov) provides not just legislation information but also links to Web pages and addresses for all members of the House and Senate. The Technology Workforce Coalition also maintains updates and background information on its Web site (techcoalition.org).

For HR professionals, the opportunities to be heard on this issue are numerous, whether through letters and e-mail to Congress or pushing for state-to-state action. "HR people should take an active role in this," said ITAA's Marjorie Bynum. "This isn't just IT legislation; it affects any organization that maintains an IT position that needs training. We advocate working with your local congressman, writing letters, and making a difference."

# 3

# TRAINING PROGRAM DESIGN

# INTRODUCTION TO TRAINING PROGRAM DESIGN: SECTION 3

Training program design has been front and center in numerous publications this year. Many companies of all sorts have now had solid experience in creating online training, in working with technology and instructional design vendors for help, in networking in new ways within their organizations for design collaborations, in figuring out how to blend the best of classroom training with the promise of Web-based training, and in making mistakes. In this section, we provide articles and other entries to help you make sense of the profusion of action in the design area.

### BUILDING A LEARNING INFRASTRUCTURE

The foundation of discussion of all of the design issues is the issue of building a learning infrastructure. This fundamental concern is given heightened awareness this year because of the essential difference between online learning and classroom learning. Adding to the pressures on trainers is the push from vendors and consultants who offer design help, from information technology departments who often see online training design initiatives as competition for corporate funds, from marketers and executives who want their companies to be seen as embracing the latest trends.

Those responsible for building a new learning infrastructure are finding that it takes time, money, talent, resources, and support. Today's training program designers first need to figure out ways to work within these constraints and find internal and external design partners in many different places. The environment today in which instructional designers work is vastly more complex than the focus on course design for classroom delivery of just a few years ago.

### DESIGN CONCEPTS FOR E-LEARNING

In this subsection, we focus on the design concepts for e-learning. The year 2000 marked great strides in designing for Web-based and other kinds of online learning, now mostly referred to as "e-learning." Instructional designers, having had some solid experience in e-learning design, are beginning to publish results of their experiences and are articulating some of the important ideas in this kind of instructional design. Four entries, three article reprints and one book review, illustrate the breadth and depth of thinking about the design concepts for e-learning.

### DESIGN FOR SKILLS IMPROVEMENT

In this subsection, we've chosen four entries that highlight some specific design skills discovered or developed in response to learners' needs for the kind of blended computerized-and-classroom training. These four entries represent a range of organizations and learning challenges typical of our times. Our entries also represent a range of corporate goals: productivity, profit, quality, safety, and the more personal goals of improved basic skills and computer literacy, better communication, and the motivation for continual learning. We've chosen entries that focus on various how-to techniques and skills.

### DESIGN TECHNOLOGIES FOR E-LEARNING

This final subsection of Training Program Design focuses more on the features and effects of learning technologies and provides ideas and techniques for solving some of the problems experience has defined over the last year. "Learning technologies" is a broad term, encompassing the design systems such as the Instructional System Design (ISD) system or its adaptation, the Performance Technology System; including traditional and newer models of cognition and communication; and especially focusing on the characteristics of the Internet, the World Wide Web, CD-ROMs, and all sorts of video—technical and hardware characteristics as well as design and software characteristics. "Technologies" mean various things to those responsible for using them.

Perhaps a brief report on learning research projects newly funded by Hewlett-Packard found in *TechLearn TRENDS* newsletter from The MASIE Center, June 16, 2000 can illustrate best the current interest in and range of definitions of design technologies for e-learning. HP's new projects include

- *How adult learners acquire knowledge in Net-centric environments*; research grant to University of Texas Austin in collaboration with Norwegian University of Science and Technology

- *Models for integrating technology into problem-based learning*; research grant to University of Oslo, Norway

- *Best practices in designing a Web-based curriculum*; research grant to University of Lige, Belgium

- *Exploring the applications of mobile phones for e-learning*; research grant to the Global Learning Center of Tokyo Metropolitan Institute of Technology

- *Effectiveness of e-learning among working adults*; research grant to the India Management Association.

In this subsection we deal with some of the design challenges inherent in the use of learning technologies.

# 3A. BUILDING A LEARNING INFRASTRUCTURE

## ABSTRACT

## CRITICAL FUNCTIONS OF A DIGITAL BUSINESS

*Editor's Comment*: With so much talk this year about knowledge management systems, managers, information technology specialists, and instructional designers are experimenting with database and communications tools in new and promising ways. At the foundation level of the system design for knowledge management is a need for collaboration and, yes, even marketing in order to build a learning infrastructure in organizations and throughout companies.

The global enterprise is demanding a digital learning infrastructure. A recent Conference Board Study (Report #1262-00-RR) indicated that 80 percent of the survey's 200 executives from 158 large multinational companies had some sort of knowledge management program underway, although a much smaller percentage (6 percent) could call their program "organization-wide."

Trainers who seek a role in creating a learning infrastructure in their companies are being constantly prodded to focus on business results, and to devise systems within which to work that lead to a valued business outcome because of the quality of learning and the value of a knowledge asset. Internet-based learning systems are being defined that include front-end design processes and delivery, back-end administration and support, feedback, service, and follow-up communication and help on demand. Many business and training publications this year have ventured into suggesting the designs for such digital learning infrastructure. Creating the learning environment is at least as important as designing the individual training. Learning is being both pulled and pushed into a digital business framework.

One interesting and clear representation of a digital business system is that created by graphics company xplane.com in the February 2000 issue of the computer magazine, *Business 2.0*. The detailed and bright graphic covers two pages in the magazine. The focus of this "digital assembly line" is a representation of the key functions of the "ecommerce engine," a system that is similar in many ways to a digital learning system. These are the eight key functions:

1. *Attract:* The system must have a function whose sole purpose is to bring customers (or learners in the case of a learning system) into an electronic marketplace.

2. *Inform:* Once customers (or learners) are at a Web site, they need to find relevant content; content mediators or agents can assist.

3. *Customize:* Order, assemble, fulfill, and deliver—these are the old-economy functions of getting product to consumer. They are also the functions of a customized and self-controlled new-economy way of doing things. Think of the Dell Computer model of configuring your own PC; configuring your own training based on mix-and-match components is the same design process. Digital learning technologies enable much more intelligent self-designed, and useful, learning opportunities.

---

*Source:* "The New eCommerce Engine" graphic by xplane in *Business 2.0*, February 2000, pp. 114–115. *Business 2.0* is published by Imagine Media, Inc., Brisbane, CA. Xplane can be reached at *www.xplane.com*.

4. *Transact:* Salesmen throughout the history of commerce have sought to perfect the process of closing of the deal. E-commerce this year particularly has shown the world several viable transaction models: auctions, barter, catalogs, and, of course, discount coupons for online transactions. Builders of the learning infrastructure also need to be thinking of analogous transaction drivers—closers of the deal of engaging in learning.

5. *Pay:* When the deal is closed, the money exchanges hands. This is true in purchasing products or services online, and it should be true for purchasing training online too. An e-commerce model just might be a useful way to at last get training out of the doldrums of being a cost center, and finally turn it into being a profit center.

6. *Interact:* After the customer is on board with an e-commerce product in hand, customer support begins. Customers need reassurance, information, advice, problem solving, and follow-up of many kinds. Help desks, call centers, live online customer service are all adaptable to a learner's situation as a new "leaning customer." Trainers can learn some lessons from e-commerce product support and customer interaction processes.

7. *Deliver:* Order fulfillment and supply/demand forecasting are typical product processes. These are more and more being handled by electronic agents that collect and interpret data from sales. Training administration and testing software programs are often performing these functions; the processes are similar, but have more business cachet when seen as part of a digital business system.

8. *Personalize:* Electronic profiling can be used for good or for ill; in the context of enabling the provider of service (including learning service) to analyze the behavior patterns and/or needs of the customer (or learner) in the name of being able to provide more personalized, efficient and effective service the next time.

## CASE STUDY

### A DOWNSIZED AETNA FIGURES IT OUT

*Editor's Comment*: A few years ago, Aetna's famed Institute for Corporate Education had a staff of 130 educators and support staff responsible largely for management training throughout the Hartford-based company. Now, a downsized and changed management development effort has a staff of 8 educators (p. 36). This is a short case study of the new management training at Aetna Financial Services. These are some of the ways in which the necessary work is still getting done, with a different focus to the learning infrastructure and a boost from technology.

### CHOOSING FROM THE MENU

Instead of the typical linear curriculum of management courses, Aetna decided to offer a menu of learning opportunities to be chosen by managers as they needed them.

### WHAT AND HOW

Aetna's managers can now choose not only the specific content they need—and no more— but they can also choose how they want to participate in learning activities.

### MIX AND MATCH

The new perspective is to offer a combination of traditional book- or classroom- learning and technology-mediated learning. Among the list of opportunities are:

- e-mailed case studies for managers to study and discuss via conference call or online chat
- reading groups for leaders in which managers discuss current articles and business books
- 1-hour issue groups, presenter-led or discussion, on various current human resources issues
- handbooks and toolbooks on new concepts and techniques
- half-day workshops on traditional management soft skills
- supervisory network meeting 40 hours over the course of 1 year
- online documentation of all programs for individual review at any time

### ONGOING SUPPORT

Learning support includes individual needs assessment for managers, mentoring from persons within the company, coaching from outside, management support networks as needed.

*Source:* "Building Better Bosses" by Shari Caudron in *Workforce*, May 2000, pp. 32–39, especially the case study of Aetna Financial Services, pp. 36–37. Shari Caudron is a Contributing Editor for *Workforce*.

# CASE STUDY

## QUALCOMM'S $5,200 ANNUAL PER-PERSON LEARNING ALLOWANCE

*Editor's Comment*: QUALCOMM is a 6,000 employee company which invented CDMA, code division multiple access, technology that's used in digital wireless communication. The company is the winner of *Workforce*'s "Optimas 2000 Award for Service." It is a company with an unusually high commitment to continual learning. "Training, employee self-service, and competency management" are what gives QUALCOMM its competitive advantage, according to its human resources leaders. This article provides details of this company's broad and deep approach to training.

## Keyboard Courses at Work or Home

### by Samuel Greengard

Inside the offices of QUALCOMM Inc., San Diego, a senior electrical engineer is sitting in a cubicle tapping away on a computer keyboard. At the moment, she's not calculating complex formulas or designing the next generation of wireless chips. She's simply viewing her personnel records and taking stock of her accomplishments via the company intranet. With the click of a mouse, she can review the courses and training modules she has already completed, and see what's required for a promotion. The information is customized for her specific position.

After spending a few minutes perusing course descriptions, the engineer clicks on an e-form to make a selection: she opts for a business management course that's conducted through the corporate intranet. In an instant, she's able to receive course materials, including videos, slides, and interactive quizzes. What's more, she is able to log on from home or while on the road. It's efficient, it's painless, and it is helping QUALCOMM dial into the 21st century.

It's no secret that many organizations have turned to computer-based training (CBT) and distance learning over the last few years. According to some estimates, it's now in excess of a $1.5 billion industry. But few have focused their energies as ambitiously as QUALCOMM, the inventor of code division multiple access (CDMA) technology that's used for digital wireless communication throughout the U.S. and beyond.

The 6,000-plus-employee firm—which also sells Eudora e-mail software and until recently manufactured digital mobile phones—now offers more than 250 course modules online. These range from basic word processing to technical design and engineering. QUALCOMM also offers employees the opportunity to obtain an MBA through San Diego State University and a master's in electrical engineering through the University and a master's in electrical engineering through the University of Southern California's distance learning program.

"Because our founders come from an academic background," says Dawn Ridz, a human resources specialist at QUALCOMM, "we've always been committed to education through continual learning and training. The organization's entrepreneurial spirit, which focuses on education and learning, is essential within such a highly competitive arena. Over the years, that philosophy has become deeply ingrained in the mindset and culture."

That you can credit to Irwin M. Jacobs, a 66-year-old former Massachusetts Institute of Technology engineering professor who co-founded the company in 1985 and has built it into a telecommunications industry powerhouse. Jacobs, the firm's chief executive, believes that ongoing learning and profits go hand in hand. And who's to argue? Last year, QUALCOMM's sales topped $3.9 billion, with an 85 percent profit increase. The firm's digital technology has been adopted as a global standard for next-generation wireless cell phones. It receives a license fee almost every time a digital phone is sold.

## THEY KNOW THEIR STUFF

At QUALCOMM's sprawling campus of 18 buildings near UC San Diego, that might seem like reason to celebrate. But within the firm's offices, labs, and research facilities, it's business as usual. And in this case that means employees taking courses. Lots and lots of courses. Last year, the firm tallied just shy of 94,000 hours of classroom training and tens of thousands of hours more of online instruction.

Employees—including those at offices in Boulder, Indianapolis, Winston-Salem, Portland, and Santa Clara, and in Israel—learn about an array of business and technical topics, including finance for non-finance managers, goal setting, negotiation, conflict resolution, business writing, creativity and innovation, and a slew of technical and engineering topics.

The program falls into four general categories:

1. Technical CDMA courses, which total 10 topics (9 classroom based and 1 CD-ROM)

2. Computer training-engineering courses, 61 total topics (49 classroom based and 33 online)

3. Manufacturing courses, 17 total topics (17 classroom based and 2 online)

4. Professional/management development, 37 total topics (36 classroom based and 12 online).

From the beginning, QUALCOMM's goal has been to provide cutting-edge training that fits different learning schedules, says Ridz. That meant making some courses available online 24/7. It meant addressing different learning styles by providing conventional classrooms as well as computers. And it meant customizing the online instruction to fit QUALCOMM's culture and critical business needs. Ridz notes that classroom instructors are top experts in their fields and that CBT and other training materials are viewed as alternatives to classroom learning. Consequently, some courses are offered both online and in the classroom.

Managing courses and content is not simple matter, however. That's why QUALCOMM uses so-called Learning Specialists to track the needs of various business units. These individuals monitor staff meetings, meet regularly with senior management, and conduct group needs assessments. Once specialists identify a new training need, they work with vendors and management to define a course and create appropriate and unique content. "Material that's covered in a course is specifically tailored to QUALCOMM," Ridz explains.

Then, it's up to employees to boost their skills and competencies. Leaders of various business units determine which courses, if any, are mandatory (most required courses center on business management, and supervisors offer advice, suggestions, and coaching along the way.

"If a supervisor feels that an employee's presentation skills or database skills could use improvement, then it's likely that he or she will suggest that the individual sign up," Ridz explains.

However, many courses are entirely optional and help build expertise that can benefit the person on the job and in a career. As an added incentive, QUALCOMM offers an annual education allowance of $5,200 per employee.

But QUALCOMM doesn't stop there. One thing that makes the program so effective is that it is tightly integrated into a competency management initiative. Early on, QUALCOMM introduced MySource, an intranet-based self-service tool that lets employees access their records and analyze their skills and accomplishments. By viewing requirements for specific positions, individuals can map out career options and then partake of the appropriate training leading up to the promotion.

Managers, on the other hand, benefit from being aware of the learning needs of individuals, teams, and entire departments. It's then possible to slot employees into specific classes. The MySource system—built in-house by QUALCOMM—ties into a PeopleSoft database to track the information across the corporation. That also lets supervisors use the information for performance appraisals, strategic planning, and deploying personnel.

Sitting at a computer, employees typically log on to the corporate intranet, surf through course offerings, and, with a few clicks, enroll in the desired classes. There's no cumbersome registration process and no paperwork. MySource automates everything and even provides assistance about what courses might be relevant, on the basis of a person's job title or skills. A portion of the system called My Development displays a list of classes in which an employee is already enrolled and courses already passed, along with the dates.

Yet the program offers enough flexibility to let employees obtain training material on a just-in-time basis. Instead of a manager signing up for a course on coaching or conflict resolution and waiting three weeks, he can access a short-course and obtain valuable information on the spot.

Says Ridz: "By dealing with issues as they arise, it's possible to resolve things far more effectively. If there's too long a delay getting needed information or knowledge, a manager can be at a tremendous disadvantage."

The objective, says Ridz, "is to make things easier for employees while providing the level of information and learning that the organization requires." Like many other companies, QUALCOMM has discovered that centralized training often isn't cost effective. Fly hundreds of employees a year into a central training site, put them up in hotels, bury them with binders filled with paperwork, and the cost can easily run into millions of dollars.

According to Brandon Hall, editor and publisher of *Multimedia and Internet Training Newsletter*, it's not uncommon for online training to slash the cost of a program by 50 to 70 percent. "Traditional training is labor and capital intensive. Although it can provide a huge payoff, it doesn't come without a tremendous amount of corporate resources," he explains.

QUALCOMM's online coursework harnesses the power of the Web along with the ability of PCs to provide an interactive experience. For example, hyperlinks let employees jump through complex documents and obtain definitions and more information, when appropriate. Text, photographs, illustrations, videos, audio, and quizzes help employees master a set of skills or specific knowledge before moving on to another topic.

And so that QUALCOMM can continually refine the program, participants fill out online evaluations at the completion of a module or course. The most common questions become part of FAQs (frequently asked questions), and content is continually tweaked. "We're constantly looking for ways to refine and improve the overall program," Ridz points out.

One of the biggest advantages for employees, she adds, is that online coursework doesn't set arbitrary limitations about time. QUALCOMM's employees increasingly are attending courses in the evenings, on weekends, and while traveling—allowing them to better juggle their daily workloads and balance work-life issues. And because the program offers "information on demand," workers aren't subjected to sitting in a classroom simply because an instructor and classroom were available at a particular time. They can take breaks, cope with interruptions, and learn as needed.

## EVERYBODY WINS IN THE END

Make no mistake, QUALCOMM is doing all it can to ensure that its employees are wired for the future. In an era when knowledge is key, it's unlocking the full potential of its workforce through training, employee self-service, and competency management.

"Ongoing learning is one of the things that gives us a competitive advantage," Ridz explains. "It offers enormous benefits for QUALCOMM and all the company's employees. It has played a large role in defining the company and leading to our success."

# ABSTRACT

## THE UNITED NATIONS' MILLENNIUM PROCLAMATION OF UNIVERSAL ACCESS

*Editor's Comment*: In September 2000, leaders from all over the world met at the United Nations in New York for a "Millennium Summit." Among the many reports and proclamations that were made was one by a panel of experts to the full Assembly that the international community had the capability to reverse the alarming trend of the growing "digital divide" between have- and have-not nations. The report challenged the world to ensure universal connectivity by the year 2004, and recommended $500 million in funding from governments and other entities to accomplish this. "Reasonable" public access to computers is the goal, not necessarily through a computer in every home, but rather through access in public institutions open to the public at large such as libraries and government extension offices.

The panel recommended that the United Nations proclaim . . . *"the right of universal access to information and communications services such as the Internet as an important new component of the United Nations principles and conventions on human rights and development."*

Following are some of the statistics reported by the panel of experts:

- As of March 2000, approximately 276 million people were users of the Internet.

- Approximately 150,000 new persons per day are added to the list of users.

- Web pages total about 1.5 billion, with 2 million new pages per day added.

- Web commerce is expected to exceed $7 trillion by 2004.

- As of March 2000, about 220 million devices were accessing the World Wide Web, and this number has been growing by 200,000 new devices daily.

*Source:* "U.N. Urged to Proclaim Net Access a Human Right" (no author given), in *Distance Education Report* newsletter, July 15, 2000, p. 8. It is published by Magna Publications Inc., Madison, WI. *www.magnapubs.com*

# 3B. DESIGN CONCEPTS FOR E-LEARNING

## ARTICLE REPRINT

## AN ACADEMIC'S VIEW OF NEW DESIGNS

*Editor's Comment:* This fine essay by Edward Tenner helps to set the tone for the three design entries that follow it. As Tenner suggests, in times like these turn-of-the-Millennium days of explosive growth of innovation, the challenges of new ideas are many and unforeseen. He suggests that along with the material side of innovation, that is, technology, there is " a more elusive but equally important behavioral side, or technique." Because we are human as we devise new designs, we are influenced politically, socially, culturally, personally, and simply by the laws of chance so that we often "transform inventions" in ways we cannot foresee. Like others before him who advocate "never throw away your boomerang," Tenner subscribes to the "first rule of intelligent tinkering," which is to "save all the pieces" (p. 76). Tenner's insights apply to innovation in learning design, and provide an excellent conceptual view for today's instructional designers.

## WE THE INNOVATORS

### *by Edward Tenner*

Life must be lived forward but understood backward, declared Kierkegaard. Science and technology are no exception. The way to verify our sense of what will be is to live long enough to experience it. In the here and now, our only recourse is to look to the past, groping for analogies. Hindsight shows us that a theory may spark a brilliant stroke—the next transistor, for example—or launch a fiasco like the Soviet discovery in the 1960s of a new state of $H_2O$ called polywater. An idea could be as fundamental as movable type—or as evanescent as the mimeograph.

The explosive growth of new ideas makes these comparisons harder rather than easier. Of hundreds or thousands of concepts that promise to be revolutionary, most will have some hidden flaw or excessive cost. Of the remainder that are technically sound, some will fail polit-

ically, socially, or culturally. And of the rest that could work, only a few will have a major, lasting influence on our lives. Personality and chance may count for more than elegance or effectiveness. They are qualities that can tip the scales. Scientific and technical life can be unfair.

**First came Sears.** Julius Comroe, a physician and medical historian, pointed to the value of the past with the wonderful word "retrospectroscope." Not long ago at a library sale, I found a book that brought home the meaning of that term: a facsimile reprint of the Sears, Roebuck & Co. catalog of 1897, all 786 pages of it. It is a mirror not only of how Americans lived a hundred years ago but of how we see our future today. Sears was the Web merchant of its day, claiming to process between 10,000 and 20,000 letters a day. It had risen just as quickly: It had

---

*Source:* "We the Innovators" as essay by Edward Tenner in *U.S. News & World Report*, January 3/January 10, 2000, pp. 74–6. Edward Tenner is a visiting researcher in the geosciences department at Princeton University, Princeton, NJ, and the author of a book, *Why Things Bite Back* (Knopf.). Reprinted with permission of *U.S. News & World Report*, copyright January 2000, *U.S. News & World Report*. Visit is at our Website *www.usnews.com* for additional inforation.

been incorporated only two years earlier in 1895. Like today's start-ups, it fought ingeniously against its older competitors. The Sears catalog was formatted, for example, to be slightly smaller than that of Montgomery Ward, so that consumers would stack the one atop the other. Sears appealed to consumers in the very same ways that we see in today's television and print advertising for electronic commerce. Just as some of our Web-based businesses lampoon their conventional rivals as seedy, overpriced bumblers, Sears decried the "unreasonable" profits of conventional retailers. It accused jewelers, for example, of spending their days gossiping with neighbor merchants and reading newspapers when they were not "cleaning and polishing . . . the old shopworn goods" to deceive customers. Sears promised absolute honesty and superior service by a staff of up to 700. The catalog, which Sears called "The Consumers' Guide," even suggested that most merchandise would be ordered direct by mail in the near future. Behind this claim was a communication revolution comparable to the Web a hundred years later: While shipments over 4 pounds had to travel by railroad express or freight, catalogs and correspondence could now travel inexpensively throughout the United States, thanks to rural free delivery, inaugurated in 1896. (Even globalization is not new. Sears claimed many international orders.) Like today's Amazon.com, Sears loved to boast about the size of its inventory, in Sears's case a five-story building occupying a whole Chicago city block. Sears claimed to offer "everything in books." Its cavernous stockrooms adorn the catalog pages. Sears even sold a large line of groceries. The people of 1897 believed they were shutting out intermediaries, going directly to the cornucopia of consumer goods that, on the catalog cover, poured out onto the American farmland.

We are no longer living in a mainly rural country where "every farmer, ranchman, and mechanic can be his own blacksmith" (and cobbler and harness maker), as the catalog promised. But many of the controversies of this turn of the century are already visible. Doubtful medical information and addictive drugs? There were pages of patent remedies and even tincture of opium (laudanum). Cheap firearms on the street? The "Department of Revolvers" offered the Defender ("safe and reliable") for 68 cents plus a dime for postage.

But what of all the vast changes over a century and those to come? For these, too, an old catalog can help ask the central question: Why do the great innovations turn out to be such surprises? It is not because the science or technology is necessarily new. It is because along with the material side of innovation, technology, there is a more elusive but equally important behavioral side: technique. Objects don't materialize and change life. Rather, people find unexpected ways of using new things, ones the inventors might not have taken seriously. There is no saxophone among the catalog's musical instruments, though it had been invented in France decades earlier, mainly for military bands and symphony orchestras. Swing and jazz musicians reinvented the sax. And many brilliant ideas remain curiosities because they require exceptional technique. The theremin, a 1920s electronic instrument that ultimately led to today's advanced music technology, had no moving parts but demanded such perfect pitch that only a few musicians could ever use it for concerts.

Communicating, like making music, demands techniques that change over time. All the instruments in the catalog were still acoustical, but telephones were also on sale there. Of course there were constant refinements, but users were already developing techniques for using a phone—the unwritten conventions and etiquette of conversations—which have not changed radically since then. These techniques remain even more important than the technological possibilities of communication. For example, the video telephone, already imagined by the French science fiction writer Albert Robida in 1883, was demonstrated as early as the 1964 World's Fair in New York. Home units were available early in the 1990s, and there are now inexpensive cameras and microphones that make Web conversations possible. But there is still no stampede to use them. Why? The camera would add an unwelcome burden to the technique of conversation. You would need to look your best, be careful about facial expressions (you're being recorded), and perhaps be forced to tidy up the visible background.

Automobiles existed in 1897 but do not appear in the catalog; they were still for wealthy urbanites. Henry Ford's genius was less in the technology than in the technique of car manufacture and design. He not only organized new workers to assemble the cars; he turned automobiles into tough, versatile powerhouses of rural America, with drive shafts that could work wonders with farm machinery. The Model T and other easily serviceable cars in turn helped educate a generation of Americans to be master tinkerers. Today some bold people still tweak automotive software for improved performance, but unlike Henry Ford, manufacturers now frown on modifications that might expose them to liability. The world of Ford, and of the Sears catalog, was amazingly open. There was even a page of watchmaking tools. The early 21st century at least will be a time of opaque assemblies, components that can only be diagnosed and swapped, not fixed or improved. Today's major applications-software packages are written by teams often so large that no single person fully understands them.

The relationship of technology to technique is not limited to how people use and change things. Even more important can be the new and unexpected patterns of living that arise because of them. Thomas Edison's incandescent electric light—now the archetype of the brilliant ideas—appears nowhere in the catalog, but central stations and wiring had already been spreading through the world's great cities for over a decade. The light bulb seemed to be a cleaner and safer alternative to gas jets and oil lamps, but in time it was much more. Just as the railroad was closing America's spatial frontier, the electric light was opening a temporal frontier, as the sociologist Murray Melbin has observed. Before it, the high cost of illumination dictated the rhythms of day and night and ensured that most people slept between nine and 10 hours a day. Shift work was rare.

**Sleep deprived.** The electrical age that Edison inaugurated opened up the night for new kinds of entertainment, from the cinema to the Internet. According to the National Sleep Foundation, Americans are getting 20 percent less sleep than they did a century ago. The Web encourages long hours even more than television because it is fastest late at night. And the pace of competition requires more people to support the 24-hour, 7-day-a-week style of electronic commerce. Most of the hot firms' employees are not affluent technical staff but front-line warehouse and customer support workers. A memo announcing a midnight e-mail-answering marathon at one of these

companies bore the headline "You Can Sleep When You're Dead." High school and college students are chronically sleep deprived, but that did not prevent one Ivy League career services director from recommending a Web recruiting site as "a valuable resource for students, who, if they so choose, can do all their job searching at 3 a.m." And as technology promotes sleeplessness, it also makes it more dangerous, whether in medical staff, equipment operators, or drivers. Today's $300 clock radios may be more polite buglers than Sears's $1.40 "Must Get Up" alarm clock of 1897, but the message is the same.

The revolution of the workplace does not seem evident in the Sears book, which has no fountain pens, let alone typewriters. Still, the catalog portends our time, and at least the near future: It ushers in the great age of paper. Early in the personal-computer era, futurists dreamed of paperless offices. Some still believe the Web will save trees. But they did not reckon with the techniques that arise in response to electronic technology. IBM passed up a chance to invest in the Xerox Corp. because its consultants saw dry copiers as replacements for the relatively small number of Photostat machines and did not realize the hundreds of new applications that users would find, including new genres of art. Laser and inkjet printers, the latest incarnations of dry copying, are used to process only a tiny proportion of all electronic data. But because the data are expanding so fast, more and more sheets are printed. High-contrast, flat-screen monitors are on their way, but it is not clear that any design will ensure both sharp text and bright color soon. More people will be getting their financial statements online, but they will want to run paper copies just to be safe. And one of the fastest-growing categories of computer products is premium-priced decorated and textured paper for promotional advantages missing in a Web site on a monitor.

Technique makes a vast difference among designers as well as among users. The products in the Sears catalog had to be designed with drafting instruments like the ones it sold. Today's electronic tools, computer-assisted design (CAD) and computer-assisted manufacturing (CAM), make possible objects and structures that would have astounded the people of 1897, from Chuck Hoberman's spiky polyhedrons that miraculously self-expand into spheres to Frank Gehry's stunning buildings. The crucial element is not the machine but the creative ability to get the machine to do something new, something the machine's inventor probably did not think of. And innovation is often best when necessity or luck brings people into new fields. Consider the sneaker, early versions of which Sears was already selling. Many of the people who transformed athletic shoes in the 1970s and 1980s were strangers to the footwear industry. Nike's rise, for example, depended not only on Steve Prefontaine and Michael Jordan but also on coaches (Bill Bowerman), biologists (Ned Frederick), aerospace engineers (Frank Rudy), and architects (Tinker Hatfield). This is not new; Samuel Morse was a renowned painter before he turned to invention. But design revolutions are likely to be even more feasible in the future—and more perilous. It's one thing for a radically new running shoe to break down prematurely, as many early models did. It's another for new bridges and buildings to fail after a decade or two because simulations could not anticipate long-term changes in materials, uses, or environmental conditions.

The hidden long-term risks of new designs remind us that the Web economy is still so new that it is hard to say how robust it is. The original 1897 Sears catalog and other 19th-century reading materials have been crumbling because the hidden price of cheap paper was excessive acidity, which slowly destroys it. But even the poorly printed image has staying power. In the mid-1960s a history professor tracked down a rare remaining copy of the catalog and arranged a reprint edition. Now there are again thousands of copies, each of which might be a master for a new reprinting. Microfilming and photocopying to archival-grade materials can preserve images for 300 years or longer. But can we say the same of documents of the Web economy? The electronic world, unlike the printed record, is evanescent. In 1996 I participated in a Discovery Channel online summit on technology and design, produced by a gifted interviewer and marvelous designers. By 1998 it was unavailable on the Discovery Channel Web site. There is a commercial Web archive that downloads millions of Web pages and deposits tapes with the Library of Congress. The symposium may or may not be on one of the tapes or the company's servers. Suppose it is. Who will pay for accessing tapes? If copyrighted photographs were originally licensed by the sites for only a year or two, as those of the summit reportedly were, is it even legal to put them back on line? (Imagine a printed book with self-destructing illustrations and footnotes.)

**Links to nowhere.** What will happen when online formats and browsers change, and then change again? Knowledge is imploding as well as exploding. Of course, some of the process is social forgetting; today's *Encyclopaedia Britannica* is not much longer than its predecessor listed a hundred years ago in the Sears book, partly because some subjects have been dropped to make way for others. But technological oblivion is a different and newer threat. No more hardware exists for some old tape formats. Devices only a few years old, like my Avatar Shark removable drive, can be suddenly orphaned when their makers go out of business. Floppy disks, magnetic tape (including video recordings), and even CD-ROMs are all decaying insidiously. Old software for converting archaic, i.e., 20-year-old, file formats won't work on current machines; their clock speeds are much too high. Commercial data archivists and librarians are discussing ways out, but they are far from a solution. Indeed, at least one prominent site devoted to the preservation of Web data has several links to vanished pages.

Why wring our hands about the fate of obsolete information at the beginning of a new millennium? It's because we never can anticipate what posterity will want to know. The rediscovery of a text of Archimedes—visible thanks to new imaging technology—excites not just historians but mathematicians, who find inspiration in his methods. Yesterday's codes and ciphers offer ideas for today's and tomorrow's cryptographers. The treatises of 19th-century biologists are vital for preserving the genetic diversity that we will need for the next millennium's crops and pharmaceuticals. The technologies and techniques of the future will almost certainly continue to need small but crucial parts of our heritage. My Sears catalog reprint will always remind me of the naturalist Aldo Leopold's dictum: The first rule of intelligent tinkering is to save all the pieces.

# ARTICLE REPRINT

## THE INTERNATIONAL SPACE STATION'S CASE FOR LINEAR NAVIGATION

*Editor's Comment:* Accuracy, clarity, and choice: These are the criteria for NASA's Space Flight Center lesson maps, based on a linear and 'just-in-time' Web-based instructional design for its International Space Station training. We include this article here because it is bravely in defense of linear organization and minimal interactivity.

## NAVIGATION FOR "JUST-IN-TIME" WEB-BASED TRAINING

### *by Liz Stagg*

For most Web-based training environments, conventional wisdom dictates that the more interactivity and branching options included in a course, the better. Drag and drop exercises, drill and practice, question and answer, hypertext, and hypermedia are among the strategies used by experienced instructional designers to reinforce learning by actively engaging trainees in course content. In contrast, courses developed with a linear organization and minimal activity are often dismissed as being little more than electronic books. Such courses may be described with a degree of scorn as being mere "page-turners." However, one type of training that benefits from having a serial pattern of instruction with limited interactivity is just-in-time training.

Just-in-time training must be structured such that it provides the exact content the learner needs, delivered precisely at the time it is needed. For this type of instruction, ease of navigation, rather than extensive branching and interactivity, has the greater impact on training effectiveness. For example, immediately before technicians in the field must execute a unique maintenance operation, they need to be able to

access the precise procedure to do the job. Once the technician selects the process from a Web-based menu, the monitor displays instructional text supported by a demonstration in the form of a videoclip. Users must feel confident that they will be able to find what they need without having to wade through layers of menus and submenus. Quizzes and interactive exercises are not necessary because the trainee will apply the information immediately after the training has occurred.

## NAVIGATIONAL CONCEPT FOR INTERNATIONAL SPACE STATION TRAINING

Because linear navigation is intuitive, astronauts being trained for operations on the international space station (ISS) provide another argument for linear just-in-time training. The extended duration of each stay in orbit may require ISS crew members to learn how to operate an experiment or maintain a system without benefit of previous training. Astronauts will rely on Web technology to show them precisely what to do at a

*Source:* "Navigation for 'Just-in-Time' Web-Based Training" by Liz Stagg in *Performance in Practice*, Winter 1999–2000, pp. 1–2. Liz Stagg is Project Manager and Lead Instructional Designer for Teledyne Brown Engineering's Training Services Group located in Huntsville, AL. Reprinted with permission of ASTD. Copyright 2000. All rights reserved. *www.astd.org*

moment's notice. According to crew member Lee Morin, who represents the astronaut corps in establishing Web-based training standards, "Ease of navigation is crucial. We have seen poorly designed training with hyperlinks that take you so far from the core lesson that it is impossible to find your way back. For use on the station, primary lessons will be presented in a linear fashion. All the information the crew needs to perform an operation will be included in these primary lessons. Supplemental information and interactivity, such as optional pop-up text, audio, video, and animations must be accessible from within the primary lesson page."

An Onboard Training Working Group is in the process of publishing standards for developing this training. At the heart of these requirements is a navigational scheme that can be intuitively followed to reach all portions of the

lesson. According to Bryan Barley of NASA's Marshall Space Flight Center, "A lesson map will be readily available so that astronauts can select any topic or operation they need. Crew members will never have to view unnecessary information or backtrack through previously viewed information, except by choice." Also, the current location in the course and the past navigational history will be displayed.

In the context of just-in-time training, having a linear organization structure and limited interactivity in no way diminishes instructional effectiveness. As long as the lesson content is accurate and it is presented clearly, learners are empowered to choose what content is needed and when it is delivered to meet objectives that they have determined. In this way, the trainee assumes control of the training outcome and the results are likely to be positive.

## BOOK REVIEW

## WEB-BASED TRAINING USER INTERFACE DESIGN ISSUES

*Editor's Comment*: This is a book for training managers or high-level instructional designers with broad responsibility for building a Web-based training program. The book addresses many of the critical issues facing instructional leaders who want the best of e-learning for their companies but who aren't sure how to create the best opportunities. This particular book reflects the uncertainties of the present state of the art of instructional design. In this review, we have chosen to focus primarily on the book's Chapter 6, "Presentation Principles," because it is the design issues surrounding the user interface (UI) that contain so much of the confusion, frustration, and obstacles to decision-making about e-learning in general.

We begin by highlighting some of the book's important features, setting its context for our focus on user interface. Nine chapters are presented in the traditional instructional system design (ISD) framework, beginning with assessment of organizational needs and training "audience" assessment and concluding with course evaluation and testing. Conrad and her colleagues follow but adapt and elaborate on the traditional systematic approach to instructional design.

Three excellent appendices contributed by TrainingLinks colleagues Judi Schade, Jay Erikson, and Kreg Wallace, a 17-page glossary, and a resource-based CD-ROM add to the book's usefulness. Appendices cover 42 pages and include:

Schade: Overview of Instructional Design

Erikson: Course Hosting and Training Management Systems

Wallace: Creating Graphics for the Web

---

*Source: Instructional Design for Web-based Training* by Kerri Conrad and TrainingLinks, Amherst, MA: HRD Press, 2000. Kerri Conrad is a Principal with TrainingLinks a Colorado-based corporate education and instructional technology consulting company. *www.traininglinks.com*

Throughout the book, charts, checklists, and tables help to present useful information in easy-to-follow formats. The style and formatting of the book work together for a practical result.

The focus throughout is on adaptation of traditional ISD to Web-based design. For example, Table 1.3, Training Skill Characteristics Suitable to WBT, in Chapter 1 on Assessing the Appropriateness of Web-Based Training, contains the following guidelines regarding objectives:

"The objective level should be achievable within a Web environment and the specified target design.

- For example, a multiple-choice quiz and a 'drag and drop' exercise each allow learner to *recognize* or *identify*, but not necessarily to *discuss*."

Table 1.3 also contains this guideline regarding feedback:

"The training should not require immediate, frequent, and detailed instructor feedback on learner performance.

- Synchronous WBT is possible, but often is less practical and more expensive than asynchronous delivery."

Conrad's Chapter 6 on Presentation Principles elaborates on the design concepts of instructional blueprints and web circuits, which she calls "virtual classroom carpentry." The chapter spells clearly out the options in negotiating the often difficult terrain of project managers, development teams, instructional designers, graphic designers, and Web programmers, all of whom claim a piece of the WBT territory. She comes up with three very simple rules for WBT designers: "be consistent, keep it simple and avoid screen clutter, and design for the target learner and no one else" (p. 139). She urges WBT designers to focus on communication issues, and to put themselves in the learner's communication context, being aware of the learner's favorite expressions and patterns of communication. One of her first rules is for the designer to "be conscious of the WBT interface as a communication system"; she suggests that WBT designers create the interface to "appeal to the users' unconscious reliance on inductive reasoning" (p. 140). Learners need ease of navigation, the comfort of consistent controls and clear indication of where they are within a course, and in general an intuitive navigational process without the need for detailed instructions.

The chapter develops through steps in creating content and integration of text, graphics, and course management. The author advocates a development team approach to design, and suggests reviews of developed materials and modules at many points before students uses them. This chapter concludes with a summary and a reference sheet of user interface guidelines and of writing guidelines (p. 164).

# ARTICLE REPRINT

## 6 DIMENSIONS AND 4 LEVELS OF WEB DESIGN

*Editor's Comment:* This article is a detailed description of the organization of today's Web-design components and the levels of expertise required to design learning within them. It is also a representation of the design skills that must be mastered before moving on to the next higher level of expertise. The article is written from the perspective of a teacher, but should be read from the point of view of a learner.

## THE FOUR LEVELS OF WEB SITE DEVELOPMENT EXPERTISE

### *by Albert L. Ingram*

Just a few years ago, when educators were just beginning to use the World Wide Web, it was much simpler than it is now. Hyper-Text Markup Language (HTML) was the only technology available for developing Web sites, and its capabilities were limited. Because of that, the Web was essentially a way to send and display static pages of simple text and graphics from a server to a browser. Multimedia, interactivity, two-way communications, and page customization were not yet available. Two consequences were that (1) there was less to learn in order to become an expert at Web development, and (2) those of us who taught Web development had much less to teach on the subject.

Today, the situation is far different. Many more technologies are available. HTML itself has expanded, and Dynamic HTML (DHTML) takes us beyond even those changes. Forms have been added to allow information to move in both directions on the Web, and a variety of languages and technologies are available to process incoming information at the server end. Java-Script (and to a lesser extent VBScript) have provided simple programming languages to increase responsiveness and interactivity on the client side. Java (not to be confused with JavaScript) offers a full-fledged programming language designed for more complex tasks on the Web. Pages can now connect to databases so that they are no longer static; instead, they can present information and activities specific to those who are viewing them. They can change on the fly according to such variables as specific users, time of day, location of the user, particular requests and histories, and many others.

New technologies now coming online promise to continue these trends. Active Server Pages (ASP) from Microsoft are making it easier to present customized information. Extensible Markup Language (XML) may broaden the possibilities even further. Other more specific programs from many different companies are providing an incredible variety of options. These by no means exhaust the possibilities, and by the time this article is published there will undoubtedly be many others.

The types of information that we can present on the Web also have changed drastically. While text and GIF and JPG images are still the mainstay of most Web sites, we have many

*Source:* "The Four Levels of Web Site Development Expertise" by Albert L. Ingram in *Educational Technology*, May–June 2000, pp. 20–28. Albert L. Ingram is with the Instructional Technology Program, College of Education, Kent State University, Kent, OH. Reprinted with permission of Educational Technology Publications, Englewood Cliffs, NJ. Copyright 2000. All rights reserved.

other choices. Animated GIFs were the first step away from stationary images. It is relatively easy to insert sounds and video clips now. Streaming audio and video are possible so that we can receive broadcasts over the Internet. Special plug-in programs allow Web surfers to view Flash animations, Director movies, Authorware programs, virtual reality (VR) environments, and many others.

At the same time, our understanding of how to design Web pages and sites has also grown, although perhaps not as quickly as the technologies available. Key questions about visual design, site organization, usability design, file and database structure, and many other issues are becoming increasingly central to how we design and use the Web. For educators, questions of instructional design and integrating the Web into our instructional systems are also important. Finally, a key concept for educators is interactivity, which most agree is vital to good instruction on the Web (e.g., Gilbert & Moore, 1998).

In sum, there is a great deal to learn when one begins to produce Web sites. It is impossible to "cover" all the technologies, knowledge, and skills one needs in a single course or even in two or three. No one starts out knowing all there is to know, and we all must move through a series of steps or stages in order to develop expertise. Beyond that, everyone who develops Web sites must continually learn more, upgrading his or her skills to keep up with the technology—hardware, software, and development processes. Ultimately, none of us will be able to keep up completely or hope to do all the tasks in a complex Web development project.

How should we organize our understanding of Web development and how to teach it? There are many people, especially in education, who are just beginning to learn to design and develop pages and sites. There are others who are gaining knowledge and skills in all or parts of the process. If we are to design curricula or course sequences that take students from novice abilities to higher levels of expertise, then we must look at the kinds of things that must be learned and the order in which they can or should be taught. Here we make a first attempt at doing so.

The purpose of this article is to propose a four-level model of Web development expertise. These four levels can serve as a curriculum overview or as a plan for an individual's professional development. Although the four levels

do seem to capture the current state of the technology (at the time of writing), there is no expectation that these levels will remain static. As new technologies come along and old ones are supplanted, this scheme will have to be revisited. In addition, as one progresses through the levels, it is likely that one will begin to specialize. Undoubtedly, the levels will have to be changed and updated regularly.

The four levels described here are labeled the Basic, Intermediate, Advanced, and Expert levels. They are not meant to be definitive, but they do represent a reasonable progression of skills that one could learn in becoming conversant with Web site development. In addition, we describe six major dimensions of expertise that may differ from level to level. As with the levels, the dimensions are not necessarily completely mutually exclusive. They do represent, however, a reasonable description of the types of things one must know in order to develop Web sites successfully. The six dimensions are as follows:

- Page Design
- Media Use
- Client-Side Processing
- Server-Side Processing
- Site Structure
- Development Processes

First, we describe the six dimensions, and then we explain what someone should be able to do at each level in all of them. Obviously, it is possible for an individual to have skills at different levels within different dimensions. This is especially true at the upper levels; at the lower levels a good developer will probably have skills in all dimensions. Again, the levels should be viewed more as a framework than as a set of mutually exclusive categories. However, people who are significantly more advanced along one dimension than along the others are unlikely to have a complete grasp of the Web or of its possibilities.

## SIX DIMENSIONS

### *Page Design*

Page design is the most basic dimension of expertise in Web development. It has been central to the process since the beginning of the Web. At first, people developing Web pages had to know HTML to develop even simple Web pages. The only way to make a page was to use a text editor or word processor to write the HTML code directly, complete with tags, paired brackets, and all the other paraphernalia involved. However, it didn't take long for more capable Web page editing software to be developed. The first ones helped ease the process by inserting fully formed tags when the user made corresponding menu choices. All the user had to do was insert text, graphics filenames, and hyperlink Uniform Resource Locators (URLs). The first WYSIWYG (What You See Is What You Get) page editor was PageMill for the Macintosh, although, given the differences among computers, screens, and browsers, no editing software can be entirely WYSIWYG. Currently there are any number of editors that make the technical process of developing individual Web pages little different from word processing. Any of them will suffice for making basic and intermediate level pages. To move beyond such basic formatting, more complex (and usually more expensive) editors can produce DHTML, Active Server Pages, and other advanced technologies.

### Media Use

The workhorses of media on the Web are GIF (Graphics Interchange Format) and JPG (or JPEG—Joint Photographic Experts Group) graphics. At the basic and intermediate levels of Web development, one should be able to insert such images into a page as well as use them as backgrounds. More advanced media choices, which may require extra steps or coding in development, include inserting sounds and video clips, animations, and streaming media. To use such media effectively on the Web one must have both the skills to produce and edit them and the ability to put them on the Web and integrate them with other Web elements. One should also be able to use graphics as hyperlinks.

### Client-Side Processing

The Web (and the Internet in general) works on a *client-server model*. The core of most Internet-based services consists of *server* computers and software, which offer information, processing,

and transmission abilities. People access the servers through *clients*, which again are specific software programs running on individual computers. For example, we may send and receive e-mail through specific e-mail client programs such as Eudora, Outlook, or Pegasus on our personal computers. To do so, however, we must connect to e-mail servers, which handle such chores as transmitting our messages to the destination servers and holding incoming messages until our client programs request them. The Web itself consists of a huge number of WWW servers scattered around the world. These range in size from the author's server software running on his office computer, to the massive computer banks that serve the Netscape, Microsoft, or Yahoo Web sites. We all access those servers through the client software we have come to call browsers. Here the key point is that, with computers and software on both sides of each Web transaction, we have the ability to process information in various ways on either end. This allows a skilled Web developer the choice of deciding where the processing will be most effective and efficient. For example, frequently the servers are much busier than the clients, since the latter spend a great deal of time waiting for a single user to enter commands. Thus, often it can be more efficient and responsive to have the server downloading processing tasks to the client. In other situations, where key information is stored on large databases on the server side, the processing must take place there.

With the advent of Web scripting languages, especially JavaScript and VBScript, the Web developer has gained the ability to create pages that are more interactive and responsive to users without changing the essential nature of the Web and its browsers. Scripts are snippets of programming code that are embedded, much like HTML, in the Web pages that are sent to the client's browser. The last several browser versions from both Netscape and Microsoft have included the ability to interpret and execute these scripts from within the page. The advantage to this scheme is that it minimizes both server load (no extra processing takes place on the server side) and the bandwidth needed to transmit the code (scripts are simply ASCII text that is interpreted on the client side, just like HTML itself). More complex scripts can be used to communicate with the originating server as well, allowing even more flexibility, interactivity, and responsiveness. The ability to use and write scripts is an increasing part of good Web page development, especially in instruction, where scripting can allow more meaningful interactivity. There are large numbers of scripts available for downloading from the Web, so one does not have to become a highly skilled programmer in order to make good use of this technology. Other programs are available to write scripts for you, for example, to produce the code needed to present simple tests and quizzes. Another client-side processing technology is the programming language *Java*, which increases the bandwidth requirements but does put complex processing tasks on the client side. Some have suggested that Java, or something like it, will provide a way to run large-scale applications over the Web.

### Server-Side Processing

For more complex interactivity, the client side of the Web (the browser) and the server side must work together. Whenever one searches a database for information, submits personal or professional information to an organization, or participates in an online Web-based conference, there is likely to be processing taking place on both ends. The first innovation to allow the two-way exchange of information on the Web (rather than just one way from the server to the client) was the online *form*. Forms consist of the text boxes, radio buttons, checkboxes, and, especially, "Submit" buttons that we are all familiar with. Forms are remarkably easy to develop on the client side, as part of a basic Web page. However, the key question in using them effectively concerns what happens when the user clicks the Submit button. Some of the basic things that can happen are:

(1) the form results can be e-mailed to someone;

(2) the form results can be posted to a Web page automatically (this occurs in online asynchronous discussions, for example);

(3) the form results can be sent to a text file or database file on the server, where it can be stored and used to aid subsequent decisions; and

(4) the server can have other special programs to deal with form results or almost anything else.

In order to take any of these actions, the server must have programs installed to handle them. Often these programs are CGI (Common Gateway Interface) programs. The programs themselves may be written in a variety of languages, since CGI is not itself a programming language but instead a standard interface among programs on Web servers. PERL has been the most popular CGI language, especially on Unix servers, but many others, such as Visual Basic and C, are used as well. Server-side scripting with JavaScript is also an option now. No matter which language is used, a CGI program allows the server to process form results and do other tasks that can increase the interactivity and responsiveness of the Web to the users. The ability to use existing programs (such as those that e-mail form results) effectively as well as to write programs to perform more complex processing is an important part of being a good Web developer.

### Site Structure

Small Web sites often have little or no structure, and they may not need any. With only a few pages, a small Web site can be linked on an *ad hoc* basis, with little regard to consistency and navigation issues. After all, how lost can one get in a few pages? With larger sites, the need for a planned structure becomes evident in at least two ways. First, in order to maintain and update the site, those working on it need to have a clear idea of where things are, where new material should be entered, and so on. As we move toward more database-driven sites, the structure of the site and the database must be specified early in the development process. At the same time, site users probably will find it easier to navigate and use the site if there is a clear structure to it. Any complex Web site might be organized in many different ways, so the emphasis through the four levels is on ensuring that structure exists, rather than on adhering to any particular structure. There are also several prototypical Web structures that can provide rough templates for a site, such as linear, hierarchical, or Web-like. At the same

**FIGURE 1. THE FOUR LEVELS OF WEB SITE DEVELOPMENT EXPERTISE**

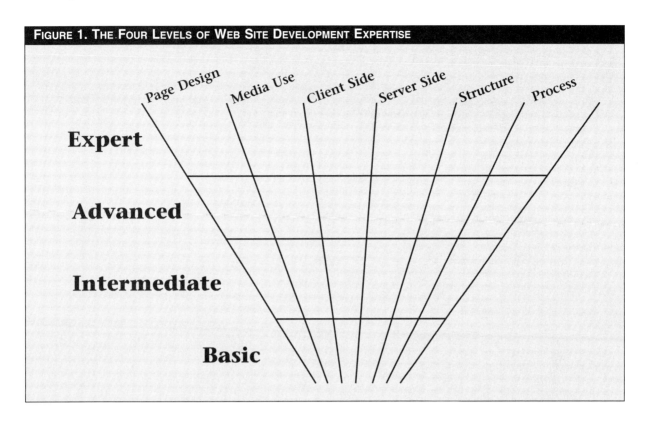

time, there is evidence that the structure and navigation of a site is intimately bound up with the information that is presented (Spool, Scanlon, Schroeder, Snyder, & DeAngelo, 1999).

### Development Processes

Finally, it is not enough just to have good technical skills in order to do Web development. As sites expand to dozens, hundreds, and thousands of pages, they are taking on the characteristics of large-scale instructional development or software engineering projects rather than smaller, craft-style designs (Powell, Jones, & Cutts, 1998). Nowadays, teams of people develop good sites, since it is unlikely that any individual will have all the skills, let alone the time, to do all parts of a project. Therefore, one of the key skills in Web development is the ability to plan and follow a systematic development process. Such a process is the best way to ensure a high quality site that is developed on time and on budget. Expertise in this area can help us define Web development expertise more generally. A variety of areas can contribute to the processes used, including project management, instructional development,

usability engineering, software engineering, and many others (see Figure 1).

## LEVELS OF WEB DEVELOPMENT EXPERTISE

Now we describe the four levels of Web development expertise with reference to the six dimensions. The levels are summarized in Tables 1 through 4. Here we will discuss the levels from the point of view of someone learning (or being taught) the skills necessary to progress from one to the next.

### Basic Level

The Basic Level is the first step for someone just starting out in Web development and is characterized by beginner-level skills (at best) in all dimensions. The pages and sites developed by those at the Basic Level tend to be personal sites, practices, and perhaps hobbyist ones. Little information is given, and little attention is paid to who will want to receive it. Someone at the Basic Level is able to enter text, perform basic format-

| TABLE 1. BASIC LEVEL | |
|---|---|
| **Page Design** | • Text entry and formatting (at least these options: fonts, sizes, styles, colors, alignment, headers)<br>• Background colors and graphics<br>• Inline graphics<br>• Internal and external text links |
| **Media** | • GIFs and JPEGs |
| **Client Side Processing** | • None |
| **Server Side Processing** | • Page Serving only |
| **Site Structure** | • *Ad hoc* structure based on small number of pages |
| **Development Processes** | • *Ad hoc*, organic, evolutionary, rapid prototyping |

| TABLE 2. INTERMEDIATE LEVEL | |
|---|---|
| **Page Design** | • Text formatting (options: lists, special html formats, indentations)<br>• Tables for more complex page formatting<br>• Graphics as links<br>• Links to anchors (same page, other pages)<br>• Image Maps for links |
| **Media** | • Background sounds<br>• PNG files<br>• Animated GIFs |
| **Client Side Processing** | • Copy and use (preferably legally!) scripts from other pages with changes<br>• Write own scripts |
| **Server Side Processing** | • Forms processing using canned programs (e.g., e-mail and storing in text files) |
| **Site Structure** | • Planned and deliberate: hierarchical, linear, Web, combination<br>• File structure taken into account |
| **Development Processes** | • Basic planning, analysis, and design processes. Structure/flow charts and storyboards |

ting tasks, use graphics, and so forth. A relatively small number of guidelines can improve these pages immensely (e.g., Maddux, 1998). The media he or she uses are primarily GIF and JPG files for backgrounds and inline graphics. A person at the Basic Level is unlikely to have any expertise whatsoever in either client-side or server-side processing, so the pages and sites developed will consist of static pages served individually with no information returned to or acted upon by the server. The site structure, from my experience in teaching beginners in Web development, is likely to be nonexistent unless individuals are forced to consider the issue. Most sites produced by those at the Basic Level are likely to be very small, however, so the structure is not critical. Finally, individuals at the Basic Level are unlikely to use any systematic development processes, since they are probably more concerned with merely completing the pages reasonably well and linking them together.

### *Intermediate Level*

The Intermediate Level takes people a step beyond the basics in several areas. People at this level are more likely to produce sites that are actually useful to others. The sites probably look better and are at least somewhat interactive, compared to those produced by those at the Basic Level. People at this level, perhaps from experience, start paying attention to the site structure, to navigation, to the file structure on the server, and to other issues. They have probably discovered the need for some planning and development processes, although they may not be skilled in them as yet.

At the Intermediate Level, page design skills are more or less complete. Developers are skilled at using most or all of the standard HTML features. Nowadays, of course, they probably access those features through one or more of the available WYSIWYG editors, not through learning and editing HTML directly. In an HTML page, the most common means of gaining control over the format of a Web page is through the use of tables (DHTML is changing that, however). Therefore, at the Intermediate Level, one key skill is to use tables effectively for page layout. Image Maps are another element that can be quite useful in instruction (for identifying the parts of an object being studied, for example), so they appear at this level as well. These technologies can be especially important for developing Web-based learning materials (El-Tigi & Branch, 1997). Among the media used, going beyond GIFs and JPGs, are PNG files (a relatively new graphic format for the Web), animated GIFs (popular, but difficult to use effectively), and background or embedded sounds.

An intermediate Web developer is at least starting to learn about client-side scripting, most likely using JavaScript. The first step in learning Web scripting is usually to download and modify scripts from other pages or from sites offering large numbers of free scripts. Given the availability of scripts to do almost anything, this is a useful strategy for bringing some instructional interactivity to a site without too much effort. Even so, doing this may entail learning a significant amount about the language. On the server side, someone at the Intermediate Level can likewise use canned programs to engage in simple forms handling. Many servers have CGI program libraries available with the ability to perform common server-side tasks. In addition, some Web editors, notably FrontPage, include server extensions that provide such functions.

The site structure is likely to be planned more carefully at the Intermediate Level, with choices made about overall organization (for example linear, hierarchical, or Weblike). The file structure also starts becoming important at this level, because the size of the sites developed is increasing, and the developer needs to be able to find pages and information quickly and easily. In order to produce a coherent structure, a consistent navigational plan, and a useful file structure, the developer must do some serious initial planning and design. Thus, the need to analyze the requirements of the site, design it, and follow that design becomes evident. Some of the tools that he or she might use include charts like structure charts or flow diagrams as well as storyboards for planning the visual look of the site. Often, the most useful design process is to develop a quick prototype of a few pages before committing to the final look and feel of the site. The relative ease of producing and changing Web pages makes this course especially viable.

In summary, the Intermediate Level represents the current state of Web development for large numbers of people who are not professional developers but who develop small to medium-size sites for personal, educational, or professional use. Much useful information has been placed on the Web at this level. However, to be a more advanced Web developer, one must go beyond these two levels. The Advanced and Expert Levels represent much more complex Web development, which approaches the state of the art at the time of this writing.

### Advanced Level

The Advanced Level of Web development moves us into some of the latest technologies on the Web. More important, especially for education, this level includes a significantly greater level of interactivity. Not only is this the level at which one must operate to be a professional Web developer, but to get here it is much more likely that many of us will require formal training rather than purely self-instructional efforts.

In Page Design, there are several important elements that are more advanced. Frames have been a part of HTML for several browser generations, but are difficult to use effectively. Done poorly, they can be confusing and disruptive to users; done well, they can help people find their way around a site. DHTML, mentioned earlier, is still a young technology and not standard across browsers. Even so, it now allows precise placement of graphics, text, and other elements in layers that normal HTML does not allow. In addition, the elements can be moved, changed, and made to appear and disappear under user or script control. All of these features make possible much more dynamic, interactive, and responsive Web pages. In addition, Cascading Style Sheets allow the developer to have greater control over fonts, sizes, colors, and styles than that allowed by HTML alone. At the Advanced Level, developers are likely to be able to make good use of video and audio clips to convey information and tone, as well as a variety of specialized media that might require "plug-ins"—small programs that are added to the browser to increase its functionality.

| TABLE 3. ADVANCED LEVEL | |
|---|---|
| **Page Design** | • Frames |
| | • Dynamic HTML |
| | • Cascading Style Sheets |
| | • More complex tables (e.g., tables within tables) |
| **Media** | • Audio and video clips |
| | • Files requiring plug-ins |
| **Client Side Processing** | • Write complex scripts from scratch |
| | • Use and modify Java programs |
| **Server Side Processing** | • Supplying intermediate CGI to do customized tasks |
| | • Connecting to databases for publishing and possible updating |
| **Site Structure** | • Complex |
| | • Fully designed up front |
| | • Information architecture and usability considerations |
| | • File structure planned and specified |
| **Development Processes** | • Good analysis and design process drawing on instructional design and incorporating some other elements from other disciplines |

Both client-side and server-side processing take on increased importance at the Advanced Level. On the client side, an advanced developer should be able to write significant scripts as well as begin to use Java programs in various ways. On the server side, the developer might design and program CGI programs. In addition, he or she should begin to connect Web pages to databases to make the sites more individually responsive. These connections can be used for a variety of tasks, from delivering the results of simple information searches to creating all the pages on a site on-the-fly. While this strat-

egy takes more planning, design, and programming, it can also make updating and maintaining a site much easier.

At this level the advanced Web developer should pay close attention to the structure of both the site and the file system that stores it. It is likely to be a much larger site and the addition of such complex technologies makes it difficult to keep track of what is going on from both the user's and the developer's points of view. Haphazard linking and development will likely ensure that visitors to the site will come away confused and frustrated. When the time comes, as it will almost immediately, for the site to be maintained and upgraded, early attention to structure will pay off handsomely.

Perhaps one of the more important ways that an Advanced developer can differ from those at the earlier levels is in her/his use of more systematic analysis, design, and development procedures. Whether from software engineering, instructional design, or other disciplines, the procedures allow the designer to be sure that he or she is solving the right problems and to design a site to solve them well. These relatively well-established processes also allow better project management, enabling the developers to estimate time and budget more accurately and to meet project goals more reliably. Other disciplines that start to become important at this level as well as the Expert level include information architecture (Rosenfeld & Morville, 1998), usability engineering (Nielson, 1993), software engineering (Powell, Jones, & Cutts, 1998), and many others.

### *Expert Level*

At the Expert Level of Web site development, practitioners are fully capable of using the latest and most effective Web technologies. However, at this level it is unlikely that any individual will be expert in all the technologies. Usually, development at this level demands a team of people, making it even more imperative that the site structure be well-specified early and that good development processes be used.

In Page Design, Expert Level Web development involves dynamically generated pages that are based on database-driven information, instantiated into page layout templates. This allows a high degree of customization, interactivity, and responsiveness in the Web site (Gar-

| TABLE 4. EXPERT LEVEL | |
|---|---|
| **Page Design** | • Dynamically generated pages based on database-driven information, page layout, etc. |
| | • Very complex interactive elements |
| | • Active Server Pages |
| **Media** | • Streaming audio and video |
| **Client Side Processing** | • Full scripting skills |
| **Server Side Processing** | • Full database interconnectivity, complex server-side processing, programming |
| **Site Structure** | • Based on abstract model that is instantiated on the fly |
| **Development Processes** | • Full planning, analysis, and design process combining instructional design and development with relevant concepts from software engineering, usability engineering, and project management, etc. |

At this level, the structure of a Web site has probably moved beyond one based on linking individual pages in various ways. Instead, there is most likely an abstract model of the site which is instantiated on-the-fly from databases. This is an efficient, effective strategy for producing, upgrading, and maintaining a site but requires a great deal of front-end analysis, planning, and design before any programs are developed or information entered. The development processes used at this level thus include full processes to plan and manage the project, procedures for analyzing such things as the systems and requirements, the instructional needs, and the learners or audiences, and design methods that allow the team to specify exactly the structure and processes on the site. These last may include such techniques as data flow diagrams from software engineering, as well as Rapid Application Development processes that can result in prototypes that can be tried out with members of the target audience. This moves us far beyond the rudimentary Web pages of the Basic Level.

## CONCLUSIONS

Just a few years ago, when the author began teaching Web site development to graduate students in instructional technology, students learned how to produce simple pages and link them together. For many, that in itself was a significant step forward and had potential educational advantages. Even though many people still have to learn the rudiments of Web page development to have a significant effect on education and training, instructional Web sites need to go beyond that. Intermediate level development skills are now necessary to produce sites with even minimal importance for education. If mere information presentation is the goal, there are likely to be no end of sites that one can find and link to where students can find information on almost any topic. The small ones produced by teachers and others at the Basic Level and even at the Intermediate Level are increasingly less likely to add much to that cacophony. To be genuinely useful, instructional sites must go beyond those levels. They should be interactive and present significant learning challenges to students. They should be responsive, adapting the information

rison & Fenton, 1999). Active Server Pages, a Microsoft technology, allow one to produce such pages, and there are other possible technologies as well. Although such sites are currently most likely to be produced for e-commerce sites, as education begins to use them, we should see more sites that adapt to the needs and wants of individual users and students. As far as media go, at this level, sites may include any media that might be transmitted on the Web, including streaming audio and video.

An individual who is expert at client side processing will have full scripting skills and/or full programming skills in a language like Java. These allow her or him to create highly interactive and capable pages that do far more than simply present static information. On the server side, expert level developers are able to produce sites with full database connectivity with complex server-side processing using scripts and programs.

and activities to the actions and inputs of the students And they should be customizable, presenting an interface and the content needed by the individual students.

To accomplish these goals, educational Web developers will need to move up through the levels outlined here. Most people in the field can readily move beyond the Basic Level to the Intermediate Level quite quickly. To help people move beyond these, we will need to offer advanced training in a variety of Web technologies, which are fast replacing more traditional computer-assisted instruction development technologies. Clearly these technologies include scripting, programming tools, and database systems. The levels outlined here provide a framework for organizing and approaching that training. As Web technologies advance, the four levels will have to be modified, but the overall structure might remain useful for a longer period of time. In addition, it is important to stress that the levels involve more than just technical skills. Understanding, using, and producing complex site structures is increasingly important as our sites grow in size and complexity. The use of good development processes is one thing that will distinguish professional and effective Web developers from those who merely produce pages.

This need for technical skills in developing Web sites is certainly changing. Already there is less pressure to learn HTML than there was just a few years ago. Although some still argue that direct HTML coding is necessary to produce the best, most efficient, and most customized pages, fewer people see the tradeoff in time and effort to be worth it. We can expect to see other aspects of Web page development automated as well, including education-specific elements. For example, it is now possible to add testing or online discussions to educational Web sites without any significant knowledge of scripting or programming.

Increasingly, instructors and others who develop sites are using pre-packaged systems, such as WebCT (http://www.webct.com/), Top-Class (http://www.wbtsystems.com), Web Course in a Box (http://www.madduck.com/), and many others to organize and enter the information and other elements in their classes. These systems offer page and site templates into which an instructor can insert the content of a course. In addition, they may include such things as quiz and test systems, synchronous and asynchronous communications, and other elements that would be difficult for most educators to program on their own. One tradeoff in using these systems is likely to be a less customized course. An implication for this article is that these systems lessen the need for expertise in the page design and scripting dimensions, while perhaps increasing the need for good media design and development, site structures, and development processes, especially some form of instructional design.

Another potential trend for the development of educational Web sites is to contract with outside agencies and companies for such services. Such groups could bring to the project a varied set of skills that individuals, small schools and colleges, and others may not have. At the same time, however, the sites produced would still have to be maintained and upgraded, a process that can be more time-consuming and expensive than the initial development, so either the contract must be an ongoing one, or in-house skills are still needed.

## REFERENCES

El-Tigi, M., & Branch, R. B. (1997, May–June). Designing for interaction, learner control, and feedback during Web-based learning. *Educational Technology, 37*(3), 23–29.

Garrison, S., & Fenton, R. (1999, July–August). Database driven Web systems for education. *Educational Technology, 39*(4), 31–38.

Gilbert, L., & Moore, D. R. (1998, May–June). Building interactivity into Web courses: Tools for social and instructional interaction. *Educational Technology, 38*(3), 29–35.

Maddux, C. D. (1998, September–October). The World Wide Web: Some simple solutions to common design problems. *Educational Technology, 38*(5), 24–28.

Nielson, J. (1993). *Usability engineering.* New York: Academic Press.

Powell, T. A., with Jones, D. I., & Cutts, D. C. (1998). *Web site engineering: Beyond Web page design.* Upper Saddle River, NJ: Prentice-Hall.

Rosenfeld, L., & Morville, P. (1998). *Information Architecture for the World Wide Web.* Sebastopol, CA: O'Reilly and Associates.

Spool, J. M., Scanlon, T., Schroeder, W., Snyder, C., & DeAngelo, T. (1999). *Web Site Usability: A Designer's Guide.* San Francisco: Morgan Kaufmann Publishers.

# 3C. DESIGN FOR SKILLS IMPROVEMENT

## CASE STUDY

## BOEING AND UNION PARTNER FOR HARD AND SOFT SKILLS TRAINING

*Editor's Comment*: One of the most important words of year 2000 was "partnership." In the human resources literature, and especially the training literature, partnering among all company stakeholders was seen as a great boon to learning and to the bottom line. Trainers particularly have been hounded in recent years to align training with business goals and deliver results that matter to profit and growth. This short case study shows how one company, Boeing, and its International Association of Machinists (IAM) union collaborated in training program design, partnering for quality, productivity, safety, and profit. A report of this partnering was part of the presentation at the April 25th conference in Chicago, the Federal Mediation and Conciliation Service's 10th National Labor-Management Conference. The focus here is on the Boeing/IAM "Quality Through Training Program" (QTTP).

What's unique about the QTTP is its concentration on both hard skills and soft skills training. The program's goals are to improve the "technical, professional, and personal skills of Boeing employees" in order to develop into "more effective human beings" (p. 1). The program's methods include both training and counseling activities. QTTP includes Boeing's educational assistance program and its career planning activities. Some of the soft skills included in the training program are: conflict resolution, humor in the workplace, building self-esteem, and stress management.

Program administrators have program evaluation data that indicate these kinds of program components have directly contributed to a 54% reduction in defects, a 51% reduction in inventory, and a 4% improvement in lost workdays due to safety problems. This is a particularly interesting program design because of its quality umbrella and because of its hard and soft skills focus.

---

*Source:* "Speakers Credit IAM/Boeing Partnerships with Boosting Productivity, Skills, and Profits" in *BNA Inc. Union Labor Report* weekly newsletter, May 4, 2000, p. 1, published by The Bureau of National Affairs, Inc., Washington, DC.

# ARTICLE REPRINT

## VOLVO'S S80 LONG-DISTANCE DESIGN TEAM LEARNING SECRETS

*Editor's Comment*: This is the story of how Volvo's model S80 design team worked together in real time across two continents and nine time zones to create an automobile that customers love. Surprisingly, the central tool for collaborative learning was a computer-based virtual; whiteboard communication system. Read this article to see how technology mediated an outstanding learning environment for designing a car. Those who design training teams across continents and time zones could adopt Volvo's approach.

## GOING THE DISTANCE

### *by Michael J. McDermott*

In 1994 a group of engineers and designers at Volvo Car Corp. undertook a challenge that, on the surface, seemed fairly straightforward: to create a new standard in aerodynamic efficiency for the company's S80 model, which debuted in late 1998. What made their task particularly challenging was the fact that key participants in the project were located on two continents nine time zones apart, in Sweden and California. Making the most of a corporate culture that encourages collaborative thinking, the group not only met its engineering goals—coming up with a drag coefficient of 0.28 for the S80, a value that ranks among the best in all cars of its class—but also developed processes and techniques for working together across long distances that are now being adopted throughout the entire company.

"As the work started, we were encouraged by management to search for ways to improve our work philosophy and practices," says engineer Pawel Seremak, who quarterbacked the team of aerodynamicists from his home base at Volvo in Gothenburg, Sweden. As a result of the improvements, he says, his team helped create a better car: "The aerodynamic elements of the S80 make a strong contribution to the image the car projects to customers."

Consumers are responding overwhelmingly to the S80. Volvo had never sold more than 30,000 cars annually in the S80's segment; as of mid-December 1999, sales of the S80 alone had climbed to 75,000 for the year.

Aside from the basic desire to improve their product, Seremak and his team of scientists were inspired by the company's goal of reducing fuel consumption of its cars by 25 percent between 1990 and 2005. Achieving that goal requires increasing the overall efficiency of the car—and improving the car's aerodynamics is just one means to that end. "Roughly one third of the power delivered by the engine is used against air resistance," Seremak says. "This shows clearly that to minimize consumption of energy needed to move from one spot to another, improving aerodymanics should be one of the main strategies."

For the S80 design project, the scientists took as a starting point Volvo's Environmental Concept Car (ECC), a forward-looking design incorporating the latest in automobile technology, such as the hybrid-electric drive train. Too costly for large-scale production, the ECC is a visionary prototype developed in 1990 at the Volvo Monitoring and Concept Center (VMCC) just outside Los Angeles. Scientists at the VMCC monitor market and cutting-edge technical trends in the automotive industry and create new concepts that ultimately might be developed into cars and trucks for Volvo.

Under the direction of designer Doug Frasher and then-chief engineer Bill Mason, engineers at the VMCC created the early designs for the S80 by utilizing a variety of powerful analytical tools such as wind-tunnel testing, virtual wind tunnels and computational fluid dynamics, a computerized version of wind-tunnel testing. The charge for the product team in Sweden was to translate those concepts from drawings to the finished product, all the while working closely with the California team to determine how changes to the design would affect the aerodynamics—and hence the fuel efficiency—of the S80.

The logistical issues raised by the prospect of collaborating across such a distance were, to say the least, interesting. As the project coordinator, Seremak organized meetings between the two teams—even providing creature comforts such as sandwiches and coffee for what often turned out to be late-evening meetings on the Gothenburg end. Seremak's job was made easier by the fact that Volvo's design department has a long tradition of working with computer-based data exchange.

The backbone of the long-distance collaboration proved to be a computer-based virtual whiteboard communication system, which allowed team members to contribute notes and make design changes in real time that could be seen by all other members of the team simultaneously. The virtual whiteboard was linked to Alias Studio, Volvo's ground-breaking computer-aided design system, which allows designers and engineers to view and manipulate a car design from any angle and in any location around the world. Add in e-mail (Volvo was one of the first companies to adopt an internal e-mail system, back in the late 1970s) and all the tools for the collaborative virtual meeting were in place. "The new style of team-oriented collaboration was something that developed as a result of this project," says Seremak. "It was not created beforehand to accommodate it."

Ichiro Sugioka, an aeronautical engineer at VMCC in Los Angeles, found the "virtual meeting" facet to be one of the most interesting aspects of the S80 project. Prior to joining Volvo, he had worked as a consultant to the company and had helped create the database that would be used in the car's design. "Until we started having these virtual meetings, I had never met or had any direct contact with my colleagues in Sweden," Sugioka says. "Our face-to-face introductions came through fuzzy videocam images on the virtual whiteboard system, but after about a year, we usually turned them off so we could use the extra bandwidth for the whiteboard."

One of the things that helped smooth the process considerably from Sugioka's point of view was that his colleagues were so clearly comfortable dealing with this type of computer-based communication. "The Swedish people have been early adopters of all types of communications technology," he says. "As a result, they were very understanding of the shortcomings of the technology. The courtesy and patience needed to do these conferences was already there, and that really helped make this happen."

What happened is now the talk of the automotive industry. Volvo's aerodynamic design team, which also included Mats Ramnefors, currently manager of the company's computational fluid dynamics group, and Tim Walker, now senior aerodynamicist and function analyst at the Fluid Dynamics and Computational Fluid Dynamics laboratories, created Volvo's most aerodynamic automobile to date. The design reduces the effect of wind forces that tend to lift a moving vehicle from the ground, and it minimizes the side-to-side sway drivers often feel in strong crosswinds. That makes the S80 easier to handle, especially in turbulent conditions, and imparts to the driver a feeling of safety, security and performance, while improving fuel efficiency—exactly the goals the team had been charged with achieving.

All the new cars and trucks created by Volvo design teams in the future will benefit from the aerodynamic efficiency achieved by the S80 team. "This is very much in line with Volvo's philosophy of developing environmentally conscious products," Seremak notes. But he also believes the team's contribution to the company extends beyond that. "We have succeeded in developing this teamwork methodology," he says, "bringing all the potential we have in this company together, regardless of where it is located, and showing to ourselves and others how powerful Volvo can be."

# CASE STUDY

## SELF-PACED LESSONS MOTIVATE RUTGERS UNIVERSITY FMO

*Editor's Comment*: The Facilities Maintenance Organization (FMO) at Rutgers, the State University of New Jersey, found itself in the unenviable position of having to implement several university-wide computerized programs without the technical know-how or math and reading skills that the jobs required. This is the story of a training design that produced not only higher skill levels but also the all-important motivation among employees for more learning.

Rutgers' Facilities Maintenance Organization of about 800 employees serves three regional Rutgers campuses with groundskeeping, maintenance, and repair services. Scheduling, work-order allocation, time and attendance record-keeping, and other work processes were increasingly being computerized, requiring higher skill levels and greater flexibility among workers. Rutgers chose a comprehensive work assessment tool, "Work Keys," to begin the job of designing appropriate training for FMO's hundreds of employees.

Rutgers is a public university; at least two-thirds of FMO employees are union members with close ties to the state Department of Labor. The FMO leadership early in the training design process asked the advice of the NJ Department of Labor regarding protection of workers' privacy rights during assessments and regarding the use of assessment results. Rutgers provided the right answers, promising that only aggregate assessment scores would be made public, and that assessment scores would be used for training purposes only. All involved in the program design at the front end were pleased that they had a process for finding out exactly what individuals needed in terms of skill development, and that a clear path was laid out for the development of training. The assessments provided training-needs profiles in 17 different positions.

One of the unique features of the FMO training is that it is assessment-based. That is, training per se is not required. Employees can opt out of training as long as their assessments indicate their competence. Training was designed to be self-paced, yet delivered in a classroom-like 16-station computer lab facilitated by an instructor. Learning is individualized, and students work side by side at different paces and on different skill-building lessons. Students also learn on Rutgers' time, not at home.

Program administrators are pleased with early results: improved skill levels in 300 out of 500 employees who qualified for training, and waiting lists for all courses being offered. They characterize the program as a "targeted, self-paced approach" and say that it has improved morale, bringing students into class excited to learn, to prove it, and to help themselves.

---

*Source*: "Rutgers University Creates Culture of Lifelong Learning" by Kelly Dunn in *Workforce,* May 2000, pp. 108–109. Kelly Dunn is an Editorial Assistant for *Workforce* magazine.

# ABSTRACT

## SKILLS FOR BETTER ONLINE DISCUSSION GROUPS

*Editor's Comment:* One of the most frequently expressed problems with online learning is the lack of human interface. Numerous case studies, research studies, and good design ideas to solve this problem have been reported in this year's professional literature. The article referred to here was originally written as a research paper suggesting a technique for instructional designers to improve the quality of electronic discussion groups among post-secondary school learners. There are some good ideas contained in it for corporate training designers too.

The question addressed by the paper's authors is: How do we promote substantive participation, that is, communication, in an electronic discussion group? MacKinnon and Aylward attempt to answer this question by crafting a coding technique for use online by instructors when students are engaged in electronic discussion groups. The authors base their technique model on established communication research which categorizes "good discussion" into nine categories, including such categories as acknowledging opinions, comparing, contrasting, providing an example from an idea, clarifying, and so forth. Through the use of coding devices applied during student discussion, the instructor can provide feedback to students and can discern patterns among students in the discussion group.

The authors devised special icons, created with Microsoft Word 7, representing one "good" category of discussion. They called these special coding icons "Cognates." They believe that using this Cognate system of coding and feedback improves communication skills at the same time that it encourages a rigorous exchange of ideas. They also believe that it encourages students to reserve online discussion for more than casual conversation (p. 19).

These are the 6 steps the authors suggest an instructional designer must follow in order to achieve better online discussion groups:

1. Decide upon a list of categories of "good discussion," each representing a desired communication skill.

2. Prepare a set of electronic icons to match each item in the category list.

3. Teach students (those whose discussion will be coded) what the categories and icons are by having them practice coding a sample discussion.

4. Place a value on each category/ skill; determine the value in joint dialogue with students; focus on higher-order thinking skills.

5. Prepare macros that facilitate assignment of the icons to discussion text; save the macros as a template for repeat use.

6. Capture students' discussion as an HTML file and import it into a work processing file; use the macro template to assign the icons to the student work; grade the students according to the agreed-upon value system for each icon; send the marked work to individual students as an e-mail file attachment.

*Source:* "Six Steps to Improving the Quality of Your Electronic Discussion Groups" by Gregory R. MacKinnon and Lynn Aylward in *Journal of Instruction Delivery Systems*, vol. 13 no. 4, received February 2000, pp. 17–19. Gregory R. MacKinnon is Assistant Professor of Science and Technology Education at the School of Education, Acadia University, Wolfville, Nova Scotia, Canada; Lynn Aylward was Student Placement Coordinator for Student Teaching at Acadia University.

# 3D. DESIGN TECHNOLOGIES FOR E-LEARNING

## ARTICLE REPRINT

## WBT'S UNIQUE DESIGN REQUIREMENTS

*Editor's Comment*: This article is the first of five entries dealing with technology aspects of design for e-learning. Training managers, and especially instructional designers, have had to come to grips this year particularly with taking charge of the Internet, the Web, improved software for training design and program delivery, and the ubiquity of desktop PCs for workplace learning. The operative words are "taking charge" as we speed into year 2001. How to use technology in service of learning has been a popular topic in business literature in year 2000.

In two successive issues of *Lakewood's Technology for Learning* newsletter, Margaret Driscoll and Tom Keating gave 10 good reasons why the "old rules" don't apply to Web-based training. Here we give you the second of these articles, with a summary of the first. We hear a lot about why learners bail out of self-paced, computer-delivered training—poor instructional design and lack of interpersonal connectedness are two of the most often expressed reasons. The article reprinted here is representative of many that are finally offering some help for training designers to understand the uniqueness of e-learning technologies and how to think differently about their strengths.

## WHAT TO FORGET ABOUT TRAINING

### *by Margaret Driscoll and Tom Keating*

Making the most of Web-based training requires trainers to think differently if they want to take advantage of the interactive possibilities of WBT.

Here are four more reasons the old rules don't apply:

**7. Developing Web-based training is developing software.** Typically, instructional designers and course developers working alone have developed instructor-led training and self-paced manuals. The new rules require organizations to recognize that they are in the business of creating software.

Consider some of the tasks required to create WBT: ▼ Design and write routines and modules for portability—for example, create nuggets of instruction that can be moved from one program to another, as well as mixed and matched within a program. ▼ Create consistent data types and use consistent names for variables. For example, at the start of a WBT project, define all of the directories and use file names that make it easy to identify which module and lesson each file is

*Source*: "What to Forget About Training: Four More Reasons Why the Old Rules Don't Apply to WBT" by Margaret Driscoll and Tom Keating in *Lakewood's Technology for Learning* newsletter, February 2000, pp. 6–7. Margaret Driscoll was Director of the Instructional Design Department at University of Massachusetts, Boston and now works at IBM; Tom Keating is Manager of Employee Development and Training at TAC Worldwide Cos. In Newton, MA. Reprinted with permission of Margaret Driscoll. Copyright 2000. All rights reserved.

Here are Margaret Driscoll and Tom Keating's first six reasons why the old rules don't apply:

1. Web-based training is an interactive training tool, not just another form of mass media.
2. WBT is alive. It needs to be visited everyday and updated regularly.
3. Web-based training is best suited for teaching cognitive skills.
4. Web-based training is justified in terms of strategic goals and not return-on-investment.
5. Web-based training requires new learning skills.
6. Content is the motivating factor in Web-based training.

associated with. ▼ Tune the HTML code to make it faster and smaller. If you can, save graphics as GIFs rather than JPEGs to create smaller files—but be sure the to test image quality. ▼ Manage the development team to keep the project on time and on budget. It is too easy to the let project specifications creep up, increasing the project's time and cost. ▼ An essential and often forgotten step in the software development process is end-user testing, also called human-factors engineering. This is an important part of the quality-assurance program. End-user testing is the key to the success of your WBT because different target audiences react differently to the same program. Thorough testing before launching the program eliminates surprises. Make usability testing and formative evaluation top priorities. Listen to the learners and make the program fit their needs.

**8. Web-based training requires interactivity on three levels:** Learner-to-materials, learner-to-learner, and learner-to-instructor. WBT requires well-designed interactivity. This does not mean full animations, or audio, or video streams. It means, however; that WBT must engage learners regularly during the learning.

▼ When learners interact with the materials, they should be required to do more than read a page of text, or simply click and drag.

Learner-to-material interactions are interchanges between the student and the program—reading text, following hyperlinks, responding to questions, engaging in simulations and playing an animated sequence.

In asynchronous programs, learner-to-material interactions predominate.

▼ With learner-to-learner interactions, students learn from each other. The Web offers the technology both to push and pull the learner into this kind of interactivity. Push technologies are Web technologies that reach out to users—e-mail, list servs, and PointCast.

Push technology draws learners into the interactivity, because the interactivity is pushed to the student's desktop. Pull technologies, in contrast, require users to make an effort to visit a Web site, join a chat, or contribute to threaded discussions.

▼ Learner-to-instructor interactions offer powerful facilitation opportunities. In the most straightforward mode, students can e-mail questions to the instructor as they encounter difficulties. At a more elaborate level, tools such as NetMeeting let student and instructor talk in real time and to collaborate on a software application. This two-way communication makes it possible for either the learner or the instructor to initiate the interaction.

WBT is lonely, even isolating at times. So use a variety of interactions to keep the learner engaged.

**9. Re-purposing conventional content for WBT requires significant redesign.** The tools for converting existing training materials into Web-based materials are deceptively easy to use. Presentation tools such as PowerPoint and Astound (*www.astound.com*) make it easy to change a presentation designed for the instructor-led environment into a series of HTML pages for a Web site. Likewise, a workbook or student manual can be saved as an HTML file and posted to the Web in an afternoon. simple "save as" commands mean existing materials can support WBT in short order.

The new rules, however require that programs be redesigned before posting to the Web. There are three primary aspects of redesign. ▼ The content must stand on its own. In the case of instructor-led materials, it takes a significant amount of work to complete bulleted lists, supply the anecdotal examples, and link learners to definitions or background information an in-person instructor might have provided off the top of the head. ▼ The second repurposing task focuses on chunking the information. Often the instructor-led program or workbook are designed for extended periods of study. Designers must find effective ways to chunk a five-day class into manageable online segments, and link those segments in a logical fashion. ▼ The third major issue is revising print-based, video, or workbook materials to make them Web-ready. Here the resolution of computer screens presents a challenge. Legibility sets lower limits on the size of text, and on the amount of text a computer screen supports. Streaming video presents its own technical challenges.

Moving graphics to the Web requires special attention to size of graphic files and the use of copyright material. All told, repurposing content for the Web requires significant effort.

**10. WBT must keep up with the state of your organization's tech-readiness.** Don't put WBT into a learning ghetto. If your organization's intranet is highly interactive, the train-

ing pages should be, too. Match WBT to the rest of your organization's intranet content. Typically, your information technology department has the coolest pages on the intranet. Make your WBT as cool.

Surf the Internet, see what is working best, and then emulate it—taking care, of course, not to copy things outright, except where sites explicitly allow it. Right now, e-business applications are hot. They involve gathering information from the buyer as the buyer selects items for purchase. The e-business tracks that buyers click, and from that information builds a profile of the buyer.

Translate that to WBT: You can gauge what a learner knows by gathering information with a pretest of qualification activity. When the learner chooses a module, you can track the learner's progress and skill development in the same way.

All in all, building WBT is new, exciting, and full of challenges. Continually remind yourself that you're not in Kansas anymore. You're in WBT, where the new rules have pushed out the old—and where you get to write some new rules yourself.

# RESEARCH SUMMARY

## WHAT YOU NEED TO KNOW ABOUT ONLINE LEARNERS

*Editor's Comment:* Observers have noticed that online learners behave somewhat differently from face-to-face learners. What they have noticed, however, seems to cover the entire field of communication and represents a range of positive and negative behavior, both enhancing and obstructing learning. The things noticed by instructor Jennifer Lieberman suggest instructional skills and learning design modifications in order for learners to make the most of online learning opportunities. These are some of her findings from observations of many online teachers and learners:

- Online learning appeals to shy students because they can participate anonymously.

- Online learning gives shy students more time to prepare responses; they don't need to be afraid of speaking in front of others.

- Non-shy students participate much the same way online as they do off-line.

- Therefore, because the number and quality of responses from shy students is added to the expected responses from non-shy students, the total quality of responses in online learning surpasses responses in traditional classrooms.

- Online learners often write more online than they would speak in a classroom; instructors therefore must set ground rules and limits to amount of text per person and the number of postings per person to encourage students to be guided by the "necessary and sufficient" guideline—only what's necessary but all that's sufficient makes the best response.

- To encourage quiet students, ask each student the same number of questions and make sure that each person's ideas get equal response attention from the instructor; design instruction for individuals, maximizing the advantages of the technology.

- Be prepared to spend more instructional design time as well as more instructional time in responding to students in online learning than in classroom learning.

- Respond to students in a way that encourages their interacting with each other so that they learn from each other.

*Source:* "Questions and Answers: Jennifer Lieberman, Online Teaching Guru" in *TRAINING Magazine*, March 2000, p. 25. Jennifer Lieberman teaches professors at University of Illinois-Urbana how to use online technology.

# RESEARCH SUMMARY

## MOVE OVER BALDRIGE: HERE COMES SCORM

*Editor's Comment:* Elliott Masie is known for spotting trends early. SCORM looks like one of them. He reports some early developments regarding standards for e-learning in one of his summer *Tech-Learn TRENDS* newsletters. SCORM has a "feel" to it similar to that of the Department of Commerce's Baldrige Quality Standards, so popular a decade or more ago.

This is some of the background information and some of the current activity in establishing e-learning standards; the action comes out of the U.S. Department of Defense:

- SCORM stands for Sharable Courseware Object Reference Model.

- SCORM is a specification for the reuse, redeployment, and interchangeability of learning content.

- SCORM originated in the Advanced Distributed Learning "Plugfest" project of the Department of Defense (find more information at *www.adlnet.org*).

- Objects are envisioned as large and valuable repositories of content that can be selected and moved to learners wherever they need them through a learning management system.

- Object usage is expected to be flexible, being appropriate for e-learning as well as instructor-led learning, in small chunks for a variety of delivery systems.

- The design of access to objects and their configuration are both expected to be areas ripe for development in the near future.

- A SCORM certification process is under development now.

- Professional associations, vendors, and corporations are expected to endorse the continued development of SCORM.

---

*Source:* "A Giant Step Forward for e-Learning Standards!" in *TechLearn TRENDS* online newsletter of The MASIE Center, June 26, 2000 p. 1.

## ARTICLE REPRINT

## PITFALLS OF MIX AND MATCH LEARNING OBJECT DESIGN

*Editor's Comment:* Granules, learning objects, chunks, infonuggets, mind snacks—these are some of the terms used to define the on-demand learning solutions made possible by mix and match instructional design efforts for use in online learning. Writer Dave Zielinski subtitles his article "Bumps on the road to 'granularizing' training." His insightful article alerts designers to the common mistakes about learning objects.

### OBJECTS OF DESIRE

*by Dave Zielinski*

It's late on a Friday afternoon, and the leader of a project team ruminates over e-mail just received from two key members saying they can't make a critical meeting early next week. The team uses the calendar facility in Microsoft Outlook to schedule its meetings, but the assistant who normally handles that is on vacation. The manager, who has never rescheduled a meeting, needs a crash course, but hasn't the time or patience to slog through a manual or take a course on using Outlook.

Instead, he goes online to search his company's database of reusable "learning objects." He retrieves a 10-minute minicourse that shows him how to check each team member's schedule for the next free slot. He practices the procedure a couple of times, then takes a test to ensure he can replicate what he's just done. Within minutes after hitting the panic button, he has successfully rescheduled the do-or-die meeting. Behold, the power of the learning granule. And yes, if it sounds a little like the software help screens that have been around for years, that's the direction training is headed these days as organizations adopt the concept of learning objects, also known as granules, chunks, infonuggets and even mind snacks.

Developments in the use—and reuse—of learning objects have been heralded as a boon to training and performance support. The idea is to allow employees the freedom to retrieve from online databases just the amount or combination of information and performance support they need to tackle the task at hand, leaving extraneous or time-wasting material aside. The mix-and-match capabilities of learning objects also promise greater return on the training-development dollar, since any given object could be recombined with others into a variety of training "courses." And as groups in the computer-learning industry inch closer to creating open standards for transporting learning objects across various computer platforms, the future of the modular learning block seems bright.

At the same time, there are concerns about potential trouble down the road due to misuse or misunderstanding of this promising design idea. The worriers are people who design granular content and industry professionals who've followed the evolution of learning objects. The reason they've got jitters is because an awful lot of organizations are eager to board the granular-learning train, but not so many are versed in the wise use of learning objects.

Recurring concerns about how designers can go wrong with learning objects tend to fall into four categories. We'll take them one by one.

## 1. FAULTY PRETEST QUESTIONS

The fear is that designers will mistakenly presume the validity of pretest questions that guide the learner's steps through a series of learning objects. Pretests often determine which segments of a computer-based learning program trainees need to take and which ones they can bypass or "test out" of. But the design of pretests tied to granular content is an area where a lot of "instructional malpractice" occurs, says Camille Price, director of consulting services for Allen Communication, a Sale Lake City courseware development firm (now part of a new e-learning roll-up called Mentergy).

Pretests are valid only if they measure what they're supposed to measure, accurately discriminating between those who know and those who don't. Price believes many designers use test questions that aren't valid. The result: Employees end up skipping prerequisite granules they need to take, creating learning barriers down the road.

Developers rarely take the time to validate a pretest, Price says. And even those who do often go only halfway, she adds. Many designers, seeking to avoid long pretests, write only one test question per learning objective. "It usually takes more than one question to test an objective, yet the majority of pretests out there use only one," she says. "That concerns me, especially if we're talking about something like safety training."

One cause of poor pretests, Price asserts, is graduate programs in instructional technology that don't require students to take courses in how to create valid assessments. Many of those graduates also don't receive appropriate training once on the job. "There's no lack of people out there now who can author a course in HTML, but they have trouble validating a test item," she says.

Jim L'Allier, head of research and development for NETg of Naperville, IL, a supplier of computer-skills training programs, suggests an alternative solution made possible by learning objects themselves: enhanced use of simulations as pretest assessments. While NETg does use time-honored methods such as multiple-choice, matching or sequencing pretests, L'Allier says, it only does so with learning objectives when the goal is to test basic knowledge or comprehension—say, asking employees to identify the pull-down menu under which fonts can be found in MS Word. For higher-order objectives—applying skills on the job, or information analysis, synthesis and evaluation—he says NETg often uses a more involved simulation as a pretesting tool.

Consider a pilot using an aircraft flight simulator. "The correlation between the simulator and real cockpit conditions is almost one-to-one, so by preassessing the pilot in that situation, you can almost guarantee you're spotting, or not spotting, the right behaviors," L'Allier says. Using learning objects, he continues, designers now can create simulations that accurately mimic many other real-life tasks—especially computer-related tasks. Such brief simulations can be used to find out whether learners really should be allowed to "test out" of particular modules.

## 2. MISSING LINKS IN LEARNING-OBJECT CHAINS

Designers refer to this as the "skipped gradient" problem, in which poorly sequenced or mismatched learning objects may cause the learner to skip a critical prerequisite concept, leading to gaps downstream when people haven't mastered the right building blocks. Think of missing a critical week of math class in elementary school. Math is linear in its progression; it's hard to learn multiplication if you haven't already learned addition.

Price learned the dangers of skipped gradient the hard way, while training mechanics for a truck manufacturer. The goal was to teach troubleshooting skills on the truck's fuel management and control systems, with hopes of reducing service time and overall repair costs. The curriculum was highly granular, featuring small training chunks on system components, functions, locations and troubleshooting scenarios. Price assumed in the beginning that the trainees knew how to use a multimeter, a tool that tests voltage and amperage. All of the information in the troubleshooting session presupposed that they understood how to use the tool. In fact, many of them did not. "That's classic skipped gradient," she says.

In "courses" composed of learning objects, the worry is not simply that the designer may omit a critical piece of information but that the learner can easily miss it. The danger of skipping prerequisites when navigating learning objects is especially acute when learners are beginners in a subject, tackling introductory-level material with no prior experience or foundational knowledge. Since they "don't know what they don't know," they can quickly lose their way in a forest of infonuggets.

A deceptively easy solution presents itself: Allow only designated pathways for trainees through these fields of objects. But the problem is more complex. For one thing, that solution doesn't allow for differences in learning styles. Learners tend to fall into two categories: the field-dependent "plodders" and field-independent "gracers." Plodders, who embrace being told what to do and struggle with ambiguity, don't recover as quickly from wrong turns. Usually, they prefer designated paths. Gracers thrive on the chance to explore and harvest only the content they need, enjoying the fruits of a system that presumes certain learners are the best judges of their own learning requirements.

Indeed, creating rigid learning paths rests on another sometimes-dubious design assumption, believes Ann Yakimovicz, president of Aprendio Inc., a Jonestown, TX, consultancy specializing in Web-based learning design. "The assumptions we make about what's important for learners at the time of need and what can be left behind aren't always valid, no matter how much we think we know," she says.

NETg's L'Allier believes well-conceived learning object databases play right to grazers' strength—cobbling together content on the fly. "Say I'm writing an electronic memo, and midway through I decide I want to create a graphic in the memo that's hotlinked to a spreadsheet," he says. For such a specific task, a person can search various object databases and pull the appropriate objects needed to learn how to do it. This assumes, of course, that the learning objects are sitting in some well-organized repository and are labeled clearly with metadata tags so that individual learners can find them easily and dip into them in the right sequence.

Sounds great as far as it goes, observes Price: "If you're talking about a performance-support object database, then free access isn't a problem." But the question remains, she says, "How can I hope to ensure that a trainee new to a subject area will properly perform a task if I don't mark their way through all of the steps—if I just allow them to go in and graze?"

Designers steeped in instructional systems design (ISD) learn to create hierarchies, prerequisites or enabling objectives, curriculum analyses and the like, Price says. "But when some of them start dropping learning objects into databases, it seems that caution goes out the window, and we put too much onus on the user to figure things out."

## 3. POOR FRAMES OF REFERENCE

A cousin to skipped gradient, the problem of "incomplete schema" results from a collection of learning objects that don't present a complete picture of the task or process being taught. This gives learners only a partial frame of reference with which to interpret information. That leads to low retention and confusion.

Price says one of her clients created schema problems with a granular approach in a basic sales-training course. Stages of the sales cycle—opening, qualifying leads, presenting, handling objections, closing—were broken out as individual objects and spaced over a period of weeks. Because of the long intervals between sessions, by the time trainees got to the last step of the process, they had forgotten much of what was taught regarding the early steps. They never got to experience the whole process or "schema" in one sitting. As a result, the training course was ineffective. "Trainees need a complete picture of a process early on before you can start adding granules as you go," Price says.

But at the same time, she adds, veteran salespeople embraced the bite-sized approach, since it gave them just what they needed, as they needed it, without forcing them to slog through a lot of familiar product information to get there. For Price, the experience underscored the different impact that granular-training approaches can have on beginners vs. people with experience in a topic.

## 4. ONE SIZE FITS ALL

To get the biggest bang for the design buck, learning objects often are designed for reuse by employees with very different jobs at many different levels in the organization. Then the challenge becomes tailoring them to the distinct

## THE LEARNING OBJECT DEFINED

What is a "learning object," exactly? Definitions abound. The concept generally refers to small chunks or granules of information that can be accessed individually or mixed, matched and glued together to form a variety of instructional courses or minicourses. Objects can be in the form of text, audio, video, diagrams, charts, graphics, or a combination of such. An object might be an individual wiring diagram for a built-in microwave oven, or it might be a short text-and-video demonstration of how to change a bicycle tire, complete with a multiple-choice test on the end.

When it comes to the concept's best use, many defer to a more restrictive definition used by Jim L'Allier, head of research and development for NETg, a Naperville, IL, developer of technology-delivered training in computer skills. Although NETg didn't mint the concept, the company trademarked the term "NETg learning object," or NLO, in the early 1990s, and has done a good share of the empirical research surrounding them.

An object, as L'Allier would have it, is a stand-alone unit of instruction that generally doesn't require a pre- or post-requisite, and contains this trio of elements: a measurable objective, a learning activity, and an assessment determining whether the objective has been met.

Within the software application Microsoft Excel, for example, an object might teach the singular task of learning how to draw a border around a cell. As many as 20 objects, or as few as a handful, might be strung together to make up a broader training "course."          —D.Z.

learning needs of these specific groups. In some scenarios, reusability holds water; for instance, learning objects covering an introductory portion of new-product training might be shared between sales and customer service people. But there are obvious dangers in trying to spread training material a mile wide and an inch deep.

"We always work to remind ourselves that we don't teach something, we teach someone," Price says. "When granules aren't adapted to audiences, that's a problem. Adult learners want some assurance that what they're learning matches their unique needs."

L'Allier says a concept known as "object memory" can help with the job of customizing objects to a particular audience. Suppose that a certain collection of learning objects—say, granules for mastering desktop applications or Java

design—is regularly drawn together by a particular audience (for example, C++ programmers) to solve a specific problem. In such cases, "the system can be set up to remember that combination, so over time we can build up patterns for certain audience types," he says.

The trick is to create an object database that is deep and versatile, yet focused on meaty content areas—product knowledge, for instance. In theory, those objects can be reused by a number of employee groups in different learning situations.

When it comes to learning objects, you ain't seen nothin' yet, L'Allier promises: "Whoever created the Lego block probably never imagined the possibility of a Legoland at the Mall of America [in Minneapolis] with hundreds of different configurations, all built using a simple little plastic block with a few nubs on it."

# ARTICLE REPRINT

## PRACTICAL TIPS ON HUMANIZING E-LEARNING

*Editor's Comment:* Here is an article that describes the experience of one instructor who taught the same course to 100 students, 30 of them online and 70 in the classroom. This report on his findings and conclusions gives the instructional designer some helpful tips based on experience for "humanizing" online learning in order to compensate for the lack of face-to-face interaction and capitalize on its strengths.

## HUMANIZING: HOW TO MAKE YOUR LEARNERS FEEL LESS LIKE CYBER-CYPHERS

### *Interview with Bridget Arend and Rob Valuck*

The subject was how to humanize your online course, and presented Bridget Arend, a training developer at Denver's eCollege.com, wasn't surprised that dozens of showgoers packed her room.

Online learning is a "dehumanized process," she says. "You're interacting with a computer, not a person. You're missing the non-verbal cues that exist in face-to-face interaction."

Online training is an effective way to deliver learning at a distance, to be sure. But Arend, who helps colleges and universities design online-training programs, argues that traditional settings for learning can be pretty distant as well.

### THE BACK ROW

"If you have 500 people sitting in a classroom, that's distance learning," Arend says. "Those people in the back rows can be more isolated and removed from the learning process than your sales manager in Japan who's taking an interactive online course with 20 other sales managers from around the world. It's all in the way you design the course."

Rob Valuck agrees. For three years, the assistant professor in the department of pharmacy at the University of Colorado has offered an online option for his Evidence-Based Pharmacy Practice course.

Typically, Valuck teaches the course to 100 students each semester—30 of them online, the rest in his classroom.

The courses are separate. The online students don't interact with the on-campus students.

### LIVE AND VIRTUAL

Teaching the same course at the same time both online and in the classroom lets Valuck compare the performance of both sets of students, live and virtual.

The result? "My online students perform better, and they progress more than my on-campus students do," he says.

One reason: the tendency of online students to participate more in the learning process. It's the nature of his online course for learners to be active—they don't have the traditional luxury of dozing through a lecture.

Valuck argues that, especially for shy or introverted students, online can be a better option. "The shy students do better online because they don't have to deal with issues like talking in front of a room full of people," he says. "Being online doesn't hinder them. It helps them."

It helps them if—and this is a big if—the course is designed with the human in mind. Valuck has worked with Arend and e.College to add human elements to his virtual course.

Online learners get the same content mix as on-campus students. "On campus, the course consists of two-thirds lecture, one-third discussion," Valuck says. "For my lectures, I use PowerPoint slides. With the online course, I just put the PowerPoint presentation online so the online students can see and hear the lectures."

## WORK ON IT

Arend and Valuck agree that online courses can be more interactive and involving than classroom-based instruction—but in order for that to happen, you have to work on it. Because of its solitary nature, WBT can be isolating. Only through concerted effort on the part of the facilitator can it become human.

Humanizing an online course is the key to successful online learning, says Arend.

▼ **Reach out to students** before the course begins. The concept of online learning is more familiar to trainers, but it's brand new to many trainees. They know what to expect from a classroom, and they may know what to expect from computer-based training via CD-ROM. But online learning, with interaction from other learners, is new.

Before the course begins, e-mail participants a list of the basics—what to expect of the course, what they should be doing and when, a schedule of real-time chat sessions. You want them to know the process so they can focus on content.

▼ **Make use of multimedia.** Students expect it. Many have played media-rich video games. But in humanizing the course, how can multimedia help? "Start off the course with a three-minute video clip of yourself explaining the course and welcoming learners," Arend says.

Or incorporate a slide show of photographs of course participants. This kind of multimedia presentation keeps people interested.

▼ **Focus on learners.** Include trainee-specific information in both the course and your instructions. When scheduling a time for an online chat session, for example, include various participants' time zones. "For Jean in California, it's noon. For John and Sarah in Iowa, it's 10 a.m."

▼ **Create informal communication opportunities.** Online students don't partake of the small talk and after-class socializing that classroom-based learners take for granted. Create surrogate opportunities online by setting up informal discussion areas where students can talk about anything—from their awful weekend to what they think of you as a facilitator.

▼ **Try to be funny.** And involve participants with humor. Encourage them to share anecdotes and stories from their experiences related to course material. It happens spontaneously in the classroom, but you'll need to nudge it along online. That way, students will get to know some personal details about their virtual coursemates, and about you.

▼ **Emote with emoticons.** They might be a bit silly, but they substitute for the kinds of nonverbal cues people pick up face to face, and they can prevent hurt feelings and misunderstandings. The statement: "This is the last time I'll ever do that for you," takes on a different feeling when punctuated with a smiling emoticon.

▼ **Require frequent interaction** between students and content. Use the interactivity that online courses provide to create group projects that require group interaction. That way, they'll have to work together instead of staying isolated behind their computer screens.

▼ **Relate to real life.** People want to learn what's relevant to them. So ask trainees to relate their best and worst experiences in training, and ask how they might transfer the good experiences to the online course.

▼ **Let them learn from each other.** This happens in classrooms all the time, but it's often left out of online courses. Ask students how they've dealt with a situation pertinent to course information. Share it with the others via e-mail or online chat. You might learn something, too.

▼ **Celebrate.** Simple, silly things like online cards, virtual gold stars and other encouragements add a sense of celebration on meeting a goal. It's not exactly beer and pizza at the end of a course, but you can do that online, too. Set up a time in which all course participants order pizza, and have a live chat session—either about the course itself or about nothing at all.

## INTRODUCTION TO TRAINING PROGRAM DELIVERY: SECTION 4

For years, the training community has been dealing with the delivery paradigm of "the sage on the stage," working hard to involve learners in dialogue, focus groups, teams, workshops, and other more democratic ways of being on the "receiving end" of training—working hard to fit not only the content but also the delivery method to the needs of individual learners. In recent years, the focuses on communities of practice, online chat rooms and electronic networking, mentoring, coaching, employee empowerment, the ubiquity of information, and self-directed learning all reinforce an evolutionary trend in training delivery, namely, that the trainer who initiates the delivery of training functions more as a "guide on the side" to individuals, and not "the sage on the stage" in front of the multitudes, within a newer, more facilitative delivery paradigm.

### FOCUS ON INDIVIDUAL LEARNING

In this first subsection, we give you four entries that address individual learning from the point of view of several typical delivery systems for individual learning: technology, tutorials, the home, and coaching. A common thread running through these entries is that efficiency of training, as in increasing the headcount of bodies moving through the corporate curriculum, is no longer the model most revered for learning. We present four very different entries, each with some light to shed on individual learning. Per-person/per-classroom hour metrics and the linear movement through predetermined course delivery seem like an Industrial-Age, not Information-Age, way of doing things.

### DISTANCE LEARNING

In this subsection on distance learning, we reflect the current maturing of this delivery format. Distance learning has been around for several decades, propelled into corporate consciousness when satellite transmission for the masses became possible. Numerous mainstream universities were quick to put college courses into a distance learning format, and new distance-only degree- and certificate-granting institutions sprang up throughout the country. Corporate universities, too, jumped on the distance learning bandwagon. It is here, in the university context that we see the most advances in and maturation of distance learning. This year especially, we have seen numerous articles about some of the deeper learning issues associated with various delivery systems we have come to recognize as distance-learning delivery. We've selected a representative number of entries to focus on these issues.

### WEB-BASED TRAINING DELIVERY

The business of training delivery has generally come to be associated with the term *Web-based training*. A huge number of new Web-based companies offer all sorts of online learning through their Websites at your desktop. The ease of global communications, especially e-mail, and the power of technology have made work, including workplace training, become a 24-hour-per-day, 7-day-per-week enterprise. In spite of work/life balance programs, humane corporate policies, and even legislation, the 24/7 nature of today's work has overtaken the workplace and provided incentives for profit-seeking Web-based training delivery companies to get into the fray. Web-based training has often gotten a bad reputation for being ill-designed and delivered as entertainment and not learning, responding to the carrot of big money to be made and the schtick of selling to companies who don't want to be left out of the Web-based training revolution.

The numbers are staggering, and hardly worth printing because they are changing so fast. For example, ASTD's brochure advertising the June 2000 "TechKnowledge" conference in Indianapolis quoted International Data Corporation (IDC) in a sidebar on p. 4 as finding that corporations spent $870 million dollars on e-learning in 1999; and by year 2003, IDC predicts that e-learning will dwarf all other learning methods. Elliott Masie, e-learning guru and entrepreneur, has engaged Tom Peters to deliver a keynote address at his Orlando conference, "TechLearn," in November 2000. Peters' topic is "Reinventing Training." Masie's online newsletter, *TechLearn TRENDS*, on Monday, June 12, 2000, reported in a quick survey of readers that only about 1/5 of employees are willing to "take an important e-learning event" at home. In addition, only about 15 percent of employees found it easy to concentrate on e-learning at their desks at work, and that interruptions from colleagues, phone calls, and checking e-mail made it difficult to concentrate on e-learning at work (91 percent of responses). This informal study during mid-May 2000 by The Masie Center of 2,474 respondents begs the question: If employees are reluctant to take e-learning courses at home on their own time and find it difficult to do so at work, just exactly when and where can e-learning take place? The vision of anytime/anyplace sometimes sounds like no time and no place.

To be sure, Web-based training delivery has much potential and many advantages. Some of the positive developments we've seen recently include a differentiation of e-learning into discrete products ("objects") such as components of courses not only complete courses, "just-in-time" content modules, better links to research and other information resources, better navigation, better video, and better use of built-in electronic performance supports (EPS).

An interview in the September 2000 *TRAINING* magazine with Jaron Lanier and others, reports on a 160-university "Tele-immersion" consortium that is working on fusing in-person and online learning through new concepts and technologies in virtual reality in order to make Web-based learning more naturally communicative (p 74). A clarification of terms and more experience with the best of Web-based training delivery is happening. Like the e-book revolution of Stephen King and year 2000, Web-based training reminds us that we need to separate the delivery mechanism from the content and develop and evaluate each according to its own standards. In this subsection, we focus on mini-case studies and resources in Web-based training delivery.

## CLASSROOMS AND GROUP LEARNING

For a variety of reasons and in spite of the promise and potential of technology-based training delivery, classroom training remains an overwhelming choice of delivery system worldwide. A study published by ASTD in January 2000, excerpts of which begin our final subsection in Section 4, suggests that in the U.S. as well as numerous other countries, various technology-based systems have been tried over the past five years and often abandoned. Usage has fluctuated from year to year, not making a steady trend line upwards as might be expected. Rather, ASTD concludes that ". . . the leveling off in the use of learning technologies suggests that organizations are encountering obstacles in implementing technology-based training" (*Training & Development*, January 2000, sidebar, p. 42). On page 11 of ASTD's *2000 International Comparison Report* the study reinforced the conclusion that "most firms around the world continued to believe that learning technologies will play an increasingly important role in the future, but have discovered the difficulty of making their contribution a reality." As we begin year 2001, the classroom delivery model persists, but more and more companies have experience with technology-based delivery systems and are pausing to evaluate the delivery method with both optimism and caution. This year we can expect more definitive studies of delivery systems based on experience in the professional training and learning literature.

The important effect on classroom training of experimentation with technology-based training is that traditional classroom trainers have been forced to examine and evaluate the nuances of classroom training methods. Guide on the Side, not Sage on the Stage is the newer representation of classroom trainer. Facilitation, workshop, collaboration, and blending are terms at least as common today as are the terms "lecture" or "seminar."

The Society for Human Resource Management (SHRM) has an excellent 6-page "White Paper" on "Matching Group Needs to Training Methods" by Carol Auerbach, on its Website. (Members can access this white paper at *www.shrm.org/whitepapers/documents/61315.asp.*) In it, she examines nine typical alternatives in delivering group training. These nine methods are the ones she defines as making group training more participative and more facilitator-led: print materials, multimedia materials, formal presentations, informal discussion groups, classroom training, experiential training, CBT (Computer-Based Training), WBT (Web-Based Training), and Distance Learning. Her paper examines each of these in terms of how each can be made more active to meet the needs for content and cost. If you are in the process of rethinking your own classroom or group training, this SHRM paper is worth downloading. SHRM's Information Center's phone number is 1-800/283-7476.

In this subsection on classroom and group learning, we give you six entries that represent the range of influences on corporate classrooms. Specifically, we consider new dimensions in corporate universities as they adapt to changing times, we show you Gateway's entry into customer training and profit as an example of how classroom training can bring in the money instead of draining it from the training center's bottom line, we report on the Defense Department's crackdown on "PowerPoint Rangers," we show you how Ryder teamed up with the public education system for the benefit of its employees, and we show you how some college classrooms—the bastion of the Sage on the Stage delivery method—are succeeding in blending their delivery methods to include technology-based delivery while retaining the best of their classrooms.

# 4A. FOCUS ON INDIVIDUAL LEARNING

## ARTICLE REPRINT

## IS TECHNOLOGY "TRANSFORMATIVE"?

*Editor's Comment:* This is a thoughtful and provocative article on the role of technology in learning. Professor Jonassen suggests that a newer and transformative view of technology in education is needed. He takes off from the point of view that each of us constructs his or her own reality, and that a constructivist view of knowledge is the goal. He examines the effects of technology on this view of learning.

## TRANSFORMING LEARNING WITH TECHNOLOGY

### *by David H. Jonassen*

### THE PROMISE OF TECHNOLOGY

Technology is modern. Throughout the industrial age, technology has promised to improve the lives of those who used it. Technology can produce faster, better, and more efficiently. During the 20th century, education has embraced technology. Technology has promised smarter, happier, better educated, and more fulfilled learners. Technology has always been zealously promoted as a modern solution for the problems of education—lack of productivity, inefficiency, and lack of focus. During the twentieth century, each new technology emerged as the panacea for education's socio-cultural problems. Unfortunately, each new technology has failed to deliver on its promise. In this article, I argue that:

- Modern and post-modern conceptions of technology impede the emergence of personal identities and learning.

- We must redefine the relationships between learners and technology in order to transcend modern promises and post-modernists' cynical fears and to truly empower learning.

In order to support this position, I will contrast modern and post-modern views of technology and suggest a newer, transformative view of technology in education in an effort to explain why technology has failed and to provide a vision for how it could work.

What is the future of educational technology? I do not know. At best, I can contrast a number of visions that have been promulgated during the latter part of this century. Since each of us constructs his or her own understanding of reality, these views can provide options for reflecting one's personal view. Since we also socially co-construct meaning, these visions can also provide a focus for conversation as we predict and hopefully co-determine our own future with technology.

### MODERN VIEWS OF TECHNOLOGY

During this century, technology has become the voice of society. In education, its role has been to transmit knowledge, culture, and meaning.

*Source:* "Transforming Learning with Technology: Beyond Modernism and Post-Modernism or Whoever Controls the Technology Creates the Reality" by David H. Jonassen in *Educational Technology*, March-April 2000, pp. 21-25. David H. Jonassen is a Contributing Editor of *Educational Technology* and Professor of Instructional Systems at Penn State University. Reprinted with permission of Educational Technology Publications, Englewood Cliffs, NJ. Copyright 2000. All rights reserved.

### Triumph of Technology: A Technophilic View

For the past two centuries, technology has represented the vehicle to the future. From mechanical advantage to information edge, learning how to harness the power of various technologies has provided the pipeline to future success. The use of technology for social and material advancement has been a major goal of these two centuries. For many, technology is the modern salvation to societal problems. In the nineteenth century, technology supplanted our physical work. In the twentieth century, it tamed time by transporting us faster. Moving into the 21st century, technology will fulfill our knowledge needs by thinking for us. Technologies are becoming more intelligent, with fuzzy logic controllers adjusting the performance of washing machines to accommodate the dirtiness of our clothes. We are increasingly represented by intelligent agents in our interactions with the world. They, of course, interact with other intelligent agents on our behalf rather than with us. HAL, the ascendant computer in Clark's *2001*, is waiting for us around the corner. In this technophilic view of technology as the answer to nearly every material and social problem, we began the abdication of personal identity, responsibility, and authority that matured in post-modern conceptions (discussed below).

Technophilia began in education with the highly specialized vocational education and home economics courses of the early twentieth century that sought to fulfill current vocational needs. However, the technophilic view of technology was best instantiated in the 1980s by an intense focusing on computer literacy. Computer literacy assumed that computers provided completely new symbol systems or formalisms to mediate knowledge sharing. It also assumed that computers could be more than symbol systems; they should be the *object* of instruction. Computers should be studied as technological phenomena. Unfortunately, what too many students learned on the way to becoming computer-literate was how to memorize the parts of a computer based on the "strong belief that vocabulary implies knowledge" (Bork, 1985, p. 34). We zealously believed that it was essential for students to embrace and understand this silicon-mediated reality.

### Technology as Teaching Medium: Educational View

Since their inception, modern educational technologies have been conceived most frequently as instructional communicators, mediated teachers, and knowledge conveyers. Information is encoded visually or verbally in the symbol systems afforded by various technologies. During the "instructional" process, students perceive the messages encoded in the technology. A generation of research and teaching averred that information-based messages that are more effectively designed and encoded will naturally produce better communication, and so result in greater learning gains. Generations of instructional television and computer-based instruction operationalized learning in terms of presentation of information on screens to students, whose understanding or memory would occasionally be assessed by making pre-scripted responses to the technology. This view of "communication as transmission centers on the ancient practice of transmitting messages over long distances in order to exert control" (Pea, 1994). Technologies (books, teachers, slates, pictures) have been used for centuries to more efficiently transmit socially acceptable beliefs and values, that is, to exert intellectual authority over learners.

This transmissive role for technology was intended to ameliorate the job of teaching to predictably control the learning of students. Unconsciously, the role of teachers was also being usurped. Technology as transmitter is based on an Aristotelian world view which relies on two essential components of reality—objectivity and causality—both integral components of Western consciousness (Jonassen, 1983). Educational communications rely on objectivity to define the physical world (determine reality), which is transmitted to learners so that they can acquire the same objective reality. Educational communications also assume that we can isolate cause-effect relationships so that we can be sure that our instructional interventions will affect learning predictably. To the degree that these beliefs are deemed true, technologies will work as information transmitters. And if we assume that information assimilation is a meaningful form of learning, the technologies do enhance learning. However, from a critical perspective, this view of technology is both naive and ungrounded.

## POST-MODERN VIEWS OF EDUCATIONAL TECHNOLOGY

Post-modern conceptions of technology augur the further erosion of personal identity, responsibility, and authority because they are most concerned with power relationships. Their view is that technology represents a focus for power, a lever to lull society into believing again in democracy, when, in reality, technology, like any other value-laden tool, benefits some (those in power) more than others.

### Technology as Power: Controlling the Masses

The eminent French post-modern philosopher Michel Foucault believed that thought can be instantiated in buildings. In *Discipline and Punish*, Foucault described the Panopticon, a circular building with a tower at its center, with windows into each cell surrounding the tower. All that was needed was to put a supervisor in the middle and populate each cell with prisoners, workers, or school children, enabling the supervisor to see and control everything. Each individual "is the object of information, never a subject in communication" (Foucault, 1977, p. 200).

The Panopticon is about power. The residents of the Panopticon are constantly reminded that they can be watched but never know when they are. In addition to surveillance, the Panopticon can function as a laboratory to try out experiments on its inhabitants. The Panopticon is "a generalizable model of functioning; a way of defining power relations in terms of the everyday life of men."

Modern learning technologies, especially networked computers, have the potential to become Panopticons from which we can be observed in the daily conduct of our lives. In a post-modern critique of some of my research (provided in a blind-review process), unknown authors argued that technologies such as hypertext and hypermedia, like prisons, observe, discipline, regulate, and control their users. When learners interact with technology, they are told what to think,

observed for what they do, and then evaluated for their understanding of the lessons.

The Internet has the potential of becoming the ultimate electronic Panopticon. It not only collects information about the habits of every user, it also deposits "cookies" onto their computers to observe them when they are not connected.

### Technoglobalism: The Commoditization of Education

Another post-modern view of technology is provided by David Noble (1998), a Canadian professor of political science. He is one of the most outspoken critics of modern universities that seek to extend their influence through distance education technologies. Why are universities investing so heavily in distance technology infrastructure? Noble argues that in addition to the fear of getting left behind, there are the modern pressures of progress. However, technology is a Trojan horse that is not intended so much to bring education to the masses anytime, anywhere as it is the commercialization and commoditization of higher education—the acts of "transforming courses into courseware, the activity of instruction itself into commercially viable proprietary products that can be owned and bought and sold in the market." He argues that it stands to reason that publishers and hardware and software manufacturers, who have the most to gain, are the most ardent supporters of this movement. As universities become larger and more entrepreneurial in order to grow (their modern imperative), this transformation of higher education is being initiated and implemented from the top down without any input from faculty or students. Its goal is economic advantage: technoglobalism. Its result, post-modernists argue, is the further erosion of personal identity, responsibility, and authority.

As more professors put their course materials online in an effort to appear innovative, they are being duped, because the goal of this commoditization is to control or eliminate the need for professors, Noble claims. Once courses go online, administrators gain greater direct control over faculty performance and course content (a higher education Panopticon). Once the knowledge is owned by the institution, the professors become redundant, and so they are outsourced, according to Winner (1997), and thus universities reduce their direct labor and plant maintenance costs, making them more efficient (their modern imperative). Technology is the new medium for administrative scrutiny, supervision, regimentation, discipline, and even censorship, Noble argues. The result will be a reduction of faculty autonomy, independence, and control over their work. Once the professors' ideas and identities become commodities, there will be no need for the real professors. Just like in other skilled industries, faculty activity is being restructured by technology in order to discipline, deskill, and displace the labor force, and place as much control as possible into the hands of the administration.

Paranoid or prescient? Noble and Winner prophesy fundamental changes in education, as universities compete in the global information market and new educational companies bid against school districts for the privilege of educating their children. As society increasingly accepts the minimalization of education as information transmission and credentialing, we have less need for publicly held, publicly supported educational systems. When that happens, we accede power to corporations (including universities) who use technology as the medium for acquiring and using power.

### *Reflections on a Post-Modern World*

What have we learned in our post-modern world? In the 20th century, we have witnessed the meltdown of the nuclear family. Parents have abdicated their responsibilities for caregiving and transmission of cultural values to technology (especially commercial television and now the Internet) to educate their offspring. What have children learned from these technologies? Obsessions with sex and violence; personal wealth is the only goal worth pursuing; peers are the only arbiters of reality (certainly not parents or teachers); education is unfulfilling and worthless; and knowledge is a commodity that can be charged on a credit card when you need it, as evidenced by the incredible growth of the knowledge management industry. The values that are conveyed by commercial technologies are violent, lurid, avaricious, petty,

vapid, vulgar, and dumb. Are these the symptoms of social changes or the means for centralizing corporate power? Who is responsible for the degeneration of social values? The fabric of society is being rewoven with a substantively different warp, but who is controlling the loom?

Are there solutions? Can we reform society? What roles, if any, can technologies play in any solutions? Can we wrest control of the technologies from corporate managers? Can technologies foster and support change?

In the next section, I describe a different vision for how to use technologies to empower learners and to transform the relationship of learners and technologies. Transformative technologies can foster meaning-making and strong identity-formation among students, parents, and teachers who believe that learning is the construction, expression, and negotiation of personal beliefs, conceptions, and identities rather than the inculcation of doctrine. When no one has the right idea, but some have better ideas, and the best ideas emerge from social co-construction of reality, transformative technologies can help to transform the educational society in which those people exist.

## TRANSFORMATIVE VIEWS OF EDUCATIONAL TECHNOLOGY

Pea (1994) argued that in order to transcend the transmissive view of education, it is necessary to adopt a transformative view of technologies as resources for transforming existing practice by providing new ways of thinking, knowing, and acting in education. How can that happen? Rather than transmitting information more efficiently and (hopefully) effectively, and rather than controlling the thoughts and behavior of learners, it is necessary to allow learners to reflect on and represent what they know and believe and to use technology to support and amplify those activities. Why? Because whoever controls the technology creates the reality.

### *Technology as Intellectual Partner*

Students do not learn *from* technology (or teachers, for that matter). Rather, students learn from thinking in meaningful ways. Thinking naturally results from meaningful activity, such as representing what students know, rather than memorizing what teachers and technologies tell them. When learners use technologies to represent what they know, they are learning *with* technologies rather than *from* technologies. In this way, learners enter into an intellectual partnership *with* the technology. When students work *with* computers, for instance, they enhance the capabilities of the computer, and the computer in turn enhances their thinking and learning. The result of this partnership is that the whole of learning becomes greater than the potential of learner and computer alone. Learners use technologies as intellectual partners in order to:

- articulate what they know (i.e., representing their knowledge);
- reflect on what they have learned and how they came to know it;
- support the internal negotiation of meaning-making;
- construct personal representations of meaning and
- support intentional, mindful thinking.

Learning *with* technologies transforms the role of the learner from receiver (classic, communications conception of learners) to producer, creator, and sender.

Technologies that are particularly effective for students to learn with include:

- semantic organization tools (databases, semantic networks) for organizing what they know;
- dynamic modeling tools (expert systems, spreadsheets, systems modeling tools) for building simulations and representing mental models;
- microworlds for exploring and experimenting with phenomena;
- synchronous and asynchronous conferencing environments for socially co-constructing meaning;
- knowledge construction environments (hypermedia, multimedia, Web publishing);
- information interpretation tools (visualization tools, information search engines) for better understanding information encountered; and

- video for visualizing the range of ideas that students generate.

These technologies function as cognitive tools for helping learners to elaborate on what they are thinking. See Jonassen, Peck, and Wilson (1999) and Jonassen (2000) for descriptions and examples of these tools.

The key to meaning-making is ownership of the ideas that are created. When technologies are used as the tools for organizing, creating, and expressing those ideas, learners are learning with the technologies and necessarily engaged in meaningful learning.

### *Mediating the Social Co-Construction of Reality*

Modern, transmissive views of technology have always assumed the objectivity of knowledge. Knowledge can be transmitted to individual learners who acquire the same objective reality. The process of learning is like filling up your automobile. The higher the octane of the fuel and the bigger the tank, the better the learning. This view has nearly always conceived of learning as an individual, acquisitive process. Teachers and technologies tell students what they know; students acquire what they know.

Contemporary conceptions of learning in discourse communities, communities of practice, learning communities, and knowledge-building communities challenge this individual, acquisitive conception of learning as filling up students' knowledge tanks. Rather, they see learning "as a social phenomenon constituted in the experienced, lived-in world, through legitimate peripheral participation in ongoing social practice" (Lave, 1991, p. 64). When a goal is really important, people collaborate to socially co-construct shared meaning and negotiate shared responsibilities. Authority is socially mediated rather than dictated. Although these processes naturally occur in non-formal situations, they are seldom allowed in formal educational processes, because that would require an abdication of power and intellectual authority. However, if we are serious about using technologies to transform existing practice, then we need to focus on how to use technologies to support the social negotiation and co-construction of knowledge.

New computer networks that facilitate immediate access to the world's information and nearly instantaneous communication with anyone anywhere have provided a level of global connectivity that was inconceivable a mere decade ago. This connectivity is redefining culture. Rather than being constrained by simultaneous location, communication is being redefined by need and interest. Computer networks have evolved to support discourse communities through different forms of computer conferences. Thousands of chat rooms and multi-user dungeons (MUDs) connect millions of users who daily converse about their lives, their dreams, and their interests. The number of active and interactive discourse communities has expanded exponentially in the past five years.

In education, networked technologies have fostered the development of knowledge-building communities. The goal of knowledge-building communities is to support students to "actively and strategically pursue learning as a goal," that is, intentional learning (Scardamalia, Bereiter, & Lamon, 1994, p. 201). Using Computer-Supported Intentional Learning Environments (CSILEs), students produce their own knowledge databases in their own knowledge-building community of students. Thus, student knowledge can be "objectified, represented in an overt form so that it [can] be evaluated, examined for gaps and inadequacies, added to, revised, and reformulated" (p. 201). Through KIDLINK, the Global Schoolhouse, Learning Circles, and many other educational telecommunications projects, students are forming global learning communities where participants conduct research (reading, studying, viewing, consulting experts), share information in the pursuit of a meaning, and reflect on the knowledge that they have constructed and the processes used to construct.

These communications technologies are capable of transforming the culture of education as well. By empowering students to negotiate their own beliefs and ideas, the balance of power is shifted from the educators to the students. I am not arguing here for a complete abdication of teacher responsibility. That would be destructive. Rather, I am arguing for a shift in the balance of power, new supportive roles for teachers, and more amplifying roles for technology.

## CONCLUSION

In this brief article, I have reviewed modern, post-modern, and transformative conceptions of educational technology. I do not presume that these are the only views of technology that can inform our deliberations, but they do provide a rich set of options.

We live in a post-modern world. Values that were endemic to the modern world—progress and efficiency—have dissolved in a cultural cynicism. This is especially prevalent among our youth, who constantly question why they have to do anything that is not immediately self-aggrandizing. Modern solutions, using technology to transmit cultural values more efficiently, will no longer affect today's youth. They are cynical about the goals of the institutions that seek to control their lives. They are post-modern, after all. However, educators who seek to transform education, to reorganize its foundational goals and values, can emancipate learners from the obligation to regurgitate that which has no relevance to them, to empower them to reflect on and represent what is important to them. Technology can support that goal. When used as tools for personal and social reflection, articulation, and creation, technology can help to transform learning and learners—to help them to become independent, self-regulated, life-long seekers and constructors of knowledge.

The future of technology in education will depend on who controls the technology and what their goals, values, beliefs, needs, and purposes are. Educators must reflect on their own beliefs and answer questions, such as:

- Who should control when, where, and how technologies in schools and universities should be used: corporations/institutions, teachers/professors, or students/learners?

- Whose knowledge and ideas are more important for learning: corporate and institutional agendas; teachers/professors know best; or learners define their own purposes for learning, convey their own beliefs, and create their own reality?

- What is the true mission of education—to transmit knowledge and values; to exert power over students; or to empower learners to reflect, construct, and express their own knowledge and beliefs?

**Acknowledgment:** Many thanks to Ali Carr, a valued colleague and friend, for her incisive review and recommended changes.

## REFERENCES

Bork, A. M. (1985). *Personal computers for education.* New York: Harper & Row.

Foucault, M. (1977). *Discipline and punish: The birth of the prison.* New York: Pantheon.

Jonassen, D. H. (1983, Winter). The tenuous relationship between research and policy making: Lessons from the new physics. *Media Management Journal, 2*, 32–33.

Jonassen, D. H. (2000). *Computers as mindtools for schools: Engaging critical thinking.* Columbus, OH: Merrill/Prentice-Hall.

Jonassen, D. H., Peck, K., & Wilson, B. G. (1999). *Learning with technology: A constructivist perspective.* Columbus, OH: Prentice-Hall.

Lave, J. (1991). Situating learning in communities of practice. In L. B. Resnick, J. M. Levine, & S. D. Teasley (Eds.), *Perspectives on socially shared cognition.* Washington, DC: American Psychological Association.

Noble, D. (1998). Digital diploma mills: The automation of higher education. *Educom Review, 33*(3).

Pea, R. (1994). Seeing what we build together: Distributed multimedia learning environments for transformative communications. *Journal of the Learning Sciences, 3*(3), 285–299.

Scardamalia, M., Bereiter, C., & Lamon, J. (1994). The CSILE Project: Trying to bring the classroom into World 3. In K. McGilly (Ed.), *Classroom lessons: Integrating cognitive theory and classroom practice* (pp. 201–228). Cambridge MA: MIT Press.

Winner, L. (1997). The handwriting on the wall: Resisting technoglobalism's assault on education. In M. Moll (Ed.), *Tech high: Globalization and the future of Canadian education.* Ottawa: Fernwood.

# ABSTRACT

## CHARACTERISTICS OF THE TUTORIAL LEARNING PARADIGM

*Editor's Comment:* Professor Bork makes the point early in his long article, referenced here, that learning is an individual thing, often independent of teaching. He says, "teaching is interesting only if it leads to learning, and learning often occurs without teachers" (p. 74). He argues that all of the world's 6 billion people should have accessible learning opportunities in order to solve our persistent challenges of poverty and conflict.

Bork's article unfolds with a history of technology in the various "learning" paradigms throughout our study and experience of education. The knowledge transfer paradigm and the communication paradigm are two that receive most of his attention. He is, of course, an advocate of breaking this "paradigm paralysis" into which our history has tended to bind us, in the cause of creating the kind of problem-solving "learning for all" which he espouses in this article.

The way to create this kind of learning, according to Bork, is to adopt a new learning paradigm, that of "tutorial learning." A willing learner and a highly skilled tutor forms Bork's ideal learning paradigm for the future. Further, he notes that computer technology, by its accessibility and power, can be an often acceptable substitute for a tutor. He acknowledges that the computer tutor can "never approach the excellent human tutor," but that it "can constitute a giant step forward from the information-transfer learning paradigm" (p. 78).

These are the characteristics of the new tutorial learning paradigm, facilitated by computer technology, which Bork identifies (pp. 78ff):

- Highly interactive
- Individualized, especially addressing unique difficulties
- Adaptive to each learner's needs
- Mastery, including continuous assessment
- Creative learning, based on constructivist and discovery perspectives
- Learning content changes away from memory toward problem solving
- Distance learning through tutorial sessions, anytime anywhere
- Peer learning through small electronic learning circles
- New production techniques focused on solving specific student problems
- Experimental studies, including formative and summative evaluations
- Development and testing of new personal "learning appliances"

Bork concludes by challenging organizations such as the World Bank, UNESCO, and USAID to invest in the problems of learning worldwide. He is hopeful, and believes that improved and affordable learning for all—through the tutorial paradigm, computer facilitated—is possible.

*Source:* "Learning Technology" by Alfred Bork in *Educause Review*, January/February 2000, pp. 74–81. Alfred Bork is Professor Emeritus of Information and Computer Science, and Physics, at the University of California, Irvine. *www.ics.uci.edu/~bork>*

# RESEARCH SUMMARY

## WHAT WE'VE LEARNED FROM HOME SCHOOLING

*Editor's Comment:* With comments like "home schooling breeds enterprising people" and reports of research studies showing that key elements in "effective education" are small class size, individualized instruction, and a disciplined, nurturing environment, Daniel Golden reports on a variety of sources showing that the home-schooling movement in American education is changing college education. The effects could be expected to spill over into workplace education too.

The best estimates are that between one million and 1.5 million U.S. students are currently being home schooled. This is contrasted with the approximately 400,000 students enrolled in charter schools, against a total of about 50 million students in schools nationwide. Recent episodes of gun violence at schools has caused more parents to opt for home schooling, especially in U.S. cities. In Chicago, for example, at the start of school year 2000, the number of registered home-schooled students rose by more than ten percent (p. 1). Religious reasons are not the only ones driving parents toward home schooling.

One unusual statistic has surfaced regarding the home-schoolers who take the ACT or SAT college-entrance tests. The approximately 2,700 home-schoolers (out of 1,000,000) who took the college entrance tests over the last three years have bettered the national averages, scoring higher than their traditionally schooled peers. On the ACT, home-schoolers scored an average of 22.7 compared with traditionally schooled peers at 21, on a scale of 1 to 36. Home-schoolers did especially well in English (23.4) and Reading (24.4). On the SAT, the home-schoolers surpassed the national average by 67 points. On nine out of ten SAT2 achievement tests in specific subjects, the home-schoolers also bettered the national averages. Once in college, the data show that the home-schoolers do better than the traditionally schooled students in terms of Grade Point Average, and many assume student leadership positions. Stanford University in school year 1999–2000 accepted 27 percent of home-schooled applicants, nearly double its overall acceptance rate. Sixty-eight percent of colleges now accept parent-prepared portfolios of home-schooled students' work in place of high school diplomas and institutional transcripts. Scholarships and financial aid incentives are increasing in order to recruit home schoolers (p. 16).

Family demographics of home-schooled students are also interesting. Home-schooling parents have more education than the national norm, and they contradict the previous stereotype of white, rural, fundamentalist Christian. Four percent are black, and another 4 percent are Hispanic. Family incomes are about $10,000 lower than the national averages, contradicting another firmly held belief that educational achievement and higher test scores are positively correlated with family income (p. 1).

What we are seeing is a sizeable number of bright and motivated individual learners making a definite mark in U.S. colleges and universities, and moving into our workplaces. As one home-schooler said, "we home-schoolers tend to be very vocal and talk to professors directly"; they are disciplined and motivated learners, enjoy experienced-based learning, and are quick to criticize the dumbing-down of many public schools (p. 16). What we're learning from home-schoolers is that the principles of learning and the methods of teaching that the movement embodies have big payoffs in the quality of learner that results. That Daniel Golden's article was featured in a prime position on page 1 of *The Wall Street Journal* should make corporate America stand up and take notice too.

---

*Source:* "Home-Schooled Pupils are Making Colleges Sit Up and Take Notice" by Daniel Golden in *The Wall Street Journal*, February 11, 2000, pp. 1, A16. Daniel Golden is a Staff Reporter of *The Wall Street Journal*.

# BOOK REVIEW

## EXECUTIVE COACHING

*Editor's Comment:* During the past year, there have been dozens of books published on mentoring and coaching, a favorite delivery system for learning during most of the last decade. During year 2000, the number of "executive coaches" has proliferated; so many people are functioning as coaches that at any social gathering of business persons one can usually find someone who is either being coached or working as a coach. I have even seen one commentator say that those who are not so engaged will be guilty of mismanaging a crucial corporate asset.

I have chosen Mary Beth O'Neill's book, *Executive Coaching with Backbone and Heart* because of its comprehensiveness of content, its dual focus of "backbone and heart", and most of all, its clarity of instructions for would-be executive coaches. Her systems approach makes the book's layout logical and understandable, and her toolbook-like way of writing makes the book approachable and useful.

For example, she challenges the reader with step-by-step kinds of instructions: ". . . identify a next step . . . focus the leader on . . . ask the leader questions that . . . ensure the leader's strategy takes into account . . . help the leader anticipate the . . . invite the leader to . . . weigh the three criteria for . . . determine with the client the range of . . . assist the leader in preparing a. . . ." Each of her ten chapters elaborates on ideas and techniques, uses personal stories and situations to illustrate various points, and concludes with a one or two-page "Chapter Highlights" review in outline form.

She devotes considerable space to techniques of consulting, including contracting, entering into a one-to-one client relationship, and planning—all of which are useful to consultants of all sorts and not only to coaches. My own particular favorite sections of the book are Chapter 7, "Live-Action Coaching: Strike When the Iron is Hot" and Chapter 8, "Debriefing: Define a Learning Focus." She has a particularly

useful list of management competencies in Chapter 8, complete with several observable behavioral criteria supporting each competency. The list of competencies is:

- Strategic thinking
- Customer relations
- Vision
- Project management
- Facilitating meetings
- Decision making
- Utilizing staff in change agent role
- Promoting conversations
- Coaching
- Performance management
- Advocacy
- Team coherence
- Systems functioning.

The book concludes with three action-oriented, practical Appendices: (1) Assessing Your Coaching Effectiveness, complete with a self-assessment rating scale on 16 items; (2), Questions for Clients; and (3), Combining Coaching and Consulting for Powerful Results.

An article in the June 2000 issue of *HR Magazine* (SHRM) notes that experts estimate that there are 10,000 corporate coaches worldwide;

---

*Source: Executive Coaching with Backbone and Heart: A Systems Approach to Engaging Leaders with Their Challenges* by Mary Beth O'Neill. San Francisco: Jossey-Bass Publishers, 2000. $30.00. Mary Beth O'Neill is a Senior Consultant for LIOS Consulting Corporation at the Leadership Institute of Seattle at Bastyr University.

membership in the International Coach Federation (ICF), headquartered in Washington, DC, has grown 600 percent since 1997, currently adding 100 new members per month. According to a recent survey by Manchester Inc., a human resources consulting firm in Jacksonville, Florida, 59 percent of organizations currently offer coaching to their managers and executives (p. 96). Coaching is seen as both a recruitment and a retention tool, as well as a career-building tool that replaces the lost career ladder resulting from downsizings of the last decade. Books such as this one by Mary Beth O'Neill can help coaches develop their own careers.

# 4B. DISTANCE LEARNING

## ABSTRACT

## DISTANCE LEARNING CHALLENGES ASSUMPTIONS

*Editor's Comment:* This long article is of particular interest to adult educators, especially at the university level, and to businesses who collaborate with them in providing distance education services. It is a comprehensive exposition of issues which the authors define as the "foundation" of distance education. These include: higher education as a market, rationales for distance education; learner segments; institutional readiness for distance education; alternative delivery models; partnerships and collaborations of all sorts; and assumptions. We focus here on the last issue, assumptions.

To be sure, higher education is seeing itself as a marketplace these days, and distance education is certainly the hottest trading commodity by many accounts. The article referenced here begins with numbers to back up this phenomenon: a Department of Education 1999 estimate that it is a $225-billion-a-year market out of a total education market of $665 billion a year. Work done by International Data Corporation (IDC) estimates big growth in both the academic and corporate distance education markets over the next 3 years, pegged at around a 33 percent growth. IDC notes that demand for distance will increase from a current 5 percent of students to 15 percent of students by 2002 (p. 32). The article notes that venture capital is being invested heavily at both the university and the corporate levels.

All the money talk at the opening of the article frames it to challenge the financial formulations of a print-on-paper based institution. Digital technology helps to facilitate new organizational and new budgeting structures, more market-based and less department-based. The point throughout the article is that with distance education and other Internet phenomena, our long-held educational assumptions about learner motivation, locus of services, the nature of teaching, how students learn, and many other institutional and organizational issues are turned upside down. The authors advocate challenging these existing assumptions in order to see the alternative models more clearly:

Perhaps we should no longer assume that:

1. Most students want a degree or credential of some kind,

2. Professors and teachers understand what students prefer,

3. Student credit hour and full-time equivalent are the best units of measure,

4. Higher education should provide all components of the educational value chain,

5. The best guarantee of institutional longevity is high quality, which will drive out low quality,

6. For-profit providers of educational services are inferior,

7. Traditional institutional models can be easily transferred to an e-learning system,

8. Distance education is a viable option for all post-secondary institutions.

*Source:* "Distance Learning: Are We Being Realistic?" by Diana Oblinger and Jill Kidwell in *Educause Review*, May/June 2000, pp. 30–39. Diana Oblinger is Vice President for Information Resources and Chief Information Officer for the 16-campus University of North Carolina system; Jill Kidwell is a Partner at Pricewaterhouse-Coopers LLP.

# RESEARCH SUMMARY

## A SAMPLE OF WHAT'S AVAILABLE

*Editor's Comment:* Year 2000 has seen a proliferation of online courses, many of the traditional distance-learning format featuring multimedia, highly reputable instructors and professors, and opportunities for online dialogue with fellow students. Here we list a small sample of what seems to be out there at year's end, providing a glimpse of the many directions in which the distance-learning delivery system is expanding. We have chosen some magazines, some commercial vendors, some universities (both old and new), and some professional organizations—all of which are reporting, promoting, or offering distance-learning programs and e-learning that has evolved from such programs.

The list is meant to be a representative sample, although small. Its purpose is to encourage you to look in these kinds of places for what's new in distance-learning opportunities. We list our sources here with Web addresses and the focus of the program we selected as an example of each source. Most sources have many distance-learning programs; this is only a "tip of the iceberg" listing. Together these sources form an overview of what's going on in distance-learning.

**Babson College**
*babson.edu*

Entrepreneurship; dotcom executive education.

**Fuqua School of Business***
Duke University
*fuqua.duke.edu*

Broad executive education; new B2B (Business-to-Business) courses.

**Harvard Business School***
*exed.hbs.edu*
*hbsworkingknowledge.hbs.edu*

High-tech, high-growth executive education offered through new Silicon Valley campus.

Harvard Business School also offers an online management information service, a kind of online magazine that includes interviews, research reports, tools, tips, and current articles in topics such as e-commerce, finance and investment, innovation and change.

**Kellogg School***
Northwestern University
*kellogg.nwu.edu*

Executive education, current focus: Winning Strategies for e-Business.

---

*Sources:* "Teaching New Executives Some Old Tricks" by Mica Schneider in *Business Week*, April 3, 2000, pp. 151–152; "The World's Finest" top 20 elite business schools listed by the *Financial Times* in *Across the Board*, June 2000, p. 37; *CCH Incorporated*, 4025 West Peterson Ave., Chicago, IL 60646; *J.J. Keller & Associates, Inc.*, 3003 W. Breezewood Lane, PO Box 368, Neenah, WI, 54957; *Capella University*, 330 Second Ave. S. Suite 550, Minneapolis, MN 55401; *Harvard Business School* "HBS Working Knowledge," *hbsworkingknowledge.hbs.edu*; *National Technological University (NTU)*, PBS Business & Technology Network, 1330 Braddock Pl., Suite 201, Alexandria, VA 22314; *New York University* "the Virtual College" *scps.nyu.edu/online/p12*, School of Continuing and Professional Education, 7 East 12th St., 11th Floor, New York, NY 10003; American Society for Training & Development (ASTD), *ASTD.org*; The MASIE Center, *masie.com.*; *onlinelearning2000.com*; and *TRAINING* (Bill Communications), *trainingsupersite.com/traininglive*.

| | |
|---|---|
| **University of Michigan Business School*** <br> *bus.umich.edu* | Executive education for high-growth companies; collaboration with Amazon.com in course design. |
| **Thunderbird American Graduate School of International Management** <br> *t-bird.edu* | Global e-commerce courses. |
| **Capella University** <br> School of Education and Professional Development <br> *capellauniversity.edu* | Instructional Design for Online Learning; Teaching and Training Online MS and PhD programs; online courses and certificates; many other programs. |
| **NTU National Technological University (PBS)** <br> Public Broadcasting System, Business & Technology Network <br> ntu.edu | NTU delivers about 400 seminars and short courses per year via satellite and Web technology, primarily in business and management, information technology, and engineering. NTU collaborates with professional associations such as AMA, the Federal Training Network, and universities such as MIT. Current titles include: Internet Security Hacking; E-Business 2001: Predictions and Projections; IT Retention: Retraining, Retaining, or Detaining; The Rookie Manager; and numerous other titles. |
| **The Virtual College** <br> New York University <br> *scps.nyu.edu/online/p12* | NYU's School of Continuing and Professional Studies (SCPS) offers an array of online courses including undergraduate, graduate, certificate programs, and non-credit courses. A sample of courses includes: Cybertext and the New Media; Introduction to Screenwriting; Environmental Law; Legal Issues in Electronic Commerce; Auto Cad. |
| **CCH Shared Learning** <br> *elearning.cch.com* | CCH programs focus on workplace law. Current offerings include: Sexual Harassment Prevention; Violence in the Workplace; Interviewing/Hiring; Discipline/Termination; and E-mail and Internet Use. Spanish language versions are also available online. |
| **J.J. Keller & Associates** <br> *jjkeller.com* | This vendor offers safety courses delivered by Interactive CD-ROM, a delivery format considered by many as the first and best "distance learning." OSHA and DOT regulatory compliance topics are offered, including driver safety, laboratory safety, right-to-know topics regarding facilities management, fire prevention, first aid, ergonomics, lead, contamination, and VDT safety, among many other topics. Trainee testing and course administration documentation are provided with the CD-ROMs. |
| *astd.org* | ASTD TechKnowledge 2000 Conference and Preconference Workshops, September 19–22, 2000, Indianapolis, IN featured about 100 sessions on a wide range of topics organized into these four tracks: Designing and Developing Training for the Desktop, Analyzing and Evaluating Training Programs, Training Management in the Digital Age, and Web-Based Training. Contact ASTD for tapes and other post-conference materials. |

*masie.com*

The MASIE Center, run by Elliott Masie, e-learning networker and technology guru, sponsored a conference, TechLearn 2000 and e-Learning Congress, in Orlando, FL, November 12–15, 2000. Topics included: e-Learning Hype and Reality, Digital Collaboration, Standards for e-Learning, e-Assessment and Evaluation Strategies, The Learner in e-Learning, and many more. The Conference featured "Expo in a Suitcase," a rolling resource extra piece of luggage for participants to take home, chock full of information, CDs, brochures, and other advertising material from more than 100 sponsors of the event. Contact The MASIE Center for post-conference information, and subscribe to its free periodic online newsletter, *TechLearn TRENDS*.

*onlinelearning2000.com*

A September 23–27, 2000 Conference and Expo in Denver, CO known as OnLine Learning 2000 including Performance Support 2000 is closely associated with *TRAINING* and former Lakewood Communications publications, sponsored by the commercial design and e-learning delivery company, *click2learn.com*. The conference brochure promised 230 plus skill-building sessions and 70 plus hands-on labs. Learning objects, streaming media, and performance support are key topics.

*trainingsupersite.com*

Bill Communications, publisher of *TRAINING* magazine, has a comprehensive Website with many links to learning resources. Among the resources is the TRAINING 2001 Conference and Expo, March 5–7, 2001, Atlanta, GA. Check *lakewoodconferences.com* for specific information. Also check *trainingsupersite.com/traininglive* for free interactive online programs of timely topics for trainers.

*Note:* These graduate business schools were chosen by the *Financial Times* newspaper as among the 20 of the world's elite business schools, reported in *Business Week*, April 3, 2000, p. 152.

# ABSTRACT

## UNIONS SAY IT'S MORE WORK WITH LESS PAY

*Editor's Comment:* There is growing concern among thoughtful persons that online delivery might not actually reduce learning time, that is, the time actually spent learning or mastering a new skill or knowledge. Critics also express concern about the high learner dropout rate (for example, Dave Zielinski, *TRAINING Magazine*, February 2000, pp. 38–39; Roger Schank and Donald Norman in *TRAINING Magazine*, September 2000, pp. 62–77). Yet eager training managers tout the time and travel savings of not having to ship bodies around the country to training centers and hotels, and they boast that anytime-anywhere training is a boon to workplace learners everywhere.

This online article in *The New York Times on the web* addresses the concerns of college and university faculty members as well as public school teachers who are members of the National Education Association (NEA). The author uses several sources, Florida State University, Tallahassee, and Bergen Community College in New Jersey to frame the issues in workload and compensation that distance-learning developers and instructors encounter as they work in this delivery system.

Among these issues are:

- Instructors are finding that distance learning courses are writing-intensive, and that much more time is required for the instructor to answer all students' questions submitted online;

- The traditional on-campus classroom size of 40 students needs to be reduced to 25 students in order for instructors to serve all students in the online course;

- Many instructors get into distance-learning because of the challenge of trying something new, not realizing that distance learning takes more preparation time and more response time, causing workload and pay inequities with other faculty;

- Schools and colleges are finding creative ways of compensating distance-learning faculty by reducing teaching load (4 instead of 5 courses), or waiving requirements of campus residency while teaching online;

- Surveys of members conducted by the NEA found that members felt that they needed equitable compensation for the extra time that distance learning was proving to require. More work with less pay might be more fun, but it is less fair.

The many dichotomies apparently inherent in the current practice of distance learning from the learner's point of view, the manager's point of view, and the instructor's point of view will need to be smoothed out in order for the delivery system to continue to flourish. The good news is that many thoughtful persons are tackling these and other difficult issues—issues that only surface with deeper experience with and new thinking about distance learning.

---

*Source:* "Instructors Say Online Courses Involve More Work at Same Pay" by Rebecca S. Weiner in *The New York Times on the web*, June 21, 2000, pp. 1–4. *nytimes.com/library/tech/00/06/cyber/education/21education.html*. The "Education" column is published online every Wednesday in the section on Technology Cybertimes.

# ARTICLE REPRINT

## MAINSTREAM CULTURE CLASH WITH VIRTUAL U'S

*Editor's Comment:* Last year, the number of degree-granting accredited distance-learning programs has more than doubled (34% in 1999 versus 15% in 1998), and the corporate e-learning market is expected to grow by more than ten times by year 2003, (a $1 billion market in 1999 to an $11.4 billion market in 2003), according to the article reprinted here. Universities are struggling with seeing themselves as a brand name, part of the American capitalist scene. Many are fighting back and bucking the flow of e-learning and distance learning; some are figuring out ways to jump into the torrent. This article fills in the details.

## A MATTER OF DEGREE

### *by Ann Grimes*

Perhaps nowhere is the pinch between the old way of doing business and the new being felt more acutely than in the very birthplace of the Internet: the hallowed halls of academia.

Some $6 billion in venture capital has flowed into the education sector since 1990—almost half of it since last year, when Cisco Systems Inc.'s John Chambers dubbed education "the next big killer application on the Internet." Analysts expect new investment of $4 billion in the sector this year.

From notHarvard.com to UniversityAccess.com to Medschool.com, the Internet landscape is now dotted with learning ventures offering everything from corporate training to software designed to improve the ways schools run to long-distance learning. With so many entrepreneurs out to chip away at their brick-and-mortar souls, colleges and universities of all stripes are defending their turf—and what analysts estimate to be a $250 billion market.

As a result, universities are moving more quickly than many industry observers expected to show that Virtual U's—such as Kaplan College, Capella University, or Apollo Group Inc.'s University of Phoenix Online (which claims a virtual student body of 60,000)—aren't all they're cracked up to be. While maintaining a stranglehold over degree granting and intellectual property, traditional schools are also carving out a space for themselves in the for-profit education world, trumping some e-learning companies at their own game.

"I do not think the highest-quality brick-and-mortar universities are directly threatened by this set of initiatives—the online universities," says Columbia University President George Rupp. "But that doesn't mean it's not a threat."

### THE WORLD HAS CHANGED

Indeed, universities now realize that the world has changed, says Michael B. Goldstein, head of the educational-institutions practice at Dow, Lohnes & Albertson, a Washington, D.C., legal firm. "They've discovered capitalism," he says. "They are creating for-profit engines without becoming for-profit."

All over the country, distance learning has taken off. Of the 1,028 accredited two- and four-year institutions surveyed recently by Market Data Retrieval, 72% offered online courses last year, up from 48% the year before. Meanwhile, 34% offered an accredited distance program, compared with 15% in 1998.

And many e-learning efforts, including those at New York University, Cornell and the University of Maryland—which has offered distance-learning classes to the military for 50 years—are being spun off as for-profit ventures. NYUonline announced plans this year to go public. And Maryland hopes to tap venture capital to help with development costs and the marketing of hundreds of online courses.

"The best defense is a good offense," says Dr. Rupp, who has spearheaded Columbia's online efforts. In May, the university announced plans to offer nondegree continuing-education courses—initially such basics as computer classes and English as a second language, but more traditional academic offerings later on. The university also launched Columbia Innovation Enterprises, which will speed faculty ideas to market and hopefully prevent top professors from being picked off by for-profits eager to market their courses. Earlier this year, the university launched an independent for-profit company, Fathom.com, which will distribute the intellectual property of Columbia and other institutions online.

"Universities are knowledge entrepreneurs, and intellectual capital is a huge resource for them," says Ann Kirchner, Fathom.com's chief executive. "They are world-renowned brands."

## CAPITALISM SPOKEN HERE

But they are also bureaucratic organizations that move at what by Internet standards is a glacial pace. Fortunately, Columbia "made the determination to put its best competitive foot forward to attract a team that understands the sensibility of the university but that is bilingual—in academics and capitalism," Ms. Kirchner says.

Other universities are trying to do the same. The University of Illinois has launched an independent venture-capital fund, dubbed iVentures, designed to fuel campus start-ups and hang on to faculty entrepreneurs. The university will own a stake in new companies and

plow its share of profits back into the fund to seed more start-ups.

After years of watching some of Silicon Valley's hottest start-ups take shape on its campus, Stanford University this spring launched its first for-profit company: e-Skolar Inc., a search engine for health-care professionals developed at the medical school. The university will hold a 60% equity stake.

Stanford is also becoming more aggressive about protecting its "brand." In March, the university sued Stanford Microdevices Inc., a Sunnyvale, Calif., electronics company, for trademark infringement. Proximity to Silicon Valley and opportunities in the marketplace "make it more important to protect the value of Stanford's name and reputation and not allow others to use it," says Debra Zumwalt, the university's acting general counsel. Both Columbia's and Stanford's for-profit ventures are typical in that they target "lifelong" learners, not the traditional core students, Mr. Goldstein says: "They are using technology on campus, substantially—but these investments are primarily to reach out to adult learners." And to make money.

Only one in six of the nation's 15 million college students fits the stereotype of "youth-centered education"—students ages 18–22 who live on campus and attend school for four consecutive years. The number of adult students is expected to increase as baby boomers age. Meanwhile, the corporate e-learning market totaled about $1 billion in revenue in 1999 and will reach $11.4 billion by 2003, according to International Data Corp., a Framingham, Mass., research firm. The online market in higher education totals $1.2 billion and is expected to grow to $7 billion by 2003, according to Merrill Lynch.

## INVESTORS TAKE NOTE

All that plus the successful initial public offerings of education companies such as Saba Software Inc. and Digital Think Inc. have caught the attention of high-profile investors. Microsoft Corp. co-founder Paul Allen has backed Click2Learn.com, an e-learning portal, while Oracle Corp. Chief Executive Larry Ellison has teamed up with former junk-bond king Michael Milken to start Knowledge Universe Inc., which focuses on lifelong learning.

"It's a nascent market," says Thomas Weisel analyst Fred McCrea. "Strategies are in flux, and a lot of questions out there haven't been answered yet."

Among them: What happens to the many middle- and lower-tier schools that survive through cross-subsidies? Patrick Clinton, editor of University Business magazine, says they lose money on their traditional, core programs—on educating undergraduates—and they pay for them in part by making money on business and professional courses. "Colleges may well keep their traditional students but lose their cash-cow students," he says.

Observers such as Mr. Clinton also envision a loss of students through what he calls "unplug-and-play" educators. Such freestanding companies would "unplug" the basics—big lecture courses like History 101—from a university and teach it online for credit, with technical support, for less cost. "These companies can come in and teach it as well or even better for a third of the cost, streaming information like video-tapes and documents over the Internet," Mr. Clinton says.

Duke University in Durham, N.C., offers a 19-month online M.B.A. program called Global Executive for high-potential managers who live anywhere in the world. Tuition for the program, which mixes classroom and Internet-mediated learning: $89,700. (That compares with $57,470 for Duke's typical on-campus M.B.A.)

In 1995 Stanford began offering complete video-based courses on the Internet, and in 1998 it became the first major research university to offer online a master's degree in engineering. "Engineers have a consumer mentality," says Andy DiPaolo, executive director of Stanford's Center for Professional Development. "They want to test-drive this like a car. Before signing up, they ask, 'Will this course meet my needs?'"

That consumer mentality explains the attraction of a University of Phoenix or Capella University for people who want a career-relevant degree that they can take to an employer to prove competency, experts say. "A principal who wants to become a superintendent needs a Ph.D., not a Columbia Ph.D.," says Joshua Lewis, a general partner with New York investment firm Forstmann Little & Co., which recently invested $35 million in Capella, a Minneapolis-based education company.

Meanwhile, schools such as Stanford and the University of California at Los Angeles have formed partnerships with for-profit companies to develop courses for the online world. Both partnerships—Stanford with Unext Learning Systems, Deerfield, Ill., and UCLA with Online Learning.net, Los Angeles—develop online, nondegree versions of top-tier courses, yet neither company has degree-granting authority. Outgoing Stanford President Gerhard Casper has described his school's alliance with Unext.com as "fairly low-risk."

The University of Pennsylvania has a similar alliance going with Pensare, Inc., a Los Altos, Calif., e-learning company, to develop business-management education programs for its online initiative, Wharton Direct. Wharton also is launching a five-week, Web-based class with professor Jeremy Siegel, a well-known market analyst. "We have to learn how to do this," says Wharton Dean Patrick T. Harker. "The only way is by doing."

## FACULTY OPPOSITION

Not surprisingly, the move online has met resistance from some faculty suspicious of for-profit ties. "There is no evidence that significant numbers want virtual education, any more than they want virtual anything else when they can have the genuine article," says Scott Rice, an English professor at San Jose State University who is writing a book about online education.

Faculty members at Williams College in Williamstown, Mass., are hotly debating a proposal by Global Education Network—an education company backed by investor Herbert Allen—to put their humanities courses online. Says Williams humanities professor Mark C. Taylor, who has taken a leave to consult with GEN: "In many instances there's resistance to technology, especially by faculty in the arts and humanities who feel what they do can't be duplicated online."

But, says Mr. Taylor, "all this stuff is coming—it's a question of whether institutions can be involved and profit from it and continue to do the thing they do well, at a time when it is increasingly costly." The challenge for colleges like Williams, he says, is to support e-learning in a way that "allows educators to retain quality control over what's occurring."

# CASE STUDY

## GETTING CERTIFIED TO DISTANCE TEACH

*Editor's Comment:* We have chosen the University of Wisconsin–Madison's distance-learning program on distance-learning instructor certification as an example of training delivered in this format. In this entry, we focus on parts of the brochure describing the program. This certificate program has been offered since 1993, one of the first in the field.

### FEES AND PROGRAM DURATION

Enrollment fee is $2,500. The core requirement courses are scheduled online from early October to late June of the academic year. Elective modules equating to 7 CEUs must also be completed at any time and at the student's own pace.

### CEUS AND CERTIFICATION

A CEU (Continuing Education Unit) is defined as 10 hours of study time. This program requires 20 CEUs for certification, made up of the following distribution:

| | |
|---|---|
| 0.5 CEUs | Orientation Planning |
| 12 CEUs | Four required core modules of 3 CEUs each |
| 7 CEUs | Electives |
| 0.5 CEUs | Capstone Report |

### FEATURES OF THE COLLABORATIVE ONLINE TRACK

- A group learning experience where participants work together via the Internet/Web to complete the required core courses;

- Highly interactive online learning activities that stimulate analysis and application through discussion, debate, case studies, small group projects, and exercises;

- High-quality course materials and Web resources;

- Online facilitation and individual advising from the University professional team;

- Choice of electives that use Internet, audio conferencing, or print formats;

- No travel requirements;

- An online learning center for access to a variety of resources to support learning.

### CORE REQUIREMENTS

Orientation (2-hour audio conference)
Course: Learning at a Distance (5 weeks)
Course: Distance Education Technology
      (5 weeks)
Course: Instructional Systems Design (5 weeks)
Course: Evaluation in Distance Education
      (5 weeks)
Capstone Report

### ELECTIVES

Students select from among these modules to equal 7 CEUs, or 70 hours of study time.

Learner Support Services
Learning Contract
Introduction to Online Learning
Group Processes for Online Learning
Designing for Online Learning
Designing for Interactive Audio
Interactive Strategies for Video Courses
Issues in Using Multimedia
Managing Distance Education in Corporate
   Settings
Managing Distance Education in Higher
   Education
Annual Conference on Distance Learning

*Source:* Brochure advertising "Professional Development and Certification in Distance Education." Fall 2000, from University of Wisconsin–Madison, Graduate Program in Continuing and Vocational Education. *wisc.edu/depd/.*

## ARTICLE REPRINT

## MAYBE YOU NEED A LEARNING PORTAL

*Editor's Comment:* Acquiring tools to do the job and skills for career self-management are two important reasons for workplace learning. Advocates of distance learning say that this learning can be done better online. But online students are often frustrated by technology problems and long for the human touch while they learn. This article suggests that one way companies can help maximize the advantages and overcome the problems is through a "learning portal." Samuel Greengard's research here tells you how to think about a learning portal and take the first steps in creating one.

## GOING THE DISTANCE

### *by Samuel Greengard*

You know the drill. Your firm's employees spend countless hours sifting through publications, attending trade conferences, and mining Websites in search of all the news and information required to stay up-to-date. They sign up for courses and fly off to far-flung locales to boost their level of knowledge on, say, compensation or online recruiting. And, at the end of the day, they feel as though they've been smacked in the face by the entire process. Not only is it a struggle to stay informed, but it's also nearly impossible to manage their careers effectively.

Welcome to the digital revolution. If one basic fact defines today's technology, it's that any advance in capabilities and tools brings additional complexity to our lives. Yes, it's wonderful to click to a Website and glance at news that's specifically tailored to our needs. It's equally incredible to sit at a PC and engage in interactive learning—without flight delays and really bad hotel beds. But as we attempt to make the leap from old-line processes and thinking to an Information Age economy, managing all these various components can become a full-time job.

Increasingly, human resources finds itself at the center of this maelstrom. Over the last few years, many organizations have begun to provide online coursework and other tools to help employees improve their expertise and to better manage their careers. Within this emerging framework, HR is spearheading the effort to develop corporate learning centers—sometimes referred to as universities—that ratchet up an organization's knowledge and competitive ability. In many respects, this technology is revolutionary rather than evolutionary.

Putting a dozen people from all across the country or the world into the same virtual classroom creates opportunities that simply didn't exist in the past. It can help incubate new ideas and eliminate time and money spent on travel. Combine this with specific tools, such as videoconferencing, live chat, document sharing, streaming video and audio, and Web-based learning, and an individual can receive the exact information that's needed at the exact moment it is needed. No long delays waiting to receive the latest computer-based training program. No hassles for the HR department ensuring that everyone is viewing the latest and correct material.

As Mark Koskiniemi, Vice President of Human Resources at Buckman Laboratories International Inc., a Memphis-based specialty chemicals manufacturer, explains: "Distance learning can provide significant advantages for everyone involved. It cuts costs, boosts productivity, and fits the need to dispense information and knowledge quickly." In fact, Buckman Labs first turned to distance learning in 1997, when Koskiniemi realized that it was a way to build a stronger, and better, organization.

But lost in the shuffle is a simple truth. Unless HR takes steps to simplify and streamline the various processes associated with professional learning, most employees will wind up feeling like they're running through mud. They might dutifully attend classes, read news, and attempt to use competency-based systems, but they are likely to feel completely taxed and overloaded by the process. And, in the end, all the good intentions and gee-whiz technology in the known universe cannot guarantee success.

The solution? Establish a learning portal, which can serve as a centralized place to turn for news, information, course listings, and materials, as well as various tools designed to boost the abilities and capabilities of individuals within an enterprise. Streamlining access to a variety of components through a simple, easy-to-use interface will make workers less inclined to feel like laboratory rats being poked, probed, and overstimulated—all in the name of progress or greater profits.

## PAYING ATTENTION
## TO FUNCTIONALITY

Here's how it works: An employee logs on to the corporate intranet and views a personalized page or a link to a page that displays relevant information. Just as Yahoo! or Excite aggregates diverse information on the Web, a MyCareer or WorkCentral page can plug in the information that's needed to manage professional development. That might include an ability to click a link and view courses already taken or those that need to be taken for a promotion, enroll in a class, obtain course materials, and read company and outside news.

The power of the portal is that it puts everyone at one central, easily navigable spot. Several Web services, most notably Individual.com,

provide filtering tools that can help an employee track news based on specific interests. After setting up an account, it's simple to choose particular areas of importance—everything from payroll to sexual harassment—in order to stay informed about industry events as well as what competitors are doing. Likewise, organizations as diverse as Institute of Management and Administration (IOMA) and International Human Resources Information Management Association (IHRIM) offer subscription and member services that can provide valuable news and information.

In reality, the possibilities are unlimited. The remarkable thing about the Internet is that it opens the door to all sorts of options that weren't even imaginable a mere decade ago. However, it's up to an organization, including the HR department, to leverage these capabilities to maximum advantage. Just like a car, computer, suitcase, or phone, success is wrapped up in the overall design and functionality. Built an outstanding product, and you will have to battle to keep up with the demand. Develop a dog, and you will find yourself running around in circles.

Of course, as with most other technology tools, establishing an effective learning portal is easier said than done. For one thing, it requires a fundamental conceptual understanding of the underlying technology that drives many of these systems—intranets, e-mail, Web-based video and audio, discussion groups, news feeds from third-party sites, and more. Although it's not necessary to understand the bits and bytes (that's best left to the propeller heads in IT), it is crucial to be able to communicate what's needed and comprehend how various systems work in the real world.

For another, it's essential to take the employee's perspective and understand exactly how real people use and view the system, and what improvements or capabilities they feel would help them better manage their careers. As I've said before in this column, there's a huge difference between self-service and self-serving. What benefits an organization doesn't necessarily help employees. And any lopsided attempt to introduce clunky or complex technology in the name of efficiency is doomed to failure. Employees will simply revert to old or inefficient ways of doing things, and the desired change is unlikely to take root.

Developing a first-rate learning portal requires a combination of excellent technology, streamlined systems, and desktop tools that can bring it all together. Today, most ERP packages and a slew of third-party products can provide the muscle power to create an effective learning portal. By teaming with IT to develop and fine-tune these systems, it's possible to put industrial-strength learning and professional development tools in the hands of employees.

## CHARTING THE COURSE

To be sure, many organizations, including Microsoft, MCI-WorldCom, QUALCOMM, Charles Schwab, Cisco Systems, Raytheon, and Buckman Laboratories, have embraced the concept without hesitation. In fact, at San Diego-based QUALCOMM, a leading wireless communications company, a learning portal has become an entrenched part of the workplace and culture (QUALCOMM was a recipient of a WORKFORCE Optimas Award earlier this year). Not only can employees view past accomplishments and completed courses—both internal and external—online, but they can also monitor their career paths and take a proactive approach to lifelong learning through the firm's MySource service. "The system improves everyone's ability to coordinate learning and professional development," says Dawn Ridz, a human resources specialist at QUALCOMM.

In fact, QUALCOMM offers more than 45 professional-development training modules and numerous skills-development courses online.

The training is available 24 hours a day, seven days a week so that employees can learn at their own pace, regardless of their work schedules.

Employees also can use the intranet to sign up for classroom training, find other learning resources (such as books and videos), and ferret out just-in-time job aids. In addition, the company has teamed with the University of Southern California to offer an on-site Master's in Electrical Engineering program, and with San Diego State University to offer an on-site MBA program. QUALCOMM's Website offers a single streamlined view of the entire assortment of tools and capabilities.

At Buckman Labs, meanwhile, employees can view course descriptions, make selections, and obtain materials online. Using their browsers, they can then read articles and coursework, take tests, collaborate on assignments, and engage in online discussions—all under the watchful eye of an instructor. An assessment manager that's built into the system allows instructors to oversee quizzes, schedules, surveys, and performance. In addition, employees can share knowledge and information through the intranet.

All of this is changing the way people manage knowledge, learning, and their careers. To be sure, you can put information at people's fingertips, but you can't force them to use it effectively. That, in the end, requires systems that can make it easy to keep track of All Things Relevant. If you want to go the distance, a learning portal might just be the shortest and most direct route to success.

# 4C. WEB-BASED TRAINING DELIVERY

## CASE STUDIES

### THREE CASE STUDIES IN DELIVERING E-LEARNING: PRICE-WATERHOUSE-COOPERS, INTEL, AND STORAGE TECHNOLOGY

*Editor's Comment:* These three case studies written by Brandon Hall tell the story of three very different companies who struggled with some of the knotty e-learning startup issues. We excerpt these case studies from a longer article that appeared in *e-Learning* magazine in January 2000.

### HOW TO EMBARK ON YOUR E-LEARNING ADVENTURE: MAKING SENSE OF THE ENVIRONMENT

*by Brandon Hall*

By 2003, 50 percent of all training may be online. Where does your company stand? If you are in the training profession or industry, are you poised to survive and thrive during this revolution, or die off with the old guard?

Education and training worldwide is becoming a huge business. It is estimated that education and training from pre-school to retirement is a $2 trillion marketplace. In the United States, it is 8 percent of the gross domestic product, second only to healthcare. One company, Cisco, has invested $20 million in television advertising that demonstrates e-learning for children and adults.

E-learning is taking off like wildfire around the globe. Organizations are finding ways to save 50 percent of the time invested in training, and cut one-third to one-half the cost. The advantages loom large, yet understanding what needs to happen to pave the way for e-learning in your organization can be overwhelming. The technology changes daily, as do the training needs.

You are not alone as you grapple with issues about the latest methods and tools; in fact you are in good company. In this article, we will look into some case studies of companies that are adopting e-learning into their corporate culture. We will share advice on how to integrate e-learning into your training; how to build a business case for e-learning; how to evaluate e-learning; how to understand packaged training systems for e-learning that are on the market today; and a key to understanding some of the buzzwords in the industry.

---

## BUILDING A BUSINESS CASE: SUCCESS STORIES OF COST-SAVINGS

One way to build a business case for e-learning and how it can help your organization is to look at case studies of success. PriceWaterhouse-Coopers is a firm that provides accounting and business consulting services. Prior to the merge, Price Waterhouse created a multimedia program entitled Terminal RISK to train the professional audit staff. Employees take the course during the third year of training. Terminal RISK serves as a prerequisite for further training, and more than 7,000 people in 50 countries have taken advantage of this training. To evaluate the program, Price Waterhouse conducted a training effectiveness review. These were the findings: compared to traditional classroom training, the multimedia program reduced by 50 percent the time needed for learners to attain the same level of knowledge.

Price Waterhouse followed up the evaluation with a return-on-investment analysis for the course, in comparison to traditional instructor-led training. The company examined the total cost for development and delivery over five years. The cost per learner for the technology-based training was $106—as opposed to $760 per learner for the instructor-led training version of the course.

Another example can be found at Intel Corp., where the focus of business is to design, manufacture and market microprocessors for personal computers. The Logistics Systems training group previously offered traditional classroom instruction to the 800 employees for learning new applications. The training group figured out how to provide embedded, technology-based training in the applications themselves, thus eliminating the need for classroom-led training.

In a comparison of hours off-the-job for training on one particular project of this group at Intel, traditional training would have required up to 12 hours, while embedded training required up to two hours. A 10-hour savings multiplied by 800 employees amounts to a lot of productivity recaptured.

The third case study involves Storage Technology, a company that reaped 47 percent cost savings. Storage Technology provides large storage hardware for mainframe computers. The cost-per-unit for this equipment can approach one-half million dollars.

Storage Technology employs a field force of 1,500 technicians to provide technical support. The company previously trained the technicians using a lecture and lab format in which the technicians traveled to Colorado for a four- to ten-day training session. Several years ago, the company began to convert the format of the training from lecture and lab to technology-based training in which the technicians received training at their local offices on a computer. The savings from this conversion were substantial.

Cost savings for Storage Technology was due to two factors in particular: compression of training time and reduction in travel expenses. A comparison of total training costs over three years at Storage Technology for development and delivery of a program showed costs for the lecture/lab format at $3,291,327 vs. costs for the technology format at $1,748,327.

## TO BUILD A BUSINESS CASE FOR YOUR ORGANIZATION, WE RECOMMEND THAT YOU:

- Examine the cost-savings possible with technology-based training;
- Review case studies and research findings for similar courses or industries;
- Determine how to evaluate your return on investment;
- Complete a cost comparison spreadsheet on a course you plan to convert; and
- Identify advantages for your workforce beyond cost savings, including convenience of anytime, anyplace access to courses via the Web, or your intranet.

## ADVANTAGES AND OBSTACLES TO E-LEARNING

Now that we have shown you some case studies, you may want to think about the advantages of e-learning for your workforce:

Courses available via intranets or the Internet are easily accessed without additional software (just a browser);

Training can be self-paced, so learners can go at their own chosen speed;

Training is available at any time and any place;

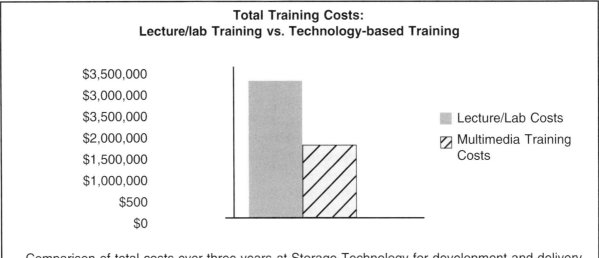

**Total Training Costs:**
**Lecture/lab Training vs. Technology-based Training**

$3,500,000
$3,000,000
$3,500,000
$2,000,000
$1,500,000
$1,000,000
$500
$0

- Lecture/Lab Costs
- Multimedia Training Costs

Comparison of total costs over three years at Storage Technology for development and delivery of another course in Lecture/lab format ($3,291,327) vs. technology-based format ($1,748,327).

Training can be less expensive;

No more travel to and from classes;

Updates can be achieved quickly by posting changes to the Web, intranet, or company network; and

The time required for learning can be shortened by 50 percent.

When you are looking into the advantages, you may want to also take a look at the obstacles to achieving success. Here is a snapshot of a few common problems: Lack of bandwidth can slow interactivity; Audio and video may be forbidden on your network; Some courses are not appropriate for technology delivery, or will still benefit by a mix of instructor-directed and e-learning; and e-learners need to be fairly self-directed, or otherwise motivated to complete courses.

## GETTING STARTED IN YOUR OWN ENVIRONMENT

So, you've looked at the options and you're ready to get going. How can you start? You'll want to make an assessment of your own skills and abilities, as well as an assessment of what is currently in place in your organization.

Some things to examine within the culture of your organization, or the organization you plan to assist:

How ready is the organization to embrace e-learning?

Is training already a part of the corporate culture?

Do employees and managers take it seriously?

Does every employee who needs training have access to a computer?

Will learners have access to your intranet or to the Internet?

Identify the courses most of the employees in a particular area need.

Will packaged courseware available today meet the organization's needs?

Does the timeline for new training rollout allow for development of e-learning? (Creating online courses typically takes longer than creating instructor-led training courses.)

To further evaluate your needs, you may benefit from Advisor 3.0, available from BNH Expert Software. It helps evaluate delivery, selection and cost savings.

Once you have begun to know your organization's needs and readiness to take advantage of the latest technology as part of the training picture, you're ready to get started. If you believe it will take time to convince management, or if your culture isn't ready technologically, you may want to start with a course that many employees need to take; or that a particular group, for instance, field sales, can benefit quickly from e-learning, due to the fact the whole team is rarely in one place, and sales people usually hate to take time off to go to a workshop!

# RESEARCH SUMMARY

## A SAMPLE OF WEB-BASED LEARNING DIRECTORIES

*Editor's Comment:* This list of sources for Web-based learning is meant to be a sample of the kinds of help out there. The list of Web addresses is purposely broad, but not deep, designed to entice you to look for more sources on your own.

**Hungry Minds**
*hungryminds.com*

Large resource for distance-learning courses, including an e-book feature that allows you to purchase only the chapters you need, and a tool known as Universal Notebook to keep all course notes in one place.

**EduPoint.com**
*edupoint.com*

Lists about 500,000 courses, mainly at traditional bricks-and-mortar institutions.

**Youachieve.com**
*youachieve.com*

Offers about 350 online learning sessions created by 180 different web-based learning gurus; programs come in 60-minute workshops, 20-minute clinics, and 5-minute articles.

**The Corporate University**
*corporate-u.com*

Universities and colleges that offer business courses and degree programs form the basic database of nearly 2000 programs accessible on the CourseFinder Web; printed guides are also available, for example, a guide to management seminars, and an evaluation guide to executive programs.

**Click2learn.com**
*click2learn.com*

An online education clearinghouse of courses from many different companies; also has software products for online course design, and has course administration tools.

**TrainingNet**
*trainingnet.com*

Aggregates technology and business training offerings from more than 1,000 providers categorized by format (classroom, online, video, CD-ROM, etc.).

**AthenaOnline.com**
*athenaonline.com*

Offers a host of inexpensive short courses online, for example, Dealing with Difficult People, Coaching for Excellence, Communication Skills—courses typically take 45–60 minutes each.

---

*Sources:* "Get Your Career in Site" by Gina Imperato in *Fast Company*, March 2000, pp. 318–329; personal correspondence from Bo Sean Hensley, VP of Sales, The Corporate University, June 9, 2000; "Get All Your Work Done in Half the Time, Be the Office Hero, and Go Home Early" by Leslie Ayers in *www.PCCOMPUTING.com*, March 2000, pp. 128–144.

# RESEARCH SUMMARY

## OBSTACLES AND CONCERNS OF WEB-BASED TRAINING

*Editor's Comment:* In this summary of various articles expressing concerns about and describing obstacles to Web-based training, we extract a range of negatives, or potential problems, that managers will have to deal with before viable Web-based training can flourish. Again, we give you a representative sample—in this case, a sample of opinions—about Web-based training success indicators and failure traps.

Inequality of access to high-quality Web connection. (*The Wall Street Journal*)

Loss of camaraderie during classroom food breaks. (*The Wall Street Journal*)

Difficulty in figuring out the right mix of face-to-face and Web-based training. (*The Wall Street Journal*)

Uneven levels of learner-readiness and skill in using computer technology. (*The Wall Street Journal*)

Getting adequate bandwidth to remote employee workstations (*The Wall Street Journal*)

Management expectations for Web-based training that are too high. (*The Wall Street Journal*)

"Yet another technology-fueled incursion of the workplace into home life." (*The Wall Street Journal*)

Learner aggravation with CD-ROM applications software, difficult installation of software instructions, huge downloads, and inconsistent support for learners struggling to get audio, video, whiteboard, and virtual classroom characteristics in order to learn via their PCs with "Thick Client" technology (*ASTD Learning Circuits*)

"Thin Client" synchronous technology's immature burst onto the scene. (*ASTD Learning Circuits*)

Tendency of the market to overhype the advantages of new technologies. (*ASTD Learning Circuits*)

Lack of organizational support for online learners. (*TechLearn TRENDS*)

Does browsing and taking course segments count as taking a course? (*TechLearn TRENDS*)

By what metric should organizations charge back e-learning by organization members? How does the training department account for e-learning expenditures and results? (*TechLearn TRENDS*)

Will excellent classroom instructors still be available, or will classroom instruction become stigmatized because of the hype of e-learning? (*TechLearn TRENDS*)

Where does e-learning fit organizationally? In training? In IT? On its own? (*TechLearn TRENDS*)

The "Digital Divide" and "Racial Ravine" in per-household Internet connection: 36% Asian, 30% white, 13% Latino, 11% black (*Across the Board*)

Underestimating the real social and economic value of universal connectivity. (*Across the Board*)

Negotiating the "land grab" regarding Internet companies' rush to patent processes like one-click buying (Amazon.com) or computer footnote generation (IBM); a new rush to patent ideas, which is vastly different from the Internet's early days of open-source software; how to adjust to the change. (*The Economist*)

---

*Sources:* "The New Dress Code for Corporate Training: Slippers and Pajamas?" E-World column by Thomas E. Weber in *The Wall Street Journal*, January 21, 2000, p. B1; "Thinking Thin: The Race for Thin-Client Synchronous E-Learning" by Tom Barron in *ASTD Learning Circuits* online newsletter (*learningcircuits.org/jun2000/barron.html*), June 2000, pp. 1–6; "Organizational Issues for e-Learning" by Elliott Masie in *TechLearn TRENDS* online newsletter published by The MASIE Center (*masie.com*), August 28, 2000, pp. 1–2; "The Digital Divide in PC Use" by Research Roundup column by Thomas Cavanaugh in *Across the Board*, April 2000, p. 55; "The Knowledge Monopolies: Patent Wars" in *The Economist*, April 8, 2000, pp. 75–78; "Closer to Godhead" by Steven Johnson in *Brill's Content*, May 2000, pp. 63–67.

Web organization: New concerns that the chaos of the Web will lead not to intelligence, but to confusion and abandonment; can the Web spontaneously generate structure as it matures? Does higher intelligence require both connectedness and organization? (*Brill's Content*)

## CASE STUDY

## ONLINE LEARNING INCENTIVES AND REWARDS AT PARK AVENUE BANK

*Editor's Comment:* "If we treat employees right, they'll treat customers right" is the belief of Park Avenue Bank's management. In this case, the bank moved from CD-ROM "check out" training to Internet training. This article explains how and why they did it. Of particular interest is the fact that the training manager's responsibility also includes marketing, and that a customer focus drives the new training format, performance incentives, and rewards.

### GEORGIA BANK FINDS SOLUTIONS IN E-TRAINING

#### *by Roy L. Karon*

Until 10 months ago, training at the Park Avenue Bank (Valdosta, Ga.) involved giving employees a diskette-based program that had to be checked out and shared. It could take days or even weeks for an individual to complete just one course.

The training schedule for the entire institution could be put in jeopardy, since the diskettes might not be available when they were needed. Training was a slow process at the bank, even though it was mandated by bank policy.

Today, a library of 94 courses, available over the Internet, has replaced the diskettes. The online library provides training in a variety of areas, including security and compliance, regulations, lending, teller skills, sales skills, product knowledge, customer service, operations and management and motivation.

This year, each employee is required to take two courses on telephone etiquette in addition to those courses required in their work areas. That is

exciting news for Emily Anderson, the bank's program director for marketing and training.

"In this fast-paced world in which we live, anything that saves time, saves money," Anderson explains. "Since going online, our employees are taking courses at their convenience 24 hours a day, 7 days a week. That's real-time in today's world."

Online learning solves a number of timing and scheduling problems for the bank's 92 employees at its four locations. Since most employees have access to the Internet, they no longer need to search for a laptop and the appropriate training diskette. They can just use their user ID and password to access the library at an appropriate time during working hours—before work, during lunch or after work—even from home—from any computer that offers Internet access.

At the Park Avenue Bank, training is mandatory and is tied to an employee incentive pro-

*Source:* "Georgia Bank Finds Solutions in e-Training" by Roy L. Karon in *e-Learning*, May–June 2000, pp. 32, 34. Roy L. Karon is President and CEO of BVS Performance Systems. Reprinted with permission of *e-Learning*, published by Advanstar Communications Inc., Duluth, MN. Copyright 2000. All rights reserved.

gram. Those who do not complete the required training before their annual review face a financial reduction.

## ONLINE TRAINING RIDS COMPLAINTS

Anderson says that since the switch to online learning she no longer hears complaints from employees about training. "Our old method of training was not convenient for our employees. We had accessibility problems. There were always some complaints." Convenience for employees is a major consideration for the Park Avenue Bank. That factor influenced the decision to move to online training.

"Our philosophy is that if we treat our employees right, they'll treat our customers right. It has a trickle down effect. When our employees are doing their work they don't need extra problems or obstacles to overcome. Access to online training that's available 24 hours a day just makes the employee's job that much easier," Anderson adds. "It all goes back to the bank's founder."

James L. Dewar, Sr. started the bank in 1956, and at 88, he still works every day. Dewar insists that this bank would be one that cares about people. Many decisions at the bank are based on a concern for the convenience of its employees because of Dewar's long-standing philosophy. That personal concern, in turn, is passed along to customers.

## INTERNET SAVVY BANKERS

"Our image theme is 'We're staying one step ahead of the future.' That image concept, along with implementation of online training, drove us to bring the Internet into the bank. We believe in using technology, the Internet and our human resources to provide the best banking experience possible for our customers," Anderson says.

"I would estimate that when we started online training, perhaps five percent of our employees were knowledgeable about the Internet and how to use and navigate it. Some of our executives and branch managers had access to the Internet, but that was all. Today, everyone at the bank undergoes some form of online training, and they all know how to access the library and take a course."

Anderson supplements the online training with live presentations on customer service and sales training by a consultant on an as-needed basis. She feels this approach provides employees with general industry, product and regulatory information, as well as very specific and targeted training that fits the bank's own philosophy and image.

## IMPLEMENTING ONLINE LEARNING

How did Anderson make the changeover to Internet-based learning? First, she worked with the information technology department to help deliver the Internet to employees' desktop PCs. She then met with all department heads to explain how the online training worked, how it could be accessed, what constituted a passing score, and which courses were required for everyone in the bank. For example, since the Y2K issue was on the top of everyone's mind in 1999, each employee (including all management personnel) was required to take the course "Surviving Y2K: Keeping Customers."

Anderson developed an eight-page guide that managers could use to explain the online learning system to their staff. It included background on the online library, a section on how to get started, an explanation of user ID and password usage, and a complete list and description of courses.

Managers are responsible for choosing the courses appropriate for their staff members and seeing to it that they are integrated into each employee's annual review.

## BENEFITS OF E-TRAINING

Thus far, employees at the $244 million bank have completed more than 700 online courses and Anderson is solidly sold on this method of learning. She sold the online concept to her management team as a way to ensure employees were being properly trained in a manner that was more convenient for them.

She identifies five major reasons for her support of online training:

- It makes employees use the Internet and builds their technology skills—something the bank believes is a big part of its future;

- It makes training more accessible, 24/7—from any Internet-enabled computer;

- It is self-paced. Anderson does not care whether it takes an employee 25 or 45 minutes to complete a course and take a test—as long as the employee takes it and passes it;

- It removes Anderson as a potential training bottleneck, because once the required courses are identified and assigned to the employees by the managers, she takes on the job of training monitor. The online program maintains a database that lets her see which employee has completed which course—at the headquarters, branch or bank-wide level; and

- It is so easy to implement that Anderson can devote her time to her other, non-training responsibilities, such as marketing.

"I am so pleased we made the switch to Internet training," Anderson concludes. "On the whole, the transition was rather painless. It has turned a once onerous task that was not working well into a bright, productive effort in our bank."

# 4D. CLASSROOMS AND GROUP LEARNING

## RESEARCH SUMMARY

### THE GLOBAL PERSISTENCE OF CLASSROOMS

*Editor's Comment:* ASTD has distinguished itself as a professional organization over the last few years by its conduct of wide-scale benchmarking and industry-wide studies. Although the 2000 reports actually report data from studies conducted during year 1999, and are made public at the beginning of year 2000, these studies contain trend-worthy data and information. These are the latest available data from these ASTD studies.

Of particular interest is the trend that 3-year projections for technology-delivered training are more cautious than last year's 3-year projections, and that firms in highly developed countries actually delivered less training via learning technologies than their counterpart firms in less well-developed countries. The use of technology-delivered training seems to have slowed somewhat in years 1999 and 2000.

Together with this trend is the trend toward increased use of the classroom as a delivery format. ASTD's Benchmarking Study in 1998 showed that participating leading-edge firms delivered 77.6 percent of its training via classrooms; and, in 1999, the last year of available data, that number actually increased to 78.5 percent of firms, indicating a trend line opposite of that expected by ASTD observers. Technology-delivered training in these leading-edge firms of ASTD's Benchmarking Study decreased during these same time periods from 9.1 percent to 8.5 percent, reflecting the difficulties encountered in implementing technology-based training. Flying in the face of these date, other predictions are that by 2001, 17 percent of all training will be delivered by technology (*ASTD 2000 International Comparisons Report*, p. 11). These trends and projections are being watched closely.

ASTD surveyed firms in six regions: Australia/New Zealand, Asia, Japan, Canada, United States, and Europe. Across these regions, ASTD found that instructor-led training in traditional classrooms remained remarkable high, at between 78 and 80 percent of all training, with classroom training in Japan actually rising 10 points from 79 to 89 percent by year 1999.

*Sources:* "The 2000 ASTD International Comparisons Report" by Mark E. Van Buren and Stephen B. King, supplement to *Training & Development*, January 2000, pp. 10–11; and "Findings at a Glance" sidebar of key findings from the 2000 ASTD State of the Industry Report, in *Training & Development*, January 2000, p. 42.

# ARTICLE REPRINT

## THE CORPORATE UNIVERSITY: MORE THAN TRAINING

*Editor's Comment:* Today's common cry by technology-based companies is the familiar one that training is the killer app of the next few years. It is somewhat of a surprise, then, that the corporate university—that typically classroom-based institution—is also saying this, but perhaps for a different reason and certainly from a different perspective. This article is one that focuses on leadership and learning skills, not only job skills. The bricks-and-mortar corporate university has impressive numbers to its credit: 400 of them in existence in 1988; more than 1,600 of them today. At that growth rate, soon corporate universities will outnumber traditional universities, of which there are around 3,700. This article describes the traditional and changing structures known as corporate universities.

## CORPORATE UNIVERSITIES 101

### *by Russell V. Gerbman*

Employees coming into companies or moving into management are probably accustomed to visiting the HR department, filling out paperwork and receiving a packet of information welcoming them to their new positions. They may have even received a *War and Peace*-sized handbook explaining their new duties or watched a company video.

But these days, they also may have been sent to corporate universities—a growing aspect of employee training at both large and small companies.

On-the-job training has changed over the years—but never so drastically as in the past five years. Business is moving at the speed of light, thanks to technology and a booming economy. Corporations and even small businesses not only have a vested interest in recruiting the best for their companies, they also need to keep employees working at the top of their games once they are hired.

And one of the most fundamental and cost-effective ways to do this is to train the employee at a corporate university.

The shortened shelf-life of information, which can expire with two clicks of a mouse, has forced corporations to take on new roles, says Jeanne Meister, author of *Corporate Universities: Lessons in Building a World-Class Work Force* (McGraw-Hill, 1998) and president of Corporate University Xchange, a corporate education consultant firm in New York.

"The corporation is becoming more of the educator," Meister says. "By the time you get out of school, you need a whole new set of skills in order to make it in the workplace. The corporation has to step up and become the educator of the workforce."

A recent college graduate can't be expected to have a confident handle on the changing world of business the moment he enters the workforce because the rules are being rewritten daily. Meister sees the new role of educator for corporations as crucial to their survival.

Corporate University Xchange helps companies build or revitalize their corporate training and teaching programs. In her experience, a good university is built around the premise of using it as a conduit for broad knowledge, in contrast to orientations and training programs that teach specific skills.

## WHAT'S THE DIFFERENCE?

A conduit for broad knowledge? Isn't that just putting window dressing on your old-fashioned training program? In some ways it is because employees still have to go through training classes and orientation modules. But, the corporate university model is designed to promote learning and to cultivate a sense of the company's vision for its employees, says Meister. The corporate university is focused on creating organizational change and providing employees with a clear understanding of what the company's vision is for the future and how their hard work will effectively move the company to that goal.

In other words, corporate universities focus on being proactive while training programs are more reactive. Corporate universities strive to be more strategic in scope, while training programs tend to be more tactical. University outcomes are more often aimed at overall increased performance, while training program outcomes often lean toward increased job skills.

"The corporate university embraces the vision of the leadership, not just the skill required for the execution of the job," says Carrie Rowland, director of education worldwide at the public relations firm Burson-Marsteller in New York.

"The role of the university is not to get [employees] thinking alike but to give them the analytical tools and skills and [to] encourage them to think differently and to challenge," says Steven Kirn, vice president of innovation and learning development at Sears Roebuck & Co. in Hoffman Estates, Ill. "Training gives you skills, but it doesn't ask you to think differently."

No one says that the corporate university is the be-all, end-all of training. In fact, there should be a balance, experts agree. Corporate universities are often umbrella programs that cover all aspects of training in the company, says Kirn. Sears University, for example, is the umbrella organization for educational development activities in Sears; but it does not encompass technical training such as auto shop programs or appliance repair programs, which are taught separately.

## EVOLUTION OF CORPORATE UNIVERSITIES

Corporate universities are not a new idea. General Motors was the leader, developing the General Motors Institute in 1927. But no one really followed suit until the late 1950s when a number of corporate universities were developed, says Meister.

General Electric introduced Crotonville Management Development Institute, and Walt Disney developed Disney University in that decade. Corporate universities did not see another resurgence until the 1990s. In 1988, there were about 400 corporate universities, says Meister. Now she estimates there are more than 1,600. If future growth continues at that pace, corporate universities soon will outnumber traditional universities, which currently total around 3,700.

To explain the role of today's corporate universities, Meister refers to the three C's: Corporate Citizenship, Contextual Framework and Core Workplace Competencies. The goal of a university is to communicate the company's vision to all employees, from the clerical staff to the CEO, and to help employees understand the company's values and culture so they know what the company is trying to achieve and how they can help the company succeed.

Just 10 years ago, companies focused on teaching their employees the skills they would need to do their job properly, without giving them a sense of how they and their jobs were valuable to the company and its future. Without this reference to the company and its goals and ideas, the employee can feel disconnected and less motivated. With this reference, or the three C's, employees can see a clear link between what they are doing and how they are helping the company to move toward its goals.

"People are doing their jobs without seeing the big picture," says Meister. "If we give them the big picture, you have redefined the orientation from a one-time event program to a strategic learning process for the individual."

## CREATING A CORPORATE UNIVERSITY

Most large companies, such as McDonalds, Target, Saturn, Intel, and Motorola have their own universities; some have their own campuses and renowned training programs that other companies emulate or even attend.

Meister says that if a company wants to stay competitive it will have to institute a corporate university of some sort. This means building a team to take charge of a program that entails moving all training courses throughout the company under the university's umbrella. Most companies do not have the resources for a physical campus, but they find some type of learning institution to hold the classes. This can be tricky if your company is global, with multiple offices in different countries.

Steven Tallman is vice president of training at Bain and Co., a management consulting firm with 26 locations in 20 countries. To help centralize its learning center, the company created a virtual university on the Web.

"We've had over 1.2 million hits," says Tallman. "On average, we are getting 50 hits per month per consultant."

More than 160 different training modules are online, and each consultant has the virtual university on his or her desktop for easy access. The modules cover everything from strategic management tools to cash flow models, people development and teaching and mentoring, says Tallman. It's been in operation for 18 months. Tallman also notes that the company puts its employees through formal classroom training as well.

Kirn notes that Sears's curriculum for middle managers is designed to improve the managers' abilities. Some examples of classes taught are advanced finance and team building for the first-time manager.

Amie Malkin, director of brand marketing practice, is also a learning coach at the Burson-Marsteller university. She volunteers her time to help teach and supervise classes at the university. One of the major components of the curriculum is a mock business case that is followed through from the first class to the last, says Malkin.

"It's a fictional case that is based on fact," says Malkin. "Many things are dead on with day-to-day experiences. It's so close to the real thing it's almost not theoretical."

Not only does the case touch on the large picture of solving problems, but it also helps students gain skills such as client relationship management, staff development, and confidence to make judgment calls, adds Rowlands. It's a way of teaching them new skills in a day-to-day format that will be more relevant to actual experiences in the real world.

## SMALL COMPANIES AREN'T OUT OF THE RACE

Should smaller companies develop a corporate university? Yes, says Adam Eisenstat, director of communications at Corporate University Xchange.

"A corporate university is a state of mind," says Eisenstat. "Strategic training is not limited to the big players."

Managed Business Solution, a data processing consulting firm in Boulder, Co., and GlobalNet, a global translation service in Pittsburgh, are two examples of smaller companies that have initiated corporate universities.

"We are a small company," says Burson-Marsteller's Rowland. "We have 2,000 employees. We all recognize how important this is. Smaller businesses are crazy not to do this."

Rowland adds that a small company with just a few employees would not want to create a formal university. Instead, he recommends adapting the format and principles. Let workers see the company's goals and how they can effectively help the company achieve those goals, he advises.

"We spend about 3 percent of our payroll on learning costs," says Rowland. "We are very lucky; most companies will only commit 1 percent."

## WHAT A CORPORATE UNIVERSITY NEEDS TO BE

The key to a successful corporate university is flexibility. Without flexibility of teaching methods, scheduling and modes of learning, the venture may be short-lived or ill-effective. Employees are busier than ever and, without a flexible learning environment, employees will not only find it hard to learn, they will be unable to apply what they have learned to their jobs, says Meister.

"Companies recognize that as everybody's job is changing so fast, they are going to expect you to learn on your own time," Meister says.

"They are going to give you the opportunities that are as flexible as possible and let the learning be decided by you and how you want to go through the program."

Sears has various ways for the employee to learn, says Kirn, including CD-ROM programs set up in all the stores and audio and video-tapes with workbooks that employees may check out of its library.

Each type of company will dictate the modes, different courses and curriculums that its university offers, according to the easiest and most efficient way for its employees to learn. Should the company have a number of different classes for different level managers? Should it only be on the Internet? Should you have both of those methods available? These questions are all answered differently. A great deal depends on the company's already established learning programs.

The choice may be to build upon those, to use those as a supplement to a new program or to start all over. This is where consultants can help, or companies can also go to other corporate universities, some of which market themselves and their knowledge.

Although flexibility gives freedom to employees, it may also be tricky if the company is unionized. Meister recommends working with the union, which may mean making them part of the education board in the company, to help smooth over rough patches related to employees learning on their own time.

## POTENTIAL PITFALLS

Flexibility is just as important to the core curriculum as it is to the modes of learning.

"You have to stay fresh," says Rowland. "If we don't stay in touch with the company and the business world, the program will lose its vitality and credibility. It constantly evolves."

Another item to consider is oversight of the program. According to Meister, 63 percent of all corporate universities report to a senior HR person; the others often report to the chairman, CIO or CFO of the business. Identifying the overseer of the program as well as determining how to integrate the current training program with the corporate universities can be stumbling blocks. One solution is to develop a team in charge of the corporate university and to have them envelop the other training programs during construction of the university.

# CASE STUDY

## GATEWAY'S NEW CLASSROOMS

*Editor's Comment:* For years, training managers have been trying to make money for their training departments, adopting a profit-center perspective rather than a cost-center one. Savvy training managers have always known that customer training can be a viable way to become a profit center. Gateway just happened to have an investment in "physical plant" that could be tapped for more than a locus for retail sales.

In summer 2000, computer manufacturer and retail merchant Gateway Inc. started a public training operation aimed at broadening the PC-using public's understanding and skills about PC operation and applications. Not incidentally, Gateway Inc. figured out a way to bring more customers and potential customers into Gateway retail stores.

Gateway has nearly 300 retail stores across the U.S., where customers typically browse showrooms of Gateway computers and place orders. Gateway's research indicated that most PC users were "unidimensional" users, and also that most of these single-purpose users would be interested in learning other applications. The company also found that only 15% of its customers felt that computers deliver on everything they promise.

Gateway began by offering free clinics for its PC users/customers in the Gateway store showrooms and through OfficeMax kiosks; then decided to build on classrooms to the showrooms and begin a full-fledged training program. By late August 2000, Gateway had room for 5,000 students in its classrooms and was selling courses at a price of between $49 and $175. Other computer manufacturers faced obstacles in their lack of real estate; Gateway was poised to leap ahead.

---

*Source:* "Gateway Aims to be Computer Trainer" by The Associated Press in *The New York Times on the Web*, August 24, 2000, pp. 1–2.

# ABSTRACT

## "BEWARE THE POWERPOINT RANGERS!"

*Editor's Comment:* The "larding" of Department of Defense briefings with "electronic slides of booming tanks and spinning pie charts" made the first page of *The Wall Street Journal* in April 2000, with a report that Chairman of the Joint Chiefs of Staff, General Hugh Shelton, gave orders to the U.S. Military around the globe to get rid of the bells and whistles and quit hogging classified bandwidth.

Apparently the culprit taking up so much internal computer space and military audiences' time is PowerPoint, and the technician/presenters' desire not to be outdone by his or her military peers. "All we need is information," said the General. Jazzy but incoherent described the presentations. One survey of junior officers at Ft. Benning, Georgia, suggested that the "ubiquity of the PowerPoint Army" so turned them off that they were leaving the military for good. Army Secretary Louis Caldera suggested that PowerPoint presentations were alienating lawmakers. Some critics have even charged that the military's PowerPoint Ranger is nothing more than a bureaucrat far more adept at sitting at a computer making slides than at tossing grenades.

Military sociologists contend that today's endless PowerPoint presentations are a product of the zero-defect culture perpetuated by the U.S. Military; or that in the absence of a real enemy, the outstanding graphics capability of PowerPoint gives presenters the illusion of control over an adversary. Pentagon top brass reportedly are trying to figure out ways to interrupt the overly complex PowerPoint presentations.

Greg Jaffe's lively article, of course, raises the age-old question plaguing classroom instructors for many decades, the question of the medium becoming the "message" as Marshall McLuhan would say, or the answer that media should always support instruction, not supplant it. Classroom instructors need to be reminded of these things, as technology makes it so simple to put on a show.

*Source:* "What's Your Point, Lieutenant? Just Cut to the Pie Charts" by Greg Jaffe in *The Wall Street Journal*, April 26, 2000, pp. 1; A6. Greg Jaffe is a Staff Reporter of *The Wall Street Journal*.

# CASE STUDY

## CAPITALIZING ON CHARTER SCHOOLS AT RYDER

*Editor's Comment:* "Tired of the education status-quo" has been a familiar mantra, especially during the presidential election year of 2000. Both major party candidates, numerous legislators, and plenty of governors have joined the chorus of complaints about our nation's public schools. Schools, like businesses, are looking for ways to boost performance—learner and worker performance. Businesses, like schools, are looking for payoffs for doing things differently and/or better.

*U.S. News & World Report*, September 11, 2000, focuses on charter schools as the most obvious success story of recent years in public education, citing bureaucratic independence, encouragement of innovation, and performance measurement and accountability as reasons for the current remarkable growth in charter schools across the country. According to the Center for Education Reform in Washington, DC, more than 519,000 students started school in Fall 2000 at a charter school. That's a 20 percent increase over school year 1999. More than 2,000 charter schools are in operation this year as an alternative to traditional public schools (p. 38). Charter schools are classroom-based and teacher-led, but with a mandate for innovative practices and accountability on the part of teachers and students.

Ryder System Inc., headquartered in Miami, Florida, chose to get in on the charter-school revolution in the name of its employees and their children. Ryder was the first company in Florida to build a charter school on its property, in 1999, after the Florida legislature passed legislation allowing workplace charter schools. It is called Ryder Elementary Charter School and will grow by 100 students each year, reaching a projected 500 students for school year 2002–2003 in grades kindergarten through fifth grade. The school is open first to children of Ryder employees, and then to children from employees of neighboring businesses.

Ryder believes that their charter school is one way to give back to the community. Parents with children in the school are expected to volunteer 20 hours per year at the school. Before-school and after-school programs are also offered there. A Ryder spokesman said that Ryder employees' response to the school was "fantastic," and said that the school provided an incentive to work for Ryder (*BNA newsletter*, April 6, 2000, p. 110). Being identified with learning, innovation, and community service are not all bad from a bottom-line business perspective either! Ryder apparently discovered that this kind of classroom has the kind of payoffs they want for their business.

*Source:* "It's Elementary: Employees Love Charter School" HR Shop Talk column in *Bureau of National Affairs newsletter*, April 6, 2000, p. 110; and "More Growth in Charter Schools" in *U.S. News & World Report*, September 11, 2000, p. 38.

## ABSTRACT

## INNOVATIVE "BLENDED" COLLEGE CLASSROOMS

*Editor's Comment:* The article referenced here is mostly about how laptop computers have transformed college classrooms, including both student and instructor behavior, as well as design and delivery of instruction. The laptop as facilitator of change in classroom instruction is not limited to influence in higher education; it works for corporate classrooms too. These are some of the ways in which the laptop has changed university classrooms.

At Wake Forest University, North Carolina, the class of 2000 was the first to receive laptops shortly after they received their acceptance letters. There, economics students sit behind laptops posting answers to the professor's questions to a virtual chalkboard; business students watch and listen to their professor on streaming video CD-ROM, expecting in class to engage in discussion and small group work; Web research and on-you-own-time quizzes are common. Physics students design their own electrical circuits and actually test them, virtually, on the Web. At Wake Forest, nearly all professors incorporate technology into their teaching. They say that students generally are putting in much more time learning and doing more homework because of the laptops.

At Clemson University, South Carolina, English classes keep their compositions in electronic portfolios posted on the Web. At Harvard Law School, Massachusetts, students respond to a question-of-the week posted on the Web, answers to which are routed to other students for analysis and comment. At Nova University's Law School, Florida, students use case-management software to file their assignments and mock-bill

for their time. Oberlin College, Ohio, keeps its university-owned laptops locked in a newly wired classroom for use in the classroom to do professor-guided historical research. One Wake Forest professor said that the laptop is an "intellectual resource," and that he would have to "dumb down" his curriculum and his teaching if he didn't have it (*The New York Times*, March 26, 2000, p. 30).

Students, naturally, still get bored in class and are tempted more than ever to do other things with open laptops in front of them—things like check stock quotes, set up dates, and e-mail their friends. Some students mourn the loss of face-to-face socialization that has naturally followed the laptop-on-every-desk revolution. Experts estimate that about 80 percent of American college freshmen bring a computer to school with them, and more and more universities and colleges are requiring that they do. Corporate trainers can learn a few things from the experiments and changes going on in college classrooms, because very soon these laptop-savvy students will enter the workforce and come to corporate classrooms expecting to continue to learn in the "blended" ways they were introduced to in college.

*Source:* "College Educators Find a Revolution Clicking Into Place" by Jodi Wilgoren in *The New York Times*, March 26, 2000, pp. 1, 30. Jodi Wilgoren is a Reporter for *The New York Times*.

## INTRODUCTION TO EVALUATION: SECTION 5

The influence of the ideas and practices of human performance technology has been felt in the training field, especially as its focus on personal and organizational improvement seems to have taken the spotlight off the strict bottom-line approach of investment, capital, and ROI. This accounting-type mindset in evaluation has been with trainers for a long time, and, over the recent decades, has devilled training managers with trying to figure out training's worth according to the traditional measures of a production economy, that is, according to the historical accountant's view of the world and the bottom line.

Over the years, Donald Kirkpatrick (1994) has tried valiantly to convince trainers and managers to "get to level 4" training evaluation, that is, training that can be directly linked to business results like documented fewer errors or more sales. Unfortunately, most trainers can't do this, because human behavior isn't easily translatable into pure number-crunching, and true cause and effect is rarely possible in a human resources field like training. Kirkpatrick himself, and many others, have stuck to the "Four Levels" framework of training evaluation, but have suggested that correlation, not causality, might be enough. Even this softening of the standards, however, has not encouraged hordes of trainers and managers to try a "level 4" evaluation.

Newer voices, Robert S. Kaplan and David P. Norton (1996), came up with their idea of a more balanced approach to defining corporate value and measuring how a company performs. They took the evaluation community by storm with the publication of their articles and book on "The Balanced Scorecard." Their scorecards included a set of measures for "learning and growth" that tried to get at the processes that are necessary to sustain a company's ability to change and improve—quite a different focus from the strict "return on investment" notion. Training evaluation as we begin year 2001 reflects this evolution.

### Measuring Performance

We begin our series of entries in this section on evaluation of training with a group of articles that advocate for measurements that are built on common sense and reality, not on some lofty or high-sounding but unrealistic standards. The very successful Benchmarking Study conducted by the American Society for Training and Development (ASTD) was chosen to lead this section because of its systematic search for standards and measures that matter in today's kind of workplace. We continue with two reviews of important books that highlight the need for clear thinking and good judgment in evaluation of people and processes. Throughout, the focus is on defining and elevating the business-critical processes that relate to customers and employees, not just to bricks, mortar, and stock price.

We conclude this first group of entries with an article abstracted from several sources all dealing with this year's very visible public discussion of school testing. As in business, so in education, we are seeing this year especially a rebellion of sorts against "the false" in standards and measures. In education, states and communities, teachers, and even students themselves are rebelling against statewide achievement tests, standardized testing, and the Scholastic Aptitude Test (SAT) which has long been a familiar hurdle to jump for many 16 and 17 year olds. *Time* magazine reported on June 19, 2000 that "protest-the-test" groups have cropped up in 36 different states (p. 34). Parents, teachers, and students complain that the tests don't represent reality, the curriculum, or even how students learn. There have been too many accounts of classroom teachers teaching to the test, giving student test takers the right answers, or falsifying results in order to look good. Several New England colleges, Bowdoin, Bates, and Mount Holyoke, announced this year that they were scrapping the SAT admission requirement (*U.S. News & World Report*, June 19, 2000, p. 12). Educators scream that testing should never upstage teaching, and the kind of "sorting" of individuals that often results from analysis of test scores runs counter to American values (*The New York Times*, Ideas & Trends column, June 18, 2000, p. WK6).

Home schooling in the United States has increased from 7 to 15 percent over the past several years, and many observers say that it is an experiment that should be encouraged. Some see this as a reaction against overzealous testers who would reduce education to comparative test scores, sacrificing personal relationships between teacher and learner. Home schoolers are justly proud of their students' accomplishments. Data show that median annual income for home-school families is $52,000, significantly higher than the $36,000 annual income for all families with children (*U.S. News & World Report*, June 19, 2000, David Gergen Editorial, p. 64). Many voices are making the point that home schooling, with its one-to-one, caring relationship, is more in tune with what learning is all about. America stood up and took notice this year when the top national spelling bee and national geography bee winners were home-schooled students. Learning at home, in schools, and at work is begging for meaningful standards of performance. Closing the gap between knowing and doing is a challenge that has been spelled out this year in many different ways; and, doing, that is, human performance, is ultimately what's important in how people and businesses grow.

## LOOKING FOR VALUE

The tantalizing and elusive notion of measuring talent, or as David Stamps says, "measuring minds," has been cropping up with increasing frequency in the training literature this year. This is in tune with a new economy that is information based, focused on knowledge acquisition and management, and increasingly rich in intellectual capital. Recruiting and retaining top talent is high priority at the start of the new millennium. This information economy places a high value on brainpower and innovation—and above all, the ability to turn knowledge into action fast. Articles in this group focus on these issues, including the development of diversity as a foundation for increased creativity (not just a legal issue) and the development of standards for online learning in order to facilitate access to and speed of learning. Workplace learning in all of its value dimensions is the subject of our next group of entries in this section on evaluation.

## THE MEANING IN NUMBERS

We conclude this section on evaluation with a set of articles on the meaning in numbers. Evaluation's foundation is validity and usefulness, but the measures of these qualities have been represented by numbers. Numbers have a way of communicating. The ideas in performance measurement contain descriptors such as skills needed, problems encountered, obstacles overcome, incidence of use, availability of access, robustness and performance over time, and many others. Evaluators typically have the job of figuring out how to represent these performance-related ideas, and, of course, how, when, and how much to measure them. To do these things, evaluators turn to numbers. Articles here shed some light on considerations regarding the meaning in numbers.

We conclude this section with some commentary about the 2000 United States Census, the ultimate task in measurement. In this commentary, we have referred to various sources about the Census process and tally, its purposes and its problems. Finally, we give you a wonderful cartoon by Istvan Banyai, which appeared in the April 10, 2000 *New Yorker* magazine, p. 50. The cartoon, which illustrated a tongue-in-cheek parody of the Census director's letter to citizens, asks the key questions, what do we count? and why? Mr. Banyai's sense of humor, social, and political commentary can help trainers think twice about what we evaluate and measure, and why.

# 5A. MEASURING PERFORMANCE

## RESEARCH SUMMARY

## FACTORS IN MEASUREMENT OF INTELLECTUAL CAPITAL AND HUMAN PERFORMANCE

*Editor's Comment:* The American Society for Training & Development (ASTD) continues this year with its Benchmarking Service. Approximately 1,300 organizations form the database on which the latest report (for year 2000) is constructed. Contact ASTD by phone or e-mail for results and other information about the study or service. The deadline for data collection was September 1, 2000. Results were expected by January 1, 2001.

ASTD's Measurement Kit is a comprehensive set of questions covering 40 pages of survey material organized in two parts, Part I on Training Investments and Part II on Training Outcomes. We reprint here excerpts from section I, specifically the questions for consideration in determining measurement of intellectual capital (Part I, pages 22–24) and factors in determining an organization's extent of management of human performance (Part I, page 13).

For our readers who are not members of ASTD nor are participants in the Benchmarking Service, these questions can serve as a guide for your own development of appropriate measures in these important training-related areas. Trainers can help improve the knowledge base in their organizations by becoming involved in these kinds of measurement studies.

*Source: ASTD 2000 Measurement Kit: Tools for Benchmarking and Continuous Improvement.* Published in March 2000 by the American Society for Training & Development, Alexandria, VA., Mark E. Van Buren, Director of Research. Four pages reprinted with permission of ASTD. Copyright 2000. All rights reserved. *www.astd.org* More information is available by telephone at 703/838-5841 or e-mail at *benchservice@astd.org*. ASTD's website is *astd.org*.

## E. INTELLECTUAL CAPITAL MEASURES (OPTIONAL)

**About this Module:** Increasingly, organizations around the world are recognizing that a large part of their value does not exist in their financial and physical capital. Rather it lies in their intellectual capital; the skills and knowledge of their people, their systems and processes, and their valued customers.

Until this time, organizations have lacked a clear and common set of metrics for measuring their intellectual capital that would allow them to see it grow over time and to compare their intellectual capital to those of other organizations. In this module, we provide a core set of intellectual capital measures that ASTD developed in conjunction with a number of leading corporations in the United States. By completing this module, your organization will be on the frontier of measuring and leveraging the most valuable part of your organization.

**General Instructions:** This module consists of two sections that differ based on the type of information collected: Section I contains questions that can be answered for your organization as a whole (as defined in the Core Module). Section II contains questions that must be answered by your employees as part of an employee survey. These questions specifically address the level of employee satisfaction and commitment in your organization. Please follow the directions provided at the start of Section II precisely.

To participate in the Module, you do *not* need to complete both Sections—you can choose to do one section only, or to do both.

**Section E-I: Intellectual Capital in Your Organization**

E-1.    **In 1999, approximately what percentage of the employees in your organization would you consider to be essential employees (i.e., those employees who are most essential to your organization)?**

_____ percent

E-2.    **During 1999, approximately what percentage of the essential employees (as you defined them above) in your organization left?**

_____ percent

E-3.    **In 1999, approximately what percentage of the openings in your organization that required either an advanced degree or 10 or more years experience were filled during that calendar year?**

_____ percent

E-4.    **In 1999, approximately what percentage of the employees in your organization had a basic level of proficiency in standard office computer applications (e.g., spreadsheets, word processing, electronic mail)?**

_____ percent

E-5.    **In 1999, on average, how much did it cost your organization to recruit, hire, and train a new employee who you considered to be one of your essential employees?**

_____

E-6.    **In 1999, approximately how much did your organization spend on conceiving and designing new products and/or services?**

_____

**E-7.** **In 1999, approximately what percentage of the full-time employees in your organization had the conception and design of new products and/or services as their primary responsibility?**

_____ percent

**E-8.** **Approximately what percentage of all products and/or services your organization had on the market in 1999 were introduced in 1997, 1998, or 1999?**

_____ percent

**E-9.** **As of the end of 1999, approximately what percentage of your organization's business-critical processes had been documented and analyzed?**

_____ percent

**E-10.** **As of the end of 1999, approximately what percentage of your organization's business-critical processes that had been documented and analyzed were being fully utilized?**

_____ percent

**E-11.** **In 1999, on average, approximately what percentage of your customers was completely satisfied with your products and/or services?**

_____ percent

**E-12.** **Approximately what percentage of the top 20 percent of customers (in sales) of your organization in 1998 ended their sales contracts in 1999?**

_____ percent

**E-13.** **In 1999, in a typical month, about what percentage of your organization's customers reported complaints about your products and/or services?**

_____ percent

**E-14.** **What is the average number of years that your existing customers have been purchasing products and/or services from your organization?**

_____ years

**E-15.** **Approximately what percentage of the customers that purchased products and/or services from your organization in the last quarter of 1999 (October through December) had previously purchased products and/or services from your organization?**

_____ percent

**E-16.** **Compared to organizations in the same primary line of business as your organization, what percent experienced a lower rate of sales growth than your organization during 1999?** (For example, 55 percent of organizations experienced a lower rate of sales growth than my organization in 1999.)

_____ percent

## SECTION E-II: EMPLOYEE SATISFACTION AND COMMITMENT

**Instructions for Section:** The following box contains nine easily-answered questions on the satisfaction and commitment of your employees. **These questions should be administered to all employees in your organization in a survey.** It is critical that they be given to employees exactly as written and that you assure all employees that their responses will be anonymous. After collecting the responses, please summarize them by completing questions E-17 to E-25 (at the end of this section).

**Text for Employee Satisfaction and Commitment Survey:**

Instructions: Please check the best response to each item.

**When you think about your company and the work you do, the people you work with, the benefits your company provides, the opportunities that are available, the current business climate, your working conditions, and other aspects . . .**

| | Very Satisfied | Somewhat Satisfied | Not Sure | Somewhat Dissatisfied | Very Dissatisfied |
|---|---|---|---|---|---|
| 1. How would you rate your company as a company to work for as compared to other companies? | ❏ | ❏ | ❏ | ❏ | ❏ |
| 2. How would you rate your overall satisfaction with your company at the present time? | ❏ | ❏ | ❏ | ❏ | ❏ |
| 3. How would you rate your overall satisfaction with your job at the present time? | ❏ | ❏ | ❏ | ❏ | ❏ |
| 4. How would you rate the training your received for your present job? | ❏ | ❏ | ❏ | ❏ | ❏ |

**To what extent do you agree with the following statements?**

| | Strongly Agree | Agree | Not Sure | Disagree | Strongly Disagree |
|---|---|---|---|---|---|
| 5. My job makes good use of my skills and abilities. | ❏ | ❏ | ❏ | ❏ | ❏ |
| 6. I am given a real opportunity to improve my skills in this company. | ❏ | ❏ | ❏ | ❏ | ❏ |
| 7. I am willing to work harder than I have to in order to see this company succeed. | ❏ | ❏ | ❏ | ❏ | ❏ |
| 8. I would take almost any job to keep working for this company. | ❏ | ❏ | ❏ | ❏ | ❏ |
| 9. I am proud to be working for this company. | ❏ | ❏ | ❏ | ❏ | ❏ |

**32. To what percentage of your organization's employees do the following human performance management practices apply?** Please check the appropriate box.

| | None | 1% to 49% | 50% to 99% | 100% |
|---|---|---|---|---|
| **(a) Annual performance reviews:** a systematic, periodic review and analysis of employee's job performance by a superior to compare that performance to a set of predetermined standards, identify strengths and weaknesses, and develop a plan to improve the employee's performance. | ❏ | ❏ | ❏ | ❏ |
| **(b) Individual development plans:** a specific course of action designed jointly by an employee and a supervisor to outline the employee's career development objectives and associated training needs. | ❏ | ❏ | ❏ | ❏ |
| **(c) Peer review of performance or 360° feedback systems:** a performance appraisal system in which an employee's work performance is evaluated (at least in part) by co-workers. | ❏ | ❏ | ❏ | ❏ |
| **(d) Skill certification:** a formal process used to ascertain and distinguish the mastery for a set of skills according to pre-defined standards. May be linked either to a particular occupation or trade, or a particular job or process. | ❏ | ❏ | ❏ | ❏ |
| **(e) Documentation of individual competencies:** a formal record of the knowledge, skills, and abilities of an organization's employees in key, pre-defined areas. | ❏ | ❏ | ❏ | ❏ |
| **(f) Training information system:** a computer-based system for assessing, tracking, and improving employee performance. Systems may include employee training history reports, training course scheduling and registration, individual development plans, and training expenditure tracking. | ❏ | ❏ | ❏ | ❏ |

# BOOK REVIEW

## MEASUREMENT THAT OBSTRUCTS JUDGMENT

*Editor's Comment:* This new book by Professors Pfeffer and Sutton could be placed anywhere in this edition of *Training & Development Yearbook.* We've chosen to frame this review in the context of evaluation ideas, because so much of what comprises the book reflects fundamental issues in measurement and evaluation. In fact, a quick look at the table of contents reminds the reader of quality guru W. Edwards Deming's famous "14 points," the classic organizational standards for building quality in as organizations develop and improve. Pfeffer and Sutton seem to have a similar focus: instead of "quality" they talk about "smart" companies; in place of "improving" they talk about "closing the knowing-doing gap." Pfeffer and Sutton, like Deming, look for simple, direct, and largely common-sense ways to create standards for and measures of positive action. Their book contains nothing revolutionary, but it is an easy-to-follow review of some current commendable corporate practices aimed at turning good words into action. My own favorite chapter is Chapter 5, "When Measurement Obstructs Good Judgment."

The book's major point of view is that most leaders know what to do, they just don't do it. In an era where both leadership and knowledge are important buzz words, it probably bears repeating that there are tried and true—and simple—ways to identify the gaps between knowing and doing. That's what this book does. It's worth reading as a common sense refresher about needs assessment, standards of behavior, measures that lead to useful action.

One of the many case studies used to illustrate various truths is that of The Men's Wearhouse, a new kind of men's clothing store. There, the nationwide retailer has developed measures of performance that are "behaviorally specific," and include things such as:

- participates in team selling,
- contributes to store maintenance and stock work,
- greets, interviews, and tapes all customers properly (p. 164).

These kinds of indicators, according to the authors, enable the company to have "in-process measures that can be taught, learned, and implemented." These kinds of measures, they suggest, are in contrast to the more typical outcome or end-of-process measures found in most companies (p. 164).

The authors also make the point that one of the problems with outcome measures is that they typically are "economic" measures. A better assumption is that individuals are "social creatures" too, and that behaviorally based measures better capture the things that really matter in working relationships (p. 157). Sharing in the process of creating knowledge is an experiential, interaction-based, face-to-face activity. Early in the book, Pfeffer and Sutton make a strong statement that knowledge management systems work best when the people who generate knowledge (through working at tasks and solving problems) are the same people as those who store it, explain it to others, and coach others to act upon it (p. 21). Throughout the book, they advocate for the active process of learning from work and from colleagues, for "rhetoric that mobilizes action" (p. 61). They caution against the temptation to reward "smart

*Source: The Knowing-Doing Gap: How Smart Companies Turn Knowledge Into Action* by Jeffrey Pfeffer and Robert I. Sutton. Boston: Harvard Business School Press, 2000. $27.50. Jeffrey Pfeffer is the Thomas D. Dee Professor of Organizational Behavior at Stanford University's Graduate School of Business. Robert I. Sutton is Professor of Organizational Behavior at Stanford University's School of Engineering. Sutton is also Co-Director of the Center on Work, Technology, and Organization.

talk" when it substitutes for action (p. 43). They tell the story of coaches at British Petroleum who intentionally spend 80 percent of their time working with people to discover how information technology can be used to make their work better, and only 20 percent of their time training people how to use systems. They make the point that at BP, people, not systems, carry information forward (pp. 219–221).

The last chapter in the book contains the authors' "recurrent themes" that guide their understanding of how to fix what they call "the knowing-doing gap." These themes are (pp. 246–262).

• Why before How: Philosophy Is Important.

• Knowing Comes from Doing and Teaching Others How.

• Action Counts More Than Elegant Plans and Concepts.

• There Is No Doing Without Mistakes. What Is the Company's Response?

• Fear Fosters Knowing-Doing Gaps, So Drive Out Fear.

• Beware of False Analogies: Fight the Competition, Not Each Other.

• Measure What Matters and What Can Help Turn Knowledge into Action.

• What Leaders Do, How They Spend Their Time and How They Allocate Resources—Matters.

# BOOK REVIEW

## COMMON-SENSE ACCOUNTABILITY

*Editor's Comment:* This rather small new book from Richard Y. Chang and co-author Mark Morgan is presented as a story about a fictional character, "Vince Sharp," Vice-President of Customer Services at the fictional company, SolvNET. Readers follow Vince's deliberations and experiences as he interacts with his staff and others in order to create meaningful measures for processes and people in his company. Characters in this serious business book help to make the difficult topic of performance measurement a bit easier to understand and provide the reader with humanized approaches that make it more comfortable to emulate SolvNET's evaluation journey into common-sense measurement.

Examples throughout the book amplify the good decisions made by Vince Sharp and his colleagues. They are small case studies mostly of previous Baldrige Award winners, with some cases from the archives of the American Productivity & Quality Center (APQC). These are familiar and useful as examples, giving the reader some real world situations and decisions taken by real people doing a good job. The book's narrative flows between the fictitious Vince and the non-fiction case studies and "expert tip" boxes scattered throughout the

*Source: Performance Scorecards: Measuring the Right Things in the Real World* by Richard Y. Chang and Mark W. Morgan. San Francisco: Jossey-Bass, A Wiley Company, 2000. $32.95. Richard Y. Chang, PhD, is President and CEO of Richard Chang Associates, Inc., Irvine, CA., a diversified consulting and publishing company. He is also past-president of the American Society for Training & Development (ASTD), and a judge for the Malcolm Baldrige National Quality Award. Mark Morgan is a Senior Consultant for Richard Chang Associates, Inc., an examiner for the Malcolm Baldrige National Quality Award, and former instructor at Florida Institute of Technology and University of Central Florida. Contact them by e-mail at *info@rca4results.com* or on their website, *richardchangassociates.com*. The Performance Scorecard Management Cycle ™ is reprinted here with permission of Jossey-Bass, Inc. a subsidiary of John Wiley & Sons, Inc. Copyright 2000.

book's 162 pages. Ample graphs and charts are clearly shown to serve as guides for the reader to use as tools in his or her own organization.

The major point made early in the book and carried throughout the work is that the quality principle of "focus on the vital few" is a far better approach to performance measurement than the typical "cover all bases" approach now in use by most organizations. The authors advocate creating various "scorecards," each uniquely designed to capture and disseminate only the things that truly make a difference to those processes or persons being evaluated. Scorecards are typically used to ". . . evaluate performance targets, monitor trends, identify strengths and weaknesses, and provide feedback on management actions" (p. xxiii).

Chang and Morgan's system of "Performance Scorecard Management" is presented as a wheel consisting of six forward-moving components: collect, create, cultivate, cascade, connect, and confirm.

These six processes used to create measures that mean something are followed throughout the book as readers are led to important decisions about what really matters to their business. As in typical performance technology approaches, knowledge, skills, and abilities—the standard province of trainers—are presented in this book as one kind of process, goal, vision, or objective among many. Trainers who are thinking as performance specialists will find this book particularly helpful. Trainers will find the steps and models useful as teaching aids in classrooms or one-on-one sessions to help learners in their charge think about measurement in a common-sense way and to create useful tools, scorecards, to keep them on track measuring things that matter and using measurement results to move their companies forward. Chang and Morgan have created a book that is useful as a performance tool and as a teaching tool.

# ABSTRACT

## TESTING AND COUNTING

*Editor's Comment:* It seems like this year, especially, the "educated public" is becoming more important than in recent past years. Several important factors are propelling the issue of education forward: (1) both Presidential candidates have made education reform a key campaign issue; (2) states have been testing selected grades with new competency tests, tests of basic skills, tests to certify competence for high school graduation, tests to certify competence to enter the teaching profession —norm-referenced and criterion referenced tests—and have seen massive numbers of failures on these state-devised tests which are polarizing the education issue; (3) the Internet and media are influencing public issues of all sorts, including education; and (4) business is pressuring public schools to produce employable graduates with skills appropriate to help support and further America's economic vitality. These factors together make us ask the questions, What are we testing and counting, and why? Using the references listed below, we consider these four factors. Trainers often must get involved in the outcomes and effects of public education. Year 2001 will probably require some visionary and astute corporate minds to make some sense of testing and counting.

1. *The Presidential Campaign factor:* Jonathan Alter's commentary in *Newsweek* suggests that the early campaign made it tough for voters to decide what positions were best in order to solve education's failure in many cities across America. Alter raises issues through the candidates' positions such as smaller classes, better buildings, parental choice, less union influence, universal pre-school, and vouchers, competition, and tuition tax breaks for parents of non-public school students. Alter suggests that maybe if the two candidates, Bush and Gore, got together on what to do, we might come up with a solid policy for real reform. He points out that public education in cities is particularly poor, citing Camden, New Jersey, where 97 percent of the poorest 8th graders failed the standardized tests, contrasting Camden with a charter middle school in Newark where test scores have skyrocketed and all students plan to go to college. Alter raises the issues of local district versus state control, and suggests that governance might be the real problem to wrestle. Businesses are being asked to be involved in the public schools; business persons who know something about process design, efficient and effective management of people, and the needs of the workforce for learning-to-learn skills can be helpful by directing the attention of public educators—and politicians—to the questions, What are we testing and counting, and why?

2. *The Statewide Testing factor:* Paula L. Park's column on standards in the Education Life supplement to the Sunday *New York Times* quotes the figure of 18 as the number of states that now have graduation requirements, certified by testing. She also notes that in every state but Iowa, statewide "standards" exist, but that these standards vary widely in quality and in speci-

*Sources:* "Al and Dubya's School Daze" by Jonathan Alter in *Newsweek*, April 10, 2000, p. 34; "The Big Blur: Vote Early and Often" by Eric Effron in *Brill's Content*, March 2000, pp. 47–48; "Next: Selling News Short" by Ilan Greenberg in *Brills' Content*, March 2000, pp. 64–65; "Work Week" column by Albert R. Karr in *The Wall Street Journal*, January 25, 2000, p. 1; "Just Say No to MCAS" letter to the editor by Sue Kohler in *Berkshire Record*, March 24, 2000, p. A4; "Squandering a Legacy" by Chris Gregor on April 14, 2000, pp. A4, 1, April 14, 2000; "Standards: A Primer" by Paula L. Park in "Education Life" supplement to *The New York Times*, April 9, 2000, p. 35; "Top 10 Educational Trends in America Today" by Lynne S. Dumas in *Family PC*, May 2000, pp. 98–103.

ficity. She also describes the broad range of performance and basic skill (language, reading, and math) tests across the country. Testing fourth and eighth graders seems to be rather common nationwide; but by what kind of test and for what reason is almost anybody's guess. She notes that "the stakes are high," elaborating that administrator and teacher pay and promotion are sometimes tied to students' test scores, and that money and prestige flowing to schools from district offices depend increasingly on a school's good showing on various tests. Some local school districts make up their own tests based on their curriculums; others buy commercially prepared tests (Iowa, CBT/McGraw-Hill, Educational Testing Service, American College Tests, etc.) and expect scores to be normed with similar scores of students across the country, and even in other countries.

In my own state of Massachusetts, a new competency test for high school sophomores called the MCAS has polarized communities across the state. Critics say that it tests isolated bits of information, and that to pass, students have to be taught in bits and bites. Some say that teachers are teaching to the tests, mostly facts that need to be memorized, to the exclusion of the kinds of learning that occurs with music, art, drama, environmental education, athletics, discussion and dialogue, team and collaborative work, and independent projects. Students and teachers have been writing letters to the editor of my small hometown paper for months. In one regional school district, a group of about 40 sophomores has organized a protest and refused to take the tests (*Berkshire Record*). Four other high schools within the area have also boycotted the MCAS tests. A Website calls this kind of testing "horserace mentality." The students have an e-mail address, *MCAS-SCAM@Hotmail.com*. The group is known as SCAM, Student coalition for an Alternative to MCAS, and they have a political agenda. The school principal is trying to use this as a lesson in civil disobedience, and says she will not punish the students for their stance against the tests.

Critics of the student critics also write letters to the editor, claiming that the students have no right to be "dictating educational standards to adults," and that the kind of "boring" education that the boycotting students say the tests test is the kind of education that has stood the "test of time" and produced the more "literate"

graduating classes of thirty years ago. Testing indeed abounds, and is surely polarizing students, teachers, communities, taxpayers, and parents; and again, the questions must be asked, What are we testing and counting, and why?

During year 2000, the nation's teachers too, not just the students, came under fire for being poorly prepared to teach. Study after study across the country pointed out large numbers of teachers who were neither certified nor prepared to teach the subjects they were in fact teaching. The rather militant teachers' union, the American Federation of Teachers, surprised the press and public by supporting higher standards for teachers, measured by, of all things, the same kind of periodic standardized tests for teachers as were being implemented for students across the country.

3. *The Internet and Media factor:* The 16 year olds in my neighborhood who boycott the Massachusetts competency tests have been using the newspapers and e-mail to recruit more students to their cause. Student leaders have gotten state legislators to meet with them, one of whom is coaching the students in how to create a bill. The school has given the boycotting students alternative ways, other than MCAS testing, to evaluate their competency (*Berkshire Record*, April 14, 2000, p. 1). The school seems determined to encourage the students to learn from their boycotting activities. The whole experience seems to beg the question of how much more learning is happening because of not taking the test.

The new media and communications magazine, *Brill's Content*, has frequently run articles about advertisements that blur into news and how entertainment and journalism often seem to have the same standards these days. Writers in this magazine often question the intent of media- and Internet-delivered messages, and between the lines of many articles ask questions about the quality of critical thinking. Eric Effron writes in the March 2000 issue about political advisor Dick Morris's *vote.com* Website, in which Morris says he expects to "transform the democratic process" by polling the world and forwarding poll results to all those who need to know. The problem, as Effron points out, is that results are easily corrupted and "playing the game" is obviously only for those online, which most folks agree is those who are affluent, well-educated, and white. Effron's article begins with, "I voted for John McCain. In fact, I liked him so much, I voted for him twice." Another article in the same issue of *Brill's Content* takes on the Internet-based news digests, popular for their immediacy and convenience. Author Ilan Greenberg poses some tough questions about the dumbing-down of standards, and asks, "Will we substitute the skimming of quickie rewrites . . . for real reading . . .? He decries the "Gimme the Gist" and "Grab the Headlines" mentality, and implies the ultimate questions of how we arrive at value and what counts.

4. *The Pressure of Business factor:* In May 2000 *Family PC* magazine ran a major article about the top 10 educational trends in the country today. Not surprising, the first trend at the top of the list was the setting of high academic standards for every child. Department of Education officials are quoted as saying that clear and rigorous standards are needed in every grade; and government felt the urgent need to be involved in facilitating students' "success" through problem solving and creative thinking. The officials quoted made clear that the success to which they were referring was success at competition in the global marketplace. Assessment and accountability for students and teachers through testing was described as the most significant trend, one that had real consequences such as school closings and teacher job loss where students failed to demonstrate competence or failed the test. This is tough talk, clearly reflective of business pressures on the public education system.

Tied to this first year 2000 "trend" is the second trend which *Family PC* calls the trend toward "Tech-Smart Curricula." To support this trend, the education establishment is calling for much more support for teachers who are expected to "integrate technology" into the entire curriculum of schools, including supports such as time to figure out how to use the technology-based resources and, of course, extra teacher training of a formal sort, in workshops, classrooms, and online. Throughout the country, universities, governments, and businesses are encouraged to help teachers be better users of computers. Another key trend is that the "digital divide" grows bigger, with households with incomes of $75,000 or more are 20 times more likely to have a computer at home, suggesting that the "technological know-how" necessary for equal opportunity in today's booming economy simply isn't there for children—and workers—from middle- and low-income households.

Developmental issues and challenges suggested by these trends in education are reflected in similar trends in the broader business community. For example, *The Wall Street Journal*, January 25, 2000, ran a clip in its first-page "Work Week" column on a new "testing and training network" sponsored by the American College Testing (ACT) group in Iowa. ACT is launching a new network of more than 200 workplace skills assessment and training centers to be located at community colleges. The article quotes the executive director of the National Association of Manufacturers' Center for Workforce Success as saying that "job-applicant testing and training is the new game in town."

Brochures and advertisements about all sorts of workplace assessment instruments come across my desk weekly. Several recent ones include Berrett-Koehler's (California) "Diversity Breakthrough! Strategic Action Series" that features, among other things, an assessment phase and an accountability phase, accompanied by an "innovative problem identification tool," for $108.15. Skillscape's (British Columbia) "Competence Manager" assessment software promises to "provide a systematic approach to assessment of an organization's knowledge capital and needs," selling for $21,200 for a 500-user license. SkillView Technologies (New Hampshire) offers a self-assessment software tool for the individual to identify and manage his or her skills and to plan their own career paths and training. This will cost a company a setup fee of $10,000 plus a monthly fee of $2–$8 per employee user. Questionmark (Connecticut) has a software product that promises be the "most powerful software for authoring, delivering and reporting on assessments." The colorful brochure, unlike the others, does not include cost information, but rather, is presented as a "newsletter" describing the many features and benefits of its products, suggesting that the reader check out its Website for more information. The message is that assessment is big, and important for business. What we test and count, how we do it, and why are fundamental issues in education and training as we blaze into the twenty first century.

# 5B. LOOKING FOR VALUE

## RESEARCH SUMMARY

## SEARCHING FOR VALUE DRIVERS

*Editor's Comment:* The group of contributors listed below have come up with what they say is a new way of measuring value in companies and workforces that conduct business in the realm of intellectual capital. Trainers for the past few years have been wrestling with how to help such companies and workers establish the right metrics for intellectual capital and then measure their organizational and personal learning against them. Peter Senge's "Learning Organization" in 1990, and Kaplan and Norton's "Balanced Scorecards" in 1992 became the foundation for a shift in corporate thinking about appropriate measures for new kinds of companies that were largely dependent on how intellectual capital, not nuts-and-bolts capital, was created and expended.

These researchers who contributed to this article here have come up with a nonfinancial set of measures which together they call the VCI, the Value Creation Index. They argue that such measures are essential to supporting growth and development in today's fast-moving companies that depend on something other than financial measures to determine their worth. The study described here contains some surprises, the most interesting of which is that innovation, and not customer satisfaction, is the highest value metric. Trainers, of course, have been developing programs of learning that emphasize self-directed learning, mentoring, high-level problem solving skills, and other process-oriented programs to encourage the development of innovation. This research summary should give trainers of this persuasion the extra validation to continue such efforts—and add a few more based on this study's results.

## INTRODUCING THE NEW VALUE CREATION INDEX

*by Geoff Baum, Chris Ittner, David Larcker, Jonathan Low,*

*Tony Siesfeld, and Michael S. Malone*

Every week, new dot-com companies go public with tiny revenues, invisible profits, and a small share of a market niche that may evaporate in an instant. Yet, within hours of the Wall Street morning bell, those companies are valued at hundreds of millions—or even billions—of dollars. So how much of that valuation is real?

Who knows? No one has yet developed a systematic means to tell us how much, say, Amazon.com is really worth; we have no accounting system that captures all the hidden values—brand, human capital, partnerships, intellectual property—embedded within the total market valuation of a company in the new economy. There have been too many nasty surprises recently to allow us to keep trusting the traditional seal of financial approval, the corporate audit. If our standard accounting system—the product of 500 years, the primary metric of the world's economy—is broken or irrelevant, we have a very large problem. And there's very little time to fix it.

Today, when intangible assets can make up a huge portion of a company's value, and when that value is remeasured every business day by stock market analysts and traders, our current system of financial measurement has become increasingly disconnected from what appears to be truly valuable in the new economy. In the current economic boom, driven by the high tech sectors, not only do intangible assets make up nearly all of the value of the hottest companies but they now may represent as much as half the value of the entire U.S. economy. If this trillion dollars of intellectual capital is a mirage, then we have a catastrophe on our hands.

We desperately need more precise metrics. But there is a reason why, after a decade of research, intellectual capital has yet to be adequately measured. Intangible assets live up to their name. They are typically amorphous, subjective, and hard to pin down. Even intangible assets that seem relatively straightforward—say, the value of a company's computer network—are complicated by, upon closer inspection, a host of other issues, such as compatibility, software, usage, and bandwidth.

In April 1999, this magazine announced that it was embarking on a joint research venture with the Ernst & Young Center for Business Innovation and the Wharton Research Program on Value Creation in Organizations to develop the first practical audit of intangible assets. We teamed up to study how managers and investors could truly evaluate nonfinancial assets—and how we at *Forbes ASAP* could establish real-life, accurate metrics that could be used in routine business by investors, managers, and analysts. We also polled you, our readers, for those nonfinancial factors you use to evaluate an investment. A year into this research project, our work has just begun. Yet our study already has begun to yield astonishing results. What follows is a chronology of our discoveries to date, including a first-ever intellectual capital-based audit of the Time Warner-AOL deal.

## COMPONENTS OF VALUE

What are the key nonfinancial factors in creating value for the modern corporation? We asked you that very question in a *Forbes Digital Tool* survey last year. The answers ranged from employees to products to company image.

Historically, most intangible asset measurements have been top-down: Investors theorize a contributing factor and then try to figure out how to measure it. Our approach was different. We applied the categories to large S&P 500 companies in the durable and nondurable manufacturing sectors. Using advanced statistical techniques, we determined the ability of each value-driver category to explain market value over and above the amount explained by traditional accounting assets and liabilities. We then combined the categories into the *Forbes ASAP/ Ernst & Young Value Creation Index* (VCI), a measurement tool that incorporates the relative importance of each key economy value driver.

Next, we examined a wide variety of intangible asset categories, which enabled us to identify the factors that are significant in creating value. Then we weighted the categories according to their importance in explaining market values, thus avoiding the arbitrary, and often incorrect, weightings frequently used to provide an overall assessment of intangible assets. What we found was surprising. Some perceived value drivers translate into market value; others do not.

HERE'S WHAT YOU SAID DRIVES
CORPORATE VALUE (IN RANK ORDER):

1. Customer satisfaction
2. Ability to attract talented employees
3. Innovation
4. Brand investment
5. Technology
6. Alliances
7. Quality of major processes, products, or services
8. Environmental performance

IN COMPARISON, HERE'S WHAT OUR RESEARCH FOUND DRIVES CORPORATE VALUE IN DURABLE MANUFACTURING (IN RANK ORDER):

1. Innovation
2. Ability to attract talented employees
3. Alliances
4. Quality of major processes, products, or services
5. Environmental performance
6. Brand investment
7. Technology
8. Customer satisfaction

Stunning, isn't it? Although our readers rated the importance of alliances relatively low, our statistical analysis shows that companies with more joint ventures, marketing and manufacturing alliances, and other forms of partnerships have substantially higher market values. It suggests that in the connected economy, connections matter. Alliances are incredibly, even decisively, important. Similarly, our results indicate that quality is not dead. Our survey respondents ranked it seventh in importance, yet in the durable sector, product quality, including the quality of the manufacturing process, remains statistically a strong predictor of corporate value. Just as surprising is the importance of environmental performance. Although most companies pay only lip service to this issue, and readers ranked it the least important of the value drivers, companies that perform better in this dimension have significantly higher market values.

Perhaps the most amazing result of our research is that two intangible asset categories—use of technology and customer satisfaction—had no statistical association with market values. That means these things, in contrast to our readers' perceptions, aren't helping companies create value at all. For all the blather over the past 10 years about the importance of customer satisfaction, it apparently has no effect on corporate value.

Why? It may be that real customer satisfaction is now inextricably tied to innovation. If your product line is at the cutting edge of technology, your customers probably are happy; if your products aren't state-of-the-art, then no

amount of call centers and training videos is going to help.

## CREATING VALUE

Once we had the different intangible asset factors appropriately weighted according to their importance, we then reapplied them to the companies under study. To do so, we computed overall VCI scores to determine which companies from our sample had the highest level of value-creating intangible assets. In validation of our work, the index correlated nicely with market value. Our statistical analysis produced an astonishing 0.9 correlation with e-commerce sector companies.

The VCI scores for technology companies in the durable manufacturing sector indicate that they have taken the lead in developing value-relevant intangible assets. However, companies in the durable manufacturing Top 10 aren't limited to computer firms. Ford Motor Co.—a traditional Rust Belt manufacturer—ranks among the leaders in intangible assets (and that was before the company decided to give computers and Internet access to all its employees). Not surprisingly, pharmaceutical and consumer product companies dominate the nondurable manufacturing sector, yet mainstream manufacturers such as 3M and DuPont also crack the Top 10, due in part to their long traditions of innovation and their strong brand names.

We tailored a whole new set of value drivers for Internet companies, because in no other industry are accounting values less relevant in explaining market capitalization. These drivers were culled from a stand-alone study we did on e-commerce firms. Here's our list, in order of importance: (1) alliances, (2) innovation, (3) eyeballs (usage traffic), (4) brand investment, (5) stickiness (minutes spent on Web pages).

Once again, the results took us aback. Three categories had substantial effects on e-commerce market values. The most important was the number of alliances and alliance partners. Investments in innovation (captured by research and development and capital expenditures) ranked close behind.

Perhaps the most widely discussed driver of e-commerce value—the number of "eyeballs" viewing a Web site—was measured by using data on a site's visitors, reach, or market share, and the number of hyperlinks to other sites. We found that a high visitor count also was strongly associated with market values, supporting the push by e-commerce companies to drive traffic through their sites at almost any cost.

Taken together, these three category relations indicate that the strength of an e-commerce company's network—both in connections to its customers and allliances within its economic web of suppliers and other partners—has a profound effect on a firm's value.

By contrast, investment in building brand awareness has no statistical association with market values. So much for those millions spent on Super Bowl ads. Big marketing campaigns may boost the egos of company executives, but our research suggests they do little to raise a firm's value. Equally surprising, "stickiness"— vaunted as the next competitive step after eyeballs—proved only a minor contributor to value.

The predictive ability of the VCI proved even higher for Internet firms than companies in the manufacturing sectors. The index alone can account for nearly 80 percent of an Internet company's market value, with a 10 percent change in the VCI associated with a 5 percent change in market value.

So what does it all mean? For managers, it provides a set of levers that, if effectively applied, can improve both corporate performance and market value. For investors, it offers a powerful new way to evaluate how a company is using its resources in creating value for its shareholders. For both groups, the VCI holds out the promise of a more efficient allocation of capital.

As time goes by, the VCI will evolve to identify new value-creation drivers, while maintaining enough flexibility to adapt to the constantly changing nature of the companies that are producing value in the connected economy. Look for more on the VCI in future issues of *Forbes ASAP*.

---

### THE VCI IN ACTION
### A CASE STUDY OF THE TIME WARNER-AOL MERGER

The Time Warner-AOL merger, announced just as the first phase of the Value Creation Index was being completed, offered a unique opportunity to conduct the first-ever real intangible assets audit.

Here's what we already knew: Both AOL and Time Warner were on our lists of top value-creating firms; AOL was No. 1 in the e-commerce category; Time Warner was No. 9 in the nondurables category. Even at first glance, it seemed likely that Time Warner would get a bump from the merger. But could a company such as AOL, already at the pinnacle of its industry, see a gain?

As a matter of fact, yes. The combined VCI score of the two companies was 99.99. After the merger, the VCI of the new combined firm climbed to 100.02. That may not seem like much, but in light of the already strong previous positions in their respective industries, it is enough to cause some repositioning among Top 10 companies.

Interestingly, the big gainer is AOL, despite already being the dominant player in its industry. The reason has to do with changes in the individual drivers. Among the things Time Warner mostly gains from the merger—technology, alliances, and innovation—the first has almost no effect on the VCI, and the latter two, while much more influential, are little changed.

By comparison, AOL, in buying credibility from the merger, enjoys a sizable jump in a middling factor: brand. That's enough to take the company to new heights in value. Steve Case, it seems, is shrewder than we thought—and the folks at Time Warner may end up thankful that AOL came courting.

# ARTICLE REPRINT

## WHO CREATES VALUE? MEASURING MINDS

*Editor's Comment:* Here's an article that challenges trainers to think differently about measuring the value of training. Here, *TRAINING Magazine*'s Senior Editor, David Stamps, urges trainers to embrace a new logic regarding measurement standards for determining the value of talent. His sidebar, "Seven Tips for Getting Measurement Right" is especially useful.

## MEASURING MINDS

### by David Stamps

Here's a trick question: What did the Chaldeans and Egyptians know 6,000 years ago that we don't today? Answer: They knew how to measure talent.

But then, of course, the "talent" measurement employed by the ancients was considerably more tangible than what we're trying to get at today when we talk about people who possess exceptional smarts or creativity. The talent was originally the weight of an Egyptian royal cubic foot of water and later a unit of monetary value. Still, it's no etymological coincidence that talent, from which derived the shekel, the drachma, the pound, and just about every other measure of value, survives today as the word we invoke to denote those who create value in an organization.

Or, more likely, those we *believe* to be the value creators. Alas, if only we could be sure which workers were worth the shekels, dollars or euros we pay them.

Unfortunately, when it comes to measuring talent we seem to be losing ground. In the Old Economy, performance could be linked to a countable output of axles, boxcars, machine screws, or what have you. In today's New Economy, value increasingly derives from intangible information. We speak of "human capital" as if it were a measurable asset, but it is far from

it. The truth be known, we're not always certain just what it is those brainy "knowledge workers" are doing or should be doing. So how the devil do we measure it?

### WHO'S SMART? WHO'S NOT?

If we *could* measure performance, surely then we would know who the true value contributors were. We would know where to focus our training and development efforts so certain workers could be even more productive. And we would know on whom to lavish top dollar, because in today's highly competitive job market you certainly don't want to let those people get away.

In fact, evidence suggests that more employers may be attempting to do just that; i.e., pay a premium for top talent. It's well-known that income varies widely by skill and education level: Those with college degrees and/or IT skills earn top money; those who don't, lag behind. What's less well-known is that income disparities can be found not only across but within almost every segment of the working population.

Labor economists traditionally look at things like differences in education, industry or regional pay scales to explain differences in compensation, explains Peter Cappelli, Wharton economics professor and author of the 1999 book *The New Deal at Work: Managing the Market-Driven Workforce* (Harvard Business School Press). Everything that can't be explained away is called the "residual." In recent years, notes Cappelli, the percentage of residual, unexplainable pay differences has been on the rise. Even more puzzling is that you can find dramatic disparities in pay within the same industries, for the same job titles within the same industries, and probably for the same job titles within the same company if you looked hard enough, Cappelli says.

In fact, employees at the New York office of Agency.com, an Internet ad agency, were surprised last September to learn that workers with identical job titles were earning quite disparate salaries. Salaries for creative directors, for instance, ranged from $65,000 to $123,000, according to a *Wall Street Journal* story, which reported that the disclosure occurred when HR accidentally e-mailed a spreadsheet with salary figures to the entire staff.

Such incidents suggest a shift in thinking about what people in HR call "compensation systems," in which some underlying logic is supposed to maintain a semblance of pay equity. Now, apparently, it's OK simply to pay some workers more than others. Not only is it OK, it may be imperative in today's talent-driven job market.

Which invites the question, By what performance measures are employers deciding who deserves the big money and who doesn't? Such a performance measure, Cappelli says, might go a long way toward explaining the income-inequality puzzle, though he doubts that such a metric exists. "My sense is that employers are taking a kind of ham-fisted approach," he says. "Performance is harder than ever to measure, and I'm not convinced measurement schemes have gotten a whole lot more sophisticated."

## NEW TOOLS FOR NEW TIMES

But that's a situation that surely can't long endure. If smart management of human capital, not financial capital or access to markets, is truly the thing that differentiates the winners from the losers in the New Economy, then managers will demand—and they will get—new tools for measuring and managing human capital.

In fact, new tools are already starting to show up. The Boston Consulting Group is reportedly working on an HR metrics system called "workonomics." Software from a company called HR Technologies will soon allow managers to specify job-performance criteria and track it over time. PricewaterhouseCoopers has developed something called the "gold knowledge standard," which it says will be used to "set a knowledge management standard throughout the firm" (translation: PricewaterhouseCoopers will very likely be selling its gold knowledge expertise to clients soon). This is by no means a complete list of firms offering new human-capital measurement tools.

James Gould, vice president of HR and compensation for Aetna Corp. in Hartford, CT, estimates that he's been approached in the past year by at least half a dozen firms selling new human-capital measurement schemes, few of which have favorably impressed him. The problem with most of them, says Gould, whose background is in both HR and finance, is that they tend to treat human capital as a static thing, an entity to be measured. That's really not much different than various competency schemes that describe attributes for specific jobs without tying them to all the various things that happen in a company to produce value, he says. Because value creation involves a complex and dynamic set of interrelated processes, measuring and managing human capital must also be dynamic, which is why Gould believes it won't be an easy thing to pull off.

And yet, Gould says he has looked at one approach that appears to show promise. It is the brainchild of John Boudreau, director of Cornell University's Center for Advanced HR Studies, and Pete Ramstad, a former CFO of Personnel Decisions International (PDI) in Minneapolis, who now serves as that firm's executive vice president of strategy.

Boudreau, who has been teaching a class on HR metrics at the Cornell center since 1983, teamed up with Ramstad five years ago to see if they couldn't turn their ideas on HR and finance into a set of tools that HR professionals can use to measure value creation in an organization. The result, which they unveiled in a series of seminars last year, if called the Human Capital Bridge. The bridge, in this case, is the conceptual link between what people, or human capi-

## SEVEN TIPS FOR GETTING MEASUREMENT RIGHT

Whatever metric you choose to measure human performance in your organization, that system must ultimately improve the decisions made regarding the use of "human capital." That, according to John Boudreau and Peter Ramstad, is the criterion of success for any human-capital measurement system.

In order to reach that goal, they suggest asking seven key questions that often are not fully considered before measurement systems are designed and implemented:

1. Are the connections between the human-capital metrics and the ultimate success of the organization clear and compelling?

2. When the organization's strategies change, do the measures identify where human-capital strategies need to change?

3. Does the measurement system support the development of human-capital strategies tailored to the organization's unique competitive advantage? (In contrast to copying "best practices" from other companies?)

4. Will the measurement system drive distinctive human-capital investment to the talent groups that have the potential to create the greatest economic impact?

5. Can the measurement system support decisions about HR programs *before* they are implemented? (In contrast to evaluating programs only after the fact?)

6. Can the measurement system reveal when HR programs should be discontinued?

7. Does the measurement framework identify how talent creates value within the organization in a way that is understandable and motivating to all employees?

—D.S.

tal, do in an organization that translates into financial capital, or value.

While their model may not let you identify value-producers down to the individual worker, it is designed to identify the critical talent pools in a company. Boiled down to essentials, it works something like this: First comes a close analysis of the value chain. How is value derived? Where can sustainable advantages be created or exploited? Where are the places where humans create value? What are the critical "talent pools" that contribute to, or constrain, the creation of value?

So far, so good, but that's just part of it—what Boudreau and Ramstad call the "north end" of the model. The south end is where, once you have identified those critical talent pools or constraints, you can start thinking about what actions to take with regard to them: Give people more training? Pay them more money? Redesign their jobs? The typical HR mistake, explains Boudreau, is to start with HR fixes such as training or pay because those are what HR knows best, and then look for places to apply them. The problem is, the critical "touch points" may be where you would least expect to find them, and the necessary fix may be something like job redesign, rather than training.

The pharmaceutical industry is a good example. Just a few years ago, the critical constraint in the value chain was the research and development time required to produce a new drug. Once a drug was produced, it was put through clinical trials. If the FDA granted approval, manufacturing could then be ramped up and the new product launched into the market. But new technologies have dramatically shortened the R&D time required to crank out new drugs. Today, the critical constraint is finding an adequate supply of human guinea pigs on whom to test new drugs, which means the ability to quickly organize and manage clinical trials takes on greater significance.

"A few years ago, a 10 percent performance advantage in clinical trials would have made very little difference in the overall scheme of things," says Ramstad. "Today, it makes a huge difference. When you analyze the value-creation chain this way, you see that improving clinical trials is an opportunity to create a sustainable advantage." Though, of course, you still have to figure out what "fixes" to apply to the clinical trials process. Training? Money? Job redesign?

## THE SWEEPERS OF MOUSELAND

This type of value-chain analysis has not been the sort of thing you'd normally find in an HR tool kit. A mathematician and economist by training, Ramstad describes how when he first joined PDI he was struck by the almost polar opposite ways in which HR and accounting look at value in an organization, and for no good reason.

Accountants look at a lot of different things that may or may not create value; they have a way of talking about value in an organization that never touches on what accounting itself does to create value. HR and training take an opposite, inward-looking approach. They tend to view value first in terms of what they do and then try to convince management that the company needs more of it. "I attended accounting conferences for 15 years and don't think I once heard the phrase 'CEO support,'" he says. "You can't spend an hour at a training or HR conference without hearing it. Either we need it or we don't have it or we're successful because we do have it."

But lest we heap too much abuse on trainers and HR folks, Boudreau likes to cite a favorite example of how humans create value in a nonintuitive way that both HR *and* accounting would typically misread.

"Ask any 10 people what made their last visit to a Disney theme park memorable and you'll hear all sorts of things," Boudreau says: "The rides, Goofy, the shuttle buses, the marching band." But, he adds, you may also hear a story about how a situation that might have turned unhappy was averted by a lowly street sweeper who appeared out of nowhere to politely direct visitors to the nearest first aid station or to a shady spot that proved an ideal vantage point for watching the parade.

"Ask yourself this question," says Boudreau: "Which would deliver the bigger boost to the value chain? Extra training for the street sweepers, or for the people who play Mickey Mouse?" HR people would likely say Mickey, since they tend to equate the critical talent pools with the more expensive talent. In this case, they'd be wrong. Disney understands that sweepers create value by creating those "all-important moments of customer delight." And for that reason Disney gives its sweepers lots of training.

Accountants, on the other hand, would make the classic mistake of looking at the sweepers in terms of cost, not the value they create, says Boudreau. And by any standard accounting measure, Disney's street sweepers are some of the most expensive in the business. Compared to other theme parks, Disney hires more of them, which means each covers a smaller area and picks up less trash. "Using the cost of trash collection as the performance yardstick is a classic example of using the wrong measure," Boudreau says. The right measure, of course, is the tally of those salvaged "moments of customer delight" that cause people to return to the park time and time again.

HR executives from several companies, including Williams-Sonoma, Dell Computer, Sun Microsystems, and Allied signal, are just starting to look at putting the Human Capital Bridge ideas to work, though few have gotten beyond "the north end of the model," if you will.

John Patterson, now vice president of talent at Priceline.com, had begun to work with the idea last year at a large bank before leaving to join the Internet start-up. A value-chain analysis at the bank showed a lack of "relationship selling" skills to be a critical constraint. His recommendations to management: Revise the compensation system to be able to attract the needed sales talent, and revise the performance-appraisal model in a way that more clearly links performance goals to key account sales.

"Neither of those things is beyond the scope of normal HR activities," Patterson says. "The difference is, we reverse-engineered the solution instead of starting with performance appraisal and then trying to sell it companywide. Instead, you find the critical touch-points where you can make the greatest difference and concentrate your efforts there."

One of the problems in even talking about measuring human capital, says Ramstad, is that in the measurement-mad business world everyone is hungry to seize upon any new measurement, and that's a mistake. "If you put the measurement piece ahead of the logic, you'll run into a wall every time," he says.

What he and Boudreau are trying to do, he explains, is give HR a new logical framework and vocabulary for thinking and talking about value in an organization. And for some training and HR professionals, that means abandoning the time-honored notion that the proper measure of a successful training function is how many people in the organization it touches. The classic expression of that belief is the hallowed notion that mandating 40 hours of training for everybody in the company, across the board, regardless of what they do, is a good thing. "In the training industry, 40 hours of across-the-board training is an applause line," Ramstad says. "In reality, it's an Old Economy way of looking at things."

# ARTICLE REPRINT

## CAUTIONS ABOUT DIVERSITY PROGRAM STANDARDS

*Editor's Comment:* Trainers at the turn of the millennium have been hearing about finding ways to make training more connected to business goals, and to set standards through training for meeting those business goals. We've been preached at, cajoled, and encouraged to adopt new ideas about measuring the things that matter in organizational programs, and to evaluate the results of organizational learning in the context of the business. We've been encouraged to throw away old and inadequate models, especially the cursory "smiles tests" rating sheets at the end of many classroom training experiences. Creating networks of information and support, seeking alignment of training with business goals, and integrating our learning of new concepts and skills with the positive flow of business are all familiar challenges for trainers. We hear the terms "balance," "customized," and scorecards," all terms that reflect our current interest in setting meaningful standards, particularly for programs and systematic organizational development efforts.

The article reproduced below is important because it raises the issue of diversity training's standards. Among other things, it cautions against adopting a legalistic or protective approach to standards, especially regarding race; it points out how, without thinking, trainers can unwittingly become involved in providing disincentives to racial harmony and opportunity. Examining diversity programs is called for.

## Is Diversity Working?

### *by Robert J. Grossman*

The Civil Rights Act of 1964 fixed a spotlight on racial issues. Then came affirmative action, attempting to bring equity to the workplace. Now diversity is the latest effort at improving interracial representation and relations at work.

But is diversity working? As it grows to include the wide variety of differences between employees—such as gender, sexual orientation, ethnicity and more—race is becoming an ever smaller piece of the pie.

While this shift is taking place, racial tensions in the workplace aren't going away, say some HR practitioners, consultants and advocacy groups. More than 30 years after the civil rights movement of the 1960s, these observers say that those who expected the most from civil rights advances—black employees—have not made the gains anticipated.

And there is concern that diversity, the latest silver bullet for race relations, isn't getting the job done. The question, then, is this: Is diversity the answer—or merely the latest answer—to race relations at work?

### HOW DID WE GET HERE?

A backlash against affirmative action is a prime reason for the current chill in race relations at work, say HR practitioners and consultants. In

---

*Source:* "Is Diversity Working?" by Robert J. Grossman in *HRMagazine*, March 2000, pp. 47–50. Robert J. Grossman is a Contributing Editor of *HRMagazine*, a lawyer and Professor of Management Studies at Marist College, Poughkeepsie, NY. The article is reprinted with permission of *HRMagazine*, published by the Society for Human Resource Management (SHRM), Alexandria, VA. Website, *shrm.org*.

many ways, diversity efforts sprang from that backlash. As a result, affirmative action and diversity are fundamentally different approaches to differences in the workplace.

David Benton, workforce policy adviser to the U.S. Coast Guard Commandant in Washington, D.C., says diversity is about equity, while affirmative action is about equality. While diversity efforts try to foster a sense of fairness, affirmative action tries to force compliance, he says.

And that's where affirmative action ran into serious problems. Its goal of increasing access to the workplace by requiring compliance was bound to meet resistance, many experts agree.

That resistance reared its head when some white employees started believing they were being displaced by less-qualified black employees. As a result, blacks who won jobs under affirmative action found that those jobs came with increased racial tension.

"Everyone [black] I ever recruited was qualified—and more qualified than whites," Benton says. "But they had to work twice as hard to get half as much back."

Nat Alston was one of those who benefited from affirmative action. Alston, vice president of the National Association of African Americans in HR (NAAAHR), credits affirmative action with launching him into HR; he has since become the vice president of HR at the State Employees Credit Union of Maryland. But it wasn't easy.

"I wasn't looking for a handout," he recalls. "I wanted a fair shot; I wanted folks to look at me as an equal in applying, being accepted and promoted on the job. But it wasn't the case. I've had to struggle against racial stereotyping for everything I've achieved."

Today, courts have upheld challenges to affirmative action, and state referenda have limited its use. Faced with growing opposition—and the reality that some people in the majority will not willingly accept policies they perceive as personally threatening—proponents of equality in the workplace have rallied instead about diversity.

## TOO DIVERSE?

Diversity, which aims to create workforces that mirror the populations and customers that organ-izations serve, seems more inclusive and possibly less threatening than affirmative action. Some say that diversity's very inclusiveness has marginalized racial issues. Others point out that diversity offers more hope than anything that came before it.

Benton sees promise in the diversity strategy, arguing that putting the spotlight back on race and pushing for compliance will only raise tensions and divisiveness. "If you continue to concentrate just on race, you'll continue to get people to be steadfastly opposed," he says. "If we continue to deal just with compliance, people will continue to sabotage the system. If you broaden the scope through diversity, you'll avoid the inevitable defensive rationalizations."

But others see big disadvantages to diversity's broader approach.

Lisa Willis-Johnson, chair of the Society for Human Resource Management's Workplace Diversity Committee, says that "any diversity person will say we don't just look at race, we look at a number of factors. This tells you they've discounted race. Race was a sacrificial lamb to launch diversity and make it palliative to corporate America. Who is corporate America? White males. And they don't want to hear about race."

Carol Kulik, a management professor at Arizona State University, in Tempe, Ariz., also feels diversity takes away from race. "If I were trying to significantly improve race relations, I would not advocate such a broad approach," she says.

George Gamble, director of the International Institute for Diversity and Cross-Cultural Management at the University of Houston, seems to take pages from both Benton and Willis-Johnson. "By broadening the scope, the diversity movement has diminished the impact of color," he says. "But at the same time, if [the diversity movement] hadn't happened, we wouldn't have had anything at all."

Alston thinks that efforts to level the playing field for racial minorities are dwindling, courtesy of the diversity movement. "You dilute [race], and you'll be pushed back down the ladder because you've got other groups that are competing for the spotlight," he says.

Some believe the argument that diversity training dilutes race is divisive. "I don't play the zero sum game, that there's only enough here for some people and others have to be out in the cold," says Sharon Parker, president of the American Institute for Managing Diversity Inc., a nonprofit research organization in Atlanta. "The reality is that all the areas need emphasis."

## WHO IS TO BLAME?

If diversity has truly turned the spotlight away from race, who is responsible? There's plenty of blame to go around, says Tracy Brown, president of Person to Person Consulting in Dallas. "We are in collusion: the diversity managers, the consultants, the companies," says Brown. "We don't go back and look at how race plays out because we're uncomfortable. We say race is no longer an issue."

One reason for the increasing diversification of diversity may be a push by those who provide training. "A vast diversity industry has sprung up," says Kulik. "You have consultants, games, videos . . . a whole catalog of products to fill these needs."

She says that the issue in diversity training today is whether to run programs geared exclusively to race relations or to broaden programs to include gender, marital status, personality clashes and more. "Race might be a real hot button for some people, but for others it might be gender or personality," she says. "Trainers think they'll get greater buy-in if they broaden their focus. Suddenly race is no more important than all the other concerns; it's diluted to make the training more acceptable to the participants."

Further, the time constraints of certain types of diversity training may be a factor. "Most workshops run two days at the most," says Kulik. "If you're trying to cover 10 or 12 diversity dimensions, how much attention are you going to pay to race?"

## EVALUATING DIVERSITY PROGRAMS

Gauging the effectiveness of diversity programs can be difficult because there is little hard data on the subject. Surprisingly, at a time when most trainers are struggling to justify the effectiveness and financial validity of their programs, there is little information on diversity training expenditures, says Jac Fitz-enz, founder and chairman of the Saratoga Institute, a Santa Clara, Calif., consulting firm that provides assessment and bench-marking data for HR. Fitz-enz has no hard information on diversity effort expenditures and can offer no benchmarking data.

However, consultants and practitioners estimate that, overall, the corporate world has put millions—maybe even billions—into diversity efforts over the years.

What do businesses have to show for it? How effective has diversity training been in dealing with race or any other aspect of diversity? Most employers simply don't know, according to Kulik. She believes that most programs are evaluated superficially at best.

"In many areas of HR, we have tools to measure how effective a training intervention is," she says. "We're not seeing those kinds of measures applied with any consistency to diversity training."

If rigorous assessments were conducted, Kulik says, the results might be disturbing. She believes that diversity training does little to change day-to-day relations at work. "How would you feel if you invested all this money and found out that it had no effect?" she asks.

Kulik says the primary evaluation of training is based on asking attendees if they like the program. "It gets them away from work for a day; the discussions are interesting," she says. "But how does it transfer to on-the-job performance? Many trainers say we're just raising awareness. But we don't settle for that in any other kind of training. There should be some standardized body of knowledge. I'd like to see accreditation for diversity trainers."

Elissa Perry, professor of psychology and education at Teachers College, Columbia University, New York, says, "there's disincentives to do evaluations. You might find out the programs are costly and not very effective."

One study suggests that this is exactly the case. The nonprofit New York-based research organization Catalyst recently asked black women if diversity programs were effective in addressing subtle racism; 64 percent said no. Only 12 percent said black women have benefited from diversity initiatives to a great or very great extent.

Such negative information won't help employers much in a court of law. Kulik says that employers may not want to know the truth—that some companies offer diversity training simply to gain legal protection and make a symbolic gesture. Perry, who has studied diversity training assessment, agrees. "Ignorance is often bliss when it comes to shielding yourself from potential lawsuits," she says. "You want to be able to show you're addressing the problem, and don't really care if you're solving it."

Brown is of a similar mind. "We don't want to correct our behavior," she says. "Most people are spending their energy trying to avoid getting into trouble."

## SOME SUCCESSES

Yet, despite the criticism, most companies are sticking with diversity. Some companies promote diversity through internal programs aimed at making minority employees feel valued and beefing up their numbers—particularly in management and executive ranks. And some claim to be having success.

IBM is one example. In 1995, IBM launched eight executive-led task forces on women, men, blacks, Hispanics, Asians, Native Americans, gays and lesbians, and employees with disabilities.

Ted Childs, vice president for global workforce diversity in Armonk, N.Y., explains: "We asked [the task forces] to look at IBM through their constituency and answer, 'What was required for your group to feel welcome and valued throughout IBM?' and 'What could we do in partnership to maximize your productivity? How could the company better approach your constituency to influence your buying decisions?'

"The intent was for us to identify anything where change would make things better. We look at recruiting, mentoring, stereotyping and external agencies we should work with," Childs says.

One task force recommendation led to the creation of local diversity network groups. These groups, also called affinity groups, enable workers with similar characteristics—such as race—to meet, in person and electronically, to support each other and focus on work-related issues that affect them.

Of the 80 network groups for IBM employees in the United States, 17 are for black employees.

Childs credits the programs and open communications with improving IBM's racial profile. "We've increased the number of African American executives from 62 to 115 from January 1996 to September 1999," Childs says. "During the same period, women of color, predominantly African American and Hispanic, have increased from 17 to 54. Overall, African Americans hold 5 percent of our executive positions."

## HOLDING MANAGERS ACCOUNTABLE

Carrier Corp., the Syracuse, N.Y.-based heating, air conditioning and refrigeration firm led by CEO John Lord, also is making race a top priority. Each of Carrier's seven business units formed diversity councils. Members run the gamut, from non-exempt staff to executives. The councils developed diversity business cases for their units, weighing the needs of customers, employees and other stakeholders.

Carrier developed its program with the assistance of John P. Fernandez, president of ARMC Consultants in Philadelphia. The program requires each business unit to develop and monitor its own diversity plan. Business unit presidents and their direct reports will sit down quarterly with Lord and Rejeans Pendleton, manager of staffing and workforce diversity, to check progress.

Among the priorities: more black executives. Currently seven of the 176 top executives, or 4 percent, are black. "We do a good job of recruiting and training people, but they get lured away," says Pendleton.

Lord plans to include diversity progress in his annual review of each top executive, Pendleton says. Lord's commitment has Pendleton optimistic about increasing the numbers. "He's holding our executives accountable for how they're making an impact, and it won't happen unless the top guy is committed."

Perry agrees that commitment at the top is vital. "There's no proof that the programs will work without management support," she says. "Often, along with being short-term training interventions, they're not tied to the rest of the organization. There's no follow-up, no tie to compensation."

## WHAT'S THE ANSWER?

Can we increase the slow assimilation of black employees into the workforce at entry levels and at leadership levels? And is diversity the best way to do it?

The experts interviewed for this article hold varying opinions on diversity programs, but most agree that today's version of these programs is not the ultimate answer.

Alston says that "diversity training is a fad. It's just somebody to punch a ticket that says we've had it and then lets us go back to business as usual."

Parker believes improvement is possible, but she says employers have to move beyond affirmative action and diversity as we know them. "You do it through organizational transformation, by changing our institutions, by managing diversity as a strategic initiative, just like total quality," she says.

Fernandez says companies should focus less on diversity programs and more on developing practices linking managers' compensation and advancement to their success at recruiting minority employees.

Employers also should stop separating diversity from other areas of HR, counsels Murray Dalziel, managing director of Organizational Effectiveness and Management Development Services at the Hay Group in Philadelphia.

"Return diversity to within the traditional management development areas," Dalziel says. "Admittedly, the legal threats make it convenient to develop a diversity sub-function, but it's potentially dangerous if it's not integrated with other aspects of leadership training."

Dalziel believes that diversity should be folded into the portfolio of the person in charge of leadership and staff development—usually, the HR chief. Having a different point person for diversity, as many corporations do, may make diversity and race more visible but also may let the employer compartmentalize these issues. Diversity and race relations then become fragmented, separated from HR's job of building an effective workforce, Dalziel says.

Margaret Simms, vice president for research at the Joint Center for Political and Economic Studies in Washington, D.C., finds hope in the nation's strong economy. "During the end of the '80s and early '90s the issue of race and equal opportunity was very divisive because of affirmative action," she says. "The opportunities for some groups appeared to be at the expense of others. But now, as we enter the 21st century, the economy is doing well. It's a good time for people to give thought to how to utilize all the talent that may be available."

For more information about Websites with diversity research and advice, see the *HR Magazine* section of SHRM online at *www.shrm.org*.

## ARTICLE REPRINT (EXCERPT)

## HOW TO EVALUATE E-LEARNING MATERIALS

*Editor's Comment:* An essential part of any training evaluation system is the evaluation of training materials. This excerpt from a longer article on e-learning program design provides ten points to consider as you evaluate materials used for online learning. It's a basic list, but one that gives you a good start as you figure out what's good and what's not so good in e-learning materials.

### EVALUATING E-LEARNING PROGRAMS

#### *by Brandon Hall, Ph.D.*

### EVALUATING E-LEARNING PROGRAMS

As you embark on incorporating e-learning into your training experiences, it is important to know what makes for great e-learning programs that you purchase packaged, or that you create. You will want to look at content, motivational level, and more.

LOOK FOR OR ANALYZE:

1. Great instructional design

2. Nice graphics

3. A simulation or metaphor

4. Great use of media

5. Motivational components

6. Network compatibility

7. Amount of space needed or bandwidth requirements

8. Navigation

9. Evaluation and record-keeping

10. Tone

1. For great instructional design, the first step will be to make sure you have in place a proper front-end analysis, including clear identifica-

tion of who will be trained, what needs to be learned, and a performance analysis of what the job requires improvement. A good instructional design can make up for poor quality of media, but it doesn't work the other way around.

2. Most internally developed programs and many off-the-shelf programs fall short in the area of good graphics. Good graphic design doesn't have to be expensive, but it does require design sensibility on the part of the project manager to value this area, and to access someone with talent if you are creating your own courseware. Good graphic design is a must.

Graphics keep the learner engaged. The graphics of a top-notch program should be at the quality level of the best printed graphics you see these days, whether it is a brochure or a business-to-business magazine ad. An analogy: when training films were first produced, videos were considered innovative, but look at the quality of professionally produced business training videos today. No serious videos are produced that don't approach broadcast quality.

3. To achieve great use of media, the program should effectively and appropriately employ animation, video, music, sound effects and special visual effects. This will work to

*Source:* "How to Embark on Your e-Learning Adventure: Making Sense of the Environment" by Brandon Hall, Ph.D. in *e-learning*, January–March 2000, pp. 14–16. Brandon Hall is an e-learning specialist, author, conference presenter, and corporate consultant. Contact him by e-mail at *brandon@brandonhall.com*. Excerpt reprinted with permission of *e-learning*, published by Advanstar Communications Inc., Duluth, MN, copyright 2000. All rights reserved.

engage the senses that help different kinds of learners learn—that is, with audio you can appeal to learners who need the spoken word; with video, you can appeal to learners who need the spoken word; with video, you can appeal to the visual learner.

4. A metaphor or simulation will provide an element that grabs the user's attention and immerses them in an environment. It may be the metaphor used for the interface, or an extended simulation. This is related to what people in the movie business call "the suspension of disbelief." Maybe we should call this "the suspension of training resistance" that occurs when the program is so interesting, or so appealing, or so intellectually stimulating that the users actually like it!

5. Motivational components include simulation and refer to any means to engage the user through novelty, humor, game elements, testing, adventure, or surprise.

6. Network compatibility is less of an issue as companies move to the intranet, where a browser typically makes the platform issue moot. But if the courseware is managed via your company's network, it is important to make sure it is compatible.

7. The amount of high-end graphics, video, and interactive content of the program will influence the space the system needs. You wouldn't want learners to be frustrated if the program runs too slowly on the network or intranet. Make sure you have enough space before purchasing a particular program.

8. Navigation is the description of how learners will move through a particular program. In a quality program, users will be able to determine their own course through the program; will always have access to an exit option; will always have access to a course map; and will find an appropriate use of icons and clear labels, so they don't have to read excessively to determine program options.

9. Evaluation and record-keeping is valuable for ongoing assessment of the course, as well as for any kind of studies regarding return on investment. In a quality course, the mastery of each section will be required prior to moving on to the next course. Section quizzes may be used,

and a quality program carries a final exam. Student performance data will be recorded, with possible tracking of time to complete the course; and of final scores. Some good programs forward data to the training manager automatically.

10. The tone for the program will need to work with your audience. You wouldn't want a course that takes on a condescending tone.

All courses online require some bandwidth, and fortunately, technology is at work every day to ease this issue that is an obstacle. Bandwidth refers to the actual speed available at the time of the transmission. The speed of transfer is determined by three variables: the server's access speed, the user's connection speed, and the size of the file.

Because of bandwidth limitations, media and interactive state-of-the-art level of Web-Based training is still at the level of sophistication that CD-ROM programs were about two years ago. While some aspects of online courses are less advanced, the ease of administration and capacity for fast, worldwide updates makes some of the technology worthwhile.

The rapidly advancing technology of the Web ensures that bandwidth limitations will be overcome in the future, paving the way for CD-ROM-like media and interactivity delivered over the Web. Future technologies promise faster access time. Multimedia applications over a company's intranet and over the Internet will soon be commonplace.

As we move into the 21st century, change is part of our lives. People are taking new jobs at a rapid pace, old jobs are changing quickly, and the training demands for every worker to simply stay in the game continues to grow.

The training needs for the current generation of the workforce may be greater than any that has gone before. E-learning is a new mechanism for training that all training professionals will need to understand to succeed. As you and others take the profession to new levels, e-learning will be embraced by a workforce determined to succeed amidst such a rapidly moving, technologically-driven society. Staying in tune with the needs of the day may be just a keyboard away, as more and more training is delivered to the desktop.

# 5C. THE MEANING IN NUMBERS

## ARTICLE REPRINT

## HOW TO MEASURE HUMAN CAPITAL: GETTING TO THE HARD NUMBERS

*Editor's Comment:* This article gives trainers some real help in getting to the hard numbers of success—formulas tied to business strategies—numbers that guarantee you respect from your company's number crunchers and bottom-line managers.

## MEASURING UP: APPROPRIATE METRICS HELP HR PROVE ITS WORTH

### *by Robert J. Grossman*

When J. Randall MacDonald joined GTE as executive vice president of HR and administration in mid-1998, the Irving, Texas-based telecommunications giant was up to its ears in cutthroat competition, fighting tenaciously for customers.

MacDonald realized that the company's carefully crafted HR strategy was critical to its success. But he also knew that the best plans are meaningless if they're not executed properly. "I need to know whether we're delivering on our strategies," he said at the time. "I need measures and metrics to make the business case that we're effective."

But the metrics weren't there, at least not ones that MacDonald could rely on. "HR would record 250,000 hours of training and conclude they must have been doing a good job," says Garrett Walker, director of human resources planning, measurement and analysis. "In fact, it indicates you were busy, not whether your [employees] were satisfied and more effective in their jobs."

MacDonald's desire to make the business case for HR led to GTE's adoption of its Balanced Scorecard, a comprehensive metrics or measurement program that assesses and quantifies HR's company-wide performance quarterly.

Today, as GTE fine-tunes the Scorecard after its first year in action, the company is among the trailblazers making HR metrics a priority. The writing is on the wall. Senior management lives or dies by the numbers and increasingly is figuring that if HR really wants to be a business partner, it must be judged by the same standards as everyone else in the organization.

### OVERCOMING METRICS PHOBIA

Yet even with mounting evidence that metrics are essential to demonstrate the value of an organization's human capital and HR practices to internal and external stakeholders, some HR practitioners are reluctant to weigh in.

*Source:* "Measuring Up: Appropriate Metrics Help HR Prove Its Worth" by Robert J. Grossman in *HRMagazine,* January 2000, pp.28–35. Robert J. Grossman is a Contributing Editor of *HRMagazine,* a lawyer and Professor of Management Studies at Marist College, Poughkeepsie, NY. The article is reprinted with permission of *HRMagazine* published by the Society for Human Resource Management (SHRM), Alexandria, VA. Website, *shrm.org.*

"Fewer than 50 percent of HR departments measure anything quantitatively," says Jac Fitz-enz, founder and chairman of the Saratoga Institute in Santa Clara, Calif.

Adds Jack J. Phillips, CEO of the Performance Resources Organization in Birmingham, Ala.: "Most *Fortune* 100 organizations and their equivalents in other countries are developing metrics programs, but even they are only allocating about 1 percent of the HR budget to the task."

Medium-size and small companies, Phillips says, are out in the cold—ignoring metrics except for statistics they are required to produce for government agencies.

Why the reluctance? For many, the idea of quantifying what's in the hearts and minds of people runs counter to their basic values. Intuitively, they feel measuring people as if they were widgets is distasteful. And unlike pure financial metrics, HR data tends to derive from softer, qualitative sources—like surveys and interviews—making it less exacting than number-crunchers would like.

"Historically, the people who migrated to HR are there for the wrong reason, or they got there for reasons that are no longer important," says Phillips. "They like people, but they aren't interested in adding value and knowing how the business operates. Part of the education process is to show them that it's a good tool that can help them, not hurt them."

HR's hesitance also can be attributed to fear of the unknown. Faced with the possibility of learning unpleasant things about their operations, HR opts for avoidance. "HR managers are worried what they'll find if their programs are measured accurately, so they claim it's too hard to do," Fitz-enz says. "I recognize it's hard, but if you set up a simple collection system, it becomes part of your routine."

If you don't, prepare to pay the price, he warns. "You can't define yourself if you don't have any data. If someone says you're taking too long to recruit key personnel, you can produce the data that shows you're in the 90th percentile."

And knowledge of measurements, basic formulas, and ratios—even if they are home-grown statistics that you have developed yourself—gives you increased credibility with line managers. "It gets you to talk like a businessperson,"

Fitz-enz adds. "You ought to spend time talking to people in the finance department. If necessary, take a course in finance for nonfinancial managers so you understand basic accounting and finance. How can you talk to people if you don't understand their language?"

## WHY MEASURE?

Forget the big picture arguments for a moment and permit a selfish thought to sneak in. A big justification for being able to trade figures with the finance folks is simple survival.

"Companies are outsourcing HR left and right, so it would seem prudent on the part of HR practitioners to become conversant in this form of analysis," says William Brown, professor of management at Marist College in Pough-keepsie, N.Y. "Metrics is a tangible way of demonstrating the value of HR to non-HR people."

But too often, line managers are wary of the numbers HR trots out in self-defense. The data may look good on the surface, but lose credibility when examined with an outsider's critical eye.

"To prove to senior management that the amount of money spent on training and development is worthwhile, HR offers 'flavor of the month' training or the HR trainer's favorite programs," explains Annie McKee, director of management development service for the Hay Group in Philadelphia.

"There's no integration, no alignment with strategy—just scrambling to get things out there. At the end, when you evaluate the program, people say they liked it. When asked if they learned something positive they can apply to their job, they say yes. HR aggregates the data and, invariably, it's positive. It's a formula for high ratings and has absolutely nothing to do with whether the learning is in the right area, whether people are actually learning something related to improving the organization's effectiveness."

McKee recalls the misleading metric generated from a *Fortune* 100 company's one-day diversity program for 12,000 workers. "At the end of the year, when they assessed their effectiveness in diversity training, they checked-off 'mission accomplished.' Wrong. It's virtually

## 10 KEY HUMAN CAPITAL METRICS

| | |
|---|---|
| 1. Revenue Factor = Revenue ÷ Total FTE | The basic measure understood by managers. The FTE number should include regular employees and contingent labor. |
| 2. Voluntary Separation Rate = Voluntary separations ÷ Headcount | Along with the time to fill jobs, this represents potential lost opportunity, lost revenue and more highly stressed employees who have to fill in for departed colleagues. |
| 3. Human Capital Value Added = Revenue – (Operating expense – [Compensation cost + Benefit cost*]) ÷ Total FTE | This is the prime measure of people's contributions to an organization. It answers the question, what are people worth? |
| 4. Human Capital ROI = Revenue – Operating expense – [Compensation cost + Benefit cost*] ÷ Compensation Cost + Benefit Cost | This is a ratio of dollars spent on pay and benefits to an adjusted profit figure. |
| 5. Total Compensation Revenue Percent = Compensation cost + Benefit cost ÷ Revenue | If you monitor pay and benefits in comparison to revenue per employee, you can see the return on your investment. |
| 6. Total Labor Cost Revenue Percent = Compensation cost + Benefit cost + Other labor cost ÷ Revenue | By looking at total labor cost vs. total compensation revenue percent, you can see the complete cost of human capital. Total labor cost revenue percent shows not only pay and benefits, but also the cost of contingent labor. |
| 7. Training Investment Factor = Total training cost ÷ Headcount | |
| 8. Cost per Hire = Advertising + Agency fees + Employee referrals + Travel cost of applicants and staff + Relocation costs + Recruiter pay and benefits ÷ Number of hires | |
| 9. Health Care Costs per Employee = Total cost of health care benefits ÷ Total employees | |
| 10. Turnover Costs = Cost to terminate + Cost per hire + Vacancy cost + Learning curve loss | |

\* Exclude payments for time not worked. Sources: Saratoga Institute; William Brown, Ph.D.

impossible to deliver meaningful diversity training in one day."

In contrast, when used prudently and interpreted by an HR professional who understands the sometimes-tenuous relationship between human capital and pure finance, metrics can lead to an exploration of deeper issues. "As an HR executive, you need to be able to justify the business case for focusing on the people in the organization—for developing their capabilities, for developing the culture," McKee says. "And for the organization's leadership to feel good about that, there has to be a bottom-line benefit."

### *Metrics for Dummies?*

Let's assume that you're persuaded to put more effort into measurements. Is there a magic formula that you can follow that will provide all the information and ammunition you'll need—an *Idiot's Guide* that will explain how to use metrics to bolster your business case, how to enhance the value of your organization's human capital? Probably not. A sound metrics strategy requires a three-pronged approach.

Begin with efficiency measures. Build in generally accepted HR metrics as tools for quantifying how you're actually using your resources and implementing your responsibilities. (See "10 Key Human Capital Metrics," on previous page.) Benchmark, at least annually, against your prior performance and others in your industry or profession.

"If your turnover rate is 10 percent higher than your competitors', it causes you to look deeper into the cause," McKee says. "You can go to senior management and say 'we need to find out why this is happening. Is it something about our culture and climate, our reward structure or some other management practice?'"

Arrange to collect and track routine data, like absenteeism, monthly or quarterly. Ideally, when inefficiencies are revealed, careful analysis of the problem should follow before expenditures are slashed.

Second, select and develop metrics geared directly to your company's mission and strategies. Metrics that are most useful need to be specially designed for each organization. HR can do this alone or with outside assistance or training.

Third, establish metrics to monitor key HR practices proven to grow human capital in a broad spectrum of businesses. Identify the keys, go to work on them, and keep close tabs.

## EFFICIENCY—THE BASIC BUILDING BLOCK

HR has been using metrics since the 1970s and, through the years, the arsenal of tools has grown substantially. In implementing a manageable metrics program, experts advise variety—consider all the possibilities and select the ones that will work best for you. Here are some suggestions from Phillips, author of *The Handbook of Training Evaluation and Measurement Methods* and *Return on Investment in Training and Performance Improvement Programs* (both from Gulf Publishing, 1997).

First, to determine how things are going in an organization, conduct an annual feedback survey of employees, administered internally or by a third party. Next, benchmark performance by cost and function either through the Saratoga Institute or industry groups or by establishing partnerships with other HR practitioners. Critical measures include: turnover, quits, and discharges as a percent of total employees, average tenure of employees in various jobs, absenteeism, employee productivity, and intellectual capital.

Although you will always track and measure against your own historical record, outside benchmarking is critical. It enables you to compare apples to apples. "One hundred percent turnover annually at McDonald's is great," Phillips says. "One hundred percent at Intel would probably kill them. At McDonald's the cost of turnover is around $2,000; at Intel it would probably average $75,000."

The Saratoga Institute is the worldwide leader in HR benchmarking, conducting a national survey of 25 industries benchmarking between 60 and 70 metrics. Results are sorted by industry, company size and geographic region. In the United States, 891 companies participate and pay about $2,000 for the annual report.

## MEASURING WHAT COUNTS—STRATEGIC METRICS

Efficiency metrics serve only as a starting point. If you're not careful they can be turned against you by financial types who believe that less is always better.

"If you're driven solely by numbers that quantify, you'll get yourself in more trouble than not measuring at all," says John Boudreau, director of the Center for Advanced Human Resource Studies at Cornell University's School of Industrial and Labor Relations in Ithaca, N.Y. "Cost ratios, costs per hire, turnover rates are linked to dollar values and carry the fundamental implication that you make them better by cutting expenditures. You get at the efficiency side of things, but it's out of context without looking at the value-creation side.

"For example, you can't really tell if a turnover rate is good or bad. Everyone knows examples go both ways. I can get my turnover rate down by hiring people who will never leave. But that's not necessarily good; you get into the efficiency mind-set and forget the value side."

Organizations into benchmarking want to prove they're in the ballpark in their industry, but it doesn't always work out. "When the benchmark numbers don't measure up, they have to start telling stories around them to explain their standing," Boudreau says. "Your cost-per-hire numbers may be high, but often you find there's a good reason. But line man-

agers won't listen. Instead, they react out of context and push to cut your costs—precluding a discussion about what HR is actually doing that may, in fact, be beneficial."

Metrics is about making things happen. Except for the relatively few measures that you're required to report, you compile most of them voluntarily. It's a waste of time, Boudreau suggests, to measure just because the data is interesting. "We want metrics that will help change happen, help us make better decisions about human capital."

It's important to focus on strategy before you settle on your measures or set out blindly to beat the benchmarks for your industry, Boudreau advises. "The business case is to think about the logic of where the organization is going, rather than the measurement."

The key is to devise unique metrics that assess strategic value and effectiveness, not just efficiency. As an example, Boudreau describes the Walt Disney Co.'s effort to design metrics to assess sweepers at Disney World. The company had to determine what they really valued in their sweepers. Along with cleaning duties, the sweepers perform valuable customer service functions that enhance Disney's strategic goal to maximize "customer delight." Had HR not taken these competencies into account when crafting the measurement criteria, sweepers would have been benchmarked against cleaners in general, neglecting an important and strategically sensitive function.

"There probably are some general benchmarks that an organization can improve on that have an across-the-board impact," Boudreau says. "But the research we have says if you're going to sustain a competitive advantage, you have to do unique things. It's important to have a general direction, but in the end, for many organizations, the real keys to value lie within the organization."

How do you do this? Saratoga's Fitz-enz says sound measurement centers around quality, efficiency and service. He suggests using a template constructed around five factors that can be applied to anything you choose to measure—the cost, the time to do it, the quantity involved, the quality involved and the human reaction. Take staffing: You can measure the costs, the time it takes to fill a position, the number of requisitions, the quality of the new hires, and the satisfaction of the hiring manager with the process.

## ROI—ON THE CUTTING EDGE

Increasingly, HR departments are turning to a variation of an established financial metric—return on investment or ROI—to demonstrate the financial vitality of their most critical and highly visible initiatives. The HR-tailored ROI ratio is calculated by assigning monetary values to an HR program and dividing the value by the program's costs. (Total program benefit divided by program costs).

There are two challenges in calculating ROI, according to Phillips. One is to determine what it is that you value about the program you'e measuring. The other is to assign a monetary equivalent to the value.

To illustrate, he describes a case study involving a sexual harassment prevention program. HR wanted to show that the program added value, and so decided to study the impact the training would have on the number of sexual harassment complaints that employees filed as well as its impact on turnover.

First, looking back a year before the program was implemented, HR determined the costs the company incurred in processing and defending complaints and the turnover costs absorbed in replacing workers who, in exit interviews, gave harassment as the reason they were departing. Once the monetary values were set, HR compared the "befores" and "afters," determining the dollar amount saved. Finally, total costs of the program were divided into the savings, yielding the ROI.

## ALL-INDUSTRY INDICATORS— THE MAGIC BULLETS

Here's the closest you'll get to the magic bullet. Consulting heavyweight Watson Wyatt recently completed a research project that found a correlation between human capital and shareholder value. The year-long study was based on an analysis of HR practices at 405 publicly traded companies with a minimum of $100 million in revenue or market value.

Survey data was matched to objective financial measures of a company's market value,

total return to shareholders, and Tobin's Q, the market value of a firm's assets divided by replacement value of the firm's assets. That ratio measures a company's ability to create economic value beyond its physical assets.

Based on the findings, Watson Wyatt researchers created a "Human Capital Index," which rates a company's effectiveness at key human resource practices that affect the bottom line. "We've identified the key human practices that make a difference vis-a-vis the bottom line," says Bruce Phau, head of Watson Wyatt's organization measurement division in New York. "If you improve in these five areas, it gives you a 30 percent increase in shareholder value."

Watson Wyatt has a measurement system and offers consulting services to help you assess and monitor yourself. If you know the five areas, you can develop your own tools. Not surprisingly, Phau cautions against it. "It's like trading your own stock portfolio. You can be your own mutual fund, but 95 percent of all investors don't do as well as a mutual fund. It's not impossible, but most can't do it." Still, if you'd like to try, here are the five areas:

**Recruiting excellence.** Do you have recruiting practices that result in new hires that hit the ground running versus new hires that require a significant amount of training? Companies that minimized the time it took to get employees up to speed scored higher in human capital.

**Collegial flexible workplace.** Do you have a flexible, high satisfaction workplace with a minimum of status or distinction, or one that focuses on hierarchy and control? Egalitarian, flatter-structured organizations build human capital.

**Communications integrity.** Do you have a communications environment where information is widely shared both upward and downward versus one where information is tightly controlled? Human capital is boosted when communications are open and two-way.

**Clear rewards and accountability.** Do you have stock-based programs that reward good performance and do you have policies and practices that provide remediation for poor performers? Companies with stock-based reward systems accrue human capital, as do those who weed out poor performers quickly and unambiguously.

**Prudent use of resources.** Do you invest in practices that conventional wisdom applauds

## HR KEEPS SCORE

Before GTE unveiled its HR Balanced Scorecard last year, most of the data that made up the 120 or so metrics was floating around the company somewhere. It took Garrett Walker, director of HR planning, measurement and analysis, his internal team and consultants from Hewitt Associates to pull it together into a state-of-the-art assessment tool. "The information was there," Walker says, "but it wasn't aligned into a relatively simple picture that measures all the things we want to accomplish."

The Scorecard links a range of indicators grouped by perspective—strategic, operational, customer and financial—which in the aggregate produce a quantitative assessment of HR's performance.

The HR team is graded for its effectiveness in responding to 17 specific questions. The 120 metrics are value-driven, springing directly from GTE's corporate mission and strategies.

### STRATEGIC PERSPECTIVE

1. Do we have the talent we need to be successful in the future?
2. Do we have the leadership bench strength we need to be successful?
3. How is HR helping GTE position to meet the customer service needs of our external customers?
4. Is HR creating an environment that encourages integration and shared vision?
5. Are we investing in growing our HR capabilities?

### CUSTOMER PERSPECTIVE

6. Is GTE viewed as a great place to work?
7. Is GTE creating an environment that engages people?
8. Is HR viewed as an enabler to attracting and retaining top talent at GTE?
9. Is HR viewed as providing effective support systems to employees?

### OPERATIONAL PERSPECTIVE

10. Are our staffing support systems fostering better recruiting and selection?
11. Are our other HR processes/transactions efficient and effective?
12. Are we using technology to improve HR efficiency?

### FINANCIAL PERSPECTIVE

13. Are we managing the cost of turnover/churn?
14. Are GTE's HR plans and programs competitive?
15. Is our HR service delivery cost effective?
16. Are we managing financial risk?
17. What is GTE's return on investment in people?

Up and running for a year now, Walker says launching the Scorecard was a daunting challenge. "When you go through a process of transformation, you have early adopters; you also have people who are resistant. But, overall, the feedback has been good."

HR distributes the Scorecard quarterly to GTE's 98,000 domestic employees. For many HR staff members, going public with their performance has been a tough adjustment. "They may not buy into their information being shared with the entire company," Walker admits. "But the wide visibility of the Scorecard has made a big difference. People are very focused on being accountable. Teamwork is crucial, because in the end it's the overall score that counts."

such as 360-degree feedback and general training programs? Surprisingly, these practices did not correlate with added value and, unlessadministered with exceptional skill and commitment, produced a decrease in human capital valuation.

## MEASURES MYOPIA

The downside of metrics is that it can lead to financial measures myopia. You may become so fixated on trying to measure financial aspects of human management that you forget to deal with the people aspects of the business. "If you become too focused on the financial measures, you may drive out creativity and innovation," says Brown, the Marist professor. "You want to maintain a balanced perspective—think of what it is you're trying to do. Will an overemphasis on financial measures change the organization's culture so as to have a negative effect?"

To make his point, Brown cites a recent study by the Saratoga Institute on personal Internet and e-mail use while at work. "Saratoga reported that a worker who spends one hour a day on personal e-mail and Internet surfing costs the company $35,000 to $45,000 per year. As a result, companies are selling software to monitor on-the-job e-mail and Internet usage. One program called Little Brother identifies Website visits deemed unproductive and other products monitor e-mail. The question is whether one one-hour-a-day figure is real or a red herring. Is monitoring or censoring e-mail via software an intangible thing that can damage culture and loyalty of employees? By measuring one thing and reacting to it, you may destroy an intangible that's of greater value."

Meanwhile, the drive for fiscal accountability and quantitative assessments continues to be a hot item for senior management teams and company boards. And the message is clear for HR. "Wherever I've gone, business leaders say the only sustainable competitive advantage will be people," says GTE's Garrett Walker, who has been describing GTE's program to executives around the country. "From the HR perspective we need to be the experts in valuing human capital. If you're not doing it, you need to get there soon."

For links to resources on the World Wide Web concerning HR metrics, see the *HRMagazine* section of SHRM online at *www.shrm.org*.

# ARTICLE REPRINT

## GETTING INTO THE "TOP 10": WHAT DOES IT MEAN?

*Editor's Comment:* For years human resources professionals have been involved in measuring work processes, how organizations learn, and other large- and small-scale group endeavors. Trainers have been working diligently to train employees and help them learn skills that are useful in improving work environments and molding work culture. Many companies "benchmark" themselves against other companies they consider worthy. Numerous survey agencies publish lists of "best places to work." Evaluation of organizations has become important to the work of trainers and performance specialists.

The article reprinted here elaborates on such organizational evaluation efforts. The authors pose the ultimate question of "use," that is, how are such evaluation results used to benefit employees and the companies for which they work. What does evaluation mean?

## TOP TEN MOST ADMIRED, MOST RESPECTED: WHO MAKES THE CALL?

### *by Christy Eidson and Melissa Master*

What's a corporate reputation worth? A great deal, it would seem, judging by the efforts spent to measure it, rank it, improve it, and promote it. But since reputation is such a porous commodity, hard evidence is especially sought after. That's the chief reason why arbiters of reputation—business publications, research firms, PR agencies—are competing so vigorously in the burgeoning field of reputation management.

*Fortune.* Burson-Marsteller. Delahaye Medialink. The *Financial Times.* The Reputation Institute. Corporate Branding LLC. Each maintains that it offers something unique in the field. To the world, they profess to be friendly competitors—most of the major players are reluctant to bad-mouth their peers' products on the record—but they are competitors nonetheless, and each is well aware of what the others are doing. Among the numerous players who measure corporate reputation—or what those from a marketing or advertising background might call

*corporate brand*—many developed their methodologies to address what some feel are the shortcomings of the oldest list: *Fortune*'s "America's Most Admired Companies."

Or so they say. It also may be that they want to get a piece of the increasingly lucrative field of reputation measurement. "Almost anyone who has ever written an ad or a press release has suddenly declared that they are a branding expert," says Don E. Schultz, professor of integrated marketing communications at Northwestern University. "It's a promotional scheme as much as anything else."

### THE BLESSING OF UNCERTAINTY

This is an ideal time for companies to throw their hats into the reputation-measurement ring. As the economy relies less on physical assets and more on intangibles—what Charles Fombrun of the New York-based Reputation Institute, a private research organization dedicated to advancing knowledge about corporate reputations, calls *cognitive assets*—public and peer perception of a company are more significant than ever. A solid reputation is a competitive advantage in terms of attracting customers, employees, and joint-venture partners, and in bolstering a company's credibility in times of crisis. At the same time, creating a solid, well-known image for your company makes it more difficult for others in your industry to imitate you.

But if you ask six different people to define corporate reputation, you're likely to get six different answers. Unlike a company's revenues or earnings, which can (creative accounting aside) be determined through a simple formula, a company's reputation is an ephemeral thing, subject to interpretation and to daily changes.

It may be this very uncertainty that leaves the door open to the many competitors who claim that they have created *the* measure of corporate reputation—a phenomenon that has some concerned. "I'm a little worried about our defining an industry of reputation," says Clarke Caywood, chairman of Northwestern University's department of integrated marketing communications. "I think that has real dangers. I'm worried that lists on lists will become a bit of a parody of itself. We have to be careful that we don't fall into a trap of reputation becoming a 'listable' thing. That's not research—that's promotion."

Nevertheless, the people wielding the reputation rulers have found a willing market for their services: 96 percent of the CEOs surveyed by Hill & Knowlton said that corporate reputation is important to them. However, only 19 percent currently take steps to measure their reputation—leaving plenty of playing field for the eager measurement specialists looking to even out those numbers.

## IRRECONCILABLE DIFFERENCES

The major point of contention among the various reputation researchers is which constituencies should be surveyed. Opinions range from the *Financial Times'* exclusive focus on CEOs to the Reputation Institute's position that the general public gives a more accurate picture of corporate reputation. Fombrun, founder of the Reputation Institute and professor of management at New York University's Stern School of Business, has conducted research showing that surveys such as *Fortune*'s, which focus solely on corporate insiders, are unfairly skewed toward financial performance. "Not surprisingly," he says, "since [the survey questions are] not being asked of employees or of consumers, who would have quite different points of view on whom they regard highly."

However, an overly broad survey population can be as problematic as an overly narrow one. Schultz warns that the general public's perception of corporate reputation may be of little value, because the survey population could consist of people who will never buy from a particular company, or even influence the purchase of its products. He thinks that the value of a reputation resides with customers, prospective customers, or others who are going to influence the organization.

*Fortune* and the *Financial Times* are quite definite on which constituencies' opinions are most valuable to their audiences. "We deliberately position this as being complete peer group approval," says Peter Barker, head of sponsorship for Europe at PricewaterhouseCoopers, which conducts the "World's Most Respected Companies" survey that is published in the *Financial Times*. He points out that the *Times'* readership consists mostly of business leaders, who value the opinions of other leaders.

"An analogy, perhaps, would be an Oscar vs. a Golden Globe, where the Oscar is a vote among the peers, and for the Golden Globe you have people voting outside of an industry and voting for their favorites," says Michael Cacace, senior list editor of *Fortune*. "The intent of the *Fortune* study is, *What do businesses think of other businesses?*"

For the most part, *Fortune* takes the attitude of a lofty older brother holding himself above this industry rife with sibling rivalry. "I see that there's an attempt to compete with us," Cacace says. "I don't think it's going to infringe on what we do."

Both surveys have come under fire from their peers for what some see as a restrictively exclusive focus. Fombrun charges: "The *Financial Times* asks chief executive officers to nominate the companies that they respect. That's obviously a similar bias to *Fortune*'s, in the sense that they're asking people who are biased to the

## SOME OF THE MAJOR PLAYERS

### World's Most Respected Companies

Conducted by: Pricewaterhouse-Coopers

Surveyed: CEOs from 75 countries

Method: Telephone and mail

Purpose: Publication

First release of global study (previously European companies): 1998

### Maximizing Corporate Reputation

Conducted by: Burson-Marsteller

Surveyed: CEOs, executives, board members, the financial community, government officials, business media, and consumers

Method: Mail

Purpose: Customized for clients

First study: 1998

### Corporate Branding Index

Conducted by: Corporate Branding LLC

Surveyed: Vice president-level executives and above in the top 20 percent of U.S. businesses

Method: Telephone

Purpose: Customized for clients

First study: 1990

### America's Most Admired Companies

Conducted by: *Fortune* and Clark Martire & Bartolomeo

Surveyed: Company officers, directors, and analysts of *Fortune* 500 companies

Method: Telephone and mail

Purpose: Publication

First release: 1983

### Reputation Quotient (RQ Gold)

Conducted by: Reputation Institute and Harris Interactive

Surveyed: General public

Method: E-mail, Website, and telephone

Purpose: Customized for clients; topline results also published in *The Wall Street Journal*

First release: 1999

### Delahaye Medialink Corporate Reputation Index

Conducted by: Delahaye Medialink

Surveyed: Print and broadcast media

Method: Media content analysis

Purpose: Sold as syndicated research

First inter-industry study: 2000

---

numbers whether a company has done well. And then [the *Financial Times*] weights the responses of each of those people by the gross national product of the corporate headquarters' country. Why? Why is a CEO's opinion from Singapore less important than a CEO's opinion from the United States?"

Fombrun also takes issue with the criteria that *Fortune* uses to determine corporate reputation, charging that nearly half of its indicators of reputation—innovativeness, quality of management, employee talent, quality of products/services, long-term investment value, financial soundness, social responsibility, and use of corporate assets—are related to financial performance. "That's fine," he says, "except that it seems to leave out certain dimensions. So we've tried to be more encompassing and use 20 attributes rather than eight." Fombrun's methodology, the "Reputation Quotient," divides these 20 attributes into six categories: emotional appeal, social responsibility, financial performance,

vision and leadership, workplace environment, and products and services.

However, *Fortune* is moving to remedy this perceived narrowness, not by changing the original survey but by creating a new one that polls a wider group of stakeholders—a methodology closer to the Reputation Quotient—and diminishes the emphasis on financial performance in measuring reputation. *Fortune* recently announced an agreement with Roper Starch Worldwide, a marketing research firm, to compile a Corporate Reputation Index that will be sold to corporations and the agencies—such as public relations and advertising—that work for them, rather than published in the magazine.

In the end, however, a survey's elements are influenced by the perspective of the surveyor. Schultz points out that surveys conducted by PR agencies tend to focus more on "perceptual value and admiration and respect," while surveys targeted to financial audiences "put much more emphasis on the evaluation of financial strength and stability," He adds, "[The surveys] tend to be put together mostly by organizations who have a particular skill that they're trying to promote."

## IS MAKING *FORTUNE* BONUSABLE?

Clearly, the lists have at least promotional value to the companies that create them. But are they meaningful to the companies that get named to them? Not surprisingly, *Fortune*'s Cacace believes they are, saying that some companies even make executives' bonuses dependent on performance in the *Fortune* survey.

"That's absolutely foolish," says Northwestern's Caywood, who feels that basing bonuses on an external judgment is tantamount to managerial irresponsibility. "That looks for a simple, easy way to judge other people's value. It's like letting somebody else determine your worth."

Any outside evaluation of your business should be taken with a grain of salt. Disney, while pleased by its regular inclusion on the lists and inclined to leverage it, doesn't go so far as to make it a factor in determining executive bonuses, or in any other business capacity. "While we reference it in various letters or speeches or presentations, I think it's more important that the readership of those publications react to it and come to us," says John Dreyer, senior vice president of corporate communications at the Walt Disney Co. "It tells us that we're doing our jobs, and that we are sustaining our reputation and our brand in what we do every day, and the products we create, and the entertainment we offer to our audiences."

The lists can be used by other audiences as well. Prospective or current shareholders can look to the lists to make an educated guess about the future value of companies' stock, and the lists give consumers the opportunity to consider reputation in their purchasing decisions. Schultz speculates that the lists probably have some value to employees, too: "Employees tend to want to work for organizations that are well respected. It's much better to go in and say, 'I work for Intel,' as opposed to, 'I work for National Semiconductor,' although they're in the same business."

Beth Comstock, General Electric's vice president of public relations, agrees that her company's placement on the list is an advantage in dealing with employees, as well as the communities where they do business. "It's something that we all get very excited about, because we use it as an opportunity to thank all the employees," she says. "It's also a way to say to the towns where we do business, 'Your local GE employees are part of this award-winning group.'"

But most of all, Schultz says, the lists are valuable to the organizations that produce them. Not only do the lists help to sell the magazines and newspapers that publish them, but some organizations produce customized lists for sale to clients, which, for example, could show a company that's too small to make the published lists how its reputation stacks up within its industry.

## WHO'S THE HORSE AND WHO'S GODIVA?

The proliferation of methodologies has raised the question of whether there should be a standard for the reputation-measurement industry. The Council of Public Relations Firms, a New York-based trade association, has already begun research into setting such a standard: Its interest is in proving that reputation is quantifiable, so that PR efforts can be translated into reputation and measured. Council president Jack Bergen believes that having too many measurements confuses people and undermines the indexes' credibility.

As useful as a standard might be, however, it's unlikely to come into existence without a struggle. First of all, the ephemeral nature of reputation leaves a lot of room for interpretation. Northwestern's Caywood says, "If you were to create some sort of standard instrument that would purport to measure reputation or corporate brand, somebody would come along in three seconds and say, 'You've forgotten this factor, your weightings are wrong, and, by the way, you forgot to take into consideration the history of XYZ.' You have to be careful about measuring complex things with simple tools."

The competitive nature of the industry raises another problem. When every magazine and consultancy is eager to market its own methodology, it's difficult to imagine any of them abandoning its proprietary numbers for someone else's. John Gilfeather, vice chairman of

**THE LATEST WORD**

World's Most Respected Companies
*Financial Times* (as of 12/99)

1. General Electric
2. Microsoft
3. Coca-Cola
4. IBM
5. DaimlerChrysler
6. Sony
7. Dell
8. Nestlé
9. Wal-Mart
10. Toyota

America's Most Admired Companies
*Fortune* (as of 2/00)

1. General Electric
2. Microsoft
3. Dell Computer
4. Cisco Systems
5. Wal-Mart
6. Southwest Airlines
7. Berkshire Hathaway
8. Intel
9. Home Depot
10. Lucent Technologies

Corporate Branding Index
Corporate Branding LLC (as of 12/99)

1. Coca-Cola
2. Microsoft
3. General Electric
4. Walt Disney
5. Johnson & Johnson
6. Campbell Soup
7. Procter & Gamble
8. FedEx
9. Harley-Davidson
10. Anheuser-Busch

Reputation Quotient (Gold List)
Reputation Institute (as of 9/99)

1. Johnson & Johnson
2. Coca-Cola
3. Hewlett-Packard
4. Intel
5. Ben & Jerry's
6. Wal-Mart
7. Xerox
8. Home Depot
9. Gateway
10. Disney

Roper Starch Worldwide, says, "I can't see any of the large advertising agencies or public-relations firms, or even some of the boutique advisers in this area, wanting to play horsie to somebody else's Lady Godiva." More importantly, however, he doesn't necessarily advocate a universal standard. "There's enough room for differences of opinion," he says. "As a matter of fact, that's what enriches this field: people continuing to look at it from different angles."

But Bergen feels that a standard measurement of reputation wouldn't detract from diversity of opinion. He points out that the value of the studies lies in the analysis, not the raw numbers: While one researcher may look at a company's reputation and recommend that it focus on its customers, another could look at the same results and advise that the company devote its attention to its shareholders.

Fombrun, whose methodology is being considered by the Council of Public Relations as a possible standard, argues that PR agencies should not be competing to establish their own measurement systems as definitive. "Their business is not measurement," he says. "Their business is doing work that changes the measure." There's also the issue of whether it constitutes severe corporate naïveté to ask the PR agency that is building your reputation to measure it, too. An industry standard would give other, less biased organizations the opportunity to measure corporate reputation as well.

Despite their differing opinions on the utility of an industry standard, both Fombrun and Gilfeather hope, naturally, to be the leader in their field. Fombrun, in fact, developed his Reputation Quotient with the goal of making it the standard; while Gilfeather, despite his appreciation for varying opinions, seems to have an eye to making the *Fortune*/Roper Starch Corporate Reputation Index so comprehensive that no other measurement of reputation will be necessary.

## THE CHICKEN OR THE EGG

Even an industry standard wouldn't resolve one of the problems with reputation measurement as it stands: that of self-perpetuation. Widely published rankings may not measure reputation as much as they feed it: The position of a company on a popular list may become part of its reputation, influencing its position on future rankings. Many of the list-makers themselves admit that, while there are changes from year to year, certain key companies consistently appear near the top of the lists.

Bergen thinks this may have something to do with the way many reputation surveys are conducted. He says he remembers filling out forms for *Fortune*'s list when he was a senior VP at Westinghouse and then at CBS. "You know, you do it very quickly," he says. "You don't sit down and analyze it all. And a lot of that top-of-mind stuff is based on how you remember the lists you've seen before."

Some charge that this is an issue especially for the *Financial Times* survey, which asks CEOs to come up with the companies they most respect off the top of their heads, rather than providing a ballot. This problem is compounded by the fact that the *Times* sometimes encloses the previous year's survey results with its letter to potential respondents. Pricewaterhouse-Coopers' Barker insists, however, that the survey elicits a lot of well-considered answers unprompted by previous results. He adds that quite a number of CEOs ask for the questions in advance of the telephone interview so they can think about their responses.

The degree of self-perpetuation can vary according to survey population: A wider respondent base, such as one that includes consumers as well as business insiders, is less likely to have been exposed to previous lists. "Not everybody reads *The Wall Street Journal*," says Joy Sever,

senior vice president at Internet research company Harris Interactive, which conducts the Reputation Quotient methodology with the Reputation Institute.

But for companies that already have great reputations, self-perpetuation is a blessing. Once a company has become entrenched in the public eye as a winner, it can be tough to knock it from its pedestal. "Perceptions tend to lag realities in the reputation arena by a couple of years," says Paul Holmes, editor of the PR trade magazines *Reputation Management* and *Inside PR*. "Reputations are easy to damage—but only by very extreme situations. And they are notoriously difficult to improve."

In fact, reputation-measurement experts seem to agree that it's easier to build a reputation from scratch than to improve one that has been badly tarnished. They contrast the overnight fame of dotcom companies to the painful process of recovery that Exxon has undergone since its PR nightmare. "I think people believe that the way companies act in crisis is a window into the soul of that company," Holmes says. "And for the most part, they're right. Companies behave the way that culturally conditioned to. So when they see an Exxon clam up, refuse to talk to the media, be generally unresponsive, they believe that that tells them a lot about what Exxon is like as an organization."

## DIGS AND DIPLOMACY

The experts that track the rise and fall of corporate reputation must, of necessity, also pay constant attention to their own. It's a fascinating exercise to hear experts in imagemaking position themselves in the industry: Listening to the listmakers talk about their competitors is like eavesdropping on a lesson in diplomacy. They speak of healthy competition and the importance of multiple viewpoints, but very few conclude an interview without at least one off-the-record dig at a competitor.

In an industry so tightly interwoven, they can't afford to snipe publicly: Today's competitors may be tomorrow's co-workers or collaborators, or vice versa. Leslie Gaines-Ross, for example, started the "Maximizing Corporate Reputation" list as chief knowledge officer of PR agency Burson-Marsteller after leaving *Fortune*, where she worked in conjunction with

## WOULD YOUR EMPLOYEES RANK YOU "BEST"?

Your company may not have a nationwide presence. It may not have astronomical revenues. But if you treat your people right, you can still get on a "best" list.

Rather than measuring what your peers or the general public thinks of your company, *Fortune*'s "100 Best Companies to Work for in America" list goes straight to those with an inside view—your employees. Two-thirds of a company's ranking depends on the evaluations of 250 randomly selected employees; the remainder is based on top management's description of the company's HR practices.

Unlike corporate-reputation lists, the "100 Best" list consists of companies that apply to be on it. The survey is conducted by Robert Levering and Milton Moskowitz, co-authors of *The 100 Best Companies to Work for in America* (Plume), with assistance from Hewitt Associates, a compensation-and-benefits consultancy based in Lincolnshire, Ill. Levering and Moskowitz include their e-mail address with the list in *Fortune*, inviting companies to apply for the next year.

Applying is only the first step: Companies that choose to go through the entire process can expect to invest about 40 hours distributing surveys to employees, filling out a 30-page questionnaire about benefits and other HR policies, and answering 10 open-ended questions about the company's work environment.

### BEST COMPANIES TO WORK FOR IN AMERICA JANUARY 2000

1. Container Store
2. Southwest Airlines
3. Cisco Systems
4. TDIndustries
5. Synovus Financial
6. SAS Institute
7. Edward Jones
8. Charles Schwab
9. Goldman Sachs
10. MBNA

Of the approximately 500 companies that initially expressed interest last year, only 236 ended up making that commitment. "It's a matter of motivation," says Hewitt managing consultant Ed Gubman. "You have to feel like this is one of your corporate priorities."

Perhaps because companies have to work to get on the list, the companies that make it use their position to their fullest advantage. Deloitte & Touche (No. 31), for example, took out full-page ads in *The New York Times* and *The Wall Street Journal* announcing that the consultancy had made the list, while Continental Airlines (No. 23) displays that information right in the cabins of its planes. Levering points out that companies leverage their position on the list not only with customers through advertising but also with shareholders by announcing it in their annual reports.

Most of all, of course, being recognized as a great company to work for is a helpful tool in recruitment and retention. "You don't have to be a great employer to be a 'most admired' company—I think the overlap between the lists is only about 35 percent," Gubman says. "But it's increasingly important for companies in getting their share of talent."

—C.E. and M.M.

Yankelovich Partners; John Gilfeather spent years at Yankelovich before leaving for Roper Starch Worldwide, which recently formed its own alliance with *Fortune*; and Pricewaterhouse-Coopers, which conducts the *Financial Times* survey, is a founding member of Charles Fombrun's Reputation Institute.

Complex alliances, in an increasingly complex industry. There's a clear departure from the original model of reputation measurement, in which *Fortune* published a static list once a year. The trend now is toward customized databases that allow for more flexibility: For example, a company can ask to be compared against others in its industry, others with similar revenues, or others in its geographic community. Furthermore, it can ask to see how it stacks up in terms of one specific element, such as social responsibility, rather than just in corporate reputation overall.

This ability to customize becomes more important as the listmakers look beyond the numbers to see why companies have received the scores that they have, and how those scores relate to performance. Going forward, this will be the consistently marketable product for the reputation measurement industry: in-depth reputation analysis that takes advantage of the measuring organization's unique strengths. More importantly, this analysis—which affords opportunity for change—is worth more to corporations than the tabletop value of a list.

# ARTICLE REPRINT

## THE USE AND MISUSE OF STATISTICS

*Editor's Comment:* Trainers, it seems, are forever under the gun to determine return on investment (ROI) of training dollars spent. In recent years, there have been some voices other than accountants who have tried to show process-based value calculations to evaluate and account for training's successes. In all investigations into return on investment (ROI), evaluators rely on the proper use of statistics to interpret results of evaluations. The article reprinted below is a good primer on the wise use of statistics.

## THE USE AND MISUSE OF STATISTICS

Are defect rates declining? Is customer satisfaction rising? You inspect the numbers, but you're not sure whether to believe them. It isn't that you fear fraud or manipulation, it's that you don't know how much faith to put in statistics.

You're right to be cautious. "The actual statistical calculations represent only 5 percent of the manager's work," declares Frances Frei, an assistant professor at Harvard Business School who teaches two-day statistics seminars to corporate managers. "The other 95 percent should be spent determining the right calculations and interpreting the results." Some guidelines for effective use of statistics, derived from Frei's seminar and other sources:

### 1. KNOW WHAT YOU KNOW—AND WHAT YOU'RE ONLY ASSERTING

"In real life, managers don't do as much number crunching as they think," avers Victor McGee, professor emeritus at Dartmouth College's Amos Tuck School of Business. "In fact, managers are primarily idea crunchers: They spend most of their time trying to persuade people with their assertions." But they rarely realize the extent to which their assertions rest on unproved assumptions. McGee recommends color-coding your "knowledge" so you know what needs to be tested. Red can represent what you know, green what you assume, and blue what you "know" because of what you assume. Assumptions and assertions—green and blue knowledge—shouldn't be taken seriously unless there is red knowledge supporting them.

### 2. BE CLEAR ABOUT WHAT YOU WANT TO DISCOVER

Some management reports rely heavily on the arithmetic mean or average of a group of numbers. But look at Figure 1, a histogram analyzing customer satisfaction survey results on a scale of

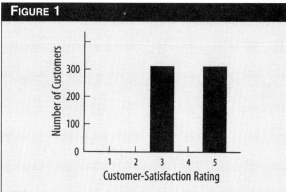

**Histogram analyzing customer satisfaction survey results.** Although the mean is 4, no one actually gave the product a rating of 4. Instead, the responses cluster around a group of very satisfied customers (the 5s) and a group of moderately satisfied ones (the 3s). The key lesson here: Know what you're looking for *before* you decide which metric to use.

1 to 5. For this data set, the mean is 4. If that's all you saw, you might figure people are pretty satisfied. But as Figure 1 shows, no one actually gave your product a rating of 4: instead, the responses cluster around a group of very satisfied customers, who scored it a 5, and moderately satisfied customers, who gave it a 3. Only by deciding beforehand that you wanted to look for subgroups within your customer base could you know that the mean would not be the most helpful metric for your search. "Ask the *direct* question," advises McGee: "What do you want to know?"

## 3. DON'T TAKE CAUSE AND EFFECT FOR GRANTED

Management is all about finding the levers that will affect performance, notes McGee. "If we do such-and-such, then such-and-such will happen." But this is the world of green and blue knowledge. Hypotheses depend on assumptions made about causes, and the only way to have confidence in the hypothetical course of action is to prove that the assumed causal connections do indeed hold.

Say you're trying to make a case for investing more heavily in sales training, and you've got numbers to show that sales revenues increase with training dollars. Have you established a

cause-and-effect relationship? No, says Frei—all you have is a correlation. To establish genuine causation, you need to ask yourself three questions. Is there an association between the two variables? Is the time sequence accurate? Is there any other explanation that could account for the correlation?

To establish the association, Frei cautions, it's often wise to look at the raw data, not just the apparent correlation. Figure 2 shows a scatter diagram plotting all the individual data points derived from a study of the influence of training on performance. Line A, the "line of best fit" that comes as close as possible to connecting all the individual data points, has a gentle upward slope. But if you remove the point Z (which represents $45,000 in training and $100,000 in sales volume) from the data set, the line of best fit becomes Line B, whose slope is nearly twice as steep as that of Line A. "When removing a single data point causes the slope of the line [of best fit] to change significantly," Frei explains, "you know that point is unduly influencing your results. Depending on the question you're asking, you should consider removing it from the analysis."

For the second question—is the time sequence accurate?—the problem is to establish which variable in the correlation occurs first. Your hypothesis is that training precedes performance, but you must check the data closely to make sure that the reverse isn't true—that it's the improved sales volume that is driving up training dollars. Question three—can you rule out other plausible explanations for the correlation?—is the most time-consuming. Is there some hidden variable at work? For example, are you hiring more qualified salespeople—and is that why performance has improved? Have you made any changes in your incentive system? Only by eliminating other factors can you establish the link between training and performance with any certainty.

But speaking of certainty, it's important to remember the following:

## 4. WITH STATISTICS, YOU CAN'T PROVE THINGS WITH 100% CERTAINTY

Only when you have recorded all the impressions of all the customers who have had an experience with a particular product can you

**FIGURE 2**

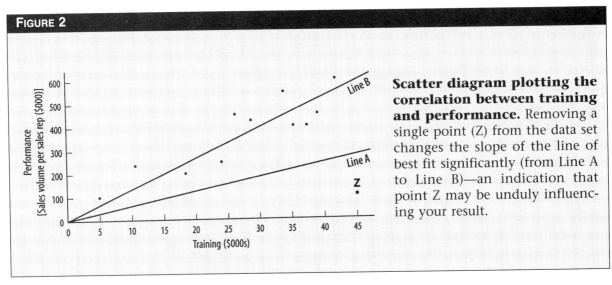

**Scatter diagram plotting the correlation between training and performance.** Removing a single point (Z) from the data set changes the slope of the line of best fit significantly (from Line A to Line B)—an indication that point Z may be unduly influencing your result.

establish certainty about customer satisfaction. But that would cost too much time and money, so you take random samples instead. A random sample means that every member of the population is equally likely to be chosen. Using a nonrandom sample is the #1 mistake businesses make when sampling, says Frei, even though a random sample is simple to generate with (for instance) Microsoft Excel.

"All sampling relies on the normal distribution and the central limit theorem," Frei continues. These principles—found in any statistics textbook—enable you to calculate a *confidence interval* for an entire population based on a sample. Say you come up with a sample defect rate of 2.8%. Depending on the sample size and other factors, you might be able to say that you're 95% confident the actual number is between 2.5% and 3.1%. The fewer defects, incidentally, the larger your sample must be to establish a 95% confidence interval. "So as you get better," says Frei, "you need to spend more on quality-assurance sampling, not less."

## 5. A RESULT THAT IS NUMERICALLY OR STATISTICALLY SIGNIFICANT MAY BE MANAGERIALLY USELESS—AND VICE VERSA

Take a customer satisfaction rating of 3.9. If you implemented a program to improve customer satisfaction, conducted some polling several months out to test the program's effectiveness,

and found a new rating of 4.1, has your program been a success? Not necessarily—you have to check the confidence interval. In this case, 4.1 might not be statistically different from 3.9 because it fell within the confidence interval. In other words, you could have no more confidence that 4.1 is the real customer rating than you could that 3.9 is correct.

Because they're unaware of how confidence intervals work, managers tend to overcelebrate and overpunish. For example, a VP might believe the 4.1 rating indicates a genuine improvement and award a bonus to the manager who launched the new customer satisfaction program. Six months later, when the number has dropped back to 3.9, he might fire the manager. In both instances, the VP would be making decisions based on statistically insignificant shifts in the data. But if new sampling produced a rating outside the confidence interval—say, 4.3—the executive could be confident that the program was having a positive effect.

Be clear about what you want to discover before you decide on the statistical tools. Make sure you've established genuine causation, not just a correlation, while keeping in mind that statistics don't allow you to prove anything with absolute certainty. And remember that not all results are statistically significant or managerially useful. Although the perspectives offered here won't qualify you to be a high-powered statistical analyst, they will help you decide what to ask of the analysts whose numbers you rely on.

# ABSTRACT

## LESSONS FROM THE CENSUS

*Editor's Comment:* During the first quarter of year 2000, the U.S. Government mailed out Census forms to all Americans, in a once-per-decade ritual that this year had critics screaming about invasion of privacy, among other things. The problem seems to have stemmed from "the long form," of the Census questionnaire, mailed to a sampling of the population, which asked many questions such as a household's availability of flush toilets and number of bedrooms. The long form became the butt of countless jokes and ridicule in the public press and airways; a poll reported in *USA Today*, April 21, 2000 indicated that 22% of the population considered it an invasion of privacy. Only about half of those long forms mailed out came back completed by the deadline date, considerably fewer than the 1990 Census's long form. Some Congressmen even found it necessary to pass legislation protecting citizens who refused to complete the forms. The more common "short form" caused much less controversy; nearly 67% of short forms were returned by the Census 2000 April 1st deadline date. The Census Bureau estimated that 500,000 personal Census Workers would be hired to go door to door in search of delinquent forms. Government advertisements for Census Workers appeared in strategic places and publications. One such ad in the April/May 2000 *Native Peoples* magazine challenges the reader to "Earn good pay and do something meaningful for our people: Call the Local Census Office now!" And, "Our community's future . . . depends on this." The Census Director hoped for a 70% overall return.

Commentators have, of course, a variety of opinions about why returns are less than expected, and about what this evaluation means to the country. One of the most thoughtful comments was that of Steven A. Holmes writing in the Sunday *New York Times* (April 9, 2000, p.5.) Holmes quotes Robert Putnam, a professor of public policy at the John F. Kennedy School of Government at Harvard University who likens the unwillingness to fill out Census forms to a general decline in community connectedness over the recent decades. Putnam cites decline in bowling leagues, decline in neighborhood bars and gathering places, decline in voting, fewer community picnics, less participation in clubs as signs of anti-community trends that began in the 1970s, well before Internet privacy issues and suspicion of government—and commercial—information gatherers. Holmes reports on focus groups sponsored by the

*Sources:* "Census Receives 'News to Celebrate'" by Haya El Nasser in *USA Today*, April 21, 2000, p. 5A; "Answer the Census. The Alternative Is Worse" by Stephen and Abigail Thernstrom in *The Wall Street Journal*, April 6, 2000, p. A22; "Down About the Count" by Steven A. Holmes in *The New York Times*, April 9, 2000, p. 5; "Privacy Concerns Threaten a 'Backlash', Census Director Fears" by Robert Pear in *The New York Times*, National Sunday, April 2, 2000, p. 15; "Why Internet Privacy Matters: The Eroded Self" by Jeffrey Rosen in *The New York Times Magazine*, cover story, April 30, 2000, pp. 46–53, 66–68, 129; and the cartoon by Istvan Banyai originally published in *The New Yorker*, April 10, 2000, p. 50. Cartoon is reprinted with permission of Istvan Banyai, illustrator.

Census Bureau in which most folks simply didn't see how the Census would *benefit* them (italics mine). The notion of "civic responsibility" seemed far from the popular consciousness in Census year 2000.

This brings us to the question of what and why we survey and count. Like any evaluation, the Census has a purpose, a use, in mind for its collected data: According to law, that purpose is to apportion congressional districts and ultimately allocate funding for programs within those districts. Aggregate data from the completed Cen-

sus will also be used by numerous entities with economic and consumer interests, as the results are made public. As the Thernstroms suggest in their *Wall Street Journal* opinion piece referenced below, "government by guesswork" is the feared result of an undercounted and inadequately described population, and that is the really scary effect of ignoring the Census. Getting assessment and evaluation right is important. Counting the things that matter is essential in a fair society. This year's Census illustrates some of the lessons in largescale evaluation.

# 6

# THE TRAINER'S ALMANAC

The *Training and Development Yearbook*'s 2001 *Trainer's Almanac* brings you the most complete reference publication available today—virtually a book-within-a-book it contains essential, verified, totally up-to-date information for human resources leaders who need to make training decisions for the important millenial calendar year 2001.

## More Ways to Find Information

This *Trainer's Almanac* contains more than 1,000 references representing the broadest range of training resources in print today, presented in easy-to-find listings with descriptive information and data you'll need for making contact with each source. Website addresses are included in our organization listings, providing a way for you to check online for the latest updates. Many organizations have online listservs for their members and sometimes for the public. Many search and registration services are free, paid for by advertisers. We've included toll-free 800-numbers, fax numbers, addresses, and Websites to give you all the motivation you need to seek the resources you want. We have verified that helpful, knowledgeable, real people are at the other end of the phone call—often a telephone call is the best place to begin your information search. We want you to see *The Trainer's Almanac* as your essential starting point for shaping and enhancing your own personal knowledge base and facilitating the growth and value of your company's intellectual capital.

Again this year, we include as Section 6.8 a 10-page listing of training Websites rated and ranked by an independent source according to completeness and usefulness to trainers. We encourage you to browse through the entire *Trainer's Almanac* to get a feel for its tremendous scope, variety of resources, and fields of data.

## A Representation of the Vitality of the Field

*The Trainer's Almanac* is designed to complement the first five narrative sections of this book which provide the current backdrop of ideas for this year's human resources programming and the business of being a professional trainer. This section, Section 6, with its eight sub-sections, contrasts with the previous five sections of text and gives you the raw resource data you'll need for the most informed training decision making for calendar year 2001.

Our choice of categories on which to focus provides you with a clear way into information and enables you to build your training operation with the extra "edge" of being able to have the whole field at hand, in one master volume. We put our decades of experience as trainers and publishers to work for you as partners in professional development.

Sections of the 2001 *The Trainer's Almanac* include:

# THE TRAINER'S ALMANAC

## PROFESSIONAL ORGANIZATIONS

We begin *The Trainer's Almanac* with an alphabetical listing of 34 professional organizations of interest to trainers.

### Membership Organizations

These are associations of professional workers with a common interest and are open to members who want to join together in like professional pursuits to advance their own professional knowledge and skills and to provide professional visibility for their companies through their membership. In Section 6.1 we list these organizations along with current key information about the organization. Many of these organizations sponsor annual conferences open to members and to the public which we further index in Section 6.2. Non-profit organizations, which are not membership associations in the usual professional sense, are included in a separate listing, Section 6.5.

### National in Scope

We have purposely included organizations that are national in scope which seek and enjoy a wide membership and which provide broad services to their members. We have checked with each professional organization listed here for their most current information. Many companies like to have their training and human resources staff join professional organizations to network and to keep up to date with changes in the field. Our Section 6.1 will give you all the guidance you need for planning the continued professionalization of your staff.

Organizations are listed alphabetically by the name of the organization, and are further indexed according to the main focus of the organization. We list 27 index terms, indicating a representation of the range of professional organizations of interest to trainers.

## INDEX TO PRINCIPAL INTERESTS OF PROFESSIONAL ORGANIZATIONS

| | |
|---|---|
| **Human resource planning** 12 | **Neuro-linguistic programming** 6 |
| **Instructional design** 5, 13, 18 | **Organization development** 4, 29, 30 |
| **Insurance industry training** 34 | **Performance improvement** 4, 5, 18 |
| **International training** 3, 5, 14, 16, 28 | **Public sector, training in** 20, 24 |
| **Juvenile justice training** 20 | **Sales training** 6 |
| **Literacy training** 1, 23 | **Technology training** 7, 11, 19, 22, 31, 33 |
| **Marketing of training** 11, 21 | **Training facilities** 15 |
| **Mentoring** 17, 27 | **Training media** 7, 11, 31 |

## 1

Name of organization:
**American Association for Adult & Continuing Education (AAACE)**
Contact information:
AAACE
1200 19th St., N.W., Suite 300
Washington, DC 20036
301/918-1913
www.albany.edu/ace
Key officers/staff:
Association Manager: Anna Darin
Membership requirements:
Open to all interested in adult and basic education, continuing education, and lifelong learning.
Size of membership:
3,000 (includes secondary and post-secondary educators, business and labor trainers, military and government, and community-based organization leaders)
Annual dues:
$115 (general)
Publications:
Adult Learning
Adult Education Quarterly
Adult Basic Education and Literacy Journal
Online newsletter
Meetings:
Annual conference
Regional and other thematic meetings

## 2

Name of organization:
**American Counseling Association**
(see also National Career Development Association)

Purpose/Mission Statement:
To promote public confidence and trust in the counseling profession.
Contact information:
American Counseling Association
5999 Stevenson Ave.
Alexandria, VA 22304
800/347-6647
703/823-9800
703/823-0252 (fax)
www.counseling.org
Key officers/staff:
Executive Director: Richard Yep
Membership requirements:
Interest in the areas of counseling and human development is the primary criterion. Candidates for membership include those who work in schools, colleges, private practice, employment, and related human service settings.
Size of membership:
approximately 51,000
Annual dues:
Approximately $100 (depends on whether you are a student or professional member) ($109, $82)
Publications:
The Journal of Counseling and Development
Counseling Today
Meetings:
Annual convention
Other benefits of membership:
Career placement, accreditation/certification programs, professional development programs, books, insurance

## 3

Name of organization:
**American Management Association International**

Purpose/Mission Statement:
AMA provides educational forums worldwide where members and their colleagues learn practical business skills and explore best practices of world-class organizations through interaction with each other and faculty practitioners. AMA's publishing program provides tools individuals use to extend learning beyond the classroom in a process of lifelong professional growth and development through education.
Contact information:
American Management Association International
1601 Broadway
New York, New York 10019–7420
212/586-8100
212/903-8329 (fax)
www.amanet.org
Key officers/staff:
President & Chief Executive Officer: Dr. George Weathersby
Corporate Vice-President & Chief Financial Officer: Viviana Gozman
Membership requirements:
Interest in the methodology and best contemporary management practices.
Size of membership:
70,000 (includes corporations, organizations, and individuals)
Publications:
AMA publishes approximately 70 business-related books each year, plus many surveys, newsletters, management briefings, self-paced courses in print and audio, as well as videos. Its flagship publication *Management Review*, is now available to members only, online only.

**Meetings:**
Annual conferences
Local/regional meetings

**Other benefits of membership:**
Gain insights at membership briefings and programs on important issues, opportunity to advance skills with management tools provided each month by AMA, network at local & regional meetings, special discounts on seminars, publications, CD-Roms, & other self-study tools, plus benefits of corporate membership.

## 4

**Name of organization:**
**The American Productivity & Quality Center (APQC)**

**Purpose:**
Founded in 1977, the American Productivity & Quality Center (APQC) is a tax-exempt entity supported by more than 500 member organizations of all sizes, across all industries. The mission of APQC and its service, the International Benchmarking Clearinghouse, is to help enterprises recognize when and why change is needed, manage it effectively, and achieve process and performance improvement along the way through benchmarking and best practices. APQC provides the tools, information, and support in areas such as knowledge management, measurement, customer satisfaction, benchmarking, strategic planning, competitive intelligence, leadership, call centers, and quality.

**Contact information:**
The American Productivity & Quality Center (APQC)
123 North Post Oak Lane, 3rd Floor
Houston, TX 77024
800/776-9676
Outside U.S. 713/681-4020
713/681-1182 (fax)
e-mail: apqcinfo@apqc.org
www.apqc.org

**Membership requirements:**
Interests in improving quality, managing change, harnessing knowledge, measuring performance, adapting best practices, and thriving in an increasingly competitive environment.

**Size of membership:**
more than 500 member organizations

**Annual dues:**
There is a one-time new-member initiation fee plus an annual fee

based on the number of employees within the organization. The initiatiom fee is U.S. tax deductible. Part of the annual fee is allocated to a bank account which can be used for purchasing additional APQC products or services. Membership is for an entire organization. All employees within member organizations can take advantage of members-only resources, content, and discounts.

**Publications:**
Best-Practice Reports (results of benchmarking studies)
Passport to Success book series
Case Studies
White papers
Conference proceedings

**Meetings:**
Conferences with members-only events
Open house
Regional seminars/presentations
Regional training programs

**Other benefits of membership:**
Membership in APQC's International Benchmarking Clearinghouse provides exclusive access to people and information, enabling you to find and adapt best practices efficiently and effectively. Clearinghouse membership gives everyone within a member organization access to knowledge and resources needed to improve productivity and quality.

## 5

**Name of organization:**
**American Society for Training and Development (ASTD)**

**Purpose:**
To provide leadership to individuals, organizations, and society to achieve work-related competence, performance, and fulfillment. Part of ASTD's mission is to link people, learning, and performance.

**Contact information:**
ASTD
1640 King St., Box 1443
Alexandria, VA 22313
703/683-8100
703/683-8103 (fax)
703/683-1523 (customer service fax)
www.astd.org

**Key officers/staff:**
President and CEO:
Susan Burnett

**Membership requirements:**
Interest in the field of workplace learning, training, technical training, and performance improvement.

**Size of membership:**
70,000 (national and chapter)

**Annual dues:**
Student $75
Senior $75
Individual membership $150
Membership Plus package $229
Group: $135 per person for 5–25 members; $120 per person for more than 25 members; 1,000 Day Membership (3 years) $360; Knowledge Plus (for training professionals) $280 per year; Organizational $350 per year

**Publications:**
Training & Development (monthly magazine)
National Report on Human Resources
Performance in Practice
Info-Line
ASTD Buyer's Guide & Consultant Directory
Technical & Skills Training (Web magazine)
Human Resource Development Quarterly (Web magazine)

**Meetings:**
ASTD International Conference & Exposition
ASTD Techknowledge℠ Conference and Exposition

**Other benefits of membership:**
Information Center, Member Information Exchange, TRAINET (electronic database), ASTD Online (online information service), representation in government, book service, audio cassettes and videotapes of national conferences.

## 6

**Name of organization:**
**Association for Business Neuro-Linguistics Training**

**Purpose:**
To make the latest findings from the behavioral and social sciences available to business and industry.

**Contact information:**
Association for Business Neuro-Linguistics Training
P.O. Box 2902
Palos Verdes, CA 90274
310/378-2666
310/378-2742 (fax)

**Key officers/staff:**
Executive Director: Dr. Donald Moine
**Membership requirements:**
Open to sales training directors and vice-presidents of marketing and human resources
**Size of membership:**
2,500
**Annual dues:**
None
**Publications:**
Newsletter
Modern Persuasion Strategies: The Hidden Advantage in Selling
Unlimited Selling Power: How to Master Hypnotic Selling Skills
The Power of Story Selling
Better Than Gold
**Meetings:**
Quarterly meetings

## 7

**Name of organization:**
**Association for Educational Communications & Technology (AECT)**
**Purpose:**
Dedicated to the improvement of instruction through the utilization of media and technology.
**Contact information:**
AECT
1800 North Stonelake Dr.
Bloomington, IN 47404
812/335-7675
812/335-7678 (fax)
www.aect.org
**Key officers/staff:**
Executive Director: Phillip Harris
**Size of membership:**
7,000
**Annual dues:**
$85 per year, plus options
**Publications:**
TechTrends
Educational Technology Research and Development
**Meetings:**
Annual Conference
Summer Leadership Conference
Professional Development Technology Conference
**Other benefits of membership:**
Low-cost insurance programs, job placement and referral services, awards program, various discounts

## 8

**Name of organization:**
**Career Planning & Adult Development Network**

**Purpose:**
The Network is designed to meet the needs of human resource specialists working with adults in a variety of settings and to keep them in touch with other human resource professionals through its publications and activities.
**Contact information:**
Career Planning & Adult Development Network
4965 Sierra Rd.
San Jose, CA 95132
408/441-9100
408/441-9101 (fax)
www.careertrainer.com
**Key officers/staff:**
Richard L. Knowdell
**Membership requirements:**
Interest in career planning and adult development
**Size of membership:**
1,200+
**Annual dues:**
$49 (U.S.); $64 (foreign); these prices for pre-paid. ($10 more for invoicing)
**Publications:**
Career Planning and the Adult Development Network Newsletter
Career Planning and Adult Development Journal

## 9

**Name of organization:**
**Council for Adult and Experiential Learning (CAEL)**
**Purpose:**
To expand lifelong learning opportunities for adults and to advance experiential learning and its assessment.
**Contact information:**
CAEL
55 East Monroe, Suite 1930
Chicago, IL 60603
312/499-2600
312/499-2601 (fax)
www.cael.org
**Key officers/staff:**
President: Pamela Tate
**Membership requirements:**
Accreditation by COPA-affiliated accrediting body for institutional membership. Any individual can join as an individual member.
**Size of membership:**
2,300
**Annual dues:**
$75 (individual); $375 (organizational); institutional dues determined by enrollment ($275–$475)

**Publications:**
Newsletter
Various books & papers
**Meetings:**
Annual conference
Spring workshops
**Other benefits of membership:**
Discounts on CAEL publications, conferences, institutes, workshops, and consultation services; access to membership commissions.

## 10

**Name of organization:**
**Distance Education and Training Council**
**Purpose:**
The Distance Education and Training Council, a voluntary association of accredited distance study institutions, was founded in 1926 to promote sound educational standards and ethical business practices within the correspondence/distance study field. The independent DETC Accrediting Commission is listed by the U.S. Dept. of Education as a "nationally recognized accrediting agency." The Accrediting Commission is also a recognized member of the Council for Higher Education Accreditation (CHEA).
**Contact information:**
Distance Education and Training Council
1601 18th St., N.W.
Washington, DC 20009-2529
202/234-5100
202/332-1386 (fax)
www.detc.org
**Key officers/staff:**
Executive Director: Michael P. Lambert
**Membership requirements:**
Accreditation of correspondence/distance study is conducted by the Accrediting Commission of the DETC.
**Size of membership:**
70 member institutions
**Annual dues:**
Less than one percent of income, estimated at $1,050 and up.
**Publications:**
DETC News
Directory of Accredited Institutions
**Meetings:**
Annual spring conference
Business Standards (every odd year)
Educational Workshop (every even year)

Other benefits of membership:
Training seminars, legislative information

## 11

Name of organization:
**Digital Learning Organization**
Purpose:
To promote the success of the training media industry by helping members protect their copyright interests, market their products more effectively, network with others in the industry, and stay current with developments in the legislative and regulatory environment.
Contact information:
Digital Learning Organization
P.O. Box 445
Western Springs, IL 60558
877/533-4914
877/533-6451 (fax)
www.digitallearning.org
Key officers/staff:
Executive Director: Joseph Drago
Membership requirements:
*Regular member:* Must be producer/distributor of training media (film, video, slides and/or print materials) or software.
*Associate member:* Must be a supplier to the industry.
Size of membership:
110 organizations worldwide
Annual dues:
Graduated according to size of company $1,000–$5,000 per year
Publications:
Quarterly Previews (newsletter)
Meetings:
Semiannual conferences
Copyright enforcement program
Management education seminars
Other benefits of membership:
Copyright protection system, Networking

## 12

Name of organization:
**The Human Resource Planning Society**
Purpose:
To increase the impact of human resource planning and management on business and organizational performance.
Contact information:
The Human Resource Planning Society
317 Madison Ave., Suite 1509
New York, NY 10017

212/490-6387
212/682-6851 (fax)
www.hrps.org
Key officers/staff:
Executive Director: Walter J. Cleaver
Membership requirements:
Senior-level human resource executives
Size of membership:
3,000 +
Annual dues:
$250 (individual); $75 (faculty); $2,500 (corporate sponsor); $1,000 (research sponsor)
Publications:
Human Resource Planning (quarterly publication)
Membership directory (online)
Meetings:
Annual conference/Biennial Research Symposium
Professional development workshops/Corporate sponsor forum

## 13

Name of organization:
**Instructional Systems Association (ISA)**
Purpose:
To enhance the development and success of member firms; to improve members' capability to serve their clients; and to expand the influence of the instructional systems industry.
Contact information:
ISA
4952 Warner Ave., Suite 243
Huntington Beach, CA 92649
714/846-6012
714/846-3987 (fax)
www.isaconnection.org
Key officers/staff:
Executive Director: Pamela J. Schmidt
Membership requirements:
Membership is open to those who produce generic and custom-designed training programs and consulting services.
Size of membership:
130
Annual dues:
Based on gross annual sales
Publications:
Intercom (newsletter, published 3 times per year)
Newswire (E-mail Newsletter)
Meetings:
Annual meeting
Fall meeting

One-day special-topic meetings
Audio conferences

## 14

Name of organization:
**International Alliance for Learning (IAL)**
Purpose:
We envision a world where everyone experiences joy and fulfillment of infinite learning. We promote and support practical implementation of accelerated learning principles.
Contact information:
IAL
P.O. Box 26175
Colorado Springs, CO 80936
800/426-2989
719/638-6153 (fax)
www.ialearn.org
Key officers/staff:
President: Nancy Omaha Boy
Membership requirements:
None
Size of membership:
700
Annual dues:
$60 (U.S.); $80 (outside U.S.)
Publications:
Journal of Accelerative Learning and Teaching
Newsletter (3 times per year)
Meetings:
Annual conference

## 15

Name of organization:
**International Association of Conference Centers (IACC)**
Purpose:
To assist members in providing the most productive meeting facilities in the world and to expand awareness of the differences between these conference facilities and other hospitality venues.
Contact information:
IACC
243 North Lindbergh Blvd.
St. Louis, MO 63141
314/993-8575
314/993-8919 (fax)
www.iacconline.org
Key officers/staff:
Executive Vice-President: Tom Bolman
Membership requirements:
Each conference center must meet the universal criteria for membership.

**Size of membership:**
450
**Annual dues:**
$700–$2,800 (based on facility size)
**Publications:**
New Publications: A Uniform System of Accounts for Conference Centers, 2000 Trends in Conference Center Industry—North America, 2000 Compass Reports: Benchmarking the North American Conference Industry.
Plus the following: Annual Membership Directory, Understanding Conference Centers, Training Room Solutions, A Conference Center by Design, The Conference Center Concept (brochure), Quarterly newsletter
**Meetings:**
Annual conference
**Other benefits of membership:**
Professional education, advisory services, networking, marketing, public relations, Internet

## 16

**Name of organization:**
**International Federation of Training and Development Organizations (IFTDO)**
**Purpose:**
IFTDO is a worldwide network committed to identifying, developing, and transferring knowledge, skills, and technology to enhance personal and organizational growth, human performance, productivity, and sustainable development.
**Contact information:**
Dr. David A. Waugh–Secretary General
IFTDO
1800 Duke St.
Alexandria, VA 22314
703/535-6011
703/836-0367 (fax)
www.iftdo.org
**Membership requirements:**
Any organization which has as a primary objective the furtherance of the science and practice of the profession of training and wishes to adopt a full voting role in the Federation may apply for full member status. This includes professional training associations, as well as multinational corporations, universities, government agencies, consulting firms, etc. Any organization wishing to be

associated with the Federation but which does not want to play a full voting part may apply as an Associate Member.
**Annual dues:**
Full members—between $300 and $900, depending on size of membership
Associate members—$300
**Publications:**
IFTDO News
**Meetings:**
Annual world conference

## 17

**Name of organization:**
**International Mentoring Association**
**Purpose:**
To provide a regular, public forum for effective mentoring, professional development activities for members, and annual conferences and workshops; to facilitate the growth of effective mentoring and the implementation and maintenance of mentoring programs; and to disseminate materials on research and practices related to effective mentoring.
**Contact information:**
Emily Jacobs
International Mentoring Association
Conferences and Seminars Division of Continuing Education
Western Michigan University
1201 Oliver St.
Kalamazoo, MI 49008-5161
616/387-4174
616/387-4189 (fax)
www.mentoring-association.org
**Key officers/staff:**
President: Mr. Danny Sledge
**Annual dues:**
$40 (student); $65 (individual); $100 (institution)
**Publications:**
The Mentoring Connection Newsletter
Membership directory
**Meetings:**
Diversity in Mentoring Annual Conference (Annual Mentoring Institutes included in)

## 18

**Name of organization:**
**International Society for Performance Improvement (ISPI)**

**Purpose:**
To increase productivity in the workplace through the application of performance and instructional technologies.
**Contact information:**
ISPI
1300 L St., N.W., Suite 1250
Washington, DC 20005-4107
202/408-7969
202/408-7972 (fax)
www.ispi.org
**Key officers/staff:**
Executive Director: Richard D. Battaglia
**Membership requirements:**
None
**Size of membership:**
6,000 international members; 5,000 local chapters not on international level
**Annual dues:**
$125 (active); $60 (student); Organizational memberships available—call for different levels of organizational membership
**Publications:**
Performance Improvement Journal (10× a year)
Performance Improvement Quarterly
Annual membership directory
**Meetings:**
Annual conference and expo
**Other benefits of membership:**
Placement service, consultants resource directory, international conference, regional chapters, Performance Technology Human Institute Seminars

## 19

**Name of organization:**
**International Society for Technology in Education (ISTE)**
**Purpose:**
ISTE is dedicated to the improvement of all levels of education through the use of computer-based technology.
**Contact information:**
ISTE
480 Charnelton St.
Eugene, OR 97401-2626
800/336-5191
541/302-3777
541/302-3778 (administrative order fax)
**Key officers/staff:**
CEO: John Vaille
**Size of membership:**
Between 7,500–8,500

**Annual dues:**
$58 (regular membership, U.S.);
$35 (student members, U.S.)

**Publications:**
Learning & Leading with
Technology
The Journal of Research on
Computing in Education
Special Interest Group (SIG) journals
The Update newsletter
plus various books and courseware
packages

**Meetings:**
NECC Annual Conference

**Other benefits of membership:**
Voting privileges, discounts on
ISTE books, discounts or com-
plimentary subscriptions to non-
ISTE professional journals and
magazines.

## 20

**Name of organization:**
**Juvenile Justice Trainers
Association**

**Purpose:**
Devoted to the development and
advancement of a specialized
system of education and training
for juvenile justice professionals.
Composed primarily of staff
development and training specialists, the association provides
a national network for sharing
information, providing technical
services and developing other
support mechanisms for juvenile
justice trainers.

**Contact information:**
Mr. Gale Smith, Executive
Director
Juvenile Justice Trainers
Association
930 Coddington Rd.
Ithaca, NY 14850
607/256-2112
607/272-4308 (fax)
www.jjta.org

**Key officers/staff:**
President: Susan Yeres
Treasurer: Margaret Davis

**Membership requirements:**
None

**Size of membership:**
250–300

**Annual dues:**
$25

**Publications:**
Quarterly newsletter

**Meetings:**
Semiannual conference (spring
and fall)

## 21

**Name of organization:**
**LERN (Learning Resources
Network)**

**Purpose:**
To provide information and
services to organizations that offer
classes for adults.

**Contact information:**
LERN
P.O. Box 9
River Falls, WI 54022
800/678-5376
715/426-9777
715/426-5847 (fax)
www.lern.org

**Key officers/staff:**
President: William A. Draves
Director of Business & Professional
Programming & Director of
Education: Greg Marsello
Vice-President of Information
Services: Julie Coates

**Membership requirements:**
Organizational membership: open
to organizations that offer lifelong
learning programs (a tier system
for organizational membership is
in the works).

**Size of membership:**
2,500 organizational members;
6,000 members

**Annual dues:**
$345 (organizational membership).
A tier system is in the works for
organizational members.

**Publications:**
Course Trends (newsletter)
Trends in Association Education
(newsletter)
Marketing Contract Training
(newsletter)
Marketing Recreation Classes
(newsletter)
Marketing Seminars and
Conferences (newsletter)
Marketing Continuing Professional
Education (newsletter)
Front Line Leadership (newsletter)
Lifelong Learning Today (newsletter)
Associations Online
Higher Education Online
Marketing Credit & Degree Programs
plus various books, pamphlets,
audiotapes, videos, and
software plus other newsletters

**Meetings:**
LERN International Conference
Regional conferences
Various seminars and institutes

**Other benefits of membership:**
Member networking, on-site
seminars, program planner

certification program, brochure
critique, customized surveys, program offering analysis, consulting,
LERN Internet services (chat
rooms, etc.), and the LERN
database.

## 22

**Name of organization:**
**The MASIE Center**

**Purpose:**
The MASIE Center is an international thinktank dedicated to
exploring the intersection of
learning and technology. It is
both a professional organization
and a commercial venture.

**Contact information:**
The MASIE Center
P.O. Box 397
Saratoga Springs, NY 12866
518/587-3522
518/587-3276 (fax)
www.masie.com

**Key officers/staff:**
President: Elliott Masie

**Membership requirements:**
Interest in learning and
technology.

**Annual dues:**
$195 for *Learning Decision*
newsletter subscription and
Website, discounts on conferences.

**Publications:**
Publications written by Elliott
Masie and copyrighted by The
MASIE Center are posted on the
Center's Website. These primar-
ily include articles on learning
and technology and TechLearn
Trends newsletter. These can be
copied and disseminated with
attribution to The MASIE Center.
A weekly letter is sent via
e-mail to members.

**Meetings:**
Annual TechLearn Conference in
Orlando, FL

**Other benefits of membership:**
The Center provides research,
perspectives, "next generation"
learning and technology solutions.

## 23

**Name of organization:**
**National Alliance of Business**

**Purpose:**
A business-led non-profit organization dedicated to building a
quality workforce that meets the
needs of employers. This objective is met through partnerships

with business and education leaders who also are committed to building an internationally competitive workforce through education reform and enhanced job training.

**Contact information:**
National Alliance of Business
1201 New York Avenue, N.W.,
Suite 700
Washington, DC 20005-3917
202/289-2888
202/289-1303 (fax)
www.nab.com

**Key officers/staff:**
President & CEO: Roberts T. Jones
Exec. Vice-President: Milton Goldberg

**Membership requirements:**
Annual dues

**Size of membership:**
5,000 (includes business, institutions, and individuals)

**Annual dues:**
Associate: $250
Associations: $500
Business: $2,500
Corporate: $5,000
Sustaining: $10,000
Leadership: $25,000 and above

**Publications:**
WorkAmerica
Workforce Economics Trends
Workforce Economics
Legislative Update
Policy Notes

**Meetings:**
Annual Workforce Conference
Annual Founder's Awards Dinner
Teleconferences/Town Meetings
Focus groups/training seminars

**Other benefits of membership:**
Member networking, monthly/ bimonthly publications, access to database, staff resources, technological trends updates

## 24

**Name of organization:**
**National Association for Government Training and Development (NAGTAD)**

**Purpose:**
To provide leadership in the training and development of public sector employees. The Association is the premier source of information on the unique needs of public sector training and development directors.

**Contact information:**
NAGTAD
167 W. Main St., Suite 600
Lexington, KY 40507

859/231-1948
859/541-9188 (fax)
www.usd.edu/nagtad

**Key officers/staff:**
President: Meredith Cash

**Membership requirements:**
Regular: Any government training and/or development official (Membership has recently been expanded to all governmental entities besides states)
There are also various levels of corporate membership

**Size of membership:**
75

**Annual dues:**
$525 (government entities with more than 2,000 employees); $250 (government entities with less than 2,000 employees); $175 (associate members)

**Publications:**
Government Training and Development Quarterly (newsletter)

**Meetings:**
Annual meeting

**Other benefits of membership:**
NAGTAD Listserv

## 25

**Name of organization:**
**National Association for Industry-Education Cooperation (NAIEC)**

**Purpose:**
NAIEC is the national clearinghouse for information on industry involvement in education. The Association believes that industry has a central role to play in helping education reshape its total academic and vocational program in a coherent, systematic manner so that it is more responsive to the needs of both students (youth and adults) and employers. Therefore, the focus for the joint efforts of industry and education is continuing school improvement, preparation for work, and human resource/economic development.

**Contact information:**
National Association for Industry-Education Cooperation
235 Hendricks Blvd.
Buffalo, NY 14226-3304
716/834-7047
716/834-7047 (fax)
www2.Pcom.net/naiec

**Key officers/staff:**
President and CEO: Dr. Donald M. Clark

**Membership requirements:**
None

**Size of membership:**
1,180

**Annual dues:**
$35 (individual); $45 (council/chapter); $100 (institutional); $250–$1,000 (corporate, based on net earnings)

**Publications:**
Industry-Education Council: A Handbook
A Guide for Evaluating Industry-Sponsored Educational Materials
NAIEC Newsletter (bimonthly)
How to Plan a Community Resources Workshop: A Handbook
Independent Education Management Audit: A System Approach
plus other books and films

## 26

**Name of organization:**
**National Career Development Association (a division of American Counseling Association)**

**Purpose:**
To advance knowledge about career development and to improve career development practice.

**Contact information:**
National Career Development Association
4700 Reed Rd., Suite M
Columbus, OH 43220
888/326-1750
614/326-1750
614/326-1760 (fax)
www.ncda.org

**Key officers/staff:**
Executive Director: Juliet Miller

**Membership requirements:**
N/A

**Size of membership:**
4,500

**Annual dues:**
$45

**Publications:**
Career Development Quarterly
Career Development Newsletter
Adult Career Development
A Counselor's Guide to Career Assessment Instruments
The Internet: A Tool for Career Planning
Learning to Work: The NCDA Gallup Survey, Experiential Activities for Teaching, Career Counseling Classes, Facilitating Career Groups

plus other single publications and media

**Meetings:**

Annual conference

**Other benefits of membership:**

Professional development & continuing education opportunities, special interest groups, and exciting learning and networking organization.

## 27

**Name of organization:**

**National Society for Experiential Education (NSEE)**

**Purpose:**

NSEE is a national nonprofit organization which supports schools, colleges and universities, government agencies, organizations, and businesses in helping students learn through meaningful work and service experiences. The purpose of NSEE is to assist institutions and organizations in the area of internships, cooperative education, service-learning, field studies, and other forms of experiential education.

**Contact information:**

NSEE
1703 N. Beauregard St.
Alexandria, VA 22311-1714
703/933-0017
703/933-1053 (fax)
www.nsee.org

**Key officers/staff:**

Executive Director: in transition

**Size of membership:**

1,800

**Annual dues:**

$50 (student); $85 (individual); $325 (institutional); $750 (sustaining). Subject to change without notice

**Publications:**

Program Evaluation, Role of Service-Learning in Education Reform, Internship as Partnership: A Handbook for site supervisors, Critical Issues K-12 Service-Learning: Care Studies and Reflections. The Experienced Hand: A Student Manual for Making the Most of an Internship, Strengthening Experiential Education within Your Institution, "Legal Issues in Experiential Education" Resource Packet, Combining Service and Learning: A Resource Book for Community and Public Service, The NSEE Quarterly

**Meetings:**

Annual national conference

## 28

**Name of organization:**

**Ontario Society for Training and Development (OSTD)**

**Purpose:**

The Ontario Society for Training and Development is Canada's largest training organization representing more than 1,500 training and human resources development practitioners. Established in 1946, the Association acts as an advocate for Training in the training industry, establishes and maintains professional standards, and serves its membership by providing certification, educational programs, annual conferences and publications.

**Contact information:**

Ontario Society for Training and Development (OSTD)
80 Richmond St. West, Suite 508
Toronto, Ontario M5H 2A4
416/367-5900
416/367-1642 (fax)
www.ostd.ca

**Key officers/staff:**

Program Manager: Lee Weisser
Executive Director: Lynn Johnston
Manager of Membership Services: Christopher Sheedy

**Membership requirements:**

Interest in training and development

**Size of membership:**

1,500

**Annual dues:**

$165 (regular); $75 initiation fee for all new members

**Publications:**

Canadian Learning Journal
Training Competency Architecture & Toolkit

**Meetings:**

Annual Conference & Trade Show

**Other benefits of membership:**

Professional Certification Group Insurance Plans

## 29

**Name of organization:**

**The Organization Development Institute**

**Purpose:**

To promote a better understanding of and disseminate information about organization development to our members and the public. Organization development is defined as the knowledge and skill necessary to implement a program of planned change using behavioral science concepts for the purpose of building greater organizational effectiveness. A secondary effort of the Institute is to provide an up-to-date listing of resources available in the field of organization development. This includes providing information on people working or studying in the field, information on other networks and organizations in the field, and information on OD/OB academic programs. The organization has written an International OD code of ethics for the field as well as a written statement on knowledge and skill necessary for competence in the field. Also, the organization has developed criteria for accreditation of OD/OB academic programs.

**Contact information:**

The Organization Development Institute
Dr. Donald W. Cole, RODC
11234 Walnut Ridge Rd.
Chesterland, OH 44026
440/729-7419
440/729-9319 (fax)
http://members.aol.com/odinst

**Key officers/staff:**

Dr. Donald W. Cole, RODC

**Membership requirements:**

Interest in organization development

**Size of membership:**

500

**Annual dues:**

$110 (regular); $80 (student); $150 (professional consultant)

**Publications:**

Organizations & Change (monthly)
Organization Development Journal (quarterly)
International Registry of OD Professionals & The OD Handbook (annual)

**Meetings:**

Annual national OD conference (annual information exchange)
Annual OD conference (world congress)
Annual international, interorganizational conference on non-violent large systems change

**Other benefits of membership:**

Information on jobs and consulting assignments, publishing opportunities, Code of Ethics, traveling to places of international interest, "Outstanding OD Consultant of the Year" award, the "Outstanding Presentation by a Student" award, the "Outstanding OD Project of the Year" award, and the "Outstanding OD Article of the Year" award.

## 30

**Name of organization:**
**Organization Development Network**
**Purpose:**
To aid the growth and development of OD practitioners; to contribute to the empowerment of the OD field; to link practitioners and their work with the needs of the world.
**Contact information:**
Richard A. Ungerer (Executive Director)
Margaret Franks Hoyer (Administrator)
71 Valley St., Suite 301
South Orange, NJ 07079-2825
973/763-7337
973/763-7488 (fax)
www.odnetwork.org
**Key officers/staff:**
Executive Director: Richard A. Ungerer
Administrator: Margaret Franks Hoyer
**Membership requirements:**
None
**Size of membership:**
4,000
**Annual dues:**
$145 (individual)—call for other membership rates
**Publications:**
The OD Practitioner
Education Resource Directory
**Meetings:**
Annual national conference
**Other benefits of membership:**
OD Network Job Exchange, professional liability insurance, discounted conference fees

## 31

**Name of organization:**
**Society for Applied Learning Technology (SALT)**
**Contact information:**
SALT
50 Culpeper St.
Warrenton, VA 20186
800/457-6812
540/347-0055
540/349-3169 (fax)
www.salt.org

**Key officers/staff:**
President: Raymond G. Fox
**Membership requirements:**
$45
**Size of membership:**
925
**Annual dues:**
$45
**Publications:**
Newsletter
Journal of Educational Technology Systems
Journal of Instruction Delivery Systems
Journal of Interactive Instruction Development

## 32

**Name of organization:**
**Society for Human Resource Management (SHRM)**
**Purpose:**
SHRM is a 50-year-old society and is also a worldwide association of human resource professionals with approximately 470+ local chapters. SHRM provides education and information services, conferences and seminars, government and media representation, online services and publications to professionals and student members all over the world.
**Contact information:**
SHRM
1800 Duke St.
Alexandria, VA 22314-3499
800/283-SHRM
703/548-3440
703/836-0367 (fax)
www.shrm.org
**Key officers/staff:**
President & CEO:
Michael R. Losey
**Membership requirements:**
Must be in human resource field and dues
**Size of membership:**
130,000+ (470+ chapters nationally)
**Annual dues:**
$160 (national dues)
**Publications:**
HR Magazine (monthly)
HR News (monthly)
The SHRM Legal Report (quarterly)
Legislative Hotline
(call-in number: 703/548-3440)
**Meetings:**
Annual Conference
Employment Law & Legislative Conference
International Conference

Employment Management Association Conference
Workplace Diversity Conference
Leadership Conference
**Other benefits of membership:**
Consumer Financial Network (888/SHRM-CFN), SHRM online, Information Center, SHRM library, SHRM store (800/444-5006)

## 33

**Name of organization:**
**Society for Technical Communication (STC)**
**Purpose:**
STC is an organization dedicated to advancing the arts and sciences of technical communication. Our work involves making technical information available and understandable to those who need it. STC also promotes the public welfare by educating its members and industry about issues concerning technical communication. Mission statement: The mission of the STC is to improve the quality and effectiveness of technical communication for audiences worldwide.
**Contact information:**
Society for Technical Communication (STC)
901 N. Stuart St., Suite 904
Arlington, VA 22203-1822
703/522-4114
703/522-2075 (fax)
www.stc-va.org
**Key officers/staff:**
Executive Director: William C. Stolgitis
Membership Director: Christopher Ruck
**Size of membership:**
23,000
**Annual dues:**
Member: $110 ($110 dues plus one-time $15 enrollment fee); Student member: $40 (no enrollment fee)
**Publications:**
Technical Communication (STC's quarterly journal)
Intercom (the society's magazine)
Proceedings (contains papers presented at annual conference)
other publications include the membership directory (which includes the STC bylaws), STC's salary survey, and the society's annual report

**Meetings:**

Annual conference

**Other benefits of membership:**

Employment information offered by many STC chapters and on STC's Internet sites, scholarships awarded to full-time undergraduate and graduate students, research grants (scientific, literary, and educational), insurance plans available at rates lower than many individual plans. Other benefits include the opportunity to network with peers and the opportunity to keep up with important developments in the field of technical communication through seminars, lectures, workshops, international symposia, and the annual conference.

## 34

**Name of organization:**

**Society of Insurance Trainers & Educators**

**Purpose:**

To stimulate the growth and professional development of its members to the benefit of their respective insurance companies and the insurance business as a whole through research and the exchange of ideas related to education and training.

**Contact information:**

Society of Insurance Trainers and Educators
2120 Market St., #108
San Francisco, CA 94114
415/621-2830
415/621-0889 (fax)

**Key officers/staff:**

Executive Director: Lois A. Markovich, CPCU, AIM

**Membership requirements:**

Interest in insurance training and education

**Size of membership:**

820

**Annual dues:**

$90 (designee member); $60 (associate member); $25 (retiree); $45 (student)

**Publications:**

Insite newsletter (bimonthly)
Journal (semiannual)

**Meetings:**

Annual conference

**Other benefits of membership:**

regional conference, SITE resource network

# THE TRAINER'S ALMANAC

## SECTION 6.2

### TRAINING CONFERENCES

Conferences are one of the trainer's principal development opportunities, and, of course, there are many to choose from during the course of a year. If you plan your conference attendance passively and wait until a brochure catches your attention, you may miss opportunities or use up your conference attendance budget on an event that might not have addressed your needs. This Section 6.2 of *The Trainer's Almanac* solves this dilemma for you by giving you a full year's most relevant conferences at a glance both in the master calendar and in the detailed conference listings that follow it.

### What Is a Conference?

As we have done in Section 6.1 with professional organizations, here, too, we have selected entries that are national in scope and open to the public. Although many conferences are designed with a particular membership organization in mind, those listed here enjoy a nationwide and often global audience and participation from exhibitors and sponsors. Most conferences have both a member price and a general admission or public price of admission (call sponsor for more information if prices are not listed). Some of the conferences listed here have pre- or post-conference workshops and seminars; many have expo sections and exhibit halls for vendors and service providers, book sellers and manufacturers to display their wares and mingle with conference attendees. Many conferences feature recruiters and career development sessions and other resources for professional advancement.

We have chosen conferences that reflect the broadening interests of trainers, and that are held in well-equipped conference centers that facilitate learning. Many conferences listed here regularly attract thousands of participants. We have also selected conferences that are typically annual conferences; many are the flagship conference of the sponsoring organization. Section 6.2 features 58 conferences. Contact information on each conference is provided in the actual listing for each conference.

### Conference Calendar

Here we provide a complete "Calendar of Training Conferences," an extensive, full year's listing of conference dates by month. This calendar will help you identify which events are being held during some particular time period, and you can easily scan the cities to find conferences that will occur in locations most attractive and convenient for you.

# Training & Development Yearbook 2001 Trainer's Almanac
## 2001 Calendar of Training Conferences

| Date | Location | # | Event |
|---|---|---|---|
| | | | **January 2001** |
| Jan. 11–14 | Orlando, FL | 26 | *IAL Annual Conference on Accelerated Learning and Teaching: One World Learning* (International Alliance for Learning) |
| Jan. 21–23 | New Orleans, LA | 34 | *Professional Education Conference North America* (Meeting Professionals International (MPI)) |
| Jan. 22–24 | Ottawa, Canada | 22 | *27th Annual National Consultation on Career Development (NATCON)* (Counseling Foundation of Canada, University of Toronto) |
| | | | **February 2001** |
| Feb. 12–16 | Orlando, FL | 9 | *14th ASLET International Training Seminar and Law Enforcement Expo* (American Society for Law Enforcement Training) |
| Feb. 17–20 | Washington, DC | 4 | *ACE 83rd Annual Meeting* (American Council on Education) |
| | | | **March 2001** |
| Mar. 5–7 | Atlanta, GA | 32 | *TRAINING '01 Conference & Expo* (Lakewood Conferences/Bill Communications) |
| Mar. 16–20 | San Antonio, TX | 5 | *ACA World Conference* (American Counseling Association) |
| Mar. 19–21 | Washington, DC | 51 | *18th Annual Employment Law and Legislation Conference* (Society for Human Resource Management (SHRM)) |
| Mar. 26–30 | Chicago, IL | 11 | *Annual Spring Conference* (Association for Quality & Participation (APQC)) |
| March | Washington, DC | 1 | *TeleCon East* (Advance Star Communication) |
| March | Chicago, IL | 30 | *Creating & Launching Learning Portals* (International Quality & Productivity Center (IQPC)) |
| March | Los Angeles, CA | 37 | *Milken Institute 2001 Global Conference* (Milken Institute) |
| | | | **April 2001** |
| Apr. 1–4 | Las Vegas, NV | 24 | *Business Growth Imperatives: New Demons, New Solutions* (Human Resource Planning Society) |
| Apr. 1–4 | Chicago, IL | 53 | *International Conference* (Society for Human Resource Management (SHRM)) |
| Apr. 2–3 | Cambridge, MA | 48 | *Managing the Difficult Business Conversation* (Program on Negotiation, Harvard University Law School) |
| Apr. 8–10 | San Francisco, CA | 23 | *Distance Education & Training Council Annual Conference* (Distance Education & Training Council) |
| Apr. 8–10 | Paris, France | 35 | *Professional Education Congress, Europe* (Meeting Professionals International (MPI)) |
| Apr. 9–12 | San Francisco, CA | 31 | *Annual Conference & Expo* (International Society for Performance Improvement (ISPI)) |
| Apr. 18–20 | Anaheim, CA | 25 | *WBT Producer Conference & Expo* (Influent Technology Group) |

| | | | |
|---|---|---|---|
| Apr. 21–26 | Las Vegas, NV | 38 | *NAB 2001: Convergence Marketplace* (National Association of Broadcasters) |
| Apr. 28–May 2 | Porto Allegre, Brazil | 29 | *30th World Conference & Expo: New Frontiers of HRD* (International Federation of Training & Development Organizations (IFTDO)) |
| April | Bowling Green, OH | 15 | *2001 Best Practices in Leading Change Conference* (Bowling Green State University (EMOD) Program) |
| Spring | San Francisco, CA | 6 | *Global Human Resources Conference* (American Management Association (AMA) International) |
| Spring | San Antonio, TX | 52 | *EMA Conference & Expo* (Employment Management Association (EMA)/ Society for Human Resource Management (SHRM)) |
| Spring | Scottsdale, AZ | 58 | *Spring Roundtable* (Work in America Institute) |

**May 2001**

| | | | |
|---|---|---|---|
| Apr. 30–May 2 | Santa Clara, CA | 44 | *intranets 2001 expo: design, build, and manage your enterprise portal* (Online Inc.) |
| May 7–9 | Charlotte, NC | 8 | *ASQ 55th Annual Quality Congress & Exhibition* (American Society for Quality) |
| May 13–16 | Chicago. IL | 55 | *48th Annual Conference* (Society for Technical Communication) |
| May 20–23 | Philadelphia, PA | 39 | *2001 Annual Conference* (National Association of Workforce Development Professionals (NAWDP)) |
| May 22–25 | Chicago, IL | 46 | *31st Annual Info Exchange: What's New in OD and HRD* (Organization Development Institute) |
| May | Contact sponsor | 7 | *6th Knowledge Management Conference* (American Productivity & Quality Center (APQC)) |
| May | Greensboro, NC | 16 | *3rd Annual Friends of the Center Conference* (Center for Creative Leadership (CCL)) |
| May | New York, NY | 18 | *13th Annual Business Ethics Conference* (The Conference Board) |
| May | Las Vegas, NV | 20 | *Corporate Universities: Benchmarks for 2001* (Corporate University Xchange) |
| May | Nashville, TN | 56 | *SITE Annual Conference* (Society of Insurance Trainers & Educators) |

**June 2001**

| | | | |
|---|---|---|---|
| May 31–June 3 | Washington, DC | 41 | *16th Annual National Conference* (National Multicultural Institute) |
| June 3–7 | Orlando, FL | 12 | *International Conference & Exposition* (American Society for Training and Development (ASTD)) |
| June 14–17 | Las Vegas, NV | 27 | *InfoComm International* (International Communication Industries Association (ICIA)) |
| June 24–27 | San Francisco, CA | 50 | *Annual Conference & Exposition* (Society for Human Resource Management (SHRM)) |
| June 25–27 | Chicago, IL | 40 | *National Education Computing Conference* (National Education Computing Association (NECA)) |
| June | New York, NY | 19 | *Leadership Development Conference* (The Conference Board) |

**July 2001**

| | | | |
|---|---|---|---|
| July 16–21 | Vienna, Austria | 45 | *21st Annual Organization Development World Congress* (Organization Development Institute) |
| July 22–24 | Las Vegas, NV | 36 | *World Education Congress* (Meeting Professionals International) |

**August 2001**

| | | | |
|---|---|---|---|
| Aug. 8–10 | Madison, WI | 57 | *17th Annual Conference on Distance Teaching & Learning* (University of Wisconsin–Madison) |
| August | Arlington, VA | 49 | *Education Technology 2001* (Society for Applied Learning Technology (SALT)) |

**September 2001**

| | | | |
|---|---|---|---|
| Sept. 10–12 | Dallas, TX | 17 | *12th Annual International Conference on Work Teams (plus Team Fair)* (Center for the Study of Work Teams, University of North Texas) |
| Sept. 23–26 | Orlando, FL | 28 | *ICSA Annual Conference* (International Customer Service Association) |

**October 2001**

| | | | |
|---|---|---|---|
| Oct. 10–12 | Charlotte, NC | 14 | *ASTD TechKnowledge(sm) Conference & Exposition* (American Society for Training and Development (ASTD)) |
| October | Orlando, FL | 42 | *NSEE Annual National Conference* (National Society for Experiential Education) |
| October | Contact sponsor | 54 | *Workplace Diversity* (Society for Human Resource Management (SHRM)) |
| Fall | Contact sponsor | 13 | *National Leadership Conference* (American Society for Training and Development (ASTD)) |
| Fall | Chicago, IL | 21 | *CAEL 2001 International Conference* (Council for Adult and Experiential Learning) |

**November 2001**

| | | | |
|---|---|---|---|
| Nov. 7–10 | Atlanta, GA | 10 | *AECT National Convention & INCITE Exposition* (Association for Educational Communication & Technology) |
| Nov. 10–14 | Vancouver, BC | 47 | *ODN Annual Conference* (Organization Development Network) |
| Nov. 12–13 | Cambridge, MA | 48 | *Managing the Difficult Business Conversation* (Program on Negotiation, Harvard University Law School) |
| November | Contact sponsor | 3 | *50th Annual Adult Education Conference* (American Association for Adult & Continuing Education (AAACE)) |
| November | Orlando, FL | 33 | *TechLearn 2001* (The MASIE Center) |

**December 2001**

| | | | |
|---|---|---|---|
| Dec. 7–11 | Denver, CO | 43 | *NSDC Annual Conference* (National Staff Development Council) |
| December | Anaheim, CA | 2 | *TeleCon West* (Advance Star Communications) |

## 1

**Sponsor:**
　**Advance Star
　Communications**
**Title:**
　TeleCon East
**Dates:**
　March 2001
**Location:**
　Washington, DC
**Contact information:**
　Advance Star Communications
　131 West 1st St.
　Duluth, MN 55802
　　800/829-3400
　　218/723-9122 (fax)
　　www.teleconexpos.com
**Cost:**
　Contact sponsor
**Exhibits:**
　Yes

## 2

**Sponsor:**
　**Advance Star
　Communicatons**
**Title:**
　TeleCon West
**Dates:**
　December 2001
**Location:**
　Anaheim, CA
**Contact information:**
　Advance Star Communications
　131 West 1st St.
　Duluth, MN 55802
　　800/829-3400
　　218/723-9122 (fax)
　　www.teleconexpos.com
**Cost:**
　Contact sponsor
**Exhibits:**
　Yes

## 3

**Sponsor:**
　**American Association for
　Adult & Continuing
　Education (AAACE)**
**Title:**
　50th Annual Adult Education
　Conference
**Dates:**
　November 2001
**Location:**
　Contact sponsor
**Contact information:**
　AAACE
　1200 19th St., NW, Suite 300
　Washington, DC 20036
　　301/918-1913
　　www.albany.edu/ace

**Cost:**
　Early Bird: $325
　Regular: $450 (members)
**Exhibits:**
　Yes

## 4

**Sponsor:**
　**American Council on
　Education**
**Title:**
　ACE 83rd Annual Meeting
**Dates:**
　February 17–20, 2001
**Location:**
　Marriott Wardman Park,
　Washington, DC
**Contact information:**
　American Council on Education
　1 DuPont Circle, NW, Suite 800
　Washington, DC 20036
　　202/939-9410
　　202/833-4760 (fax)
　　www.acenet.edu
**Cost:**
　Contact sponsor
**Exhibits:**
　Yes

## 5

**Sponsor:**
　**American Counseling
　Association**
**Title:**
　ACA World Conference
**Dates:**
　March 16–20, 2001
**Location:**
　San Antonio, TX
**Contact information:**
　American Counseling Association
　5999 Stevenson Ave.
　Alexandria, VA 22304
　　800/347-6647
　　703/823-9800
　　703/823-0252 (fax)
　　www.counseling.org
**Cost:**
　Contact sponsor
**Exhibits:**
　Yes

## 6

**Sponsor:**
　**American Management
　Association (AMA)
　International**
**Title:**
　Global Human Resources
　Conference
**Dates:**
　Spring 2001

**Location:**
　San Francisco, CA
**Contact information:**
　American Management Association
　　(AMA) International
　1601 Broadway
　New York, NY 10019-7420
　　212/586-8100
　　212/903-8329 (fax)
　　www.amanet.org
**Cost:**
　Contact sponsor
**Exhibits:**
　Yes

## 7

**Sponsor:**
　**American Productivity &
　Quality Center (APQC)**
**Title:**
　6th Knowledge Management
　Conference
**Dates:**
　May 2001
**Location:**
　Contact sponsor
**Contact information:**
　APQC
　123 North Post Oak Lane, Third
　　Floor
　Houston, TX 77024
　　800/776-9676
　　Outside U.S. 713/681-4020
　　713/681-8578 (fax)
　　www.apqc.org
**Cost:**
　Contact sponsor
**Exhibits:**
　No

## 8

**Sponsor:**
　**American Society for Quality
　(ASQ)**
**Title:**
　ASQ 55th Annual Quality Congress
　and Exhibition
**Dates:**
　May 7–9, 2001
**Location:**
　Charlotte Convention Center
　Charlotte, NC
**Contact information:**
　American Society for Quality (ASQ)
　Shirley Krentz
　611 East Wisconsin Ave., P.O. Box
　　3005
　Milwaukee, WI 53201-3005
　　800/248-1946 (customer
　　　service)
　　414/272-8575
　　414/272-1734 (fax)
　　www.asq.org

Cost:
    Contact sponsor
Exhibits:
    Yes

## 9

Sponsor:
    **American Society for Law
    Enforcement Training
    (AShLET)**
Title:
    14th AShLET International
    Training Seminar and Law
    Enforcement Expo
Dates:
    February 12–16, 2001
Location:
    Hyatt Orlando-Kissimmee
    Orlando, FL
Contact information:
    Loretta Smith
    AShLET
    121 North Court St.
    Frederick, MD 21701
        301/668-9466
        301/668-9482 (fax)
        www.ashlet.org
Cost:
    For new members:
    $375 (before 9/17/00)
    $400 (before 1/1/01)
    $450 (after that)
Exhibits:
    Yes

## 10

Sponsor:
    **Association for Educational
    Communications and
    Technology (AECT)**
Title:
    AECT National Convention &
    INCITE Exposition
Dates:
    November 7–10, 2001
Location:
    Atlanta, GA
Contact information:
    AECT
    1800 North Stonelake Dr.
    Bloomington, IN 47404
        812/335-7675
        812/335-7678 (fax)
        www.aect.org
Cost:
    Contact sponsor
Exhibits:
    Contact sponsor

## 11

Sponsor:
    **Association for Quality and
    Participation (AQP)**

Title:
    Annual Spring Conference
Dates:
    March 26–30, 2001
Location:
    Chicago, IL
Contact information:
    Association for Quality and
        Participation (AQP)
    801-B West 8th St., Suite 501
    Cincinnati, OH 45203
        800/733-3310
        513/381-1959
        513/381-0070 (fax)
        www.aqp.org
Cost:
    Approximately $1,000; Contact
        sponsor for discount.
Exhibits:
    Yes

## 12

Sponsor:
    **ASTD**
Title:
    International Conference and
    Exposition
Dates:
    June 3–7, 2001
Location:
    Orlando, FL
Contact information:
    ASTD
    1640 King St., Box 1443
    Alexandria, VA 22313
        703/683-8100
        703/683-8103 (fax) or
        703/683-1523 (customer
            service fax)
        www.astd.org
Cost:
    Contact sponsor
Exhibits:
    Yes

## 13

Sponsor:
    **ASTD**
Title:
    National Leadership Conference
Dates:
    Fall 2001
Location:
    Contact sponsor
Contact information:
    ASTD
    1640 King St., Box 1443
    Alexandria, VA 22313
        703/683-8100
        703/683-8103 (fax) or
        703/683-1523 (customer
            service fax)
        www.astd.org

Cost:
    Contact sponsor
Exhibits:
    Yes

## 14

Sponsor:
    **ASTD**
Title:
    ASTD TechKnowledge[SM]
    Conference & Exposition
Dates:
    October 10–12, 2001
Location:
    Charlotte, NC
Contact information:
    ASTD
    1640 King St., Box 1443
    Alexandria, VA 22313
        703/683-8100
        703/683-8103 (fax) or
        703/683-1523 (customer
            service fax)
        www.astd.org
Cost:
    Contact sponsor
Exhibits:
    Yes

## 15

Sponsor:
    **Bowling Green State
    University**
Title:
    Best Practices in Leading Change
    Conference
Dates:
    April 2001
Location:
    Bowling Green, OH
Contact information:
    Bowling Green State University
    EMOD Program
    40 College Park
    Bowling Green, OH 43403
        419/372-8181
        419/372-8667 (fax)
        www.cba.bgsu.edu/html/
            mod.html
Cost:
    $495
Exhibits:
    No

## 16

Sponsor:
    **Center for Creative
    Leadership**
Title:
    3rd Annual Friends of the Center
    Conference
Dates:
    May 2001

Location:
Greensboro, NC
Contact information:
Center for Creative Leadership
Client Services
P.O. Box 26300
Greensboro, NC 27438
336/545-2810
336/282-3284 (fax)
www.ccl.org
Cost:
$900
Exhibits:
No

## 17

Sponsor:
**Center for the Study
of Work Teams**
Title:
12th Annual International
Conference on Work Teams
(plus Team Fair)
Dates:
September 10–12, 2001
Location:
Fort Worth, TX
Contact information:
Charla Friday
Center for the Study of Work Teams
University of North Texas
P.O. Box 311280
Denton, TX 76203
940/565-3096
940/565-4806 (fax)
www.workteam@UNT.edu
Cost:
$995; Early Registration Dis-
counted Prices available
Exhibits:
Yes

## 18

Sponsor:
**The Conference Board**
Title:
13th Annual Business Ethics
Conference
Dates:
May 2001
Location:
New York, NY
Contact information:
The Conference Board
P.O. Box 4026
Church Street Station
New York, NY 10261
212/339-0345
212/836-9740 (fax)
www.conference-board.org/
ethics.htm

Cost:
$1,625
$810 not-for-profit organizations
Exhibits:
No

## 19

Sponsor:
**The Conference Board**
Title:
Leadership Development
Conference
Dates:
June 2001
Location:
New York, NY
Contact information:
The Conference Board, Inc.
P.O. Box 4026
Church Street Station
New York, NY 10261
212/339-0345
212/836-9740 (fax)
www.conference-board.org
Cost:
$1,525
Exhibits:
No

## 20

Sponsor:
**Corporate University Xchange**
Title:
Corporate Universities:
Benchmarks for 2001
Dates:
May 2001
Location:
Las Vegas, NV
Contact information:
Corporate University Xchange
381 Park Avenue South
New York, NY 10016
800/946-1210
212/213-8621 (fax)
www.corpu.com
Cost:
$1,295 plus $649 for pre- and
post-conference workshop
Exhibits:
Yes

## 21

Sponsor:
**Council for Adult &
Experiential Learning (CAEL)**
Title:
CAEL 2001 International
Conference
Dates:
Fall 2001
Location:
Chicago, IL

Contact information:
CAEL
55 East Monroe
Suite 1930
Chicago, IL 60603
312/499-2600
312/499-2601 (fax)
www.cael.org
Cost:
Contact sponsor
Exhibits:
Yes

## 22

Co-Sponsors:
**The Counseling Foundation of
Canada, Human Resources
Development Canada, and
Career Centre, University of
Toronto**
Title:
27th Annual National
Consultation on Career
Development (NATCON)
(Colloque National touchant le
développement de carrière)
(CONAT)
Dates:
January 22–24, 2001
Location:
Government Conference Center
Ottawa, Canada
Contact information:
NATCON Office
University of Toronto
Career Centre
214 College St.
Toronto, Ontario M5T 2Z9 Canada
416/978-8011
416/978-2271 (fax)
natcon-conet.careers.utoronto.ca
Cost:
$190 (by 12/4/00)
$230 (after 12/4/00)
$96 (daily)
$80 (full-time student)
Exhibits:
Yes (24 exhibitors)

## 23

Sponsor:
**Distance Education and
Training Council**
Title:
Distance Education and Training
Council Annual Conference
Dates:
April 8–10, 2001
Location:
San Francisco, CA

Contact information:
Distance Education and Training
Council
1601 18th St., N.W.
Washington, DC 20009-2529
202/234-5100
202/332-1386 (fax)
www.detc.org
**Cost:**
Contact sponsor
**Exhibits:**
No

## 24

**Sponsor:**
**The Human Resource
Planning Society**
**Title:**
The Business Growth Imperative:
New Demons, New Solutions
**Dates:**
April 1–4, 2001
**Location:**
Las Vegas, NV
**Contact information:**
The Human Resource Planning
Society
317 Madison Ave., Suite 1509
New York, NY 10017
212/490-6387
212/682-6851 (fax)
www.hrps.org
**Cost:**
Contact sponsor
**Exhibits:**
No

## 25

**Sponsor:**
**Influent Technology Group**
**Title:**
WBT Producer Conference & Expo
**Dates:**
April 18–20, 2001
**Location:**
Anaheim, CA
**Contact information:**
Kimberly Pais
Influent Technology Group
498 Concord St.
Framingham, MA 01702-2357
888/333-9088
508/872-2299 (fax)
508/872-9088, Ext. 348 (Kim)
www.influent.com
**Cost:**
$1,095; discounts available
**Exhibits:**
Yes

## 26

**Sponsor:**
**International Alliance for
Learning (IAL)**

**Title:**
IAL Annual Conference on
Accelerated Learning & Teaching:
One World Learning
**Dates:**
January 11–14, 2001
**Location:**
Orlando, FL
**Contact information:**
IAL
P.O. Box 26175
Colorado Springs, CO 80936
800/426-2989
719/638-6153 (fax)
www.ialearn.org
**Cost:**
Contact sponsor
**Exhibits:**
Yes

## 27

**Sponsor:**
**International Communications
Industries Association (ICIA)**
**Title:**
InfoComm International
**Dates:**
June 14–17, 2001
**Location:**
Las Vegas, NV
**Contact information:**
ICIA
11242 Waples Mills Rd., Suite 200
Fairfax, VA 22030
703/273-7200
703/278-8082 (fax)
www.icia.org
www.infocom.org
**Cost:**
Contact sponsor
**Exhibits:**
Yes

## 28

**Sponsor:**
**International Customer
Service Association (ICSA)**
**Title:**
ICSA Annual Conference
**Dates:**
September 23–26, 2001
**Location:**
Orlando, FL
**Contact information:**
International Customer Service
Association (ICSA)
401 N. Michigan Ave.
Chicago, IL 60611
800/360-ICSA (4272)
312/245-1084 (fax)
Pam Bowerman:
312/644-6610, Ext. 4743
www.icsa.com

**Cost:**
Contact sponsor
**Exhibits:**
Yes

## 29

**Sponsor:**
**International Federation of
Training and Development
Organizations (IFTDO)**
**Title:**
30th World Conference & Expo:
New Frontiers of HRD
**Dates:**
April 28–May 2, 2001
**Location:**
Porto Allegre, Brazil
**Contact information:**
Dr. David A. Waugh, Secretary
General
IFTDO
1800 Duke St.
Alexandria, VA 22314
703/535-6011
703/836-0367 (fax)
www.iftdo.org
**Cost:**
Contact sponsor
**Exhibits:**
Yes

## 30

**Sponsor:**
**International Quality &
Productivity Center (IQPC)**
**Title:**
Creating & Launching Learning
Portals
**Dates:**
March 2001
**Location:**
Chicago, IL
**Contact information:**
International Quality &
Productivity Center
150 Clove Rd., P.O. Box 401
Little Falls, NJ 07424
800/882-8684
973/256-0205 (fax)
www.iqpc.com
**Cost:**
$1,495 or $2,295 including two
workshops
**Exhibits:**
Yes

## 31

**Sponsor:**
**International Society for
Performance Improvement
(ISPI)**
**Title:**
Annual Conference & Expo

**Dates:**
April 9–12, 2001
**Location:**
San Francisco, CA
**Contact information:**
ISPI
1300 L St., NW, Suite 1250
Washington, DC 20005-4107
202/408-7969
202/408-7972 (fax)
www.ispi.org
**Cost:**
Contact sponsor
**Exhibits:**
No

## 32

**Sponsor:**
**Lakewood Conferences/**
**Bill Communications**
**(Minneapolis)**
**Title:**
Training Conference & Expo
**Dates:**
March 5–7, 2001
**Location:**
Atlanta, GA
**Contact information:**
Shannon Lynch
Lakewood Conferences
Dulles International Airport
P.O. Box 17413
Washington, DC 20041
703/318-0300
703/318-7568
800/654–8873 (fax)
www.lakewoodconferences.com
**Cost:**
Contact sponsor
**Exhibits:**
Contact sponsor

## 33

**Sponsor:**
**The MASIE Center**
**Title:**
TechLearn 2001
**Dates:**
November 2001
**Location:**
Orlando, FL
**Contact information:**
The MASIE Center
P.O. Box 397
Saratoga Springs, NY 12866
518/587-3522
518/587-3276
www.masie.com
**Cost:**
$995
**Exhibits:**
Yes

## 34

**Sponsor:**
**Meeting Professionals**
**International (MPI)**
**Title:**
Professional Education Conference,
North America
**Dates:**
January 21–23, 2001
**Location:**
New Orleans, LA
**Contact information:**
Eric Johnson or Shanna Dixon
Meeting Professionals International
(MPI)
4455 LBJ Frwy., Suite 1200
Dallas, TX 75244-5903
972/702-3000
972/702-3030 (Shanna)
972/702-3095 (fax)
www.mpiweb.org
**Cost:**
Contact sponsor
**Exhibits:**
Contact sponsor

## 35

**Sponsor:**
**Meeting Professionals**
**International**
**Title:**
Professional Education Congress
(Europe)
**Dates:**
April 8–10, 2001
**Location:**
Paris, France
**Contact information:**
Eric Johnson or Shanna Dixon
Meeting Professionals International
4455 LBJ Frwy., Suite 1200
Dallas, TX 75244-5903
972/702-3000
972/702-3030 (Shanna)
972/702-3095 (fax)
www.mpiweb.org
**Cost:**
Contact sponsor
**Exhibits:**
No

## 36

**Sponsor:**
**Meeting Professionals**
**International**
**Title:**
World Education Congress
**Dates:**
July 22–24, 2001
**Location:**
Las Vegas, NV
**Contact information:**
Eric Johnson or Shanna Dixon
Meeting Professionals International

4455 LBJ Frwy., Suite 1200
Dallas, TX 75244-5903
972/702-3000
972/702-3030 (Shanna)
972/702-3095 (fax)
www.mpiweb.org
**Cost:**
Contact sponsor
**Exhibits:**
Yes

## 37

**Sponsor:**
**Milken Institute**
**Title:**
Milken Institute 2001 Global
Conference
**Dates:**
March 2001
**Location:**
Los Angeles, CA
**Contact information:**
Milken Institute
310/998-2605
www.milken-inst.org
**Cost:**
$950
**Exhibits:**
Contact sponsor; for corporate
sponsorships phone 310/998-2632

## 38

**Sponsor:**
**National Association of**
**Broadcasters**
**Title:**
NAB 2001 The Convergence
Marketplace
**Dates:**
April 21–26, 2001
**Location:**
Las Vegas, NV
**Contact information:**
National Association of Broadcasters
1771 N St., NW
Washington, DC 20036-2891
202/429-5300
202/429-3922 (fax)
www.nab.org
**Cost:**
Contact sponsor
**Exhibits:**
Yes

## 39

**Sponsor:**
**National Association of**
**Workforce Development**
**Professionals (NAWDP)**
**(formerly Partnership for**
**Training and Employment**
**Careers)**
**Title:**
2001 Annual Conference

**Dates:**
May 20–23, 2001
**Location:**
Philadelphia, PA
**Contact information:**
National Association of Workforce
Development Professionals
(NAWDP)
1620 I Street, NW, Suite LL (lower
level) 30
Washington, DC 20006
202/887-6120
202/887-8216 (fax)
www.nawdp.org
**Cost:**
Contact sponsor
**Exhibits:**
Yes

## 40

**Sponsor:**
**National Educational
Computing Association
(formerly International
Society for Technology in
Education)**
**Title:**
National Education Computing
Conference
**Dates:**
June 25–27, 2001
**Location:**
Chicago, IL
**Contact information:**
Donella Ingham or Jessica Truhan
NECC/NECA
1244 Walnut St., Suite A
Eugene, OR 97403-2081
541/346-2834
541/201-9995
541/346-2565 (fax)
www.neccsite.org
**Cost:**
Contact sponsor
**Exhibits:**
Yes

## 41

**Sponsor:**
**National MultiCultural
Institute**
**Title:**
16th Annual National Conference
**Dates:**
May 31–June 3, 2001
**Location:**
Washington, DC
**Contact information:**
National MultiCultural Institute
3000 Connecticut Avenue, NW,
Suite 438
Washington, DC 20008

202/483-0700, ext 227
202/483-5233
www.nmci.org
**Cost:**
$750 or $900
**Exhibits:**
Yes

## 42

**Sponsor:**
**National Society for
Experiential Education**
**Title:**
NSEE Annual National Conference
**Dates:**
October 2001
**Location:**
Orlando, FL
**Contact information:**
NSEE
1703 N. Beauregard St.
Alexandria, VA 22311-1714
703/933-0017
703/933-1053 (fax)
www.nsee.org
**Cost:**
Contact sponsor
**Exhibits:**
Yes

## 43

**Sponsor:**
**National Staff Development
Council (NSDC)**
**Title:**
NSDC Annual Conference
**Dates:**
December 7–11, 2001
**Location:**
Denver, CO
**Contact information:**
Shirley Havens
National Staff Development
Council (NSDC)
P.O. Box 240
Oxford, OH 45056
513/523-6029
513/523-0638 (fax)
www.nsdc.org
**Cost:**
Approximately $600
**Exhibits:**
Yes

## 44

**Sponsor:**
**Online Inc.**
**Title:**
intranets 2001 expo: design, build,
and manage your enterprise portal
**Dates:**
April 30–May 2, 2001
**Location:**
Santa Clara, CA

**Contact information:**
Online Inc.
213 Danbury Road
Wilton, CT 06897
800/248-8466, ext 500
203/761-1444
www.intranets2001.com
**Cost:**
$595, pre- and post-conference
seminars at $195 each
**Exhibits:**
Yes

## 45

**Sponsor:**
**The Organization
Development Institute**
**Title:**
21st Annual OD World Congress
**Dates:**
July 16–21, 2001
**Location:**
a castle outside Vienna, Austria
**Contact information:**
The Organization Development
Institute
Dr. Donald W. Cole, RODC
11234 Walnut Ridge Rd.
Chesterland, OH 44026
440/729-7419
440/729-9319 (fax)
http://members.aol.com/odinst
**Cost:**
Approximately $230 (members);
$290 (non-members)
**Exhibits:**
Contact sponsor

## 46

**Sponsor:**
**The Organization
Development Institute**
**Title:**
31st Annual Information
Exchange: What's New in OD
and HRD
**Dates:**
May 22–25, 2001
**Location:**
Hickory Ridge Center
Near Chicago, IL
**Contact information:**
The Organization Development
Institute
Dr. Donald W. Cole, RODC
11234 Walnut Ridge, Rd.
Chesterland, OH 44026
440/729-7419
440/729-9319 (fax)
http://members.aol.com/odinst
**Cost:**
Approximately $230 (members);
$290 (non-members)

Exhibits:
  Contact sponsor

## 47

Sponsor:
  **Organization Development Network**
Title:
  ODN Annual Conference
Dates:
  November 10–14, 2001
Location:
  Vancouver, BC
Contact information:
  Organization Development
    Network
  71 Valley St., Suite 301
  South Orange, NJ 07079-2825
    973/763-7337
    973/763-7488 (fax)
    www.odnet.org
Cost:
  Contact sponsor
Exhibits:
  Yes

## 48

Sponsor:
  **The Program on Negotiation at Harvard Law School**
Title:
  Managing the Difficult Business
  Conversation
Dates:
  April 2–3, 2001
  November 12–13, 2001
Location:
  Cambridge, MA
Contact information:
  Center for Management Research
  55 William St., Suite 210
  Wellesley, MA 02481
    781/239-1111
    781/239-1546 (fax)
    pon.execseminars.com
Cost:
  Contact sponsor
Exhibits:
  No

## 49

Sponsor:
  **Society for Applied Learning Technology (SALT)**
Title:
  Education Technology 2001
Dates:
  August 2001
Location:
  Arlington, VA
Contact information:
  SALT
  50 Culpeper St.
  Warrenton, VA 20186

  800/457-6812
  540/347-0055
  540/349-3169 (fax)
  www.salt.org
Cost:
  Contact sponsor
Exhibits:
  No

## 50

Sponsor:
  **Society for Human Resource Management (SHRM)**
Title:
  Annual Conference and
  Exposition
Dates:
  June 24–27, 2001
Location:
  San Francisco, CA
Contact information:
  SHRM
  1800 Duke St.
  Alexandria, VA 22314
    703/548-3440
    703/836-0367 (fax)
    www.shrm.org
Cost:
  Contact sponsor
Exhibits:
  Yes

## 51

Sponsor:
  **Society for Human Resource Management (SHRM)**
Title:
  18th Annual Employment Law &
  Legislative Conference
Dates:
  March 19–21, 2001
Location:
  Washington, DC
Contact information:
  SHRM
  1800 Duke St.
  Alexandria, VA 22314
    703/548-3440
    703/836-0367 (fax)
    www.shrm.org
Cost:
  Contact sponsor
Exhibits:
  No

## 52

Sponsor:
  **Society for Human Resource Management (SHRM)**
Title:
  EMA Conference & Exposition
  (Employment Management
  Association)

Dates:
  Spring 2001
Location:
  San Antonio, TX
Contact information:
  SHRM
  1800 Duke St.
  Alexandria, VA 22314
    703/548-3440
    703/836-0367 (fax)
    www.shrm.org
Cost:
  Contact sponsor
Exhibits:
  Contact sponsor

## 53

Sponsor:
  **Society for Human Resource Management (SHRM)**
Title:
  International Conference
Dates:
  April 1–4, 2001
Location:
  Chicago, IL
Contact information:
  SHRM
  1800 Duke St.
  Alexandria, VA 22314
    703/548-3440
    703/836-0367 (fax)
    www.shrm.org
Cost:
  Contact sponsor
Exhibits:
  Yes

## 54

Sponsor:
  **Society for Human Resource Management (SHRM)**
Title:
  Workplace Diversity
Dates:
  October 2001
Location:
  TBA
Contact information:
  SHRM
  1800 Duke St.
  Alexandria, VA 22314
    800/283-SHRM
    703/548-3440
    703/836-0367 (fax)
    www.shrm.org
Cost:
  Contact sponsor
Exhibits:
  Yes

## 55

Sponsor:
**Society for Technical
Communication**
Title:
48th Annual Conference
Dates:
May 13–16, 2001
Location:
Chicago, IL
Contact information:
Society for Technical
Communication
901 North Stuart St.,
Suite 904
Arlington, VA 22203-1854
703/522-4114
703/522-2075 (fax)
www.stc-va.org
Cost:
Contact sponsor
Exhibits:
Contact sponsor

## 56

Sponsor:
**Society of Insurance Trainers
& Educators**
Title:
SITE Annual Conference
Dates:
May 2001
Location:
Nashville, TN
Contact information:
Society of Insurance Trainers and
Educators
2120 Market St., #108
San Francisco, CA 94114
415/621-2830
415/621-0889 (fax)
Cost:
Contact sponsor
Exhibits:
Yes

## 57

Sponsor:
**University of Wisconsin–
Madison**
Title:
17th Annual Conference
on Distance Teaching and
Learning
Dates:
August 8–10, 2001
Location:
Madison, WI
Contact information:
Dr. Christine Olgren, Conference
Manager
University of Wisconsin–Madison
1050 University Ave.
Room B-136
Lathrop Hall
Madison, WI 53706
608/262-8530
608/265-7848 (fax)
www.uwex.edu/disted/
conference
Cost:
Approximately $295
Exhibits:
Yes
*Also*: Pre- and post-conference
workshops

## 58

Sponsor:
**Work in America Institute**
Title:
Spring Roundtable
Dates:
Spring 2001
Location:
Scottsdale, AZ
Contact information:
Work in America Institute
700 White Plains Rd.
Scarsdale, NY 10583
914/472-9600
914/472-9606 (fax)
www.workinamerica.org
Cost:
$1,850
Exhibits:
Yes

# THE TRAINER'S ALMANAC

## SECTION 6.3

## WORLDWIDE CONFERENCE CENTERS

"Doing the conference" has become a favorite professional growth activity for more and more professionals at all levels. The big national conferences continue to attract record numbers of attendees, and the business of creating attractive and effective learning spaces to host the crowds is a competitive challenge. In Section 6.3 of *The Trainer's Almanac* we give you a state-by-state and international listing of conference centers, including details about accommodations, meeting facilities, and conference services.

### Growth Reflects Current Trends

The continuing trend this year of outsourcing and the lingering effects of widespread downsizing have led to a booming business in training conferences. The conference experience has become a kind of "one stop shopping center" for staff who still need training and an infusion of the latest information as well as for consultants and vendors who need a venue to display and advertise their services and products. Corporate training centers, eager to bring in some more revenue and share their expertise, have now often opened their doors to the public and to other companies. The practice in recent years of benchmarking best practices, and the universal need for professionals to get together socially and exchange ideas have also spurred trainers to attend conferences. University conference centers have sought more business from corporations and agencies, independent campus-like conference centers—even mansions, historic sites, country houses, and castles—have become a conference business of their own, and hotels have continued to beef up their facilities and hired conference planning staff to provide state-of-the-art spaces and services to attract trainers and trainees. As we enter year 2001, conference trends include: more satellite links, videoconferencing, networked PCs, international phone lines, modems, data ports, ergonomic furniture, printing, food, and travel services.

### A Set-up for Learning

The conference has always been an excellent vehicle for individual learning within a large group setting. Today's drive for excellence through the practice of benchmarking and the concept of life-long learning, our appetites for travel and networking with colleagues, and the impetus of frequent flyer miles and credit card bonus points have all also helped to push us toward conference-going. With smaller corporate training department staffs and a growing proliferation of training entrepreneurs, companies have found that the conference experience can deliver a lot of bang for the training buck. Public-private partnering of all sorts and an awareness of the need to assemble the building blocks of a "learning organization" bring people together to learn from each other.

### Wide Choice in Public Facilities

The International Association of Conference Centers (IACC), founded 20 years ago with 22 members, now includes more than 400 member conference facilities worldwide. You can find out more about them on IACC's Web page at *www.iacconline.org*. In our listing here, we have edited IACC's membership list to eliminate the centers that are private or for use of a single company's employees. The conference centers listed here, with permission of the International Association of Conference Centers (IACC), are from the current *Global Membership Directory*. More information about the association and about any individual center listed here is available from Steve Smith, Director of Communications, or Tom Bolman, Executive Vice President, International Association of Conference Centers (IACC), 243 North Lindbergh Blvd., St. Louis, MO 63141, telephone 314/993-8575 or on IACC's Website, *www.iacconline*. Conference centers in the following list are presented in alphabetical order by state, followed by conference centers in Canada, South America, Europe, Australia, Africa, and Asia. In the last year, IACC has had 13 new global centers and 29 new U.S. centers join its membership. Those listed here are open to the public. All have recreation facilities. Contact the center for specifics.

## ALABAMA

### Auburn University Hotel and Conference Center

**Address** 241 South College Street, Auburn, AL 36849-5645 **Phone** (800) 2AUBURN (334) 821-8200 **Fax** (334) 844-4725

**Accommodations** 248 rooms (5 handicap accessible).

**Meeting Facilities** 16 meeting rooms with maximum capacity of 700.

**Services** Full-range A/V equipment; satellite uplink and downlink capabilities; computer lab; faculty expertise identification; conference management services; and complete program planning.

### The Legends at Capitol Hill Conference and Golf Resort

**Address** 2 North Jackson Street, Montgomery, AL 36104 **Phone** (334) 223-5793 **Fax** (334) 223-5797

**Accommodations** 90 guest rooms, 74 single rooms, 2 8-bedroom villas.

**Meeting Facilities** 10 meeting rooms.

**Services** None listed.

## ARIZONA

### Tempe Mission Palms Hotel and Conference Center

**Address** 60 E. Fifth Street, Tempe, AZ 85281 **Phone** (887) 784-1748 and (408) 894-1400 **Fax** (480) 968-7677

**Accommodations** 303 sleeping rooms; phones with voice mail and lines for PC usage.

**Meeting Facilities** 14 meeting rooms with 30,000 sq. ft. of space. Outdoor rooftop terrace with fireplace. Business center, ballroom, executive boardroom.

**Services** ISDN lines for video conferencing and Internet access. Wired for fiber optic; data ports in every meeting room.

### YWCA of the USA Leadership Development Center

**Address** 9440 North 25th Avenue, Phoenix, AZ 85021 **Phone** (602) 944-0569 **Fax** (602) 997-5112

**Accommodations** Close to major hotels: Sheraton, Marriott, Holiday Inn, and the Wyndhams.

**Meeting Facilities** 52,000 sq. ft. training/conference/meeting/ banquet facility with 22 meeting spaces; 2 outdoor classroom areas; 2 auditoriums; 2,500 sq. ft. fitness area with hardwood floors, mirrored wall, showers and lockers.

**Services** Full media services; TV studio and teleconferencing capabilities. Customized meeting packages, professional conference planners. Outdoor classrooms.

## ARKANSAS

### University of Arkansas Center for Continuing Education

**Address** 2 University Center, Fayetteville, AR 72701 **Phone** (501) 575-3604 **Fax** (501) 575-7232

**Accommodations** 236 rooms at adjacent Hilton Hotel.

**Meeting Facilities** 400-theater and 70-theater seat auditoriums; 11 conference rooms seating 650 lecture style, or 400 classroom style.

**Services** Professional staff meets a full range of conference/meeting needs. Complete A/V production facilities including satellite teleconferencing.

### Winrock International Conference Center

**Address** 38 Winrock Drive, Morrilton, AR 72110 **Phone** (501) 727-5435 **Fax** (501) 727-5242

**Accommodations** 35 single or 40 double occupancy rooms

**Meeting Facilities** 4 large meeting rooms seating up to 250; 4 breakout rooms seating 10–16 persons.

**Services** Conference Service Department handles planning and on-site meeting coordination. Basic A/V equipment provided.

## CALIFORNIA

### Chaminade Executive Conference Center

**Address** One Chaminade Lane, Santa Cruz, CA 95065 **Phone** (800) 283-6569 **Fax** (408) 476-4798

**Accommodations** 152 rooms showcasing mountain and forest views; Air-conditioned rooms offer luxury accommodations including room service; 10 parlor suites with conference table and wet bar.

**Meeting Facilities** 12 meeting rooms (10 rooms with windows). The largest "Santa Cruz Room" is 2,600 sq. ft. A/V data control center.

Included in CMP: Standard A/V package (25" monitor and VCR, 16mm movie projector, 35 mm slide projector, overhead projector, flip chart with marker or white board with marker, podium, microphone).

New Business Center; conference concierge for on-site needs; fax/copy services; typing; telephone; messages; personal conference coordinators for planning details; professional A/V technicians on site.

Santa Cruz Room holds 20 8' × 10' booths. Executive Fitness Center holds 45 8' tabletop displays.

**Services** Full guest services staff, concierge and free valet parking. Two phones in each room—one modem-compatible. Gift shop.

### Davidson Executive Conference Center

**Address** 3415 S. Figueroa St., Los Angeles, CA 90089-0871 **Phone** (213) 740-5956 **Fax** (213) 740-9366 **e-mail** confrnce@usc.edu

**Accommodations** Rooms for up to 4,000 guests from May through August.

**Meeting Facilities** Newly renovated state-of-the-art center; 8 rooms with breakout capabilities, accommodating up to 400; Ergonomically designed seating with writing tables.

**Services** Concierge, business center with PC & Macintosh workstations, World Wide Web access, e-mail forwarding. Daily newspapers, parcel and postal services, self-parking adjacent to center. Satellite uplink, videoconferencing, credit card phone and self-fax capability, USC bookstore, gift department services.

### The Hayes Mansion Conference Center

**Address** 200 Edenvale Ave., San Jose, CA 95136 **Phone** (408) 362-3200; (800) 420-3200 **Fax** (408) 362-2388

**Accommodations** 135 guest rooms and suites, work/study areas with multiple phone lines, modems, voice mail, in-room safes. Historic 1905 landmark.

**Meeting Facilities** 15 meeting rooms, 15,000 sq. ft. with state-of-the-art

A/V, telecommunications, "help button" services.

**Services** Video conferencing, teleconferencing, networked computing, closed-circuit TV, secretarial services, notary public.

### Kellogg West Conference Center

**Address** 3801 W. Temple Boulevard, Bldg. 76, Pomona, CA 91768
**Phone** (909) 869-2222
**Fax** (909) 869-4214

**Accommodations** 85 guest rooms, 3 suites.

**Meeting Facilities** 12,000 sq. ft. including auditorium seating 300. Registration desk, exhibit area, all meeting rooms have scenic views.

**Services** A/V on site with technical staff and complete inventory of equipment. University Speakers' bureau available. Complimentary Ontario airport shuttle. Many University resources available.

### Kennolyn Conference Center

**Address** 8400 Glen Haven Road, Soquel, CA 95073
**Phone** (831) 479-6700
**Fax** (831) 479-6730

**Accommodations** 26 guest rooms; log cabins filled with antiques, down comforters, wood stoves.

**Meeting Facilities** 9 meeting rooms, large outdoor amphitheater. Many rooms ideal for discussion groups, set with overstuffed chairs and couches.

**Services** Customized personal services.

### Morgan Run Resort and Club

**Address** 5690 Cancha de Golf, Rancho Santa Fe, CA 92091
**Phone** (858) 756-2471
**Fax** (858) 759-2196

**Accommodations** 89 sleeping rooms.

**Meeting Facilities** 6 rooms.

**Services** None listed.

### Network Meeting Center at Techmart-Santa Clara

**Address** 5201 Great America Parkway, Suite 122, Santa Clara, CA 95054
**Phone** (408) 562-6111
**Fax** (408) 562-5703

**Accommodations** N/A (Adjacent to 500-room Westin Hotel Santa Clara).

**Meeting Facilities** 17 dedicated meeting rooms plus exhibit and event space.

**Services** Conference planning, meeting coordinators, complete A/V inventory on-site, 8-hr. chairs, videoconferencing.

### PG&E Learning Center

**Address** 3301 Crow Canyon Road, San Ramon, CA 94583 **Phone** (510) 866-7500 **Fax** (510) 866-7378

**Accommodations** 119 rooms, each with a double extra long bed.

**Meeting Facilities** 40 rooms, totalling 27,000 sq. ft., plus a 5,300 sq. ft. conference center, breakout rooms, and a 1,700 sq. ft. auditorium. Each room has standard A/V equipment and projectors.

**Services** Professional meeting planners, business center, A/V specialists, phone message center, video conferencing, dry cleaning.

### Resort at Squaw Creek

**Address** 400 Squaw Creek Road, P.O. Box 3333, Olympic Valley, CA 96146 **Phone** (800) 327-3353 **Fax** (916) 581-5407

**Accommodations** Luxurious mountain-view accommodations with 405 rooms including 204 suites.

**Meeting Facilities** 33,000-sq. ft. conf. center with 36 rooms. All rooms with multiple electrical outlets, indiv. controls for climate, sound, and 110V electricity. Rear and front screen projection. Audio conferencing. State-of-the-art A/V production capabilities.

At no charge (with CMP or CP pkg.): Standard A/V package including 25" monitor and VCR, 35 mm slide projector, overhead projector, flip chart with marker, white board with marker, podium, microphone.

Conference concierge for on-site needs; fax/copy services; typing; telephone messages; professional conference planning managers for planning details; professional A/V staff.

The Grand Sierra Ballroom has 9,525 sq. ft. of exhibit space and Squaw Peak Ballroom has 5,120 sq. ft.

**Services** Gift shops, room service, laundry, dry cleaning, ice machines, golf/ski tuning and pros,

sports locker room. Concierge, conf. concierge, valet parking.

## COLORADO

### The Aspen Institute Aspen Meadows

**Address** 845 Meadows Road, Aspen, CO 81611 **Phone** (800) 452-4240 (970) 925-4240 **Fax** (970) 544-7852

**Accommodations** 98 oversized guest rooms and suites.

**Meeting Facilities** 11,000 sq. ft., incl. state-of-the-art conference center.

**Services** Valet, business center, notary, complimentary airport transfers.

### The Inverness Hotel & Golf Club

**Address** 200 Inverness Drive West, Englewood, CO 80112
**Phone** (800) 346-4891 (303) 799-5800 **Fax** (303) 799-5874

**Accommodations** 302 guest rooms and suites.

**Meeting Facilities** 33 dedicated meeting rooms, seating 10–350, with built-in A/V.

35mm slide, 16 mm film and overhead projectors; audio systems, video cassette & audio tape players.

Professional Conference Services staff, plus A/V technicians.

30,000 sq. ft. in conference wing.

Conference Services Department handles planning and on-site meeting coordination, fully-equipped A/V department and graphics studio, executive club services, complete business center.

**Services** Secretarial, courier, photographic and graphic design.

## CONNECTICUT

### Gray Conference Center University of Hartford

**Address** 200 Bloomfield Avenue, W. Hartford, CT 06117 **Phone** (860) 768-4996 **Fax** (860) 768-5016 **e-mail** gibbs@uhavax.hartford.edu

**Accommodations** Residence halls/apartments available, accommodating 3,200 May–August.

**Meeting Facilities** Executive meeting rooms, classrooms, auditoriums, banquet facilities, theater. Capacity ranging from 8–4,600.

**Services** 4 seminar rooms, 7 breakout rooms, 225-seat auditorium, and restaurant. Housing options available at nearby hotels during the academic year. Downlink teleconference capabilities. Other campus facilities including auditorium, theater, classrooms, meeting rooms are also available.

### Hastings Hotel and Conference Center

**Address** 85 Sigourney Street, Hartford, CT 06105 **Phone** (860) 727-4200 **Fax** (860) 727-4217

**Accommodations** 271 guest rooms and suites, each equipped with a spacious work station including dataports for Internet connectivity. 5 executive suites; 12 parlor suites.

**Meeting Facilities** 50 meeting rooms for 10–500 persons. Includes 28 conference rooms, 3 amphitheaters, 13 breakout rooms, 8 conference suites; 3 PC training rooms each with 15 networked computers and an instructor's station; Complete A/V and computer-based presentation equipment.

**Services** Skilled lighting and audio technicians, A/V production including digital editing, transcribing, typesetting, computer-generated graphics in video, slide, or hard copy formats. Desktop publishing and binding services. Fully-trained conference coordinators.

### Heritage Inn, A Dolce Conference Resort

**Address** Heritage Road, Southbury, CT 06488 **Phone** (860) 264-8200 **Fax** (860) 264-6910

**Accommodations** 163 guest rooms including 5 suites.

**Meeting Facilities** 25 dedicated meeting rooms; 3 rear screen rooms; amphitheatre for 150; Conference Service Desk.

**Services** Specialty shops; shopping arcade; free parking for 200 cars.

### Prudential Center for Learning & Innovation

**Address** Weed Avenue, Norwalk, CT 06850 **Phone** (203) 852-7300 **Fax** (203) 852-7364

**Accommodations** 116 king-bedded rooms with a second telephone line and closed-circuit TV.

**Meeting Facilities** 28 meeting rooms including 2 amphitheaters, 3,600 sq. ft. multipurpose room with 24-foot rear screen. 17 breakout

rooms. Extensive A/V and computer equipment.

**Services** Expansive complete meeting package includes name badges, tent cards, and free parking.

## DELAWARE

### Conference Centers of the University of Delaware

**Address** 107 Clayton Hall, Newark, DE 19716 **Phone** (302) 831-2214 **Fax** (302) 831-2998

**Accommodations** 5–1,000 people.

**Meeting Facilities** 70 conference rooms, large auditorium. Three statewide locations.

**Services** In-house A/V equipment including satellite dish. Full-meal plans. Summer housing for 5,000 plus. Fax machine, copying, conference planners available. Free parking. Year-round housing for 38 in Virden Conference Center in Lewes, and apartment suites for 172 at Newark campus.

### Hotel du Pont

**Address** 11th and Market Streets, Wilmington, DE 19801 **Phone** (302) 594-3107 **Fax** (302) 434-3403

**Accommodations** 217 guest rooms.

**Meeting Facilities** 30 meeting rooms.

**Services** N/A.

## DISTRICT OF COLUMBIA

### Gallaudet University Kellogg Conference Center

**Address** 800 Florida Ave., NE, Washington, DC 20002 **Phone** (202) 651-6000 **Fax** (202) 651-6103

**Accommodations** 93 accessible guest rooms, including 6 suites.

**Meeting Facilities** 21 meeting and breakout rooms, seating 5–150, 274-seat auditorium, exec. boardroom, tiered classroom, ballroom for groups to 400.

**Services** Complete conference planning services and business center. Extensive A/V, incl. multilink interactive video conferencing, full TV broadcast and online editing capabilities, satellite capabilities, Internet accessibility, on-site technicians. Total accessible facility featuring TTY telephones, visual signaling devices throughout.

## FLORIDA

### The Conference Center at Dodgertown

**Address** P.O. Box 2887, 3901 26th Street, Vero Beach, FL 32961 **Phone** (561) 569-4900 **Fax** (561) 569-9209 **e-mail** ladodger@iu.net

**Accommodations** Cluster of modern, redecorated villas with 88 rooms, including 10 executive suites and 2 pool-side cabanas.

**Meeting Facilities** 20 meeting rooms with multiple electrical and microphone outlets, and controls for sound and electricity. Executive Leadership Course.

At no charge: PA system, tape recorders, portable and floor microphones, A/V replacement parts, overhead, 16mm sound, 35mm slide projectors, projection screens, remote-control cords, lecterns, podiums, blackboards, easels, and tables, on-site professional conference coordinators, A/V repairmen. At a charge: CCTV equipment, name badges, opaque projectors, and 8mm sound projectors, portable stages, duplicating machines, stenographer, musicians, A/V operators, security guards.

Jackie Robinson Room has 3,000 sq. ft. of exhibit space. Holds 25 8' × 10' or 20 10' × 10' booths.

**Services** Newsstand, sundries, gifts, and women's/men's sportswear shops; 3 min. from local hospital.

Rear screen projectors, typewriters, truck/van, messenger service, notary public, printers, photographers, carpenters, sign painters, electricians, laborers.

### University of Florida Hotel and Conference Center

**Address** 1714 Southwest 34th Street, Gainesville, FL 32607 **Phone** (352) 378-0070 **Fax** (352) 378-8141

**Accommodations** 248 rooms in 7-story highrise; 2 phone lines per room.

**Meeting Facilities** 13 meeting rooms on same floor; 7,000 sq. ft. ballroom.

**Services** Direct Internet connection, business center, conference services desk, complete A/V inventory.

## GEORGIA

### Aberdeen Woods Conference Center

**Address** 201 Aberdeen Parkway, Peachtree City, GA 30269
**Phone** (770) 487-2666 **Fax** (770) 631-4096; Sales (770) 487-3029

**Accommodations** 233 guest rooms.

**Meeting Facilities** 150-seat auditorium, 59 individual meeting rooms; 40-seat and 80-seat indoor amphitheaters; all A/V equipped.

**Services** Conference planning, A/V staff.

### Chateau Elan Resort & Conference Center

**Address** 100 Rue Charlemagne, Braselton, GA 30517
**Phone** (800) 233-WINE (770) 932-0900 **Fax** (770) 271-6005

**Accommodations** 276 Inn rooms, 14 spa rooms, 9 2- and 3-bedroom villas.

**Meeting Facilities** 25,000 sq. ft. of meeting space, including 2 ballrooms, 60-seat amphitheatre, 15 additional meeting rooms.

**Services** On-property transportation includes 2 24-passenger buses, 3 12-passenger vans, 4 VIP vehicles; room service; business center, AV staff, concierge, gift shop.

### Emory Conference Center Hotel

**Address** 1615 Clifton Road, Atlanta, GA 30329 **Phone** (404) 712-6000 **Fax** (404) 712-6025
**e-mail** sales@ecch.emory.edu

**Accommodations** 195 deluxe guest rooms, 3 spacious suites. All guest rooms include hair dryer, coffeemaker, iron/ironing board, two-line telephone with data port & voice mail. All double-bedded rooms offer double vanity sinks with two well-lit desks; 15 ADA/accessible rooms.

**Meeting Facilities** 30,000 total sq. ft. of function space. 2 amphitheaters: 1 seats 200, the other seats 70. 5,400 sq. ft. ballroom; 3,000 sq. ft. Garden Courtyard, numerous additional meeting rooms.

Ergonomic chairs and hard-top writing surfaces. Advanced A/V capabilities include satellite downlink with KU and C bands, teleconferencing, multi-image projections equipment, computer data presentation, interactive video system and dedicated fiber optic phone lines.

A/V technicians, electrician, notary public.

**Services** Concierge, conference planning, area transportation, newsstand/gift shop, ATM, business center. Complimentary garage parking for 200.

### Marriott Evergreen Conference Resort

**Address** P.O. Box 1363, One Lakeview Drive, Stone Mountain, GA 30086 **Phone** (770) 879-9900 **Fax** (770) 469-9013

**Accommodations** 250 guest rooms-suites.

**Meeting Facilities** 20 rooms; 45,209 sq. ft. of meeting and exhibit space.

**Services** Conference planning, secretarial, messenger, language, graphic services. Closed-circuit TV, teleconferencing, overhead viewgraph, tape recording, easels and blackboards, videotape recording, film and slide projectors, PC computers.

### Gold Creek Resort

**Address** One Gold Creek Drive, Dawsonville, GA 30534
**Phone** (800) 966-2441 (706) 265-2700 **Fax** (706) 265-4191

**Accommodations** 74 suites.

**Meeting Facilities** 5 rooms, 30,000 sq. ft. 2 fixed-wall meeting rooms; 3 air walls. Each meeting room has immediate access to outdoors. In-room data ports.

**Services** Full-service business center.

### Marietta Conference Center & Resort

**Address** 500 Powder Spring St., Marietta, GA 30064 **Phone** (770) 427-2500 **Fax** (770) 429-9577

**Accommodations** 200 guest rooms, 1 Presidential Suite, 8 parlor suites.

**Meeting Facilities** 20,000 total sq. ft. conf. space, 6,500 sq. ft. grand ballroom, 2 exec. boardrooms, 18 breakout rooms.

**Services** 24-hour business center, 2 conf. concierge desks, valet. 24-hour room service, airport shuttle.

### Timber Ridge Conference Center

**Address** 5601 North Allen Road, Mableton, GA 30059
**Phone** (770) 941-2176
**Fax** (770) 732-1580

**Accommodations** 22 twins, 2 singles (barrier free).

**Meeting Facilities** 5 meeting rooms accommodating 15–120 people.

**Services** All A/V included, standard A/V package, secretarial services, including typing, photocopying, and Fax. Gift shop. Owned/operated by NW Georgia Girl Scout Council.

### Wyndham Peachtree Executive Conference Center

**Address** 2443 State Hwy. 54 West, Peachtree City, GA 30269
**Phone** (770) 487-2000
**Fax** (770) 487-4428

**Accommodations** 250 contemporary conference center guest rooms and 6 suites. All rooms are soundproof and have air conditioning control, color TV, balconies and direct-dial phones. In-room coffeemakers, iron and ironing board.

**Meeting Facilities** 24 meeting rooms for 10–300 people. Two ballrooms can accommodate up to 400 for banquets and 600 for receptions; all rooms have multiple electrical/microphone/phone outlets and controls for climate and sound. 200-seat amphitheater with front and rear screen projection.

Pads, pencils, direction signs available. Installed PA system, portable stages, tape recorder/player, portable and floor microphones, duplicating machines, teleconferencing facilities.

Electrician, A/V operators, notary public, graphics department.

The Peachtree Ballroom has 5,400 sq. ft. of exhibit space.

**Services** Conference Planning, ground transportation, airline ticketing, newsstand, gift shop, concierge. Free outdoor parking, cap. 400; full Business Center.

Stenographer, translator, photographer, entertainers.

Complete Business Center for administrative services, fax, photocopies, messenger.

## ILLINOIS

### Andersen Worldwide Center for Professional Education

**Address** 1405 North Fifth Avenue, St. Charles, IL 60174 **Phone** (630) 444-4355 **Fax** (630) 584-7212
**e-mail** pam.a.zawne@awo.com

Accommodations 1,277 sleeping rooms, including 21 suites.

Meeting Facilities 135 meeting rooms, 6 auditorium bays, and 3 amphitheaters; 27,000 sq. ft. of exhibit space.

Services 1,200 personal computers incl. 750 networked with on-site support, conference planning, TV studio, teleconferencing, business TV, interactive multimedia, Outdoor Adventure Program w/30 low/high level ropes course, on-site travel agency.

### CNA2 North Conference Center

Address CNA Plaza, 2 North, Chicago, IL 60685 Phone (312) 822-6847 Fax (312) 817-3708

Accommodations Hotel rooms within walking distance.

Meeting Facilities Multi-faceted meeting rooms with built-in A/V and network capabilities. On-site A/V department.

Services Dedicated conference coordinator; conference concierge.

### Doubletree Hotel North Shore Executive Meeting Center

Address 9599 Skokie Boulevard, Skokie, IL 60077 Phone (800) 879-4458 Fax (847) 679-2385

Accommodations 364 rooms. Oversized work desks with data ports, ergonomic chairs, voice mail.

Meeting Facilities 18 rooms, 10,000 sq. ft. executive board room; fiberoptic cabling, ergonomic seating, individual temperature control, soft-seating meeting rooms, state-of-the-art A/V with dedicated staff.

Services Business Center, on-site planner, two meeting coordinators, security.

### Esplanade Conference Center

Address 2001 Butterfield Road, Downers Grove, IL 60515 Phone (630) 434-9128 Fax (630) 434-9132

Accommodations 247 guest rooms.

Meeting Facilities 20 meeting rooms, 20,000 sq. ft. of meeting space. Breakout rooms, board rooms, forum seating up to 90.

Services Suite hotel, business center.

### Harrison Conference Center at Lake Bluff

Address Green Bay Road, Lake Bluff, IL 60044 Phone (847) 295-1100 Fax (847) 295-8792 e-mail lakebluff@iacc.iacconline.com

Accommodations 5-story Mediterranean-style villa comprised of 83 guest rooms. All have climate control, color TV, oversized beds, and heat lamps.

Meeting Facilities 11 meeting rooms for 2–200. All rooms have climate control, multiple electrical/microphone outlets, 110V electricity, direct truck access.

At no charge: Reel and cassette tape recorders; overhead, 16mm sound, 35mm slide projectors; portable projection screens; podiums; chairs; blackboards, on-site professional conference coordinators, A/V repairs.

For a fee: 35mm sound; Panaboard; LCD panels; opaque projectors; typewriters; duplicating machines; CCTV equipment with guest room relay capability, stenographer, musicians, A/V operators, security guards, photographer.

The "Great Hall" is 2,450 sq. ft. and can seat 200 theater style.

Services Newsstand, sundries, laundry, dry cleaning, free outdoor parking for 200 cars.

Messenger service, print shop, notary public, carpentry shop, display builder, sign painter, plumbers, electricians, locksmith, laborers.

### Hickory Ridge Conference Centre

Address 1195 Summerhill Drive, Lisle, IL 60532-3190 Phone (800) 225-4722 (708) 971-5023 Fax (708) 971-6939

Accommodations 376 single rooms including 50 2-room suites; handicapped and non-smoking rooms available. All have individual climate control and free cable TV.

Meeting Facilities 47 conference rooms seating 10–200, with rearscreen projection systems and closed circuit TV; majority of the rooms are wired for computer training; amphitheater for up to 90 people; board room, 3 executive meeting rooms; and 75 breakout rooms.

At no charge: Doublesize flip chart w/ markers, overhead screen and projector, 35mm slide projector, lighted podium, white boards w/ markers, paper and pencils, personal conference coordinator, A/V technicians, Business Center telephone messages, Notary Public.

For a fee: VCR with rear screen video projection, recorders, video cameras, closed-circuit TV cameras, spotlights, typewriters, PCs, fax/copy services, typing, stenographer, electricians, A/V operators, developers and speakers, simultaneous translation equipment for interpreters, signs, security, graphic arts, photographer, and shipping.

Up to 20 8' × 10' booths.

Services Executive floor, message board displayed throughout building, gift shop, laundry, dry cleaning, ice and vending machines, local shuttle. Special diet menus available. Free parking.

Entertainers. Other services upon request.

### Hoffman Estates Education Center

Address 5555 Trillium Boulevard, Hoffman Estates, IL 60192 Phone (847) 645-3000 Fax (815) 753-8865 e-mail kgilmer@nie.edu

Accommodations Cooperative arrangements with local hotels as close as 5 mi. from the Center.

Meeting Facilities 4 executive training rooms with adjacent break service; 11 conference rooms; an auditorium seating 250 (hearing accessible); 2 networked computer laboratories; 4 breakout rooms; individual climate and lighting controls.

All rooms are equipped with ceilingmounted VCR or video projector, overhead projector, marker boards, flip charts, presentation rail system, and projection screens. Executive rooms and auditorium include a computerized lectern system. Other equipment includes portable video/data projection, mobile computer, video camcorder, slide projector, wireless mikes, and opaque projector. All equipment is included in room rental at no additional charge.

Conference services; in-house audio/visual/computer technology staff; phone line for laptops; business desk services including fax, transparencies, photocopying, and message boards.

**Services** Corporate rates with selected local hotels for sleeping rooms; free parking.

Musicians, florists, recreation, ground transportation.

### James L. Allen Center

**Address** 2169 N. Campus Dr., Evanston, IL 60208 **Phone** (708) 864-9270 **Fax** (708) 491-4323

**Accommodations** 150 rooms (handicap accessible).

**Meeting Facilities** 7 rooms seating 50–230, and 38 rooms seating 10–35.

**Services** Full range of A/V services; computer lab and all networked PCs in conference and study rooms.

### Oak Brook Hills Resort & Conference Center

**Address** 3500 Midwest Rd., Oak Brook, IL 60522-7010 **Phone** (630) 850-5555 **Fax** (630) 850-5569

**Accommodations** 382 elegantly appointed guest rooms including 38 suites, "business class" rooms and a concierge level with private lounge.

**Meeting Facilities** 35,000 sq. ft. of flexible meeting space including 140-seat amphitheater, 11 boardrooms and newly renovated Grand Ballroom.

**Services** Full conference planning staff, complimentary parking, concierge, full-service audiovisual, gift shop, Pro Shop, and dry cleaning.

### Summit Executive Centre

**Address** 205 N. Michigan Avenue, Chicago, IL 60601 **Phone** (312) 938-5053 **Fax** (312) 861-0324 **e-mail** 74117.444@compuserve.com

**Accommodations** Connected to 3 major hotels with over a total of 3,000 guest rooms.

**Meeting Facilities** 20,000 square ft. with 15 rooms able to accommodate groups of 3–125 people. Dedicated computer lab with

networked PCs available to accommodate groups up to 26 people.

In-house A/V staff with in-house equipment: overheads, slide projectors, flip charts, screens, VCR and monitor, cameras, LCD panels, video projectors.

Concierge to assist in access to all city amenities; professional audio visual staff; in-house caterer; business center.

**Services** Underground parking; in-house A/V technical support; concierge; conference planning; special rates at all adjoining hotels for sleeping rooms; team building program using the world's tallest indoor rock-climbing wall (located next door at the athletic club).

Computer rentals.

Parking; conference planning; resource center for educational programming ideas; training consultants.

## INDIANA

### The Marten House Hotel and Lilly Conference Center

**Address** 1801 West 86th St., Indianapolis, IN 46260 **Phone** (317) 872-4111 **Fax** (317) 415-5245

**Accommodations** 176 rooms featuring comfortable work areas, data ports.

**Meeting Facilities** Conference center features multi-layered state-of-the-art auditorium seating 220. Fully equipped breakout rooms. Hotel features 2 ballrooms, 2 boardrooms, 7 breakout rooms.

**Services** Videoconferencing, computer lab, satellite up/downlinks.

### University of Notre Dame Center for Continuing Education

**Address** Notre Dame Avenue, P.O. Box 1008, Notre Dame, IN 46556 **Phone** (219) 631-6691 **Fax** (219) 631-8083

**Accommodations** 92 rooms (handicap).

**Meeting Facilities** 70,000 sq. ft. of meeting space available; 23 conference rooms seating 8–375.

State-of-the-art translation equipment and auditorium; most rooms equipped for audio and video recording, closed-circuit television and satellite reception and broad-

casting; full audiovisual support available.

Notre Dame's Center for Continuing Education is a full-service conference center. Each conference, course or meeting is coordinated by a member of the Center's professional faculty who administers all the logistics of the program. In addition to detailed coordination by a member of the Center's professional staff, fees also include the following professional and clerical services: conference planning, marketing and evaluation; all required meeting facilities and exhibit space at the Center for Continuing Education and elsewhere on campus; advance and on-site registration, including preparation and mailing of promotional materials, confirmation of registration and preparation of name tags and rosters; full administration and accounting of program funds; secretarial support services (word processing, typing, copying, collating of handout materials); folders, maps, and other informational literature needed by program recipients.

**Services** Gift shop, dry cleaning, safety deposit boxes, room service, library, fax, and all University facilities and services by arrangement.

### University Place Conference Center and Hotel

**Address** 850 West Michigan Street, Indianapolis, IN 46202-5198 **Phone** (800) 410-MEET (317) 274-2700 (conf. ctr.), 269-9000 (hotel) **Fax** (317) 274-3878 (conf. ctr.), 231-5168 (hotel)

**Accommodations** 278-room AAA 4-diamond hotel is integrated with conference center. Includes 16 suites as well as rooms for disabled. Non-smoking rooms avail. All rooms have climate control, sprinkler system, direct-dial phones, working-size desks, lounge chairs and ottomans, voice mail, computer hook-ups, TV feature movies.

**Meeting Facilities** 28 dedicated self-contained meeting rooms ranging from 340-seat auditorium to breakout rooms; includes two tiered meeting rooms, 2 boardrooms, and 1 ballroom.

Included in package: Overhead, and slide projectors, sound system, lectern, screens, VCRs, monitors, audio recorder, white board, easel/pads/markers, conference management and meeting support, on-site registration assistance, name tags, folders, meeting room signs.

For a fee: Total turnkey conference planning from announcement brochure to final financial statement. Special A/V services—A/V production, editing, photography, teleconferencing, technicians, audience-response system, translation facilities. Office support—photocopying, transparencies, fax, notary, desktop publishing.

**Services** Business Service Center with computers available. Underground 385-car parking garage, sky walk to Indiana University Medical Center, and full-time technical staff. Services center with computers available. Web: http://www.iupui.edu/it/univplac/uplac.html

Stenographer, photographer, displays, banners, locksmiths, entertainers, decorators.

## MARYLAND

### Belmont Conference Center

**Address** 6555 Belmont Woods Rd., Elkridge, MD 21075 **Phone** (410) 796-4300 **Fax** (410) 796-4565

**Accommodations** 21 rooms, individually decorated.

**Meeting Facilities** 4 rooms, 2,100 sq. ft. Spectacular views, spacious, many windows, easy access to outdoors, plenty of break space, flexible set-ups.

**Services** Conference coordinators, business center, transportation coordinator.

### Burkshire Guest Suites and Conference Center

**Address** 10 West Burke Avenue, Towson, MD 21204 **Phone** (410) 324-8103 **Fax** (410) 830-3749 **e-mail** emke-n@toa.towson.edu

**Accommodations** 116 suites (including living/dining room and full kitchen).

**Meeting Facilities** 11,000 sq. ft. of meeting space, 19 meeting rooms seating 10–150.

**Services** Full conference planning and on-site A/V capabilities with technician services, business center, a Marriott Conference Center.

### The Conference Center at Charles County Community College

**Address** Charles County Community College, 8730 Mitchell Rd., P.O. Box 910, LaPlata, MD 20646 **Phone** (301) 934-7661 **Fax** (301) 934-7667

**Accommodations** None.

**Meeting Facilities** 12 rooms, 10,000 sq. ft. of meeting space with state-of-the-art media equipment. Teleconference auditorium with surround sound and video projection. Fiberoptic and ISDN-based teleconferencing, satellite links, Internet access.

**Services** Business center, meeting planners, technical support, notary public, exposition, and convention display support.

### The Conference Center at Sheppard Pratt

**Address** 6501 North Charles Street, Baltimore, MD 21204 **Phone** (410) 938-3906 **Fax** (410) 938-4099

**Accommodations** N/A.

**Meeting Facilities** 200-seat auditorium, 5 classrooms seating 20–70 each.

**Services** Relaxed environment located on 100 acres of beautifully landscaped grounds. Experienced catering, A/V and conference services professionals. Full range of A/V equipment and teleconferencing capabilities.

### George Meany Center for Labor Studies

**Address** 10,000 New Hampshire Ave., Silver Spring, MD 20903 **Phone** (301) 431-5417 **Fax** (301) 431-5411

**Accommodations** 115 sleeping rooms; 7 handicap accessible. Accommodations feature study desks, coffeemakers, free use of laundry room.

**Meeting Facilities** Attractive meeting room with ergonomic seating, in-house A/V and technical staff. 13 rooms seating 6–175 persons.

**Services** Campus on 47 scenic acres located 20 minutes from Washington, DC. Serves AFL-CIO union affiliates only.

### The Inn & Conference Center at University of Maryland University College

**Address** University Boulevard at Adelphi Road, College Park, MD 20740 **Phone** (301) 985-7303 **Fax** (301) 985-7445

**Accommodations** 108 hotel rooms, 3 suites; modem compatible.

**Meeting Facilities** Over 32,000 square feet of meeting space. Ballroom seats 750 for banquets, beautiful auditorium for 750, Executive Board Room, 2 equipped computer labs, 29 total meeting rooms.

Motorized screens, chalkboards in majority of rooms, PCs in computer labs, tackable wall railings, teleconferencing and satellite uplink capabilities, a built-in rear-screen projection room.

Full conference services; in-house A/V; full-time Conference Coordinator; electrician.

8,200 sq. ft. ballroom available for exhibits. Ballroom concourse holds up to 20 8' × 10's as well.

**Services** Newsstand with gift items, free newspaper for overnight guests, parking garage capacity 850, dry cleaning service, cable TV, Conference Planning, tape recording, videotaping, rear-screen capabilities.

Photographers, florists, decorators, golf lessons, entertainers, printers.

### The Learning Center

**Address** 901 Dual Highway, Hagerstown, MD 21740 **Phone** (301) 733-5566 **Fax** (301) 797-4286

**Accommodations** 210 guest rooms.

**Meeting Facilities** 3 Learning Centers with comfortable seating, excellent design, built-in A/V.

**Services** Full services, A/V, off-site dining plan.

### The Magna Center for Executive Learning

**Address** 901 Dual Highway, Hagerstown, MD 21740 **Phone** (301) 733-5566 **Fax** (301) 797-4286

Accommodations 210 guest rooms each with phone and dataport.

Meeting Facilities 12 meeting rooms including 4 Learning Centers with contiguous breakout areas and built-in A/V.

Services Business services provided.

## Maritime Institute Conference Center

Address 5700 Hammonds Ferry Road, Linthicum Heights, MD 21090
Phone (410) 859-5700
Fax (410) 859-0942;
Telex: 87-637

Accommodations 220 guest rooms; 8 suites on 80 suburban wooded acres.

Meeting Facilities 40 meeting rooms covering 41,000 sq. ft., from 204 sq. ft. to 5,100 sq. ft; 250-seat tiered auditorium; house-owned A/V; complete A/V studio.

Services 2 free laundry rooms, dry cleaning service, Ship's Store, newsstand.

## William F. Bolger Center for Leadership Development

Address 9600 Newbridge Drive, Potomac, MD 20854 Phone (301) 983-7000 Fax (301) 983-7728

Accommodations 470 rooms, including 95 new deluxe rooms and suites, cable TV, dataports.

Meeting Facilities 60 rooms with 60,000 sq. ft. Dedicated meeting rooms feature windows, business center, new furnishings. Capacity 500 persons.

Services Free nightly transportation to Bethesda, Metro, and Montgomery Mall. Complimentary computer usage and Internet access.

## Wye River Conference Center at the Aspen Institute

Address P.O. Box 222, Queenstown, MD 21658 Phone (410) 827-7400 Fax (410) 827-9295

Accommodations 3 private houses with 86 guest rooms.

Meeting Facilities Country estate setting for groups of 5–120.

Services Business services, state-of-the-art video/teleconferencing and audio/visual equipment.

# MASSACHUSETTS

## BankBoston Conference & Training Center

Address 100 Federal Street, MS 01-02-01, Boston, MA 02110
Phone (617) 434-4000
Fax (617) 434-7750
e-mail bankboston@iacc.iacconline.com

Accommodations N/A.

Meeting Facilities 16 professionally designed meeting and breakout rooms including tiered meeting rooms, built-in state-of-the-art audio/visual technology, ergonomic seating and specially designed lighting systems.

At no charge: overhead projector, slide projector, screens, VCR and monitors, audio cassette and CD player, 2 flip charts.

An on-site audio/visual technician will be available to assist each instructor with all equipment questions. Printers, computer rental.

## Batterymarch Conference Center

Address 60 Batterymarch Street, 2nd Floor, Boston, MA 02110
Phone (617) 556-8000
Fax (617) 556-9901

Accommodations 100 guest rooms in the new Wyndham Boston Hotel, in which Batterymarch Conference Center is located.

Meeting Facilities 13 meeting rooms, 9 fully-equipped meeting rooms and 4 amphitheatres. Rooms equipped with tackable walls, white boards, presentation rails, electronic screens, ceiling-mounted video/data projectors.

Services Several-day meeting package including food and full business center services.

## Bell Atlantic Learning Center at Marlboro

Address 280 Locke Drive, Marlboro, MA 01752 Phone (508) 460-4610 Fax (508) 481-3451
e-mail nynex@iacc.iacconline.com

Accommodations Modern conference complex situated on 25 wooded acres with 226 large single rooms equipped with TV, telephone, and desk.

Meeting Facilities 40 main meeting rooms, 28 additional smaller meeting rooms; 170-seat auditorium.

At no charge: many rooms offer rear-screen projection and permanently installed 35 mm slide projectors, video and audio cassette records, voice and data lines for use with computer and quality speakers and amplifiers.

An on-site audio/visual technician will be available to assist each instructor with all equipment questions.

Services Gift shop, dry cleaning, free parking.

## The Center for Executive Education at Babson College

Address Woodland Hill Drive, Babson Park (Wellesley), MA 02157
Phone (617) 239-4000
Fax (617) 239-4026
e-mail babson@iacc.iacconline.com

Accommodations Contemporary complex of low-rise buildings, including 120 rooms and 6 suites. All rooms are soundproof with climate control, direct-dial phone, color TV, and stereo.

Meeting Facilities 25 meeting rooms for 8–200. All rooms have climate control, multiple electrical and telephone outlets. Larger rooms have microphone outlets.

At no charge: Portable PA systems, cassette recorders, all microphones, A/V replacement parts, overhead and slide projectors, podiums, blackboards, easels/tables, cork boards, attendee registration.

For a fee: CCTV cameras, monitors, recorders, electrician.

Services House physician, laundry, dry cleaning, free on-site parking.

Locksmith, laborers, A/V operators, messenger, stenographer, notary, printer, photographer, carpenter, display builders, translators, painters, security, entertainers.

## Four Points Sheraton Hotel & Conference Center

Address 1151 Boston-Providence Turnpike, Norwood, MA 02062
Phone (617) 769-7900
Fax (617) 551-3552

Accommodations 126 rooms, 2 suites, air conditioning, cable TV, facilities for physically disabled, fully sprinklered.

**Meeting Facilities** 30 conference rooms for 5–125 people. All have executive seating, 2 1/2 ft. x 8 ft. conference tables, dimmer lighting, white boards, built-in projection screens. Two rooms with multiple dedicated phone lines.

**Services** Newsstand, laundry, dry cleaning, ice and business center, free parking.

### Henderson House

**Address** 99 Westcliff Road, Weston, MA 02193-1409 **Phone** (617) 235-4350 **Fax** (617) 235-5847 **e-mail** tpetrin@lynx.neu.edu

**Accommodations** Local hotels nearby.

**Meeting Facilities** 36-room mansion; 12 meeting rooms, seating to 100.

**Services** Professional conference and A/V support, complimentary standard A/V, computer projection, electronic white board, IBM/MAC compatible LCD panel; free parking on site.

### John Hancock Conference Center

**Address** 40 Trinity Place, Boston, MA 02116 **Phone** (617) 572-7700 **Fax** (617) 572-7709

**Accommodations** 64 guest rooms.

**Meeting Facilities** 12 meeting rooms, 4 function rooms, 1,100-seat auditorium.

**Services** Complete A/V, incl. teleconferencing, computer-compatible projectors, on-site technicians, dedicated conference planner.

### MIT Endicott House

**Address** 80 Haven Street, Dedham, MA 02026 **Phone** (617) 326-5151 **Fax** (617) 326-8702

**Accommodations** 50 rooms (1 handicap accessible).

**Meeting Facilities** 6 meeting rooms of varying size including a tiered amphitheater.

**Services** Standard, including 35mm, 16mm, and overhead projectors, and VCR/Monitor. Computers by arrangement.

### Tufts University Conference Bureau

**Address** 108 Packard Ave., Medford/ Boston, MA 02155 **Phone** (617) 627-3568 **Fax** (617) 627-3856

**e-mail** conferences@infonet.tufts. edu

**Accommodations** 600 rooms (handicap accessible). Overnight accommodations available on campus, May 22–August 13.

**Meeting Facilities** 35 rooms, seating 20–600.

All standard equipment including 35 mm, 16mm and overhead projectors, tape recorders, videotape equipment, PA system, blackboards and flip charts; A/V technician.

Secretarial, fax, teleconferencing, and PC or terminal hookups.

**Services** Specialization in English as a Second Language Program and international conferences in Boston and France. Conference planning assistance, full conference coordination.

### Warren Conference Center & Inn of Northeastern University

**Address** 529 Chestnut St., Ashland, MA 01721 **Phone** (508) 881-1142 **Fax** (508) 881-1515

**Accommodations** 5 guest rooms; team-living cabins for 64.

**Meeting Facilities** 8 rooms, seating to 150.

**Services** Full A/V, business services, complete conference support.

### The World Trade Center-Boston The Executive Conference Center

**Address** 164 Northern Avenue, Boston, MA 02210 **Phone** (617) 439-5084 **Fax** (617) 439-5090 **e-mail** mike.bloy@wtcb.com

**Accommodations** Hotel nearby

**Meeting Facilities** 24 rooms, 35,000 sq. ft., 24 breakout rooms, board rooms.

**Services** Video teleconferencing, business center, satellite links, VTC, full A/V, concierge, dedicated event manager.

## MICHIGAN

### Crystal Center at Crystal Mountain Resort

**Address** 12500 Crystal Mountain Drive, Thompsonville, MI 49683 **Phone** (800) 968-7686 (616) 378-2000 **Fax** (616) 378-4594 **e-mail** info@crystalmtn.com

**Accommodations** 210 sleeping rooms; hotel rooms, deluxe suites, 1-3 bedroom condominiums.

**Meeting Facilities** 6 meeting rooms with 4,800 sq. ft. of meeting space. Rear screen projection with 8′ × 10′ screen, ergonomic chairs, classroom tables, multilevel lighting, double drywall interior walls with quiet HVAC system.

**Services** Business Center, conference planning, teleconferencing, video tape recording.

### Dow Leadership Development Center

**Address** 22 Galloway Drive, Hillsdale, MI 49242 **Phone** (517) 437-3311 **Fax** (517) 437-3240 **e-mail** jo.bates@ac.hillsdale.edu

**Accommodations** 32 guest rooms; conference/meeting rooms.

**Meeting Facilities** 11 meeting rooms accommodating up to 200.

**Services** VCR, overheads, 35mm, fax machines, duplication services.

### Eagle Crest Conference Resort

**Address** 1275 South Huron Street, Ypsilanti, MI 48197 **Phone** (313) 487-0600 **Fax** (313) 484-1411

**Accommodations** 236 spacious guest rooms and suites with data ports and work areas. Concierge Level.

**Meeting Facilities** 13 conference/ seminar rms., executive boardroom, computer lab. Auditorium I seats 200; Auditorium II seats 100; 9,672 sq. ft. of flexible meeting space. Satellite downlink capabilities.

Full A/V equipment with staff technicians, rear screen projection, simultaneous translation system, PC hookups in conference and seminar rooms, closed circuit TV.

PGA golf professional, full AV support, security, on-site registration assistance, office and clerical support.

58 8 × 10 booths; 9,672 sq. ft.

**Services** Full A/V, teleconferencing, support staff, complimentary parking, business center services, full catering and banquet services, dry cleaning and laundry services.

### Fetzer Center

**Address** Western Michigan University, Kalamazoo, MI 49008 **Phone** (616) 387-3232 **Fax** (616) 387-5030

**Accommodations** N/A.

**Meeting Facilities** Auditorium seating 250; lecture hall seating 90;

6 conference rooms seating 10–80; video teleconferencing room seating 10–15.

**Services** Conference planning, all standard equipment including 35 mm, 16mm, video, overhead projectors, flip charts, as well as dual 35mm rear-screen projection, teleconferencing, video and audio recording. Computer lab.

### Genoa Woods Executive Conference & Banquet Center

**Address** 7707 Conference Center Drive, Brighton, MI 48114 **Phone** (810) 227-4030 **Fax** (810) 227-0725

**Accommodations** 90 rooms, next door to Courtyard by Marriott.

**Meeting Facilities** In-room A/V; ergonomic chairs, windows, light-blocking curtains, sound-proof walls, supply caddy, storage closet.

**Services** Secretarial; business center with all amenities; tranquil, wooded location for privacy.

### Haworth Inn & Conference Center

**Address** 225 College Ave., Holland, MI 49423 **Phone** (800) 905-9142 **Fax** (616) 395-7151

**Accommodations** 50 rooms, single and double occupancy. Complimentary *USA Today* newspaper.

**Meeting Facilities** 11 rooms, 10,000 sq. ft. Presentation boards, video conferencing, private dining room.

**Services** Complete A/V, gift shop, college library, fax, valet service, secretarial services.

### Management Education Center Michigan State University

**Address** 811 West Square Lake Road, Troy, MI 48098 **Phone** (810) 879-2460 **Fax** (810) 879-6125

**Accommodations** 10 modern hotels within minutes of the center.

**Meeting Facilities** 9 rooms seating 10–400; large lobby for social functions, cocktail receptions, and product exhibits.

**Services** The center maintains an extensive array of A/V and computer equipment, including video/computer projection and professional sound systems.

## MINNESOTA

### Daniel C. Gainey Conference Center of the University of St. Thomas

**Address** Route 2, Box 1, Owatonna, MN 55060-9610 **Phone** (507) 451-7440 **Fax** (507) 451-2705 **e-mail** aesims@stthomas.edu

**Accommodations** 35 guest rooms (handicap accessible), on 182 acres of rolling countryside.

**Meeting Facilities** Executive Board Room seating 12, main conference room seating 54, five breakout rooms seating 10 each; auxiliary facility with 4 rooms accommodating 20 people each.

**Services** Educational resources of the University of St. Thomas; conference planning services; audio/visual equipment including interactive video capabilities.

### Earle Brown Continuing Education Center

**Address** 1890 Buford Ave., St. Paul, MN 55108 **Phone** (612) 624-3275 **Fax** (612) 625-1948

**Accommodations** None.

**Meeting Facilities** 12 seating 10–440.

**Services** Computer laboratory equipped with 20 IBM PCs; Novell Netware; in-house technical staff; satellite downlink capability; 1 meeting room designed and equipped to serve as an origination point for live video teleconferences. In-house A/V. Professional staff.

### Madden's on Gull Lake

**Address** 8001 Pine Beach Peninsula, Brainerd, MN 56401 **Phone** (800) 247-1040 **Fax** (218) 829-6583

**Accommodations** Cottages, hotel rooms, suites (300 room capacity).

**Meeting Facilities** 18,000 sq. ft. Town Hall Conference Center, plus 30 additional various-size meeting rooms totalling 36,092 sq. ft.

**Services** Complete in-house property-owned A/V inventory.

### The Northland Inn and Executive Conference Center

**Address** 7025 Northland Drive, Brooklyn Park, MN 55428 **Phone** (800) 441-6422 (612) 536-8300 **Fax** (612) 536-8790

**Accommodations** An all-suite executive conference center with 231 units. All suites include two work/study areas, whirlpools, color TVs and two phones.

**Meeting Facilities** 25 conference rooms (42,000 sq. ft.). All rooms have solid wall construction, ergonomic swivel chairs, climate controls, call buttons, projection screens, A/V feed, and multiple phone jacks.

State-of-the-art A/V equipment.

Conference concierge services, personal conference managers, A/V staff.

**Services** Laundry/dry cleaning, sundry shop, free parking.

Props, special transportation, carpenters, electricians, stage hands, entertainers, simultaneous translation equipment.

### Oak Ridge Conference Center

**Address** One Oak Ridge Drive, Chaska, MN 55318 **Phone** (612) 368-3100 **Fax** (612) 368-1494

**Accommodations** 147 guest rooms, including handicap facilities.

**Meeting Facilities** 36 conference rooms (36,000 sq. ft.). All rooms have solid walls, windows, individual climate controls, multiple phone/computer jacks.

State-of-the-art A/V equipment. Complete on-site inventory.

Personal conference coordinator. Professional A/V staff.

**Services** Professional A/V staff, personal conference services coordinator, fax/copy service, dry cleaning, transportation.

### Radisson Hotel & Conference Center Minneapolis

**Address** 3131 Campus Drive, Plymouth, MN 55441 **Phone** (612) 559-6600 **Fax** (612) 559-7516

**Accommodations** 243 rooms, 25 are jr. suites.

**Meeting Facilities** 32 meeting rooms. Auditorium, ballroom, boardrooms.

**Services** Full conference center facilities.

## MISSISSIPPI

### Whispering Woods Hotel & Executive Conference Center

**Address** 11200 E. Goodman Road, Olive Branch, MS 38654

**Phone** (601) 895-2941
**Fax** (601) 895-1590

**Accommodations** Modern, 4-story complex offers 181 guest rooms, including 6 suites.

**Meeting Facilities** 24 meeting rooms, concentrated on the first and mezzanine levels. All rooms have multiple electrical/microphone outlets and individual controls for climate.

**Services** Safety deposit boxes, laundry and dry cleaning. Gift shop offering gifts, books and sundry items. Free outdoor, self parking.

## MISSOURI

### Anheuser-Busch Conference & Sports Centre

**Address** One Soccer Park Rd., Fenton, MO 63026 **Phone** (314) 343-5347 **Fax** (313) 343-8340

**Accommodations** None listed.

**Meeting Facilities** 3 rooms with 4,418 sq. ft. of meeting space. Professional meeting managers. State-of-the-art A/V equipment, Sony projection systems, large screens, LCD projector (VGA Data & Video Active). Teleconferencing, on-site A/V technician.

**Services** Professional staff can plan theme/special events. Full service food and beverage staff.

### Doubletree Hotel & Conference Center

**Address** 16625 Swingley Ridge Road, St. Louis, MO 63017 **Phone** (800) 222-TREE (314) 532-5000 **Fax** (314) 530-1149

**Accommodations** Contemporary high-rise tower with 223 guest rooms and delivery.

**Meeting Facilities** 15 conference rooms for 15–350, 21 breakout rooms for 4–12. All rooms have swivel chairs, flexible control lighting. Peoples Theater features stationary rear screen projection, sound booth stage, tiered SR seating for 50–150.

On-site service management, PA systems, tape recorders/players, microphones, overhead, 35mm slide projectors, 16mm sound, remote controls, screen, electronic podiums, lecterns, CCTV equipment, spotlights, duplicating machines, typewriters.

Fax, transparencies, photocopying, secretary support, message delivery, A/V technicians, computer rental, laborers, musicians.

The "Great Room" holds 30, 8 ft. × 10 ft. booths piped and draped, direct truck access.

**Services** Conference center service desk, club operations service desk, pro-shop rentals, concierge, valet, free outdoor parking. Express check-in/check-out and on-site car rental office.

Bus transportation, photographers, print shop, sign shop, security, translators.

### Eric P. Newman Education Center—St. Louis

**Address** 660 S. Euclid, Campus Box 8209, St. Louis, MO 63110 **Phone** (314) 747-MEET (6338) **Fax** (314) 747-2000

**Accommodations** 200 rooms available at nearby hotels with wide range of amenities and prices.

**Meeting Facilities** 450-seat auditorium, 2 tiered seminar rooms seating 55 and 101, 10 breakout rooms and a divisible multipurpose room seating up to 168 classroom style.

Flip charts, marker boards, pointers, easels, microphones, network connections, telephones, teleconferencing, system annotating device, modem outlets, overhead, 35mm and video projectors, VCRs. All rooms have hard writing surface tables, ergonomic chairs.

Fax, transparencies, photocopying, secretarial service, security, message center and audio/visual technician on site. Satellite and interactive video teleconferencing.

Lobby, Mezzanine, Promenade exhibit areas.

**Services** Business Center, exceptional catering, listening assisted devices. Professional meeting planners to help with theme parties and other special needs.

Florist, photographers, printers, sign makers/decorators, computer rentals, ground transportation.

### Innsbrook Conference Center

**Address** 1 Innsbrook Estates Drive, Wright City, MO 63390 **Phone** (314) 745-3000 **Fax** (314) 745-8855

**Accommodations** 100 bedrooms in 1-, 2-, or 3-bedroom condominiums overlooking 140-acre lake.

**Meeting Facilities** 9 meeting rooms (7,900 sq. ft.) for groups of 5–150, adjustable upholstered armchairs, additional breakout rooms, individual climate control.

**Services** All standard A/V equipment, fax machine, secretarial services, theme dinners and parties. Airport shuttles. Conference planners; client business office.

### St. Louis Executive Conference Center at America's Center

**Address** 801 Convention Plaza, St. Louis, MO 63101 **Phone** (314) 342-5050 **Fax** (314) 342-5053

**Accommodations** One block from the Doubletree Mayfair Suites and the Holiday Inn Convention Center, two blocks from the Drury Inn-Gateway Arch. Many other excellent hotels with wide range of amenities and prices nearby.

**Meeting Facilities** 3 private meeting suites, each with general session room, lounge, and adjacent breakout rooms. Also, an Executive Board Room and 4 additional conference rooms. Individual climate and lighting controls.

General session rooms are equipped with microphone, modem outlets, overhead projector, 35mm, VCR and video projector, projection screens. All rooms have hard writing surface tables, ergonomic executive chairs, and phones, in addition to a presentation rail system with flip charts and marker boards.

Fax, transparencies, photocopying, secretarial service, security, message boards and audio/visual technicians on site. Satellite and interactive video teleconferencing.

Lobby, atrium and rotunda areas can be used for exhibiting. Additional space at America's Center up to 20,000 sq. ft.

**Services** Conference Services Desk. Professional meeting coordinators can plan theme parties, spouse activities, etc.

Florist, photographers, sign makers/decorators, computer rentals, ground transportation.

## MONTANA

### The Center at Salmon Lake

**Address** H.C. 31, Box 800 South, Seely Lake, MT 59868
**Phone** (888) 773-2643
**Fax** (406) 677-3846

**Accommodations** 11 suites for up to 25 people, some with fireplaces. 8,000 sq. ft. deck, satellite TV; bathrobes, slippers, hair dryers, turn-down service.

**Meeting Facilities** 4 rooms, 3,200 sq. ft. Executive tilt-swivel chairs, big-screen TV, casual overstuffed furniture or formal setup, huge windows.

**Services** Exclusive use of entire center at all times. Continuous refreshment service, business center, A/V equipment, one contact for all planning needs; airport transportation; full-service conference center for upscale retreats, strategic planning, or board of directors' meetings.

## NEBRASKA

### Arbor Day Farm Lied Conference Center

**Address** 2700 Sylvan Road, Nebraska City, NE 68410 **Phone** (800) 546-LIED (5433) for reservations (402) 873-8733 **Fax** (402) 873-4999

**Accommodations** 96 guest rooms in a relaxed, warm and rustic atmosphere. Nestled on a 260-acre national historic landmark amidst apple orchards and nut trees, the facility uses wood as a source of all heating and cooling. An active recycling program produces a lesson in environmental stewardship, reflecting the philosophy of its parent organization, The National Arbor Day Foundation.

**Meeting Facilities** 10 conference rooms seating up to 400; 14,000 sq. ft. of meeting space with windows and distinctive natural wood themes, upholstered ergonomic chairs, computerized lighting and individual climate control.

In-house audio/visual with teleconferencing and computer network capabilities, rear screen projection.

Conference management and meeting support, registration assistance.

**Services** Conference planning, coordination, clerical support, teleconferencing, in-house A/V staff, environmental tours and activities available.

### Clifford Hardin Nebraska Center for Continuing Education

**Address** University of Nebraska, 33rd and Holdrege Sts., Lincoln, NE 68583 **Phone** (402) 472-3435 **Fax** (402) 472-8207

**Accommodations** 96 sleeping rooms with choice of beds; complimentary continental breakfast.

**Meeting Facilities** 14 meeting rooms with 16,500 sq. ft. of space; tiered auditorium seating 600; complete A/V capabilities, broadcast quality TV and radio studio connections; Internet connection; large lobby for exhibits.

**Services** Videoconferencing, teleconferencing, computer lab, satellite links, Internet access.

## NEW HAMPSHIRE

### New England Conference Center

**Address** 15 Stafford Avenue, University of New Hampshire, Durham, NH 03824 **Phone** (603) 862-2712 **Fax** (603) 862-4351 **e-mail** bhm@hopper.unh.edu

**Accommodations** 115 rooms (handicap accessible), non-smoking.

**Meeting Facilities** 11 rooms seating 2–270.

**Services** Transportation services to/from airports. Complete conference center support on-site, A/V, teleconferencing via satellite. Programming support available.

## NEW JERSEY

### Chauncey Conference Center

**Address** Rosedale and Carter Roads, Princeton, NJ 08541 **Phone** (609) 921-3600 **Fax** (609) 683-4958

**Accommodations** 100 spacious guest rooms with executive-sized desks, task lighting, color TVs; most overlook the rural countryside from balconies or terraces; suites; handicap rooms.

**Meeting Facilities** 13 dedicated conference rooms, 1 with rear screen

projection, all individually climate controlled seating up to 200; ergonomic chairs; complete computer capabilities and A/Vs including CCTV, teleconferencing, and satellite downlink. Experiential Teambuilding course.
XENO• Learning. Laurie House Executive Retreat—a private, self-contained, restored 19th century farm house for senior-level executive groups of up to 15.

Conference Coordinator assigned to group, Conference Services desk, fax, secretarial support, transparencies, photocopying, message delivery.

**Services** CMP includes guest rooms, continuous refreshment breaks, meeting space, A/V services and use of recreational facilities. Collaborative Courseware[SM] offers the most advanced training resources in strategic alliance with the leading management education providers to meeting and training professionals.

### The Executive Meeting Center at the Doubletree Hotel—Somerset

**Address** 200 Atrium Drive, Somerset, NJ 08873
**Phone** (732) 469-2600
**Fax** (732) 509-4527

**Accommodations** 360 newly renovated guest rooms, including 6 deluxe suites.

**Meeting Facilities** 12 rooms, including 2 telephone rooms with speaker phones; 7,000 sq. ft. of meeting space.

**Services** Full business center; 2 self-service computer stations with print capabilities and Internet access.

### Doral Forrestal at Princeton

**Address** 100 College Rd. East, Princeton, NJ 08540 **Phone** (609) 452-7800 **Fax** (609) 452-7883

**Accommodations** 291 rooms (handicapped accessible), including 10 suites.

**Meeting Facilities** 36 rooms seating 12–400.

Included in CMP price: monitor, VCR, flip charts, 35mm projector, overhead projector, pads/pens.

Fax, photocopying, secretarial, Business Center.

**Services** Fully equipped A/V department. Complete travel services, conference services, meeting planning, expanded executive services, party planning.

Conference Services handles planning and on-site meeting coordination. Audio/visual specialist on staff. In-house florist, professional catering staff, staff photographer, entertainment director.

### Hamilton Park
### A Dolce Conference Center

**Address** 175 Park Avenue, Florham Park, NJ 07932 **Phone** (201) 377-2424 **Fax** (201) 377-6108

**Accommodations** 209 deluxe guest rooms including 13 suites.

**Meeting Facilities** 40 dedicated meeting rooms, 3 rear screen rooms, computer lab, teleconferencing, video taping, indiv. climate control, soundproofing, natural lighting.

**Services** Room service, same-day laundry and valet, free parking, local shopping.

### KPMG Center for Leadership Development

**Address** 3 Chestnut Ridge Road, Montvale, NJ 07645 **Phone** (201) 307-7317 **Fax** (201) 307-8037

**Accommodations** Within walking distance of 2 major hotels.

**Meeting Facilities** 25,000 sq. ft., 17 meeting rooms for 2–125 people. Climate control, amphitheatre, rear screen projection, 2 computer rooms. Built-in screens. In-house audio/visual staff and equipment.

**Services** Professional conference coordinator and A/V technical support. On-site parking.

### The Merrill Lynch Conference and Training Center

**Address** 900 Scudders Mill Road, Plainsboro, NJ 08536 **Phone** (800) HCC-MEET (609) 282-1000 **Fax** (609) 282-2126 **e-mail** merrilllynch@iacc.iacconline.com

**Accommodations** 343 guest rooms, includes 50-room Executive Center.

**Meeting Facilities** 34 meeting rooms, auditorium seating 316. Small breakout rooms to large classrooms, will accommodate any size group with any set-up requirements.

In-house staff provides rear screen, overheads, 35mm projectors, video cameras, monitors, phone labs, key pad response system, closed-circuit broadcast capabilities, satellite dish for downlink communications with guestroom relay capabilities; PA system, computer projector & monitors.

Personal conference planner, complete conference services staff and A/V technicians, copy services, fax services, package handling, messages, writing pads, pencils, supplies.

3,136 sq. ft. exhibit space.

**Services** Gift Shop with newsstand, laundry, dry cleaning, shoe shine, vending machines, on-site free parking. French and Spanish-speaking employees.

Notary, print shop, photo lab.

### Sheraton Meadowlands Hotel and Conference Center

**Address** 2 Meadowlands Plaza, East Rutherford, NJ 07073 **Phone** (201) 896-0500 **Fax** (201) 507-2825

**Accommodations** 425 guest rooms, 5 with New York City skyline view. 66 Club Level rooms with private Club Lounge. All rooms with voice mail and data ports. Fully ADA compliant.

**Meeting Facilities** 9 meeting rooms in 4,300 sq. ft. conference center. Amphitheater, 40 executive boardrooms, 6 classrooms; 18 meeting rooms in hotel, 22,252 sq. ft.; 10 additional conference rooms; 2 ballrooms 11,520 sq. ft. and 5,200 sq. ft.

**Services** Full service Business Center, video conferencing packages available. New York City shuttle.

## NEW YORK

### Arden Conference Center: Arden House/Arden Homestead

**Address** Columbia University, Harriman Campus, Harriman, NY 10926 **Phone** (914) 351-4715 **Fax** (914) 351-4561 **e-mail** LisaP@tuxedo.ny.frontiercomm.net

**Accommodations** Total 97: Arden House (80), Arden Homestead (17).

**Meeting Facilities** Total 15: Arden House (12), Arden Homestead (3). Seating 6–125.

Overhead projectors, flip charts, personal computers, computer lab, VCRs, 35mm slide projectors, computer projection.

Concierge service, conference planner, A/V computer technician on site. Graphics capability in house.

**Services** Laundry and dry cleaning.

North America's largest factory outlet mall nearby. Florists, barbershops, historical museums, craft village, antique shopping, outdoor sculpture museum nearby.

Faxing; duplicating; special events planning; free outdoor parking.

### Beaver Hollow Conference and Training Center, NY

**Address** 1083 Pit Road, Java Center, NY 14082 **Phone** (800) 964-7903 (716) 457-3700 **Fax** (716) 457-9348

**Accommodations** 43 rooms, including 7 villa suites.

**Meeting Facilities** 5 rooms, seating 5–60.

**Services** Wide selection of A/V equipment. Ropes course, climbing wall. Experiential education facilitators on staff.

### Chase Conference Center at Chase Manhattan Plaza

**Address** One Chase Manhattan Plaza, 28th Floor, New York, NY 10081 **Phone** (212) 552-5000 **Fax** (212) 552-7200

**Accommodations** None listed.

**Meeting Facilities** 44 multipurpose designed meeting rooms; 63,000 sq. ft. of meeting space.

**Services** A full range of audio/video and computer equipment is available. Including teleconferencing, video and audio recording/playback. Audio conferencing, digitized recording, 35 mm and overhead projectors. Podiums and dedicated control equipment. Wireless microphones. PCs with on-site technical support for standard applications and laserjet printers. Networked setup and loading of standard software available. Video and audio duplication. Internet accounts available.

### Chase Conference Center at 600 Fifth Avenue

**Address** 600 Fifth Avenue, 2nd floor, New York, NY 10020 **Phone** (212) 332-4144 **Fax** (212) 332-4143

**Accommodations** None listed.

**Meeting Facilities** 13 multipurpose designed meeting rooms ranging in size from 300 to 1,300 sq. ft. Total of 7,000 sq. ft. of meeting space.

**Services** Wide selection of A/V equipment including overhead projectors, CD or audio cassette playback equipment, easels and white boards, pads & pencils, videotape recording and playback, PCs, laser printers, Polycomm speakerphones, Barco projection system, limo and messenger services, conference service aides, business services desk, in-house A/V technician.

### The Coleman Center

**Address** 810 Seventh Avenue, 23rd Floor, New York, NY 10019 **Phone** (212) 541-4600 **Fax** (212) 541-4232

**Accommodations** N/A. Hotel reservations at special rates.

**Meeting Facilities** Our only business and sole concentration of our staff are to contribute to improved meeting success. Variety of rooms to hold 10–150 attendees.

**Services** Extensive inventory of every type of audiovisual equipment, fax, duplicating, reproduction of handouts and collation of workbooks. Limousine service, theater tickets, messenger service. Hotel reservation at special rates.

### Doral Arrowwood

**Address** Anderson Hill Road, Rye Brook, NY 10573 **Phone** (914) 939-5500 **Fax** (914) 939-8311

**Accommodations** 272 guest rooms.

**Meeting Facilities** 36 purpose-designed rooms, 120-seat amphitheatre.

Full A/V and technical support, computer lab.

Conference Services desk, administrative support, dedicated conference management.

**Services** Concierge service, valet parking, 24-hr. room service,

newsstand, laundry and dry cleaning.

Project Excel, adventure-based team-building courses.

### Edith Macy Conference Center

**Address** Chappaqua Road, Briarcliff Manor, NY 10510 **Phone** (914) 945-8098 **Fax** (914) 945-8009

**Accommodations** 46 rooms.

**Meeting Facilities** 200-seat auditorium plus 5 meeting rooms and 10 breakout areas. Steelcase highback chairs. Outdoor educational learning available.

**Services** A/V technician on site, full-conference planner to ensure guest satisfaction. Secretarial assistance available.

### Executive Conference Center at the Sheraton New York

**Address** 811 Seventh Avenue, New York, NY 10019 **Phone** (212) 841-6560 **Fax** (212) 841-6445

**Accommodations** 1,750 rooms, corporate club rooms with fax, copier, data port, 2-line phones.

**Meeting Facilities** 12 conference rooms; 1 executive boardroom.

**Services** Videoconferencing, Internet access, conference concierges, meeting-planning offices.

### Harrison Conference Center at Glen Cove

**Address** Dosoris Lane, Glen Cove, NY 11542 **Phone** (800) HCC-MEET (Nat'l Sales) (516) 671-6400 **Fax** (516) 671-6490 **e-mail** PGJERPEN@aol.com

**Accommodations** Two-story estate with 198 modern guest rooms including 4 executive suites. All rooms have air-conditioning control, color cable TV, 2 direct-dial phones, clock radio, voice mail and dataports.

**Meeting Facilities** 30 meeting rooms for 2–225. All have multiple electrical/microphone outlets, recessed lighting, climate controls, 110V electricity.

At no charge: Tape recorders, microphones, overhead, 16mm sound, 35mm slide projection screens, podiums, blackboards, easels (one

per main meeting room), Conference coordinators.

For a fee: A/V operators, stenographers, full business center services.

The "Embassy" has 2,850 sq. ft. of exhibit space.

**Services** Gift shop, laundry and dry cleaning, free outdoor parking for 200 cars.

Computer rental and technical service, notary public, messenger services, print shop, photographer, carpenters, display builders, sign painters, locksmiths, laborers.

### Millennium Conference Center

**Address** 145 West 44th Street, New York, NY 10036 **Phone** (800) 317-3186 (212) 768-4400 **Fax** (212) 789-7630

**Accommodations** 627 luxury guest rooms, incl. 9 suites, and 72 upgraded club rooms.

**Meeting Facilities** 33 meeting rooms accommodating up to 125 each; 17,000 sq. ft. of exhibit space; Hudson Theatre accommodating 700.

**Services** Professional conference coordinators, business center, graphics center. On-site production manager.

### Minnowbrook Adirondack Conference Center

**Address** Maple Lodge Road, Blue Mountain Lake, NY 12812 **Phone** (315) 443-4900 **Fax** (315) 443-4902

**Accommodations** 32 guest rooms with pine tongue-in-groove walls. Main Lodge and Greenhouse each have 10 double bedrooms. Lawn House has 4 double bedrooms. Two hillside cabins each have 4 rooms with queen-sized beds. Shared baths.

**Meeting Facilities** 2 meeting rooms including a 75-seat classroom. Several smaller seminar rooms for up to 56 persons.

**Services** Full A/V equipment, digital projection units, wired for Internet.

### Palisades Executive Conference Center

**Address** Route 9W, Palisades, NY 10964 **Phone** (914) 732-6000 **Fax** (914) 732-6571

**Accommodations** 206 guest rooms, each with IBM network station, queen-size bed, iron & board, hair dryer, bathrobe, and full amenities.

**Meeting Facilities** 43 meeting rooms with 47,000 sq. ft. multipurpose room. Interactive multimedia center, IBM PS/Z computer, extensive audio/visual package.

**Services** Business center/concierge.

### Tarrytown House, A Dolce Conference Hotel

**Address** East Sunnyside Lane, Tarrytown, NY 10591 **Phone** (914) 591-8200 **Fax** (914) 591-4014

**Accommodations** 148 guest rooms.

**Meeting Facilities** 30 meeting rooms; 30,000 sq. ft. of dedicated conference space. New ballroom for up to 400 people.

**Services** Gift shops; free parking; same-day dry cleaning.

### White Eagle Conference Center

**Address** P.O. Box 679, West Lake Moraine, Hamilton, NY 13346 **Phone** (800) 295-9322 (315) 824-2002 **Fax** (315) 824-6799 **e-mail** White_Eagle@iacc.iac-conline.com

**Accommodations** 60 private guest rooms in a rustic setting overlooking beautiful Lake Moraine, three executive suites.

**Meeting Facilities** 8 meeting rooms, up to 18 breakout areas; 2 stand-alone executive-training sites; theater-style seating to 200.

**Services** Full A/V capabilities, projectors, VCRs, cameras, monitors, recorders, fax, copiers, notary public.

## NORTH CAROLINA

### Conference & Education Facility, North Carolina Biotechnology Center

**Address** 15 T.W. Alexander Drive, P.O. Box 13547, Research Triangle Park, NC 27709 **Phone** (919) 541-9366 **Fax** (919) 990-9544 **e-mail** yvonne_patton@ ncbiotech.org

**Accommodations** Coordinated with major hotels, 5-10 min. from facility.

**Meeting Facilities** 170-seat auditorium. Large multipurpose room (opens to garden) holds from 90–150 in various configurations, or exhibits.

**Services** Complete conference capabilities, catering, A/V services, teleconferencing.

### R. David Thomas Executive Conference Center

**Address** One Science Drive, Durham, NC 27708 **Phone** (919) 660-6400 **Fax** (919) 660-3607 **e-mail** tmartin@mail.duke.edu

**Accommodations** 113 rooms including 2 suites (all guest rooms are supported by independent modem line for computer access).

**Meeting Facilities** 15 Thomas Center meeting rooms seating 18–75, 21 breakout rooms; 11 Fuqua School meeting rooms seating 30–450, 20 breakout rooms.

**Services** On-site conference planning and audio/visual technical support.

### The Sanderling Inn Resort & Conference Center

**Address** 1461 Duck Road, Duck, NC 27949 **Phone** (800) 701-4111 (919) 261-4111 **Fax** (919) 261-1638 **e-mail** 74161.41@compuserve.com

**Accommodations** 87 rooms and suites, oceanfront and sound side, private balconies.

**Meeting Facilities** Private conference facility—meetings up to 100 people; 5 meeting rooms; breakout rooms available.

8-hr. ergo chairs; hard writing tables; tackable walls; fully controllable heating/AC/lighting; standard AV on property—other AV available on request.

Conference Concierge (if needed); fax and copying.

**Services** Concierge; fax and copying; private dining; theme parties.

## OHIO

### Dana Conference Center

**Address** Medical College of Ohio, P.O. Box 10008, Toledo, OH 43699 **Phone** (419) 381-4090 **Fax** (419) 381-4025

**Accommodations** 213 rooms (handicap accessible).

**Meeting Facilities** 19 rooms seating 10–450.

**Services** Teleconference equipment, CCTV, video recorders (3/4" or 1/2"), projection TV or monitors, video cameras, slide projectors, overheads, flip charts, X-ray view

boxes. CD or audio cassette playback equipment, A/V technicians. Connected to the Toledo Hilton by walkway; hotel offers complimentary airport shuttle.

### The Forum Conference & Education Center, Inc.

**Address** 1375 East 9th Street, Cleveland, OH 44114 **Phone** (216) 241-6338 **Fax** (216) 241-2583 **e-mail** ForumCC@aol.com

**Accommodations** Adjacent to 3 full service hotels.

**Meeting Facilities** 12 rooms; 400-seat auditorium; 22,000 sq. ft. of meeting space.

**Services** Advanced A/V and video presentation capabilities, satellite downlink in all rooms, interactive video conferencing, conference planning, business services, in-room data lines.

### George S. Dively Building Case Western Reserve University

**Address** 10900 Euclid Ave., Cleveland, OH 44106-7166 **Phone** (216) 368-0020 **Fax** (216) 368-0200 **e-mail:** mam56@po.cwru.edu

**Accommodations** Nearby quality lodging.

**Meeting Facilities** 6 meeting rooms seating up to 100. 7,625 sq. ft. of meeting space. First class amenities include complete catering and meal services; access to a full complement of audiovisual equipment; connections to the University's fiberoptic network and electronic distance-learning capabilities.

**Services** Full range of conference services. Degree and non-degree executive education programs available through the Weatherhead School of Management, Case Western Reserve University.

### Kingsgate Conference Center

**Address** 151 Goodman Drive, Cincinnati, OH 45219 **Phone** (513) 487-3800 **Fax** (513) 487-3810

**Accommodations** 206 guest rooms, oversized desks, adjustable chairs, high-speed Internet connections, 2 phone lines per room.

**Meeting Facilities** 23 rooms, 20,000 sq. ft. including 5,355 sq. ft. ballroom accommodating 576 theater style; 396 for banquet. Two boardrooms, 2 amphitheaters, ISDN lines, A/V communications among meeting rooms and guest rooms.

**Services** Dedicated conference staff, A/V technicians, 24-hour business center.

### Marcum Conference Center & Inn

**Address** Miami University, Oxford, OH 45056 **Phone** (513) 529-6911 **Fax** (513) 529-5700 **e-mail** finkll@hdgs.muohio.edu

**Accommodations** 92 elegantly appointed guest rooms.

**Meeting Facilities** 11 rooms seating 4–250, flexible set-up, complimentary audiovisual, networked computer room.

**Services** Free parking, laundry and dry cleaning, access to university facilities; complimentary newspapers.

### Professional Education and Conference Center

**Address** Kent State University Stark Campus, 6000 Frank Avenue NW, Canton, OH 44720 **Phone** (330) 499-9600

**Accommodations** None.

**Meeting Facilities** 16 meeting rooms, corporate theatre, state-of-the-art communications, computer, and A/V technology.

**Services** Multimedia staff and conference center planners.

### Xavier University Conference Center

**Address** 3800 Victory Parkway, Cincinnati, OH 45207 **Phone** (513) 745-3394 **Fax** (513) 745-4307

**Accommodations** None.

**Meeting Facilities** 8 meeting rooms.

**Services** N/A.

## PENNSYLVANIA

### The Desmond Great Valley Hotel and Conference Center

**Address** One Liberty Boulevard, Malvern, PA 19355 **Phone** (610) 296-9800 **Fax** (610) 889-9869

**Accommodations** 195 rooms (handicap accessible, non-smoking).

**Meeting Facilities** 16 rooms, seating up to 375; state-of-the-art amphitheater.

**Services** Full range of A/V, program coordinators, banquet facilities.

### Eagle Lodge Conference Center & Country Club

**Address** Ridge Pike and Manor Road, Lafayette Hill, PA 19444 **Phone** (800) 523-3000 (610) 825-8000 **Fax** (610) 940-4344

**Accommodations** 120 deluxe guest rooms, including 3 Jr. suites, 6 handicap-accessible; each room has private balcony/patio, cable TV, in-room movies/games; computer hook-up, comfortable work area.

**Meeting Facilities** 32 dedicated meeting rooms, incl. 3 tiered amphitheaters; seating to 250. 15-station computer learning center.

Leather, ergonomic armchairs; zoned lighting, rear screen projection, built-in VCR monitors, flip charts, tackable walls, blackboards, pads/pens, microphones, overheads, podiums, individual computer rentals, other equipment on request.

Professional conference planners; PGA golf professionals, full A/V support, business concierge (faxing, typing, photocopying, messenger, reservations, etc.), security, notary public.

**Services** All standard A/V equipment supplied including VCR, monitor. Business concierge, bell service, social event planning, golf shop, golf lessons/clinics, recreation director. TDD equipment. Complimentary newspapers. Free parking.

### Gregg Conference Center at The American College

**Address** 270 Bryn Mawr Avenue, Bryn Mawr, PA 19010 **Phone** (215) 526-1208 **Fax** (215) 526-1156

**Accommodations** 50 rooms (handicap accessible).

**Meeting Facilities** 15 rooms seating 10–300, 25 breakout rooms, 225-seat auditorium.

**Services** Conference planning, in-house A/V Department, complete equipment and personalized services, teleconferencing, concierge, graphics department, video/audio recording, closed-circuit broadcast system, front and rear screen projection, 2 rooms w/multiple dedicated phone lines.

### Hidden Valley Resort Conference Center

**Address** 1 Craighead Drive, Hidden Valley, PA 15502 **Phone** (800) 833-9308 (814) 443-8000 **Fax** (814) 443-1907

**Accommodations** 225 bedrooms consisting of efficiency bedrooms, parlor, and one-bedroom suites, two and three bedroom condos and townhomes, all with color cable TV, many with kitchens and fireplaces.

**Meeting Facilities** 21 dedicated conference rooms, expertly designed for executive comfort for up to 350; amphitheater for 100. All rooms with Vecta swivel chairs and Johnson custom work surfaces.

Portable PA systems, projection screens, remote control cords, lighted lecterns, podiums, blackboards, cork boards; tape recorders, sound mixers, rear screen, video cameras, computer monitors.

Notary public, first aid, repairmen, stenographer, electricians, A/V operators.

**Services** Conference center concierge, newsstand and sundry shops, free outdoor parking. Babysitting, doctors on call.

Multilingual translation, entertainment and musicians, direction signs, trucks/vans, photographer, paint shop, laborers.

### Manufacturer's Association of Northwest Pennsylvania Conference Center

**Address** 2171 West 38th Street, Erie, PA 16508 **Phone** (800) 815-2660 **Fax** (814) 836-0819

**Accommodations** N/A.

**Meeting Facilities** 9 meeting rooms with 20,000 sq. ft. incuding 85-seat auditorium.

**Services** All rooms equipped with A/V capability. Conference services provided.

### Park Ridge at Valley Forge

**Address** 480 N. Gulph Road, King of Prussia, PA 19406 **Phone** (800) 337-1801 (610) 337-1800 **Fax** (610) 337-4506

**Accommodations** 265 guest rooms including 19-room VIP concierge level; 1 bi-level Presidential Suite and 2 executive suites.

Meeting Facilities 14,796 square feet of meeting space. Including 24 conference rooms seating 12–600 people; 3 boardrooms; 4,864 sq. ft. ballroom.

Included in CMP price: VCR, flip charts, overhead projector, executive note pads.

Complete conference planning services available.

5,000 sq. ft. plus exhibit space.

Services Fully equipped AV department, conference planning and conference concierge.

### Penn Stater
### Conference Center Hotel

Address 215 Innovation Blvd., Penn State Research Park, State College, PA 16803 Phone (814) 863-5000 Fax (814) 863-5003

Accommodations 150 deluxe guest rooms; 5 suites.

Meeting Facilities 38 dedicated meeting rooms from 336–2,203 sq. ft., computer labs, forum meeting room.

Included in CMP price: Monitor, VCR, flip charts, 35 mm projector, overhead projector, pads/pens.

Fax, photocopying, secretarial, and graphics.

19,661 sq. ft. available exhibit space.

Services Conference Services handles planning and on-site meeting coordination. Audio/visual specialist on staff.

Flowers; University recreation, sports.

Gift shop, same-day dry cleaning, in-room movies.

### Sugarloaf
### Albert M. Greenfield
### Conference Center

Address 9230 Germantown Avenue, Philadelphia, PA 19118 Phone (215) 242-9100 Fax (215) 242-8362

Accommodations 50 recently refurbished, well-appointed double rooms. Handicap rooms available.

Meeting Facilities 20 distinctive meeting and conference rooms for groups from 10–200 in country manor setting on 40 acres of rolling hills on this university-owned estate. Rooms are capable of a variety of arrangements and functions. Ample free parking.

Services Full-time conf. specialists assist with any and all aspects of your meeting. Full range A/V. Office support services.

### The Villanova Conference Center

Address 601 Countyline Road, Radnor, PA 19087 Phone (610) 523-1776 Fax (610) 523-1779

Accommodations 58 guest rooms, each with spacious work area, phone, data line, private balcony.

Meeting Facilities 24 rooms combining early 20th century elegance with 21st century technology.

Services Conference planners, broad range of A/V services.

### Wildwood Conference Center

Address One HACC Drive, Harrisburg, PA 17110-2999 Phone (717) 780-2678 Fax (717) 780-3273

Accommodations Local hotels, motels within minutes.

Meeting Facilities 9,000 sq. ft of meeting space, large dining room, state-of-the-art A/V equipment, large prefunction areas.

Services Full range, professional staff; satellite downlink in all rooms; free parking.

## RHODE ISLAND

### Whispering Pines
### Conference Center

Address University of Rhode Island, 401 Victory Highway, West Greenwich, RI 02816-9772 Phone (401) 397-3361 Fax (401) 397-6540

Accommodations 64 in double rooms (handicap accessible).

Meeting Facilities 4 rooms seating 18–100.

Services Conference and meeting planners, PA system, video cameras, flip charts, overhead projector, VCR monitors, 16-mm projectors.

## TENNESSEE

### The Centre at Millennium Park

Address 2001 Millennium Place, Johnson City, TN 37604 Phone (423) 232-2001 Fax (423) 232-2002

Accommodations 1,200 sleeping rooms within 5 minutes.

Meeting Facilities 15 rooms, including 2 auditoriums seating 85 and 125; 8 classrooms, 3 meeting rooms, executive lounge, boardroom.

Services Cutting-edge A/V with video and teleconferencing, satellite downlink, distance learning center, computer training room.

### The Chattanoogan
(Opening April 2001)

Address 1253 South Market Street, Suite 100, Box 4, Chattanooga, TN 37402 Phone (423) 757-2023 Fax (423) 757-2025

Accommodations 202 guest rooms.

Meeting Facilities 20 meeting rooms; Conference Center features a 7,500 sq. ft. ballroom, 84 seat amphitheater, 5 general session rooms for 20–100 persons, and 12 breakout rooms.

Services Superior technology throughout including pre-wired high speed Internet access in all meeting and public spaces as well as in guest rooms. LAN capabilities; full A/V; data projection services. Full service conference concierge and Business Center.

### The Fogelman Executive Center

Address University of Memphis, Memphis, TN 38152 Phone (901) 678-3700 Fax (901) 678-5329

Accommodations 51 single rooms, queen beds.

Meeting Facilities 16 meeting rooms for 12–400 including 3 auditoriums.

Services As part of the CMP: overhead projectors, flip charts, slide projectors, VCR/monitors, video cameras, PA systems, in-room A/V booths with Barco projectors, satellite downlink, van service, conference concierge, A/V technician, conference and meeting planners.

### MeadowView Conference Resort

Address 1901 Meadowview Parkway, Kingsport, TN 37660 Phone (423) 378-0100 Fax (423) 378-3669

Accommodations 196 guest rooms, 73 rooms designed specifically for business travelers.

Meeting Facilities 35,000 sq. ft. convention center, 2 ballrooms (10,000 sq. ft, 4,000 sq. ft), 96-seat amphitheatre, 8 meeting rooms, 2 boardrooms.

Services Conference concierge, complete conference planning services, A/V staff. Golf professionals for tournament organization. Airport transportation.

### Willis Conference Center

**Address** 26 Century Blvd., Nashville, TN 37214 **Phone** (615) 872-6400 **Fax** (615) 872-6429

**Accommodations** Adjacent to 3 full-service hotels.

**Meeting Facilities** A non-smoking facility with 17 rooms seating 4–100, ampitheatre with permanent tiered schoolroom seating for 175. All rooms have solid wall construction, climate controls, ergonomic chairs.

**Services** State-of-the-art A/V equipment, complete conference planning services, video conference equipment, flourescent and incandescent lighting.

## TEXAS

### American Airlines Training & Conference Center

**Address** 4501 Highway 360, Fort Worth, TX 76155 **Phone** (817) 967-1000 **Fax** (817) 967-4867

**Accommodations** 300 sleeping rooms. Single and double occupancy.

**Meeting Facilities** 8 amphitheaters seating 75 each (full audio/visual), 300-seat auditorium (built-in rear screen projection); 31 breakout rooms, 4 computer labs (Windows and Macintosh), 7 cabin simulators (F100, MD80, MD11, DC10, B727, B757, B767, Cargo Compartment).

**Services** Conference planners, support staff, audio/visual technicians, business center, airfare arrangements, full catering and banquet services, dry cleaning and laundry services, tour operations.

### Del Lago Waterfront Conference Center & Resort

**Address** 600 Del Lago Blvd., Montgomery, TX 77356 **Phone** (800) 833-3078 **Fax** (409) 582-4918

**Accommodations** 488 sleeping rooms incl. 302 hi-rise tower suites and 8 penthouses, 45 golf-course cottages and 13 waterfront villas.

**Meeting Facilities** Over 45,000 sq. ft. of function space—all first floor, no load limit.

**Services** Valet, concierge.

### Garrett Creek Ranch Conference Center

**Address** Route 2, Box 235, Paradise, TX 76073 **Phone** (214) 680-8679 **Fax** (214) 690-9318

**Accommodations** 45 rooms.

**Meeting Facilities** Meeting rooms for 10–80.

**Services** Offers the combination of a working ranch and conference center. Complete inventory of A/V equipment, professional meeting planning services, porches with rocking chairs, personalized service.

### Hilton DFW Lake Executive Conference Center

**Address** 1800 Highway 26 East, DFW Airport (Dallas), TX 76051 **Phone** (817) 481-8444 **Fax** (817) 481-3160

**Accommodations** Two 9-story towers comprised of 400 comfortable guest rooms and 4 VIP suites. All have air-conditioning control, 26" color TV, oversized work/study area, direct-dial phone, message alert.

**Meeting Facilities** 40,000 sq. ft. meeting space; 40 meeting rooms for 10–500; 3 tiered amphitheaters. All have climate control.

**Services** Newsstand, gift shop, bookstore.

### Lakeway Inn A Dolce Conference Resort

**Address** 101 Lakeway Drive, Austin, TX 78734-4399 **Phone** (800) LAKEWAY (512) 261-6600 **Fax** (512) 261-7322

**Accommodations** 137 inn rooms; plus 25 villa rooms.

**Meeting Facilities** Austin Room with rear screen for up to 360 attendees; 9 other meeting rooms plus workshop suites.

**Services** Gift shop, pro shop for each golf course, conference planning, and A/V as needed.

### Rough Creek Lodge & Executive Conference Center

**Address** P.O. Box 2400, Glen Rose, TX 76043 **Phone** (800) 864-4705 **Fax** (817) 571-3988

**Accommodations** 39 rooms, 7 suites including a presidential suite.

**Meeting Facilities** 4 rooms, 3,570 sq. ft. boardroom for 16; 3 meeting rooms with front/rear screen projection capabilities.

**Services** Guest rooms have executive desks with dataports. Business center with fax, copier. Complete in-house A/V, gift shop, personalized service.

### The San Antonio Learning Center

**Address** 711 Navarro Street, Suite 100, San Antonio, TX 78205 **Phone** (210) 226-4600 **Fax** (210) 226-4027

**Accommodations** None listed.

**Meeting Facilities** 4 rooms, 10,000 sq. ft., 2 large computer classrooms seats 19 and 22; 2 other meeting rooms seats 20 and 80 with flexible setup.

**Services** 41 networked PCs and workstations; videoconferencing; multimedia presentation; Internet; satellite downlink, on-site technical and meeting planning staffs, food and beverage services.

### The San Luis Resort & Conference Center

**Address** 5222 Seawall Blvd., Galveston, TX 77551 **Phone** (409) 744-1500 **Fax** (409) 744-7545 **e-mail** SanLuisRst@aol.com

**Accommodations** 244 rooms including 2 penthouse suites.

**Meeting Facilities** 22 meeting rooms include the 6,000 sq. ft. Argosy Ballroom and 12 dedicated conference rooms.

**Services** Business services include: personal computers, private offices, copy and facsimile machines. Multilingual staff.

### Sheraton Austin Hotel Executive Meeting Center

**Address** 500 North I-35, Austin, TX 78701 **Phone** (512) 480-8181 **Fax** (512) 480-8633

**Accommodations** 254 guest rooms, each with voice mail and dataports.

**Meeting Facilities** 9 meeting rooms for 5–100 persons, each room features tackable walls, white boards, built in screens, in-room house phone, multiple floor power and data jacks, cherry conference table, meeting supply kit.

**Services** Business Center and staff, trained technicians.

### Star Brand Ranch Executive Retreat

**Address** P.O. Box 660, Kaufman, TX 75142 **Phone** (214) 932-2714 **Fax** (214) 932-7606

**Accommodations** Comfortably appointed guest rooms with amenities, housing up to 40 double occupancy.

**Meeting Facilities** 3 rooms serving group up to 40; multiple breakout rooms, ergonomic chairs, climate controls.

**Services** A/V equipment, write-on, wipe-off, magnetic walls; conference planners; modem connections; business center with fax, copies, and transparencies at no charge.

### The Woodlands Resort & Conference Center

**Address** 2301 N. Millbend Drive, The Woodlands, TX 77380 **Phone** (800) 433-2624 (713) 367-1100 **Fax** (713) 364-6338

**Accommodations** 268 guest rooms, including 79 suites.

**Meeting Facilities** 36 dedicated conference rooms encompassing 44,000 sq. ft. of space.

Complete in-house A/V production equipment supply and staffing is available.

Notary public, first aid, A/V repair, and conference concierge.

18,000 sq. ft. indoor exhibit space.

**Services** Retail shopping, airport transportation, tennis and golf professionals for tournament organization.

Printing, painting, signs, musicians, translation equipment, and other transportation.

## UTAH

### The Inn at Prospector Square Conference Center & Athletic Club

**Address** P.O. Box 1698, Park City, UT 84060 **Phone** (801) 649-7100 **Fax** (801) 453-3812

**Accommodations** Hotel rooms, studios, 1-, 2-, 3-bedroom condos.

**Meeting Facilities** Largest room approx. 500 theater-style seats, 10 breakouts.

**Services** Concierge, bell service, athletic club.

### Snowbird Conference Center at The Cliff Lodge

**Address** Snowbird, UT 84092 **Phone** (800) 882-4766 (801) 742-2222 **Fax** (801) 742-3342, Telex (910) 240-0389

**Accommodations** 532-room, full-service Cliff Lodge includes deluxe bedrooms and suites, room service.

**Meeting Facilities** 22 rooms seating 10–900, deluxe exec. boardroom, built-in rear-screen projection in 3 sections of ballroom. Ballrooms accommodate 43 8′ × 10′ booths. Seasonal (June–Oct.) Event Center seats 2000.

**Services** Concierge, laundry, dry cleaning, day-care facility, business center.

## VERMONT

### Stoweflake Resort & Conference Center

**Address** P.O. Box 369, Stowe, VT 05672 **Phone** (800) 253-2232 (802) 253-7355 **Fax** (802) 253-4419

**Accommodations** Elegant Vermont countryside inn and modern townhouses offer a total of 94 guest rooms.

**Meeting Facilities** 10 multi-purpose meeting rooms.

**Services** Conference planning, gift shop, room service.

## VIRGINIA

### Airlie Conference Center

**Address** Route 605, Airlie, VA 22186 **Phone** (800) 288-9573 (703) 347-1300 **Fax** (703) 347-5957

**Accommodations** 160 rooms, single or double.

**Meeting Facilities** Conventional-style meeting rooms for up to 200 participants, other buildings for special sessions, many with fireplaces and beautiful views.

**Services** 3,000-acre estate in the heart of the Virginia hunt country offers a blend of retreat and meeting facilities, special events areas. Site tours are encouraged.

### Donaldson Brown Hotel & Conference Center

**Address** Virginia Polytechnic Institute & State University, Blacksburg, VA 24061-0104 **Phone** (540) 231-8000 **Fax** (540) 231-3746 **e-mail** lisae@vt.edu

**Accommodations** 100 rooms (handicap accessible).

**Meeting Facilities** 10 rooms, seating 12–600; complete line of slide, overhead, video equipment and accessories; sound equipment, and trained technical staff.

### The Founders Inn

**Address** 5641 Indian River Rd., Virginia Beach, VA 23464 **Phone** (800) 926-4466 (757) 424-5511 **Fax** (757) 366-5785

**Accommodations** 249 sleeping rooms. Elegant period decor, Georgian architecture, AAA 4-diamond rating.

**Meeting Facilities** 28 meeting rooms with 32,000 sq. ft. of meeting space. 70-seat amphitheater, high-speed data lines throughout.

**Services** Business Center, videoconferencing, teleconferencing, Internet access.

### The Hotel Roanoke & Conference Center

**Address** 110 Shenandoah Avenue, Roanoke, VA 24016 **Phone** (540) 985-5900 **Fax** (540) 853-8290

**Accommodations** A 4-diamond hotel, listed in the National Register of Historic Places.

### Kingsmill Resort & Conference Center

**Address** 1010 Kingsmill Road, Williamsburg, VA 23185 **Phone** (800) 482-2892 (804) 253-1703 **Fax** (804) 253-3993

**Accommodations** 352 guest rooms; 1-, 2-, or 3-bedroom suites in villas.

**Meeting Facilities** 16 meeting rooms seating 10–550.

**Services** Complete A/V including overhead projectors, video, monitors.

### Lansdowne Resort

**Address** 44050 Woodridge Parkway, Leesburg, VA 20176 **Phone** (800) 541-4801 (703) 729-8400 **Fax** (703) 729-4096

**Accommodations** 305 rooms; 14 suites.

**Meeting Facilities** 45,000 sq. ft. of executive conference space with 25 dedicated conference rooms. Facility also includes 124-seat tiered amphitheater. All rooms have multiple electrical outlets and individual controls for climate, sound, and lighting. Rear/front screen projection. Audio conferencing. Audio and video production capabilities.

At no charge: Standard A/V package including 26″ monitor and VCR, 16mm film projector, 35mm slide projector, overhead projector, flip chart, and white board with marker, podium, microphone.

At a charge: Translation equipment, camcorders, computer monitors, projectors/screens, CCTV equipment, typewriters, direction signs, name card printers, etc.

Conference concierge for on-site needs; fax/copy services, typing, phone messages, personal conference planning manager for planning details, professional A/V staff.

15,500 sq. ft. of exhibit space is available. (9,525 sq. ft. of exhibit space available in Lansdowne's ballroom.)

**Services** Pro Shop, sundries, valet, laundry, dry cleaning, doctor on call, free parking, massage, salon and spa services.

Stenographer, printers, photographer, carpenters, display builders, translators, painter, plumber, musicians.

### Westfields Marriott

**Address** 14750 Conference Center Drive, Chantilly, VA 22021 **Phone** (800) 635-5666 (703) 818-0400 **Fax** (703) 818-3655

**Accommodations** 335 guest rooms.

**Meeting Facilities** 40,000 sq. ft. of dedicated meeting space including 30 meeting rooms, amphitheatre.

**Services** Media center, full-time A/V staff, business center, simultaneous translation booths, broadcast studio.

### Xerox Document University

**Address** P.O. Box 2000, Leesburg, VA 22075 **Phone** (703) 729-8000 **Fax** (703) 729-5382

**Accommodations** 800 rooms, 60 suites.

**Meeting Facilities** 125 rooms, seating 8–400.

**Services** Conference package includes meeting facilities and most services such as A/V equipment, chalkboard, easels, etc. On-

site coordinators assigned to assist each group.

## WASHINGTON

### Bell Harbor International Conference Center

**Address** Pier 66, 2211 Alaskan Way, Seattle, WA 98121-1604 **Phone** (206) 441-6666 **Fax** (206) 441-6665

**Accommodations** Preferred arrangements available with local hotels.

**Meeting Facilities** 4 waterfront conference rooms, large auditorium, 5,000 sq. ft. exhibit hall.

**Services** Business services center, A/V support.

### Hilton Seattle Airport & Conference Center

**Address** 17620 Pacific Highway South, Seattle, WA 98188 **Phone** (206) 244-4800 **Fax** (206) 248-4495

### Skamania Lodge

**Address** 1131 SW Skamania Lodge Way, Stevenson, WA 98648 **Phone** (800) 982-9095 **Fax** (509) 427-2548

**Accommodations** 195 sleeping rooms featuring views of Columbia River Gorge or forest; 34 deluxe rooms with fireplaces.

**Meeting Facilities** 11 meeting rooms with 12,000 sq. ft. of meeting space. Two ballrooms totaling 11,500 sq. ft. Each is divisible into breakout space by state-of-the-art acoustical walls. Complete A/V equipment and conference services staff.

**Services** Forest Service information center in Hotel lobby provides directions to local points of interest including day trips to Mt. Hood and Mt. St. Helens.

## WEST VIRGINIA

### Summit Conference Center

**Address** 129 Summers Street, Charlston, WV 25301 **Phone** (888) 224-0515 **Fax** (304) 343-5114

**Accommodations** 3 major hotels in walking distance; shuttle service available.

**Meeting Facilities** 5 rooms seating 2–100 persons.

**Services** None listed.

## WISCONSIN

### Minnesuing Acres

**Address** 8084 S. Minnesuing Acres Dr., Lake Nebagamon, WI 54849 **Phone** (612) 540-5205 **Fax** (612) 449-1150

**Accommodations** 40 comfortably appointed rooms, including 1 VIP suite. Private lodge situated on 100 wooded acres booked to only one group at a time—no transient business.

**Meeting Facilities** 4 meeting rooms with a total of 3,500 sq. ft. of meeting space. New main meeting room with state-of-the-art A/V, capable of seating 100; 3 smaller meeting rooms.

**Services** Transportation to and from Duluth airport at nominal charge.

### University of Wisconsin Extension Conference Centers

**Address** 702 Langdon Street, Madison, WI 53706 **Phone** (608) 262-1122 **Fax** (608) 262-8516

**Accommodations** 153 guest rooms including 2 suites; handicapped accessible.

**Meeting Facilities** 34 rooms, seating 15–500.

**Services** A/V on-site with technical staff, complete inventory of equipment including CCTV, teleconference, computer lab; registration, and full conference planning services.

### Wingspread

**Address** 33 East Four Mile Road, Racine, WI 53402 **Phone** (414) 639-3211 **Fax** (414) 681-3327

**Accommodations** Nearby hotels.

**Meeting Facilities** 12 rooms. Meetings are held at Wingspread, designed by Frank Lloyd Wright in the late 1930s for the H. F. Johnson family.

**Services** The Johnson Foundation provides ground transportation, meals and conference support for conferences that meet Wingspread guidelines.

## GLOBAL CENTERS

## CANADA

### The Banff Centre

**Address** Box 1020, Station 11, Banff, Alberta T0L 0C0 **Phone** (403) 762-6204 **Fax** (403) 762-7560

**Accommodations** 414 rooms, featuring a variety of types, including deluxe suites.

**Meeting Facilities** 60 rooms, accommodating 8–1,000.

**Services** Full meeting planning, off-site activities, full A/V department.

### The Metropolitan Centre

**Address** 333 Fourth Avenue, Southwest, Calgary, Alberta, T2P 0H9 **Phone** (403) 266-3876 **Fax** (403) 233-0009

**Accommodations** Connected to the Westin-Calgary, with easy access to other major downtown hotels.

**Meeting Facilities** 8 rooms, 15,000 sq. ft. The Centre offers 5,200 sq. ft. conference hall, 250-seat tiered lecture theatre, 3 dedicated meeting rooms to accommodate a variety of set-up styles.

**Services** State-of-art A/V, video and teleconferencing services, satellite downlink, ISDN, fibre optics, ergonomic seating, individually climate controlled rooms, underground parking. Full-service executive catering.

### Morris J. Wosk Centre for Dialogue

**Address** Simon Fraser University, 515 West Hastings Street, Vancouver, BC V6B 5K3 Canada **Phone** (604) 291-5800 **Fax** (604) 291-5060

**Accommodations** 150 guest rooms.

**Meeting Facilities** 14 meeting rooms.

**Services** N/A.

### Donald Gordon Centre

**Address** Queen's University, Kingston, Ontario K7L 3N6 **Phone** (613) 545-2221 **Fax** (613) 545-6624

**Accommodations** 75 single rooms (1 handicap).

**Meeting Facilities** 1 seminar room seating 100; 1 tiered lecture theater seating 50, 10 meeting/breakfast rooms seating 10–25.

**Services** 35mm, 16mm and overhead projectors, video recording and playback on 1/2″ VHS tape, video/computer image projection available.

### Eaton Hall Inn & Conference Center

**Address** 13990 Dufferin Street, King City, Ontario L7B 1B3 **Phone** (905) 833-4500 **Fax** (905) 833-1760 **e-mail** gbaker@ehalladm.senecac.on.ca

**Accommodations** 44 rooms, accommodating up to 67 guests in lakeside chalets or the historic Villa Fiori, a short stroll from the Hall.

**Meeting Facilities** 9 meeting rooms, focusing on comfort, are well-lit, climate controlled, equipped with comfortable armchairs.

**Services** Full range of A/V.

### J. J. Wettlaufer Executive Development Center

**Address** Richard Ivey School of Business, 6450 Kitimat Rd., Mississauga, ON L5N 2B8, Canada **Phone** (905) 819-8380 **Fax** (905) 819-8613

**Accommodations** None.

**Meeting Facilities** 10 rooms.

**Services** None.

### Kempenfelt Conference Centre Georgian College

**Address** R.R. #4, Barrie, Ontario L4M 4S6 **Phone** (705) 722-8080 **Fax** (705) 721-3395

**Accommodations** 77 rooms.

**Meeting Facilities** 22 meeting and seminar/breakout rooms seating 5–200.

**Services** Complete inventory of A/V and support equipment with on-site services, including LCD boards, rear screen video/slide, teleconferencing, 3/4″ and 1/2″ VCR, color cameras and monitors, 35mm and 16mm projection.

### NAÝ CANADA Training & Conference Centre

**Address** 1950 Montreal Road, Cornwall, ON K6H 6L2 **Phone** (613) 936-5000 **Fax** (613) 936-5010

**Accommodations** 620 sleeping rooms.

**Meeting Facilities** 50 meeting rooms with 50,000 sq. ft. of meeting space.

**Services** Business center, computer lab, interactive video, videoconferencing, teleconferencing, satellite up/down links, Internet access.

### Spencer Hall

**Address** 551 Windermere Road, London, Ontario N5X 2T1 **Phone** (519) 679-4546 **Fax** (519) 645-0733

**Accommodations** 130 rooms (handicap accessible).

**Meeting Facilities** Seats 8–130.

**Services** Extensive A/V inventory, resident A/V technician, resident photographer, satellite conferencing.

### White Oaks Conference Resort & Spa

**Address** 253 Taylor Road, Niagra-on-the-Lake, Ontario L0S 1J0 **Phone** (800) 263-5766 **Fax** (905) 688-2220

**Accommodations** 150 rooms, including luxury suites and standard rooms. Standard, king-size and double beds. Smoking and non-smoking rooms available.

**Meeting Facilities** 18 meeting rooms with 15,000 sq. ft. of meeting space. Amphitheatre, grand event ballroom. Nonsmoking, new conference center added in 1998. Business center.

**Services** Dining, fitness, photocopying, faxing, room service, handicap accessible.

### Hotel du Parc Le Centre de Conférence de Montréal

**Address** 3625 Avenue du Parc, Montreal, Quebec H2X 3P8 **Phone** (514) 288-6666 **Fax** (514) 288-2469

**Accommodations** 445 deluxe rooms and suites.

**Meeting Facilities** 29 banquet and meeting rooms. Accommodating 8–900 people.

**Services** Full convention and meeting planning services. Assistance in all off-site activities.

## SOUTH AMERICA

### World Trade Center Curacao

**Address** P.O. Box 6005, Piscadera Bay, Curacao **Phone** 59 9-9-636100 **Fax** 9-9-624408

Accommodations 500 hotel rooms across the street.

Meeting Facilities 11 rooms, including 325-seat auditorium and small exhibition hall.

Services Full range of A/V, conference planning, marketing services, secretarial services.

## IACC EUROPE

## DENMARK

### Bymose Hegn Kursuscenter

Address Bymosegardsvej 11, DK 3200 Helsinge, Denmark Phone 45 48-79-84-00 Fax 48-79-80-74

Accommodations 113 rooms (handicap accessible).

Meeting Facilities 30 conference rooms.

Services Complete inventory of equipment and services.

### Hindsgavl Slot

Address Hindsgavl Alle 7, DK 5500 Middelfart, Denmark Phone 45 64-41-88-00 Fax 64-41-88-11

Accommodations 73 rooms.

Meeting Facilities 13 rooms.

Services Conference planning, secretarial and technical services, overhead/viewgraph, tape recorder, videotape recording, film and slide projectors.

### Klarskovgaard Conference Center

Address Korsoer Lystskov, DK 4220 Korsoer, Denmark Phone 45 53-57-23-22 Fax 53-57-35-41

Accommodations 104 rooms.

Meeting Facilities 24 conference rooms seating 8–200.

Services Full range, trained technicians on staff.

### Munkebjerg Hotel

Address Munkebjerg 125, Vejle 7100 Denmark Phone 45 76-42-85-00 Fax 45 75-72-08-86

Accommodations 148 rooms in 4-star hotel, 125 standard rooms; 23 luxury rooms.

Meeting Facilities 14 meeting rooms with 45,000 sq. ft. Largest room accommodates up to 500. New conference center area.

Services Business center, conference services, technical support.

### Pharmakon

Address 42 Milnersvej, DK 3400 Hilleroed, Denmark Phone 45 42-26-50-00 Fax 42-26-51-60

Accommodations 138 rooms.

Meeting Facilities 28 conference rooms seating 8–200.

Services Full range of A/V, computer lab with 12 networked PCs.

### Scanticon Comwell Helsingor a/s

Address Norrevej 80, DK-3070 Snekkersten, Denmark Phone 45 42-22-03-33 Fax 42-22-03-99

Accommodations 149 rooms.

Meeting Facilities 33 rooms.

Services Conference planning, secretarial services, messenger service, language services, graphic services, closed-circuit TV, teleconferencing, overhead/viewgraph, tape recorder, videotape recording, film and slide projectors.

### Scanticon Comwell Kolding a/s

Address Skovbrynet 1, P.O. Box 53, DK 6000 Kolding, Denmark Phone 45 75-50-15-55 Fax 75-50-15-68

Accommodations 160 rooms.

Meeting Facilities 24 rooms, seating 10–1,200.

Services Graphics workshop, conference secretariat, travel and excursion service. Overhead projectors, slide projectors, wide-screen projector, PA systems, cassette video and audio playback units, CCTV, simultaneous translation, teleconference facilities, personal computers, trained technicians on staff.

### Schaeffergaarden

Address Fondet for Dansk-Norsk Samarbejde; Jaegersborg Allé 166, DK 2820 Genteofte, Denmark Phone 45 39-65-60-65 Fax 39-65-05-46 e-mail schaef@inet.uni-c.dk

Accommodations 74 rooms.

Meeting Facilities 1 auditorium, seating up to 130; 8 meeting rooms seating 2–50; 10 group rooms seating 2–12.

Services Overhead projectors 400/250 watt, projection screens, flip charts, video (VHS/U-Matic, Pal), LCD projector, tape recorders, special conference staff.

### Toruplund

Address Torupvejen 90, 3390 Hundested, Denmark Phone 45 47-98-70-98 Fax 45 47-98-70-22

Accommodations 42 rooms.

Meeting Facilities 9 rooms seating 6–100.

Services Conference planning, language services, overhead-viewgraph, tape and video recording, VHS editing suite, video and slide projectors, PCs. Offices for conference staff.

## FRANCE

### Fregate

Address Route de Bandol, R.N. 599, 83270 St. Cyr Sur Mer, France Phone 33 94-29-39-39 Fax 94-29-39-40

Accommodations 133 four-star hotel rooms, including a Presidential suite and 38 junior suites. All have outdoor terraces and views of the sea.

Meeting Facilities Seating up to 140.

Services Rear-screen SVGA projection, drop screens, video projection capabilities, PCs.

## NETHERLANDS

### Congresscentre Koningshof

Address Locht 117, 5504 RM Veldhoven, The Netherlands Phone 31 40-253-7475 Fax 31 40-254-5515

Accommodations 440 guest rooms.

Meeting Facilities 70 meeting rooms, seating 7–700 persons; 2,400 sq. meters exhibition space.

Services All technical facilities available. Technical and secretarial department on permanent standby.

## NORWAY

### Klekken Hotell

Address N3500 Hønefoss, Norway Phone 47 32-13-22-00 Fax 32-13-27-93

Accommodations 116 rooms.

Meeting Facilities 27 rooms.

Services Conference planning, messenger service, all technical equipment including videotape recording.

### Leangkollen Hotel og Konferanse Senter

**Address** Bleikerasen 215, N-1370 Asker, Norway
**Phone** 47 66-78-23-65

**Accommodations** 102 guest rooms.

**Meeting Facilities** 20 rooms, seating 10–100.

**Services** Overhead projectors, tape recorders, easels, blackboards, film and slide projectors, video equipment.

### Vettre Hotel Konferansesenter

**Address** Konglungveien 201, N-1392 Vettre, Norway **Phone** 47 66-90-22-11 **Fax** 66-90-28-30

**Accommodations** 76 rooms, 152 beds (handicap accessible).

**Meeting Facilities** 24 rooms, seating 6-300.

**Services** Full range, including overhead projector, videos and monitors, special conference staff.

### SWEDEN

### Best Western Hotel Riverton

**Address** Stora Badhasgatan 26, Göteborg, S-411-21 Sweden
**Phone** 46 31-750-1000
**Fax** 46 31-750-1001

### Best Western Hotell Södra Berget

**Address** Box 858, S-851-24 Sundsvall, Sweden **Phone** 46 60-123000 **Fax** 60-151034

**Accommodations** 180 rooms.

**Meeting Facilities** 24 rooms, seating 10–360.

**Services** Full range, including overhead projector, videos, monitors.

### Engsholm Castle

**Address** S-153-93 Holo, Sweden
**Phone** 46 8-55-15-51-00
**Fax** 55-15-50-07

**Accommodations** 53 single rooms.

**Meeting Facilities** 17 rooms.

**Services** Overhead, tape recorder, video VHS, slide projector. Most needs met on request.

### Foresta Hotel & Conference Center

**Address** Box 1324, Lidingö, 18125 Sweden **Phone** 46 87-65-27-00 **Fax** 46 87-67-75-42

**Accommodations** 96 sleeping rooms; newly renovated large rooms and suites.

**Meeting Facilities** 8 meeting rooms, seating 10–400; 8 breakout rooms, seating 5–15; 600 sq. meters of exhibit space.

**Services** Overhead projectors, LDC, video, TV.

### Hotel Strandbaden

**Address** Havsbadsallen, Falkenberg, S-311-42, Sweden
**Phone** 46 346-71-49-00
**Fax** 46 34-61-61-11

**Accommodations** 135 sleeping rooms.

**Meeting Facilities** 7 meeting rooms plus 9 breakout rooms, each with white board, overhead projector, flip chart.

**Services** Conference services, business services, A/V technicians, ISDN lines, Internet connectivity.

### Hotel Tylösand

**Address** Box 643, S-301 16 Halmstad, Sweden **Phone** 46 3-53-05-00 **Fax** 46 3-53-24-39 **e-mail** tylosand@info.se

**Accommodations** 230 rooms.

**Meeting Facilities** 27 rooms, seating up to 550.

**Services** Full range, overhead projector, videos, ISDN, monitors.

### Lustikulla Konferens

**Address** Box 47095, S-100-74 Stockholm, Sweden **Phone** 46 8-744-45-40 **Fax** 8-19 82 85

**Accommodations** N.A.

**Meeting Facilities** 15 rooms, seating 10-225.

**Services** Complete inventory of equipment and services.

### Nordkalotten Hotell & Konferens

**Address** Lulviksvägen 1, S-972-54 Luleå, Sweden **Phone** 46 92-08-93-50 **Fax** 46 92-01-99-09 **e-mail** info.nordkalotten@sweden-hotels.se.html

**Accommodations** 171 rooms, including 65 minisuites with private sauna.

**Meeting Facilities** 30 rooms, seating 6–345.

**Services** Full range, including overhead projector, videos, monitors.

### Nova Park Hotel ar

**Address** Gredelbyleden, S-741-71 Uppsala/Arlanda, Sweden
**Phone** 46 18-34-90-00 **Fax** 46 18-34-92-92

**Accommodations** 119 rooms.

**Meeting Facilities** 9 rooms, seating 10–125.

**Services** Full range, including overhead, projector, videos, monitors, computer connection, Internet (credit card terminal).

### Romantic Hotel Söderköpings Brunn

**Address** Box 44, S-614-21 Soderkoping, Sweden **Phone** 46 121-10900 **Fax** 121-13941

**Accommodations** 103 rooms, including 8 suites.

**Meeting Facilities** 17 rooms, seating 8–200.

**Services** Complete inventory of equipment and services.

### Rosenön Conferens Center

**Address** S-13054 Dalaro, Sweden **Phone** 46 8 501 53700 **Fax** 8 501 53801 **e-mail** rosenon@iac.iac-conline.com

**Accommodations** 87 guest rooms.

**Meeting Facilities** 25 rooms, seating 8–120.

**Services** Complete inventory of equipment and services.

### Selma Lagerlöf Hotel & Spa

**Address** Box 500, S-686-28 Sunne, Sweden **Phone** 46 565-166-00, SPA 565-166-21 **Fax** 565-166-20

**Accommodations** 340 rooms.

**Meeting Facilities** 16 conference rooms, 16 breakout rooms, seating 5–400.

**Services** Full range, including overhead projector, videos, monitors.

### Skogshem & Wijk Conference Centers

**Address** Box 1213, S-181-24 Lidingo, Sweden **Phone** 46 8-731-42-00 **Fax** 8-731-42-04

**Accommodations** 189 rooms.

**Meeting Facilities** 16 rooms, seating 10–200.

**Services** Latest technical equipment, computer center.

### Steningevik Konferens

**Address** Steninge allé, Märsta/
Arlanda, S-195-91, Sweden
**Phone** 46 8-591-231-50
**Fax** 46 8-591-127-31

**Accommodations** 51 sleeping rooms,
all 2-bed doubles.

**Meeting Facilities** 14 meeting rooms
seating 6–100; 8 breakout rooms.

**Services** Full range A/V services
including overhead projector, LCD
projector, video monitors, computer connections, Internet and
ISDN lines.

### Strand Hotell, Borgholm

**Address** P.O. Box 41, S-387-88
Borgholm, Sweden **Phone** 46
485-888 88 **Fax** 485-124- 27
**e-mail** strandhotell@borgholm-
strand.se

**Accommodations** 125 rooms.

**Meeting Facilities** 9 rooms, seating
10–300.

**Services** Full range, including overhead 16mm, 35mm slide projectors, PA systems, video and audio
playback units. Special conference
and technical staff.

### Vildmarks Hotellet

**Address** Kolmården S-618-93, Sweden
**Phone** 46 11-15-71-00
**Fax** 46 11-39-50-84

**Accommodations** 213 rooms.

**Meeting Facilities** 10 meeting rooms.

**Services** N/A.

### Ystads Saltsjöbad

**Address** Saltsjöbadsvägen 6, S-271-39
Ystad, Sweden **Phone** 46 41-11-
36-30 **Fax** 46 41-15-58-35

**Accommodations** 108 double rooms.

**Meeting Facilities** 15 rooms, 1
convention hall, seating 10–325.
Program for approx. 40 social
activities.

**Services** Full range, including overhead projectors, videos, all technical facilities including ISDN.

## UNITED KINGDOM

### Ashridge Management College

**Address** Berkhamsted, HP4 1NS
Hertfordshire, England **Phone** 44
1442-841027 or 841029 **Fax** 1442-
841036

**Accommodations** 173 rooms.

**Meeting Facilities** 15 rooms seating
12–150; syndicate rooms.

**Services** Conference planning,
secretarial, graphic, fixed closed-circuit TV, TV and radio studio, over-
head/viewgraph, tape recorders,
videotape recording, camcorders,
film and slide projectors, PCs, flip
charts, black or white boards.

### Barnett Hill Conference & Training Centre

**Address** Wonersh, Guilford, Surrey
GU5 ORF England **Phone** 44
1483-893361 **Fax** 44 1483-892836

**Accommodations** 53 rooms, contemporary and well-equipped.

**Meeting Facilities** 8 rooms, seating
20–70. Sophisticated conference
suites equipped with state-of-the-
art presentation systems, ISDN
links, data projection, overhead
projector, flip charts, A/V, closed-
circuit TV.

**Services** Secretarial services, translation services. Unique outdoor,
intellectually challenging exercises
can test teamwork.

### Barony Castle

**Address** Eddleston by Peebles, EH45
8QW Peeblesshire, Scotland
**Phone** 01721 730395 **Fax** 01721
730275

**Accommodations** 78 guest rooms.

**Meeting Facilities** 8 rooms, 8
syndicate rooms.

**Services** Complete range of equipment and services.

### Branksome

**Address** Hindhead Road, Haslemere,
GU27-3PU, Surrey, England
**Phone** 44 1428-664600
**Fax** 44 1428-664699

**Accommodations** 59 rooms.

**Meeting Facilities** 22 meeting rooms,
9 syndicate rooms.

**Services** Complete range of equipment and services.

### Burleigh Court

**Address** Loughborough University,
Loughborough, LE11-3TD Leices-
tershire, England **Phone** 44 1509-
211515 **Fax** 1509-211508

**Accommodations** 118 rooms.

**Meeting Facilities** 20 meeting rooms.

**Services** Conference planning, secretarial services, language transla-
tions, closed-circuit TV, overhead/
viewgraph, tape recorder, videotape recording, film and slide projectors, computer link.

**24-Hour Reception fax:** 44-1509-
211569.

### Cranage Hall

**Address** Knutsford Road, Cranage,
Holmes Chapel, Cheshire CW48E0,
England **Phone** 44 1477-536666
**Fax** 1477-536787

**Accommodations** 120 double and
twin ensuite rooms with T/C, TV,
satellite, voicemail and tea/coffee-
making facilities.

**Meeting Facilities** 29 rooms, seating
2–300. Largest is 3,200 sq. ft. All
are air conditioned.

**Services** Beauty salon.

### Durdent Court

**Address** Tilehouse Lane, Denham,
UB9-5DU Buckinghamshire,
England **Phone** 44 1895-833338
**Fax** 1895-832156

**Accommodations** 83 rooms.

**Meeting Facilities** 20 rooms, seating
8–150.

**Services** Conference planning, secretarial services, CCTV, slide projectors, audio conferencing, data and
video projection, computers,
dedicated conference technicians.

### Elvetham Hall Ltd. Conference Centre

**Address** Hartley Wintney, RG27-8AR
Hampshire, England **Phone** 44
1252-844871 **Fax** 1252-844161

**Accommodations** 72 rooms.

**Meeting Facilities** 17 meeting rooms.

**Services** Conference planning, closed-
circuit TV, camcorders, overhead/
viewgraph, tape recorder, videotape recording (VHS and U-matic),
film and slide projectors, video/
data projector. On-site technicians.

### Ettington Chase Conference Centre

**Address** Ettington, Stratford upon
Avon, CV37 7NZ Warwickshire,
England **Phone** 44 1604-821666
**Fax** 1604-821596

**Accommodations** 113 guestrooms.

**Meeting Facilities** 29 meeting rooms.

**Services** Conference planning, secretarial services, language translators, closed-circuit TV, overhead/viewgraph, tape recorder, videotape recording, personal computers, film and slide projectors, video conferencing.

### Gorse Hill

**Address** Gorse Hill, Hook Heath Road, Woking, GU22 Surrey, England **Phone** 44 1483-747444 **Fax** 1483-747454

**Accommodations** 50 rooms.

**Meeting Facilities** 7 meeting rooms, 10 syndicates.

**Services** CCTV, OHP, LCD, Barco, PCs, Lite Pro.

### Harben House

**Address** Tickford Street, Newport Pagnell, MK16 9EY Buckinghamshire, England **Phone** 44 1908-215600 **Fax** 1908-215610

**Accommodations** 140 rooms.

**Meeting Facilities** 14 meeting rooms, 28 syndicates, theatre seating 200.

**Services** CCTV, OHP, LCD, Barco, PCs.

### Hartsfield Manor

**Address** Sandy Lane, Betchworth, RH3 7AA Surrey, England **Phone** 44 1737-842821 **Fax** 1737-842965

**Accommodations** 50 rooms.

**Meeting Facilities** 7 meeting rooms, 10 syndicates, theatre seating 100.

**Services** CCTV, OHP, LCD, Barco, PCs.

### Highfield Park

**Address** Heckfield, Hook, RG27 OL9 Hampshire, England **Phone** 44 118-9328-369 **Fax** 118-9326-500

**Accommodations** 60 rooms.

**Meeting Facilities** 12 meeting rooms.

**Services** CCTV, OHP, LCD, Barco, PCs.

### Highgate House Conference Centre

**Address** Creaton, NN6-8NN Northamptonshire, England **Phone** 44 1604-505505 **Fax** 1604-505656

**Accommodations** 95 rooms.

**Meeting Facilities** 30 meeting rooms.

**Services** Conference planning, secretarial services, language trans-

lations, CCTV, LCD, ISDN, overhead/viewgraph, tape recorder, videotape recording, personal computers, film and slide projectors.

### Horsley Management Centre

**Address** Ockham Road South, East Horsley, KT24 6DU Surrey, England **Phone** 44 1483-284211 **Fax** 44 1483-285812

**Accommodations** 126 rooms.

**Meeting Facilities** 35 meeting rooms.

**Services** CCTV, OHP, LCD, Barco, Lite Pro.

### Horwood House

**Address** Little Horwood, Milton Keynes, Buckinghamshire, MK 17 OPQ England **Phone** 44 1296-722100 **Fax** 44 1296-722300

**Accommodations** 120 rooms, ensuite, single study with TV, voicemail, tea/coffeemaking facilities.

**Meeting Facilities** 29 rooms, with capacity of 2–90. Fully equipped with the latest presentation technology, including OH projector and screen, 35 mm projector, flipchart, white board. Also available: light projector, TV, video, rear screen projector.

**Services** None listed.

### Hunton Park

**Address** Essex Lane, Kings Langley, WD4 8PN Hertfordshire, England **Phone** 44 1923-261511 **Fax** 1923-267537

**Accommodations** 60 rooms.

**Meeting Facilities** 6 meeting rooms, 12 syndicates.

**Services** CCTV, OHP, LCD, Barco, PCs.

### Latimer House and Conference Center

**Address** Latimer, Chesham, HP5 1UD Buckinghamshire, England **Phone** 44 1494-764422 **Fax** 1494-765704

**Accommodations** 135 rooms.

**Meeting Facilities** 20 meeting rooms.

**Services** CCTV, OHP, LCD, Barco, PCs, videoconferencing.

### Latimer Mews Training and Conference Centre

**Address** Latimer, Chesham, HP5-1UD Buckinghamshire, England

**Phone** 44 1494-764466 **Fax** 1494-765891

**Accommodations** 53 rooms.

**Meeting Facilities** 4 meeting rooms, 10 syndicates.

**Services** CCTV, OHP, LCD, Barco, PCs.

### The Mill and Old Swan Conference Centre

**Address** Minster Lovell, OX8 5RN Oxfordshire, England **Phone** 44 01993-77441 **Fax** 01339-702002

**Accommodations** 60 guest rooms.

**Meeting Facilities** 5 rooms, 8 syndicates.

**Services** OHP, monitor and video, Barco, CCTV, PCs, 35mm projector.

### Milton Hill

**Address** Milton Hill, Abingdon, Oxfordshire OX13-6AF, England **Phone** 44 1235-831474 **Fax** 44 1235-825796

**Accommodations** 79 rooms.

**Meeting Facilities** 7 meeting rooms, 14 syndicate rooms.

**Services** Complete range of equipment and services.

### The Moller Centre for Continuing Education

**Address** Storey's Way, CB3 ODE Cambridge, England **Phone** 44 (0) 1223-465530 **Fax** (0) 1223-46554 **e-mail** jmd12@cam.ac.uk

**Accommodations** 70 ensuite guest rooms.

**Meeting Facilities** Lecture Theatre with racked seating; 14 meeting rooms ranging in size to cater for 1:1 training to 140.

**Services** Conference planning, overhead projectors, white boards, flip charts, slide projectors, Barco, TV/VCR sets, computer data projection, computer network facilities.

### New Place Management Centre

**Address** Shirrell Heath, Southampton, S032 2JH Hampshire, England **Phone** 44 1329-833543 **Fax** 1329-833259

**Accommodations** 110 guest rooms.

**Meeting Facilities** 2 conference suites; 13 meeting rooms; 22 syndicate rooms.

**Services** Lite Pro, CCTV, OHP, LCD, Barco, PCs.

### Radcliffe House

**Address** University of Warwick, CV4-7AL Coventry, Warwickshire, England **Phone** 44 1203-474711 **Fax** 1203-694282

**Accommodations** 154 rooms.

**Meeting Facilities** 11 lecture rooms; 28 syndicate rooms.

**Services** Conference planning, overhead projector film and slide projector, closed-circuit TV, videotape recording, tape recording, computer data projection, U-Matic recording.

### Scarman House Training and Conference Centre

**Address** University of Warwick, Coventry, CV4-7AL Warwickshire, England **Phone** 44 1203-221111 **Fax** 1203-520362

**Accommodations** 200 rooms.

**Meeting Facilities** 52 meeting rooms.

**Services** Conference planning, overhead/viewgraph, film and slide projectors, closed-circuit TV, video tape recording, tape recording, computer data projection, U-matic recording.

### Sedgebrook Hall

**Address** Pitsford Road, Chapel Brampton, NN68BD Northhampton, England **Phone** 44 1604-821666 **Fax** 1604-821596

**Accommodations** 102 guest rooms.

**Meeting Facilities** 23 meeting rooms.

**Services** Conference planning, secretarial services, language translators, closed-circuit TV, overhead/viewgraph, tape recorder, videotape recording, personal computers, film and slide projectors, video conferencing.

### Staverton Park

**Address** Staverton, NN11 61T Northamptonshire, England **Phone** 44 1327-302000 **Fax** 1327-311428

**Accommodations** 100 rooms.

**Meeting Facilities** 7 rooms, 12 syndicates.

**Services** CCTV, OHP, LCD.

### Sundridge Park

**Address** Plaistow Lane, Bromley, BR1-3TP Kent, England **Phone** 44 1313-3131 **Fax** 1313-7500

**Accommodations** 150 rooms.

**Meeting Facilities** 11 meeting rooms.

**Services** Conference planning, secretarial services, overhead/viewgraph, tape recorder, videotape recording, film and slide projectors.

### Theobolds Park Conference Centre

**Address** Bulls Cross Ride, Cheshunt, Herts, EN7 5HW, England **Phone** 44 1992-633375 **Fax** 1992-634212

**Accommodations** 42 guest rooms.

**Meeting Facilities** 15 conference rooms.

**Services** Full range of A/V equipment and specialist staff.

Expansion plans include 8 more conference rooms seating up to 120, and 26 additional guest rooms.

### Uplands

**Address** Four Ashes Road, Cryers Hill, High Wycombe, HP15 6LA Buckinghamshire, England **Phone** 44 1494-716473 **Fax** 1494-713318

**Accommodations** 77 rooms.

**Meeting Facilities** 8 meeting rooms, 10 syndicates.

**Services** CCTV, OHP.

### Warbrook House

**Address** Eversley, RG27 OPL Hampshire, England **Phone** 44 1189-732174 **Fax** 1734-730472

**Accommodations** 60 rooms.

**Meeting Facilities** 4 meeting rooms, 17 syndicates.

**Services** CCTV, OHP, LCD, Barco, PCs.

### Wokefield Executive Centre

**Address** Mortimer, Reading, RG7 3AG Berkshire, England **Phone** 44 0118 9332391 **Fax** 0118 9333558

**Accommodations** 200 double ensuite guest rooms, 65 single ensuite guest rooms.

**Meeting Facilities** Extensive meeting rooms for 2–350, ample syndicate space.

**Services** Video projection, CCTV, OHP, LCD, Barco, PCs and secretarial service.

### Wokefield Mansion

**Address** The Mansion House, Mortimer, Reading, Berkshire RG7-3AG, England **Phone** 44 1189-332391 **Fax** 44 1189-334401

**Accommodations** 97 rooms.

**Meeting Facilities** 4 meeting rooms, 14 syndicate rooms.

**Services** Complete range of equipment and services.

## IACC AUSTRALIA

### Bentinck Country House

**Address** 1 Carlisle Street, Woodend, Victoria, 3442, Australia **Phone** 61 05427-2944 **Fax** 054272232

**Accommodations** 28 rooms (24 ensuite/4 shared facility).

**Meeting Facilities** 2 rooms each 80 sg. mtrs.; 4 breakout rooms; office; full equipment inventory.

**Services** Conference planning, secretarial, messenger, and A/V services including video recording, data and video projection, and electronic whiteboard.

### Blythewood Grange Conference Centre

**Address** CNR Morgan and Grant Streets, Sebastopol, Ballarat, Victoria, 3356, Australia **Phone** 61 5335-8133 **Fax** 83361550

**Accommodations** 58 rooms.

**Meeting Facilities** 3 conference rooms and 9 syndicate rooms catering from 2-200 in exclusive dedicates area.

**Services** Full conf. planning and on-site support, secretarial, fax, copying, TV-video recording, electronic white board, direct projector, OHP including Zoom OHP, flip chart, slide projector, ergonomic furniture, climate control systems.

### Campaspe House Executive Retreat

**Address** Goldie's Lane, Woodend, Victoria, 3442, Australia **Phone** 61 354-272-273 **Fax** 61 534-271-049 **e-mail** campaspe@hitech.net.com

**Accommodations** 20 single rooms. Accommodates up to 34 people on a single and twin-share basis. Sole occupancy for all groups.

**Meeting Facilities** Main conference rooms with syndicate room and 3 breakout areas.

**Services** Full conference planning and on-site service. Electronic white board, OHP projectors, slide projector, video monitors, flip charts, copying, fax, climate-control systems.

### The Country Place

**Address** Olinda Creek Road, Kalorama, Victoria, 3186, Australia
**Phone** 61 03-9728-1177
**Fax** 03-9728-6260

**Accommodations** 42 elegantly appointed ensuite double rooms, including 16 twin share, accommodating up to 60.

**Meeting Facilities** 5 rooms, seating 10–80.

**Services** Secretarial support, photocopier, fax, conference planning and services, TV-video recording, electronic white board, flip charts, slide projector, ergonomic furniture, black-out facility, overhead projectors, screens, climate-control systems, high and low rope outdoor experiential learning circuit, laundry, photographer and hospitality lounge.

### The Cumberland Marysville

**Address** 34 Murchinson St., Marysville, Victoria, 3779, Australia
**Phone** 61 35-963-203
**Fax** 61 35-963-458

**Accommodations** 43 rooms, ensuite, with color TV, air conditioning, and heating.

**Meeting Facilities** 5 rooms, equipped with ergonomic chairs, electronic white boards, great lighting and garden views.

**Services** Full secretarial.

### Deakin Management Centre

**Address** Deakin University, Geelong, Victoria, 3217, Australia
**Phone** 613 5227-3000
**Fax** 613 5227-3101

**Accommodations** 57 sleeping rooms including 30 twin share rooms and 2 facilitator suites.

**Meeting Facilities** 2 meeting rooms plus 7 syndicate rooms. Centre is designed for up to 100 delegates.

**Services** Full conference planning and secretarial services. Networked computers, laser printers, overhead projector, video, audio system/ AMP/cassette/CD player, white board, flip chart, blackout facility.

### Edmund Barton Centre

**Address** 488 South Road, Moorabbin, Victoria, 3189, Australia
**Phone** 61 392-095-929 **Fax** 61 392-095-907 **e-mail** mwithers@ barton.vic.edu.com.html

**Accommodations** 50 rooms, executive style, incl. 3 executive lounges.

**Meeting Facilities** 19 rooms, state-of-the-art A/V, abundance of natural light in all rooms.

**Services** Full catering and banquet services, free parking for 600 cars, professional conference management.

### Green Gables Conference Centre

**Address** Gable Lane, Warburton, Victoria, 3799, Australia
**Phone** 61 05-966-2077
**Fax** 05-966-5382

**Accommodations** 38 ensuite rooms accommodating up to 70 people.

**Meeting Facilities** 4 productive conference rooms, 4 syndicate rooms, catering for 12–160 participants.

**Services** Full conference planning support, secretarial, fax, photocopier, TV/video, white boards, flip charts, OH projectors and screen, ergonomic furniture, climate-controlled systems.

### Killara Inn

**Address** 480 Pacific Highway, Killara, NSW, 2071, Australia
**Phone** 61 02 9416-1344
**Fax** 61 02 9416-6347

**Accommodations** 39 sleeping rooms.

**Meeting Facilities** 5 meeting rooms, full video conferencing facilities in all rooms.

**Services** N/A.

### Kyarra Business Retreat

**Address** 63-111 Mangans Road, Lilydale, Victoria, 3140, Australia
**Phone** 61 39-739-5611
**Fax** 3-97396913

**Accommodations** 48 double rooms.

**Meeting Facilities** 5 conference rooms, 20 syndicate rooms.

**Services** Secretarial support, photocopier, fax, laundry, photographer, conf. planning and services, hospitality/recreation room, TV/ video, electronic whiteboard, flip charts, slide proj., ergonomic furniture, outdoor experimental course, blackout facility, overhead proj., screens, conf. rooms individually fully air conditioned.

### Lancemore Hill Conference Center

**Address** Kilmore-Lancefield Rd., Kilmore, Victoria, 3764, Australia
**Phone** 61 57-822-009
**Fax** 57-822-371

**Accommodations** 71 ensuite rooms, sleeping capacity 130.

**Meeting Facilities** 4 rooms (seating to 130), 18 syndicate rooms.

**Services** Secretarial support, copier, fax, conf. planning, 52″ monitors computer graphics and standard, vhs, pal, ntsc, u-matic 1/2 & 3/4, video cameras, overhead projectors and screens, carousel projectors.

### Macquarie Graduate School of Management

**Address** Macquarie University, New South Wales, 2109, Australia
**Phone** 61 298-509-004 **Fax** 61 298-508-595 **e-mail** pat.mcdonald@mq.edu.au

**Accommodations** 40 double ensuite rooms, with queen-size beds, 2 facilitator suites available on requests. Rooms are fully serviced daily and feature individually controlled a/c and heat, hair dryers, complimentary tea and coffee-making facilities, complimentary soft drinks, ISD-STD international direct dial phones.

**Meeting Facilities** 33 meeting rooms in total, comprised of 21 syndicate rooms, 4 tiered theatres, 8 flat floor rooms.

**Services** Full A/V in meeting rooms, business centre. Guest services include laundy and dry cleaning, reading room, fully licensed bar, 24-hr. reception, TV and video hire, safety deposit, souvenir-promotional items, free parking.

### The Management Centre

**Address** Deakin University, Geelong, Victoria, 3217, Australia **Phone** 61 52-273-000 **Fax** 52-273-101

Accommodations 57 well-appointed dbl. rooms, including 30 twin share, and 2 facilitator suites.

Meeting Facilities 2 main conf. rooms and 7 specialized syndicate rooms. The centre is designed for up to 100 delegates.

Services Full conf. planning and secretarial services. All conference and syndicate rooms include networked multi-compatible computer, laser printer, overhead projector, video, audio system/AMP/ cassette/CD player, white board, flip chart, blackout facility.

### Marylands Country House

Address 22 Falls Road, Marysville, Victoria, 3779, Australia
Phone 61 59-63-3204
Fax 59-633-251

Accommodations 42 double rooms accommodating up to 100 persons.

Meeting Facilities 3 main rooms with syndicate rooms available. All standard A/V and display equipment is available together with video recording facilities and computer modem connections.

Services Fax, photocopying, word processing, computer usage, laundry, event coordination, conference planning.

### Monash Mt. Eliza Business School

Address Kunyung Road, Mt. Eliza, Victoria, 3930, Australia
Phone 61 392-151-100 Fax 61 392-875-139 e-mail conf@mteliza.edu.au.html

Accommodations 97 spacious single rooms.

Meeting Facilities 20 rooms, 9,160 sq. ft. Datashow and video-data projectors, slide projectors, PAL/NTSC/VHS videos and monitors, video cameras.

Services A/V equipment and support, conference planning and administrative services. Local area network with PCs in every meeting and syndicate room, offering a wide range of applications. Secretarial support available.

### O'Shannassy Lodge

Address 1025 Woods Point Road, East Waburton, Victoria, 3799,

Australia, Phone 61 59-668-521
Fax 59-668-490

Accommodations 16 ensuite double bedrooms.

Meeting Facilities 1 room with syndicate rooms.

Services Standard A/V equipment, conference planning, secretarial support. Outdoor experiential learning course with in-house corporate fitness leaders. Professional stress management programs.

### Portsea Village Conference Resort

Address 3765 Point Nepean Rd., Portsea, Victoria, 3944, Australia
Phone 61 359-848-484
Fax 61 359-844-686

Accommodations 56 apartment-style accommodations with 1, 2, or 3 bedrooms. Twin share is a 2-bedroom, 2-bathroom apartment.

Meeting Facilities 2 rooms, seating 50 and 15 people. Executive lounge rooms available for small meetings.

Services CMP includes standard A/V equipment, stationery, and audio equipment.

### The Shearwater Conference Centre

Address Cape Schanck Resort, Boneo Road, Cape Schanck, Victoria, 3939, Australia Phone 61 3-5950-8000
Fax 61 3-5950-8

Accommodations 58 rooms. Designed for today's conference market with international direct-dial phones and modem lines, TV, radio, fridge, AC, heating, private balcony with ocean view.

Meeting Facilities 8 rooms, with automated rear projectors, multimedia facilities incorporating video and slide presentation, computer display, theatre-quality sound.

Services Courtesy shuttle available, parking, full secretarial support, fax, photocopier, user-friendly technical facilities, complete in-house coordination.

### Stonelea

Address Connelly's Creek Road, Acheron, 3714, Australia,
Phone 61 57-722-222
Fax 57-722-210

Accommodations 47 Boutique Australian Colonial, with ensuite,

AC, mini bar and STD/ISD telephones.

Meeting Facilities 2 main conference rooms and several breakout rooms, 110 total capacity theatre style.

Services Lecterns, P.A. system, tape deck and recording facilities, electronic white board, video projection cameras, monitors, VHS/Hi-FI/VCR, slide and overhead projectors, screens, flip charts, white boards, fax, copying, secretarial services.

## IACC JAPAN

### The Tokyo Conference Center

Address 3-22-20 Iidabashi, Chiyoda-ku, Tokyo, 102-0072, Japan
Phone 81 3-3841-0791
Fax 81 3-3841-0790

Accommodations 200 rooms in nearby hotels. Reservations can be arranged.

Meeting Facilities 14 rooms, including 12 conference rooms seating 12–60; 1 boardroom, divisible large hall seating up to 900 theater style.

Services On-site A/V manager, professional conference coordinators to assist with all aspects of a meeting.

## MALAYSIA

### The Signature International Conference Center

Address The Palace of the Golden Horses, The Mines Resort City, 43300 Seri Kembangan, Selangor Daral Eshan, Malaysia
Phone 60 3-943-2333
Fax 60 3-943-2666

Accommodations 665 rooms at Palace of the Golden Horses (403 rooms, 82 suites) and The Mines Beach Resort, a 180-room, 4-star hotel with smaller ballrooms and 5 meeting rooms.

Meeting Facilities 14 rooms, including a 250-seat theatre. Each conference room is equipped with soundproofing, glare-free lighting, tackable wall surfaces, ergonomic seating.

Services None listed.

## NIGERIA

### The Conference & Training Centre

Address Elephant House, 16th and 17th floors, 214 Broad Street, Lagos, Nigeria, Africa

**Phone** 234 41-266-7329 41-264-3737 **Fax** 234 41-266-3442

**Accommodations** Non-residential.

**Meeting Facilities** 18 rooms; 18,000 sq. ft. Flexible floor arrangements. Meeting rooms for 10–15; seminar rooms for 20–25; lecture theatre seats 120.

**Services** Lounges, bookstore.

# THAILAND

## U-Thong Inn & Executive Conference Center

**Address** 210 Rojana Road, Ayutthaya, 13000, Thailand **Phone** 66 35-242236 **Fax** 66 35-242235

**Accommodations** 208 rooms. New tower features junior suites, executive suites and royal suite (2 bedrooms with large parlor).

**Meeting Facilities** 14 rooms with 20,000 sq. ft. of meeting space, featuring ballroom for up to 700. Ergonomic chairs for meeting rooms, climate control.

**Services** Full range of A/V with feeds to/from all meeting rooms.

# THE TRAINER'S ALMANAC

## SECTION 6.4

## TRAINING FOR TRAINERS

The latest trends in training have significantly broadened the field of opportunity for the trainer's own on-the-job training. The broader ideas of workplace learning challenge those who do training to look around for more and better opportunities to foster learning for individuals, teams, and organizations. Our representative listing also reflects the trend toward the role of instructor being done by managers, supervisors, mentors, coaches, and colleagues of all titles. It is our hope that all persons who need to function as "trainer" in today's lively workplace will find this section 6.4 of *The Trainer's Almanac* particularly useful. The listing is a unique reflection of what's happening in the year 2001; Prentice Hall does not endorse any provider of services. Inclusion here in *The Trainer's Almanac* illustrates the range of services available and is meant to reflect the breadth of the field in warm-body, eyeball-to-eyeball, shoulder-to-shoulder, bricks-and-mortar training.

Our section 6.8 contains a listing of online learning opportunities with Web addresses. Our sections 3, *Training Program Design*, and 4, *Training Program Delivery*, also contain numerous references to learning opportunities other than seminars and workshops where people gather face to face.

### A Representation of Current Trends

Outsourcing, again this year, has meant that training consultants and vendors of training services of all sorts are thriving as corporations, non-profits, and the government are all hiring training outsiders to do work inside. This trend alone means that training providers, especially outsiders, need to pay attention to their own professional development as businesspersons and as trainers who are aware and up on the latest changes in the field. Downsizing, of course, has worked with outsourcing to provide both a supply of independent training workers as well as a demand for services as reduced staffs continue to want and need to provide services. Trainers who are still employed full time need to be aware of and skilled in many more executive and management functions, yet competent in all of the traditional training jobs including needs assessment, instructional design and development, training presentation techniques and delivery systems, and evaluation for return on investment. Mentoring, coaching, and Web-based design and delivery skills are also required of today's trainers.

Trainers, inside organizations as well as on the outside, are being both pushed and enticed by the possibilities of the performance improvement focus in human resources and organization development. The broadening of the trainer's view to encompass personal and organizational performance has opened up a host of knowledge, skill, and attitude requirements for the savvy trainer. Keeping up with the latest issues and developmental challenges in Web-based training and distance learning is also an opportunity for training for trainers. Building leadership and collaborative alliances are hot topics this year.

And finally, facilitation skills of all sorts are required of trainers because of new ways of working in teams and in flatter and less formal organizations. The classroom is not always the delivery venue of choice, and trainers need to know more about facilitating learning online and across distances, and within different social structures with an increasingly global, multicultural, and diverse trainee population. Section 6.4's representative listing of resources for continuous learning reflects these current trends as well as indicates the field's grounding in more traditional train-the-trainer topics. Training is still in evolution, not revolution.

**Our Approach to Indexing**

In our approach to indexing these 179 representative training opportunities we chose 34 indexing terms or keywords that describe the major thrust of the seminar or workshop described in the listing. In some cases, an entry is indexed under more than one keyword. As you leaf through this section, you'll quickly see that the 179 seminars and workshops are listed alphabetically by the name of the vendor or company providing the service. Leafing through and scanning the section first will give you a good idea of the breadth of topics and the range of current interest. Using the index of keywords will help you with depth of coverage and focus on specific areas. You'll also see that we have indexed the 84 vendors and service provider companies by the geographic area of the headquarters office, and that we have a good representation from all four geographical areas. You'll see, too, that we have listed these vendors and service providers alphabetically in a separate listing, since in the seminar listing some providers have more than one listing for seminars or workshops. In this alphabetical listing of providers, we include website addresses and note that some offer discounts for Web registration. Most training providers post their schedules on their Websites. Check them for dates and locations. Our indexing philosophy is to be representative, fair, and broad, including opportunities that are truly nationwide. Costs quoted are for one person; however, most providers offer a discount for teams or more than one person.

**A Focus on Public Seminars and Workshops**

We have also chosen to focus on training for trainers that is open to the public. Most provider companies also offer on-site or customized training. Many offer certification programs. If this is what you want, be sure to telephone the contact number to inquire about individualized company programs. In our listing we have also deliberately not included all training offered by a particular provider. We have been selective and guided by a philosophy of being representative rather than inclusive of every seminar or program offered by a particular company. We believe we have given you enough information to whet your appetite for learning and to understand how to get in touch with a vendor for more information. We have also tried to find relevant programs throughout the country, so that our listing is truly nationwide. In addition, we cite a wide variety of training for beginning trainers as well as for those at manager and executive levels.

What you will not find here is specific training in computer software products, nor will you find programs offered by professional associations only for their members. We have also not included community college outreach programs, and although we do include some business school continuing education programs, these are not inclusive but rather are meant to encourage you to investigate further into these kinds of sources in your own local area.

We have carefully made phone calls to verify the information included here, and have used information from the latest vendor brochures. We have listed the public's price for one attendee; in many cases, the service provider offers a discount for more than one attending from a company. We are not endorsing any company listed here. As in the purchase of any product or service, you as the buyer of a training program must choose carefully so that your objectives for learning match the product or service being offered. We have tried to include programs at varying prices and for durations of one day to several weeks. Our listing can help you comparison shop, at least. We can honestly say that we are the most truly representative, trainer-focused index of training opportunites available from any publisher. To get the most out of your search through section 6.4, we suggest that you first review the list of providers on the next four pages. Web addresses are provided for you to search complete information.

# GEOGRAPHIC INDEX OF SEMINAR AND WORKSHOP PROVIDERS

**Northeast**
2, 6, 9, 12, 22, 24, 25, 35, 37, 38, 41, 42, 49, 51, 52, 54, 65, 67

**Mid-Atlantic/South**
1, 5, 11, 17, 18, 19, 28, 29, 30, 36, 39, 44, 45, 48, 56, 59, 64, 66, 68, 71, 75, 79, 83

**Midwest**
4, 8, 10, 14, 16, 23, 26, 31, 32, 40, 46, 53, 55, 60, 62, 76, 77, 78, 80, 81, 82, 84

**West**
3, 7, 13, 15, 20, 21, 27, 33, 34, 43, 47, 50, 57, 58, 61, 63, 69, 70, 72, 73, 74

---

## 1

Achieve Global, Inc.
8875 Hidden River Parkway,
   Ste 400
Tampa, FL 33637
800/291-2752
888/662-7692 (fax)
www.achieveglobal.com

## 2

American Management Association
   International
P.O. Box 169
Saranac Lake, NY 12983
800/262-9699
518/891-0368 (fax)
www.amanet.org

## 3

American Productivity & Quality
   Center (APQC)
123 N. Post Oak Lane
Houston, TX 77024-7797
713/681-4020
800/776-9676
www.apqc.org

## 4

American Society for Quality (ASQ)
P.O. Box 3066
Milwaukee, WI 53201
800/248-1946
414/272-1734 (fax)
www.asq.org

## 5

American Society for Training &
   Development (ASTD)
1640 King Street, Box 1443
Alexandria, VA 22313
800/628-2783
703/683-8103 (fax)
www.astd.org

## 6

Babson School of Executive
   Education
Babson Park, MA 02457
781/239-4354
781/239-5266 (fax)
www.babson.edu/see

## 7

Behavioral Science Technology,
   Inc.
417 Bryant Circle
Ojai, California 93023
800/548-5781
805/646-0328 (fax)
www.bstsolutions.com

## 8

The Bob Pike Group
7620 West 78th Street
Minneapolis, MN 55439
800/383-9210
952/829-0260 (fax)
www.bobpikegroup.com

## 9

Boston University Corporate
   Education Center
72 Tyng Road
Tyngsboro, MA 01879
800/288-7246
978/649-2162 (fax)
www.butrain.bu.edu

## 10

Bradley University
Foster College of Business
   Administration
Peoria, IL 61625
309/677-4420
309/677-4421 (fax)
www.bradley.edu/ldc

## 11

Brainstorm Dynamics, Inc.
Reproducible Training Programs
12 Brocster Court, Suite 200
Phoenix, MD 21131
888/825-8434
410/561-9050
410/592-9156 (fax)
www.brainstormdynamics.com

## 12

Bryant College
Center for Management
   Development
1150 Douglas Pike
Smithfield, RI 02917-1283
401/232-6200
401/232-6704 (fax)
www.bryantcollege.edu

## 13

California Institute of Technology
Industrial Relations Center 1-90
Pasadena, CA 91125
626/395-4043
626/795-7174 (fax)
www.irc.caltech.edu

## 14

Capella University
330 Second Avenue South, Suite 550
Minneapolis, MN 55401
612/239-8650
888/227-3552
612/337-5396 (fax)
www.capellauniversity.edu

## 15

Career Track/Fred Pryor Seminars
P.O. Box 2951
Shawnee Mission, KS 66201
800/334-6780
918/665-3434 (fax)
www.careertrack.com

**16**

Center for Accelerated Learning
1103 Wisconsin Street
Lake Geneva, WI 53147
414/248-7070
414/248-1912 (fax)
www.execpc.com/~alcenter

**17**

Center for Applications of
   Psychological Type, Inc.
2815 N.W. 13th Street, Suite 401
Gainesville, FL 32609
800/777-2278
904/378-0503 (fax)
www.info@capt.org

**18**

Center for Creative Leadership
One Leadership Place
P.O. Box 26300
Greensboro, NC 27438-6300
336/545-2910
336/282-3284 (fax)
www.ccl.org

**19**

The Center for Effective
   Performance, Inc.
2300 Peachford Road, Ste. 2000
Atlanta, GA 30338
800/558-4237
770/458-9109 (fax)
www.cep.worldwide.com

**20**

Center for Management &
   Organization Effectiveness
P.O. Box 21103
Salt Lake City, UT 84121
801/943-6310
801/569-3449 (fax)
www.thecoach.com

**21**

Center for the Study of Work
   Teams
University of North Texas
P.O. Box 311280
Denton, TX 76203
940/565-3096
940/565-4806 (fax)
www.workteams.unt.edu

**22**

Columbia University Teachers
   College
Center for Educational Outreach
   and Innovation
525 West 120th St., Box 132
New York, NY 10027
212/678-3987
212/678-4048 (fax)
www.tc.columbia.edu~academic/
   ceoi/

**23**

Comp Ed
Rockhurst University
Continuing Education Center, Inc.
P.O. Box 419107
Kansas City, MO 64141
800/258-7248
800/258-7246
913/432-0824 (fax)
www.natsem.com

**24**

The Conference Board
845 Third Avenue
New York, NY 10022
212/759-0900
212/980-7014 (fax)
www.conference-board.org

**25**

Cornell University, School of
   Industrial and Labor Relations
Management Development and
   Human Resources Programs
16 East 34th St.
New York, NY 10016
212/340-2863
212/340-2890 (fax)
www.ilr.cornell.edu/mgmtprog

**26**

Crisis Prevention Institute, Inc.
3315-K North 124th Street
Brookfield, WI 53005
800/558-8976
414/783-5906 (fax)
www.crisisprevention.com

**27**

Darryl L. Sink & Associates, Inc.
60 Garden Court, Suite 101
Monterey, CA 93940
800/650-7465
831/649-3914 (fax)
www.dsink.com

**28**

Disney Institute
P.O. Box 10093
Lake Buena Vista, FL 32830
407/828-4411
407/828-2402 (fax)
www.disneyseminars.com

**29**

Eckerd College
Management Development
   Institute
4200 54th Avenue South
St. Petersburg, FL 33711
800/753-0444
813/864-8996 (fax)
www.eckerd.edu

**30**

Educational Resources, Inc.
45064 Underwood Lane,
   Ste. 200
Dulles, VA 20166
703/904-1800
703/904-1856 (fax)
www.educationalres.com

**31**

Emerging Technology Consultants,
   Inc.
2819 Hamline Ave. North
St. Paul, MN 55113
651/639-3973
651/639-0110 (fax)
www.emergingtechnology.com

**32**

FKA Friesen, Kaye and Associates
3448 Richmond Road
Ottawa, ON, Canada K2H8H7
800/FKA-5585
613/829-0845 (fax)
www.fka.com

**33**

FranklinCovey
360 West 4800 North
Provo, UT 84604
800/972-4321
801/229-1233 (fax)
www.franklincovey.com

**34**

The Gallup Organization
The Gallup School of Management
300 South 68th Street Place
Lincoln, NB 68510
800/360-2801 ext. 7686
402/489-8700
www.gallup.com

**35**

The Global Institute for Leadership
    Development
One Forbes Road
Lexington, MA 02173
781/402-5451
781/862-2355 (fax)
www.linkageinc.com

**36**

Global Knowledge
P.O. Box 1039
Cary, NC 27512
800/268-7737
919/461-8600
919/461-8646 (fax)
www.globalknowledge.com

**37**

Harvard University
John F. Kennedy School of
    Government
The Leadership Education Program
79 JFK Street
Cambridge, MA
617/496-5920
617/495-3090 (fax)
www.ksg.harvard.edu/exceed

**38**

Harvard University Law School
Program on Negotiation for Senior
    Executives
Center for Management Research
55 William Street
Wellesley, MA 02181
781/239-1111
781/239-1546 (fax)

**39**

Hay Group
229 South 18th Street
Philadelphia, PA 19103
215/861-2000
215/875-2891 (fax)
www.haygroup.com

**40**

Human Synergistics International
39819 Plymouth Rd. C8020
Plymouth, MI 48170
800/622-7584
734/459-5557 (fax)
www.humansyn.com

**41**

Information Mapping, Inc.
41 Waverly Oaks Rd.
Waltham, MA 02154
800/463-6627
617/906-6400 (fax)
www.infomap.com

**42**

Innovation Associates
Acorn Park
Cambridge, MA 02140
617/498-5700
617/498-5701 (fax)
www.innovationassociates.com

**43**

Institute for Applied Management
    and Law, Inc.
610 Newport Center Drive,
    Ste. 1060
Newport Beach, CA 92660
949/760-1700
949/760-8192 (fax)
www.iaml.com

**44**

Institute for Professional
    Education
2200 Wilson Boulevard, Ste. 406
Arlington, VA 22201
703/527-8700
703/527-8703 (fax)
www.theipe.com

**45**

International Quality and
    Productivity Center
150 Clove Road
P.O. Box 401
Little Falls, NJ 07424
800/882-8684
201/256-0205 (fax)
www.iqpc.com

**46**

J.L. Kellogg Graduate School of
    Management
Northwestern University
James L. Allen Center
Evanston, IL 60208
847/467-7000
847/491-4323 (fax)
www.kellogg.nwu.edu

**47**

Keye Productivity Center
11221 Roe Avenue
Leawood, KS 66211-1748
800/821-3919
800/914-8879 (fax)
www.amanet.org

**48**

Otto Kroeger Associates
3605-A Chain Bridge Road
Fairfax, VA 22030-3245
703/591-6284
703/591-8338 (fax)
www.typetalk.com\oka

**49**

Langevin Learning Services
P.O. Box 1221, 420 Ford Street
Ogdensburg, NY 13669
800/223-2209
800/636-6869 (fax)
www.langevin.com

**50**

LERN (Learning Resources Network)
1550 Hayes Drive
Manhattan, KS 66502
800/678-5376
888/234-8633 (fax)
www.lern.org

**51**

Liberty Mutual Group
Loss Prevention, M.S. 8F
P.O. Box 140
Boston, MA 02117
800/320-7581
617/695-9216 (fax)
www.lmig.com

**52**

Linkage Inc.
One Forbes Road
Lexington, MA 02173
781/862-3157
781/862-2355 (fax)
www.linkageinc.com

**53**

Management Education Consulting
    Company of America (MECCA)
40 W. 919 Elodie Drive
Elburn, IL 60119
630/584-0164
630/584-0184 (fax)

**54**

Massachusetts Institute of
    Technology
The Sloan School of Management
55 William Street
Wellesley, MA 02181
781/239-1111
781/239-1546 (fax)

**55**

National Businesswomen's
    Leadership Association
P.O. Box 419107
Kansas City, MO 64141
800/258-7246
913/432-0824 (fax)
www.natsem.com

**56**

National MultiCultural Institute
3000 Connecticut Avenue, NW,
    Suite 438
Washington, DC 20008
202/483-0700
202/483-5233 (fax)
www.nmci.org/nmci/

**57**

NLP University
Dynamic Learning Center
P.O. Box 1112
Ben Lomond, CA 95005
408/336-3457
408/336-5854 (fax)
www.nlpu.com

**58**

Novations Group, Inc.
2155 N. 200 West, Suite 200
Provo, UT 84604
801/375-7525
801/377-5440 (fax)
www.intranet.novations.com

**59**

NTL Institute
1240 N. Pitt Street, Suite 100
Alexandria, VA 22314
703/548-1500
703/684-1256 (fax)
www.ntl.org

**60**

Numerof Associates
11457 Olde Cabin Road, Ste. 350
St. Louis, MO 63141
314/997-1587
314/997-0948 (fax)
www.nai-consulting.com

**61**

The Padgett-Thompson Division
    of the American Management
    Association International
Padgett-Thompson Building
P.O. Box 8297
Overland Park, KS 66208
800/255-4141
913/451-2900
800/914-8879 (fax)
www.amanet.org/seminars/public

**62**

Perrone-Ambrose Associates, Inc.
2 North Riverside Plaza, Ste. 1433
Chicago, IL 60606
800/648-0543
312/648-0622 (fax)
www.mentors2000.com

**63**

Practical Management
    Incorporated
3280 West Hacienda Avenue,
    Ste. 205
Las Vegas, NV 89118
800/444-9101
702/795-8339 (fax)
www.practmgt.com

**64**

Professional Society for Sales &
    Marketing Training
P.O. Box 995
Fayetteville, GA 30214
770/719-4SMT
770/719-8SMT (fax)
www.smt.org

**65**

Rensselaer Learning Institute
Rensselaer at Hartford
275 Windsor Street
Hartford, CT 06120-2991
800/306-7778
860/548-7999 (fax)
www.rh@edu

**66**

Rollins College
Corporate Learning Institute
1000 Holt Avenue - 2728
Winter Park, FL 32789
800/494-4253
407/646-1503 (fax)

**67**

Situation Management Systems, Inc.
195 Hanover Street
Hanover, MA 02339
617/826-4433
617/826-2863 (fax)
www.smsinc.com

**68**

Society for Human Resource
    Management (SHRM)
1800 Duke Street
Alexandria, VA 22314
800/283-SHRM
703/535-6490 (fax)
www.shrm.org/seminars

**69**

The Sony Video Institute
3300 Zanker Road
San Jose, CA 95134
408/955-4231
408/955-5340
www.sony.com/training

**70**

Stanford Business School
Office of Executive Education
Stanford University
Stanford, CA 94305
650/723-3341
650/723-3950 (fax)
www-gsb.stanford.edu/eep

**71**

TechLink Training
P.O. Box 226
Fanwood, NJ 07023
908/789-2800
908/789-2811 (fax)
www.tltraining.com

**72**

TeleTraining Institute
1524 West Admiral
Stillwater, OK 74074
800/755-2356
405/744-7511 (fax)
www.teletrain.com

## 73

Thunderbird
The American Graduate School of
    International Management
15249 North 59th Avenue
Glendale, AZ 85306
602/978-7635
602/439-4851 (fax)
www.t-bird.edu

## 74

The Training Clinic
645 Seabreeze Drive
Seal Beach, CA 90740
800/937-4698
310/430-9603 (fax)
www.apc.net/trainu

## 75

Training Resources Group,
    Inc.
909 N. Washington Street,
    #305
Alexandria, VA 22314-1555
703/548-3535
703/836-2415 (fax)

## 76

University of Chicago
Graduate School of Business
450 N. Cityfront Plaza Drive
Chicago, IL 60611
312/464-8732
312/464-8731 (fax)
www.gsb.uchicago.edu/programs/
    exec-ed

## 77

University of Michigan
The Michigan Business School
Executive Education Center
Ann Arbor, MI 48109
734/642-3109
734/764-4267 (fax)
www.bus.umich.edu

## 78

University of Minnesota
Employer Education Service
430 Management and Economics
    Building
271-19th Avenue South
Industrial Relations Center
Minneapolis, MN 55455
800/333-3378
612/626-7747 (fax)
www.csom.umn.edu/csom/ees

## 79

University of Richmond
Management Institute
Special Programs Building
Richmond, VA 23173
804/289-8019
804/289-8872 (fax)
www.richmond.edu./mgmt.institute

## 80

University of Wisconsin–Madison
Engineering Professional
    Development
432 North Lake Street
Madison, WI 53706
800/462-0876
800/442-4214 (fax)
www.epd.engr.wisc.edu

## 81

University of Wisconsin–Madison
Management Institute
Grainger Hall
975 University Ave.
Madison, WI 53706
800/292-8964
800/741-7416 (fax)
800/292-8964 (program info)
608/262-4617 (fax)
www.wisc.edu/mi

## 82

University of Wisconsin–Stout
Technical Instructor Institutes
102 Communication Technologies
    Building
Menomonie, WI 54751
715/232-3289
715/836-5263 (fax)

## 83

Walden Institute for Learning and
    Leadership
24311 Walden Center Drive, 3rd
    floor
Bonita Springs, FL 34134
800/237-6434
941/498-7821 (fax)
www.waldeninstitute.com

## 84

Xavier University Consulting Group
3800 Victory Parkway
Cincinnati, OH 45207
513/745-3396
513/745-4307 (fax)
www.xavierconsulting.com

## INDEX TO SEMINAR AND WORKSHOP TOPICS TDY2001

The following listing of seminars and workshops of interest to trainers is comprehensive as well as representative of learning opportunities available in calendar year 2001 to any trainer with the interest and the funds available to attend.

In order to have been chosen for inclusion in the *Training & Development Yearbook 2001,* a seminar or workshop met some or all of the following criteria: a track record or history of being of service to a training audience; a new content focus; and a popular current leading edge topic. In addition, each provider listed has been a reputable and accessible sponsor, responsive to our inquiries about their programs. In several instances, programs delivered in a nontraditional format are also included in this listing because they are particularly interesting or timely. This year's listing of seminars again reflects the proliferation of service providers as downsized human resources employees around the country are striking out on their own to offer vendor and consulting services. New entries in 2001 also, in many instances, represent new ideas in team development, leadership, Web- and technology-based delivery, and organizational and human performance. Most programs listed are given in several locations throughout the United States.

Most training providers who offer public seminars and workshops also are happy to develop custom, in-house, or on-site adaptations of their public programs listed here. Costs given here are current costs for programs open to the public; customized programs vary in cost. Costs listed are training costs only; in general, travel, food, and lodging are extra. In many cases, a toll-free telephone number is given in the listing for more information. Providers listed are prompt with faxed information in response to your request. Their fax numbers are also listed for those who prefer to communicate this way. Website addresses are provided in the alphabetical listing of providers beginning on page 6.4.3. Websites are provided for 84 different training providers, with verified, current, useful information.

The following Index is a topical index to the 179 seminars and workshops we have chosen to represent the field in year 2001.

## INDEX TO SEMINAR AND WORKSHOP TOPICS TDY2001

**analyzing needs**

8, 14, 54, 68, 101, 104, 111, 112, 117, 130, 132, 135, 140, 154, 164, 167, 169, 175, 179

**benchmarking, quality, best practices**

9, 12, 13, 41, 44, 65, 111, 112, 174

**business strategy**

34, 50, 88, 94, 106, 113, 115, 139, 143, 145, 151, 152, 155, 161, 174

**coaching, mentoring**

24, 49, 59, 110, 111, 119, 122, 128, 134, 136

**communication, documentation**

35, 38, 39, 83, 84, 85, 88, 105, 141, 154

**conflict resolution, negotiation, problem solving, stress reduction**

6, 28, 37, 52, 61, 68, 79, 108, 116, 117, 144, 177

**consulting**

26, 70, 76, 80, 93, 106, 109, 113, 118, 125, 126, 140, 157

**creativity, critical thinking, innovation**

22, 39, 53, 60, 68, 78, 137, 139, 169, 177

**customer service, sales**

1, 65, 131, 133, 139, 146

**evaluation, measurement**
15, 45, 62, 77, 81, 92, 96, 100, 120, 124, 130, 133, 135, 164, 170, 179

**executive education**
4, 42, 44, 56, 90, 94, 98, 138, 145, 151, 152, 162, 174

**facilitation skills**
2, 20, 22, 31, 42, 46, 54, 76, 117, 124, 135, 137, 139, 140, 144, 153, 155, 160, 165, 169

**global and multicultural issues**
98, 138, 151, 152

**instructional design**
5, 8, 18, 25, 33, 36, 47, 54, 63, 64, 79, 82, 100, 102, 103, 114,
117, 124, 131, 132, 154, 166, 167, 170, 171, 176, 179

**knowledge management, intellectual capital**
11, 12, 58, 74, 88, 94, 152

**leadership**
20, 30, 32, 42, 43, 72, 73, 76, 78, 87, 88, 111, 116, 117, 139, 140, 143, 145, 162

**management and supervisory training**
21, 28, 50, 56, 59, 71, 72, 77, 88, 90, 91, 99, 101, 108, 114, 115, 127, 134,
136, 139, 143, 145, 156, 161, 163, 164

**managing the training operation**
7, 29, 48, 58, 69, 81, 91, 94, 96, 106, 107, 129, 130, 138, 155, 159, 172

**organization development**
19, 23, 50, 86, 89, 100, 106, 115, 136, 138, 159, 163, 166

**performance evaluation, feedback**
10, 15, 50, 52, 68, 71, 77, 81, 96, 124

**performance technology**
14, 15, 16, 17, 18, 19, 22, 23, 77, 81, 91, 112, 113, 157

**presentation skills and technologies**
2, 8, 22, 46, 100, 124, 131, 135, 137, 141, 150, 154, 158, 164, 167, 168, 169, 170, 176, 178, 179

**self-directed learning, self-development**
4, 28, 39, 42, 72, 118, 120, 124, 133, 135, 154, 173

**team development**
27, 28, 40, 50, 51, 52, 66, 121, 123, 127, 136, 142, 152, 153, 165, 177

**technical skills**
17, 33, 35, 55, 67, 101, 102, 131, 136, 138, 141, 143, 145, 154, 164, 170, 172, 175

**web-based training, online learning**
35, 36, 57, 63, 67, 75, 82, 94, 95, 97, 102, 132, 147, 148, 149, 175, 178

**1**

Title:
**Achieving Extraordinary Customer Relations**
Sponsor:
AchieveGlobal, Inc.
8875 Hidden River Pkwy., Ste. 400
Tampa, FL 33637
800/291-2752
888/662-7692 (fax)
Length:
2 days
Cost:
$730
Location:
Boston, Chicago, San Francisco, Tampa, Washington DC
Description:
The focus of this workshop is how to strategically manage each customer's experience; and that includes the learner as "customer." With today's emphasis on self-directed and individualized learning, this workshop's "personalized service" message is in tune with trainers' needs.

**2**

Title:
**Tools for Trainer Excellence**
Sponsor:
AchieveGlobal, Inc.
8875 Hidden River Pkwy., Ste. 400
Tampa, FL 33637
800/291-2752
888/662-7692 (fax)
Length:
3 days
Cost:
$995
Location:
Various cities throughout the U.S.
Description:
This skill-based workshop for new and experienced trainers is one of AchieveGlobal's most popular offerings. It is highly interactive and designed to turn good trainers into great trainers. The focus is on improving the speed and quality of learning with material from any source.

**3**

Title:
**Critical Thinking: A New Paradigm for Peak Performance**

Sponsor:
American Management
Association International
P.O. Box 169
Saranac Lake, NY 12983
800/262-9699
518/891-0368 (fax)
Length:
3 days
Cost:
$1,525
Location:
Various cities throughout the U.S.
Description:
This seminar focuses on ways to come to better conclusions and decisions more often, to challenge assumptions, and encourage innovation.

**4**

Title:
**Executive Effectiveness Course**
Sponsor:
American Management
Association International
P.O. Box 169
Saranac Lake, NY 12983
800/262-9699
518/891-0368 (fax)
Length:
Two 4½ day units
Cost:
$3,750
Location:
Hilton Head, SC; Williamsburg, VA; San Francisco; Boston
Description:
The time-lapse format of this 9-day training program is one of its key features. Both units incorporate the input and support of other seminar attendees. Self-awareness and a workable plan for future action are program goals. The second unit occurs 2–6 months after the first and builds upon insights learned from experience. Throughout, the focus is on strengths and resources.

**5**

Title:
**Instructional Design for Trainers**
Sponsor:
American Management Association
International
P.O. Box 169
Saranac Lake, NY 12983

800/262-9699
518/891-0368 (fax)
Length:
3 days
Cost:
$1,595
Location:
Washington, DC
Description:
This seminar teaches how to create effective training programs that meet the learning needs of employees and the goals of the company. Topics include: conducting micro-needs analysis; getting top management to approve a proposal; tapping into resources; the 4-step method of training; refining a program; writing the lesson plan; designing useful and flexible leader's guides and participant manuals; preassignments and integrative post-assignments for trainee evaluation systems; how to implement a program; presentation of a program.

**6**

Title:
**Managing Emotions in the Workplace**
Sponsor:
American Management Association
International
P.O. Box 169
Saranac Lake, NY 12983
800/262-9699
518/891-0368 (fax)
Length:
2 days
Cost:
$1,395
Location:
Various cities throughout the U.S.
Description:
This seminar emphasizes self-awareness as participants learn skills to deal with difficult people and work situations.

**7**

Title:
**Managing the Training Function**
Sponsor:
American Management
Association International
P.O. Box 169
Saranac Lake, NY 12983
800/262-9699
518/891-0368 (fax)

**Length:**
4¹/₂ days
**Cost:**
$1,925
**Location:**
Various cities throughout the U.S.
**Description:**
This seminar is for those who are newly responsible for a training function. Topics include: alignment with corporate goals, training budgets, outsourcing vs. internal training, partnering and forming alliances.

## 8

**Title:**
**Training the Trainer**
**Sponsor:**
American Management Association International
P.O. Box 169
Saranac Lake, NY 12983
800/262-9699
518/891-0368 (fax)
**Length:**
5 days
**Cost:**
$1,925
**Location:**
Various cities throughout the U.S.
**Description:**
Designed for trainers with less than three years' experience, this course covers the importance of training, needs analysis, setting objectives, course development, training methods, and presentation skills.

## 9

**Title:**
**Applying Benchmarking Skills**
**Sponsor:**
American Productivity & Quality Center (APQC)
123 N. Post Oak Lane
Houston, TX 77024
800/776-9676
713/681-3705 (fax)
**Length:**
2 days
**Cost:**
$945
**Location:**
Houston, TX; Chicago, IL
**Description:**
This seminar focuses on a systematic process for using the findings

of benchmarking studies. This and other APQC seminars are offered primarily as an adjunct to APQC's annual conference.

## 10

**Title:**
**Establishing Performance Measures**
**Sponsor:**
American Productivity & Quality Center (APQC)
123 N. Post Oak Lane
Houston, TX 77024-7797
800/776-9676
713/681-3705 (fax)
**Length:**
1 day
**Cost:**
$595
**Location:**
Houston, TX; Chicago, IL
**Description:**
Individuals responsible for designing performance measures will benefit from this seminar, which offers a step-by-step facilitator's guide that shows you how to lead an in-house staff in the design and implementation of effective performance measures. As an added highlight of the seminar, you will explore the crucial role of measurement group reward systems and benchmarking.

## 11

**Title:**
**Knowledge Management Overview**
**Sponsor:**
American Productivity & Quality Center (APQC)
123 N. Post Oak Lane
Houston, TX 77024-7797
800/776-9676
713/681-3705 (fax)
**Length:**
¹/₂ day
**Cost:**
$375
**Location:**
Houston, TX; Chicago, IL
**Description:**
This intensive half-day session will provide participants with a strategic perspective on how to evaluate and use the principles and strategies collectively called "Knowledge Management" to add value to your

bottom line, customers, and employees. Other seminars and forums on knowledge management are also available.

## 12

**Title:**
**Transfer of Knowledge and Best Practices**
**Sponsor:**
American Productivity and Quality Center (APQC)
123 N. Post Oak Lane
Houston, TX 77024
800/776-9676
713/681-3705 (fax)
**Length:**
2 days
**Cost:**
$945
**Location:**
Houston, TX
**Description:**
This seminar introduces a proven transfer methodology that focuses on logistical, structural, and cultural issues, showing how to identify and close knowledge gaps. Participants must have a TQM background. APQC's Benchmarking and Knowledge Management Overview courses are part of this seminar.

## 13

**Title:**
**Foundations in Quality Self-Directed Learning Series**
**Sponsor:**
American Society for Quality (ASQ)
P.O. Box 3066
Milwaukee, WI 53201
800/248-1946
414/272-1734 (fax)
**Length:**
8 self-study modules;
600 pages of text reinforced by computer-based testing, practice, and exercises
**Cost:**
$345
**Location:**
Your home or office pc, IBM-compatible, 486 or higher 4 MEG of RAM, 8 MEG free hard disk space, Microsoft Windows 3.1 or higher
**Description:**
Also known as Q101. This unique quality foundations course

includes 8 modules of focused study: quality standards, organizations and their functions, quality needs and overall strategic plans, customer satisfaction and focus, project management, continuous improvement, human resource management, and training and education. A demonstration program is available free of charge through the ASQ Website.

## 14

Title:
**Analyzing Human Performance**
Sponsor:
American Society for Training and Development (ASTD)
1640 King Street, Box 1443
Alexandria, VA 22313
800/628-2783
703/683-8103 (fax)
Length:
3 days
Cost:
$1,150
Location:
Various universities throughout the U.S.
Description:
This seminar is part of a recently-developed ASTD Human Performance Improvement Certificate Program. Topics include: performance and cause analysis, organizational scanning, workflow/work process analysis, and ergonomic analysis. Five other related seminars listed here are offered in the Certificate Program.

## 15

Title:
**Evaluating Performance Improvement Interventions**
Sponsor:
American Society for Training and Development (ASTD)
1640 King Street, Box 1443
Alexandria, VA 22313
800/628-2783
703/683-8103 (fax)
Length:
3 days
Cost:
$1,150
Location:
Various universities throughout the U.S.
Description:
This seminar is part of a recently-developed ASTD Human Perfor-

mance Improvement Certificate Program. Topics include: measuring learning, behavior, and results; the value and limitations of various evaluation models; cost-benefit analysis; measuring the intangibles; and linking behavior and performance. Five other related seminars listed here are offered in the Certificate Program.

## 16

Title:
**Human Performance Improvement in the Workplace**
Sponsor:
American Society for Training and Development (ASTD)
1640 King Street, Box 1443
Alexandria, VA 22313
800/628-2783
703/683-8103 (fax)
Length:
3 days
Cost:
$1,150
Location:
Various universities throughout the U.S.
Description:
This seminar is part of a recently-developed ASTD Human Performance Improvement Certificate Program. Topics include: exploring a variety of training and non-training interventions, role-specific competencies and outputs, developing a change plan for an HPI intervention, stakeholder support, and Human Performance Technology's link to systems. Five other related seminars listed here are offered in the Certificate Program.

## 17

Title:
**Learning Technologies for Improving Performance**
Sponsor:
American Society for Training and Development (ASTD)
1640 King Street, Box 1443
Alexandria, VA 22313
800/628-2783
703/683-8103 (fax)
Length:
3 days
Cost:
$1,150

Location:
Various universities throughout the U.S.
Description:
This seminar is part of a recently-developed ASTD Human Performance Improvement Certificate Program. Topics include: determining appropriate technologies for your organization, justifying the move to technology, and creating a transition plan. Five other related seminars listed here are offered in the Certificate Program.

## 18

Title:
**Selecting and Designing Performance Improvement Interventions**
Sponsor:
American Society for Training and Development (ASTD)
1640 King Street, Box 1443
Alexandria, VA 22313
800/628-2783
703/683-8103 (fax)
Length:
3 days
Cost:
$1,150
Location:
Various universities throughout the U.S.
Description:
This seminar is part of a recently-developed ASTD Human Performance Improvement Certificate Program. Topics include: types and examples of interventions, assessing organizational readiness, gathering support, and implementing the intervention. Five other related seminars listed here are offered in the Certificate Program.

## 19

Title:
**Transitioning to Human Performance Improvement**
Sponsor:
American Society for Training and Development (ASTD)
1640 King Street, Box 1443
Alexandria, VA 22313
800/628-2783
703/683-8103 (fax)
Length:
3 days
Cost:
$1,150

**Location:**
Various universities throughout the U.S.

**Description:**
This seminar is part of a recently-developed ASTD Human Performance Improvement Certificate Program. Topics include: deciding to make the transition, organizational readiness; stakeholders, peer and management buy-in; organizing the new HPI department; keeping the change alive. Five other related seminars listed here are offered in the Certificate Program.

## 20

**Title:**
**Leadership and Influence: Empowerment Through Shared Responsibility**

**Sponsor:**
Babson School of Executive Education
Babson Park, MA 02457
781/239-4354
781/239-5266 (fax)

**Length:**
5 days in May or 5 days in October, with one "Reunion" day 5 months later

**Cost:**
$4,950 including meals, accommodations, materials plus $995 for the "Reunion" day

**Location:**
Babson College's Center for Executive Education, Wellesley, MA

**Description:**
This is an interactive hands-on workshop for senior managers to learn and practice effective techniques for today's "shared responsibility" workplaces. Participants learn competencies in communication, using power and influence, building commitment, dealing with conflict, developing collaboration, and teaching and coaching. A one-day followup session is optional.

## 21

**Title:**
**Enhancing Supervisor Effectiveness in Safety**

**Sponsor:**
Behavioral Science Technology, Inc.
417 Bryant Circle
Ojai, CA 93023

800/548-5781
805/646-0328 (fax)

**Length:**
2 days

**Cost:**
$845; $795 early registration

**Location:**
St. Louis, MO

**Description:**
This unique seminar focuses on the behavioral aspects of leadership as it applies to workforce safety. Seminar leaders include front line safety managers, training and education leaders, and psychologists. Topics include implementation planning, accountability, leadership vs. management, and where safety activities fit into the bigger corporate picture.

## 22

**Title:**
**Creative Training Techniques**

**Sponsor:**
The Bob Pike Group
7620 West 78th Street
Minneapolis, MN 55439
800/383-9210
612/829-0260 (fax)

**Length:**
2 days

**Cost:**
$895

**Location:**
Various cities throughout the U.S.

**Description:**
This program is for the trainer who wants more out of training efforts, a more exciting training routine, and faster results. Participants receive a 140-page manual with charts, samples, checklists, tips, and insights. Discussion on the course covers: (1) methods for motivating adults, (2) building the "middle" of one's presentation, (3) kindergarten lessons that enhance adult learning, (4) "Ten Deadly Sins" that kill presentations, (5) incorrect ways to use audiovisuals, (6) creating personal accountability, and more.

## 23

**Title:**
**The Performance Solutions Institute**

**Sponsor:**
The Bob Pike Group
7620 West 78th Street
Minneapolis, MN 55439

800/383-9210
952/829-0260 (fax)

**Length:**
2 days, with optional add-on customized sessions

**Cost:**
$895

**Location:**
Minneapolis or customized on-site

**Description:**
The Institute is run as a conference, with two tracks from which to choose. It is built upon master trainer, Bob Pike's, creative training techniques program expanded to encompass strategic organizational content more in line with the performance shift in training. Phone the Bob Pike Group for customization, on-site options, and group discounts.

## 24

**Title:**
**Coaching People to Work at Peak Performance**

**Sponsor:**
Boston University
Corporate Education Center
72 Tyng Road
Tyngsboro, MA 01879
800/288-7246
978/649-2162 (fax)

**Length:**
2 days

**Cost:**
$995

**Location:**
Various locations in the Boston, MA area

**Description:**
This is a skills-based workshop for anyone who needs to be a coach. Self assessment and clarification of managing, supervising, and coaching are stressed.

## 25

**Title:**
**Instructional Design I and II**

**Sponsor:**
Boston University
Corporate Education Center
72 Tyng Road
Tyngsboro, MA 01879
800/288-7246
978/649-2162 (fax)

**Length:**
3 days

**Cost:**
$1,295

**Location:**
Various locations in the Boston, MA area

**Description:**
This interactive workshop is designed to give the participant an opportunity to increase his or her abilities in developing and designing a training program either for a classroom situation or for one-on-one training. Active participation is essential for meeting training and learning objectives. Course I is a recommended prerequisite to Course II. Both courses focus on learner-focused and performance-based instructional design. The courses use a systematic instructional design methodology and provide trainees with skills for design of performance-based competency objectives.

## 26

**Title:**
**Internal Consulting Skills**
**Sponsor:**
Boston University
Corporate Education Center
72 Tyng Road
Tyngsboro, MA 01879
800/288-7246
978/649-2162 (fax)
**Length:**
2 days
**Cost:**
$995
**Location:**
Various locations in the Boston, MA area
**Description:**
This seminar addresses the new position many trainers are assuming, that of internal consultant. Balancing task and process, analysis skills, and communication skills for collaborative training are covered. The seminar is based on the work of Peter Block.

## 27

**Title:**
**Leading & Managing Successful Teams**
**Sponsor:**
Boston University
Corporate Education Center
72 Tyng Road
Tyngsboro, MA 01879
800/288-7246
978/649-2162 (fax)

**Length:**
3 days
**Cost:**
$1,295
**Location:**
Various locations in the Boston, MA area
**Description:**
This workshop uses the MBTI (Myers-Briggs Type Indicator) for analysis of individual styles and team dynamics. The workshop focuses on securing commitment to team, consensus-building techniques, negotiation skills, communication and leadership skills.

## 28

**Title:**
**Women's Institute for Managerial Excellence**
**Sponsor:**
Boston University
Corporate Education Center
72 Tyng Road
Tyngsboro, MA 01879
800/288-7246
978/649-2162 (fax)
**Length:**
3 days
**Cost:**
$1,295
**Location:**
Various locations in the Boston, MA area
**Description:**
This intensive and skill-focused workshop is limited to 20 participants. Motivation, conflict resolution, style assessment, and team building are key topics.

## 29

**Title:**
**Partnering Skills for Outsourcing**
**Sponsor:**
Boston University
Corporate Education Center
72 Tyng Road
Tyngsboro, MA 01879
800/288-7246
978/649-2162 (fax)
**Length:**
1 day
**Cost:**
$695
**Location:**
Various locations in the Boston, MA area
**Description:**
This practical seminar provides a toolkit of essential strategies and

skills to maximize the productivity of outsourcing and vendor relationships. Customers and their service providers are encouraged to attend together.

## 30

**Title:**
**Foundations of Leadership**
**Sponsor:**
Bradley University
Foster College of Business Administration
Peoria, IL 61625
309/677-4420
309/677-4421 (fax)
**Length:**
3 days
**Cost:**
$2,900
**Location:**
The Leadership Development Center, Bradley College, Peoria, IL
**Description:**
This is an experience-based course for leaders and emerging leaders, part of the expanded program of The Center for Creative Leadership. Among the key topics are: leadership and influence, leadership and collaboration, and communication, and consultation. Analysis of case studies and a personal plan of action are part of the program.

## 31

**Title:**
**Facilitation Skills**
**Sponsor:**
Brainstorm Dynamics, Inc.
Reproducible Training Programs
12 Brocster Court, Suite 200
Phoenix, MD 21131
888/825-8484
410/561-9050
410/592-9156 (fax)
**Length:**
2 days
**Cost:**
$149.95
**Location:**
A training room in your company
**Description:**
This is one of 10 workshops available for in-house trainers to copy and use within your own company. Brainstorm Dynamics workshops come in CD-ROM and/or print form. A Facilitator's Guide and a Participant's Workbook come with the full 2-day program. Topics include: managing structure, not content; key criteria to

"client" contracts; developing the structure and process; encouraging participation; listening and questionning; and closing meetings.

## 32

**Title:**
**Practical Leadership**
**Sponsor:**
Brainstorm Dynamics, Inc.
Reproducible Training Programs
12 Brocster Court, Suite 200
Phoenix, MD 21131
888/825-8484
410/561-9050
410/592-9156 (fax)
**Length:**
2 days
**Cost:**
$149.95
**Location:**
A training room in your company
**Description:**
This is one of 10 workshops available for in-house trainers to copy and use within your own company. Brainstorm Dynamics workshops come in CD-ROM and/or print form. A Facilitator's Guide and a Participant's Guide come with the full 2-day program. Topics include: identifying leadership and followership; skills of an effective leader; management versus leadership; positioning and presenting ideas; learning how to gain followers; dealing with negative emotions in others; and handling challenges to leadership.

## 33

**Title:**
**Tools for Technical Trainers**
**Sponsor:**
Bryant College
Center for Management
Development
1150 Douglas Pike
Smithfield, RI 02917-1283
401/232-6200
401/232-6704 (fax)
**Length:**
1 day
**Cost:**
$325
**Location:**
Smithfield, RI
**Description:**
In this program, participants learn to develop more effective technical training, and they learn the basics of instructional design. There are opportunities to practice four dif-

ferent types of training exercises, and participants learn how to develop materials that are aimed at the different types of students they will encounter. The program includes examples of proven technical training courses in major corporations, and participants have the chance to work on developing a program of their own.

## 34

**Title:**
**Integrated Strategic Planning**
**Sponsor:**
California Institute of Technology
Industrial Relations Center 1-90
Pasadena, CA 91125
626/395-4043
626/795-7174 (fax)
**Length:**
2 days
**Cost:**
$1,745
**Location:**
Pasadena, CA
**Description:**
This program is applicable to small, medium, and large companies and to all industries manufacturing, service, distribution, and retail. It will assist companies diversifying into new markets and products as well as those consolidating their present position. Participants will build *key elements of their own strategic plans* after moving through process, strategic thinking, a case study and planning forms with both lecture and workshop activities. Trainers moving into performance management will find this a useful perspective.

## 35

**Title:**
**Certificate in Teaching and Training Online**
**Sponsor:**
Capella University
330 Second Avenue South, Ste. 550
Minneapolis, MN 55401
612/239-8650
888/227-3552
612/337-5396 (fax)
**Length:**
Certificate program averages 1 year, or 3 months per course; doctoral program averages 3–4 years
**Cost:**
$3,700, or $925 each for 4 courses; PhD Seminar residence fees: $350

Focused Seminar; $890 Two-Week Extended Seminar
**Location:**
Online; residence in MN; courses begin in January, April, July, and October
**Description:**
This online program is one of several certificate programs offered by Capella University. It is made up of 4 courses: Critical Skills for Facilitating Online Learning, Tools and Techniques for Online Learning, Strategies for Building Online Learning Communities, and Practical Applications for Online Teaching and Training. Each course can be taken separately and can be transferred into a Capella University masters degree or doctoral program. Courses may be taught in a "Directed Study" format, matching a tutor or mentor with a learner. The option of seminar extensions in residence are also provided.

## 36

**Title:**
**How to Build a Successful Website**
**Sponsor:**
Career Track/Fred Pryor Seminars
P.O. Box 2951
Shawnee Mission, KS 66201
800/334-6780
918/665-3434 (fax)
**Length:**
1 day
**Cost:**
$199
**Location:**
Many cities throughout the U.S.
**Description:**
Essentials of Website design including applications of online catalogs, newsletters, chat rooms; includes overview of Website tools and software and new ideas in graphics.

## 37

**Title:**
**Getting It All Done**
**Sponsor:**
Career Track/Fred Pryor Seminars
P.O. Box 2951
Shawnee Mission, KS 66201
800/334-6780
918/665-3434 (fax)
**Length:**
1 day
**Cost:**
$149

**Location:**
Many cities throughout the U.S.
**Description:**
This seminar focuses on managing priorities, deadlines, and pressure. Time management, setting priorities, maintaining control, and unclogging bottlenecks are all covered.

## 38

**Title:**
**How to Become a Great Communicator**
**Sponsor:**
Career Track/Fred Pryor Seminars
P.O. Box 2951
Shawnee Mission, KS 66201
800/334-6780
918/665-3434 (fax)
**Length:**
1 day
**Cost:**
$149
**Location:**
Many cities throughout the U.S.
**Description:**
This seminar includes how to communicate in tough situations, work within team communication styles, how to increase personal power through communication, how to listen with purpose, and how to communicate to be trusted and respected.

## 39

**Title:**
**Accelerated Learning Training Methods**
**Sponsor:**
The Center for Accelerated Learning
1103 Wisconsin Street
Lake Geneva, WI 53147
262/248-7070
262/248-1912 (fax)
**Length:**
3 days
**Cost:**
$995
**Location:**
Various cities throughout the U.S.
**Description:**
This workshop teaches skills and theory of "accelerated learning" with a goal of enhanced integration of new knowledge and skill. Topics and skills include: using the whole body to learn, using imagery and mnemonics, informa-

tion mapping, collaborative learning, and learning in context.

## 40

**Title:**
**Using Type in Team Performance**
**Sponsor:**
Center for Applications of Psychological Type, Inc.
2815 N.W. 13th Street, Suite 401
Gainesville, FL 32609
800/777-2278
904/378-0503 (fax)
**Length:**
2 days
**Cost:**
$375
**Location:**
Raleigh, NC; St. Louis, MO; San Francisco, CA
**Description:**
This workshop is designed for professional MBTI users who wish to apply type concepts and structured team assessment techniques to their client teams, and who want a systematic way to approach the management of their own work teams. Participants learn (1) to relate type concepts to a diagnostic model, (2) to increase their predictive and explanatory capabilities in team development, and (3) to put type concepts into perspective for overall team effectiveness.

## 41

**Title:**
**Benchmarks Certification Workshop**
**Sponsor:**
Center for Creative Leadership
One Leadership Place
P.O. Box 26300
Greensboro, NC 27438-6300
336/545-2810
336/282-3284 (fax)
**Length:**
2 days
**Cost:**
$1,200
**Location:**
Greensboro, NC; Colorado Springs, CO; San Diego, CA
**Description:**
To certify human resource managers, career development professionals, and consultants to give one-on-one feedback using the *Benchmarks* instrument. Participants

are certified to use *Benchmarks* as either a stand-alone instrument or in conjunction with other management development programs.

## 42

**Title:**
**Developing the Strategic Leader: Thinking, Acting, and Influencing**
**Sponsor:**
Center for Creative Leadership
One Leadership Place
P.O. Box 26300
Greensboro, NC 27438-6300
336/545-2810
336/282-3284 (fax)
**Length:**
5 days
**Cost:**
$4,700
**Location:**
Colorado Springs, CO
**Description:**
This is a recently revamped workshop focusing on strategic skills for executive effectiveness. It features considerable one-on-one instruction and learning.

## 43

**Title:**
**Leadership Development Program**
**Sponsor:**
Center for Creative Leadership
One Leadership Place
P.O. Box 26300
Greensboro, NC 27438-6300
336/545-2810
336/282-3284 (fax)
**Length:**
6 days
**Cost:**
$5,200
**Location:**
Greensboro, NC; Colorado Springs, CO; San Diego, CA
**Description:**
This is the flagship workshop of the Center for Creative Leadership. Training emphasizes the practical skills and knowledge required for creative leadership and effective management. Resources of the Center's research and publishing efforts are available as guides for effective assessment, development, and practice.

## 44

**Title:**
**Tools for Developing Successful Executives**

**Sponsor:**
Center for Creative Leadership
One Leadership Place
P.O. Box 26300
Greensboro, NC 27438-6300
336/545-2810
336/282-3284 (fax)

**Length:**
3 days

**Cost:**
$2,900

**Location:**
San Diego, CA

**Description:**
The workshop is designed for human resource executives, line managers, and professionals who are responsible for establishing and operating career and executive development systems in their organizations. By evaluating a selection of assessment techniques and instruments, participants learn to design and implement career development systems. All the tools introduced during this program are research-based and free standing. Participants have the opportunity (1) to practice and evaluate using each of the tools presented and (2) to discuss applications to specific situations back home. The Center offers a *Benchmarks Certification* option following the "Tools for Developing Executives" program at its Greensboro, San Diego, and Brussels locations. This certification allows human resource professionals to use *Benchmarks* within their own organizations. The fee for this optional certification is $600.

## 45

**Title:**
**Criterion-Referenced Instruction**

**Sponsor:**
The Center for Effective Performance Inc.
2300 Peachford Road, Ste. 2000
Atlanta, GA 30338
800/558-4237
770/458-9109 (fax)

**Length:**
10 days (This self-paced workshop takes a maximum of 2 weeks to complete. Participants may attend for only one week to complete selected sections of the course.)

**Cost:**
$2,600

**Location:**
Atlanta, GA; Chicago, IL

**Description:**
This new edition of Robert Mager's self-paced workshop gives participants the skills to excel in a state-of-the-art training and performance improvement effort. Participants learn to: (1) reduce total training time, (2) make training results measurable, (3) use training only where it is needed, (4) guarantee that each qualified trainee reaches competence, and (5) provide substantial dollar savings in training costs. The workshop allows participants to progress at a rate comfortable to them, and apply their new skills to a course they are currently working on to use immediately back on the job.

## 46

**Title:**
**Mastering the Art of Instructor-Led Training**

**Sponsor:**
The Center for Effective Performance Inc.
2300 Peachford Road, Ste. 2000
Atlanta, GA 30338
800/558-4237
770/458-9109 (fax)

**Length:**
4 days

**Cost:**
$1,650

**Location:**
Atlanta, GA; Phoenix, AZ

**Description:**
This four-day workshop is designed to sharpen presentation skills of both newcomers and veterans. More than 75 percent of the workshop time is devoted to practice in an environment that is positive, constructive, and non-threatening. Participants use their own course material to prepare and conduct presentations and receive constructive feedback from an expert practitioner. The workshop features a new media module.

## 47

**Title:**
**Instructional Module Development**

**Sponsor:**
The Center for Effective Performance Inc.
2300 Peachford Road, Ste. 2000
Atlanta, GA 30338
800/558-4237
770/458-9109 (fax)

**Length:**
10 days

**Cost:**
$2,400

**Location:**
Atlanta, GA; Chicago, IL

**Description:**
This program is for course writers, designers, developers, and instructors who write their own instruction. Using the prerequisite skills learned in Robert Mager's "Criterion-Referenced Instruction," participants learn to develop instructional material, speed development time, and save training costs. Using their own objectives, participants go through each step of the development process. They leave the workshop with two modules of their own instruction that have been developed and tested.

## 48

**Title:**
**Training Manager Workshop**

**Sponsor:**
The Center for Effective Performance Inc.
2300 Peachford Rd., Ste. 2000
Atlanta, GA 30338
800/558-4237
770/458-9109 (fax)

**Length:**
5 days

**Cost:**
$2,475

**Location:**
Washington, DC; Orlando, FL

**Description:**
For new or experienced training managers, Robert Mager's workshop gives participants the skills to manage a modern training function with confidence. Participants learn: (1) to recommend appropriate solutions to performance problems, (2) to review and evaluate instruction, media choices, project proposals, and vendor proposals, and (3) how to respond to, and stimulate, requests for services. The workshop is performance-based and self-paced.

## 49

Title:
**Coaching Skills Workshop**
Sponsor:
Center for Management &
Organization Effectiveness
P.O. Box 21103
Salt Lake City, UT 84121
801/943-6310
801/569-3449 (fax)
Length:
2 days
Cost:
$495
Location:
Various cities throughout the U.S.
Description:
This workshop helps develop skills
which can be used to improve the
performance, productivity, and
growth of employees. It shows (1)
how to maximize employee performance through the "Eight-Step
Coaching Model", (2) how to deal
with and manage differences and
employee resistance while building
morale and motivation, (3) how to
conduct a motivational coaching
session to make the average
employee a better contributor to
the team, and (4) how to coach
employees to support the changes
necessary to keep the organization
competitive.

## 50

Title:
**Integrating Business Strategy,
Team Performance Measure-
ment, and Incentives**
Sponsor:
Center for the Study of Work
Teams
University of North Texas
P.O. Box 311280
Denton, TX 76203
940/565-3096
940/565-4806 (fax)
Length:
2 days
Cost:
$790
Location:
Denton, TX
Description:
This 2-day workshop is a skill-
based workshop on how to
develop performance measurement
systems, incorporating feedback
practices and incentives. Uses

Excel spreadsheet, modified for
team applications. One of 10 workshops in the CSWT's "Workshop
Series," most of which are taught
by recently published authors on
various aspects of teams.

## 51

Title:
**Need to Improve Team
Results?**
Sponsor:
Center for the Study of Work
Teams
University of North Texas
P.O. Box 311280
Denton, TX 76203
940/565-3096
940/565-4806 (fax)
Length:
1 day
Cost:
$395
Location:
Denton, TX
Description:
This workshop focuses on team
pay as the best motivator for
improving team results. It uses
many examples of what works and
what doesn't work and why. One
of 10 workshops in the CSWT
Workshop Series.

## 52

Title:
**Team Problem Solving**
Sponsor:
Center for the Study of Work Teams
University of North Texas
P.O. Box 311280
Denton, TX 76203
940/565-3096
940/565-4806 (fax)
Length:
1 day
Cost:
$395
Location:
Denton, TX
Description:
This is a hands-on workshop that
presents a 6-step problem-solving
process immediately applicable to
any organization's actual problems
with teams. Presented by the
"Xerox Hi-Rockers," an award win-
ning systems service Team from
Xerox.

## 53

Title:
**Developing Critical Thinkers**
Sponsor:
Columbia University
Teachers College
Center for Educational Outreach
and Innovation
525 West 120th Street, Box 132
New York, NY 10027
212/678-3987
212/678-4048 (fax)
Length:
2 days
Cost:
$195
Location:
New York, NY
Description:
In this workshop, participants
explore the ways in which adults
learn critical thinking, and they
experience different techniques to
teach critical thinking. They also
learn about blockages to critical
thinking and how to help learners
overcome them. The format of
the workshop is a combination
of presentations and small group
exercises.

## 54

Title:
**Helping Adults Learn**
Sponsor:
Columbia University
Teachers College
Center for Educational Outreach
and Innovation
525 West 120th Street, Box 132
New York, NY 10027
212/678-3987
212/678-4048 (fax)
Length:
2 days
Cost:
$195
Location:
New York, NY
Description:
Some of the questions explored by
this workshop will be as follows:
How do adults experience learning? What characteristics do adult
learners value in educators? What
are some of the most typical
dilemmas which educators of
adults face, and how might they
be resolved? In addition to presentations by the workshop

leader, participants will work in small groups to explore different approaches to helping adults learn.

## 55

Title:
**Troubleshooting, Fixing, and Upgrading PCs for Non-Techies**
Sponsor:
CompEd
P.O. Box 419107
Kansas City, MO 64141
800/258-7246
800/258-7248
913/432-0824
Length:
2 days
Cost:
$395
Location:
Various cities throughout the U.S.
Description:
This is a hands-on workshop for non-technical persons who need to know more about what makes a PC run. Topics include: installing and removal of hardware components such as motherboard, CPU, hard drive, CD-ROM drive, fax/modem and video cards; how to prevent problems between system parts; how to protect data; memory, speed, performance, and maintenance.

## 56

Title:
**Succession Planning and Top Talent Development**
Sponsor:
The Conference Board
845 Third Avenue
New York, NY 10022
212/759-0900
212/980-7014 (fax)
Length:
1 day
Cost:
$845
Location:
Chicago, IL; Atlanta, GA; Dallas, TX; New York, NY
Description:
Designed for senior executives and human resources leaders, this intensive seminar is led by CEOs and senior executives. Development of top talent for senior level positions is a key focus. One of many semi-

nars and learning opportunities offered by The Conference Board.

## 57

Title:
**HR on the Internet**
Sponsor:
Cornell University, School of Industrial & Labor Relations Management Development and Human Resources Programs
16 East 34th St.
New York, NY 10016-4328
212/340-2863
212/340-2822 (fax)
Length:
1 day
Cost:
$595
Location:
New York, NY; Ithaca, NY; Melville, NY
Description:
This workshop focuses on the basics of internet/intranet use, including the Web, list servs, search engines, employment law, online recruiting and career management, and training.

## 58

Title:
**Building a Diversity Program**
Sponsor:
Cornell University, School of Industrial & Labor Relations Management Development and Human Resources Programs
16 East 34th St.
New York, NY 10016-4328
212/340-2863
212/340-2822 (fax)
Length:
2 days
Cost:
$795
Location:
New York, NY; Ithaca, NY
Description:
This is an innovative workshop on building a diversity program and making it work. Special features include a live theater presentation exploring workplace diversity issues, and keynote speakers discussing tough issues such as how to train and evaluate training, respond to backlash, demographics and EEO/AA laws, and diversity's place in globalization efforts.

## 59

Title:
**Manager as Coach**
Sponsor:
Cornell University, School of Industrial & Labor Relations Management Development and Human Resources Programs
16 East 34th Street
New York, NY 10016-4328
212/340-2863
212/340-2822 (fax)
Length:
2 days
Cost:
$795
Location:
New York, NY; Ithaca, NY
Description:
This workshop focuses on a coach's "Toolbox" for building a successful coaching program to motivate people, change problem behavior, and boost individual and team behavior.

## 60

Title:
**Thinking Outside the Box: Creativity and Innovation**
Sponsor:
Cornell University, School of Industrial & Labor Relations Office of Management & Executive Education
Room 220, Garden Ave., ILR Conference Center
Ithaca, NY 14853-3901
607/255-9212
607/255-3274 (fax)
Length:
2 days
Cost:
$995
Location:
Ithaca, NY; New York, NY
Description:
This workshop focuses on discovery of the trainee's own personal creativity and features development and a Creativity Workout Plan.

## 61

Title:
**Nonviolent Crisis Intervention**
Sponsor:
Crisis Prevention Institute, Inc.
3315-K North 124th Street
Brookfield, WI 53005

800/558-8976
414/783-5787
414/783-5906 (fax)
**Length:**
1 or 2 days
**Cost:**
$295 or $545
**Location:**
Various cities in the U.S. and
Canada
**Description:**
Day 1 focuses on preventing physical violence at work, nonverbal techniques for controlling disruptive behavior, dealing with fear and anxiety, and verbal crisis resolution. Day 2 includes when and how to restrain disruptive persons, staff and spectator safety, team intervention, and tension reduction after intervention. Videotapes and publications are also available. A 4-day program leading to instructor certification is also available for $995.

## 62

**Title:**
**The Criterion-Referenced Testing Workshop**
**Sponsor:**
Darryl L. Sink & Associates, Inc.
60 Garden Court, Suite 101
Monterey, CA 93940
831/649-8384
800/650-7465
831/649-3914 (fax)
**Length:**
2 days
**Cost:**
$749
**Location:**
Various cities throughout the U.S.
**Description:**
This program is for trainers, training managers, and course developers who want to design or redesign the measurement of training results. Participants practice writing all kinds of test items used to evaluate what learners need on the job. Topics include writing checklists, testing at the correct level, developing a testing plan, and issues in Web-based testing.

## 63

**Title:**
**Designing Instruction for Web-Based Training**

**Sponsor:**
Darryl L. Sink & Associates, Inc.
60 Garden Court, Suite 101
Monterey, CA 93940
800/650-7465
831/649-8384
831/649-3914 (fax)
**Length:**
3 days
**Cost:**
$1,199
**Location:**
Various cities throughout the U.S.
**Description:**
This is an intensive workshop for instructional designers, training managers, and supervisors. Participants receive over 50 job aids and a 300-page guide for use back on the job. Topics include: site maps, Web development models, navigation, active responding, types of authoring tools, domain and content types, templates and prototypes, writing Web-based instruction, creating engaging instruction, implementation strategies, usability, formative evaluation, review and feedback, and identifying and assessing business need for Web-based training.

## 64

**Title:**
**The Instructional Developer Workshop**
**Sponsor:**
Darryl L. Sink & Associates, Inc.
60 Garden Court, Suite 101
Monterey, CA 93940
831/649-8384
800/650-7465
831/649-3914 (fax)
**Length:**
3 days
**Cost:**
$899
**Location:**
Various cities throughout the U.S.
**Description:**
This course moves the learner through the basic techniques of course development, as well as through more advanced skills in instructional design. Examples include Web-based and computer-based training. Includes course-writed software.

## 65

**Title:**
**The Disney Approach to Quality Service**

**Sponsor:**
Disney University/Disney
Institute
P.O. Box 10,093
Lake Buena Vista, FL 32830
407/828-4953
407/828-2402 (fax)
**Length:**
3$^{1/2}$ days
**Cost:**
$3,295
**Location:**
Walt Disney World, Orlando, FL
**Description:**
This seminar uses the Walt Disney World Resort as a "living classroom" to learn how Disney creates "magic moments" for customers. Visits to behind-the-scenes operations, presentations by Disney managers, and extensive take-home materials focus on ways to maximize delivery systems.

## 66

**Title:**
**Teamwork in Action**
**Sponsor:**
Eckerd College
Management Development
Institute
4200 54th Avenue South
St. Petersburg, FL 33711
800/753-0444
813/864-8996 (fax)
**Length:**
3 days
**Cost:**
$2,600
**Location:**
St. Petersburg, FL
**Description:**
Teamwork in Action features two powerful "feedback from colleagues" instruments. The Systematic Multiple Level Observation of Groups® (SYMLOG) enables participants to examine in detail those aspects of their behavior which enhance teamwork and those which may be interfering with it. The second instrument, the Leadership Effectiveness Analysis® 360° (LEA), allows participants to measure leadership behaviors as perceived by superiors, peers, and direct reports. The results help participants assess their impact on others and their ability to inspire team commitment. Additional features include confidential one-on-one feedback with a professional

staff member, peer learning, and action planning.

## 67

**Title:**
**Interactive Multimedia Training: Introduction to CD-ROMs**
**Sponsor:**
Emerging Technology Consultants, Inc.
2819 Hamline Ave. North
St. Paul, MN 55113
651/639-3973
651/639-0110 (fax)
**Cost:**
$1,000 per day
**Description:**
This workshop is designed to be conducted on-site by client organization personnel using a kit of training materials (outline, 4 CD-ROMs, masters for overheads, and participant workbooks) provided by Emerging Technology Consultants. The program provides participants with a working knowledge of CD-ROM terminology, an overview of hardware, and detailed hands-on activities that lead to successful CD-ROM integration. Participants explore the capabilities of CD-ROMs using a variety of prepackaged CD-ROMS, and then they create their own CD-ROM-enhanced lessons. The program is designed for participants with little or no prior multimedia knowledge or experience.

## 68

**Title:**
**The 7 Habits of Highly Effective People**
**Sponsor:**
FranklinCovey
360 West 4800 North
Provo, UT 84604
801/817-1776
801/229-1233
**Length:**
3 days
**Cost:**
$1,495
**Location:**
Various cities throughout the U.S.
**Description:**
This workshop is based on the best-selling book of the same title by Stephen R. Covey. One month prior to the workshop, anonymous feedback is gathered from supervisors, associates, peers, and those who report to you. During the workshop, you receive confidential, computerized feedback along with an Action Planning Guide.

## 69

**Title:**
**Managing the Training Function**
**Sponsor:**
FKA Friesen, Kaye and Associates
3448 Richmond Rd.
Ottawa, ON, Canada
800/FKA-5585
613/829-0845 (fax)
**Length:**
2 days
**Cost:**
$895
**Location:**
Various cities in the U.S.; also in Ottowa, Toronto, and Vancouver, Canada
**Description:**
Managing the Training Function examines the critical components necessary to ensure that training initiatives in organizations are linked to business needs, and provide measurable results. The program assesses the training function through a series of highly interactive applications, facilitated by Michael Nolan, President of Friesen, Kaye and Associates.

## 70

**Title:**
**Performance Consulting Skills**
**Sponsor:**
FKA Friesen, Kaye and Associates
3448 Richmond Rd.
Ottawa, ON, Canada
800/FKA-5585
613/829-0845 (fax)
**Length:**
2 days
**Cost:**
$895
**Location:**
Various cities in the U.S.; also in Ottawa and Toronto, Canada
**Description:**
The Performance Consulting Skills Workshop is a comprehensive program which addresses the development needs of trainers and HRD professionals. The workshop offers participants, whose roles are evolving into consultancy, the opportunity to build the skills necessary to link training and other interventions to business needs. Participants practice the concepts and skills learned in the workshop through highly interactive applications of the consulting process.

## 71

**Title:**
**High Impact Management: Maximizing Performance by Building on Strengths**
**Sponsor:**
The Gallup Organization
The Gallup School of Management
300 South 68th Street Place
Lincoln, NB 68510
800/288-8593
402/486-6369 (fax)
**Length:**
$2^1/_2$ days
**Cost:**
$2,500
**Location:**
Lincoln, NB; London, England
**Description:**
This highly interactive workshop is limited to 15 participants. Each participant benefits from a 360° assessment study conducted by the Gallup Organization prior to the workshop at each participant's work location. The workshop is built upon Gallup's "18 themes of excellent management" developed from 25 years of research involving executives, managers, and employees. The reality base of the workshop includes results of 40,000 executive interviews and 250,000 manager/employee interviews.

## 72

**Title:**
**Leadership Institute: Leveraging Individual Talent for Organizational Excellence**
**Sponsor:**
The Gallup Organization
The Gallup School of Management
300 South 68th Street Place
Lincoln, NB 68510
800/360-2801 ext. 7686
402/486-6369 (fax)
**Length:**
5 days
**Cost:**
$4,800

Location:
 Lincoln, NB; London, England
Description:
 This intensive full week of learning
 begins with a social time on
 Sunday evening, and continues
 through Friday. Prior to the Institute, the Gallup research staff
 administers a 360° information
 and feedback instrument to colleagues, superiors, and direct
 reports of Institute participants.
 Enrollment is limited to 15 persons. Research conducted by
 The Gallup Organization is used
 throughout the Institute.

## 73

Title:
 **The Emerging Leader Program**
Sponsor:
 Global Institute for Leadership
  Development
 One Forbes Road
 Lexington, MA 02173
  781/402-5451
  781/862-2355 (fax)
Length:
 6 days
Cost:
 $5,500
Location:
 San Diego, CA
Description:
 This is an accelerated leadership pro-
 gram for high-potential employees.
 It features 360-degree assessment
 profiles, a faculty of world-renowned
 business leaders, individual coaching
 from Learning Team Leaders, and
 follow-up development through an
 Internet connection.

## 74

Title:
 **Data Warehousing and
 Mining**
Sponsor:
 Global Knowledge
 P.O. Box 1039
 Cary, NC 27512
  919/461-8600
  800/268-7737
  919/461-8646 (fax)
Length:
 3 days
Cost:
 $1,600
Location:
 Various cities throughout the U.S.

Description:
 This is a new workshop for those
 interested in information sharing
 and knowledge management. The
 workshop focuses on what works
 and what doesn't, how to maximize the profits and value of data
 warehouses, and how to build a
 data warehouse. Tuition financing
 is available.

## 75

Title:
 **Web Development
 Fundamentals**
Sponsor:
 Global Knowledge
 P.O. Box 1039
 Cary, NC 27512
  919/461-8600
  919/461-8646 (fax)
Length:
 3 days
Cost:
 $1,595
Location:
 Various cities throughout the U.S.
Description:
 In this workshop, participants learn
 to install and configure Web
 servers. Topics include: Web com-
 ponents (clients, servers, protocols);
 product overviews, and various
 server installation and configura-
 tion options. Global Knowledge
 Network, Inc. is a certified
 Microsoft trainer, and UNIX trainer.
 Phone for extensive software, hardware, and Internet courses. Course
 financing is also available as a student service.

## 76

Title:
 **Leadership Education: An
 Advanced Program for
 Professional Trainers,
 Educators, and Consultants**
Sponsor:
 Harvard University
 John F. Kennedy School of
  Government
 The Leadership Education
  Program
 79 JFK Street
 Cambridge, MA 02138
  617/496-5920
  617/495-3090
Length:
 10 days, May 14–25, 2001

Cost:
 $6,700, including lodging, materi-
 als, meals, use of Harvard's
 libraries and athletic facilities;
 some scholarship aid is available.
Location:
 Cambridge, MA
Description:
 This is an intensive and highly
 interactive program taught by Harvard faculty. It focuses on skills
 analysis and improvement, refine-
 ment of leadership tools, organizational politics surrounding
 leadership, and mobilizing people
 to do good things. The program is
 designed to engage the participant
 as a learner, a teacher, and a leader.

## 77

Title:
 **Managing People for
 Maximum Performance**
Sponsor:
 Harvard University
 John F. Kennedy School of
  Government
 Center for Management Research
 55 William Street
 Wellesley, MA 02181
  781/239-1111
  781/239-1546 (fax)
Length:
 2 days
Cost:
 $1,950
Location:
 Cambridge, MA
Description:
 Faculty from Harvard University
 are presenters and facilitators in
 this program for executives and
 senior managers. Its focus is deci-
 sion making and building toward
 long-term improvement. Topics
 include how and why people work,
 making good performance pay off,
 setting goals, and tracking results.
 Case studies on improving performance are analyzed. Part of a series
 of programs on leadership.

## 78

Title:
 **Promoting Innovation &
 Organizational Change**
Sponsor:
 Harvard University
 John F. Kennedy School of
  Government

Center for Management Research
55 William Street
Wellesley, MA 02181
781/239-1111
781/239-1546 (fax)

**Length:**
2 days

**Cost:**
$1,950

**Location:**
Cambridge, MA

**Description:**
Faculty from Harvard University are presenters and facilitators in this program for executives and senior managers. The focus of the seminar is how to promote innovation that is manageable and measurable, including small improvements, major changes, and strategic breakthroughs. Topics include strategies for generating innovative alternatives, building an innovation-friendly workplace, and developing suggestion systems that rake in spontaneous creativity. Lessons from both public and private sectors are used as examples. Part of a series of programs on leadership.

## 79

**Title:**
**Teaching Negotiation in the Corporation**

**Sponsor:**
Harvard University Law School Program on Negotiation
Center for Management Research
55 William Street
Wellesley, MA 02181
781/239-1111
781/239-1546 (fax)

**Length:**
$1^1/_2$ days

**Cost:**
$1,475

**Location:**
Cambridge, MA

**Description:**
This seminar teaches a new negotiation process and offers the opportunity to get a behind-the-scenes view of the strategies and objectives which the faculty at the Program on Negotiation at Harvard Law School have developed for teaching that process to senior executives. The course was designed to provide strategies, tools, and techniques needed to develop the participants'

own curriculum training objectives. It is part of a major program on various aspects of negotiation.

## 80

**Title:**
**Consulting Skills for the HR Professional**

**Sponsor:**
The Hay Group
229 South 18th St.
Philadelphia, PA 19103
215/861-2000
215/875 2891 (fax)

**Length:**
2 days

**Cost:**
$995

**Location:**
Dallas, TX; New York, NY; Newport Beach, CA

**Description:**
This intensive two-day workshop helps HR professionals develop competence and expertise in partnering with line managers and other internal clients. The session introduces a consulting framework for participants to apply to their interactions; provides tools and templates to back their work; and offers opportunities for participants to practice what they've learned.

## 81

**Title:**
**Training Leaders Workshop**

**Sponsor:**
Human Synergistics International (HSI)
39819 Plymouth Rd. C8020
Plymouth, MI 48170
800/622-7584
734/459-5557 (fax)
International affiliates throughout the world

**Length:**
$4^1/_2$ days

**Cost:**
$995

**Location:**
Plymouth, MI

**Description:**
This workshop focuses on producing measurable, cost-effective improvement in individuals, groups, and organizations, especially in productivity, quality, and cultural change. Participants use sponsor-developed tools for customizing

their own measurement-based systems, including how to administer and interpret assessments. HSI staff provides post-workshop follow-up assistance at no extra charge.

## 82

**Title:**
**Designing Information for the Web**

**Sponsor:**
Information Mapping, Inc.
41 Waverly Oaks Road
Waltham, MA 02154
800/463-6627
781/906-6400 (fax)

**Length:**
2 days

**Cost:**
$1,225

**Location:**
Various cities throughout the U.S.

**Description:**
This seminar focuses on the design of information and its organization for the Web and Internet. The emphasis is on accessibility and usability of information. One of several Web seminars.

## 83

**Title:**
**Developing Procedures, Policies, and Documentation**

**Sponsor:**
Information Mapping, Inc.
411 Waverly Oaks Rd.
Waltham, MA 02154
800/463-6627
781/906-6400 (fax)

**Length:**
4 days

**Cost:**
$1,395

**Location:**
Various cities throughout the U.S.

**Description:**
This seminar is for trainers, developers, and managers who need a standard approach to documentation. The program teaches how to create consistent, high-quality materials. It can be applied to a variety of types of manuals and business documentation.

## 84

**Title:**
**Mapping Business Communication**

**Sponsor:**
Information Mapping, Inc.
411 Waverly Oaks Rd.
Waltham, MA 02154
800/463-6627
781/906-6400 (fax)
**Length:**
2 days
**Cost:**
$895
**Location:**
Various cities throughout the U.S.
**Description:**
This is a seminar of particular usefulness to persons who have already been trained in Information Mapping. It focuses on how to structure and organize mapped information for electronic environments as well as reports and proposals.

## 85

**Title:**
**Structuring User Documentation**
**Sponsor:**
Information Mapping, Inc.
411 Waverly Oaks Rd.
Waltham, MA 02154
800/463-6627
781/906-6400 (fax)
**Length:**
3 days
**Cost:**
$1,325
**Location:**
Various cities throughout the U.S.
**Description:**
This seminar focuses on creating user guides for paper and online distribution.

## 86

**Title:**
**Foundations for Organizational Learning**
**Sponsor:**
Innovation Associates
Acorn Park
Cambridge, MA 02140
617/498-5700
617/498-5701 (fax)
**Length:**
3 days
**Cost:**
$2,450; Team rates available
**Location:**
Various cities throughout the U.S. and Canada
**Description:**
This program provides grounding in The Five Disciplines of The

Learning Organization, based on the work of Peter Senge. The program shows participants how to move organizations into a learning mode by applying these tools.

## 87

**Title:**
**Leadership and Mastery**
**Sponsor:**
Innovation Associates
Acorn Park
Cambridge, MA 02140
617/498-5700
617/498-5701 (fax)
**Length:**
3 days
**Cost:**
$2,450; Team rates available
**Location:**
Various cities throughout the U.S. and Canada
**Description:**
This program enables leaders to clarify and communicate a realizable vision of the future for themselves as leaders and for their organizations. Both intuitive and analytical skills are taught. The concepts of Shared Vision and Personal Mastery are explored.

## 88

**Title:**
**Systems Thinking**
**Sponsor:**
Innovation Associates
Acorn Park
Cambridge, MA 02140
617/498-5700
617/498-5701 (fax)
**Length:**
3 days
**Cost:**
$2,450; Team rates available
**Location:**
Various cities throughout the U.S. and Canada
**Description:**
This program is an in-depth introduction to the discipline of Systems Thinking. It includes a focus on leverage points and communication strategies, including system "stories" and archetypes.

## 89

**Title:**
**Mastering Systems Thinking**
**Sponsor:**
Innovation Associates

**Length:**
3 days
**Cost:**
$2,450; Team rates available
**Location:**
Boston, MA
**Description:**
This program is for managers who want to apply Systems Thinking to real problems while simultaneously deepening technical skills. This is a new public seminar as of June 2000.

## 90

**Title:**
**Employment Relations Law**
**Sponsor:**
Institute for Applied Management and Law
610 Newport Center Drive, Ste. 1060
Newport Beach, CA 92660
949/760-1700
949/760-8192 (fax)
**Length:**
4$^1$/2 days
**Cost:**
$1,825
**Location:**
Various cities throughout the U.S.
**Description:**
This seminar covers all facets of employment law, taught by employment law attorneys from leading law firms. The focus is practical, providing participants with information that can help companies avoid litigation. The first 2 days cover labor law; the second 2 days focus on employment discrimination law. The final day focuses on special issues in employee relations law. Other seminars on specific laws are also available.

## 91

**Title:**
**Essentials of Human Resource Management**
**Sponsor:**
Institute for Applied Management and Law
610 Newport Center Drive, Ste. 1060
Newport Beach, CA 92660
949/760-1700
949/760-8192 (fax)
**Length:**
4$^1$/2 days
**Cost:**
$1,725

Location:

Various cities throughout the U.S.

Description:

This seminar focuses on human resource management and the law. The first half of the seminar is presented by employment law attorneys; the second half focuses on topics such as performance-based management, taking the chaos out of change, and training the trainers.

## 92

Title:

**Designing Effective Program Evaluations**

Sponsor:

Institute for Professional Education
2200 Wilson Blvd., Ste 406
Arlington, VA 22201
703/527-8700
703/527-8703 (fax)

Length:

3 days

Cost:

$1,250

Location:

Washington, DC; San Francisco, CA

Description:

This seminar is designed for program managers and others interested in assessing the efficiency, effectiveness, and responsiveness of programs and policies. The course will outline step-by-step procedures for conducting effective evaluation research utilizing examples from business, education, criminal justice, and health.

## 93

Title:

**Improving Consulting Effectiveness**

Sponsor:

Institute for Professional Education
2200 Wilson Blvd., Ste. 406
Arlington, VA 22201
703/527-8700
703/527-8703 (fax)

Length:

3 days

Cost:

$1,250

Location:

Washington, DC

Description:

This intense, pragmatic seminar enables participants to improve their overall effectiveness in con-

sulting. The seminar provides participants with strategies and skills in four areas:

- tools to better understand the consulting role, its opportunities and limitations, and to use that understanding to design the role for maximum impact
- human relations tools to better understand the diverse people they must work with
- strategies to design effective, collaborative consulting relationships
- everyday communications skills to work more effectively, one-on-one, with all kinds of clients

## 94

Title:

**Corporate University Week**

Sponsor:

International Quality & Productivity Center
150 Clove Rd.
P.O. Box 401
Little Falls, NJ 07424
800/882-8684
201/256-0205 (fax)

Length:

2 days plus pre- and post-conference workshops

Cost:

$1,499 conference only; $500 extra per workshop

Location:

Scottsdale, AZ

Description:

Based on the premise that corporate training functions will undergo dramatic growth and change in the coming years, this program focuses on the "corporate university" as the vehicle of that change. Delivered in a conference format, the program consists mostly of presentations of the experiences of various organizations with the corporate university format. Included is information about putting the corporate university online. The principal thrust of the program, however, is how to establish, organize, manage, and empower a corporate university as a focal point for an organization's training and development activity.

## 95

Title:

**Creating & Launching Learning Portals: The Next**

**Wave in Web-Based Distance Learning**

Sponsor:

International Quality & Productivity Center
150 Clove Road
P.O. Box 401
Little Falls, NJ 07424
800/882-8684
201/256-0205 (fax)

Length:

2 days of conference; plus 2 days of workshop

Cost:

$1,495 conference only; $500 extra per workshop

Location:

Several locations; phone for specifics

Description:

This training features a panel of experts from leading companies who have been successful with online learning. Benefits of learning portals, communities of learning, pros and cons of outsourcing, and technical topics concerning software architecture, bandwidth, marketing, and financing are included.

## 96

Title:

**Performance Measurements for Training**

Sponsor:

International Quality & Productivity Center
150 Clove Road
P.O. Box 401
Little Falls, NJ 07424
800/882-8684
201/256-0205 (fax)

Length:

2 days of workshops in conjunction with a 2-day conference on the same topic

Cost:

$1,499; conference only
$500 extra per workshop

Location:

Various cities throughout the U.S.

Description:

Participants learn how to define, measure, and improve the results of training. Topics include budgeting, determining return on investment, and collaborative tracking of the impact of training. Case studies of numerous successful companies are presented in conference format; workshops supplement the conference and deal with details.

## 97

Title:

**Web-Based Training
Performance Support**

Sponsor:

International Quality &
Productivity Center
150 Clove Road
P.O. Box 401
Little Falls, NJ 07424
800/822-8684
201/256-0205 (fax)

Length:

2 days

Cost:

$1,495

Location:

Various cities throughout the U.S.

Description:

Participants focus on how Web-based systems support today's workers with advice, know-how, tools, references, and training exactly at the required time and place of need. The seminar deals with specific development skills, desktop learning, multimedia deployment over the Internet, and cost structures for Web-based training. Case studies are included.

## 98

Title:

**Executive Development
Program**

Sponsor:

J.L. Kellogg Graduate School of
Management
Northwestern University
James L. Allen Center
Evanston, IL 60208
847/467-7000
847/491-4323 (fax)

Length:

20 days

Cost:

$16,900, includes food, lodging, all
materials

Location:

Evanston, IL

Description:

For those with at least 10 years experience with senior management potential who want to lead or contribute to organizational change initiatives. Topics include investing and customer service in addition to global competition opportunities, interaction of various functions, improved strategic thinking and analytical skills for

better decision making and problem solving. Other 3- and 4-day seminars are also available.

## 99

Title:

**Basic Supervision**

Sponsor:

Keye Productivity Center/AMAI
11221 Roe Ave.
Leawood, KS 66211
800/821-3919
800/914-8879 (fax)

Length:

1 day

Cost:

$169

Location:

Various cities throughout the U.S.

Description:

This is one of many one-day seminars of Keye Productivity Center, affiliated with The American Management Association International. Topics include basic supervisory skills, specific skills such as coaching and counseling, how to motivate and discipline employees, effective communication, boosting productivity, and solving problems.

## 100

Title:

**How to Develop and Deliver
Powerful Employee
Orientation Programs**

Sponsor:

Keye Productivity Center/AMAI
11221 Roe Ave.
Leawood, KS 66211
800/821-3919
800/914-8879 (fax)

Length:

1 day

Cost:

$169

Location:

Various cities throughout the U.S.

Description:

This seminar focuses on skills for helping new employees fit into new jobs. The emphasis is on program development, presentation, and evaluation.

## 101

Title:

**OSHA Basics of Accident
Prevention and Compliance**

Sponsor:

Keye Productivity Center/AMAI
11221 Roe Avenue
Leawood, KS 66211
800/821-3919
800/914-8879 (fax)

Length:

1 day

Cost:

$169

Location:

Various cities throughout the U.S.

Description:

This workshop focuses on content and techniques for creating and delivering safety training. Topics include: identifying training requirements for each worker, finding and using resources, presentation techniques, legal issues, personal protective equipment, machine operations, and confined spaces training.

## 102

Title:

**Designing Computer-Based
Training**

Sponsor:

Langevin Learning Services
P.O. Box 1221, 420 Ford St.
Ogdensburg, NY 13669
800/223-2209
800/636-6869 (fax)

Length:

3 days

Cost:

$1,499

Location:

Various cities throughout the U.S.;
Ottawa and Toronto, Canada

Description:

This is a practical workshop in all elements of design and production of Computer-based Training (CBT). Topics include: designing linear tutorials, designing branching tutorials, developing a structure plan, designing frames and storyboards, applying motivational techniques in lesson design, constructing pre-tests, and choosing an authoring system.

## 103

Title:

**Instructional Design for
New Designers**

Sponsor:

Langevin Learning Systems
P.O. Box 1221, 420 Ford St.
Ogdensburg, NY 13669
800/223-2209
800/636-6869 (fax)

**Length:**
3 days

**Cost:**
$999

**Location:**
Various cities throughout the U.S.; Ottawa, Toronto, and Vancouver, Canada

**Description:**
This skills-based workshop is for those new to instructional design with no formal training in design. Major sections of the workshop include: work plans and estimating design time, learner analysis including dealing with diversity among learners, task analysis and sequencing content, how to write measurable objectives, and designing tests. A 6-month post-workshop edit service is included for all participants. An advanced workshop is also available.

## 104

**Title:**
**Training Needs Analysis**

**Sponsor:**
Langevin Learning Services
P.O. Box 1221, 420 Ford St.
Ogdensburg, NY 13669
800/223-2209
800/636-6869 (fax)

**Length:**
1 day

**Cost:**
$399

**Location:**
Various cities throughout the U.S.; Ottawa, Toronto, and Vancouver, Canada

**Description:**
This practical, "how to" workshop includes planning a needs analysis, data collection, data analysis, cost-benefit analysis, and dealing with politics surrounding needs analysis. Participants receive a diskette of templates to use back on the job, and receive unlimited telephone consultation for one year post-workshop.

## 105

**Title:**
**Writing Skills for Trainers**

**Sponsor:**
Langevin Learning Services
P.O. Box 1221, 420 Ford St.
Ogdensburg, NY 13669
800/223-2209
800/636-6869 (fax)

**Length:**
1 day

**Cost:**
$399

**Location:**
Various cities throughout the U.S.; Ottawa and Toronto, Canada

**Description:**
This workshop is for course designers, training analysts, instructors, and managers of training who want to improve the effectiveness of their written materials. It is also intended for anyone involved in training who wants more polished writing skills. Topics include: how to develop content, options in structure of writing, grammar and usage for clarity and completeness, and how to develop style in writing.

## 106

**Title:**
**Contract Training Institute**

**Sponsor:**
LERN (Learning Resources Network)
1550 Hayes Dr.
Manhattan, KS 66502
800/678-5376
888/234-8633 (fax)

**Length:**
4 days

**Cost:**
$1,195

**Location:**
Minneapolis, MN

**Description:**
Designed for professionals who conduct programs for business and industry, this institute covers topics such as personal selling, telemarketing, direct e-mail promotions, etc. as they relate to contract training, seminars, and business courses.

## 107

**Title:**
**Program Management Institute**

**Sponsor:**
LERN (Learning Resources Network)
1550 Hayes Dr.
Manhattan, KS 66502
800/678-5376
888/234-8633 (fax)

**Length:**
4 days

**Cost:**
$1,195

**Location:**
Minneapolis, MN

**Description:**
In sessions led by a 4-person faculty, a maximum of 10 program managers, coordinators, and directors receive intensive training in the management of programs for adult education, continuing education, corporate training, etc.

## 108

**Title:**
**Workplace Violence Prevention and Conflict Resolution**

**Sponsor:**
Liberty Mutual Group
175 Berkeley Street, M.S.8F
P.O. Box 140
Boston, MA 02117
800/320-7581
617/695-9216 (fax)

**Length:**
2 days

**Cost:**
$500

**Location:**
Various cities throughout the U.S.

**Description:**
This seminar is designed to provide attendees with the principles and procedures for control of exposures to workplace violence. Topics include: OSHA guidelines and enforcement policy, developing a loss control program, outside workplace violence assistance, employment-related prevention measures, intruder-related prevention measures, and major types of workplace exposures and risk factors for workplace violence.

## 109

**Title:**
**Consulting Skills for Human Resource Professionals**

**Sponsor:**
Linkage, Inc.
One Forbes Rd.
Lexington, MA 02173
781/862-3157
781/862-2355 (fax)

**Length:**
2 days

**Cost:**
$1,095

**Location:**
Lexington, MA, and other cities throughout the U.S.

**Description:**

This workshop provides participants with the knowledge and skills necessary to increase their consulting role with internal clients and customers. It examines the variety of roles that consultants perform and the appropriateness and applications of each. Participants practice applying a step-by-step consulting (problem-solving) methodology which provides them with a practical tool for immediate application on the job. An advanced workshop is also available.

## 110

**Title:**

**Developing a Coaching and Mentoring System**

**Sponsor:**

Linkage, Inc.
One Forbes Rd.
Lexington, MA 02173
781/862-3157
781/862-2355 (fax)

**Length:**

2 days

**Cost:**

$1,095

**Location:**

Lexington, MA; Chicago, IL; New York, NY; Washington, DC

**Description:**

This workshop helps participants identify the best options for building an environment to support coaching and mentoring and use the best tools for developing the program.

## 111

**Title:**

**Global Institute for Leadership Development**

**Sponsor:**

Linkage, Inc.
One Forbes Rd.
Lexington, MA 02173
781/862-3157
781/862-2355 (fax)

**Length:**

5 days

**Cost:**

$5,495

**Location:**

San Diego, CA

**Description:**

This is an intensive institute for leadership development featuring topics in assessment, training, coaching, and benchmarking within a global needs model. The Institute's mission is "to accelerate the development of emerging leaders through focused learning around core leadership competencies, knowledge areas, and skills." The 50-hour program features more than 50 CEOs, COOs, internationally known thought leaders, authors, and facilitators. An action learning model is used for work in teams during the Institute.

## 112

**Title:**

**Introduction to Competency-Based Systems**

**Sponsor:**

Linkage, Inc.
One Forbes Rd.
Lexington, MA 02173
781/862-3157
781/862-2355 (fax)

**Length:**

2 days

**Cost:**

$1,095

**Location:**

Lexington, MA; Princeton NJ

**Description:**

In this program, participants learn to analyze the skills and competencies demonstrated by the top performers in their business. They get training in competency and workforce analysis that will enable them to articulate the critical development issues in their company's future, and they develop skills in interviewing, running focus groups, performing data analysis, and building models.

## 113

**Title:**

**Strategic HR and Training: Linking to Performance**

**Sponsor:**

Linkage, Inc.
One Forbes Rd.
Lexington, MA 02173
781/862-3157
781/862-2355 (fax)

**Length:**

2 days

**Cost:**

$1,095

**Location:**

San Francisco, CA; Lexington, MA; New York, NY; Chicago, IL

**Description:**

How to demonstrate results is the focus of this workshop. Models from performance consulting and "balanced scorecards" are used. Financial and evaluation tools are also used.

## 114

**Title:**

**How to Build a Complete Management Training Curriculum**

**Sponsor:**

Management Education Consulting Company of America (MECCA)
40 W. 919 Elodie Dr.
Elburn, IL 60119
630/584-0164
630/584-0184 (fax)

**Length:**

1 day

**Cost:**

$495

**Location:**

Various cities throughout the U.S.

**Description:**

This program shows trainers how to develop a "just-in-time" management training curriculum. It teaches how to properly sequence and configure management training into an integrated curriculum for new supervisors, experienced supervisors, managers of supervisors, and executives. Sample curricula from several companies are presented.

## 115

**Title:**

**System Dynamics for Senior Managers**

**Sponsor:**

MIT
Massachusetts Institute of Technology
Sloan School of Management
55 William Street
Wellesley, MA 02181
781/239-1111
781/239-1546 (fax)

**Length:**

2 days

**Cost:**

$1,950

**Location:**

Wellesley, MA

**Description:**

For senior managers interested in a systems framework supporting high performance. Topics include: project management, integrated growth strategies, organizational change, process improvement, supply chains, competitive response, cultural conflict, system archetypes, and simulation modeling. Part of MIT's Executive Series on Management and Technology.

## 116

Title:
**Leadership and Supervisory Skills for Women; Life Balance and Stress Reduction Solutions**
Sponsor:
National Businesswomen's Leadership Association
P.O. Box 419107
Kansas City, MO 64141
800/258-7246
913/432-0824 (fax)
Length:
2 days
Cost:
$113; one day only, $69
Location:
Numerous cities throughout the U.S.
Description:
An intensive two days focused on typical problems and how to solve them. Topics include: how to lead and supervise, build teamwork and cooperation, position yourself as credible and authoritative, communicate with groups and one-to-one, handle conflict, reduce stress, and prevent burnout.

## 117

Title:
**Training of Trainers: Developing Cultural Diversity Programs for the Workplace**
Sponsor:
National MultiCultural Institute
3000 Connecticut Ave., NW, Suite 438
Washington, DC 20008
202/483-0700
202/483-5233 (fax)
Length:
4 days
Cost:
$900
Location:
Washington, DC
Description:
The purpose of this program is to enable participants to design and

deliver a basic, one-day "Valuing Cultural Diversity Workshop" for the workplace. It focuses on design, facilitation skills, exercises, and lecturette material. After an introduction to several fundamental workshop components, participants have the opportunity, in small groups, to design and present a one-day workshop and to facilitate an exercise. The session combines didactic and experiential teaching techniques. This program is for experienced trainers in the government, corporate, and non-profit sectors who have participated in personal cultural awareness training, but who have limited experience in facilitating diversity workshops.

## 118

Title:
**NLP Trainer & Consultancy Certification (400)**
Sponsor:
NLP University
Dynamic Learning Center
P.O. Box 1112
Ben Lomond, CA 95005
408/336-3457
408/336-5854 (fax)
Length:
20 days
Cost:
$6,110 including lodging and meals
Location:
University of California, Santa Cruz
Description:
The program is oriented around helping individuals explore the multiple levels involved in training—the *what, how, why,* and *who.* A core element of the training is to create a context in which participants can discover their missions and visions related to training. For individuals to learn effectively, learning material must be anchored to personal reference experiences and then directed to specific objectives and results. Thus, the basic goals of all training are to (1) establish and (2) activate patterns or programs within the nervous system of the learner. This involves two fundamental interactions between instructor and learner:
1. Instructor: Delivering Cognitive Packages

Learner: Widening Perceptual Maps
2. Instructor: Activating Reference Experiences for Cognitive Maps
Learner: Connecting Reference Experiences to Cognitive Maps

## 119

Title:
**Coaching for Contribution**
Sponsor:
Novations Group, Inc.
2155 N. 200 West, Suite 200
Provo, UT 84604
801/375-7525
801/377-5440 (fax)
Length:
2 days
Cost:
$795
Location:
Provo, UT
Description:
This workshop gives participants the tools and skills needed to coach others. Skills covered include establishing a climate for learning, identifying learning needs, promoting discovery and self-reliance, providing feedback, leveraging the talents of others, and providing others with opportunities to grow in their current jobs. Includes 12-rater 360° feedback for participants.

## 120

Title:
**Managing Career Development**
Sponsor:
Novations Group, Inc.
2155 N. 200 West, Suite 200
Provo, UT 84604
801/375-7525
801/377-5440 (fax)
Length:
2 days
Cost:
$795
Location:
Provo, UT
Description:
This workshop is centered on the research-based "Four Stages" model of careers. It offers participants a "tool-kit" of practical career development techniques—including intensive skill building as career coaches, and candid, confidential performance feedback. Includes 12-rater 360° feedback for participants.

## 121

Title:
**Advanced Team Building**
Sponsor:
NTL Institute
1240 N. Pitt St., Suite 100
Alexandria, VA 22314-1403
703/548-1500
703/684-1256 (fax)
Length:
7 days
Cost:
$1,999
Location:
Bethel, ME
Description:
This experiential workshop emphasizes diagnosis, instruments, application skills, and interventions
with a particular focus on: roles,
vision, mission, problem solving,
decision making, interpersonal
relations, conflict, and resistance
to change. Participants (1) develop
a file of team-building activities,
simulations, and readings, (2)
create strategies for elite team
building with executives and top
management groups, and (3) learn
how to "sell" team building to the
organization.

## 122

Title:
**The Art of Coaching
Employees**
Sponsor:
NTL Institute
1240 N. Pitt St., Ste. 100
Alexandria, VA 22314-1403
703/548-1500
703/684-1256 (fax)
Length:
4 days
Cost:
$1,500
Location:
Clearwater, FL
Description:
This program is designed to help
managers and other leaders
develop staff through coaching
and mentoring. Participants assess
their styles and learn how to create
an effective coaching climate.

## 123

Title:
**Team Building: Developing
and Maintaining Excellence
in Teams**

Sponsor:
NTL Institute
1240 N. Pitt St., Suite 100
Alexandria, VA 22314-1403
703/548-1500
703/684-1256 (fax)
Length:
7 days
Cost:
$1,800
Location:
Bethel, ME
Description:
This program examines how teams
evolve, how they are constituted,
how they function, and how they
differ from other small groups. Participants (1) practice team building
skills and get candid feedback, (2)
learn to diagnose the nature of
tasks, structures, and norms of
work teams, and (3) expand their
confidence and ability to work as a
third-party agent in the process.

## 124

Title:
**Trainer Skillshop**
Sponsor:
NTL Institute
1240 N. Pitt St., Suite 100
Alexandria, VA 22314-1403
703/548-1500
703/684-1256 (fax)
Length:
7 days
Cost:
$1,900
Location:
Bethel, ME
Description:
This workshop is a hands-on, skills
training course for instructors and
trainers who feel they have not
had adequate preparation for activities like preparing course outlines
and materials, giving presentations, creating a good learning climate, and evaluating other adults.
This workshop helps improve participants' ability (1) to use a variety of training techniques, (2) to
effectively use questioning, listening, and feedback skills, (3) to
manage course time, difficult students, and difficult situations, (4)
to diagnose their own strengths
from peer and video feedback,
using behavioral checklists, (5) to
write plans for continued self-
development, and (6) to evaluate
training sessions and programs.

## 125

Title:
**The Advanced Consultant**
Sponsor:
Numerof & Associates, Inc.
11457 Olde Cabin Rd., Ste. 350
St. Louis, MO 63141
314/997-1587
314/997-0948 (fax)
Length:
3 days
Cost:
$1,495
Location:
Various cities throughout the U.S.
Description:
This workshop focuses on managing large scale organizational
change. Participants bring examples
from their own work to share with
the group which is limited to 10
persons. The focus is on self-assessment, diagnostic skill development,
and use of tools proven valuable for
consultants. One hour of telephone
consultation with staff consultants
is included with the workshop fee.

## 126

Title:
**Internal Consulting**
Sponsor:
Numerof & Associates, Inc.
11457 Olde Cabin Rd., Ste. 350
St. Louis, MO 63141
314/997-1587
314/997-0948 (fax)
Length:
2 days
Cost:
$1,195
Location:
Various cities throughout the U.S.
Description:
This workshop focuses on consul-
tative skill development, particularly in problem diagnosis, needs
assessment, and intervention. Program attendance is limited to 15
persons. One hour of telephone
consultation with staff consultants
is included with the workshop fee.

## 127

Title:
**How to Motivate, Manage,
and Lead a Team**
Sponsor:
The Padgett-Thompson Division of
the American Management
Association International

Padgett-Thompson Building
P.O. Box 8297
Overland Park, KS 66208
   800/255-4141
   800/914-8879 (fax)
**Length:**
   1 day
**Cost:**
   $130
**Location:**
   Various cities throughout the U.S.
**Description:**
   This program focuses on the fundamental skills needed for effective leadership and management of teams. Topics include problem analysis, elimination of obstacles, strengthening and motivational tools. Focus on "how to" throughout the seminar.

## 128

**Title:**
   **Establishing Your Mentoring System**
**Sponsor:**
   Perrone-Ambrose Associates, Inc.
   2 North Riverside Plaza, Ste. 1433
   Chicago, IL 60606
      800/648-0543
      312/648-0622 (fax)
**Length:**
   1 day
**Cost:**
   $1,000
**Location:**
   Chicago, IL; New York, NY
**Description:**
   The focus of this workshop is how to establish strategic goals and plans for implementing a mentoring system. Topics include how to watch mentors and mentees, and how to sustain and measure progress and results. A workshop outcome is a system "layout." Perrone-Ambrose also has a full range of job aids and mentoring books and products, and provides mentoring services. A workshop on sharpening mentoring skills is also available.

## 129

**Title:**
   **Managing the Training Function**
**Sponsor:**
   Practical Management Incorporated
   3280 West Hacienda, Ste. 205
   Las Vegas, NV 89118
      800/444-9101
      702/795-8339 (fax)

**Length:**
   2 days
**Cost:**
   $595
**Location:**
   Various cities throughout the U.S.
**Description:**
   This course first leads participants through the process of building a training philosophy for their organization. Next, they cover how to: (1) improve relations with line management, (2) respond to their needs, and (3) analyze training requests. Other topics include: (a) the hierarchy of objectives, (b) the strategic training plan, (c) the buy-vs.-build decision, (d) working effectively with outside resources, and (e) analyzing the training department's contribution. The workshop culminates with participants preparing their own action plan.

## 130

**Title:**
   **Needs Analysis, Evaluation, and Validation**
**Sponsor:**
   Practical Management Incorporated
   3280 West Hacienda, Ste. 205
   Las Vegas, NV 89118
      800/444-9101
      702/795-8339 (fax)
**Length:**
   3 days
**Cost:**
   $995
**Location:**
   Various cities throughout the U.S.
**Description:**
   This program is for trainers, training analysts, and training managers. Through a combination of participative instructional techniques and application exercises, attendees participate in the development of a training plan that combines the major training functions—from needs analysis through evaluation to the validation process.

## 131

**Title:**
   **Teaching Technical Topics**
**Sponsor:**
   Practical Management Incorporated
   3280 West Hacienda, Ste. 205
   Las Vegas, NV 89118
      800/444-9101
      702/795-8339 (fax)

**Length:**
   3 days
**Cost:**
   $995
**Location:**
   Various cities throughout the U.S.
**Description:**
   This program is for technical trainers or for customer service reps, supervisors, and employees with teaching duties—in particular those who teach technical subjects or sales programs. Relying heavily on practice and application, this course begins by reviewing the common failure points of technical instruction and the keys to effective training, including the use of questions, written materials, visual aids, and ice-breakers. Participants are taught the use of objectives and lesson plans, and they practice new skills using the specifics of courses currently taught by them or those which they are preparing to teach.

## 132

**Title:**
   **Web-Based Training**
**Sponsor:**
   Practical Management Incorporated
   3280 West Hacienda, Ste. 205
   Las Vegas, NV 89118
      800/444-9101
      702/795-8339 (fax)
**Length:**
   3 days
**Cost:**
   $1,695
**Location:**
   Various cities throughout the U.S.
**Description:**
   This program is for individuals who use personal computers in developing and delivering training. It covers each aspect of the design of CBT, including: (1) selection of hardware options, (2) course authoring alternatives, (3) design steps, (4) lesson flow alternatives, and (5) validation. Hands-on practice is provided throughout the program. New developments in Web-based and intranet-based training are featured.

## 133

**Title:**
   **Sales Manager's Workshop**
**Sponsor:**
   Professional Society for Sales &
      Marketing Training
   P.O. Box 995
   Fayetteville, GA 30214

770/719-4SMT
770/719-8SMT (fax)
**Length:**
3 days
**Cost:**
$1,495
**Location:**
Grand Rapids, MI
**Description:**
This is a workshop for sales managers with little or no experience in management skills training or development. The program includes self-assessment, 360° feedback, and a Sales Leadership Profile. Topics include: monitoring competencies, identifying perform-ance gaps, creating sales vision, motivating a sales team, and how to do field coaching for improved performance.

## 134

**Title:**
**Coaching Skills for Managers and Supervisors**
**Sponsor:**
Pryor Seminars (Career Track/ Fred Pryor)
P.O. Box 2951
Shawnee Mission, KS 66201
800/255-6139
918/665-3434 (fax)
**Length:**
1 day
**Cost:**
$195
**Location:**
Various cities throughout the U.S.
**Description:**
This program focuses on skills required for enhancing your own management potential as well as unleashing the talent of individual employees. It features how to generate the desire to win, to end mediocrity, to inspire teamwork, and to redirect the program employee through effective one-to-one coaching. See also listings under Career Track.

## 135

**Title:**
**Training the Trainer**
**Sponsor:**
Pryor Seminars (Career Track/ Fred Pryor)
P.O. Box 2951
Shawnee Mission, KS 66201
800/255-6139 or
918/665-3434 (fax)
**Length:**
1 day

**Cost:**
$195
**Location:**
Various cities throughout the U.S.
**Description:**
This train-the-trainer program comes from an organization that itself trains 50,000 people per week. The seminar concentrates on key professional skills, including tips, techniques, and strategies to make the participant a more effective trainer. The 7 principal topics of the program are: (1) Pinpoint Your Training Needs, (2) Understand the Adult Learning Process, (3) Plan and Develop Super Powerful Programs, (4) Produce Innovative Materials and Presentations, (5) Encourage Maximum Learning and Participation, (6) Master One-on-One Training, and (7) How to Evaluate Training Effectiveness. See also listings under Career Track.

## 136

**Title:**
**Strategies for Success—The Role of Management and Technology**
**Sponsor:**
Rensselaer Learning Institute
Rensselaer at Hartford
275 Windsor Street
Hartford, CT 06120-2991
800/306-7778
860/548-7999 (fax)
**Length:**
1 day preview
**Cost:**
Complimentary; contact sponsor
**Location:**
Hartford or Waterbury, CT
**Description:**
Rensselaer Learning Institute is a Network Associate of the Center for Creative Leadership and a Licensee of Zenger Miller Programs. Highlights include: leadership programs, management skills training, team-building, and executive coaching. The Institute also offers a full range of technical, database, and mainframe courses. Preview seminars are offered on various programs throughout the year.

## 137

**Title:**
**Beyond Train-the-Trainer**
**Sponsor:**
Rollins College
Corporate Learning Institute

1000 Holt Avenue - 2728
Winter Park, FL 32789
800/494-4253
407/646-1503 (fax)
**Length:**
2 days
**Cost:**
$695
**Location:**
Winter Park, FL
**Description:**
An advanced workshop created by Ed Jones, master trainer, this program features limited enrollment, small group, and hands-on work. Special topics include facilitation skills, designing and using case studies, and designing creative games that encourage learning. Prerequisite to attending this workshop is at least 2 years of classroom training experience.

## 138

**Title:**
**Transnational Human Resources: Best Practices**
**Sponsor:**
Institute for International Human Resources
Society for Human Resource Management (SHRM)
1800 Duke Street
Alexandria, VA 22314
800/283-SHRM
703/535-6490 (fax)
**Length:**
1 day
**Cost:**
$225
**Location:**
New York, NY
**Description:**
This seminar is jointly organized by the Institute and Fordham University's Graduate School of Business. SHRM members and Fordham Alumni receive substantial discount on tuition. Topics include: Best Practices in China, Managing the Expatriate Function, Global Compensation in a Fiercely Competitive Market, and Transnational Information Technology Recruiting.

## 139

**Title:**
**The Walt Disney Approach to Leadership Excellence for HR Professionals**

**Sponsor:**
Society for Human Resource
Management (SHRM)
1800 Duke Street
Alexandria, VA 22314
800/283-SHRM
407/828-4411
703/535-6490 (fax)
**Length:**
4 days
**Cost:**
$2,995 includes lodging, meals,
course materials
**Location:**
Orlando, FL
**Description:**
Especially designed for HR professionals who are middle managers
and change agents. Topics include:
strategies for employee involvement, accountability, organization
and culture, improvement strategies, character, and the power of
story. The program is focused on
Disney's successful strategies and
practices. Cost includes theme park
admission and free use of the
Park's transportation system.

## 140

**Title:**
**Positive Power and Influence
Program**
**Sponsor:**
Situation Management Systems
195 Hanover Street
Hanover, MA 02339
781/826-4433
781/826-2863 (fax)
**Length:**
3 days
**Cost:**
$1,675
**Location:**
Various cities throughout the U.S.
**Description:**
This program helps participants to
develop and refine skills required
to influence others in a positive
and constructive manner. Mastery
over several influence styles is the
key to achieving effective results.
Participants learn appropriate
tactics to analyze situations and
achieve their influence objectives.

## 141

**Title:**
**Introduction to Video
Production**

**Sponsor:**
Sony Video Institute
3300 Zanker Road
San Jose, CA 95134
408/955-4231
408/955-5340 (fax)
**Length:**
3 days
**Cost:**
$1,600
**Location:**
Various cities throughout the U.S.
**Description:**
This program covers the elements of
preproduction, production, and
postproduction, as well as operational, organizational, and marketing concepts. In the 20-step
approach, "Progressive Video Programming," students learn essentials
of preparation and execution of
"film-style" on-location taping and
editing. Participants gain confidence
handling equipment in actual
"shooting" and "editing" exercises,
using state-of-the-art video equipment. Subjects include: program
design, content qualification, behavioral objectives, brainstorming, budgeting, client presentation,
composition, storyboarding, scripting, shot selection, movement,
audio and lighting, staging and
blocking, rehearsal, talent releases,
makeup, interviews, directing, postproduction, graphics, logging, editing, validation, and marketing.

## 142

**Title:**
**Managing Teams for
Innovation and Success**
**Sponsor:**
Stanford Business School
Office of Executive Education
Stanford University
Stanford, CA 94305
650/723-3341
650/723-3950 (fax)
**Length:**
1 week, March
**Cost:**
$6,300
**Location:**
Stanford, CA
**Description:**
This is especially for the executive
who is new to managing teams
and for teams of up to six mem-
bers. The focus is on how to
increase organizational respon-
siveness and foster innovation
through teams and groups.

## 143

**Title:**
**Managing Technology and
Strategic Innovation**
**Sponsor:**
Stanford Business School
Office of Executive Education
Stanford University
Stanford, CA 94305
650/723-3341
650/723-3950 (fax)
**Length:**
1 week, February
**Cost:**
$6,300
**Location:**
Stanford, CA
**Description:**
This program was designed specifically for managers in high-technology industries such as computers,
software, telecommunications,
pharmaceuticals, and chemicals,
who are concerned with managing
innovation in fast-changing environments. Besides targeting general
managers, the program will be
of interest to managers in charge
of R&D or technical product
development.

## 144

**Title:**
**Negotiation and Influence
Strategies**
**Sponsor:**
Stanford Business School
Office of Executive Education
Stanford University
Stanford, CA 94305
650/723-3341
650/723-3950 (fax)
**Length:**
1 week, April
**Cost:**
$6,300
**Location:**
Stanford, CA
**Description:**
This is a challenging and interactive
program for executives who want
to improve their skills in negotia-
tion and increase their influence.
Topics include: social networks,
cross-cultural influence, ethical con-
cerns, power, and getting things
done through other people.

## 145

**Title:**
**Strategic Uses of Information
Technology**

**Sponsor:**
Stanford Business School
Office of Executive Education
Stanford University
Stanford, CA 94305
  650/723-3341
  650/723-3950 (fax)
**Length:**
1 week, April
**Cost:**
$6,300
**Location:**
Stanford, CA
**Description:**
Sharing a wealth of expertise gained in part from Stanford's long connection to nearby Silicon Valley, this program will help executives integrate technology, operating procedures, and people into a cohesive strategy for the future. It is designed for senior managers with responsibility for the strategic direction of their companies.

## 146

**Title:**
**Managing a Customer Support Help Desk**
**Sponsor:**
TechLink Training
P.O. Box 226
Fanwood, NJ 07023
  908/789-2800
  908/789-2811 (fax)
**Length:**
2 days
**Cost:**
$995
**Location:**
Various cities throughout the U.S.
**Description:**
This workshop presents practical, innovative tips and techniques for helping customers learn just-in-time what they need to do better work. Topics include selecting technology, adding value, problem solving, and change management.

## 147

**Title:**
**The Academy**
**Sponsor:**
TeleTraining Institute
1524 West Admiral
Stillwater, OK 74074
  800/755-2356
  405/744-7511 (fax)

**Length:**
10 days, 8:30 A.M.-5:00 P.M. with some evening computer labs
**Cost:**
$3,500
**Location:**
Stillwater, OK (online); adjacent to campus of Oklahoma State University
**Description:**
An extensive immersion course in distance education, this is the most comprehensive course offered by the Teletraining Institute. It is for educators, corporate trainers, and government instructors who are responsible for designing a course for delivery at remote sites, adapting existing training programs to a new distance education format, or implementing new techniques for interest or cost-effectiveness. Focus on video and Web-based instruction.

## 148

**Title:**
**Distance Education Boot Camp**
**Sponsor:**
TeleTraining Institute
1524 West Admiral
Stillwater, OK 74074
  800/755-2356
  405/744-7511 (fax)
**Length:**
1 day
**Cost:**
$295
**Location:**
Stillwater, OK
**Description:**
This is an informational and motivational workshop focusing on the implementation and management of distance education. Topics include: designing, equipping, and operating a distance education network.

## 149

**Title:**
**The TeleTrainer's Toolkit**
**Sponsor:**
TeleTraining Institute
1524 West Admiral
Stillwater, OK 74074
  800/755-2356
  405/744-7511 (fax)
**Length:**
1 day
**Cost:**
$295

**Location:**
From Stillwater, OK, to any organizational site
**Description:**
This 2-day workshop is delivered at a distance via ISDN. Participating sites can enroll up to 30 individuals and may charge an additional participant fee. The workshop covers the basics of how to teach in this environment.

## 150

**Title:**
**Train the (Tele)Trainer**
**Sponsor:**
TeleTraining Institute
1524 West Admiral
Stillwater, OK 74074
  800/755-2356
  405/744-7511 (fax)
**Length:**
5 days
**Cost:**
Call for quote: includes site license and materials to train persons within the purchaser's organization
**Location:**
Stillwater, OK
**Description:**
This program is for trainers to learn how to train others within their organization to effectively design and deliver a learning program at a distance using a live, interactive, video-based medium. Student presentations to others in the program are required.

## 151

**Title:**
**Globalization: Merging Strategy with Action**
**Sponsor:**
Thunderbird
The American Graduate School of
  International Management
15249 North 59th Avenue
Glendale, AZ 85306
  602/978-7635
  602/439-4851 (fax)
**Length:**
6 days
**Cost:**
$5,200 includes lodging, meals, course materials
**Location:**
Glendale, AZ
**Description:**
This program focuses on how to combine functional areas of a business across the globe and develop

a strategic plan of action to meet global goals. Participants stay at a new Executive Conference Center on campus.

## 152

Title:

**Leadership: Leading the Global Organization**

Sponsor:

Thunderbird
The American Graduate School of
   International Management
15249 North 59th Avenue
Glendale, AZ 85306
   602/978-7635
   602/439-4851 (fax)

Length:

6 days

Cost:

$5,200 includes lodging, meals, course materials

Location:

Glendale, AZ

Description:

This program is for leaders at many levels and in many positions within organizations that need help in becoming a global organization. The program focuses on how to structure a global organization, how to lead global teams, and how to meet the needs of persons working together from many cultures. Participants stay at a new Executive Conference Center on campus.

## 153

Title:

**Facilitation Skills for Trainers and Team Leaders**

Sponsor:

The Training Clinic
645 Seabreeze Dr.
Seal Beach, CA 90740
   800/937-4698
   310/430-9603 (fax)

Length:

1 day

Cost:

$349

Location:

Numerous cities throughout the U.S.

Description:

A one-day workshop for classroom trainers who want to encourage group participation and for team leaders who need to help groups become productive. Major topics covered are: (1) What is facilita-

tion? (2) facilitation skills, (3) Group dynamics and group functions, and (4) Facilitator issues.

## 154

Title:

**How to Design Effective Training Programs**

Sponsor:

The Training Clinic
645 Seabreeze Dr.
Seal Beach, CA 97040
   800/937-4698
   310/430-9603 (fax)

Length:

2 days

Cost:

$699

Location:

Numerous cities throughout the U.S.

Description:

This is a hands-on workshop in the theory and practice of effective training program design. The program begins with the issue of assessing training needs, including the avoidance of unnecessary training, assessment techniques, and task analysis. After reviewing the reasons for and the techniques behind developing behavioral objectives, the program proceeds to the basics of program design, including consideration of: (1) adult learning principles, (2) the selection of methods, (3) the use of case studies, (4) the use of audiovisual support, and (5) the design of handout materials. The next topic is four methods of program evaluation, and the program concludes with a survey of training applications: classroom instruction, on-the-job training, self-paced instruction, small group learning, and technical training.

## 155

Title:

**How to Transfer Learning to the Workplace**

Sponsor:

The Training Clinic
645 Seabreeze Dr.
Seal Beach, CA 90740
   800/937-4698
   310/430-9603 (fax)

Length:

1 day

Cost:

$349

Location:

Numerous cities throughout the U.S.

Description:

This workshop is an overview of issues in training transfer: the Trainer's Role, Manager's Role, and Trainee's Role. Skills for effective transfer from learning situation to the job are demonstrated and discussed.

## 156

Title:

**Make New Employee Orientation a Success**

Sponsor:

The Training Clinic
645 Seabreeze Dr.
Seal Beach, CA 90740
   800/937-4698
   310/430-9603 (fax)

Length:

1 day

Cost:

$399

Location:

Numerous cities throughout the U.S.

Description:

This workshop is based on research of the most productive orientation methods in use today. Participants learn how to design and conduct a successful orientation program—setting objectives, selecting content and methods, and evaluating the program. Some of the points covered in the workshop are: (1) the benefits of orientation, (2) how to make it more self-directed, (3) how to eliminate boredom, and (4) how to deal with new company start-ups, mergers, and other special situations. Supplemental text included at no charge.

## 157

Title:

**Performance Consulting Skills for Trainers**

Sponsor:

The Training Clinic
645 Seabreeze Dr.
Seal Beach, CA 90740
   800/937-4698
   310/430-9603 (fax)

Length:

1 day

Cost:
$349
Location:
Numerous cities throughout the U.S.
Description:
This workshop helps participants actively plan training events to resolve issues in their organization. It is intended for training managers, coordinators, course designers and instructors, and especially the "department of one" trainer. The major sections of the program are titled: (1) Analyze your role in the organization, (2) How to shift gears for different projects, (3) Who is your client? (4) What skills do you need to be a performance consultant? and (5) Change agent vs. trainer vs. consultant.

## 158

Title:
**Survival Skills for the New Trainer**
Sponsor:
The Training Clinic
645 Seabreeze Dr.
Seal Beach, CA 90740
800/937-4698
310/430-9603 (fax)
Length:
1 day
Cost:
$349
Location:
Numerous cities throughout the U.S.
Description:
The special concerns of the new trainer are addressed in this workshop. Participants are shown how to relate to the learner—building rapport, maintaining pace, giving and getting feedback, etc. They are also taught classroom assertion skills, including (1) how to avoid manipulation, (2) how to get along with difficult people, (3) what to do when they are wrong or don't know an answer, and (4) how to act assertively without acting aggressively. Another major topic of this workshop is the new trainer's self-image and specific techniques for building confidence and projecting an image of confidence.

## 159

Title:
**Today's Effective Training Coordinator**
Sponsor:
The Training Clinic
645 Seabreeze Dr.
Seal Beach, CA 90740
800/937-4698
310/430-9603 (fax)
Length:
1 day
Cost:
$349
Location:
Numerous cities throughout the U.S.
Description:
Addressed to the training coordinator, human resource administrator, or HR secretary who must administer the detail work in the training function, this workshop begins by exploring the training coordinator's role. After considering the marketing of training programs, the workshop reviews the basics of various training recordkeeping systems: course registration, tuition reimbursement, budget—as well as considering the advisability of automated systems. Participants are then shown how to evaluate needs and either select training resources (people or programs) externally or make the most of internal experts. Finally, a variety of additional practical considerations are raised: scheduling, room set-up, use of external facilities, and purchasing of supplies.

## 160

Title:
**Facilitator Training Program**
Sponsor:
Training Resources Group, Inc.
909 N. Washington St., #305
Alexandria, VA 22314-1555
703/548-3535
703/836-2415 (fax)
Length:
3 days
Cost:
$995
Location:
Alexandria, VA
Description:
Designed for full-time trainers/facilitators or other professionals with similar responsibilities. Participants have the opportunity to design experiential sessions, write case studies and role plays, learn to facilitate group activities, practice giving and receiving feedback, develop stand-up delivery and recovery skills, and receive video-based feedback on their skills.

## 161

Title:
**Financial Analysis for Nonfinancial Managers**
Sponsor:
University of Chicago
Graduate School of Business
450 N. Cityfront Plaza Drive
Chicago, IL 60611
312/464-8732
312/464-8731 (fax)
Length:
5 days
Cost:
$4,650
Location:
Chicago, IL
Description:
This program is one of seven in the University's "Finance Series." It is particularly of interest to training directors and managers responsible for determining training's financial value to a company. Topics include: analyzing historical performance, forecasting financial performance, the firm's internal information systems, activity-based costing and management systems, profitability and strategy, and planning, control, and evaluation systems.

## 162

Title:
**Leading Change: Creating Transformational Competencies**
Sponsor:
University of Michigan
The Michigan Business School
Executive Education Center
Ann Arbor, MI 48109
734/763-1000
734/764-4267 (fax)
Length:
5 days
Cost:
$5,900
Location:
Ann Arbor, MI

Description:

This seminar focuses on the role of leadership in change. It provides participants with tools and methods to effectively manage change initiatives. It is designed to engage the participant in the application of change methodology.

## 163

Title:

**Designing Employee Orientation Programs**

Sponsor:

University of Minnesota
Employer Education Service
430 Management and Economics Building
271-19th Ave. South
Industrial Relations Center
Minneapolis, MN 55455
    800/333-3378
    612/626-7747 (fax)

Length:

1 day

Cost:

$195

Location:

Minneapolis, MN

Description:

Participants learn what to include in an orientation program, how to include it, and when to present it. They also discover ways to get others involved in and committed to the orientation process. The course is designed for anyone with orientation responsibilities who is either starting an orientation program from scratch or revising an existing program. The course covers: (1) understanding the major objectives and potential pay-offs of orientation, (2) designing an orientation program that meets the needs of the organization, (3) incorporating organizational values and goals into the orientation program, (4) sharing responsibility for orientation, and (5) monitoring, evaluating, and updating the orientation process. Participants receive a notebook with checklists and other helpful information.

## 164

Title:

**Public Sector Training and Development**

Sponsor:

University of Minnesota
Employer Education Service
430 Management and Economics Building
271-19th Ave. South
Industrial Relations Center
Minneapolis, MN 55455
    800/333-3378
    612/626-7747 (fax)

Length:

1 day

Cost:

$195

Location:

Minneapolis, MN

Description:

This program is designed for public sector personnel practitioners and managers. It is a survey course that presents an overview of the practices and theories in training and development. Topics covered include: needs assessments, skill-building methods and techniques, team building and quality of working life, training and motivating "seasoned" employees, computer-based instruction, getting a return on investment in training, retention of learning, and career and job development. Phone sponsor for other seminars in the "public sector" series.

## 165

Title:

**The Skilled Team Facilitator Intensive Workshop**

Sponsor:

University of North Texas
Center for the Study of Work Teams
P.O. Box 311280
Denton, TX 76203
    940/565-3096
    940/565-4806 (fax)

Length:

5 days

Cost:

$2,225

Location:

Chapel Hill, NC; Denton, TX

Description:

This is a skills- and values-based intensive workshop for experienced facilitators who want to upgrade their effectiveness as agents of change in working with teams. It is limited to 28 participants and requires completion of assignments prior to the workshop.

## 166

Title:

**How Adults Learn: 15 Practical Tips**

Sponsor:

University of Richmond
Management Institute
Special Programs Building
Richmond, VA 23173
    804/289-8019
    804/289-8872 (fax)

Length:

1 day

Cost:

$375

Location:

Richmond, VA

Description:

Participants in this seminar gain a working understanding of Malcolm Knowles' work on "andragogy" (how adults learn), while discovering what motivates adult learners and how to do it most effectively. Participants also learn instructional techniques that work best with adult learners and how to tap their life experiences to help them relate to the material at hand. The seminar includes group involvement methods and specific tips for designing workshops for adults. The program also explicitly covers the special case of retraining the older worker.

## 167

Title:

**Planning, Designing, and Evaluating Training Programs**

Sponsors:

University of Richmond
Management Institute
Special Programs Building
Richmond, VA 23173
    804/289-8019
    804/289-8872 (fax)

Length:

2 days

Cost:

$750

Location:

Richmond, VA

Description:

Participants in this program learn: (1) three necessary components of instructional outcomes, (2) how to use the C.A.P. model for identifying instructional goals, (3) nine ways of identifying training needs, (4) ten creative points to keep in mind when designing training programs, (5) how to write measurable instructional objectives, and (6) how to design effective training strategies. Participants are encouraged to bring materials with them which they can use in designing a training program for "back home" use. Some of the other topics covered in the workshop include: giving on-the-job instruction, using handouts, effective lecture techniques, and classroom arrangements.

### 168

Title:
**Proven Classroom Training Techniques**
Sponsor:
University of Richmond
Management Institute
Special Programs Building
Richmond, VA 23173
804/289-8019
804/289-8872 (fax)
Length:
2 days
Cost:
$750
Location:
Richmond, VA
Description:
This workshop begins by exploring creative ideas for providing effective training inexpensively. Then the focus turns to specific platform skills: holding the group's interest, making the subject matter interesting, getting participants involved, dealing with negative learners, employing visual aids effectively, using questions, maintaining a motivational learning climate, and wrapping up the presentation. Also covered is the development and use of lesson plans. Participants make their own 10-minute presentation, which is videotaped (for them to keep) and critiqued by the instructor and fellow participants.

### 169

Title:
**Train-the-Trainer**
Sponsor:
University of Richmond
Management Institute

Special Programs Building
Richmond, VA 23173
804/289-8019
804/289-8872 (fax)
Length:
5 days
Cost:
$1,595
Location:
Richmond, VA
Description:
Participants learn to (1) choose when to train and when to facilitate learning; (2) apply the 18 characteristics unique to a facilitator; (3) design a results-oriented case study for the general classroom instructor, as well as for the technical trainer; (4) plan and use a results-oriented game; (5) employ easy-to-use techniques that avoid time wasters in a training session; and (6) practice creative problem-solving techniques.

### 170

Title:
**Advanced Training Skills for Instructors**
Sponsor:
University of Wisconsin–Stout
Technical Instructor Institutes
102 Communication Technologies
Building
Menomonie, WI 54751
715/232-3289
715/836-5263 (fax)
Length:
4 days
Cost:
$1,000
Location:
Menomonie, WI
Description:
This institute provides a mix of theory and practice in developing effective technical presentations: (1) principles and practices which facilitate the learning process are examined; (2) help is provided in setting objectives, lesson planning, and evaluation; and (3) elements of good technical presentations are discussed. The participant's technical presentation is videotaped and professionally critiqued.

### 171

Title:
**Instructional System Design**
Sponsor:
University of Wisconsin–Stout
Technical Instructor Institutes

102 Communication Technologies
Building
Menomonie, WI 54751
715/232-3289
715/836-5263 (fax)
Length:
5 days
Cost:
$1,000
Location:
Menomonie, WI
Description:
This "systems approach" institute was developed for trainers who are concerned with design and implementation of total training programs—from needs analysis through evaluation. All elements of the closed-loop system approach are discussed to help participants design instruction based on job tasks their prospective students must be able to perform.

### 172

Title:
**Managing Technical Training**
Sponsor:
University of Wisconsin–Stout
Technical Instructor Institutes
102 Communication Technologies
Building
Menomonie, WI 54751
715/232-3289
715/836-5263 (fax)
Length:
4 days
Cost:
$1,000
Location:
Menomonie, WI
Description:
This institute is for those who are responsible for directing the work of technical instructors. The instructors discuss practical applications for managing a training department, providing a base for the process of selecting, training, and updating instructors. They also cover techniques for managing training projects that help in the crucial area of selling the training function to management.

### 173

Title:
**Training One-on-One Instructors**
Sponsor:
University of Wisconsin–Stout
Technical Instructor Institutes

102 Communication Technologies
Building
Menomonie, WI 54751
715/232-3289
715/836-5263 (fax)
**Length:**
4 days
**Cost:**
$1,000
**Location:**
Menomonie, WI
**Description:**
This workshop is concerned with several distinct tasks that a senior instructor may encounter. Team building, and inter-group communication techniques are discussed to help establish the effective work relationships necessary for successful training one on one. Participants gain knowledge and skill in making tough decisions regarding training value and instructional strategies with peers and across levels as a one-on-one instructor.

## 174

**Title:**
**Competitive Intelligence**
**Sponsor:**
University of Wisconsin–Madison
Management Institute
Grainger Hall
975 University Avenue
Madison, WI 53706-1323
800/348-8964
800/741-7416 (fax)
**Length:**
2 days
**Cost:**
$1,045
**Location:**
Madison, WI
**Description:**
This workshop shows participants how to use competitive intelligence as a foundation for more profitable corporate strategies. Topics include: data collection, project staffing, features and benefits of information products.

## 175

**Title:**
**Effective Distance Education**
**Sponsor:**
University of Wisconsin–Madison
Engineering Professional
Development
432 North Lake Street
Madison, WI 53706

800/462-0876
800/442-4214 (fax)
**Length:**
3 days
**Cost:**
$895
**Location:**
Madison, WI
**Description:**
Participants learn how to assess their training and education needs to see if distance education methods will solve their problems. They also learn how to organize their distance education program to make the most effective use of the tools and technology they now have or may acquire. The course features demonstrations and discussions of all applicable technology, as well as case studies from a variety of public and private organizations.

## 176

**Title:**
**Instructional Skills for New Trainers**
**Sponsor:**
University of Wisconsin–Madison
Management Institute
Grainger Hall
975 University Ave.
Madison, WI 53706-1323
800/348-8964
800/741-7416 (fax)
**Length:**
3 days
**Cost:**
$1,095
**Location:**
Madison, WI
**Description:**
Increasing change is forcing many organizations to use internal staff—those who know a subject, concept, or process—as instructors. This program is designed for these people. An effective trainer must know how to create a learning climate, build a lesson plan, present knowledge and ideas, and evaluate a presentation. This workshop gives new trainers the opportunity to practice the skills that instructors need. It features numerous suggestions, tips, and personal counsel to improve participants' effectiveness and build their confidence as instructors. Lodging available at the new Fluno Center for Executive Education.

## 177

**Title:**
**Problem Solving, Process Improvement, and Reinvention: A Systematic Team Approach**
**Sponsor:**
University of Wisconsin–Madison
Management Institute
Grainger Hall
975 University Ave.
Madison, WI 53706-1323
800/348-8964
800/741-7416 (fax)
**Length:**
3 days
**Cost:**
$1,275
**Location:**
Madison, WI
**Description:**
Participants will form teams, each of which will select a problem-solving or process-improvement project. Topics include identifying needs, collecting data, determining root causes, and developing and testing alternatives. This workshop is part of the "Quality Management Certificate Series."

## 178

**Title:**
**Online Instructor Program: Corporate Training Track**
**Sponsor:**
Walden Institute for Learning and Leadership
24311 Walden Center Drive, 3rd floor
Bonita Springs, FL 34134
800/237-6434
941/498-7821 (fax)
**Length:**
12 weeks, online; Programs begin in June, September, March, and December.
**Cost:**
$995
**Location:**
online
**Description:**
This is one example of an online professional development program for trainers. This one offers "an online classroom" and "a learning community." This is considered an overview of online learning. Topics include online tools and their purposes, instructional design theory and techniques, distance-based evaluation, quality assurance in

online learning, and Collaborative learning communities. Program completion results in an Online Instruction Certificate.

## 179

Title:
**Train-the-Trainer**
Sponsor:
Xavier University Consulting Group
3800 Victory Parkway
Cincinnati, OH 45207

513/745-3396
513/745-4307 (fax)
Length:
5 days
Cost:
$1,600; or 1 day $395; 2 days $745
Location:
Cincinnati, OH; Boston, MA
Description:
This is a 5-day comprehensive workshop of particular interest to new trainers. It is made up of 3 shorter workshops, each of which can be taken separately. These are:

How Adults Learn, 1 day; Planning Designing, and Evaluating Training, 2 days; and Proven Classroom Training Techniques, 2 days.

# THE TRAINER'S ALMANAC

## SECTION 6.5

### NON-PROFIT ORGANIZATIONS

Organizations listed in this section hold non-profit status. These organizations conduct research, hold meetings and conferences, publish newsletters, reports, and books, have online services, and provide various other customized services to trainers. They particularly represent potential partnering possibilities for businesses who want to expand their networks and collaborate with the non-profit sector.

### Training-Related Services Worth Investigating

Listing these organizations here differentiates them from the professional associations in Section 6.1 who seek membership and charge dues, and from the traditional "vendor" training suppliers listed in Section 6.4. The often unique and specialized services of these non-profit organizations are frequently overlooked in other directories of training providers; we provide them here because they are an excellent source of research-based information and a complement to commercial training sources. We list 22 non-profit organizations.

## INDEX TO PRINCIPAL INTERESTS OF NON-PROFIT ORGANIZATIONS

**Accreditation programs**
1, 11, 20

**Advancement of Women**
4

**Career development**
3, 4, 9, 20

**Co-operative education programs**
17

**Continuing education**
1, 9

**Distance learning**
21

**Diversity, training for**
18

**English language training**
16

**Ethics**
5

**Higher education**
2, 14

**Leadership**
6, 10

**Literacy in the workplace**
15, 16

**National training needs/policy**
10, 12, 14, 22

**Research in training/development**
7, 10, 11, 13, 14, 15, 22

**Team training**
8

**Technical training**
7, 19, 20

**Testing**
11, 19, 20

**Vocational training**
7, 17, 19, 20

## 1

**Name of organization:**
   **Accrediting Council for**
   **Continuing Education &**
   **Training**
**Purpose:**
   The Accrediting Council for Con-
   tinuing Education & Training
   (ACCET) is a voluntary group of
   educational organizations affiliated
   for the purpose of improving
   continuing education and training.
   Through its support of an indepen-
   dent Accrediting Commission, the
   ACCET membership promulgates
   and sustains the Standards for
   Accreditation along with policies
   and procedures that measure and
   ensure educational standards of
   quality.
**Contact information:**
   ACCET
   1200 19th St., NW, Suite 200
   Washington, DC 20036
       202/955-1113
       202/955-1118 (fax)
       www.accet.org
**Key officers/staff:**
   Executive Director: Roger J.
   Williams
**Funded by:**
   Sustaining organizations
**Publications:**
   Annual Accredited Schools'
   Directory
**Seminars/conferences:**
   Accreditation workshop
   Annual convention

## 2

**Name of organization:**
   **American Council on**
   **Education, Center for Adult**
   **Learning and Educational**
   **Credentials**
**Purpose:**
   An independent, non-profit
   organization founded in 1918, the
   American Council on Education is
   the umbrella organization for the
   nation's college and universities.
   ACE's Center for Adult Learning
   administers the General
   Educational Development (GED)
   and National External Diploma
   (EDP) testing programs, which
   allow adults to earn a high school
   credential. It also evaluates
   courses offered by business and
   industry, labor unions, associations, government agencies, and

the military services and makes
college credit recommendations
where appropriate.
**Contact information:**
   American Council on Education
   One DuPont Circle, Suite 250
   Washington, DC 20036–1193
       202/939-9475
       202/775-8578 (fax)
       www.acenet.edu
**Key officers/staff:**
   President: Stanley Ikenberry
**Parent Organization:**
   American Council on Education
**Funded by:**
   Membership dues, fees for services,
   federal contracts, private support
**Publications:**
   The following ACE publications are
   the standard reference tools used by
   the majority of U.S. colleges and
   universities to award credit for learn-
   ing attained outside the classroom:
   • The National Guide to
     Educational Credit for
     Training Programs, 1998
   • Guide to Educational Credit
     by Examination, 1996
   • Guide to the Evaluation of
     Educational Experiences in
     the Armed Services, 1998
   A catalog of nearly 100 other titles
   in the ACE/Orxy Press Series on
   Higher Education is available by
   calling 800/279-6799.
**Seminars/conferences:**
   ACE Annual Meeting
   "All of One Nation" a conference
   on minorities in higher educa-
   tion, every 2 years
**Other activities:**
   Other ACE activities are the
   Business-Higher Education Forum,
   which provides an opportunity for
   interchange among corporate and
   academic chief executives, and the
   Labor-Higher Education Council,
   which is conducted in cooperation
   with the AFL-CIO.

## 3

**Name of organization:**
   **Career Planning & Adult**
   **Development Network**
**Purpose:**
   The Career Planning and Adult
   Development Network is a non-
   profit international organization of
   professionals who work with adults
   in career transition. The Network
   offers a professional certification
   program for Job and Career

Transition Coaches, conferences,
meetings, workshops, and
publications.
**Contact information:**
   Career Planning and Adult
   Development Network
   4965 Sierra Rd.
   San Jose, CA 95132
   408/441-9100
   408/441-9101 (fax)
   www.careertrainer.com
**Key officers/staff:**
   President: Richard Knowdell
**Funded by:**
   Annual memberships
   $49 U.S. addresses
   $69 foreign addresses
**Publications:**
   • Monthly newsletter
   • Quarterly Journal
**Seminars/conferences:**
   International Career
   Development Conference
   California Career Conference
**Other activities:**
   List of local area referral sources
   throughout the U.S.

## 4

**Name of organization:**
   **Catalyst**
**Purpose:**
   Catalyst is a non-profit research
   and advisory organization working
   to advance women in business and
   the professions. Catalyst works
   with corporations and professional
   firms to effect change for women
   through the workplace.
**Contact information:**
   Catalyst
   120 Wall Street
   New York, NY 10005
       212/514-7600
       212/514-8470 (fax)
       www.catalystwomen.org
**Key officers/staff:**
   President: Sheila Wellington
**Publications:**
   Perspective (newsletter)
   Research Studies (check website)
   Other publications available—check
   website for more details
**Seminars/conferences:**
   The Catalyst Awards gala
   Check website for updates on
   future events
**Other activities:**
   Catalyst issue specialists and senior
   staff members of the organization's
   research and advisory service teams
   are regularly on the road across the

country, spreading the word about their research findings at many types of venues. Speakers can deliver presentations on every issue affecting working women.

## 5

**Name of organization:**
**Center for Business, Religion and Public Life**
**Purpose:**
The purpose of the Center for Business, Religion and Public Life is to initiate ethics awareness and provide a forum for discussion of ethical issues in the workplace at the highest corporate level. The center was created in the mid-1980s by corporate leaders from Westinghouse Electric Corporation and Pittsburgh Theological Seminary. The center is currently dealing with issues of child care, communications, genetic alteration, downsizing, corporate giving, trust, and integrity.

**Contact information:**
Center for Business, Religion and Public Life
Pittsburgh Theological Seminary
616 No. Highland Drive
Pittsburgh, PA 15206

**Key officers/staff:**
Seminary President: Samuel Calian
412/362-5610, Ext. 2100

**Publications:**
- Quarterly Newsletter
- Audiotape Library
- Listing of Symposia

**Other activities:**
Forums, customer seminars, conferences, consulting, collaborative programming

## 6

**Name of organization:**
**Center for Creative Leadership (CCL)**
**Purpose:**
The Center for Creative Leadership is a non-profit educational institution offering open enrollment and custom programs. Its mission is "to advance the understanding, practice, and development of leadership for the benefit of society worldwide."

**Contact information:**
Center for Creative Leadership
One Leadership Place
P.O. Box 26300
Greensboro, NC 27438

336/545-2810
336/282-3284 (fax)
www.ccl.org

**Key officers/staff:**
President: John R. Alexander
**Funded by:**
Grants and donations from foundations, corporations, and individuals
Tuition, royalties, fees for services
Sales of products

**Publications:**
Books, reports, papers on wide variety of leadership topics
Catalogs of publications
Periodic newsletter, *Leadership in Action*

**Seminars/conferences:**
Numerous conferences, seminars, workshops, and colloquia

**Other activities:**
Research, assessment instruments, simulations
Educational facilities in Brussels, Belgium; Colorado Springs, CO; San Diego, CA; and Greensboro, NC

## 7

**Name of organization:**
**Center for Occupational Research and Development**
**Purpose:**
The Center for Occupational Research and Development (CORD) is a nonprofit public service organization. CORD helps educators in schools and industry address the technical education, training, and retraining needs of workers. CORD's primary areas of operation include technical assistance for Tech Prep, school-to-work transition, and worksite learning, contextual academic curriculum development, advanced technologies curriculum development, and *Transformations* adult training program implementation assistance. CORD also administers the National Tech Prep Network and the National Coalition for Advanced Technology Centers.

**Contact information:**
Gwen Burnham
Center for Occupational Research and Development (CORD)
601 Lake Air Drive
P.O. Box 21689
Waco, TX 76702–1689
800/972-2766
254/772-8972 (fax)
www.cord.org

**Key officers/staff:**
President & Chief Executive Officer: Daniel M. Hull
**Publications:**
CORD is best known for having developed applied academic course materials in mathematics, biology, chemistry, and physics. In addition to these materials, CORD publishes educational planning guides, research studies, reports, and books.

**Other activities:**
In 1993, CORD formed the CORD Foundation, a nonprofit educational foundation, and CORD Communications, Inc., a publishing subsidiary, to better serve the needs of the educational community. The 3 organizations work together to provide quality educational materials and services for students, educators, and employers.

## 8

**Name of organization:**
**Center for the Study of Work Teams**
**Purpose:**
The Center for the Study of Work Teams is a center for research and education on collaborative work systems. Center staff and associates include faculty and graduate students from the Department of Psychology, the College of Business, College of Education, and School of Community Service. The center features corporate sponsors at annual conferences.

**Contact information:**
Center for the Study of Work Teams
Claims Accounting
University of North Texas
P.O. Box 310499
Denton, TX 76203
940/565-3096
940/565-4806 (fax)
www.workteams.unt.edu

**Key officers/staff:**
Director: Michael Beyerline
**Publications:**
Proceedings from International Conference, Quarterly Newsletter, Books

**Other activities:**
Annual international conference, advanced concepts conference, strategies and skills for effective teaming conferences, seminars, forums, team assessment, corporate sponsors, research projects

## 9

Name of organization:
**Clearinghouse on Adult, Career, & Vocational Education**

Purpose:
ERIC/ACVE is one of 16 clearinghouses in the U.S. Department of Education-sponsored ERIC system. ERIC is a national education information service that identifies, selects, processes, and disseminates information in all areas of education. The ERIC Clearinghouse on Adult, Career, and Vocational Education covers adult and continuing education, career education, and vocational and technical education and training.

Contact information:
Clearinghouse on Adult, Career, and Vocational Education
Center on Education and Training for Employment
Ohio State University
1900 Kenny Rd.
Columbus, OH 43210–1090
800/848-4815
614/292-4353
614/292-1260 (fax)
www.ericacve.org

Key officers/staff:
Director & Adult Education Specialist: Susan Imel
User Services Specialist: Cheryl Grossman

Parent organization:
Center on Education and Training for Employment, The Ohio State University

Funded by:
Office of Educational Research and Improvement, U.S. Department of Education, under Contract No. RI88062005

Publications:
ERIC Digests
Trends and Issues Alerts
Practice Applications Briefs
Information brochures
Newsletter

Seminars/conferences:
Training workshops offered on a cost-recovery basis

## 10

Name of organization:
**The Conference Board**

Purpose:
The Conference Board is the world's leading business membership organization, connecting companies in more than 60 nations. Founded in 1916, the Board's twofold purpose is to improve the business enterprise system and to enhance the contribution of business to society. A not-for-profit, non-advocacy organization, The Conference Board's membership includes over 3,000 companies and other organizations worldwide in 67 countries.

Contact information:
The Conference Board
845 Third Avenue
New York, NY 10022
212/759-0900
212/980-7014
www.conference-board.org

Key officers/staff:
C. R. Shoemate, Chairman, President, and CEO

Funded by:
Corporate and organization associate memberships; colleges and universities

Publications:
Research reports
Conference proceedings
*Across the Board*, monthly magazines

Seminars/conferences:
Meetings and conferences are held weekly throughout the year. The focus for all meetings is actual business experience shared by executives, providing a superior level of networking with peers.

Other activities:
Research centers located in New York City

## 11

Name of organization:
**Educational Testing Service (ETS)**

Purpose:
Educational Testing Service (ETS) is a private, nonprofit corporation devoted to measurement and research, primarily in the field of education. Testing programs are used for school and college admission, student guidance and placement, awarding degree credit for independent or advanced learning, and continuing education.

Contact information:
Educational Testing Service
Rosedale Road, P.O. Box 6736
Princeton, NJ 08541
609/921-9000
www.ets.org

Key officers/staff:
President: Nancy Cole

Funded by:
Most ETS programs are conducted under contract with independent client agencies or organizations.

Publications:
Numerous publications of all sorts related to testing. Well-known trademarks of ETS include: The Graduate Record Examinations (GREs), The Praxis Series, Strategies for Teaching Critical Thinking, Worklink, and others.

Seminars/conferences:
Periodic seminars and conferences sponsored by various ETS clients and partners

Other activities:
Software, films, videos; The Center for the Assessment of Educational Progress (CAEP) is a division of ETS which administers The National Assessment of Educational Progress.

## 12

Name of organization:
**Hudson Institute**

Purpose:
Hudson Institute is a private, not-for-profit research organization founded in 1961 by the late Herman Kahn. The institute analyzes and makes recommendations about public policy for business and government executives, as well as for the public at large. It does not advocate an express ideology or political position. However, more than thirty years of work on the most important issues of the day has forged a viewpoint that embodies skepticism about the conventional wisdom, optimism about solving problems, a commitment to free institutions and individual responsibility, an appreciation of the crucial role of technology in achieving progress, and an abiding respect for the importance of values, culture, and religion in human affairs.

Contact information:
Hudson Institute, Inc.
5395 Emerson Way
Indianapolis, IN 46226
317/545-1000
317/545-9639 (fax)
Offices also in Washington, DC; Madison, WI; San Antonio, TX; and Montreal, Canada
www.hudson.org

**Key officers/staff:**
President: Herbert London
Vice President/COO: Curt Smith
Director of Research: Edwin
Rubenstein
**Funded by:**
Foundation and private gifts
**Publications:**
Quarterly newsletter, *Visions*
Monthly monographs
Monthly research reports
Book: *Workforce 2000* (1987)
Book: *Workforce 2020* (1997)
Healthcare 2020

## 13

**Name of organization:**
**The Human Resource**
**Planning Society**
**Purpose:**
The Human Resource Planning
Society is a not-for-profit associa-
tion committed to "improving
organizational performance by cre-
ating a global network of individu-
als who function as business
partners in the application of strate-
gic human resource management
practices."
**Contact information:**
The Human Resource Planning
Society
317 Madison Ave., Suite 1509
New York, NY 10017
212/490-6387
212/682-6851 (fax)
www.hrps.org
**Key officers/staff:**
Executive Director: Walter J.
Cleaver
President: Marilyn Buckner
**Funded by:**
More than 3,300 individual mem-
bers and 200 corporate and
research sponsors.
$250 - individual
$2,500 - corporate
$1,000 - research
**Publications:**
Quarterly publication, Human
Resource Planning
Price: $120
**Seminars/conferences:**
Annual conferences
Professional development monthly
seminars
**Other activities:**
Corporate sponsor forum annually
Research symposium biennially

## 14

**Name of organization:**
**RAND Education**

**Purpose:**
This institute was established: (1)
to conduct research, analysis, and
technical assistance that will
improve policy and practice at all
levels and in all sectors that provide education and training in the
United States; and (2) to train
policy analysts in this field of
research. It has developed a comprehensive program of policy
analysis in these areas: educational
assessment and accountability,
alternative institutional reform
concepts, response to new fiscal
limits, preparation for work, educational technology, and the social
context of education and training.
This "integrative" approach
ensures that a major theme in all
these areas is educational access,
equity, and achievement for poor
and minority students.
**Contact information:**
RAND Education
P.O. Box 2138
Santa Monica, CA 90407–2138
310/393-0411
310/393-4818 (fax)
www.rand.org
**Key officers/staff:**
Director: Dominic Brewer
**Parent organization:**
RAND; Chairman: Paul H. O'Neill
**Funded by:**
Multiple governmental and non-
governmental sources (National
Science Foundation, and other
foundations)
**Publications:**
RAND Research Review; various
reports, issue papers, and policy
briefs
**Seminars/conferences:**
Occasional conferences and
seminars

## 15

**Name of organization:**
**Institute for the Study**
**of Adult Literacy**
**Purpose:**
The Institute for the Study of Adult
Literacy's goals include (1) development and dissemination of a sound
conceptual and research base in
adult literacy, (2) improvement of
practice, and (3) leadership and
coordination of comprehensive
approaches to the delivery of adult
literacy services. Projects address
interrelated themes, such as: workplace literacy, technology in adult

literacy, intergenerational literacy,
special needs populations, cus-
tomized materials development,
and staff development/training.
The Institute is nationally recog-
nized for its work in literacy
research, development, and dis-
semination activities.
**Contact information:**
Institute for the Study of Adult
Literacy
Pennsylvania State University
102 Rackley Building
University Park, PA 16802–3202
814/863-3777
814/863-6108 (fax)
www.ed.psu.edu\isa\
**Key officers/staff:**
Director and Professor of
Education: Eunice N. Askov
Assistant Director: Barbara H. Van
Horn
**Parent organization:**
College on Education, The
Pennsylvania State University
**Funded by:**
Grants and contracts
**Publications:**
Newsletter *The Mosaic*
Other publications available
**Seminars/conferences:**
Project staff presents workshops
and seminars on selected topics
in adult literacy via contracted
services.
**Other activities:**
Project staff provides consulting
services via contract

## 16

**Name of organization:**
**National Clearinghouse for**
**ESL Literacy Education (NCLE)**
**Purpose:**
The National Clearinghouse for ESL
Literacy Education (NCLE), an
adjunct ERIC Clearinghouse, provides information, referral, and
technical assistance on literacy education for limited-English-proficient
adults and out-of-school youth. As
the only national clearinghouse for
adult ESL literacy, NCLE primarily
serves researchers, literacy instructors, and program administrators.
**Contact information:**
NCLE
Center for Applied Linguistics
4646 40th Street, NW
Washington, DC 20016-1859
202/362-0700
202/362-3740 (fax)
www.cal.org/ncle

**Key officers/staff:**
Director: Joy Peyton
Associate Director: Miriam Burt
**Parent organization:**
Center for Applied Linguistics
**Funded by:**
Office of Vocational and Adult
Education, U.S. Dept. of Education
**Publications:**
NCLE Notes newsletter (semiannual), books, ERIC digest and
annotated bibliographies, issue
papers, and resource guides
**Other activities:**
NCLE maintains a resource center
that is open to the public and has
materials on ESL and native language literacy. NCLE has produced
a series of videos for staff development, documenting effective ESL
and adult literacy programs. NCLE
moderates a listserv for adult ESL
educators, NIFL-ESL.

## 17

**Name of organization:**
**National Commission for
Cooperative Education**
**Purpose:**
Founded in 1962, The National
Commission for Cooperative
Education is a non-profit higher
education organization and advo-
cacy group. NCCE's mission is to
advance the concept of cooperative
education as an educational strat-
egy, integrating classroom curricu-
lum with related work experience.
**Contact information:**
National Commission for
Cooperative Education
360 Huntington Ave.
Boston, MA 02115–5096
617/373-3770
617/373-3463 (fax)
www.co-op.edu
**Key officers/staff:**
President: Paul J. Stonely
**Funded by:**
Corporations, foundations, and
higher education institutions
**Publications:**
Informational brochures
Newsletters, booklets
**Seminars/conferences:**
Annual meeting (June)
**Other activities:**
Public awareness activities in col-
laboration with employment and
educational organizations; profes-
sional outreach and training for
educators and employers.

## 18

**Name of organization:**
**National MultiCultural
Institute**
**Purpose:**
The National MultiCultural
Institute's mission is to increase
communication, understanding,
and respect among people of dif-
ferent racial, ethnic, and cultural
backgrounds. NMCI is a non-profit
training and development and
consulting organization.
**Contact information:**
National MultiCultural Institute
3000 Connecticut Ave., NW,
Suite 438
Washington, DC 20008–2556
202/483-0700
202/483-5233 (fax)
www.nmci.org/nmci/
**Key officers/staff:**
President: Elizabeth P. Salett
**Funded by:**
Contracts, fees for service, founda-
tion grants, and corporate and
individual contributions
**Publications:**
Educational materials
Videos
Training manuals
Books
**Seminars/conferences:**
Annual national conference
Training courses
**Other activities:**
Mental health counseling and
referral service

## 19

**Name of organization:**
**National Occupational
Competency Testing Institute
(NOCTI)**
**Purpose:**
NOCTI is America's foremost
developer of high-quality validated
written and performance occupational competency assessments and
testing materials. NOCTI's products and services are purchased by
businesses, industry, educational,
and government agencies. NOCTI
is a not-for-profit educational consortium dedicated to facilitating
development of national workforce
standards.
**Contact information:**
National Occupational
Competency Testing Institute
500 N. Bronson Avenue
Big Rapids, MI 49307

800/334-6283
616/796-4699 (fax)
www.nocti.org
**Key officers/staff:**
President/CEO: Ray Ryan
**Funded by:**
Clients who purchase assessment
products and services
**Publications:**
Individual occupational competency assessments built around
a job and task analysis which
defines occupational competencies, knowledges, skills, worker
traits, and attitudes.
Newsletter, *NOCTI Network*
**Seminars/conferences:**
National conference, biennial
**Other activities:**
Partnerships with diverse individuals, organizations, businesses,
industries, government associations, and communities to facilitate national workforce standards
and to improve the assessment of
occupational competency.

## 20

**Name of organization:**
**National Skill Standards Board
(NSSB)**
**Purpose:**
The NSSB is building a voluntary
national system of skill standards,
assessment and certification that
will enhance the ability of the
United States to compete effectively in a global economy. These
skills are being identified by indus-
try in full partnership with educa-
tion, labor, civil rights, and
community-based organizations.
The standards will be based on
high performance work and will be
portable across industry sectors.
**Contact information:**
National Skill Standards Board
1441 L Street, NW, Suite 9000
Washington, DC 20005
202/254-8628
202/254-8686 (fax)
www.nssb.org
**Key officers/staff:**
Executive Director: Edie West
**Parent organization:**
U.S. Congress
**Funded by:**
U.S. Congress; U.S. Department of
Labor, 1994 National Skill
Standards Act
**Publications:**
Newsletter, annual report,
brochures, electronic

Clearinghouse of Skill Standards in academic education, occupation-specific areas, and for employability, database of certification and apprenticeship programs

**Seminars/conferences:**
Staff regularly functions as presenters at various national conferences of many other organizations. Check the NSSB Website for updates.

**Other activities:**
Partnerships with K–12 educators, vocational educators, community- and four-year colleges and job training organizations

# 21

**Name of organization:**
**United States Distance Learning Association**

**Purpose:**
To promote the development and application of distance learning to education and training, including K–12, higher education, continuing education, and corporate training.

**Contact information:**
USDLA
P.O. Box 376
Watertown, MA 02471
   800/275-5162
   617/924-1308 (fax)
   www.usdla.org

**Key officers/staff:**
Executive Director: John G. Flores

**Publications:**
*ED—Education at a Distance*
Annual report on data and funding sources
Policy forum report

**Seminars/conferences:**
IDLCON—International Distance Learning Conference

**Other activities:**
Summer board meeting, annual meeting

# 22

**Name of organization:**
**Work in America Institute, Inc.**

**Purpose:**
The mission of Work in America Institute is to study and promote high performance work systems that improve productivity and the quality of worklife. Founded in 1975, the Institute is a nonpartisan, multipartite organization with a board composed of corporate, labor union, government, and academic leaders. In its action-oriented research and its events, the Institute serves as a catalyst for change in the human resources practices of American corporations and unions.

**Contact information:**
Work in America Institute, Inc.
700 White Plains Road
Scarsdale, NY 10583–5058
   914/472-9600
   914/472-9606 (fax)
   www.workinamerica.org

**Key officers/staff:**
CEO/Chairman: Jerome M. Rosow
Senior VP: Diane Epstein
Vice-President, Policy Studies Jill Casner-Lotto
Vice-President, Client Services & Programs: Marty Cohen

**Funded by:**
Major foundations, membership fees, sale of publications, contributions

**Publications:**
National Policy Studies (e.g., *Strategic Partners for High Performance*; *New Roles for Managers*; *Training for New Technology*; *Job-Linked Literacy*)
Books (e.g., *Employment Security in a Free Economy*; *The Innovative Organization*)
Studies in Productivity

**Seminars/conferences:**
10–15 Site Visits annually
Productivity Forum Roundtables
Network Meetings
Train the Facilitator conferences

# THE TRAINER'S ALMANAC

## SECTION 6.6

### TRAINING RESEARCH AND REFERENCE SOURCES

This section of *The Trainer's Almanac* lists sources of sources; that is, references listed here are tools to lead you forward into finding more sources and expanded information in each specific category presented.

**Variety and Focus**
Resources listed here are in many formats: books, catalogs, directories, audiotapes, videos, CD-ROMs, and online databases. Services referenced here are delivered through many formats, too: telephone, Website, diskette, multimedia, Internet communication, registration, referral, and consulting services.

Entries here are listed only once, although several of the entires could be listed in more than one category; for example, *ASTD's Buyer's Guide and Consultant Directory* could be listed in the categories "Training Suppliers," "Consultants," and "Online Services." We've chosen the category that made the most sense to us. However, be sure to read the individual descriptions carefully to understand the complete nature of each entry. The Websites *astd.org* and *trainingsupersite.com* are comprehensive training Websites and good places to begin a search for references.

**Eight Categories**
In this section we list 57 reference sources, including new listings for Annuals, Compendia, and Directories; and separate listings for "Handbooks" and for "Toolbooks." These references are the latest versions of the resource; all have been published within the last 5 years, most within the last 2 years. The following categories are included for the year 2001:

|  | item numbers |
|---|---|
| • Annuals, Compendia, and Directories | 1, 2, 3, 4, 5, 6, 7, 8, 9, 10, 11, 12, 13 |
| • Consultants | 14, 15, 16, 17 |
| • Handbooks | 18, 19, 20, 21, 22, 23, 24 |
| • Online Services | 25, 26, 27, 28, 29, 30, 31, 32 |
| • Seminar Databases | 33, 34, 35, 36, 37, 38, 39 |
| • Toolbooks | 40, 41, 42, 43, 44, 45, 46, 47, 48, 49 |
| • Training Suppliers | 50, 51 |
| • Videos, Films, Audiotapes | 52, 53, 54, 55, 56, 57 |

## Annuals, Compendia, and Directories

### 1

Title:
**ASTD's Guide to Learning Organization Assessment Instruments**
Authors:
Mark E. Van Buren and Lisa Lucadamo
Publisher:
American Society for Training and Development (ASTD)
1640 King Street, Box 1443
Alexandria, VA 22313
703/683-8100
410/516-6998 (fax)
Publication data:
1996, 24 pages, $35.00
Description:
This two-part guide summarizes key features of 36 assessment instruments. A comprehensive table lists levels of learning—individual, team, and organization. A detailed descriptive second part follows the Table. Instruments are categorized according to: learning level, content, validation, method of assessment administration, time frame, intended audience, and clients served. Other evaluation publications are available from ASTD.

### 2

Title:
**The ASTD Training Data Book**
Authors:
Laurie J. Bassi, Anne L. Gallagher, and Ed Schroer
Publisher:
American Society for Training and Development (ASTD)
1640 King Street, Box 1443
Alexandria, VA 22313
703/683-8100
410/516-6998 (fax)
www.astd.org
Publication data:
1997, 133 pages, $69.00
Description:
This research study summarizes what is known about formal training provided by private sector employers within the United States. The book includes an overview of basic training statistics, a look at who is getting what

training, and how corporations are using technology. It includes sections on operational data and a sampling of practices for performance improvement. At year's end, the *ASTD State of The Industry Report* is also available.

### 3

Title:
**The ASTD Training and Performance Yearbook**
Authors:
James W. Cortado and John A. Woods, Editors
Publisher:
ASTD/McGraw-Hill
ASTD Publishing Service
P.O. Box 4856
Hampden Station, Baltimore, MD 21211
410/516-6949
www.astd.org
Publication data:
2000, book, $99.95
Description:
The book consists of articles reprinted from training magazines and chapters of books by the authors. A directory of contact information is included.

### 4

Title:
**BLS Handbook of Methods**
Editor/Author:
Bureau of Labor Statistics (BLS)
Publisher:
U.S. Government Printing Office
Superintendent of Documents
Mail Stop M
732 N. Capitol St., N.W.
Washington, DC 20402
202/512-1800
202/512-2250 (fax)
Publication data:
250 pages
published in 1997
$23
Description:
The *Handbook* explains BLS data preparation in the areas of employment and unemployment, compensation and working conditions, occupational safety and health, productivity and technology, economic growth and employment projections, and prices and living conditions. Tables, three appendixes, and an index.

### 5

Title:
**The Women Executives' Desk Set**
Type of resource:
Book set
Publisher:
Catalyst
120 Wall Street
New York, NY 10005
212/514-7600
212/514-8470 (fax)
www.catalystwomen.org
Price:
$250
Description:
This set of 3 major directories includes The *Catalyst Census of Women Board Directors of the Fortune 500* and the *2001 Catalyst Census of Women Corporate Officers and Top Earners*, as well as *Women in Corporate Leadership: Progress and Prospects*. The books list where the women are and tell how they got there. Company comparisons are provided. Catalyst provides many other research reports.

### 6

Title:
**The 2000 Higher Education Directory**
Type of resource:
Book, 812 pages
Publisher:
Higher Education Publications, Inc.
6400 Arlington Blvd., Suite 648
Falls Church, VA 22042
703/532-2300
703/532-2305 (fax)
www.hepinc.com
Price:
$60
Description:
This directory is a listing of all postsecondary, degree-granting institutions that are accredited by agencies recognized by the U.S. Secretary of Education and the Council of Higher Education Accreditation. It contains information regarding tuition reimbursement, assistance, and career development.

### 7

Title:
**Off-Site Meetings 2000/2001 Marketplace Directory: Training Meeting Facilities**

Type of resource:
   Directory of meeting facilities in
   U.S. and Canada, 75 pages
Provider:
   Bill Communications
   TRAINING Directories
   50 South Ninth St.
   Minneapolis, MN 55402
      800/707-7749
      612/333-0471
      612/333-6526 (fax)
Price:
   Free with subscription to TRAIN-
   ING Magazine. $6 cost to non-
   subscribers.
Description:
   This directory lists approximately
   350 facilities that are available
   for off-site training meetings.
   Information on each listing
   includes: number of meeting
   rooms and their capacity, number
   of guest rooms, whether or not
   they belong to the professional
   association IACC, audiovisual
   capabilities, recreation and fitness
   facilities, and distance to airport
   and other transportation and
   travel notes.

**8**

Title:
   **Leadership Directories, The
   "Yellow Books" and
   Leadership Library**
Type of resource:
   Catalog of directories, or CD-ROM,
   and Internet
Publisher:
   Leadership Directories, Inc.
   104 Fifth Avenue
   New York, NY 10011
      212/627-4140
      212/645-0931 (fax)
      www.leadershipdirectories.com
Price:
   Semi-annual subscription per direc-
   tory, approximately $235;
   All 14 directories on CD-ROM, plus
   Internet subscription, $2,910
   annually
Description:
   14 directories of leaders in various
   segments of society; described as a
   Who's Who in leadership of the
   United States. Each directory fea-
   tures clear data in chart form
   in a variety of fields and includes
   a photo of each person listed.
   Directory titles include:
   Congressional, Federal, State,
   Municipal, Federal, Regional,

Judicial, Corporate, Financial,
News Media, Associations, Law
Firms, Government Affairs, Foreign
Representatives, and Nonprofit
Sector. The compilation of all
individual directories is called
"Leadership Library."

**9**

Title:
   **Complete Games Trainers
   Play, vol. II**
Type of resource:
   Looseleaf binder
Authors:
   Edward Scannell, John Newstrom,
   Carolyn Nilson
Publisher:
   McGraw-Hill
   11 West 19th Street
   New York, NY 10011
      800/2-McGRAW
      614/759-3644 (fax)
Publication data:
   1998, 724 pages, $110
Description:
   This is a compendium of nearly
   300 short training games and
   exercises to increase creativity
   and focus on learning. Binder
   format allows easy copying for
   class handouts. All are field tested,
   can be used in less than 30 minutes, and are inexpensive or free
   to implement. Best-selling vol. I is
   also available.

**10**

Title:
   **The Pfeiffer Annuals**
Editor:
   Elaine Beich, Consulting Editor
Publisher:
   Pfeiffer & Company
   8517 Production Ave.
   San Diego, CA 92121-2280
      800/274-4434
Publication data:
   2 volumes, $79.95 (paper); $169.95
   (looseleaf)
Description:
   Material from hundreds of authors
   is organized into experiential
   learning activities; inventories,
   questionnaires, and surveys; pre-
   sentation and discussion resources;
   and theories and models in
   applied behavioral science.
   Updated annually.

**11**

Title:
   **Stern's SourceFinder®:
   The Master Reference
   to Information Resources
   for Leadership, Strategy,
   Organization, and Human
   Resource Management**
Type of resource:
   Book (1998, 815 pages) and
   database, 2 volume set
Publisher:
   Michael Daniel Publishers
   P.O. Box 3233
   Culver City, CA 90231–3233
      310/838-4437
      310/838-2344 (fax)
Price:
   $239.95 for book and hotline
Description:
   This reference covers the whole field
   of human resource management—
   including training and development. Of the 46 chapters (which
   cover compensation, benefits, law,
   etc.), about one-third are related to
   the various aspects of human
   resource development. The 5,000
   plus entries include books, directories, professional journals, databases,
   information services, associations,
   libraries, government agencies, and
   research services—among other
   resources. Each entry consists of the
   name of the item, the address and
   phone of its source, price, date,
   length, and a 25- to 50-word
   description. There is a subject
   index (with over 9,000 entries),
   as well as indexes for titles and
   authors. Update available in 2002.

**12**

Title:
   **Soundview Executive Book
   Summaries**
Type of resource:
   Periodic book reviews of current
   business books
Publisher:
   Soundview Executive Book
      Summaries
   10 LaCrue Avenue
   Concordville, PA 19331
      800/521-1227
      800/453-5062 (fax)
Price:
   Annual subscription, $89.50
Description:
   Extensive book reviews (8 pages
   each) of current business books are

mailed monthly to subscribers. Reviewed books may also be purchased through Soundview Executive Book summaries. A large binder is provided with tabs for easy organization into categories of interest.

## 13

**Title:**
   **Business References Catalog**
**Type of resource:**
   Catalog of government publications
**Publisher:**
   U.S. Government Printing Office
   Superintendent of Documents
   Mail Stop SM
   732 N. Capitol Street, NW
   Washington, DC 20402-0003
      202/512-1800
      202/512-2250 (fax)
      www.access.gpo.gov/su_docs/
         sale/prf/prf.html
**Price:**
   Free
**Description:**
   This is a 28-page catalog of selected references of particular interest to businesses. Large databases are represented; all publications are described; many are illustrated. A sample of titles includes: The Census Catalog and Guide (344 pages); Statistical Abstract of the United States (1,044 pages); Congressional Directory including Internet and e-mail addresses (1,193 pages); Health Information for International Travel (220 pages); Education and the Economy Report (134 pages); Defense Acquisition Deskbook on CD-ROM; and Foreign Labor Trends (60-issue subscription). Prices vary for listed publications.

## Consultants

## 14

**Title:**
   **The Training Consortium**
**Type of resource:**
   Website service linking trainers to seminar providers.
   www.trainingconsortium.com
**Publisher:**
   Andrew E. Schwartz & Associates
   P.O. Box 228
   Waverly, MA 02179

617/926-9111
617/926-0660 (fax)
www.aeschwartz.com
**Price:**
   Free
**Description:**
   This service is an international link between individuals and resources including bulletin boards, e-mail, events calendar, career postings, and a variety of service providers. The site features 70 different languages, 37 types of industry including social service, education, and government, and 100 categories of expertise.

## 15

**Title:**
   **The Consulting Exchange**
**Type of resource:**
   Referral service
**Provider:**
   The Consulting Exchange
   1770 Massachusetts Avenue
   Cambridge, MA 02140
      617/576-2100
      www.cx.com
**Price:**
   Free to inquirer
**Description:**
   Covering the northeastern U.S., this firm provides referrals to consultants in all fields, but especially general management consultants, computer consultants, expert witnesses, and, of course, training consultants. The user of the service is interviewed over the phone (or on-site) to determine the need, which is then compared to information maintained in a free-text database of the capabilities of the listed consulting firms and sole practitioners. Referred consultants pay a service fee.

## 16

**Title:**
   **Consultants and Consulting Organizations Directory, 22nd Edition**
**Type of resource:**
   Book (3 volumes–4,000 pages) and database
**Publisher:**
   Gale Research Inc.
   835 Penobscot Bldg.
   645 Griswold Street
   Detroit, MI 48277-0748

   800/877-GALE or
      313/961-2242
   313/961-6083 (fax)
**Price:**
   $770 for 3-volume set
**Description:**
   This book covers 25,000 firms in over 200 fields. The data provided on each includes: name, address, phone, fax, telex, branch offices, principals, size of staff, organizational purpose, markets/clients/regions served, and services provided. There are special notations for organizations that serve the U.S. government, that serve a particular industry, and that offer international counsel. Seminars/workshops that might be offered by the firm are also noted. Four indexes are provided. The content of this directory is available online through "The Human Resource Information Network" and on diskette or magnetic tape. This reference is revised annually, and *New Consultants and Consulting Organizations* is issued 6 months after publication to update each year's directory. Published in August.

## 17

**Title:**
   **National Consultant Referrals, Inc.**
**Type of resource:**
   Referral service
**Provider:**
   National Consultant
      Referrals, Inc.
   8445 Camino Santa Fe,
      Suite 207
   San Diego, CA 92121
      800/221-3104
      619/552-0111
      619/552-0854 (fax)
      e-mail: Kline@referrals.com
      www.referrals.com
**Price:**
   Free to inquirer
**Description:**
   Representing an international network of consultants, this organization takes information from the inquirer by phone or fax. The inquirer describes the problem or project, and the NCR staff searches their database for a match. After they identify the best candidate, they call the consultant or consulting organization to confirm the fit before notifying

the inquirer. Consultants in the database are validated and verified (reference checked) beforehand and evaluated after the engagement.

# Handbooks

## 18

**Title:**
**The Trainer's Handbook, Third Edition**
**Author:**
Gary Mitchell
**Publisher:**
AMACOM
P.O. Box 1026
Saranac Lake, NY 12983
518/891-5510
**Publication data:**
1998, 428 pages, $75
**Description:**
This is a pragmatic, basic survey of training, written in a personal style. Chapters are titled: (1) The Function of Training, (2) The Object of Training, (3) The Structure of Training, (4) The Role of the Trainer, (5) Preparing a Needs Analysis, (6) Evaluating Your Effectiveness, (7) Researching the Subject Matter, (8) Writing the Training Program, (9) Alternatives to Writing Programs, (10) Setting the Physical Environment, (11) Aids to Training, (12) Computer-Based Training and Interactive Videodisc Instruction, (13) Setting the Physical Environment, (14) Managing the Training Department, (15) Special Problems in Training, (16) Marketing the Training Function, (17) Negotiations and Training, and (18) Issues in Training.

## 19

**Title:**
**1997 Computer-Based Training Report**
**Type of resource:**
Book
**Provider:**
Bill Communications
50 South Ninth Street
Minneapolis, MN 55401
800/323-4329
612/333-0471
www.ittrain.com

**Price:**
$295
**Description:**
The 1997 Computer-Based Training Report is a comprehensive study of CBT and the future of multimedia as an instructional delivery system. Based on a sample survey of over 1,100 CBT professionals, it provides answers for anyone who is responsible for producing, managing, or delivering training technology.

Topics covered include: CBT usage and budgets for different organizations, subjects taught with CBT, CBT delivery platforms, satisfaction ratings of courseware vendors and authoring systems.

## 20

**Title:**
**Handbook of Leadership Development**
**Editor/Author:**
C. D. McCauley, R. Moxley, and E. Van Velsor
**Publisher:**
Center for Creative Leadership
One Leadership Place, P.O. Box 26300
Greensboro, NC 27438
336/286-4011
336/288-3999 (fax)
www.ccl.org
**Publication data:**
1998, $65
A CCL Jossey-Bass publication
**Description:**
As a result of almost three decades of work with thousands of leaders, the Center has refined a view of leadership development that can be simply stated: it is an ongoing process, grounded in personal development and embedded in experience, and it can be facilitated by interventions that are woven into those experiences. This handbook provides strategies and practices for people responsible for or interested in the not-so-simple task of facilitating this process. Updates and leadership research report.

## 21

**Title:**
**The Complete Guide to Teams**
**Author:**
Human Technology Inc.

**Publisher:**
HRD Press
22 Amherst Rd.
Amherst, MA 01002
800/822-2801
413/253-3490 (fax)
www.hrdpress.com
**Publication Data:**
1999, 250 pages, $99.95
**Description:**
Contains over 70 tools and, resources for teams including assessments, job aids, worksheets, and troubleshooting tips.

## 22

**Title:**
**The Computer Training Handbook, Second Edition**
**Author:**
Elliott Masie
**Publisher:**
Bill Communications
50 South Ninth St.
Minneapolis, MN 55402
800/707-7769
612/340-4819 (fax)
**Publication data:**
1996, book, 286 pp., $49.00
**Description:**
This is a resource textbook providing solutions to computer training problems and hundreds of tips to help trainers with technology-based training. Check www.masie.com for current publications.

## 23

**Title:**
**The McGraw-Hill Handbook of Distance Learning**
**Authors:**
Alan Chute, Burton Hancock, Melody Thompson
**Type of Resource:**
Book
**Publisher:**
McGraw-Hill
11 West 19th Street
New York, NY 10011
800/2-McGRAW
614/759-3644 (fax)
**Publication data:**
1998, 350 pages, $39.95
**Description:**
This book shows you how to get started with videoconferencing, internal online networks, satellite broadcasting, and virtual training rooms. It includes tips and guide-

lines regarding: technology options, costs, staffing, technical support requirements, and program development and evaluation tips.

## 24

Title:
**Occupational Outlook Handbook 2000**
Editor/Author:
U.S. Department of Labor
Publisher:
U.S. Government Printing Office
Superintendent of Documents
Mail Stop M
732 N. Capitol St., N.W.
Washington, DC 20402
202/512-1800
202/512-2250 (fax)
Publication data:
560 pages, paper $49, cloth $51
Description:
This is the latest version of the classic government publication on jobs, occupations, and hiring trends. It contains detailed descriptions of more than 250 occupations—covering what the work entails, working conditions, education and training needed, earnings, job outlook, advancement potential, and related occupations. Includes 10- to 15-year projections of the labor force, economic growth, industry outlook and employment, and occupational employment.

## Online Services

## 25

Title:
**ASTD Website: astd.org**
Type of resource:
Website
Provider:
American Society for Training and Development (ASTD)
1640 King Street, Box 1443
Alexandria, VA 22313
703/683-8122
703/683-8103 (fax)
www.astd.org
Price:
Free
Description:
In addition to chat groups, job bank, and networking opportunities online, this service provides full Internet/www access and help guides developed specifically for trainers. The database includes training news, a training library of

more than 10,000 references, policy studies, information on performance improvement and technical training, buyer's guide, and job bank. This is the most comprehensive Website for trainers. See section 6.8 of this yearbook for other sites. Chapter 4 "Training Delivery" also features Websites.

## 26

Title:
**TRAINET.com**
Type of resource:
Website information center
Provider:
Linton Publishing Company
1011 First Street South
Hopkins, MN 55343
612/936-2288
www.trainet.com
Price:
Access is free
Description:
This Website is a complete and up-to-date training and development information center on the World Wide Web designed to offer a variety of information for the training professional.

Included are numerous databases allowing trainers to freely browse and locate resources as well as post requests to training consultants for products and services. Directories previously published as books are now available online. These include: Corporate Human Resources and Personnel Directory, Recommended Training Supplier and Consultant Directory, and Linton's Top 5,000 U.S. Industry Directory.

## 27

Title:
**Training Newsletters Online**
Type of resource:
Online and e-mail newsletters
Provider:
Dartnell/LRP
360 Hiatt Drive
Palm Beach Gardens, FL 83418
800/621-5463
561/622-2423
www.dartnellcorp.com
Price:
Prices vary
Description:
This is a new service of Dartnell, publisher of audios, videos, and books on sales, customer service, and teamwork. This new service is

an online newsletter service, available through e-mail or on diskette. Titles include: Teamwork, From 9 to 5, Customers First, Quality 1st, Salesmanship, Effective Telephone Techniques, Communication at Work, Small Office/Home Office Solutions, Getting Along, Successful Supervisor, and others.

## 28

Title:
**TRAINING Website: trainingsupersite.com**
Type of resource:
Website of training resources
Provider:
Lakewood Publications
50 South Ninth St.
Minneapolis, MN 55402
800/707-7769
612/340-4819 (fax)
www.trainingsupersite.com
Price:
Free
Description:
This Website is a comprehensive collection of human performance and productivity resources. Key features are a commercial center called the "Training Mall" where training products and programs are sold, and a "Learning Center" through which more than 1,000 courses can be taken and conference presentations accessed. A link to the SIS seminar and conference database is available through The Learning Center. The usual books and publications of Bill Communications and Lakewood Publications are also available for purchase online.

## 29

Title:
**TRAINSEEK.com**
Type of resource:
Online product catalog
Provider:
TrainSeek.com
University of Utah Research Park
295 Chipeta Way, 1st Floor
Salt Lake City, UT 84108
888/799-3030
801/303-3901 (fax)
Price:
Free online previews
Description:
This is an online catalog of training products and services, annotated and reviewed for easy

comparison among vendors. Videos, CD-ROMS, and instructor-led programs are featured.

## 30

Title:
**VIRTUAL LEARN.COM**
Type of resource:
Online product catalog
Provider:
Virtual Learn
1611 Telegraph Ave, Ste. 500
Oakland, CA 94612
510/302-6100
Price:
Free searching
Description:
This Website contains thousands of products and services and features peer and expert reviews of listings. Streaming video previews are available. Virtual Learn's vision is "to be the largest provider of out sourced training services worldwide."

## 31

Title:
**Enhanced academic journals**
Publisher:
MCB University Press
P.O. Box 10812
Birmingham, AL 35201
888/622-0075
205/995-1588 (fax)
www.mcb.co/uk
Type of resource:
Journals enhanced with CD-ROM Abstract and Archive site licenses, Internet Continuous Publishing Domain name licenses, and Full Internet Archive capability.
Price:
Enhanced journals range in price from $300 to $6,000
Description:
Academic journals of interest to training and development professionals are electronically enhanced to provide researchers with instant access to journal editions as far back as 1993. Document delivery of full text articles is included in the purchase price. The CD-ROM archive permits interactive search by subject, type of material, and quality level. Journal titles include: *Industrial & Commercial Training, Journal of European Industrial Training, Journal*

*of Management Development, Leadership & Organization Development Journal, Training for Quality*, and *Training & Management Development Methods.*

## 32

Title:
**ERIC® (Educational Resources Information Center)**
Provider:
U.S. Department of Education
Office of Educational Research and Improvement
ERIC ACVE/Center on Employment
1900 Kenny Road
Columbus, OH 43210-1090
800/848-4815
614/292-4353
614/292-1260 (fax)
www.cete.org
www.ericacve.org
Type of resource:
Online information service
Description:
Begun in 1966 as a project of the U.S. Dept. of Education and converted into an online database in 1972, *ERIC* houses about 700,000 records. These consist of abstracts from 800 education and education-related journals, as well as conference proceedings, papers, research materials, and other unpublished documents. The number of access points to *ERIC* is increasing. In addition, there are several access points to *ERIC* via the Internet. For instructions and a current list, call ACCESS ERIC at 800/538-3742 or send a message to askeric@ericir. syr.edu.

## Seminar Databases

## 33

Title:
**Leadership Education: A Source Book, 8th edition**
Type of resource:
Book
Publisher:
Center for Creative Leadership
P.O. Box 26300
Greensboro, NC 27438-6300
336/288-7210
336/288-3999 (fax)
www.ccl.org
Price:
Vol. 1 $40, Vol. 2 $40, 2-vol. set $70

Description:
Designed as a complete reference to leadership education, nearly half of this book is devoted to detailed descriptions of leadership courses and programs offered by colleges, universities, and other selected organizations. Another section of the book covers instruments, exercises, simulations, and games for leadership education. A Leadership Bibliography gives summaries of 1,000 books and journal articles, and there is also a directory of 130 films and videos. Some 300 professionals in the field are profiled in a Resource Persons Directory, and 80 organizations (associations, institutes, foundations) are described in a Resource Organizations Directory. The final directory lists dozens of annual leadership events. Extensive detail is provided for each item in the directory, and indexes provide subject, author, name, and institutional access to all sections.

## 34

Title:
**The 2001 Corporate University Evaluation Guide to Executive Programs**

**The 2001 Corporate University Guide to Management Seminars**
Type of resource:
Binder manuals, 500+ pages each
Publisher:
The Corporate University Press
P.O. Box 2080, 504 N. 4th St.
Fairfield, IA 52556
800/255-1261
515/472-7105 (fax)
Price:
$295 per binder
Description:
These guides cover training seminars in the U.S. and worldwide provided by universities and independent seminar providers. Programs are categorized into approximately a dozen fields and provide evaluative comments from program participants and others. The same information is available on CD-ROM or through the web page www.hrsoft.com. at $400 per user per year. Quantity discounts are available.

## 35

Title:
**SMART OPTIONS**
Type of resource:
Seminar Registration and
Accounting Service
Provider:
First Seminar
175 Cabot St.
Lowell, MA 08154
978/452-0766
978/441-2755 (fax)
www.firstseminar.com
Price:
Free information; $250 application
fee
Description:
Preferred Customers of First
Seminar's SMART OPTIONS
Service are provided full and
unlimited access to its Database of
instructor-led training, National
Registration Center, and a single
source for payment on all training
processed through First Seminar.

First Seminar adds to and
updates its SMART OPTIONS database on a daily basis. Information
includes over 250,000 training
offerings being sponsored by
nearly 1,000 of the nation's best
companies. Searches can be conducted by any of 7,000 keywords
or topics, time frame, and location
of choice. Once an employee
chooses the training best suited for
their needs, First Seminar will
process the enrollment and confirm the registration through its
National Registration Center.

First Seminar also provides a
consolidated billing system.
Streamlining the accounting
process directly saves resources
and time for preferred companies
Accounts Payable Departments.

## 36

Title:
**Bricker's International
Directory: University-Based
Executive Programs 2001**
Type of resource:
Book
Publisher:
Peterson's Thompson Learning
202 Carnegie Center
P.O. Box 2123
Princeton, NJ 08543–2123
800/338-3282 or
609/243-9111
609/243-9150 (fax)

Price:
$395
Description:
This guide appears annually in
October, presenting information on
some 720 university-based executive development programs (from
92 institutions) for mid- to upper-
level executives, ranging from 2
days to up to a year in length. Each
program is described in at least a
page, covering data such as the
sponsoring organization, location,
dates/duration, course objectives,
key topics, methods of instruction,
profile of participants, faculty, facilities, program contact, and special
features offered.

## 37

Title:
**Seminar Clearinghouse
International Inc.**
Type of resource:
Telephone service, database, and
seminar registration service
Provider:
Seminar Clearinghouse
International Inc.
P.O. Box 1757
St. Paul, MN 55101-0757
612/293-1044
612/293-0492 (fax)
800/927-0502
Price:
$55 per search; $27 each for 100 or
more
Description:
Clients of this service can get
information on seminars,
videos/training films and consultants over the phone, or by fax.
In providing this personal service,
SCI draws on a number of information resources to meet a client's
particular training resource need.
In SCI's databases, there is information on about 29,000 seminar
titles (including public and on-site
seminars) comprising about
60,000 events. The most significant part of the firm's service
is the database of seminar
evaluations (plus instructor/
speaker evaluations) contributed
by clients. SCI also offers a service, Training Information
Management System, which cen-
tralizes all external seminar
enrollments. SCI performs all
administrative responsibilities
related to attendances including
enrollment, registration fee pay-

ments, tracking, reporting, and
evaluating. It is a comprehensive,
quality-driven system that provides organizations with the tools
to manage their training costs.

## 38

Title:
**SIS Electronic**
Type of resource:
Database; CD-ROM updated every
3 months
Publisher:
Seminar Information Service, Inc.
17752 Skypark Circle, Suite 210
Irvine, CA 92714
949/261-9104
949/261-1963 (fax)
Price:
$295
Description:
This CD-ROM covers thousands of
business and technical seminars.
Both public and in-house programs
are included. They are listed by
topic (e.g. "general management:
time/stress management"), then
alphabetically by sponsor, then in
a calendar format. Data includes a
1- to 3-sentence description, the
fee, the sponsor, contact information, and the date and location.
Evaluative information is available
for selected seminars. Some
100,000 separate events from over
500 sponsors are tracked. Formerly
published in workbook format as
an annual.

## 39

Title:
**Distance Learning Directory**
Type of resource:
Book (about 225 pages in length)
8th edition, 2000
Publisher:
Virginia A. Ostendorf, Inc.
P.O. Box 2896
Littleton, CO 80161-2896
303/797-3131
303/797-3524 (fax)
Price:
$250
Description:
This directory covers scheduled
live instructional programs that are
delivered at a distance. The types
of programs include corporate
training, medical topics, K 12,
higher education, formal degree
programs, continuing education,
certification, etc. A wide variety of

technologies are represented: audiographic programs and courses, computer conferencing, and full motion video (including satellite, microwave, fiber optics, and cable delivery). Lists vendors, products, and services.

## Toolbooks

### 40

Title:
**How to Manage Training, 2nd edition: A Guide to Design and Delivery for High Performance**
Author:
Carolyn Nilson
Publisher:
AMACOM Books
P.O. Box 169
Saranac Lake, NY 12983
800/250-5308
518/891-3653
Publication Data:
1997, 304 pages, $75.00
Description:
This handbook covers the details of setting up and running a training operation. More than 100 forms and checklists, graphics, and models are presented in a looseleaf binder for easy copying and adaptation. The book includes an extensive annotated bibliography representing a historical and current view of thinkers from Deming, Bloom, Maslow, Gilbert, Gagne, Guilford to Senge, Blanchard, Kirkpatrick, Robinson, and Gery.

### 41

Title:
**Distance Learning: A Step-by-Step Guide for Trainers**
Authors:
Karen Mantyla and J. Richard Gividen
Type of resource:
Book
Publisher:
American Society for Training and Development (ASTD)
1640 King Street, Box 1443
Alexandria, VA 22313
703/683-8100
410/516-6998 (fax)
Publication data:
1997, 179 pages, $45.00

Description:
This book examines distance learning from three perspectives: the learner, the trainer, and the manager. It includes templates, checklists, and job aids for creating and managing distance learning events. Topics include interactive audio and interactive video conferencing, CBT, Internet and Intranet based training.

### 42

Title:
**How to Start a Training Program: Training Is a Strategic Tool in Any Organization**
Author:
Carolyn Nilson
Type of resource:
Book
Publisher:
American Society for Training and Development (ASTD)
1640 King Street, Box 1443
Alexandria, VA 22313
703/683-8100
410/516-6998 (fax)
Publication data:
1999, 231 pages, $32.00
Description:
This book is a practical guide to setting up a training program. It covers: creating a business plan, developing training standards and writing policy, setting budgets, and introducing the program in your company. It also includes designing and delivering training courses and programs, evaluating training, and focusing on performance. Numerous interviews and case studies illustrate and supplement the how-to ideas.

### 43

Title:
**Info-line**
Type of resource:
Series of booklets, each 16–20 pages, 8 1/2″ × 11″
Publisher:
American Society for Training and Development (ASTD)
1640 King Street, Box 1443
Alexandria, VA 22313
800/628-2783
888/628-5329 (fax)
Price:
Annual subscription $119; single issue $10; quantity discounts

Description:
The Info-line series are single-issue/topic publications produced by training practitioners throughout the year. Currently more than 150 topics are available. Many titles are available in Spanish. The series features step-by-step guidelines, how-to tips, diagrams and illustrations, job-aids, worksheets, templates, forms, checklists, reference lists, mini-case studies of practical applications. Recent topics include: knowledge management, Group Decision Making, Learning Technologies, Successful Global Training, Selecting a Coach, Training Telecommuters, Service Management, and many others. Info-line collections are also available at $75 each on a single topic, for example, evaluation.

### 44

Title:
**The ASTD Media Selection Tool for Workplace Learning**
Author:
Raymond J. Marx
Type of resource:
Book and CD-ROM
Publisher:
American Society for Training and Development (ASTD)
1640 King Street, Box 1443
Alexandria, VA 22313
703/683-8100
410/516-6998 (fax)
Publication data:
1999, 158 pages, $49.95
Description:
This book and CD-ROM on media selection includes practical job aids and questionnaires to help the trainer choose the best delivery option. Customizable spreadsheets are included for cost comparison studies. Topics include: development time, development cost, equipment and facility requirements, maintenance issues, business and financial factors in media selection, and integrated delivery. References are provided to Web resources and URL links.

### 45

Title:
**ASTD Toolkits**
Author:
ASTD editors

**Publisher:**
American Society for Training & Developing (ASTD)
P.O. Box 4856, Hampden Station
Baltimore, MD 21211
703/683-8100
410/516-6998 (fax)
**Publication data:**
$59.00 each; Publication dates range from 1990–2000
**Description:**
This is a series of books containing samples of materials used by trainers throughout the U.S. The books have been compiled by ASTD's Information Center in response to requests for original documents, forms, and job aids in actual use by trainers. Each Toolkit contains related journal articles and a bibliography. Titles include: Lesson Plans, Needs Assessment Instruments, Project Plans, Evaluation Instruments, Job Descriptions, Mission Statements, Educational Assistance Policies, and others.

## 46

**Title:**
**The Internet Trainer's Guide**
**Type of resource:**
Book
**Author:**
Diane K. Kovacs
**Publisher:**
John Wiley & Sons
605 Third Avenue
New York, NY 10158
800/225-5945
800/597-3299 (fax)
**Publication data:**
1997, $34.95
**Description:**
This is both a handbook of Internet resources for trainers and training designers and a guide book detailing how to build your own Internet training. Appendices are particularly useful and include: (A) Bibliography of training design readings, (B) Directory of Selected Internet Tutorials and Training Materials on the Internet, (C) Directory of Selected Internet Resources and Internet Resources Finding Tools, and (D) Directory of Selected Internet Software Sources. Sold with a disk included.

## 47

**Title:**
**Web-Based Training Cookbook**

**Author:**
Brandon Hall
**Type of resource:**
Book and CD-ROM
**Publisher:**
John Wiley & Sons
605 Third Avenue
New York, NY 10158
800/225-5945
800/597-3299 (fax)
**Publication data:**
1997, 482 pages, $49.99
**Description:**
This is a handbook for trainers, information technology professionals, and multimedia developers. It is organized in 4 parts: (1) Introduction to the basics; (2) Steps involved in setting up a WBT program; (3) Integration of parts 1 and 2 with working examples of WBT courses; (4) Sample proposal for WBT, evaluation criteria for WBT, and legal issues to consider in WBT. The CD-ROM with the book provides demos of an online testing program, an HTML training site, and a sample multimedia program.

## 48

**Title:**
**A Trainer's Guide to the World Wide Web: Using the Web and Intranets**
**Author:**
Wendy Webb
**Publisher:**
Bill Communications
50 South Ninth St.
Minneapolis, MN 55402
800/707-7769
612/340-4819 (fax)
**Publication data:**
1996, 175 pages, $39.95
**Description:**
The book contains case studies and advice from peers and experts on how to design training for this mode of delivery. Included are: tips for ensuring security of web pages, how to find your way around, and a complete list of design resources.

## 49

**Title:**
**The Performance Consulting Toolbook**
**Author:**
Carolyn Nilson

**Type of resource:**
Book
**Publisher:**
McGraw-Hill
11 West 19th St.
New York, NY 10011
800/2-McGRAW
614/759-3644 (fax)
**Publication data:**
1999, 259 pages, $39.95
**Description:**
This is a book of tools designed to help trainers think like performance consultants. It provides step-by-step exercises, activities, checklists, questionnaires, charts and forms for individual use in making the transition from trainer to performance consultant.

## Training Suppliers

## 50

**Title:**
**ASTD Buyer's Guide and Consultant Directory (Annual)**
**Type of resource:**
Book (350 pages)
**Publisher:**
American Society for Training and Development
1640 King St., Box 1443
Alexandria, VA 22313
703/683-8100
703/683-1523 (fax)
www.astd.org
**Price:**
$85
**Description:**
This directory lists over 700 providers of training services alphabetically with name, address, phone, and contact person. Each supplier describes its firm and its products and services in its own words, with a special notation regarding the type of media and services of subject areas in which they provide (1) consulting services, (2) off-the-shelf courseware, (3) custom-designed courseware (if any), (4) continuing education, (5) workshops/seminars, (6) equipment/supplies/furniture, and (7) training media. Some 300 subject terms are used to annotate these products and services. Suppliers are cross-indexed by geographical location, industry specialty (if any), and subject. Subjects are further annotated to indicate whether the

supplier offers: computer-based materials, correspondence/home study, games/simulations, instructor-led training, printed materials, videodisc/CD-ROM, and videotape/films. The book is published every January.

## 51

Title:
**2001 Select Guide to Human Resource Executives**
Type of resource:
Directory/Book and CD-ROM
Publisher:
Hunt-Scanlon Publishing Company
One East Putnam Ave.
Greenwich, CT 06830
    800/477-1199
    203/629-3701 (fax)
    www.hunt-scanlon.com
Price:
$245
Description:
This directory lists over 23,000 human resources executives at 9,500 leading companies in the U.S. The CD-ROM features searching by 14 different criteria, including name, title, business sector, SIC code, and others. The listing includes the title "Manager Training and Development."

## Videos, Films, Audiotapes

## 52

Title:
**TRAINING Conference Audiotapes**
Type of resource:
    Audiotapes from Lakewood's Annual TRAINING Conference
Provider:
    Audio Transcripts, Ltd.
    3660-B Wheeler Avenue
    Alexandria, VA 22304
        703/370-8273
        703/370-5162 (fax)
Price:
    $12 each tape; $2.00 shipping
Description:
    Audio Transcripts, Ltd. (ATL) produces audiotapes directly from keynote speeches and breakout sessions. Approximately 150 audiotapes are available. A complete listing is available through atltapes@aol.com.

## 53

Title:
**The Multimedia and Videodisc Compendium**
Type of resource:
    Book (208 pages) 2001 edition
Publishers:
    Emerging Technology Consultants, Inc.
    2819 Hamline Ave. North
    St. Paul, MN 55113
        651/639-3973
        651/639-0110 (fax)
Price:
    $69.95 with index diskette
Description:
    This publication covers over 5,000 titles (videodiscs, CDs, and multimedia software) from more than 350 producers. The programs included are those which are suitable for school/college and business training and healthcare purposes, and they are categorized into 24 major subject areas, including the categories of training, authoring systems, and presentation systems. Each listing includes up to a 100-word description, price, level of interactivity, audience, and producer contact information. Published in January.

## 54

Title:
**SHRM Conference Audiotapes**
Type of resource:
    Audiotapes from the Annual Conference of Society for Human Resource Management (SHRM)
Publisher:
    InfoMedia
    12800 Garden Grove Blvd., Suite F
    Garden Grove, CA 92843
        800/367-9286
        714/537-3244 (fax)
Price:
    $10 each tape; $1.00 shipping
Description:
    InfoMedia produces audiotapes directly from keynote speeches and breakout sessions. Approximately 100 tapes are available. If you buy 6 tapes, you get the 7th one free.

## 55

Title:
**The Directory of Video, Computer, and Audio Visual Products**

Publisher:
    Pacific Technologies
    9221 Flint Ave.
    Overland Park, KS 66214
        800/255-6038
        913/492-2085 (fax)
Type of resource:
    Website www.avavenue.com
Price:
    $50
Description:
    This directory covers over 250 categories of equipment with over 2,500 products, and it includes a complete glossary. Over 400 manufacturers and 800 dealers are represented. Some of the categories include: video (presentation units, monitors, projectors, cameras, VCRs), slide/transparency viewing equipment, projection/video screens, slide projectors (silent, sound, random access), overhead and opaque projectors, filmstrip projectors and viewers, sound motion picture projectors (8mm, 16mm, 35mm), multi-image (dissolves, programmers, racks), interactive video, computer-generated graphics systems, and audio equipment (mixers, sound systems, lecterns, tape duplicators and recorders). There are illustrated and unillustrated sections of the directory. In the illustrated section, the following data is provided: suggested list price, model number, weight, capacity, features, applications, accessories, and other technical details.

## 56

Title:
**Marketplace Directory: Training Presentation Products**
Publisher:
    Bill Communications
    50 South Ninth St.
    Lakewood Building
    Minneapolis, MN 55402
        612/333-0471
Type of resource:
    Magazine feature (a supplement to the November issue of *TRAINING Magazine*)
Price:
    $6 cost for non-subscribers
Description:
    The latest edition of this annual directory covers hundreds of suppliers of: audio, computer/multimedia, furniture/fixtures,

presentation aids/packaging, slides, video, visual projection, rental equipment, services, and computer software. Each of these areas is further subdivided to get 180 product categories in all. An address, phone, and contact person are provided for each vendor.

## 57

**Title:**
**ASTD Audio and Videotapes Collection**

**Type of resource:**
Audio/Videotapes from ASTD Conferences Catalog of tapes
**Publisher:**
Mobiltape Company Inc.
24730 Avenue Tibbitts,
    Suite 170
Valencia, CA 91355
    800/369-5718
    661/295-8474 (fax)
**Price:**
Audiotapes: members of ASTD $13 each, plus $1.50 shipping; non-members, $16.50 each, plus $1.50

shipping; Videotapes $69.95 each, plus shipping $4.00
**Description:**
Mobiltape Company Inc. reproduces sessions presented by conference speakers and makes them available to members and non-members of sponsoring associations. The pricing structure and reference listed here are for current ASTD conferences. Phone Mobiltape for other conferences recorded by them.

# THE TRAINER'S ALMANAC

## SECTION 6.7

## TRAINING JOURNALS, MAGAZINES, AND NEWSLETTERS

Any experienced trainer is well aware that there is a flood of training publications vying for his or her attention. In a way, this whole book is a testament to the incredible volume of HRD media, and in this section of *The Trainer's Almanac* we list the journals, magazines, and newsletters that especially serve the training field. Of course, many of the popular business magazines, such as *Business Week, Fortune, Newsweek, Fast Company*, and *Brill's Content* have articles and features of particular interest to trainers. These magazines are not listed here; these general business magazines are easy to find on newsstands and store shelves everywhere, and on the Internet. See the frontmatter pages of this book for addresses of these general business magazines and other training-focused magazines that have informed this *Training & Development Yearbook 2001.*

### Content to Lead You Forward
We have compiled the key information on each publication, including a description of its editorial thrust. One of our objectives is to simply give you enough information to contact a publication that may have been difficult to find. No doubt, also, you will discover some titles in the following directory that you were unaware of, but which may well suit your needs. We can also imagine readers using these listings to prepare subscription budgets, assess the completeness of the department library, or facilitate the development of individual trainers and trainees. All prices are for subscriptions addressed to U.S. addresses; rates for foreign subscribers are higher to reflect mailing costs. If you are interested in examining a certain publication, you will find that almost all publishers offer a complimentary sample issue.

Trends this year include a proliferation of online newsletters. Some former paper-based periodicals are now available online only and some are in transition from paper to digital format. Some online newsletters are free, others are available by subscription only. We list some of the important ones here. Check publishers' Websites to see what's new. ASTD's *Technical and Skills Training* magazine and Bill Communications' (formerly Lakewood Publications) *Training Directors Forum* newsletter are examples. AMA's *Management Review* is now a members-only publication and now only online.

Also, large management consulting companies, and some smaller ones too, are increasing their publication efforts, both online and via paper periodical newsletters, reports, and magazine-like publications. We include some of these here too. Booz-Allen & Hamilton's *Strategy and Business*, Berlitz's *Global Voice*, and Elliott Masie's *TechLearn Trends* are examples.

As the blurring of news and entertainment is on TV, so the blurring of advertisement and information in our periodicals offline and online has increased this year especially. Readers simply have to become more astute at recognizing these important points of view, and in many cases, themselves must perform the function of peer review board or editor.

### Further Indexed in 22 Categories
We present the publications in alphabetical order by title of publication. However, to help you target specific publications of interest, we have also indexed the 62 entries in this section according to their editorial content. We have not tried to index every topic a journal or newsletter typically has; instead, we have indexed according to the publication's specialty. Note, therefore, that the most widely known training journals and magazines are grouped together under "general training topics." Fifty-two publications are indexed here in 22 categories. This is the most comprehensive focused listing of periodicals in the field.

## INDEX TO EDITORIAL COVERAGE

**Career development**
4, 5, 6, 24

**Computer-based training**
11, 12, 26, 27, 29, 39, 54

**Corporate universities**
7, 8

**Distance learning**
2, 13

**Diversity**
10, 15, 16

**Executive education**
3, 14, 17, 18, 28, 30, 48, 49, 51, 52, 53

**Games**
9, 55

**General training topics**
19, 20, 21, 22, 33, 34, 35, 36,
42, 43, 44, 48, 57, 58, 61, 62

**Higher education**
13, 54

**Instructional design**
10, 11, 26, 27, 33, 34, 40, 42, 43, 60

**Internet/Intranet/Web-Based training**
28, 33, 34, 47, 60

**International/global**
12, 15, 16, 25, 47, 48, 51, 52, 62

**Knowledge management**
28, 34, 49, 51, 52

**Leadership**
1, 14, 16, 17, 18, 21, 28, 29, 30, 31, 34, 35, 36,
41, 42, 43, 49, 51, 52, 54, 57

**Literacy**
15, 50

**Management development**
3, 14, 16, 17, 18, 19, 20, 21, 28, 29, 30, 31, 32, 34, 36,
37, 38, 40, 41, 42, 43, 47, 51, 54, 56, 57, 58, 61, 62

**Multimedia**
26, 27, 29, 40, 54, 59

**Organization development**
31, 35, 38, 41, 51, 52, 53, 56, 57, 61

**Performance improvement**
23, 42, 43, 56, 61

**Research on training and learning**
2, 4, 5, 12, 13, 20, 21, 23, 24, 25, 26, 27, 43, 54

**Technical training**
33, 34, 38, 39, 47, 54, 59, 60

**Quality**
45, 46

### 1

**Publication Title:**
**Across the Board**
**Publisher:**
The Conference Board
P.O. Box 4026
Church Street Station
New York, NY 10261
212/759-0900
212/980-7014 (fax)
**Issue Frequency:**
10/yr.
**Price:**
$45
**Description:**
This magazine features articles that further the purpose of The Conference Board, that is, "to improve the business enterprise system and to enhance the contribution of business to society." Contributors are frequently high-profile business leaders. Content covers a wide range of current issues of concern to human resource leaders.

### 2

**Publication Title:**
**The American Journal of Distance Education**

**Publisher:**
Penn State University
College of Education
403 S. Allen St., Suite 206
University Park, PA 16801-5202
814/863-3764
814/865-5878 (fax)
www.ed.psu.edu/ACSDE
**Issue Frequency:**
3/yr.
**Price:**
$75 institutional; $45 personal
**Description:**
This journal's stated purpose is "to disseminate information and act as a forum for criticism and debate about research in and practice of distance education in the Americas." Defining "distance education" as "teaching-learning relationships in which the actors are geographically separated and communication between them is achieved through such media as radio and television programs, audio and video recordings, personal computers, various types of teleconferences, and correspondence texts," this journal is aimed at professional trainers, adult educators, communication specialists, and professionals in higher and continuing education and in

public schools. In addition to referred articles, each issue contains a mixture of editorials, opinion pieces by readers, interviews, and reviews of books and other media.

### 3

**Publication Title:**
**Bulletin to Management**
**Publisher:**
Bureau of National Affairs (BNA)
1231 25th Street, NW
Washington, DC 20037
800/372-1033
www.bna.com
**Issue Frequency:**
Bi-weekly
**Price:**
$225
**Description:**
This is one of a group of newsletters that focus on developments in federal legislation, regulatory agencies, and in corporate issues around what's new in Washington. Other BNA newsletters include *Policy & Practice, Union Labor Report, HR Practitioners Guide,* and others. CD-ROM and online versions are available

## 4

**Publication Title:**
**The Career Development Quarterly**
**Publisher:**
National Career Development Association
4700 Reed Rd., Suite M
Columbus, OH 43220
888/326-1750 (toll free)
800/633-4931
614/326-1760 (fax)
**Issue Frequency:**
Quarterly
**Price:**
Free to NCDA and American Counseling Association members; non-member prices $67
**Description:**
Each issue of this journal includes 7–10 articles on research, theory, and practice in the field of career development. Some of the specific areas covered include career counseling, occupational resources, labor market dynamics, career education, and work and leisure. Occasionally, special issues are published, and recent topics have been "Career Development of Racial and Ethnic Minorities" and "Work and Family Issues." The objective of the journal is to foster career development through the design and use of career interventions in educational institutions, in community and government agencies, and in business and industry settings.

## 5

**Publication Title:**
**Career Planning and Adult Development Journal**
**Publisher:**
Career Planning and Adult Development Network
4965 Sierra Rd.
San Jose, CA 95132
408/559-4946
408/559-8211 (fax)
**Issue Frequency:**
Quarterly, 4/year
**Price:**
Part of Network membership or $7.50 each
**Description:**
Addressing an audience of human resource professionals, career counselors, educators, and researchers, this journal consists of full-length articles on career planning and

development. Most issues are thematic, and recent topics have been: comprehensive career assessments, using interest assessment instruments, temperament and type in career counseling, tools for life planning and development, outplacement, the work-leisure connection, succession planning, managing a counseling practice, mentoring, and computers in career counseling. Occasionally, an entire issue is devoted to a bibliography on some aspect of career development. Many issues also include one or more book reviews.

## 6

**Publication Title:**
**Career Planning and Adult Development Newsletter**
**Publisher:**
Career Planning and Adult Development Network
4965 Sierra Rd.
San Jose, CA 95132
408/559-4946
408/559-8211 (fax)
**Issue Frequency:**
Monthly
**Price:**
Part of Network membership. $49 Free sample.
**Description:**
This 8-page newsletter is the primary communication vehicle for members of the Career Planning and Adult Development Network, an organization of career counselors, human resource professionals, educators, and researchers. Each issue highlights lengthy announcements of forthcoming workshops and seminars, as well as meetings and conferences. Other features include news of the field, job listings, book reviews, and resources for counselors. The Network publishes many career planning books. Call for catalog.

## 7

**Publication Title:**
**Corporate University Review**
**Publisher:**
H R Events
150 Clove Rd.
P.O. Box 401
Little Falls, NJ 07424
800/882-8684
973/256-0205

**Issue Frequency:**
6/yr.
**Price:**
$295
**Description:**
This is a magazine about organizational learning and performance. The particular focus of the publication is the corporate university, but articles include features on employee training programs and processes in general. Information about new products, services, and job opportunities is also included.

## 8

**Publication Title:**
**Corporate University Xchange**
**Publisher:**
Corporate University Xchange
381 Park Avenue So., Ste. 713
New York, NY 10016
212/213-2828
212/213-8621 (fax)
**Issue Frequency:**
6/yr.
**Price:**
$199/yr.; $99 for non-profit organizations
**Description:**
This newsletter is published and edited by Jeanne C. Meister, author of *Corporate Quality Universities: Lessons in Building a World-Class Work Force*. The newsletter addresses the corporate university concept in the broadest sense, dealing with all aspects of continuous intentional learning in the workplace. Some of the recent topics include: the results of the *Corporate University Xchange Annual Survey of 100 Corporate University Deans* on the future direction of corporate universities, a new paradigm for leadership development as reported in a research monograph from Penn State Institute for the Study of Organizational Effectiveness. *Corporate University Xchange* also publishes several research monographs on topics uncovered in *Corporate University Xchange Annual Survey*. Upcoming research monographs will examine best practice alliances between corporate universities and conventional universities and how to promote a commitment for individual employee self-development.

## 9

**Publication Title:**
  **Creative Training Techniques**
**Publisher:**
  Bill Communications
  50 South Ninth St.
  Lakewood Building
  Minneapolis, MN 55402
    800/383-9210
    612/333-0471
    612/333-6526 (fax)
**Issue Frequency:**
  Monthly
**Price:**
  $99 per year
**Description:**
  Edited by experienced trainer Bob Pike, this 8-page newsletter consists of practical ideas on training that don't require major redesigns or large capital expenditures. Addressed to the stand-up trainer, *Creative Training Techniques* consists of short items on classroom techniques (e.g., ice breakers, motivation, use of audiovisuals), administration, evaluation, new products, etc. There is also a "tip of the month," a book review section, and a question-and-answer column, and a new department called "Covering Technology for Learning."

## 10

**Publication Title:**
  **Cultural Diversity at Work**
**Publisher:**
  The GilDeane Group
  13751 Lake City Way, N.E.,
    Suite 106
  Seattle, WA 98125-3615
    206/362-0336
    206/363-5028 (fax)
    www.diversitycentral.com
**Issue Frequency:**
  Newsletter
  Bulletin
**Price:**
  $99/yr. (includes newsletter, bulletin, and access to interactive worldwide diversity forum)
**Description:**
  This online newsletter, subtitled "Preparing You for Managing, Training, and Conducting Business in the Global Age," explores the fabric of cultural differences in the workplace and marketplace. Each issue seeks answers to the question, "How can diverse people work together and conduct busi-

ness effectively?" Focusing on the new strategies, new skills, and new perspectives all people must acquire for a multicultural work environment, articles offer solutions from both the training and learning viewpoints. Each issue centers on a theme. Past themes include: multicultural skills for managers, diversity and cross-cultural trainers (Do they know what they're doing?), misinterpreting behavior and resolving conflict, and recruiting diverse employees. The newsletter includes practical tips and techniques for managers of diverse employees, applications of intercultural communication skills, case studies, resource reviews, and model programs. Contributing writers include diversity and cross-cultural consultants, internal diversity managers, and international human resource managers. The *Bulletin* is a monthly listing of workshops, conferences/meetings, and related announcements on diversity/cross-cultural topics and issues.

## 11

**Publication Title:**
  **Educational Technology**
**Publisher:**
  Educational Technology Publishers
  700 Palisade Ave.
  Englewood Cliffs, NJ 07632-0564
    201/871-4007
    201/871-4009 (fax)
**Issue Frequency:**
  6/year
**Price:**
  $119 ($139 overseas)
**Description:**
  This magazine deals with all aspects of the use of technology in education and training, including, but not restricted to, instructional system design, computer and video-based technologies such as interactive video, multimedia, expert systems, and artificial intelligence. The publication is directed to both the business and educational communities, and the number of articles devoted to training (as opposed to education) has risen in recent years. One unique feature of *Educational Technology* is about half of its readership is outside the U.S., and many of its articles are contributed from this international readership. The editorial content of

the magazine includes: case studies/applications, essays on the state of educational technology, reports of research, reviews of products (including software), reviews of books, organizational news, news of people in the field, and a new research section. It publishes a number of special issues each year on various aspects of work in the field.

## 12

**Publication Title:**
  **Educational Technology Research and Development**
**Publisher:**
  Association for Educational Communications and Technology (AECT)
  1800 North Stone Lake Dr., Suite 2
  Bloomington, IN 47404
    812/335-7675
    812/335-7678 (fax)
**Issue Frequency:**
  Quarterly
**Price:**
  $65
**Description:**
  This journal consists of refereed articles on research (in educational technology) and development (i.e., instructional development and other applications of educational technology). In addition, each issue features one or more formal book reviews, "international reviews" (profiles of educational technology applications from around the world), and "research abstracts" culled from the ERIC database.

## 13

**Publication Title:**
  **Educom Review**
**Publisher:**
  EDUCAUSE
  1112 16th St., NW, Ste. 600
  Washington, DC 20036
    202/872-4200
    202/872-4318 (fax)
**Issue Frequency:**
  6/year
**Price:**
  $24
**Description:**
  Articles in this magazine focus on learning, communications, and information technology. Content generally deals with issues of con-

cern to higher education and university students and faculty.

## 14

Publication Title:
**Executive Book Summaries**
Publisher:
Soundview Executive Book
Summaries
3 Pond Lane
Middlebury, VT 05753–1164
800/521-1227
800/453-5062 (fax)
Issue Frequency:
12/year
Price:
$89.50
Description:
This is a monthly publication of book reviews, two or three of which are extensive (6–8 pages) on featured current, high-interest books. In addition to the main selections, 6–10 additional books are highlighted with brief reviews. The editorial staff and board review approximately 100 books per month and choose the books they feature from among the latest proofs, manuscripts, and books on current management issues, including many of interest to trainers.

## 15

Publication Title:
**Global Voice**
Publisher:
Berlitz International Inc.
400 Alexander Park
Princeton, NJ 08540
800/528-8908
www.berlitz.com
Issue Frequency:
Quarterly
Price:
Free
Description:
This 6-page newsletter, while a promotional tool for Berlitz language services, contains good information and case studies about a variety of language training options and situations

## 16

Publication Title:
**Global Workforce**
Publisher:
ACC Communications
245 Fischer Ave., B-2
Costa Mesa, CA 92626

714/751-1883
714/751-4106
www.workforceonline.com
Issue Frequency:
12/year
Price:
Provided as a free supplement to *Workforce* magazine which costs $59 per year, or at a cost of $8 per issue
Description:
Global issues in the workforce are featured exclusively in this new magazine. These include: culture and language training, expatriate and dual-career spouse services, global competency development, workforce travel and communication, and more. Advertising within the magazine is geared to global needs.

## 17

Publication Title:
**Harvard Business Review**
Publisher:
Harvard Business Review
60 Harvard Way
Boston, MA 02163
800/988-0886
617/496-1029 (fax)
Issue Frequency:
6/year
Price:
$95 (1 yr)
Description:
*Harvard Business Review* is a publication of ideas and stories about solving business problems across a range of industries. Contributors include well-known business persons, consultants, and professors. *HBR* is often full of articles of interest to trainers and to human resources development management. Particularly popular and unique are the "Executive Summaries" of key articles, a book review section, an extensive case study with interpretations, and a Letters to the Editor section which is always worth reading.

## 18

Publication Title:
**Harvard Management Update**
Publisher:
Harvard Business School
Publishing
P.O. Box 305
Shrub Oak, NY 10588

800/988-0886
617/496-1029 (fax)
Issue Frequency:
12/year, monthly
Price:
$99
Description:
Billed as a newsletter for "people with managerial responsibilities, particularly people who are still working their way toward the corner office," this newsletter is for middle managers. Negotiating: dealing with problem employees, and getting results are some of the issues addressed by contributing writers. The publication is especially appropriate for training managers and consultants.

## 19

Publication Title:
**HR Magazine**
Publisher:
Society for Human Resource
Management (SHRM)
606 N. Washington St.
Alexandria, VA 22314
703/548-3440
703/836-0367 (fax)
Issue Frequency:
12/year, monthly
Price:
$70
Description:
This is the monthly magazine of SHRM, providing news and features of concern to the broad range of human resources specialists including training professionals. Regular features include benefits, recruitment, and technology, in addition to training and development. The magazine is also a good source of current information about legal issues and actions in topics such as diversity, affirmative action, and specific developments in legislation such as The Americans with Disabilities Act (ADA) and Family and Medical Leave Act.

## 20

Publication Title:
**Human Resource
Development Quarterly
(HRDQ)**
Publisher:
Jossey-Bass, Inc.
350 Sansome St.
San Francisco, CA 94104

800/274-4434
800/569-0043 (fax)

**Issue Frequency:**

Quarterly

**Price:**

Free online to ASTD members (www.astd.org); $57/yr. individuals; $119 libraries

**Description:**

Sponsored by ASTD and the Academy of Human Resource Development. Following on the premise that there is adequate discussion and exchange of the practice of HRD in the media, the focus of the journal is on theory and research—specifically the application of quantitative and qualitative methods of inquiry to HRD topics. The journal is interdisciplinary in concept, drawing on fields such as industrial psychology, economics, adult education, organizational behavior, instructional technology, management, and human resource development, and it is "dedicated to serving the needs of researchers, senior practitioners, and academics in the field of human resource development." To stimulate healthy debate, each issue presents a featured article and an invited reaction. In addition to a selection of peer-reviewed articles, there are book, videotape, and software reviews, and a "forum" section for reader reactions and short essays.

## 21

**Publication Title:**

**Human Resource Management**

**Publisher:**

John Wiley & Sons, Inc.
605 Third Avenue
New York, NY 10158
800/825-7550
212/850-6021 (fax)

**Issue Frequency:**

Quarterly

**Price:**

$195; $125 for members of the Society for Human Resource Management (SHRM)

**Description:**

Described as a journal of strategy and innovation, it is co-sponsored by the University of Michigan Business School, SHRM, and John Wiley & Sons, publisher. It is a combination academic journal and

report on workplace trends in human resources management, including training and learning.

## 22

**Publication Title:**

**INFO-LINE**

**Publisher:**

American Society for Training and Development
P.O. Box 1567
Merrifield, VA 22116
703/683-8100
703/683-1523

**Issue Frequency:**

Monthly

**Price:**

$10 single issue; $119/yr; quantity discounts

**Description:**

This is a series of booklets on a single training topic. Since *INFO-LINE* was introduced in 1984, over 400 topics have been covered. The content of the typical booklet covers: preliminary steps, key terms, benefits/advantages, potential implementation problems, do's and don'ts, guidelines, tips, techniques, roles/responsibilities, activities/exercises, materials, tools, evaluation standards, etc. *INFO-LINE* uses lists, diagrams, and other presentation devices extensively, and each issue includes a "job aid" and a lengthy list of references and resources (articles, books, video, and other media).

## 23

**Publication Title:**

**Journal of Applied Behavioral Science**

**Publisher:**

SAGE Publications, Inc.
P.O. Box 5084
Thousand Oaks, CA 91359
805/499-9774
805/499-0871 (fax)
www.sagepub.com

**Issue Frequency:**

Quarterly

**Price:**

$80

**Description:**

Founded and sponsored by NTL, JABS is now in its 35th year. The academic journal focuses on the effects of evolutionary and planned change, including group dynamics, organization development, and social change.

## 24

**Publication Title:**

**Journal of Career Development**

**Publisher:**

Human Sciences Press
233 Spring St.
New York, NY 10013
212/620-8000
212/463-0742 (fax)

**Issue Frequency:**

Quarterly

**Price:**

$335 (institutional); $57 (personal)

**Description:**

Each issue of this journal consists of 6–8 articles on career development theory, research, and practice—with an emphasis on the impact that theory and research have on practice. Topics covered include career education, adult career development, career development of special-needs populations, career development and the family, and career and leisure. Occasionally, issues are thematic (e.g., "Evaluating Computer-Assisted Career Guidance Systems").

## 25

**Publication Title:**

**Journal of European Industrial Training**

**Publisher:**

MCB University Press North America
875 Massachusetts Ave., Suite 82
Cambridge, MA 02139
888/622-0075
www/mcb/co.uk/customer

**Issue Frequency:**

9/yr., plus online services

**Price:**

$7,429

**Description:**

The editorial objective of this journal is "to provide all those involved in training [and] training management with current practice, ideas, news and research on major issues in organization development and employee education and training." The editors strive to provide a balance between the theory and practice of training, and they favor articles based on experience and evidence. Most issues include 5 or 6 major articles, though there are occasional special issues that consist of a single monograph. In addition, each regular issue includes new items, information about training products and services, and book reviews. Includes CD-ROM, online edition, and Internet chatrooms.

## 26

Publication Title:
**Journal of Instruction Delivery Systems**
Publisher:
Learning Technology Institute
50 Culpeper St.
Warrenton, VA 22186
   540/347-0055
   540/349-3169 (fax)
Issue Frequency:
Quarterly
Price:
$60 per year for non-members
Description:
This quarterly journal is devoted to enhancing productivity through the appropriate application of technology in education, training, and job performance. The journal's purpose is to heighten awareness of technology-based learning system capabilities, to present information on applications and issues related to technology-based learning systems, and make them accessible to all who are interested.

## 27

Publication Title:
**Journal of Interactive Instruction Development**
Publisher:
Learning Technology Institute
50 Culpeper St.
Warrenton, VA 22186
   540/347-0055
   540/349-3169 (fax)
Issue Frequency:
Quarterly
Price:
$60 for non-members
Description:
The object of this journal is to enhance quality, effectiveness, and productivity in the design of interactive instructional systems. It covers strategies and techniques of design, tools and templates, objective discussion of the facilities provided by different hardware and software systems, and commentary on issues related to interactive program design. The audience includes HRD professionals, software/course-

ware developers, designers and vendors, academic leaders, and government officials. Although a technical, scholarly publication, the journal focuses on practical approaches that can be understood by the entry-level designer.

## 28

Publication Title:
**Knowledge Management Review**
Publisher:
Melcrum Publishing Ltd.
311 South Wacker Dr., Suite 4550
Chicago, IL 60606
   877/226-2764
   312/803-1871 (fax)
   www.melcrum.com
Issue Frequency:
Bimonthly
Price:
$337
Description:
*Knowledge Management Review* is a publication that gives its subscribers a "one-stop" guide to the latest ideas and techniques in knowledge management. Knowledge Management Review provides its readers with corporate case studies, special reports, reviews and practitioners' insights as well as the following sections: Briefings, Q&A, Bookmarks, and a Calendar of all relevant conferences and KM events.

## 29

Publication Title:
**The Lakewood Report on Technology for Learning**
Publisher:
Bill Communications
50 South Ninth St.
Minneapolis, MN 55402
   800/328-4329 or
   612/333-0471
Issue Frequency:
Monthly
Price:
$291/yr.
Description:
This newsletter premiered in 1995 and is another publication among the wide variety of publications of Bill Communications, best known as the publisher of *TRAINING Magazine*. It is a newsy document in newsletter format, with articles contributed both by a "contributing editor" staff of editors and by

other writers who tell about their programs, ideas, and experiences with new training technology. Topics typically include product news, videoconferencing, electronic performance support, distance learning, multimedia, assessment models for technology-based learning, and articles about the issues of cost and implementation of technology-based systems to foster learning and enhance performance.

## 30

Publication Title:
**Leader to Leader**
Publisher:
Jossey-Bass Inc.
350 Sansome St.
San Francisco, CA 94104-9960
   888/378-2537
   800/605-2665 (fax)
   www.jbp.com
Issue Frequency:
4/year
Price:
1 year (4 issues) $149; single issues $37.25
Description:
*Leader to Leader* is a quarterly report that brings leaders together to address the strategic issues we will face in the new millennium. This publication provides a forum for world-class leaders and thinkers to meet and share insights in their own words.

## 31

Publication Title:
**Leadership & Organization Development Journal**
Publisher:
MCB University Press North
   America
875 Massachusetts Ave., Suite 82
Cambridge, MA 02139
   888/622-0075
   www/mcb.co.uk
Issue Frequency:
7/yr., plus online services
Price:
$6,599
Description:
As the editors explain, this journal undertakes to "offer a sound balance between theory and practice, with articles based on experiences and evidence rather than just philosophical encouragement." Some of the topics covered include:

organizational culture, managing change, leadership issues, consultation, team building, conflict management, politics in organizations, organization development techniques, productivity, and communication. Both readers and contributors come from experienced organization development professionals in industry and the public sector, as well as in consulting firms and academia. Most issues consist of 4 or 5 major articles, plus conference reports, book reviews, article abstracts, and news of the field. Occasionally, issues are devoted to a single monograph.

## 32

Publication Title:
**Leadership In Action**
Publisher:
Jossey-Bass, Inc.
350 Sansome St.
San Francisco, CA 94104
800/274-4434
800/569-0443 (fax)
Issue Frequency:
6/yr.
Price:
$124
Description:
Formerly *Issues & Observations*. Primarily, this publication is a communication vehicle for the non-profit Center for Creative Leadership, reporting on the Center's research, publications, and seminars. In each issue, however, there is one major article, based on Center research, on some aspect of leadership or management development. These subjects are also addressed in each issue in several other shorter articles and columns that are of interest to practitioners of management and executive development. CCL's Website is www.ccl.org/publications.

## 33

Publication Title:
**Learning Circuits**
Publisher:
ASTD (American Society for Training & Development)
1640 King St., Box 1443
Alexandria, VA 22313
703/683-8100
703/683 1523 (fax)
www.learningcircuits.org
Issue Frequency:
12 issues/year; monthly

Price:
Free
Description:
This is ASTD's new (2000) Webzine. As expected it features reports of Web-based training and online learning of all sorts. It is practical in focus and has some features available to ASTD members only. A free e-mail newsletter based on *Learning Circuits* is called *Learning Circuits Express* and is available simply by signing up.

## 34

Publication Title:
**Learning Decisions**
Publisher:
The MASIE Center
P.O. Box 397
Saratoga Springs, NY 12866
800/956-2743
www.learningdecisions.com
Issue Frequency:
11/year
Price:
$195 plus online resources
Description:
This is an interactive online newsletter featuring issues in digital learning, presentation and analysis of issues including subscriber surveys and information sharing, research summaries product and services analyses. Subscribers receive discounts to MASIE Center conferences and events.

## 35

Publication Title:
**The Learning Organization**
Publisher:
MCB University Press North America
875 Massachusetts Ave., Suite 82
Cambridge, MA 02139
888/622-0075
www/mcb.co.uk/customer
Issue Frequency:
5/yr., plus online services
Price:
$649
Description:
Published for the first time in 1994, this journal presents articles that focus on the relationship between learning undertaken by managers as individuals and the continuous learning which occurs within organizations. This recognizes the need for organizations to harness the development activity

which occurs for individuals so that the organization as a whole advances. As the economic and market conditions become more turbulent, the flexibility inherent in a learning organization will become of paramount importance. The journal publishes articles of relevance to human resource professionals, management development specialists, consultants, and individual managers who wish to grow their skills in tune with organizational requirements.

## 36

Publication Title:
**Leverage**
Publisher:
Pegasus Communications, Inc.
One Moody St.
Waltham, MA 02453
781/398-9700
781/894-7175 (fax)
www.pegasus.com
Issue Frequency:
12/yr (monthly)
Price:
$99
Description:
*Leverage* is designed to provide a forum for news, concepts, and sharing from the organizational learning community. Articles are written by academics, consultants, and managers in public and private corporations. A conference calendar is included.

## 37

Publication Title:
**Managers Edge**
Publisher:
Briefings Publishing Group
A Division of Financial Times Professional Inc.
1101 King St., Ste 110
Alexandria, VA 22314
703/548-3800
703/684-2136
www.briefings.com
Issue Frequency:
12/yr (monthly)
Price:
$97
Description:
The founding publisher of Managers Edge is *The Fred Pryor Report*. It is similar in concept and format to other Fred Pryor reports such as *Communication Briefings*.

Articles are actually selected abstracts and excerpts of current books and articles on management and leadership. Sources are provided for reader follow-up. Other "briefings" newsletters are also available. See Website or phone for other titles.

## 38

**Publication Title:**
**Marketing Contract Training**
**Publisher:**
LERN
1550 Hayes Dr.
Manhattan, KS 66502
800/678-5376
888/234-8633
**Issue Frequency:**
12/yr (monthly)
**Price:**
$145
**Description:**
This newsletter from a non-profit lifelong learning organization is focused narrowly on the contract trainer. Articles are practical and provide specific help in marketing issues of all sorts. Internet reports and other networking services are included with the subscription.

## 39

**Publication Title:**
**The Microcomputer Trainer**
**Publisher:**
Systems Literacy, Inc.
6 Saint Lo Pl.
P.O. Box 1032
Hopatcong, NJ 07843
973/770-7762
973/770-2205 (fax)
www.systemsliteracy.com
**Issue Frequency:**
11/yr.
**Price:**
$195/yr.
**Description:**
Billed as providing "practical solutions and strategies for the professional responsible for building end-user skills," this newsletter presents practical, in-depth information with "tips" on everything. There is an emphasis on what successful trainers are doing, with samples of their work in the form of lists, course outlines, models, forms, illustrations, etc. Articles, case studies, and interviews report on the work of trainers in corpora-

tions, educational institutions, government, and the computer training industry, worldwide. Also available: an online newsletter, Quick Training Tips, featuring numerous trainer anecdotes. You can request free samples of both The Microcomputer Trainer and Quick Training Tips by phone, fax, mail, or e-mail: loretta@panix.com

## 40

**Publication Title:**
**Multimedia and Internet Training Newsletter**
**Publisher:**
Brandon Hall, Ph.D.
690 W. Fremont Ave., Suite 10
Sunnyvale, CA 94087
408/736-2335
408/736-9425 (fax)
www.brandon-hall.com
**Issue Frequency:**
12/yr (monthly)
**Price:**
$189
**Description:**
This newsletter provides its readers with independent technology-based training information. You will learn about the latest industry trends and products, find out how to use technology-based training to save money and increase productivity, and read insightful editorials from industry experts. You will also have access to the following vital information:
• case studies showing viability of technology-based training
• return-on-investment studies that show how to reduce cost of training
• how to separate hype from reality using the internet and intranet for training
• instructional design for computer-based training
• interviews
• new product information
• industry trends
• program reviews
• upcoming events
• employment opportunities and more.

## 41

**Publication Title:**
**Organizational Dynamics**
**Publisher:**
American Management Association
P.O. Box 319
Saranac Lake, NY 12983-0319

800/262-9699 (U.S.)
518/891-1500 (international)
518/891-3653 (fax)
www.amanet.org
**Issue Frequency:**
Quarterly
**Price:**
$63
**Description:**
Organizational Dynamics is a quarterly journal on applying behavioral sciences in organizations. This journal presents perspectives from innovative minds in business management. Organizational Dynamics is also a publication for executives who understand that to run an organization effectively, you have to understand the inner workings that make it run. Organizational Dynamics gives the latest thinking on and practical approaches to issues such as quality, customer service, restructuring and self-managed teams, empowerment, etc.

## 42

**Publication Title:**
**Performance Improvement**
**Publisher:**
International Society for
Performance Improvement
1300 L St., NW, Suite 1250
Washington, DC 20005
202/408-7969
202/408-7972 (fax)
**Issue Frequency:**
Monthly except for combined May/June and November/December issues
**Price:**
Included in annual membership dues of $125; $69 per year for non-members
**Description:**
NSPI's official journal is dedicated to the advancement of performance science and technology. *PI* publishes practical articles, theoretical and conceptual discussions, procedural models, research reports, case studies, book and software reviews, and short essays on topics related to improving human performance.

## 43

**Publication Title:**
**Performance Improvement Quarterly**

**Publisher:**
Learning Systems Institute
Florida State University
384 Hickory Wood Drive
Crawfordville, FL 32327
904/926-5266
904/926-8694 (fax)
(Subscription information
from:)
International Society for
Performance Improvement
1300 L St., NW, Suite 1250
Washington, DC 20005–4107
202/408-7969
202/408-7972 (fax)
www.ispi.org
**Issue Frequency:**
Quarterly
**Price:**
$50/yr. non-members;
$22 students; $64 libraries
**Description:**
This is a peer-reviewed journal that publishes scholarly works on performance technology, which the editors define as "a set of methods and processes for solving problems and realizing opportunities related to the performance of people." The journal's editorial content emphasizes original work involving technologies such as front-end analysis, systems thinking and strategic alignment, process redesign, design models, problem solving, and evaluation, and interventions such as motivation, mentoring, management development, reengineering, instruction, and performance support systems. Each issue includes 5–7 articles and special features: ERIC research abstracts, tables of contents from journals of interest to readers, and/or book reviews.

**44**

**Publication Title:**
**People@Work**
**Publisher:**
Professional Training Associates, Inc.
210 Commerce Blvd.
Round Rock, TX 78664
800/424-2112
512/255-7532 (fax)
www.hardatwork.com
**Issue Frequency:**
12/year, monthly
**Price:**
$72

**Description:**
This is a newsletter full of a variety of short articles to help readers make "the most of your job and the people on your team." It is unique in its way of engaging the reader through quizzes, puzzles, and "what if" scenarios. With each issue, subscribers also receive a 4-page "in-depth" special report containing how-to guidance on a single topic. A recurring feature throughout the newsletter is "a bottom-line idea" or how-to tip.

**45**

**Publication Title:**
**Quality Digest**
**Publisher:**
QCI International
40 Declaration Dr., Ste. 100-C
Chico, CA 95973
530/893-4095
530/893-0395 (fax)
**Issue Frequency:**
12/year, monthly
**Price:**
$59
**Description:**
This magazine covers a broad range of quality issues in corporations, government, and non-profits. Articles tend to be short; advertisements are many, and provide the trainer with a good example of products available to help get the quality message out. The publication includes regular columns by A. Blanton Godfrey, Paul Scicchitano, and Ken Blanchard. Certifications and standards are common topics in most issues.

**46**

**Publication Title:**
**Quality Progress**
**Publisher:**
American Society for Quality Control (ASQC)
P.O. Box 3005
Milwaukee, WI 53201-9488
800/248-1946
414/272-8575
**Issue Frequency:**
12/year, monthly
**Price:**
$60 non-members; free to members
**Description:**
*Quality Progress* is a peer-reviewed journal with 85% of its feature

articles written by quality professionals. Many of the issues addressed in the magazine deal with performance measurement and training for continuous improvement. Human resources issues associated with The Baldrige National Quality Award and ISO 9000 certification are found in many issues of the publication.

**47**

**Publication Title:**
**Ragan's Intranet Report**
**Publisher:**
Ragan Communications, Inc.
316 N. Michigan Ave.
Chicago, IL 60610
800/878-5331
312/960-4106 (fax)
www.ragan.com
**Issue Frequency:**
12/year
**Price:**
$229
**Description:**
*Ragan's Intranet Report* is a monthly publication loaded with information on the latest technological trends, tactics, and techniques that are affecting internal communications in organizations/ companies. Ask about other Ragan newsletters.

**48**

**Publication Title:**
**Ragan's Strategic Training Report**
**Publisher:**
Ragan Communications, Inc.
316 N. Michigan Ave.
Chicago, IL 60601
800/878-5331
312/960-4106 (fax)
www.ragan.com
**Issue Frequency:**
12/year, monthly
**Price:**
$169
**Description:**
This is a Ragan newsletter targeted to the training executive. It features articles on curriculum options, measurement practices, and the latest technology. It is problem-and-solution focused. Ask about other Ragan newsletters.

## 49

**Publication Title:**
**Reflections: The SoL Journal**
**Publisher:**
Reflections: The SoL Journal
222 Third St., Ste 2323
Cambridge, MA 02142
617/492-7236
617/577-1545 (fax)
www.mitpress.mit.edu/SOLJ
**Issue Frequency:**
Quarterly
**Price:**
$50
**Description:**
This journal from Massachusetts Institute of Technology (MIT) Press is a hybrid academic journal and magazine. It is fairly broad in scope, featuring contributions from researchers, consultants, and practitioners. It also includes poetry, photography, drawing, painting, and other types of artistic reflection. It is meant to be an eclectic, international, and intellectually diverse publication on managing knowledge, learning, and change.

## 50

**Publication Title:**
**Report on Literacy Programs**
**Publisher:**
Business Publishers, Inc.
951 Pershing Dr.
Silver Spring, MD 20910–4464
800/274-6737
301/589-5103
301/589-8493 (fax)
**Issue Frequency:**
25/yr.
**Price:**
$305
**Description:**
This 8-page newsletter is designed for those who administer adult literacy programs. It provides current intelligence on the public policy debate concerning adult literacy, as well as information about programs around the country. Another feature is notice of grants, contracts, and other funding sources. There is also notice of meetings and conferences in the literacy field, as well as details on books, reports, periodicals, curricula, software, and other resource materials on basic skills education. A special benefit to subscribers is access to a service called DocuDial that allows one to order by phone faxed copies of the full text of government studies, speeches, and other documents.

## 51

**Publication Title:**
**Sloan Management Review**
**Publisher:**
MIT Sloan School of Management
77 Massachusetts Ave., E53-416
Cambridge, MA 02139-4307
617/253-7170
617/258-9739 (fax)
**Issue Frequency:**
Quarterly
**Price:**
$89
**Description:**
This is an academic journal written by management academics, consultants, and practitioners and edited for professional managers. The emphasis is on general management issues, with special focus on organizational change, management of technology, and international management. Training issues associated with these topics are frequently discussed.

## 52

**Publication Title:**
**Strategy and Business**
**Publisher:**
Booz-Allen & Hamilton, Inc.
101 Park Ave.
New York, NY 10178
888/557-5550
617/723-3989 (fax)
www.strategy-business.com
**Issue Frequency:**
4/year
**Price:**
$38
**Description:**
This is a publication of a consulting company, launched in 1995 with a mission "to provoke readers with new ideas about business." In it are best practice reports and case studies, interviews with thought leaders, articles on strategy and competition, and research reports. Book reviews and "noteworthy quotes" are features of each issue.

## 53

**Publication Title:**
**The Systems Thinker**
**Publisher:**
Pegasus Communications, Inc.
One Moody St.
Waltham, MA 02453
800/272-0945
800/701-7083 (fax)
www.pegasus.com
**Issue Frequency:**
10/year
**Price:**
$139
**Description:**
This newsletter helps managers and leaders put systems thinking to work in their organizations. It introduces readers to tools and concepts of systems thinking. It is practical in focus and encourages readers to share innovative ideas and "systems stories."

## 54

**Publication Title:**
**TechTrends for Leaders in Education & Training**
**Publisher:**
Association for Educational Communications and Technology (AECT)
1800 North Stone Lake Dr., Suite 2
Bloomington, IN 47404
202/624-9731
812/355-7675 (voice)
812/355-7678 (fax)
www.aect.org
**Issue Frequency:**
6/yr.
**Price:**
$50; free to AECT members
**Description:**
Described as being directed to "leaders in education and training," this is the official publication of the Association for Educational Communications and Technology. Although it welcomes articles "on any aspect of new technology in education and training in schools, colleges and private industry," most of the articles in this publication are by educators and for educators. All feature articles are reviewed by experts in the field before acceptance for publication. Recent issues have focused on distance learning, interactive video, CBT, CD-ROM, and hypermedia. Other features of the magazine include news of the field, interviews, abstracts from the ERIC database, descriptions of new books and software, profiles of new

hardware products, and a calendar of events.

## 55

**Publication Title:**
**Thiagi Game Letter**
**Publisher:**
Jossey-Bass/Pfeiffer
350 Sansome St.
San Francisco, CA 94104
    888/378-2537 (toll free)
    800/605-2665 (fax)
    www.josseybass.com
**Issue Frequency:**
10/year
**Price:**
$149
**Description:**
*Thiagi Game Letter* is designed to help trainers, facilitators, managers, and consultants to use interactive, experiential strategies to improve human performance. This publication provides a variety of training games, simulations, role plays, team building activities, computer games, and other creative methods to deliver results quickly and effectively.

## 56

**Publication Title:**
**Training & Development**
**Publisher:**
American Society for Training and
    Development, Inc.
1640 King St., Box 1443
Alexandria, VA 22313–2043
    703/683-8100
    703/683-8103 (fax)
**Issue Frequency:**
Monthly
**Price:**
Included in dues of national ASTD members; $85/yr. to non-members
**Description:**
As the monthly magazine of the American Society for Training and Development, this is, by definition, the flagship publication in the industry of HRD and workplace performance. Each issue includes 12–13 in-depth feature articles with practical, how-to information—written primarily by practitioners for practitioners. Departments include: "News You Can Use" with short news items covering the trends, approaches, and happenings in the field. A special section, "@work," lists current online resources. "FaxForum"

lets readers share opinions and experiences on work-related topics. "Training 101" covers the basic concepts and techniques of the profession. "Career Power" gives tips on personal and professional development. "Working Life" is a lively wrap-up of issues and anecdotes from the world of work. Other columns include reactions from readers via letter, fax, and e-mail; descriptions and contact information on new products and services; up-to-date reports on the state of technology; and "Marketplace," a one-stop shopping guide to suppliers and consultants. Global issues are often featured.

## 57

**Publication Title:**
**Training Directors' Forum**
**Newsletter (online only)**
**Publisher:**
Bill Communications
50 South Ninth St.
Lakewood Building
Minneapolis, MN 55402
    612/333-0471
    612/333-6526 (fax)
    www.trainingsupersite.com
**Issue Frequency:**
Frequent updates
**Price:**
Free
**Description:**
This online newsletter is designed as a communication vehicle among training directors and other leaders of the HRD field. It is completely experience-based, and most articles are detailed and specific descriptions of "how they do it," using input from training managers and directors. The subjects covered include every aspect of the administration of the training function, plus a wide variety of training programs, projects, techniques, etc.

## 58

**Publication Title:**
**TRAINING Magazine**
**Publisher:**
Bill Communications
50 South Ninth St.
Lakewood Building
Minneapolis, MN 55402
    612/333-0471
    612/333-6526 (fax)

**Issue Frequency:**
Monthly
**Price:**
$78 per year
**Description:**
This magazine is well-known to every professional trainer. It covers the full range of training and development topics through a mix of articles written by the magazine's staff (in their characteristically lively style) and by practicing trainers, consultants, suppliers, etc. Many issues include a special editorial supplement on a particular training subject. The supplements on off-site training meetings and on presentation technologies feature a "marketplace directory" of suppliers in these areas. Then every year in October, the magazine publishes its *Industry Report*, (available separately for $35) the results of its nationwide survey of training practices: types of training being provided, who is being trained, modes of training delivery, budgets, etc. This survey also covers salaries, and the following issue (November) reports extensively on the trainer salary information that is collected. In addition, each monthly issue of *TRAINING Magazine* includes numerous short articles (on research events, training practices, etc.), letters from readers, calendars of conferences and seminars, reviews of books and films, and extensive listings of new products.

## 59

**Publication Title:**
**Training Media Review**
**Publisher:**
TMR Publications
P.O. Box 381822
Cambridge, MA 02238-1822
    877/532-1838 (toll-free)
    617/661-1095 (editor)
    617/661-1797 (fax)
    www.tmreview.com
**Issue Frequency:**
6/yr. plus special issues
**Price:**
$79 (6 bimonthly issues and online access); e-mail edition $59
**Description:**
This newsletter features candid reviews of training videos and multimedia software. Written by working trainers, the reviews

include (1) key information about the title (producer, running time, price, supplementary materials); (2) a 200- to 1,000-word review; and (3) ratings (1 to 4 stars) on ability to hold viewer attention, acting/presenting, instructional value, production quality, value of content, portrayal and casting of women/minorities, instructional value, value for the money—and an overall rating. There are 10–12 reviews in each issue, drawn from some 200 producers monitored by the editors. Occasionally, reviews of videos on a particular subject are grouped together. Apart from the reviews, there are a variety of other features in an issue, including industry news (e.g., notes about new video releases).

## 60

**Publication Title:**
**Web Content Report**
**Publisher:**
Ragan Communications, Inc.
316 N. Michigan Ave., Ste 300
Chicago, IL 60601
800/878-5331
312/960-4105 (fax)
www.ragan.com

**Issue Frequency:**
12/year, monthly
**Price:**
$249
**Description:**
This newsletter reports on practical, effective ways various organizations have created Websites that keep audiences and users coming back. It is full of short real-life stories and designs for Websites that work. Issues are full of tips and contact persons at sites.

## 61

**Publication Title:**
**What's Working in Human Resources**
**Publisher:**
Progressive Business Publications
370 Technology Dr.
Malvern, PA 19355
800/220-5000
610/647-8089 (fax)
**Issue Frequency:**
Semimonthly except December
**Price:**
$299/year
**Description:**
This is an 8-page newsletter of short and information-rich articles. Phone numbers and specific citations are given in each article for

further exploration. Performance boosters, legal issues, and case studies on difficult issues are found in most editions. "Training & Development" is a regular feature.

## 62

**Publication Title:**
**Workforce**
**Publisher:**
ACC Communications Inc.
245 Fischer Ave., B-2
Costa Mesa, CA 92628
714/751-1883
714/751-4106 (fax)
www.workforceonline.com
**Issue Frequency:**
12/year, monthly
**Price:**
$59/year
**Description:**
This magazine focuses on issues of concern to personnel managers and others such as trainers with direct responsibility for workforce development. The magazine has a particular interest in human resources issues created by implementation and changes in employment law and by changes in the composition of the workforce. Global issues are frequently featured.

# THE TRAINER'S ALMANAC

## SECTION 6.8

### RATINGS OF TRAINING WEBSITES

Over 250 Websites have been objectively evaluated and rated by an independent rater in this study sponsored by Lakewood Publications. This listing is a download from Lakewood's TrainingSuperSite, *www.trainingsupersite.com.*

### Alphabetic Index by Category

We have chosen this listing by rank of the Web resource. Other representations of the list are available by choosing other options for viewing it on the site itself. Each item in the list here is further categorized according to the type of resource it is. The two capital letters at the beginning of each item are a key to the category of resource. These are:

| | |
|---|---|
| BP | Books and Products Sites |
| CL | Commercial Sites |
| GA | Government Agency Sites |
| JN | Journals and Newsletters Sites |
| OR | Organization Sites |
| RT | Research Tools Sites |
| TR | Training Resources Sites |
| VL | Value-Added Sites |

The list of Websites can be accessed and sorted through each of these categories, and downloaded by single category to focus your search more intentionally.

### A-B-Cs of the Site Rating

Lakewood's Master List of Links contains no sites with a rating lower than C minus, although many "D" and "F" sites were reviewed. While some of the sites on the master list are academic and somewhat tangential to training, the vast majority are readily usable. Sites which did not function as advertised were culled from the list.

### *Methodology*

*Study Purpose*
An independent research service was hired to analyze the World Wide Web and select those sites related to training, or which may prove to be (or provide links to) valuable online resources to trainers and to provide an unbiased rating system to help users get the most from the World Wide Web as a resource tool.

*Study Duration*
The study began in October 1996 and was completed in January 1997.

*Criteria for Site Identification*
No limitations were placed on the sites reviewed. None were eliminated due to competitiveness of products or services, nor included due to any special considerations.

*Scope of Study*

As with the criteria for site identification, no limitations were placed on site selection methods that were used. They include:

> *Requests for input from subscribers on three major training listservs. No indication was given that the sites were for a comparative analysis.*
>
> *C/NET, PR Newswire, Z-D Press, Business Wire and other news services were monitored daily to filter out site URL information on sites which might be of potential value for the study.*
>
> *Newsgroups such as NewsBytes, DejaNews, and others were combed weekly to find sites of interest.*
>
> *Internet-savvy trainers were polled as to what sites they used regularly.*
>
> *World Wide Web site guides (New Riders and others) were reviewed.*
>
> *Searched the World Wide Web (using two browsers: Microsoft Internet Explorer and Netscape Navigator 3.0) using a variety of search engines, indices, and directories (Lycos, World Wide Web Worm, Galaxy, Infoseek, Excite, Hot Bot, Yahoo, Webcrawler, Open Text, and hosts of others).*

*Findings*

From mid-October 1996, through January 15, 1997, 10,200 Websites out of the 600,000 plus that claimed to discuss some aspect of "training" were investigated for their value to human resource, motivation, sales, and productivity trainers.

It took very liittle time to determine "training" is a broad term encompassing weight training, baseball spring training, dog obedience, and even some mysterious aspect of hair beautification. Sites were weeded out as they slipped through the various Boolean algebraic strings used, but still several thousand site choices remained. From the remaining sites, 255 (2.5% of the original 10,200) were chosen as high-potential sites for inclusion in the study.

Undoubtedly, some sites were missed, which could have been included and others were selected, which may not have universal appeal.

*Site Classification*

For the purposes of the study, sites were divided into eight categories: (1) Books and Products; (2) Commercial Links; (3) Government Agencies; (4) Journals and Newsletters; (5) Organizations; (6) Research Tools; (7) Training Resources; and (8) Value-Added Links. All are described in more depth under SITE CATEGORIES and RATING SYSTEM.

Of the 255 sites selected, 12 are Books and Products, 36 are Commercial Links, 18 are Government Agencies, 25 are Journals and Newsletters, 39 are Organizations, 41 are Research Tools, 51 are Training Resources, and 32 are Value-Added Links.

*Ratings*

Each site has been rated according to the criteria detailed in the SITE CATEGORIES and RATING SYSTEM. Sites rated lower than a "C-" were discarded in favor of higher rated sites.

*URL Transfer*

The URL for each site appears in a field of the analysis tables. It is not a "live" link (selecting one will not take you to the site described). The links are provided for further research only. The analysis tables can be printed, and the individual sites can be accessed by typing them into a browser. The addresses can also be lifted directly from the table and pasted to the browser's address window, if desired.

## Web Traffic 2001

The numbers of web users has increased substantially during year 2000. Advertisements as well as news about Websites have filled our publications and airways. For example, a company that manages Webservers, *www.web2010.com*, ran an ad in the October 2000 issue of *ecompany.com* magazine. Conversation with the salesperson there produced these numbers: about 400 hosting companies are registered with them, each with 50,000–60,000 Websites. An article by Nicole Parianos in *Lakewood's Technology for Learning*, September 2000, p. 6 stated that by 2003 we can expect 35 million handheld Web-access devices to be in use. What's new about this year is the focus on use, not simply on listing. Year 2000 also saw the upstart *Napster* Website all over the news, reporting 20 million users by the time attorneys and copyright specialists tried to crack down on them (*Atlantic Monthly*, September 2000, p. 39). Many business and professional magazines routinely feature columns of new Websites and ratings of existing ones. To be sure, a lively business exists to attract, manage, and keep Websites users, as year 2001 begins.

For exploratory Web searching for training and other information, these are tools for getting into the resources of the Web:

**www.altavista.com**   a comprehensive and easy-to-use search tool for beginners as well as advanced searchers;

**www.google.com**   a tool that rates every Website according to the number of other Websites that link to it;

**www.metacrawler.com**   a very helpful tool that enters a query simultaneously into about a dozen search engines, ranking results from each;

**www.yahoo.com**   the original, most improved, and well-maintained Web directory, with automatic links to altavista.

For specific training-related information, we list on the following pages TrainingSuperSite's rating of Websites they have found to be of greatest interest to trainers. Find them on the Web at **www.trainingsupersite.com**.

The following chart describes the site rating system:

| | |
|---|---|
| A+ | Top level site. High level of usability. Attractive. Information packed. Current. |
| A | Excellent site. Very usable. Appealing. Plenty of information. Good interest. |
| A– | Excellent site. Minor flaw or paucity of information keeps it from an A or A+. |
| B+ | Very good site. Usable. Good information. A better-than-average site overall. |
| B | Good site. Usable. Good information. May be short on ambiance or content. |
| B– | Good site with a flaw. May have an out-of-date link. May be slow to load. |
| C+ | Average site. May be put together a little awkwardly. Still has value. |
| C | Average. A take-it-or-leave-it site. Take a higher rated site if available. |
| C– | Ho hum. OK, but just barely. Included only if info cannot be found elsewhere. |

This list of ratings of Websites in Section 6.8 of *The Trainer's Almanac* is reprinted with permission from TrainingSuperSite (*www.trainingsupersite.com*) Bill Communications. Copyright 1997–1998. Website accessed April 12, 2000.

## All Sites, Listed by Rank

Sites are listed by ranking (alphabetically within ranks).

| | | | |
|---|---|---|---|
| BP | Amazon.com Books | http://www.amazon.com/exec/obidos/subst/index2.html | A+ |
| VL | Argus ClearingHouse | http://www.clearinghouse.net/ | A+ |
| TR | Big Dog's HR Development Page | http://www.nwlink.com/~donclark/hrd.html | A+ |
| TR | CMC Information Services | http://www.december.com/cmc/info/ | A+ |
| VL | Comic Strip® | http://www.unitedmedia.com/comics/ | A+ |
| VL | Dilbert Zone | http://www.unitedmedia.com/comics/dilbert/ | A+ |
| VL | Dilbert's Daily Mental Workout | http://www.unitedmedia.com/comics/dilbert/ddmw/ | A+ |
| JN | Electronic Newsstand | http://www.enews.com/ | A+ |
| RT | EZ Connect Search Directory | http://www.ezconnect.com//home.htm | A+ |
| JN | Future Net | http://www.futurenet.co.uk/ | A+ |
| TR | Home for Intranet Planners | http://www.kensho.com/hip/ | A+ |
| RT | InfoSeek Search Engine | http://www.infoseek.com/ | A+ |
| JN | Intranet Design Magazine | http://www.innergy.com/ | A+ |
| GA | Library of Congress | http://marvel.loc.gov/ | A+ |
| RT | LISTZ Directory of E-Mail Discussion Groups | http://www.liszt.com/ | A+ |
| VL | Mercury Mail | http://www.merc.com/ | A+ |
| JN | Newsletter Library | http://pub.savvy.com/ | A+ |
| VL | Newspapers Online | http://www.newspapers.com/ | A+ |
| RT | Open Text Index | http://index.opentext.net/ | A+ |
| RT | Publicly Accessible Mailing Lists | http://www.neosoft.com/internet/paml/ | A+ |
| VL | Smart Business Super Site | http://www.smartbiz.com/ | A+ |
| GA | Superintendent of Documents | http://www.access.gpo.gov/su_docs/ | A+ |
| JN | Training Magazine | http://www.lakewoodpub.com/ | A+ |
| TR | Training Net | http://www.trainingnet.com/ | A+ |
| CL | Training Registry | http://www.tregistry.com/ | A+ |
| TR | TRDEV-L - Training and Development Home Page | http://train.ed.psu.edu/TRDEV-L | A+ |
| CL | Ultimate Industry Connection | http://www.hardware.com/complist.html | A+ |
| VL | URL Minder | http://www.netmind.com/URL-minder/ | A+ |
| GA | US Government Printing Office | http://www.access.gpo.gov/ | A+ |
| TR | World Economic & Business Development Resources | http://www.mecnet.org/edr/ | A+ |
| RT | World Fax Directory | http://infolab.ms.wwa.com/wtx/m_r.htm | A+ |
| JN | +Value: MoreValue.com | http://www.gonogo.com/ | A |
| VL | A-Word-A-Day Home Page | http://lrdc5.lrdc.pitt.edu/awad/home.html | A |
| OR | Academy of Human Resource Development | http://www.ahrd.org/ | A |

| OR | Academy of Human Resource Development | http://www.ahrd.org/ | A |
|----|----|----|----|
| RT | Access Business Online | http://www.clickit.com/touch/accbiz.htm | A |
| TR | Adult Education Collection at Syracuse University | http://web.syr.edu/~ancharte/resource.html | A |
| CL | Advanced Leadership Group | http://www.adv-leadership-grp.com/ | A |
| RT | AltaVista Search Engine | http://www.altavista.digital.com/ | A |
| VL | America's Job Bank | http://www.ajb.dni.us/ | A |
| OR | American Compensation Association | http://www.ahrm.org/aca/aca.htm | A |
| OR | American Council on International Personnel | http://www.ahrm.org/acip/acip.htm | A |
| OR | American Management Association | http://www.amanet.org/ | A |
| OR | American Productivity and Quality Center | http://www.apqc.org/ | A |
| OR | American Society for Training and Development | http://www.astd.org/ | A |
| OR | ASAE Online Association Directory | http://www.asaenet.org/gateway/ OnlineAssocDir.html | A |
| CL | Ask the Expert - Bob Pike | http://www.training-info.com/expert/pike.html | A |
| TR | AskERIC | http://ericir.syr.edu/ | A |
| OR | Association of Federal Technology Transfer Executives | http://www.datasync.com/ | A |
| RT | AT&T Toll Free Internet Directory | http://www.tollfree.dir.att.net/ | A |
| TR | Atlas Web Workshop | http://ua1vm.ua.edu/~crispen/atlas.html | A |
| VL | Awesome Lists | http://www.princeton.edu/~rcurtis/aee.html | A |
| JN | Business Week Online | http://www.businessweek.com/ | A |
| JN | Catalog Mart | http://catalog.savvy.com/ | A |
| GA | CDC National Aids Clearinghouse | http://cdcnac.org/ | A |
| OR | Center for Internet-Based Training | http://www.internet-basedtraining.com/ | A |
| CL | Center for Mgmt and Org Effectiveness | http://www.thecoach.com/ | A |
| OR | Center for the Study of Work Teams | http://www.workteams.unt.edu/ | A |
| CL | Change Technologies | http://www.city-net.com/changetech/ | A |
| VL | CNBC News | http://www.cnbc.com/ | A |
| RT | CNET Search Site | http://www.search.com/ | A |
| VL | CNN Interactive | http://www.cnn.com/ | A |
| JN | Communications Week | http://techweb.cmp.com/cw/cwi/ | A |
| TR | Computer Training Network | http://www.crctraining.com/training/ | A |
| TR | Consultant Resource Center | http://www.consultant-center.com/ | A |
| VL | Corporate Financials Online | http://www.cfonews.com/ | A |
| CL | Covey Leadership Center | http://www.covey.com/ | A |
| CL | Creative Training Techniques International, Inc. | http://www.cttbobpike.com/ | A |
| JN | Customer Service Review | http://www.csr.co.za/ | A |

| | | | |
|---|---|---|---|
| CL | Cyber State University | http://cyberstateu.com/ | A |
| RT | DejaNews News Group Search Engine | http://www.dejanews.com/ | A |
| JN | Directory of Electronic Journals and Newsletters | http://arl.cni.org/scomm/edir/ | A |
| RT | dNet Directory Central | http://www.d-net.com/ | A |
| VL | E-Minder | http://www.netmind.com/e-minder/ e-minder.html | A |
| RT | E-ZINE-LIST | http://www.meer.net/~johnl/e-zine-list/ | A |
| RT | Education Index | http://www.educationindex.com/ | A |
| JN | Educational Technology Journal | http://www.pacificrim.net/~mckenzie/ | A |
| OR | Employee Assistance Professionals Association | http://www.ahrm.org/eapa/eapa.htm | A |
| CL | Excellence in Training Corporation | http://www.extrain.com/ | A |
| RT | Excite Search Engine | http://www.excite.com/ | A |
| JN | Fortune | http://pathfinder.com/@@D9OHhw QAq24kTKSx/fortune/ | A |
| RT | FTP Search 3.3 | http://ftpsearch.ntnu.no/ | A |
| VL | Funny Bone Home Page | http://www.indirect.com/www/nunley/ bone/index.html | A |
| RT | Galaxy Search Engines (Professionals) | http://www.einet.net/ | A |
| JN | Georgia Center Quarterly | http://www.gactr.uga.edu/GCQ/gcq.html | A |
| JN | High Technology Careers | http://hightechcareers.com/ | A |
| RT | HotMail - World's Free Web-Based E-Mail Site | http://www.hotmail.com/ | A |
| TR | HR Headquarters | http://www.hrhq.com/ | A |
| BP | HRD Press | http://www.hrdpress.com/ | A |
| OR | Human Resource Planning Society | http://www.ahrm.org/hrps/hrps.htm | A |
| JN | Information Week | http://techweb.cmp.com/iw/613/ | A |
| OR | Institute for Learning Sciences | http://www.ils.nwu.edu/ | A |
| OR | Institute for Learning Technologies | http://www.ilt.columbia.edu/ | A |
| OR | International Association for Information Management | http://www.ihrim.org/ | A |
| OR | International Personnel Management Association | http://www.ipma-hr.org/ | A |
| CL | Internet and Online Industry Sourcebook Online | http://www.internetsourcebook.com/ | A |
| VL | Internet Business Connection | http://www.intbc.com/ | A |
| VL | Internet Pizza Server | http://www.ecst.csuchico.edu/~pizza/ | A |
| TR | Internet Training Center Training Links | http://world.std.com/~walthowe/tnglinks.htm | A |
| RT | INTERNIC Services Directory | http://ds.internic.net/ | A |
| JN | Intranet Journal | http://www.intranetjournal.com/ijx/ | A |
| JN | IT Training | http://www.train-net.co.uk/it/ | A |

| | | | |
|---|---|---|---|
| JN | iWorld | http://www.iworld.com/ | A |
| JN | Journal of Industrial Teacher Education | http://scholar.lib.vt.edu/ejournals/JITE/ jite.html | A |
| RT | Library of Congress Search Tools | http://lcweb.loc.gov/global/search.html | A |
| RT | Link Star Business Directory | http://www.linkstar.com/ | A |
| RT | Lycos Search Engine | http://www.lycos.com/ | A |
| CL | Masie Center | http://www.masie.com | A |
| CL | Microsoft Office | http://www.microsoft.com/office/ | A |
| CL | Microsoft Training & Certification | http://www.microsoft.com/train_cert/ | A |
| GA | NASA Online Educational Resources | http://www.nasa.gov/ nasa_online_education.html | A |
| OR | National Center on Adult Education | http://litserver.literacy.upenn.edu | A |
| GA | National Institute of Standards and Technology | http://www.nist.gov/ | A |
| GA | National Performance Review | http://www.npr.gov/ | A |
| JN | Net Smart | http://www.microsoft.com/industry/acc/ pages/intra-en.htm | A |
| CL | NeverForget | http://www.neverforget.com/ | A |
| VL | News.Com | http://www.news.com/ | A |
| OR | Organization Development Network | http://www.odnet.org/ | A |
| VL | PR Newswire | http://www.prnewswire.com/ | A |
| OR | Professional Society for Sales and Marketing Training | http://www.smt.org/ | A |
| JN | Quality Improvement Newsletter | http://www.ccc.govt.nz/Library/Connect/ 42Peters.html | A |
| TR | Resources for Internet Training | http://world.std.com/~walthowe/training.htm | A |
| TR | San Diego State University EdWeb | http://edweb.sdsu.edu/ | A |
| VL | Science in the Headlines | http://www2.nas.edu/new/newshead.htm | A |
| VL | Shareware | http://www.shareware.com/ | A |
| OR | Society for Applied Learning Technology | http://www.salt.org/ | A |
| OR | Society for Human Resource Management | http://www.shrm.org/ | A |
| OR | Society for Technical Communication | http://stc.org/ | A |
| VL | Stat-USA | http://www.stat-usa.gov/ | A |
| CL | Sterling Speakers Bureau | http://members.aol.com/speakers2u/ meetings.htm | A |
| RT | Switchboard Business Directory | http://www.switchboard.com/ | A |
| TR | Syllabus Web Top 40 Education Sites | http://www.syllabus.com/top40.htm | A |
| CL | TASL - Training and Seminar Locators | http://www.tasl.com/ | A |
| BP | Tech Expo Product and Literature Showcase | http://www.techexpo.com/home_pg.html/ | A |
| VL | Trade Show Central | http://www.tscentral.com/ | A |
| VL | Trade Show Central | http://www.tscentral.com/ | A |
| TR | TRAIN - Australian Training Information Network | http://www.opennet.net.au/partners/bvet/ train/topics.htm | A |

| TR | Training and Development Via the Internet | http://cac.psu.edu/~cxl18/trdev/ | A |
| TR | Training Forum Speakers Database | http://www.trainingforum.com/Speakers/index.html | A |
| TR | Training Net | http://www.trainingnet.com/ | A |
| TR | Training Net Magazine | http://www.trainingnet.com/magazine/magazine.html-ssi | A |
| TR | Training Resource Access Center | http://trainingaccesscenter.com/ | A |
| BP | TrainingSpace Online | http://www.trainingspace.com/ | A |
| TR | TRDEV-L Training Summaries (Pennsylvania State Univ.) | http://cac.psu.edu/~cxl18/trdev-l/summary.html | A |
| VL | UPS | http://www.ups.com/ | A |
| GA | US Department of Labor OSHA Information | http://www.osha-slc.gov/ | A |
| GA | US Federal Government Agencies | http://www.lib.lsu.edu/gov/fedgov.html | A |
| TR | Walt Howe's Internet Learning Center | http://world.std.com/~walthowe/index.html | A |
| RT | Web Search - Computer and Communication URLs | http://www.cmpcmm.com/cc/ | A |
| RT | Web Technology Super Site | http://www.techweb.com/ | A |
| RT | Webcrawler Search Engine | http://www.webcrawler.com/ | A |
| TR | Wellness on the Web | http://planet-hawaii.com/wellnet/allco2.html | A |
| RT | WhoWhere? Directory Search | http://www.whowhere.com/about.html | A |
| RT | World Pages Phone, E-Mail and Web Search | http://www.worldpages.com/ | A |
| RT | World Post Business Research | http://www.worldpost.com/research.html | A |
| VL | WWW Measurements Converter | http://www.mplik.ru/~sg/transl/ | A |
| RT | Yahoo Search Engine | http://www.yahoo.com/ | A |
| RT | Ahoy - Home Page Finder | http://ahoy.cs.washington.edu:6060/ | A– |
| OR | Association for Experiential Education | http://www.princeton.edu/~rcurtis/aee.html | A– |
| VL | Automatic Complaint Letter Generator | http://www-csag.cs.uiuc.edu/individual/pakin/complaint | A– |
| TR | Bill Communications | http://www.billcom.com/ | A– |
| JN | Career Magazine | http://www.careermag.com/ | A– |
| OR | Distance Learning Association | http://www.usdla.org/ | A– |
| GA | Education and Training (White House) | http://www.gsa.gov/ | A– |
| TR | Educom | http://educom.edu/ | A– |
| OR | EdWeb Home Room | http://edweb.cnidr.org:90/resource.cntnts.html | A– |
| CL | Employease, Inc. | http://www.employease.com/ | A– |
| OR | Ethics Resource Center | http://www.lmco.com/erc/ | A– |
| CL | ExpertSpace Speakers | http://www.expertspace.com/ | A– |
| GA | Federal Information Exchange | http://www.fie.com/ | A– |
| CL | Help Desk Institute | http://www.tregistry.com/ttr/hdi.htm | A– |
| RT | ICS Ultimate Search Page | http://www.internethub.com/search.html | A– |

| BP | IIR Technology | http://www.iir.co.za/ | A– |
|----|----------------|------------------------|----|
| RT | Inter-Link Search Engine | http://www.nova.edu/Inter-Links/ | A– |
| OR | International Organization for Standardization | http://www.iso.ch/ | A– |
| CL | International Quality and Productivity Center | http://www.iqpc.com/ | A– |
| TR | Internet Documentation and IETF Information | http://www.internic.net/ds/dspg0intdoc.html | A– |
| BP | Internet Training & Consulting Services | http://www.itcs.com/ | A– |
| BP | Internet Videos | http://www.webcom.com/~ivi/ | A– |
| RT | InterNic Directory of Directories | http://ds.internic.net/ds/dsdirofdirs.html | A– |
| RT | Meta Crawler Search Engine | http://metacrawler.cs.washington.edu:8080/ | A– |
| TR | National Centre for Vocational Education Research (Aust.) | http://www.ncver.edu.au/ncver.htm | A– |
| CL | Networked Learning | http://www.knowab.co.uk/nl.html | A– |
| TR | PC Trainer's Gateway | http://www.isitraining.com/gateway.html | A– |
| CL | Quality Improvement Newsletter | http://www.weber.edu/QualityNews/QualityNews-0296.htm | A– |
| TR | Que Education & Training | http://www.mcp.com/queet/linx0311.html | A– |
| OR | Society of Competitive Intelligence Professionals | http://www.scip.org/ | A– |
| CL | TCM - T&D Resource Center | http://www.tcm.com/trdev/ | A– |
| CL | Training Consortium Vendors | http://www.trainingconsortium.com/suppliers.shtml | A– |
| CL | Training Express | http://www.dgl.com/te/ | A– |
| TR | Training Forum Home Page | http://www.trainingforum.com/ | A– |
| BP | UC Davis Information Technology Training | http://instruction.ucdavis.edu/ | A– |
| TR | Virtual Environment Technical Training (VETT) | http://mimsy.mit.edu/ | A– |
| RT | Virtual Multi-Search Engine | http://www.dreamscape.com/frankvad/search.multi.html | A– |
| TR | Vision for Human Resource Development Network | http://www.mcb.co.uk/hrn/nethome.htm | A– |
| TR | Visual Edge Productions | http://www.vised.com/home.htm | A– |
| VL | Wall Street Journal | http://www.wsj.com/ | A– |
| TR | Web-Based-Training Information Site | http://www.multimediatraining.com/training.html | A– |
| TR | World Wide Web Virtual Library | http://tecfa.unige.ch/info-edu-comp.html | A– |
| RT | World Wide Web Worm | http://wwww.cs.colorado.edu/wwww | A– |
| RT | Yanoff's Internet Services List | http://www.spectracom.com/islist/ | A– |
| OR | International Technology Education Association | http://www.iteawww.org/ | B+ |

| GA | O-Net: Organizational Information Network | http://www1.whitehouse.gov/WH/pointers/ html/educ.html | B+ |
|---|---|---|---|
| BP | The Learning Center | http://www.tlckinkos.com/ | B+ |
| RT | US Universities and Community Colleges | http://www.utexas.edu/world/univ/ | B+ |
| VL | Anonymous Message Server | http://sp1.berkeley.edu/anon.html | B |
| TR | Benchmarking Exchange | http://www.benchnet.com/ | B |
| GA | Bureau of Labor Statistics | http://stats.bls.gov/ | B |
| OR | Center for Advanced Technology Education | http://www.cate.ryerson.ca/ | B |
| CL | Cheltenham Computer Training | http://www.cctglobal.com/ | B |
| CL | ComputerPrep | http://www.computerprep.com/ | B |
| TR | Courseware Clearinghouse | http://www.mrg.ab.ca/clear/ | B |
| RT | CyberStacks | http://www.public.iastate.edu/~CYBERSTACKS/ | B |
| JN | Educational Technology Review | http://aace.virginia.edu/AACE/pubs/etr/ etr.html | B |
| OR | Employee Benefit & Research Institute | http://www.ebri.org/ | B |
| VL | Federal Express | http://www.fedex.com/ | B |
| GA | Federal Training Mall | http://www.fedworld.gov/training/ | B |
| GA | General Services Administration | http://www.gsa.gov/ | B |
| CL | Human Resource Sofware and CBT Library | http://www.hrpress-software.com/ | B |
| BP | IETF/TERENA Training Materials Catalogue | http://www.trainmat.ietf.org/catalogue.html | B |
| TR | Interesting Listservs and Their Usage | http://www.teleport.com/~erwilson/ listserv.html | B |
| OR | International Foundation of Employee Benefits | http://www.ifebp.org/ | B |
| CL | International Education Services | http://www.iac.co.jp/~iesinfo/index.html | B |
| TR | Internet Resources | http://www.brandonu.ca/~ennsnr/Resources/ | B |
| OR | Internet Society | http://www.isoc.org/ | B |
| TR | Internet/Intranet Resources | http://www.mahesh.com/internet.html | B |
| BP | Knowledge Online | http://www.meu.edu/ | B |
| OR | National Association of Student Personnel Administration | http://www.naspa.org/ | B |
| TR | On the Horizon | http://sunsite.unc.edu/horizon/index.html | B |
| CL | Plus Style Training | http://www.es.co.nz/~meta4/ | B |
| TR | ProEd - Clearinghouse for Training and Development | http://www.proed.com/ch/ | B |
| OR | Rand Institute on Education and Training | http://www.ils.nwu.edu/ | B |
| TR | Roadmaps 96 Workshop | http://www.ultranet.com/~mobius/Roadmap/ | B |
| CL | SalesSense | http://ourworld.compuserve.com/homepages/ SalesSense/ | B |

| | | | |
|---|---|---|---|
| CL | Training and Education Resource Database | http://web20.mindlink.net/skillnet/training.html | B |
| CL | Training Broker | http://www.trainingbroker.com/ | B |
| TR | Training Forum Associations Database | http://www.trainingforum.com/assoc.html | B |
| BP | Via Grafix Software and Training Products | http://www.deerfield.com/viagrafix/training/ | B |
| OR | Vocational Evaluation and Work Adjustment Association | http://www.impactonline.org/vewaa/lists.html | B |
| VL | Web Employment Opportunities for Training | http://www.iweb.co.uk/DIRJT6.html | B |
| TR | World On-Line Internet Guide | http://toltec.lib.utk.edu/~lss/training/WebTutorial/tutor1.html | B |
| TR | Adult Education on the Internet-NetTutoring Group | http://www.oise.on.ca/~fkeller/AdultAid.html | B– |
| CL | Connect - Tom Peters | http://www.ccc.govt.nz/Library/Connect/42Peters.html | B– |
| JN | Human Resource Development Quarterly | http://www.jbp.com/hrdq.html | B– |
| CL | Learning Exchange | http://www.tcm.com/trdev/faq/index.html | B– |
| TR | Learning Styles | http://www.hcc.hawaii.edu/hccinfo/facdev/8.html | B– |
| GA | Minority Information Service (USAID) | http://www.fie.com/fedix/aid.html | B– |
| OR | National Association of Temporary Staffing Services | http://www.podi.com/staffing/ | B– |
| TR | Training Stuff Training Materials and Development | http://www.ccn.cs.dal.ca/~aa068/TrainDev.html | B– |
| RT | World College and University Home Page Links | http://www.mit.edu:8001/people/cdemello/univ.html | B– |
| GA | Alabama Industrial Development Technology | http://www.aidt.edu/ | C+ |
| GA | Advanced Technologies Applied to Training Design | http://ott.sc.ist.ucf.edu/1_2/nato.htm | C |
| OR | NewMedia Centers | http://www.csulb.edu/gc/nmc/ | C |

customer focus, 1.80
empowerment through training accounts, 1.80
Individual Training Accounts, 1.5, 1.80
One-Stop Centers, 1.5, 1.80
Workforce Investment Act, 1.5
Workgroup utilities, 1.50–51
Work/life balance study, 2.5–8
"family friendly" programs, 2.6
Hewlett-Packard/Agilent and Merck & Co. Inc., 2.6–7
Workonomics, 5.21
Workplace digital storytelling, 1.49
Work villages, 1.48
World's Most Respected Companies (survey), 5.41
Wyatt, Watson, 5.36

**X**
Xerox Corp., 1.43–45, 2.36–37, 3.14

**Y**
Yakimovicz, Ann, 3.41
Yang, Jerry, 2.3
Yardley-Jones, Tony, 2.16–17, 2.19
Yellow pages, 1.49
Youachieve.com, 4.31

**Z**
Zahn, Steve, 1.58
Zemke, Ron, 2.35
Zielinski, Dave, 3.39, 4.20
Zumwalt, Debra, 4.22
Zwart, Dale, 1.20